# Essentials of Services Marketing: Concepts, Strategies & Cases

SECOND EDITION

**K. Douglas Hoffman**
*Professor of Marketing*
*Colorado State University*

**John E. G. Bateson**
*Group Chief Executive Officer*
*SHL Group plc*

SOUTH-WESTERN
THOMSON LEARNING

Australia • Canada • Mexico • Singapore • Spain
United Kingdom • United States

**SOUTH-WESTERN**

™

**THOMSON LEARNING**

**Essentials of Services Marketing: Concepts, Strategies, & Cases, Second Edition**

K Douglas Hoffman, John E. G. Bateson

**Publisher:**
Mike Roche

**Acquisitions Editor:**
Mark Orr

**Developmental Editor:**
Debbie Anderson

**Marketing Strategist:**
Beverly Dunn

**Project Manager:**
Barrett Lackey

**Compositor:**
Graphic World

**Printer:**
Phoenix Color Corp
Hagerstown, Maryland

Library of Congress
Catalog Card Number:
2001090107

ISBN: 0-03-028892-4

*To Britty, Emmy, Maddy, and my parents*
Doug Hoffman

*For Dori, Lorna, and Jonathan*
John Bateson

# preface

The primary objective of *Essentials of Services Marketing: Concepts, Strategies & Cases* is to provide materials that not only introduce the student to the field of services marketing but also acquaint the student with specific customer service issues. The business world now demands, in addition to traditional business knowledge, increasing employee competence in customer satisfaction, service quality, and customer service, skills that are essential in sustaining the existing customer base.

*Essentials of Services Marketing: Concepts, Strategies & Cases* consists of 16 chapters, and 17 cases. This book is written in an "essentials" format for two reasons. First, due to the lack of a "true" undergraduate services marketing textbook for a number of years, many services marketing instructors have been using their own materials such as articles, cases, and videos. The "essentials" textbook provides these instructors with the means of covering the basic concepts and at the same time provides the flexibility for instructors to insert their own materials as they see fit. Second, because services marketing is relatively young as an academic field, a framework from which to study services marketing that is acceptable to all instructors has yet to emerge. Hence, the "essentials" textbook provides an initial framework that may be easily modified, as it has been in this second edition.

## STRUCTURE OF THE BOOK

*Essentials of Services Marketing: Concepts, Strategies & Cases* is divided into four main parts. The first part, "An Overview of Services Marketing," concentrates on defining services marketing and discusses in detail the fundamental concepts and strategies that differentiate the marketing of services from the marketing of tangible goods. The primary objective of Part 1 is to establish a core knowledge base that will be built upon throughout the remainder of the text.

Chapter One provides an introduction to the field of services marketing. It establishes the importance of the service sector in the world economy and the need for services marketing education. Chapter Two focuses more deeply on the fundamental differences between goods and services and their corresponding managerial implications. Chapter Three provides an overview of the service sector and focuses on the most substantial changes taking place within the sector. New concepts such as e-services and supplemental services are presented, and predicted keys to success within the service encounter are also discussed. Chapter Four focuses on consumer purchase decision issues as they relate to the services field. Consumers often approach service purchases differently than the way they approach the purchase of goods. The first part of the book concludes with Chapter Five, which takes an in-depth look at ethics in the service sector. Because of the differences between goods and services, unique opportunities arise that may encourage ethical misconduct.

The second part of the book, "Service Strategy: Managing the Service Encounter," is dedicated to topics that concern the management of the service encounter. Due to the consumer's involvement in the production of services, many new challenges are presented that do not frequently occur within the manufacturing sector. The primary topics of this part are strategic issues related to the marketing mix as well as the Servuction Model including process, pricing, promotion, physical evidence, and people (employee and customer) issues.

Chapter Six provides an overview of service operations, pinpointing the areas where special managerial attention is needed in the construction of the service process. In addition, the importance of balancing operations and marketing functions in service operations is also discussed. Chapters Seven and Eight focus on pricing and communication issues as they relate specifically to service firms. Chapter Nine examines the development and management of the service firm's physical environment. Chapter Ten discusses the many challenges associated with managing employees within the service experience. The service business, by it's very definition, is a people business and requires talented managers who can navigate the thin line between the needs of the organization, its employees, and its customers. Part 2 concludes with Chapter Eleven in which the art of managing service consumers is explored. Due to the impact of inseparability, the consumer's role in service production can both facilitate and hinder the exchange process. Hence, developing a strategic understanding of how the consumer can be effectively managed within the service encounter is critical. Chapter Eleven also introduces the fundamental components as well as the advantages and disadvantages associated with CRM systems.

The third part of the text, "Assessing and Improving Service Delivery," focuses on customer satisfaction and service quality issues. Methods for tracking service failures and employee recovery efforts as well as customer retention strategies are also presented. Ideally, assessing and improving the service delivery system will lead to "seamless service"—provided without interruption, confusion, or hassle to the customer.

Chapter Twelve presents an overview of the importance and benefits of customer satisfaction and the special factors to consider regarding measurement issues. Chapter Thirteen builds from the materials presented in Chapter Twelve and discusses conceptual and measurement issues pertaining to service quality and service quality information systems. Chapter Fourteen presents methods for tracking service failures and employee service recovery efforts. Chapter Fifteen focuses on the often forgotten benefits of customer retention and discusses strategies that maximize a firm's customer retention efforts. Chapter Sixteen concludes the text with "Putting the Pieces Together: Creating the Seamless Service Firm." Chapter Sixteen is dedicated to pulling the ideas in the book together in a manner that demonstrates the delivery of flawless customer service.

Part 4 of the book, "Cases," consists of cases that are specifically relevant to each of the chapters and also integrate other topics discussed throughout the text. The cases are to be used at the instructor's discretion to give students "real-world" practice in using the concepts presented in the textbook. Many of these cases have been purposely written to include an international and/or e-business flavor to reflect the changing business climate and the wide variety of issues that face service marketers today.

## WHAT'S NEW IN THE SECOND EDITION?

- Updated text, PowerPoint slides, Instructor's Manual and Test Bank
- 300+ PowerPoint slides available on-line
- New chapter on "Managing Service Consumers"
- More e-business examples
- More international examples
- Over 50 Services In Action boxes integrated throughout the text
  - many e-business–related
- New Sections
  - Millennial themes of how technological advances, demographic changes, and competitive pressures have continued to fuel the growth of the service sector
  - The role of supplemental services as they relate to the "service imperative"
  - Special considerations of service pricing as it relates to demand, cost, customer, profit, product, and legal considerations
  - An introduction to E-Services
  - An introduction to the fundamental components of CRM Ecosystems
  - Outcomes associated with CRM practices
  - Perceived justice as it relates to Service Recovery Evaluations
- New Cases
  - More cases
  - More variety in length
  - Many internationally-based
  - Many e-business–related
- Overall:
  - Same crispness to core content
  - Better domestic and international examples
  - Much more material relating to e-business
  - Better support materials
- The total package for any Services Marketing class

## INSTRUCTORS' RESOURCES

The Instructor's Manual with Test Bank and Transparency Masters, written by the authors, includes instructors' materials collected by the authors from professors all over the world. In addition, all test questions are available as computerized test banks on 3.5-inch disks in DOS, Windows, and Macintosh versions.

South-Western may provide complimentary instructional aids and supplements or supplement packages to those adopters qualified under our adoption policy. Please contact your sales representative for more information. If as an adopter or potential user you receive supplements you do not need, please return them to your sales representative or send them to:

Attn: Returns Department
Troy Warehouse
465 South Lincoln Drive
Troy, MO 63379

## ACKNOWLEDGMENTS

Many thanks are owed to family, friends, and colleagues for their assistance, continued patience, and encouragement. The first two editions have benefited greatly from the quality of reviewers' comments. We are very appreciative of the insightful comments of the following colleagues:

Kenneth D. Bahn, James Madison University
Julie Baker, University of Texas, Arlington
Rita Cossa, McMaster University
Ken Crocker, Bowling Green State University
Ronald E. Goldsmith, Florida State University
Scott Kelley, University of Kentucky
Rhonda Walker Mack, College of Charleston
Gene W. Murdock, University of Wyoming
Kim Snow, York University
Susan Stites-Doe, SUNY-Brockport
Stephen Tax, University of Victoria
Louis Turley, Western Kentucky University

Special thanks also go to the staff. A number of people have played a major role in the creation and production of this text, including Debbie Anderson, developmental editor; Barrett Lackey, Project Manager; Bev Dunn, Marketing Strategist; Mark Orr, Acquisitions Editor; and Linda Blundell, Picture and Rights Editor. We would especially like to thank our case contributors: Jochen Wirtz, Stephan Martin, S. Mohan, Brian Wansink, Jeanette Ho Pheng Theng, Aliah Hanim M. Salleh, Eric Cannell, Richard A. Engdahl, and Judy Siguaw. Jochen, thank you for your consistent interest in this second edition!

In closing, we hope that you enjoy the book and your services marketing class. It will likely be one of the most practical courses you will take during your college career. Education is itself a service experience. As a participant in this service experience, you are expected to participate in class discussions. Take advantage of the opportunities provided to you during this course, and become an integral component of the education production process. Regardless of your major area of study, the services marketing course has much to offer.

We would sincerely appreciate any comments or suggestions you would care to share with us. We believe that this text will heighten your sensitivity to services, and because of that belief, we leave you with this promise: We guarantee that after completing this book and your services marketing course, you will never look at a service experience in the same way again. This new view will become increasingly frustrating for most of you, as you will encounter many experiences that are less than satisfactory. Learn from these negative experiences, relish the positive encounters, and use this information to make a difference when it is your turn to set the standards for others to follow. As apostles of services marketing, we could ask for no greater reward.

Doug Hoffman
Professor of Marketing
Marketing Department
Colorado State University
Fort Collins, Colorado 80523
(970) 491-2791 (office)
(970) 491-5956 (fax)
*doug.hoffman@colostate.edu*

John Bateson
SHL Group plc
The Pavilion
Thames Ditton
Surrey KT7 One
United Kingdom

+44(020) 8335 8000 (office)
+44(020) 8335 7000 (fax)
*john.bateson@shlgroup.com*

# about the authors

**K. Douglas Hoffman** is a Professor of Marketing at Colorado State University. Over the last fourteen years, Doug has taught courses such as Services Marketing, E-Marketing, Principles of Marketing, Retail Management, and Marketing Management. His primary teaching and research passion is in the Services Marketing area in which he has started the first Services Marketing classes at Mississippi State University, The University of North Carolina at Wilmington, and Colorado State University. He has also taught the services course as a Visiting Professor at the Helsinki School of Economics and Business Administration in Helsinki, Finland.

Doug has been formally recognized for Teaching Excellence and is a past Education Coordinator for the Services Marketing Special Interest Group of the American Marketing Association. He has published a variety of articles in academic and practitioner journals such as the *Journal of Retailing, Journal of Business Research, European Journal of Marketing, Journal of Personal Selling and Sales Management, Journal of Business Ethics, Journal of Services Marketing, Journal of Professional Services Marketing, Journal of Marketing Education,* and *Marketing Education Review.* He is also the co-author of three textbooks:

*Essentials of Services Marketing, Second Edition,* The Dryden Press
*Managing Services Marketing, Fourth Edition,* The Dryden Press
*Marketing: Best Practices, First Edition,* The Dryden Press

Prior to his academic career, Doug was actively involved in his family-owned golf course business, a distribution analyst for Volkswagen of America, and a research analyst for the Parker Hannifin Corporation. Doug's current research and consulting activities are primarily in the areas of customer service/satisfaction and services marketing education.

**John E. G. Bateson** is a Group Chief Executive Officer of SHL Group plc, and was previously with the Gemini Group as a Senior Vice-President and Practice Leader in Gemini Consulting. He was Associate Professor of Marketing at the London Business School, England, and a visiting associate professor at the Stanford Business School. Prior to teaching, he was a brand manager with Lever Brothers and marketing manager with Philips.

Dr. Bateson holds an undergraduate degree from Imperial College, London, a master's degree from London Business School, and a Ph.D. in marketing from the Harvard Business School. He has published extensively in the services marketing literature, including the *Journal of Marketing Research, Journal of Retailing, Marketing Science,* and *Journal of Consumer Research.* He is also the author of *Managing Services Marketing: Text and Readings* (Dryden) and *Marketing Public Transit: A Strategic Approach* (Praeger).

Dr. Bateson was actively involved with the formation of the services division of the American Marketing Association. He served on the Services Council for four years and has chaired sessions of the AMA Services Marketing Conference. He also serves on the steering committee of the Marketing Science Institute. Dr. Bateson consults extensively in the services sector.

# contents in brief

# contents

· · · · · · · · · · · · · · · · · · · · · · · · · · · · · · · · · · · · · · · · · · · · · · · · · · · · · · · · · · · · · · · · ·

*part two*

# part three

*part four*

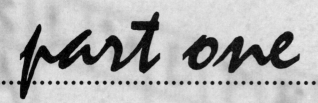
*part one*

# AN OVERVIEW OF SERVICES MARKETING

*Essentials of Services Marketing: Concepts, Strategies and Cases* is divided into four main parts. Part I, An Overview of Services Marketing, concentrates on defining services marketing and discusses in detail the fundamental concepts and strategies that differentiate the marketing of services from the marketing of tangible goods. The primary objective for Part I is to establish a core knowledge base that will be built upon throughout the remainder of the text.

# chapter 1

# An Introduction to Services

## CHAPTER OBJECTIVES

This chapter provides an introduction to the field of services marketing. It establishes the importance of the service sector in the world economy and the need for services marketing education.

After reading this chapter, you should be able to:

- Discuss the basic differences between goods and services.
- Discuss the factors that influence the customer's service experience.
- Understand the driving forces behind the increasing demand for services marketing knowledge.

"Economic value, like the coffee bean, progresses from commodities to goods to services to experiences."

Joseph B. Pine II &
James H. Gilmore
*The Experience Economy*

# Introduction

Services are everywhere we turn, whether it be a visit to the doctor, a church service, a trip to our favorite restaurant, or a day at school. As indicated by the table displayed on the inside cover of this text, the global service economy is booming. More and more the so-called industrialized countries in particular are finding that the majority of their gross national products are being generated by their service sectors. However, the growth of service sector does not just lie within traditional service industries such as health care, financial services, and insurance. Traditional goods producers such as automotive, computer, and numerous other manufacturers are now turning to the service aspects of their operations to establish a differential advantage in the marketplace as well as to generate additional sources of revenue for their firms. In essence, these companies, which used to compete by marketing "boxes" (tangible goods), have now switched their competitive focus to the provision of unmatched, unparalleled customer services.

Ample evidence exists documenting this transition from selling "boxes" to service competition. Traditional goods-producing industries such as the automotive industry are now emphasizing the service aspects of their businesses such as low APR financing, attractive lease arrangements, bumper-to-bumper factory warranties, low maintenance guarantees, and free shuttle services for customers. Simultaneously, less is being heard about the tangible aspects of vehicles such as gas mileage, acceleration, and leather seats in these firm's marketing communications. Similarly, the personal computer industry promotes in-home repairs, 24-hour customer service, and leasing arrangements. In addition, the satellite television industry is now boasting the benefits of digital service, pay-per-view alternatives, and security options to prevent children from viewing certain programming.

Overall, this new "global services era" is characterized by economies and labor force figures that are dominated by the service sector; more customer involvement in strategic business decisions; products that are increasingly market focused and much more responsive to the changing needs of the marketplace; the development of technologies that assist customers and employees in the provision of services; employees who have been provided with more discretionary freedom to develop customized solutions to special customer requests and solve customer complaints on the spot with minimal inconvenience; and the emergence of new service industries and the **service imperative,** in which the intangible aspects of the product are becoming the key features that differentiate products in the marketplace.

**service imperative**
Reflects the view that the intangible aspects of products are becoming the key features that differentiate the product in the marketplace.

It is clear that the service sectors in many countries are no longer manufacturing's poor cousin. Services provide the bulk of the wealth and are an important source of employment and exports for many countries. In addition, there are countless examples of firms using the service imperative to drive their businesses forward to profit and growth. Many of these are highlighted in the Services in Action boxes located throughout the remainder of the text.

In the near future, the service boom looks set to continue. It seems unlikely that there will be a successful business that does not make service the foundation of its competitive strategy. The growth in the importance of services is also being reflected in the changing role of the service department within organizations. In the not-so-distant past the service department tended to be viewed as a necessary evil—it was the place that fixed the "box" and made good on failed production promises. As service has become a primary source of differentiation, the service department has grown in importance. Often, it's the firm's reputation for service excellence that enables the firm to charge premium prices in the market—if the premium price of a Dell machine is justified by the quality of the service, then the importance of the service department becomes much greater. Consequently, the service department is now the place to be, rather than a punishment as once it may have been.

## WHAT IS A SERVICE?

Admittedly, the distinction between goods and services is not always perfectly clear. In fact, providing an example of a pure good or a pure service is very difficult. A pure good would imply that the benefits received by the consumer contained no elements supplied by service. Similarly, a pure service would contain no goods elements.

In reality, many services contain at least some goods elements, such as the menu selections at a fine dining restaurant, the bank statement from the local bank, or the written policy from an insurance company. Also, most goods at least offer a delivery service. For example, simple table salt is delivered to the grocery store, and the company that sells it may offer innovative invoicing methods that further differentiate it from its competitors.

The distinction between goods and services is further obscured by firms that conduct business on both sides of the fence. For example, General Motors, the "goods" manufacturing giant, generates 20 percent of its revenue from its financial and insurance businesses, and the carmaker's biggest supplier is BlueCross BlueShield, not a parts supplier for steel, tires, or glass, as most people would think.[1]

**goods**
Objects, devices, or things.

**services**
Deeds, efforts, or performances.

**product**
Either a good or a service.

Despite the confusion, the following definitions should provide a sound starting point in developing an understanding of the differences between goods and services. In general, **goods** can be defined as objects, devices, or things, whereas **services** can be defined as deeds, efforts, or performances.[2] Moreover, note that when the term **product** is mentioned, it refers to both goods and services and is used in such a manner throughout the remainder of this text. Ultimately, the primary difference between goods and services is the property of intangibility—lacking physical substance. As a result of the difference in intangibility, a host of services marketing problems evolve that are not always adequately solved by traditional goods-related marketing solutions. These differences are discussed in detail in Chapter 2.

**scale of market
entities**
The scale that displays a range of products along a continuum based on their tangibility.

## THE SCALE OF MARKET ENTITIES

Another way of looking at the differences between goods and services is provided by the **scale of market entities.** The scale of market entities presented in

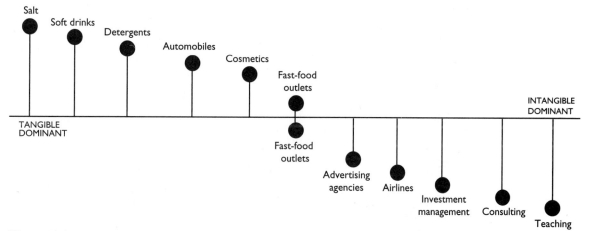

**Figure 1.1**     **Scale of Market Entities**
Source: Adapted from G. Lynn Shostack, "Breaking Free from Product Marketing,"
*The Journal of Marketing* (April 1977), p. 77.

Figure 1.1 displays a range of products based on their tangibility. Pure goods are **tangible dominant,** whereas pure services are **intangible dominant.** Businesses such as fast food, which contain both goods and services components, fall in the middle of the continuum. Firms that manufacture goods and ignore, or at least forget about, the services (intangible) elements of their offering are overlooking a vital component of their businesses.

By defining their businesses too narrowly, these firms have developed classic cases of **marketing myopia.** For example, the typical family pizza parlor may myopically view itself as being in the pizza business. However, a broader view of the business recognizes that it is providing the consumer with a reasonably priced food product in a convenient format surrounded by an experience that has been created for the consumer. Interestingly, adding service aspects to a product often transforms the product from a commodity into an experience, and by doing so increases the revenue-producing opportunities of the product dramatically (see Services in Action 1.1).

According to the scale of market entities, goods are tangible dominant. As such, goods possess physical properties that can be felt, tasted, and seen prior to the consumer's purchase decision. For example, when purchasing a car, the consumer can kick the tires, look at the engine, listen to the stereo, smell that "new car smell," and take the car for a test drive before making the actual purchase. The same cannot be said for the purchase of services—services are intangible dominant.

In contrast to goods, services lack the physical properties that can be sensed by consumers prior to purchase. As a result, a number of marketing challenges immediately become evident. For example, how would you (1) advertise a service that no one can see; (2) price a service that has no cost of goods sold; (3) inventory a service that cannot be stored; and (4) mass-merchandise a service that needs to be performed by an individual (e.g., dentist, lawyer, physician)? Clearly,

**tangible dominant**
Products that possess physical properties that can be felt, tasted, and seen prior to the consumer's purchase decision.

**intangible dominant**
Products that lack the physical properties that can be sensed by consumers prior to the purchase decision.

**marketing myopia**
The practice of too narrowly defining one's business.

SERVICES 1.1

IN ACTION

### Combating the Commodities Trap of the Internet: Developing the Experience Economy

Given the onslaught of e-service companies such as E*TRADE, Priceline. com, and others, many traditional service firms are concerned that their industries are being transformed into commodities. Many of today's Internet companies would like to convince customers that personal service is out and price is the only factor that really matters. For example, commissions for stock trades range from $200 for full-service firms to $8 on the Internet— who needs a broker! For many Internet companies, convincing customers that self-service on the Net is the only way to go is a full-time endeavor— and in many instances it seems to be working.

The servuction model provides the means to develop "compelling experiences" that can be used as a competitive weapon in the war against service commoditization. For example, when priced as a raw *commodity,* coffee is worth little more than $1 per pound. When processed, packaged, and sold in the grocery store as a *good,* the price of coffee jumps to between 5 and 25 cents a cup. When that same cup is sold in a local restaurant, the coffee takes on more *service* aspects and sells for 50 cents to $1 per cup. However, in the ultimate act of added value, when that same cup of coffee is sold within the compelling *experience* of a five-star restaurant or within the unique environment of a Starbucks, the customer gladly pays $2 to $5 per cup. In this instance, the whole process of ordering, creation, and consumption becomes "a pleasurable, even theatrical" experience. Economic value, like the coffee bean, progresses from *commodities* to *goods* to *services* to *experiences.* In the above example, coffee was transformed from a raw commodity valued at approximately $1 per pound to $2 to $5 per cup—a markup of as much as 5000 percent.

Creating "experiences" for customers is not a new idea. The entertainment industry and venues such as Disney have been doing it for years. Others, particularly in the hospitality sector, have recently picked up on the idea and have introduced "experience" product concepts such as Hard Rock Cafe, Planet Hollywood, and Dick's Last Resort. The question facing many other types of service providers is how to transform their own operations into memorable experiences for the customer. One unique example involves a computer repair firm based in Minneapolis, Minnesota. This team of crack technicians, formally called the "Geek Squad," are purposely dressed in white shirts, thin black ties, pocket protectors, and badges. In this instance, a mundane service has been transformed into a memorable event that's fun for the customer. Other profit opportunities have opened up for the firm as demand for "geek memorability" increases.

Source: Joseph B. Pine II and James H. Gilmore, *The Experience Economy* (1999). Harvard Business School Press: Boston, MA.

ERVICES *1.2*
IN
ACTION     **The Challenge of Running a Service Firm**

The American Customer Satisfaction Index (ACSI), which measures customer satisfaction across a variety of sectors, demonstrates the added complexity of managing a service firm. All the top ten firms are traditional goods manufacturers. In contrast, those scoring lowest on the ACSI are service firms (scores are out of a possible 100).

## Top Ten

| | | |
|---|---|---|
| 1. | DaimlerChrysler | 87 |
| 2. | Maytag | 87 |
| 3. | Colgate Palmolive | 86 |
| 4. | GM-Buick | 86 |
| 5. | GM-Cadillac | 86 |
| 6. | Hershey Foods Corporation | 86 |
| 7. | Whirlpool Corporation | 86 |
| 8. | Cadbury Schweppes | 85 |
| 9. | Ford-Lincoln Mercury | 85 |
| 10. | H.J. Heinz Company | 85 (tie) |
| 10. | Kenmore | 85 (tie) |

## Bottom Ten

| | | |
|---|---|---|
| 1. | Wells Fargo & Company | 65 |
| 2. | KFC | 64 (tie) |
| 2. | Police service (metro) | 64 (tie) |
| 2. | Taco Bell | 64 (tie) |
| 2. | US West Inc. | 64 (tie) |
| 3. | American Airlines | 63 |
| 4. | Continental Airlines | 62 |
| 5. | Northwest Airlines | 62 |
| 6. | United Airlines | 62 |
| 7. | USAir Group, Inc. | 62 |
| 8. | McDonald's | 61 |
| 9. | Unicom | 59 |
| 10. | Internal Revenue Service | 51 |

Source: http://www.acsi.asq.org/results.html

managing a service operation seems to be much more complicated than managing a firm that primarily produces and markets goods. Findings from the latest American Customer Satisfaction Index support the added difficulties and challenges associated with managing a service firm (see Services in Action 1.2).

## THE MOLECULAR MODEL

**molecular model**
A conceptual model of
the relationship
between tangible and
intangible components
of a firm's operations.

Another method to understand the differences between goods and services and
gain an appreciation for how they relate to one another is provided by the molecular model. The **molecular model** reinforces our understanding that virtually all
products have both tangible and intangible elements.[3] One of the primary benefits
obtained from developing a molecular model is that it is a management tool that
offers the opportunity to visualize a firm's entire market entity (product). Figure
1.2 provides examples of two such entities: airlines and automobiles. Airlines differ from automobiles in that typically consumers do not physically possess the airline. Consumers in this case purchase the benefit of transportation and all the
corresponding tangible (denoted by solid circles) and intangible elements
(denoted by dashed circles) that are associated with flying. In contrast, a consumer
who purchases an automobile primarily benefits by ownership of the physical possession that renders a service—transportation.

The diagrams provided in Figure 1.2 are oversimplifications of the mix of elements that ultimately comprise the airline experience and car ownership. From
a managerial perspective, an elaboration of these models would identify the tangible and intangible components that need to be effectively managed. For example,
the successful airline experience is not just determined by the safe arrival of

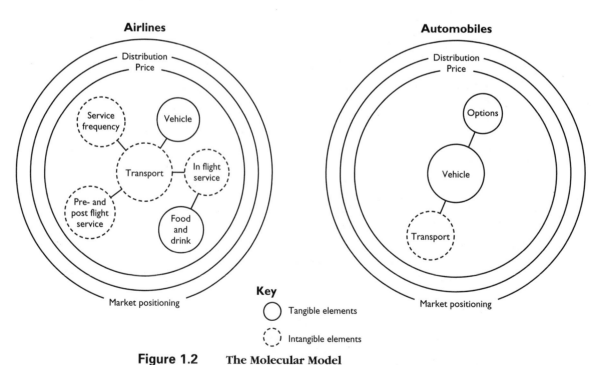

**Figure 1.2**    **The Molecular Model**
Source: Adapted from G. Lynn Shostack, "Breaking Free from Product Marketing,"
*The Journal of Marketing* (April 1977), p. 76.

passengers to their selected destinations. The airline molecular model could easily be expanded to include:

* long-term and short-term parking (intangible element)
* shuttle services (intangible element)
* rental car availability (intangible element)
* flight attendants (tangible element)
* gate attendants (tangible element)
* baggage handlers (tangible element)

Similarly, the automobile model could be expanded to include:

* salespersons on the showroom floor (tangible element)
* financing arrangements (intangible element)
* finance manager (tangible element)
* maintenance and repair services (intangible element)
* mechanics and service representatives (tangible element)

The point of developing molecular models is to develop an appreciation for the intangible and tangible elements that comprise market entities. Once managers understand this broadened view of their products, they can do a much better job of understanding customer needs, servicing those needs more effectively, and differentiating their product offering from competitors. The molecular model also demonstrates that consumers' service "knowledge" and goods "knowledge" are not obtained in the same manner. With tangible dominant products, goods knowledge is obtained by focusing on the physical aspects of the product. In contrast, consumers evaluate intangible dominant products based on the experience that surrounds the core benefit of the product. Hence, understanding the importance and components of the service experience is critical.

## THE SERVICE EXPERIENCE

Because of the dominance of intangibility, service knowledge is acquired differently than knowledge pertaining to goods. For example, consumers can sample soft drinks and cookies prior to purchase. In contrast, a consumer cannot sample a haircut, a surgical procedure, or a consultant's advice prior to the actual purchase. Hence, service knowledge is gained through the experience of receiving the actual service. Ultimately, when a consumer purchases a service, he or she is actually purchasing an experience!

All products, be they goods or services, deliver a bundle of benefits to the consumer.[4] The **benefit concept** is the encapsulation of these benefits in the consumer's mind. For a good such as Tide, for example, the core benefit concept might simply be cleaning; however, for other individuals, it might also include attributes built into the product that go beyond the mere powder or liquid, such as cleanliness, whiteness, and/or motherhood (it's a widely held belief in some cultures that the cleanliness of children's clothes is a reflection on their mother). The determination of what the bundle of benefits comprises—the benefit concept purchased by consumers—is the heart of marketing, and it transcends all goods and services.

**benefit concept**
The encapsulation of the benefits of a product in the consumer's mind.

In contrast to goods, services deliver a bundle of benefits through the experience that is created for the consumer. For example, most consumers of Tide will never see the inside of the manufacturing plant where Tide is produced; they will most likely never interact with the factory workers who produce the detergent or with the management staff that directs the workers; and they will also generally not use Tide in the company of other consumers. In contrast, restaurant customers are physically present in the "factory" where the food is produced. These customers do interact with the workers who prepare and serve the food as well as with the management staff that runs the restaurant. Moreover, restaurant customers consume the service in the presence of other customers, and they may all influence one another's service experience.

# FRAMING THE SERVICE EXPERIENCE: THE SERVUCTION MODEL

**servuction model**
A model used to illustrate the factors that influence the service experience, including those that are visible to the consumer and those that are not.

One particularly simple but powerful model that illustrates factors that influence the service experience is the servuction model depicted in Figure 1.3. The **servuction model** is constructed of two parts: that which is visible to the consumer and that which is not. The visible part of the servuction model consists of three parts: the inanimate environment, contact personnel/service providers, and other customers (denoted as Customer B in Figure 1.3). The invisible component of the model consists of the invisible organization and systems.

## The Inanimate Environment

**inanimate environment**
All the nonliving features that are present during the service encounter.

The **inanimate environment** consists of all the nonliving features that are present during the service encounter. Because services are intangible, they cannot be objectively evaluated as can goods. Hence, in the absence of a tangible product,

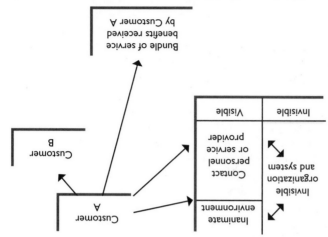

**Figure 1.3** The Servuction Model

Source: Adapted from E. Langeard, J. Bateson, C. Lovelock, and P. Eiglier, *Marketing of Services: New Insights from Consumers and Managers*, Report No. 81-104 (Cambridge, Mass.: Marketing Sciences Institute, 1981).

consumers look for tangible cues that surround the service on which to base their service performance evaluations. For example, you might partially assess the teaching competence of a professor by observing the contents of his or her office. The inanimate environment is full of tangible cues such as furniture, flooring, lighting, music, odors, wall hangings, countertops, and a host of other inanimate objects that vary according to the service being provided. Because of the importance of the physical evidence in consumer perceptions of service performance, Chapter 9 is devoted to the management of the physical evidence.

## Contact Personnel/Service Providers

**Contact personnel** are employees other than the primary service provider who briefly interact with the customer. Typical examples of contact personnel are parking attendants, receptionists, and hosts and hostesses. In contrast, **service providers** are the primary providers of the core service, such as a waiter or waitress, dentist, physician, or college instructor.

Unlike the consumption of goods, the consumption of services often takes place where the service is produced (e.g., dentist's office, restaurant, and hair style salon) or where the service is provided at the consumer's residence or workplace (e.g., lawn care, house painter, janitorial service). Regardless of the service delivery location, interactions between consumers and contact personnel/service providers are commonplace. As a result, the impact of contact personnel and service providers on the service experience can be profound, if not peculiar, at times (see Services in Action 1.3). Because of the importance of service providers and other contact personnel within the service encounter, Chapter 10 is devoted to the management issues of hiring, training, and empowering service personnel.

**contact personnel**
Employees other than the primary service provider who briefly interact with the customer.

**service providers**
The primary providers of a core service, such as a waiter or waitress, dentist, physician, or college instructor.

Contact personnel are extremely important in service interactions, even if they interact only briefly with the customer, just as this supermarket employee is assisting a customer.

SERVICES 1.3

ACTION     **The Girl Obviously Needed a Break!**

Understanding the power of the servuction model comes easily as ample examples exist in the marketplace of how the factors that make up the model impact the customer's overall service experience. The impact of customer contact personnel becomes immediately apparent. My own trip to a fast food restaurant one evening was particularly bizarre, and I am sure that most services marketing students have their own stories to tell about "crazed" service providers.

I entered the popular fast-food restaurant around 8 P.M. There was a young female employee standing behind the counter who I greeted with a "How's it going?" as I approached to place my order. She just looked at me and said, purposely loud enough for the rest of the staff behind her to hear, "I need a break!" I replied, "You do?" She responded, "Yep, I need a break!" She continued, "Do you see that one-eight-hundred number up there on the board to call customer service at corporate headquarters? Would you please call and tell them that I NEED A BREAK!" I smiled and ordered my food, which she gave to me at no charge, announcing, "I need a BREAK!"

As I went to take a seat, I noticed that there were only a few other customers seated in the dining area. We all looked at each other and started to laugh a little. The woman behind the counter then began bouncing on her toes and in a "sing-songy" voice began chanting, "I need a break!" "I need a break!" "I need a break!" At this point, the dining area was in hysterics and watched the next unsuspecting customer come in the door and approach the counter. The employee's greeting to the new customer: "I need a break!" The girl apparently really did need a break!

Source: K. Douglas Hoffman, Co-author: *Essentials of Services Marketing: Concepts, Strategies and Cases.*

## Other Customers

**Customer A**
The recipient of the bundle of benefits that is created through the service experience.

**Customer B**
Other customers who are part of Customer A's experience.

To complete the visible portion of the servuction model, we need to introduce Customers A and B. **Customer A** is the recipient of the bundle of benefits that is created through the service experience. In other words, Customer A is one who most would think of as the customer who actually purchases the service. In contrast, **Customer B** represents all other customers who are part of Customer A's experience. The consumption of services is often described as a "shared experience" because it often occurs in the presence of other customers. Examples include eating at a restaurant, seeing a show at a movie theater, or being a spectator at a sporting event. As is the case with the other visible components of the servuction model, other customers can impact Customer A's service experience.

For example, while eating at a fast food restaurant, a customer was startled when his wife clutched her chest and exclaimed, "Don't look, don't look!" Believing that his wife was experiencing some sort of health-related difficulty, the husband hastily inquired about the reason for the horrific expression now appar-ent on his wife's face. Still clutching her chest, she explained, "Somebody is getting sick over there." Upon hearing this unappetizing news, the husband and wife stared at one another so as to not look in the direction of Customer B's problem while deciding on their next course of action.

In this case, Customer B had indeed made a significant impact on all the restau-rant's customers. In fact, Customer B's actions practically cleared the entire restau-rant in under 60 seconds. Particularly frustrating for the restaurant, it could not have foreseen the "upcoming event" and was unable to take any action that would have minimized its consequences. What's particularly interesting about this sce-nario is that even though the restaurant had no control over Customer B's actions, the event profoundly influenced the couple's future purchase intentions. As a result of their vivid memories of the event, the couple was unable to eat in any of the restaurant's franchises for more than a year and a half.

As a rule, Customer B's influence on Customer A's experience can be active or passive and positive or negative. Unruly customers in a restaurant or movie theater are likely to affect other customers' experiences. Children who cry at church or run through restaurants are also likely to affect others. More passive examples might include customers who show up late for appointments, making each sub-sequent appointment late; an individual who has "big hair" or wears a hat in a movie theater and sits directly in front of another customer; or simply being part of a crowd that as a collective group increases the waiting time for the service being sought for everyone else. In contrast, sporting events and dining experiences are generally more enjoyable when other customers are present.

## Invisible Organization and Systems

Thus far the servuction model suggests that the benefits derived by Customer A are influenced by the interaction with (1) the inanimate environment, (2) contact personnel and/or service providers, and (3) other customers. The benefits are therefore derived from an interactive process that takes place throughout the ser-vice experience. Of course, the visible components of service firms cannot exist in isolation, and indeed, they have to be supported by invisible components. For example, Jim Kelly, the CEO of UPS, attributes much of the firm's success to the behind-the-scenes activities that the customer seldom sees:

> We have 12 mainframes capable of computing 5 billion bits of information every second. We have 90,000 PCs, 80,000 hand-held computers to record driver deliveries, the nation's largest private cellular network and the world's largest BD-2 database designed for package tracking and other customer ship-ping information. To give you an idea of how valuable information has become to our company, that database actually has more storage capacity than the repositories of the U.S. Census Bureau.[5]

The **invisible organization and systems** reflect the rules, regulations, and processes on which the organization is based. As a result, although they are invisi-ble to the customer, they have a profound effect on the consumer's service experi-ence. The invisible organization and systems determine factors such as information

**invisible organization and systems**
That part of a firm that reflects the rules, regulations, and processes on which the organization is based.

forms to be completed by customers, the number of employees working in the firm at any given time, and the policies of the organization regarding countless decisions that may range from the substitution of menu items to whether the firm accepts American Association of Retired Persons (AARP) identification cards for senior citizens' discounts.

The servuction system is what creates the experience for the consumer, and it is the experience that creates the bundle of benefits for the consumer. Perhaps the most profound implication of the model is that it demonstrates that consumers are an integral part of the service process. Their participation may be active or passive, but they are always involved in the service delivery process. This has a significant effect on the nature of the services marketing task and provides a number of challenges that are not typically faced by goods manufacturers.

## WHY STUDY SERVICES?

Over the last 30 years, substantial changes have taken place in the global business environment. Emerging service sectors (profit and nonprofit) are now dominating economies that were once known for their industrial manufacturing strength. Coinciding with the tremendous growth in the global service economy, the demand for individuals who command services marketing expertise is also greatly expanding (see Services in Action 1.4). Practitioners in the services field have quickly learned that traditional marketing strategies and managerial models, with roots based in the goods-producing manufacturing sector, do not always apply to their unique service industries. More specifically, the demand for services marketing knowledge has been fueled by:

- the tremendous growth in service-sector employment
- increasing service-sector contributions to the world economy
- the deregulation of many service industries
- a revolutionary change of managerial philosophy of how service firms should organize their companies

### Service Sector Employment

Throughout the world, the shifting of economies to services is evident.[6] The service industries not only have grown in size, but along the way they also have absorbed all the jobs shed by traditional industries, such as agriculture, mining, and manufacturing. The Bureau of Labor Statistics expects service occupations to account for all net job growth through the year 2005. And the same pattern is being repeated in the European Community and Japan. In 1990 services accounted for 58 percent of gross domestic product (GDP) in Japan and 60 percent of total GDP in the European Community. The service sector employs 133 million persons, or 60 percent of the workforce, in the European Community, whereas industrial employment has declined steadily to 32 percent. Only in Japan has industrial employment continued to increase.[7]

In 1900, 30 percent of the United States' workforce was employed in the service sector; by 1984, service industries employed 74 percent of the workforce; and

SERVICES *1.4*
IN ACTION    **Marketers: The New "It" People in Silicon Valley**

In the fast-paced business world of the Internet, technological and financial smarts are still important, but not as important as a strong background in marketing. According to a recent cover story in *USA Today,* "Pocket protectors are out, [and] marketing skills are in at tech start-ups." Labeled as the new rock stars of the Internet, marketers are in great demand at Internet firms. "This is absolutely a great time for people who have a real interest in marketing," says Paul Ray of Ray & Berenson Recruiting. Other recruiters agree. Powell Recruiting notes that in the early days of the Internet, the big recruiting efforts were geared toward those who understood the infrastructure of the systems. "The pipeline had to get laid." Now, "emerging e-commerce companies [are] looking for CEOs or vice presidents of marketing." The former CEO of MVP.com, John Costello, agrees: "Technology is important, but it is a means to an end. The key to success is building a brand that meets customer needs better than anybody else."

Examples of the power of marketing as it relates to the Internet are numerous. Bob Pittman, who previously had helped launch MTV and was the former CEO of Century 21, is now co-COO of the combined AOL Time Warner. Pittman was able to use his marketing savvy to escalate AOL to one of the most valuable brands in the world. Similarly, William Razzouck, CEO of PlanetRx, recognizes the value of bringing marketers to his company. "The CEO knows how to run a business. But somewhere in the organization you need to have someone who knows marketing." Marketing jobs on the Internet are not just for Fortune 500 refugees. Karen Edwards, a 32-year-old Harvard MBA, became employee number 17 at Yahoo. Karen was one of the early marketing pioneers of the Internet and firmly established the importance of marketing by creating one of the most recognized names on the Internet.

One of the most attractive aspects of marketing on the Internet is the e-commerce attitude toward marketing. Traditionally, marketing has been looked at as a cost—a necessary evil. Within the world of the Internet, marketing is viewed as an investment and marketers do not have to fight to obtain increases in the marketing budget to get the job done.

Source: "Sales Smarts Rule Internet," *USA Today,* January 19, 2000, pp. 1B, 2B.

by the mid-1990s that figure had risen to nearly 80 percent. At the same time, the proportion of the workforce engaged in agriculture declined from 42 percent to just 3 percent.[8] In 1948, 20.9 million persons were employed in goods production of all kinds in America, and 27.2 million persons were employed in services; by the mid-1990s employment in goods production was 19.9 million (with no increase in more than two decades), whereas service employment (including wholesale and retail trade and financial services) had risen to 81.1 million, far more than the total number of persons employed in all sectors 30 years earlier.[9]

a. Employment in manufacturing

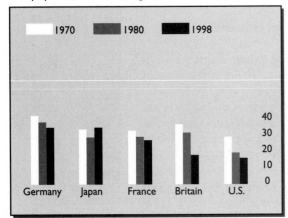

b. Employment in services

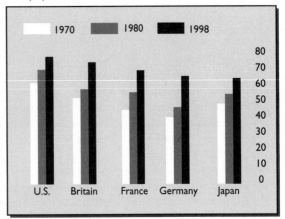

**Figure 1.4**    **Worldwide Changes in Employment**
Source: "The Manufacturing Myth, "*The Economist,* March 19, 1994, p. 91. Adapted
from OECD, National Statistics; and *The World Factbook 1999,* published by the
Central Intelligence Agency (www.odci.gov/cia/publications/factbook/index.html).

Even these numbers conceal the true contribution of services to economic
growth, because service employees on direct payroll of goods companies are
counted as goods industry employees. The service division of IBM, one of the largest
worldwide service organizations, is counted as being in the goods, not the services,
sector because IBM's core business is computers and electronics. A truer picture
can be obtained by looking at the combination of persons employed formally in
the services sector, such as independent architectural or accounting firms, and the
persons employed in those same jobs but working for firms based in the goods sector. Statistics reveal that the number of the latter rose from 4.7 million to 12.7 million between 1948 and 1978. These numbers suggest that the value added to the
economy by "service providers in the goods sector" alone exceeded the value
added by all of manufacturing in 1977, and this is without counting the formal service sector and its value.[10]

One of the consequences of this transformation has been a change in the
shape of the workforce itself. For example, the bulk of new jobs created in America
over the last 30 years have been white-collar jobs in higher-level professional, technical, administrative, and sales positions. Experts monitoring the American economy note that as services have replaced goods as the most dominant force in the
economy, human capital has replaced physical capital as the most important source
of investment. "Americans must unshackle themselves from the notion that goods
alone constitute wealth, whereas services are nonproductive and ephemeral. At
the same time, they should act on Adam Smith's understanding that the wealth of
a nation depends on the skill, dexterity, and knowledge of its people."[11]

## Economic Impact

Worldwide economic growth has fueled the growth of the service sector, as
increasing prosperity means that companies, institutions, and individuals increasingly have become willing to trade money for time and to buy services rather than

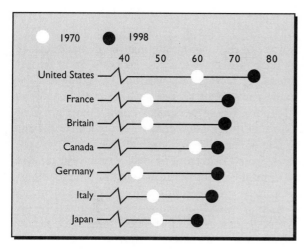

**Figure 1.5**   Service Sector Contributions to Gross Domestic Product by Country (As % of GDP)
Source: "The Final Frontier," *The Economist,* February 20, 1993, p. 63; and *The World Factbook 1999,* published by the Central Intelligence Agency (www.odci.gov/cia /publications/factbook/index .html).

spend time doing things for themselves. New technology has led to considerable changes in the nature of many services and in the development of new services. Higher disposable incomes have led to a proliferation of personal services, particularly in the entertainment sector. Growth has meant an increase not only in the overall volume of services, but in the variety and diversity of services offered.

The result has been phenomenal growth in service industries, shown clearly in economic and trade statistics (Figures 1.4 and 1.5). In economic terms, the service sector now accounts for 58 percent of worldwide gross national product (GNP); in 1980 service business worldwide was valued at $350 billion and accounted for 20 percent of all world trade, whereas by the 1990s that figure had nearly tripled to $1000 billion.[12] All developed economies now have large service sectors, and Japan and Germany in particular have service economies at least as developed as that of the United States. Many service firms now operate internationally, and exports of services are also increasing. The United States remains the world's leading service exporter, with exports valued at $148.5 billion, or 10.5 percent of total worldwide service exports in 1991; service imports amounted to $100 billion in the same year. Given that the American balance of payments deficit in manufactured goods is nearly $130 billion per year, the $50 billion trade surplus in services is obviously vital to the American economy.[13]

The difference in trade figures shows distinctly the growing importance of services and the parallel decline of manufacturing. In 1970 manufacturing accounted for 26 percent of American GDP; by 1991 it accounted for only 21 percent. Even more dramatic declines can be seen in the other two traditional manufacturing nations: In the former West Germany, manufacturing as a percentage of GDP fell from 41 percent in 1970 to 28 percent in 1991, and in Japan the figures show a drop from 36 percent to 29 percent. Yet the idea that an economy cannot survive without relying on manufacturing to create wealth continues to dominate business and political thinking in the West. *The Economist* magazine noted in 1993, "That services cannot thrive without a strong manufacturing 'base' is a claim rarely challenged. The opposite argument—that manufacturing needs services—is hardly ever put."[14] Today it is hard to avoid the conclusion that it is services, not manufacturing, that are the real creators of wealth in many countries.

## The Impact of Deregulation

The growth of the service sector is not the only reason that the demand for services marketing knowledge has increased. Over the past 20 years an increasing interest in the marketing problems of service organizations has paralleled the emergence of competition in many parts of the service sector. The emergence of the need for professional services marketing personnel could then rightly be explained by the lack of a need for it in times when demand exceeded supply and competitive pressures were few. Deregulation has changed all that!

During the 1980s deregulation forced many American service industries such as airlines, financial services, telecommunications, and trucking into the competitive arena for the first time. These industries were forced to be competitive not only with existing firms within their industry, but also with new firms that were permitted to enter the industry due to deregulation. The new firms were leaner, more focused, and extremely competitive.

As competitive pressures increased within the deregulated industries, the need for services marketing knowledge became apparent. In addition to facing new competitors, the deregulated industries found themselves with excess supply and inadequate demand. In an effort to attract more customers, many of the companies began slashing prices. In response, the competition matched or lowered prices even further. Price wars erupted and the consequences for companies that were unprepared were devastating.[15] During the first 12 years of deregulation the U.S. airline industry declined from 36 operators to 11. The number of trucking companies that failed during the 1980s was more than the previous 45 years combined, and the number of commercial banks declined by 14 percent.

It became apparent that competing on pricing alone was leading to devastating results. Services marketing knowledge was needed in nonprice strategy areas such as customer service, customer retention, service differentiation, service quality, image enhancement, and the transformation of public contact employees into marketing-oriented personnel. Service industries such as the health care industry, which in its recent past considered marketing a dirty word and beneath the dignity of its personnel, now embrace marketing techniques as a means for their firms' survival; however, even in the health care field, the transformation remains incomplete. If you ask a room full of health care workers to identify their primary customer, the majority of the room will still answer "the physician," or perhaps more disturbing, "the insurance companies."

**industrial management model** An approach to organizing a firm that focuses on revenues and operating costs and ignores the role personnel play in generating customer satisfaction and sustainable profits.

**market-focused management model** A new organizational model that focuses on the components of the firm that facilitate the firm's service delivery system.

## The Services Revolution: A Change in Perspective

Without a doubt, the world economy is experiencing the most substantial period of change since the industrial revolution. Accompanying this change has been a shift in the philosophy of how service firms should organize their businesses. Many feel that the management model currently in place, the **industrial management model**, needs to be replaced by a **market-focused management model** if service companies are to survive and thrive.[16] Service marketing professionals who understand the pros and cons of both models will be needed to make the necessary changes.

## The Industrial Management Model

The industrial management model, which has its roots in the manufacturing sector, is still employed today by many service organizations. Organizations that follow this approach believe that (1) location strategies, sales promotions, and advertising drive sales revenue; and that (2) labor and other operating costs should be kept as low as possible. In sum, the industrial model focuses on revenues and operating costs and ignores (or at least forgets) the role personnel play in generating customer satisfaction and sustainable profits. Given the role that people play throughout the service encounter, it is sadly ironic that the industrial model continues to be embraced by many of today's companies.

Followers of the industrial model believe that good employees are difficult to find and support the view that "all things being equal, it is better to rely on technology, machines, and systems than on human beings."[17] Followers of this approach believe that most employees are indifferent, unskilled, and incapable of fulfilling any duties beyond performing simple tasks. Consequently, jobs under the industrial model are specifically narrowly defined to leave little room for employees to exercise judgment. Moreover, employees are held to low job performance expectations, their wages are kept as low as possible, and few opportunities for advancement are available.

As opposed to valuing front-line employees, the industrial model places a higher value on upper and middle managers while viewing the people who deliver service to the customer as the "bottom of the barrel." The industrial approach assumes that only managers can solve problems; consequently, resolving customer problems quickly becomes almost impossible as additional steps are built into the service delivery process.

In sum, the industrial model by definition guarantees a cycle of failure because service failures are designed directly into the system. As a result of its lack of support for front-line personnel, the industrial approach, albeit unintentionally, actually encourages front-line employees to be indifferent to customer problems. In essence, the system prohibits the front-line employee from taking any action even if the employee wants to assist in correcting the problem. Customer reactions to this type of treatment are not surprising. Two thirds of customers who defect from their former suppliers do so not because of the product, but because of the indifference and unhelpfulness of the person providing the service.[18]

Adding insult to injury, in further attempts to reduce operating costs, many firms that embrace the industrial model have replaced their full-time personnel with less experienced and less committed part-time personnel. These individuals are paid less than full-time personnel and receive few, if any, company benefits (Table 1.1). In some instances, companies routinely release workers before mandatory raises and other benefits begin, in an attempt to keep operating costs down. Managerial practices such as this have created a new class of migrant worker in the United States—16 million people now travel from one short-term job to another.

The consequences associated with the industrial model in regard to service organizations have been self-destructive. The industrial model has produced dead-end front-line jobs, poor pay, superficial training, no opportunity for advancement, and little, if any, access to company benefits. Moreover, the industrial approach has

## T|A|B|L|E| *1.1*

### Temporary Worker Facts (United States)

Temporary workers earn an average 40% less per hour than full-time workers
55% do not have health insurance
80% work 35 hours a week
25% are under age 25
53% are women; in the total workforce, 47% are women
60% of the women have children under 18
22% of the temp workforce is African American; 11% of the total workforce is African
  American

Source: Modified from "Temporary Workers Getting Short Shrift," *USA Today*, April 11, 1997, p. B1.

led to customer dissatisfaction, flat or declining sales revenues, high employee turnover, and little or no growth in overall service productivity. In sum, many believe that the industrial approach is bad for customers, employees, shareholders, and the countries in which this philosophy continues to be embraced.

## The Market-Focused Management Model

In contrast to the industrial management model, proponents of the new market-focused management model believe that the purpose of the firm is to serve the customer.[19] Consequently, logic suggests that the firm should be *organized in a manner that supports the people who serve the customer*. By following this approach, service delivery becomes the focus of the system and the overall differential advantage in terms of competitive strategy.

**services triangle**
The framework that supports the market-focused management model by depicting the relationships among the systems, the service strategy, and the people, with the customer in the center of the triangle, interacting with each group.

The framework that supports this change in philosophy is based on the services triangle presented in Figure 1.6.[20] The **services triangle** depicts six key relationships. First, the firm's service strategy must be communicated to its customers. If superior service is the focus of the organization and the key point of differentiation on which it distinguishes itself from competitors, the customer needs to be made aware of the firm's commitment to excellence. Second, the service strategy also needs to be communicated to the firm's employees. Good service starts at the top, and management must lead by example. If top management is not committed to the process, front-line employees who interact with the firm's customers will be ineffective at best.

The third relationship depicted within the triangle focuses on the consistency of the service strategy and the systems that are developed to run the day-to-day operations. The systems, like those discussed as the invisible components of the servuction model, should flow logically from the service strategy and enhance the service encounter for employees and customers alike. The fourth relationship involves the impact of organizational systems on customers. Interactions with the firm's systems should facilitate the customer's service experience. Too often, systems are designed for the sole purpose of keeping a small minority of customers

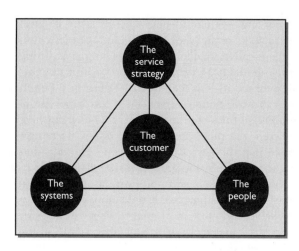

**Figure 1.6**    The Service Triangle
Source: Adapted from Karl Albrecht and Ron Zemke, *Service America* (Homewood, Ill.: Dow Jones-Irwin, 1985), pp. 31–47.

from taking advantage of the company. Meanwhile, the majority of honest customers are forced to suffer through systems and policies that treat them as suspects instead of valued assets.

The fifth relationship within the services triangle pinpoints the importance of organizational systems and employee efforts. Organizational systems and policies should not be obstacles in the way of employees wishing to provide good service. For example, a frustrated Sam's Club (a division of Wal-Mart Stores) employee informed a customer that policy dictated that he was not permitted to help customers load merchandise into their vehicles. His frustration stemmed from the firing of an employee who, a week earlier, turned down a woman's request for assistance. It later became apparent that the employee was fired not so much for his refusal, but due to the content of his response: "Hey, lady, this ain't Food Lion [a grocery store]!" Finally, the last relationship is perhaps the most important of them all—the customer/service provider interaction. These interactions represent **critical incidents** or **"moments of truth."** The quality of this interaction is often the driving force in customer satisfaction evaluations.

**critical incidents ("moments of truth")** The customer/service provider interaction that is often the key in customer satisfaction evaluations.

The market-focused management model, supported by the services triangle, is based on the belief that employees, in general, want to do good work. Hence, proponents of this model are more optimistic regarding their faith in human nature. As such, the market-focused management approach encourages investing in people as much as it does investing in machines. For example, the primary purpose of technology is viewed as a means to assist front-line personnel, not to replace them or monitor and control their activities. In addition, data once collected and controlled by middle managers is now made readily available to front-line personnel.

## A COMPARISON OF THE TWO APPROACHES

In contrast to the industrial model, the market-focused management model recognizes that employee turnover and customer satisfaction are clearly related. Consequently, the market-focused management model emphasizes the recruitment and training of front-line personnel and ties pay to performance at every level throughout the organization. The benefits of superior training and compensation programs are clear. For example, the turnover rate for employees not participating in training programs at Ryder Truck Rental is 41 percent. In comparison, employees who did participate in training turned over at the rate of 19 percent.[21] Better-trained and better-paid employees provide better service, need less supervision, and are more likely to stay on the job. In turn, their customers are more satisfied, return to make purchases more often, and purchase more when they do return.

Past studies have also indicated that the correlation between customer satisfaction and employee turnover is also affected by the proportion of full-time to part-time employees.[22] As you might expect, the higher the proportion of full-time to part-time employees, the more satisfied the customers. Full-time employees tend to be more knowledgeable, more available, and more motivated to satisfy customers.

In further contrast to the industrial management model philosophy, proponents of the market-focused management model refuse to sacrifice competent and motivated full-time personnel in the name of lower operating costs. The benefits of maintaining a highly motivated full-time staff are clear. As evidence, companies that pay their employees more than competitors pay often find that, as a percent of sales, their labor costs are actually lower than industry averages.

One final difference between the industrial management model and the market-focused management model is that the latter attempts to utilize innovative data to examine the firm's performance by looking beyond generally accepted accounting principles. Traditional accounting principles reflect the sales orientation of the old industrial management model. New accounting measures that reflect the focus on customer orientation need to be developed and refined. The new measures of interest include the value of customer retention as opposed to obtaining new customers, the costs of employee turnover, the value of employee training, and the monetary benefits associated with service recovery—making amends with the customer when the service delivery system fails.

Given what has been presented thus far, it should be clear that the field of services marketing is much broader than what is discussed in a traditional marketing class. As such, many of the concepts and strategies presented in this text have their origins in management science, human resources, and psychology as well as marketing. Ultimately, services marketing is about managing the compromising relationships that must exist among marketing, operations, and human resources.

## SUMMARY

Services permeate every aspect of our lives; consequently, the need for services marketing knowledge is greater today than ever before. The distinction between goods and services is often unclear. In general, goods are defined as objects, devices, or things, whereas services are defined as deeds, efforts, or performances. Very few products can be classified as pure services or pure products. The scale of market entities and the molecular model presented in Figures 1.1 and 1.2 illustrate how various goods and services vary according to their tangibility.

When a consumer purchases a service, he or she purchases an experience. The four components of the servuction system create the experience for the consumer—the inanimate environment, service providers/contact personnel, other customers, and the invisible organization and systems. In turn, the service experience that is created delivers a bundle of benefits to the consumer. In contrast to the production of goods, the servuction model demonstrates that service consumers are an integral part of the service production process.

Recent developments have fueled the demand for services marketing knowledge. First, tremendous growth has occurred in service-sector employment and in the service sector's contribution to many countries' gross domestic product. For example, experts suggest that by the year 2020, 90 percent of the United States labor force will be employed in service or service-related industries. The demand for services marketing knowledge has also increased as a result of the deregulation of many service industries. Many of these industries are facing situations in which supply exceeds demand, combined with fierce competitive pressures for the first time.

The demand for services marketing knowledge has also been fueled by a change in perspective in how service firms should manage their companies. Organizations that follow the traditional industrial model believe that (1) location strategies, sales promotions, and advertising drive sales revenue; and (2) labor and other operating costs should be kept as low as possible. The industrial model focuses on revenues and operating costs and ignores, or at least forgets, the role personnel play in generating customer satisfaction and sustainable profits.

In contrast, proponents of the new market-focused management model believe that the purpose of the firm is to serve the customer. Consequently, logic suggests that the firm should organize itself in a manner that supports the people who serve the customer. By following this approach, service delivery becomes the focus of the system and the overall differential advantage in terms of competitive strategy. The basic concepts and outcomes associated with the market-focused management approach are illustrated in the services triangle depicted in Figure 1.6.

# Key Terms

| | |
|---|---|
| Benefit concept | Marketing myopia |
| Contact personnel | Molecular model |
| Critical incidents | Product |
| Customer A | Scale of market entities |
| Customer B | Service imperative |
| Goods | Service providers |
| Inanimate environment | Services |
| Industrial management model | Services triangle |
| Intangible dominant | Servuction model |
| Invisible organization and systems | Tangible dominant |
| Market-focused management model | |

## Discussion Questions

1. Why is it difficult to distinguish between many goods and services?
2. Define the following terms: goods, services, products.
3. Discuss the relevance of the scale of market entities to marketing myopia.
4. Develop a molecular model for your College of Business.
5. Discuss the consequences of the industrial management model.
6. What benefits are associated with better-paid and better-trained personnel?
7. Discuss the relevance of the services triangle to the market-focused management model.
8. What is meant by the chapter's opening quote: "Economic value, like the coffee bean, progresses from commodities to goods to services to experiences." (Hint: see Services in Action 1.1).

## Notes

1. "The Final Frontier," *The Economist,* February 20, 1993, p. 63.
2. Leonard L. Berry, "Services Marketing Is Different," *Business Magazine* (May-June 1980), 24–29.
3. This section adapted from G. Lyn Shostack, "Breaking Free from Product Marketing," *Journal of Marketing* 41 (April 1977), 73–80.
4. This section adapted from John E. G. Bateson, *Managing Services Marketing,* 2nd ed. (Fort Worth, Tex.: The Dryden Press, 1992), 8–11.
5. Jim Kelley, "From Lip Service to Real Service: Reversing America's Downward Service Spiral," *Vital Speeches of the Day,* 64, no. 10 (1998), 301–304.
6. "The Manufacturing Myth," *The Economist,* March 19th, 1994, p. 91.
7. Sernos, *Annual Statistics 1990, Eurostat,* 1993.
8. See Peter Mills, *Managing Service Industries* (Cambridge, Mass.: Ballinger, 1986), 3.
9. *Statistical Abstract of the United States,* 1993.
10. Eli Ginzberg and George J. Vojta, "The Service Sector of the U.S. Economy," *Scientific American* 244, no. 3 (March 1981), 31–39.
11. Ibid.
12. "The Final Frontier," p. 63.
13. *International Trade* 1991/1992 (1993).
14. *The Economist,* Feb. 20, 1992.
15. Leonard L. Berry and A. Parasuraman, "Building a New Academic Field—The Case of Services Marketing," *Journal of Retailing,* 69 (Spring 1993), pp. 1, 13.
16. Leonard A. Schlesinger and James L. Heskett, "The Service-Driven Service Company," *Harvard Business Review* (September-October 1991), 71–75.
17. Ibid., 74.
18. Ibid., 71.
19. Ibid., 77.

20. Karl Albrecht and Ron Zemke, Service America (Homewood, Ill.: Dow Jones-Irwin, 1985), 31–47.
21. Schlesinger and Heskett, "The Service-Driven Service Company," 76.
22. Ibid.

# chapter 2

# Fundamental Differences Between Goods and Services

## CHAPTER OBJECTIVES

This chapter discusses the basic differences between goods and services, the marketing problems that arise due to these differences, and possible solutions to the problems created by these differences.

After reading this chapter, you should be able to:

- Define the characteristics of intangibility, inseparability, heterogeneity, and perishability.
- Discuss the marketing problems associated with intangibility and their possible solutions.
- Discuss the marketing problems associated with inseparability and their possible solutions.
- Discuss the marketing problems associated with heterogeneity and their possible solutions.
- Discuss the marketing problems associated with perishability and their possible solutions.
- Discuss the impact of intangibility, inseparability, heterogeneity, and perishability on marketing's relationship to other functions within the service organization.

"It is wrong to imply that services are just like goods 'except' for intangibility. By such logic, apples are just like oranges, except for their 'appleness.' "

G. Lynn Shostack

# Introduction

In the beginning the work toward accumulating services marketing knowledge was slow. In fact, not until 1970 was services marketing even considered an academic field. It then took 12 more years before the first international conference on services marketing was held in the United States in 1982.[1] One of the reasons the field of services marketing was slow to grow within the academic community was that many marketing educators felt the marketing of services was not significantly different from the marketing of goods. Markets still needed to be segmented, target markets still needed to be sought, and marketing mixes that catered to the needs of the firm's intended target market still needed to be developed. However, since those early days, a great deal has been written regarding specific differences between goods and services and their corresponding marketing implications. The majority of these differences are primarily attributed to four unique characteristics—intangibility, inseparability, heterogeneity, and perishability.[2]

Services are said to be intangible because they are performances rather than objects. They cannot be touched or seen in the same manner as goods. Services are produced by people; consequently, variability is inherent in the production process. Rather, they are experienced, and consumers' judgments about them tend to be more subjective than objective. Inseparability of production and consumption refers to the fact that whereas goods are first produced, then sold, and then consumed, services are sold first and then produced and consumed simultaneously. For example, an airline passenger first purchases a ticket and then flies, consuming the in-flight service as it is produced.

Heterogeneity refers to the potential for service performance to vary from one service transaction to the next. This lack of consistency cannot be eliminated as it frequently can be with goods. Finally, perishability means that services cannot be saved; unused capacity in services cannot be reserved, and services themselves cannot be inventoried.[3]

The sections that follow focus on each of these four unique characteristics that service industries share and that differentiate their marketing from the marketing of goods. Because services fall in many places along the continuum that ranges from tangible dominant to intangible dominant, as described by the scale of market entities in Chapter 1, the magnitude and subsequent impact that each of these four characteristics has on the marketing of individual services will vary.

## INTANGIBILITY: THE MOTHER OF ALL UNIQUE DIFFERENCES

Of the four unique characteristics that distinguish goods from services, **intangibility** is the primary source from which the other three characteristics emerge. As discussed in Chapter 1, services are performances, deeds, and efforts. As a result, services cannot be seen, felt, tasted, or touched in the same manner as tangible goods can be sensed.

For example, compare the differences between purchasing a movie ticket and purchasing a pair of shoes. The shoes are tangible goods, so the shoes can be objectively evaluated before the actual purchase. You can pick up the shoes, feel

**intangibility**
A distinguishing characteristic of services that makes them unable to be touched or sensed in the same manner as physical goods.

Subway passengers purchase a ticket for the intangible benefit of transportation.

the quality of materials from which they are constructed, view their specific style and color, and actually put them on your feet and sample the fit. After the purchase, you can take the shoes home, and you now have ownership and the physical possession of a tangible object.

In comparison, the purchase of a movie ticket entitles the consumer to an experience. Because the movie experience is intangible, it is subjectively evaluated. For example, consumers of services must rely on the judgments of others who have previously experienced the service for prepurchase information. Because the information provided by others is based on their own sets of expectations and perceptions, opinions will differ regarding the value of the experience. For example, if you ask five moviegoers what they thought about the film *American Beauty*, they are likely to express five different opinions ranging from "I loved it!" to "I hated it!" After the movie the customer returns home with a memory of the experience and retains the physical ownership of only a ticket stub.

As a result of the intangibility of services, a number of marketing challenges arise that are not normally faced when marketing tangible goods. More specifically, these challenges include the lack of service inventories, the lack of patent protection, the difficulties involved in displaying and communicating the attributes of the service to its intended target market, and the special challenges involved in the pricing of services. The following sections address many of these challenges and offer possible solutions to minimize their effects.

## Marketing Problems Caused by Intangibility

### LACK OF ABILITY TO BE STORED

Because of their intangibility, services cannot be inventoried. As a result, supplies of services cannot be stored as buffers against periods of high demand. For example, physicians cannot produce and store physical exams to be used at a later date; movie seats that are not sold for the afternoon matinee cannot be added to the theater for the evening show; and the Auto Club cannot inventory roadside service to be distributed during peak periods. Consequently, customers are commonly forced to wait for desired services, and service providers are limited in how much they can sell by how much they can produce. The bottom line is that the inability to maintain an inventory translates into constant supply and demand problems. In fact, the lack of service inventories presents so many challenges to marketers that it has earned its own name—perishability. Specific problems associated with perishability and the strategies associated with minimizing its effects are discussed in much greater detail later in the chapter.

## LACK OF PROTECTION BY PATENTS

Because of the property of intangibility, services are not patentable. What is there to patent? Human labor and effort are not protected. Firms sometimes advertise that their processes are patented; however, the reality is that the tangible machinery involved in the process is protected, not the process itself. One challenge faced by the lack of patent protection is that new or existing services may be easily copied. Consequently, it is difficult to maintain a firm's differential service advantage over attentive competitors for long periods.

## DIFFICULTY IN DISPLAYING OR COMMUNICATING SERVICES

The promotion of services presents yet another set of special challenges to the service marketer and is discussed in greater detail in Chapter 8. The root of the challenge is this: How do you get customers to take notice of your product when they cannot see it? As an example, consider the insurance industry. Insurance is a complicated product for many people. As customers, we cannot see it, we are unable to sample it prior to purchase, and many of us do not understand it. Insurance seems to cost an awful lot of money, and the benefits of its purchase are not realized until some future time, if at all. In fact, if we do not use it, we are supposed to consider ourselves lucky. Why should spending thousands of dollars a year on something the customer never uses make them feel lucky? To say the least, due to intangibility the task of explaining your product's merits to consumers is highly challenging.

## DIFFICULTY IN PRICING SERVICES

Typically products' prices are based on cost-plus pricing. This means that the producing firm figures the cost of producing the product and adds a predetermined markup to that figure. The challenge involved in the pricing of services is that there is no cost of goods sold! The primary cost of producing a service is labor.

As an example, let's say you are very competent in the field of mathematics. Taking notice of your expertise in the field, a student who is struggling with his math assignments wants to hire you as a tutor. What would you charge per hour? What are the costs involved?

Based on feedback from other services marketing classes faced with this example, students usually begin laughing and indicate that they would engage in price-gouging and charge the student $100 per hour. After reality sets in, students quickly realize that it is very difficult to place a value on their time. Specific considerations usually emerge, such as how much money the tutor could make doing something else and the opportunity costs associated with not being able to lie around the apartment and enjoy free time. Typically the consensus is that the tutor should charge something comparable to the charges of all the other tutors. The problem with this response is that it still does not answer the original question, that is, how was this competitive-based price originally calculated?

## Possible Solutions to Intangibility Problems

### THE USE OF TANGIBLE CLUES

**physical evidence/
tangible clues**
The physical
characteristics that
surround a service to
assist consumers in
making service
evaluations, such as the
quality of furnishings,
the appearance of
personnel, or the quality
of paper stock used to
produce the firm's
brochure.

Given the absence of tangible properties, services are evaluated differently from goods. In many instances, consumers look at the **physical evidence** or tangible clues that surround the service to assist them in making service evaluations. **Tangible clues** may include such evidence as the quality of furniture in a lawyer's office, the appearance of the personnel in a bank, and the quality of paper used for an insurance policy.

Tangible clues are also often used in services advertising. As previously discussed, because of intangibility, firms often find it difficult to effectively communicate their service offerings to consumers. Returning to the insurance example, the major challenge of an insurance firm is to communicate to consumers in a 30-second television commercial what the specific firm has to offer and how the firm is different from every other insurance firm. One strategy embraced by many service firms is to use some form of tangible clues in advertising. Prudential uses "the rock" and promises "rock-solid protection." AllState shows us "helping hands" and promises that "you're in good hands with AllState." The list goes on and on—Merrill Lynch has "the bull," Nationwide promotes "blanket-wide protection," Kemper has "the cavalry," Travelers utilizes "the umbrella," and Transamerica promotes the shape of its office building as "the power of the pyramid." The lesson that all these companies have learned over time is that the services they sell are abstract to the consumer and therefore difficult for the average consumer to understand. The answer to this challenge was to provide tangible clues that were easily understood by the public and directly related to the bundle of benefits the services provided. For example, State Farm's credo of "Like a good neighbor, State Farm is there" reinforces the firm's commitment to looking after its customers when they are in need.

### THE USE OF PERSONAL SOURCES OF INFORMATION

Because consumers of services lack any objective means of evaluating services, they often rely on the subjective evaluations relayed by friends, family, and a variety of other opinion leaders. For example, when moving to a new town and seeking a family physician, consumers will often ask co-workers and neighbors for referrals. Hence, in purchasing services, personal sources of information become more important to consumers than **nonpersonal sources** such as the mass media (e.g., television, radio, Yellow Pages, etc.).

**nonpersonal sources**
Sources such as mass
advertising that
consumers use to
gather information
about a service.

**personal sources**
Sources such as friends,
family, and other
opinion leaders that
consumers use to
gather information
about a service.

**Personal sources** of information are a source of word-of-mouth advertising. One strategy often used to stimulate word-of-mouth advertising is to offer incentives to existing customers to tell their friends about a firm's offerings. Apartment complexes often use the incentive of a free month's rent to encourage tenants to have their friends rent vacant units. Service firms sometimes simulate personal communication while using the mass media. Mass advertising that features customer testimonials simulates word-of-mouth advertising and can be very effective. Examples include hospital advertisements featuring former recipients of major surgery who are now living normal and happy lives and insurance companies that feature victims of hurricanes, fires, and earthquakes who were satisfied with their insurance protection when they needed it most.

## CREATION OF A STRONG ORGANIZATIONAL IMAGE

Another strategy utilized to minimize the effects of intangibility is to create a strong organizational image. Because of intangibility and the lack of objective sources of information to evaluate services, the amount of perceived risk associated with service purchases is generally greater than their goods counterparts. In an attempt to combat the higher levels of perceived risk, some service firms have spent a great deal of effort, time, and money in developing a nationally known **organizational image.** A well-known and respected corporate image lowers the level of perceived risk experienced by potential customers and, in some instances, lowers the reliance on personal sources of information when making service provider choices. As an example, the consumer who is moving to a new town may bypass personal referrals and automatically seek out the nearest Nationwide Insurance agent for home and auto insurance needs based on the firm's organizational image. In this case, the national firm, through image development and subsequent brand awareness, has developed a differential advantage over small, local firms of which the consumer is unaware.

**organizational image**
The perception an organization presents to the public; if well-known and respected, lowers the perceived risk of potential customers making service provider choices.

# INSEPARABILITY

One of the most intriguing characteristics of the service experience involves the concept of inseparability. **Inseparability** refers to (1) the service provider's physical connection to the service being provided; (2) the customer's involvement in the service production process; and (3) the involvement of other customers in the service production process. Unlike the goods manufacturer, who may seldom see an actual customer while producing the good in a secluded factory, service providers are often in constant contact with their customers and must construct their service operations with the customer's physical presence in mind. This interaction between customer and service provider defines a **critical incident.** Critical incidents represent the greatest opportunity for both gains and losses in regard to customer satisfaction and retention.

**inseparability**
A distinguishing characteristic of services that reflects the interconnection among the service provider, the customer involved in receiving the service, and other customers sharing the service experience.

**critical incident**
A specific interaction between a customer and a service provider.

## Marketing Problems Caused by Inseparability

### PHYSICAL CONNECTION OF THE SERVICE PROVIDER TO THE SERVICE

For the production of many services to occur, the service provider must be physically present to deliver the service. For example, dental services require the physical presence of a dentist or hygienist, medical surgery requires a surgeon, and in-home services such as carpet cleaning require a service provider to complete the work. Because of the intangibility of services, the service provider becomes a tangible clue on which at least part of the customer's evaluation of the service experience becomes based.

As tangible clues, service providers are particularly evaluated based on their use of language, clothing, personal hygiene, and interpersonal communication skills. Many service firms have long appreciated the impact that public contact personnel have on the firm's overall evaluation. For example, wearing uniforms or conforming to dress codes is often required of service employees to reflect professionalism.

Other service firms such as restaurants often place their most articulate and attractive personnel in public contact positions such as wait staff, host/hostess, and bartender. Personnel who do not have these skills and traits are often employed in areas that are invisible to the consumer, such as the kitchen and dish room areas.

Face-to-face interactions with customers makes employee satisfaction crucial. Without a doubt, employee satisfaction and customer satisfaction are directly related. Dissatisfied employees who are visible to customers will translate into lower consumer perceptions of the firm's performance. The importance of employee satisfaction within service firms cannot be overemphasized. Customers will never be the number one priority in a company where employees are treated poorly. Employees should be viewed and treated as internal customers of the firm. This issue is discussed in much greater detail in Chapter 10.

## INVOLVEMENT OF THE CUSTOMER IN THE PRODUCTION PROCESS

The second defining characteristic of inseparability is that the customer is involved in the production process. The customer's involvement in the production process may vary from (1) a requirement that the customer be physically present to receive the service, such as in dental services, a haircut, or surgery; (2) a need for the customer to be present only to start and stop the service, such as in dry cleaning and auto repair; and (3) a need for the customer to be only mentally present, such as in participation in college courses that are transmitted via the Internet. Each scenario reflects different levels of customer contact, and as a result each service delivery system should be designed differently.

Unlike goods, which are produced, sold, and then consumed, services are first sold and then produced and consumed simultaneously because of inseparability. For example, a box of breakfast cereal is produced in a factory, shipped to a store where it is sold, and then consumed by customers at a place and time of the customer's choosing. In contrast, services are produced and consumed simultaneously, so consumption takes place inside the service factory. As a result, service firms must design their operations to accommodate the customer's presence (see Services in Action 2.1). Inseparability makes the service factory become another tangible clue that consumers consider when making service quality evaluations.

Overall, as customer contact increases, the efficiency of the operation decreases. The customer's involvement in the production process creates uncertainties in the scheduling of production. More specifically, the customer has a direct impact on the type of service desired, the length of the service delivery process, and the cycle of service demand. Attempting to balance consumer needs with efficient operating procedures is a delicate art.

Regarding the cycle of demand, restaurants would be more efficient if consumers would smooth their demands for food throughout the day as opposed to eating primarily during breakfast, lunch, and dinner hours. As one frustrated, senior-citizen McDonald's employee told a customer, "These people would get better service if they all didn't show up at the same time!" Further complications arise as consumers also dictate the nature or type of service needed. This is particularly frustrating for health care workers who provide services to waiting emergency-room patients. Every patient has a different need, some needs are more immediate than

SERVICES *2.1*
IN
ACTION

### Health Care Industry: Embracing Rapid Response Program

Generally, when someone from the health care industry starts talking about rapid response programs, most of us would think that it pertained to how fast the ambulance could get to the scene of the accident. However, in this instance, "rapid response" refers to how quickly the health care institution can identify customer service problems and resolve them. Hospitals are a good example of how the unique characteristic of inseparability affects everyday operations by being an integral component of production process.

When the University of Chicago Hospital opened its Center for Advanced Medicine in 1996, it also implemented a customer satisfaction initiative that has been copied by several other hospitals since. As part of the center's rapid response program, all patients are encouraged to complete detailed customer satisfaction surveys. The surveys are then processed and sent to the unit involved within 24 hours. Managers are then strongly encouraged to respond to any issues that need to be addressed as quickly as possible. The Center for Advanced Medicine and its enlightened counterparts have learned much from the patient satisfaction surveys. Some of the improvements that have been implemented in these various health care institutions include the following:

- Outdoor bike racks were added.
- More wheelchairs were made available.
- Clerical staff were trained in telephone etiquette.
- Patient parking prices were reduced.
- Efforts to reduce waiting time were implemented.
- Employee award programs were started to reward extra kindness to patients.
- A noisy nurses station was moved away from patient rooms.
- Room service was started for a maternity ward.
- Patients were given prepaid phone cards to encourage them to complete customer satisfaction forms.

The bottom-line for many of these institutions is that "clinical excellence" is not enough to succeed in a competitive health care market. Listening and responding to customer feedback that pertains to areas other than their medical needs is just as important. This type of philosophy is an amazing turnaround for an industry that not too long ago recognized no long-term value in regard to marketing.

Source: Adapted from Dave Carpenter, "Fast Fixes for Bad Service," *Hospitals & Health Networks* 16, no. 74 (March, 2000), 16.

others, and you never know what the next ambulance will deliver. Obviously, this scenario is frustrating for waiting patients as well as for the health care providers. Finally, even when consumer needs are the same, some consumers ask more questions and/or need more attention than others, thereby affecting the length of demand. As a result, fixed schedules are difficult to adhere to without delays.

During the customer's interaction with the service provider, the customer provides inputs into the service production process. As such, the customer often plays a key role in the successful completion of the service encounter. For example, a patient who feels ill must be able to accurately describe his or her symptoms to a physician to receive proper treatment. Not only must the symptoms be described accurately, but the patient must also take the recommended dosage of medicines prescribed. In this case, the customer (the patient) becomes a key player in the service production process and can directly influence the outcome of the process itself. Failure of the patient to follow recommended instructions will likely lead to a dissatisfactory service experience. The customer will probably blame the service provider, even though the service provider fulfilled his or her part of the transaction.

Another issue directly related to the consumer's presence in the service factory concerns the appearance of the service factory itself. Service factories must be built with consumers' presence in mind. Consequently, the service factory not only provides the service, but in and of itself becomes a key tangible clue in the formation of consumer perceptions regarding service quality. The design and management of the service factory is discussed in much greater detail in Chapter 9.

## INVOLVEMENT OF OTHER CUSTOMERS IN THE PRODUCTION PROCESS

The presence of other customers during the service encounter is the third defining characteristic of inseparability. Because production and consumption occur simultaneously, several customers often share a common service experience. This "shared experience" can be negative or positive.

The marketing challenges presented by having other customers involved in the production process generally reflect the negative aspects of their involvement (see Services in Action 2.2). Restaurants once again provide an ideal setting for examples of negative events, including smokers violating the space of nonsmokers and vice-versa, families with young children sharing the same space with adult couples seeking a quiet dining experience, drunk customers interacting with sober ones, and the occasional lovers' quarrel that spills over into the aisles. Overall, the primary challenge concerns effectively managing different market segments with different needs within a single service environment.

The impact of "other customers" is not always negative. On the positive side, audience reaction in the form of laughter or screams of terror often enhances the show at a movie theater. Similarly, a crowded pub may facilitate the opportunity for social interaction, and a happy crowd may make a concert an even more pleasurable event. As social creatures, humans tend to frequent places of business and feel more comfortable in places that have other customers in them. In fact, the lack of other customers may act as a tangible clue that the impending experience may be less than satisfactory. For example, would you rather eat at an unfamiliar restaurant

SERVICES 2.2
IN
ACTION          **Passenger-Induced Turbulence**

The service encounter is often a shared experience where customers can have a profound impact on each other's overall experience. Nowhere is this more evident than sharing an airplane with hundreds of "other customers." During the late 1990s and into the second millennium, the popular press has been full of stories that describe incidents of "air rage" or "passenger-induced turbulence." Areas known to contribute to disruptive behavior include alcohol abuses, sexual misconduct, smoking in nonsmoking areas, failure to follow boarding instructions, violating carry-on baggage restrictions, and a variety of other confrontations dealing with lapses in creature comforts, crew training, and food quality.

Clearly the airlines are concerned and are part of the problem. During the summer of 2000, the CEO of United Airlines publicly apologized to the airline's customers during United's stalled contract negotiations with employees. Numerous flights were canceled or delayed. United admitted in television commercials that their airline had failed to deliver on its basic promise—to service its customers. The voice of the customer is being heard loud and clear as customers are letting the airlines know when violations of customer service occur. Air traveler complaints are up 25 percent, and the number of incidents involving passengers interfering with flight crews has more than tripled over the last 10 years. However, the airlines themselves are not totally to blame for what's going on in the skies up above. Clearly, some customers are out of control.

One of the more recent problems deals with increasing numbers of passengers having sex in their seats or in airplane restrooms. "It's uninhibited up there these days," says psychologist Christina Lawrence, a former United Airlines flight attendant. Airline consultant Agnes Huff agrees: "People used to be discreet. But more and more passengers these days are pushing the limits." In one case involving a South African Airways jumbo jet, a couple disrobed and began having sex in full view of other customers. Flight attendants summoned the captain, who was quoted as saying, "This plane is not a shag house!"—South African slang for bordello. In another incident, numerous members of a company sales group became intoxicated and began to expose themselves to other passengers. One couple, who was part of the group, consummated their office romance on the plane while being cheered on by other members of the group. The captain cut off liquor sales, but the group continued to drink by opening their own personal bottles of liquor, which were purchased at the duty-free shop before boarding. In yet another incident, the flight attendant of a Delta Airlines flight felt compelled to knock on the door of the plane's bathroom. Inside, a Southern California woman was having sex with her boyfriend. After the passenger responded that she "would be out in a second," the frustrated flight attendant began citing federal rules that restrict the plane from landing until all passengers are seated.

> The policing of customer misconduct aboard planes is a tricky issue. According to one flight attendant, "At 37,000 feet, you don't have the option of throwing people out like you can in a cocktail lounge." In training sessions dealing with air rage, flight attendants are advised to be tactful, address passengers by name, and communicate on an eye-to-eye level and in a non-threatening tone.

Source: Adapted from Asra Q. Nomani, "In the Skies Today, A Weird New Worry: Sexual Misconduct," *Wall Street Journal,* June 10, 1998, p. A1; Frances Fiorino, "Passengers Who Carry Surly Bonds of Earth Aloft," *Aviation Week and Space Technology* 149, no. 5 (December 28, 1998), 123.

that had no cars in the parking lot, or would you choose to eat at a restaurant down the street with a full parking lot? In the absence of other information, which restaurant would potential customers believe would be the better dining experience?

## SPECIAL CHALLENGES IN MASS PRODUCTION OF SERVICES

One final obstacle presented by inseparability is how to successfully mass produce services. The problems pertaining to mass production are twofold. First, because the service provider is directly linked to the service being produced, an individual service provider can produce only a limited supply. Consequently, the question arises: How does one provide enough service product to meet the demand of the mass market? The second problem directly relates to the consumer's involvement in the production process. Consumers interested in a particular provider's services would have to travel to the provider's location. If goods were constrained by inseparability, every consumer in the world who was interested in purchasing a Chevrolet Corvette would have to travel to the Corvette's production facility in Bowling Green, Kentucky, to purchase a vehicle. Hence, one of the problems associated with inseparability is how to sell intangible products to a geographically widespread target market.

### Possible Solutions to Inseparability Problems

#### EMPHASIS ON SELECTING AND TRAINING PUBLIC CONTACT PERSONNEL

Just as customers are part of the service process, contact personnel are part of the service experience as well. Contact personnel, unlike goods, are not inanimate objects, and being human, they exhibit variations in behavior that cannot be controlled by the service process. Moreover, the attitudes and emotions of contact personnel are apparent to the customer and can affect the service experience for better or worse. This is evident in Services in Action 1.3, where the employee tells everyone willing to listen that she "needs a break." Surly or unhappy employees can affect both customers with whom they come into direct contact and other employees. On the other hand, a bright, highly motivated employee can create a more pleasant service experience for everyone who comes into contact with that person.[4]

As a result of the frequency and depth of interactions between service providers and consumers, **selection** of service personnel with superior communication and public relations skills is a must. In addition, **training** personnel once they are on the job is also necessary. A case in point is UPS. UPS handles more than 3 billion packages and 5.5 percent of the United States' GNP annually. The behind-the-scenes activities of hiring, training, and rewarding employees is directly related to how well customers are served. UPS believes in building trust and teamwork and making employees loyal to the company's mission. The company spends more than $300 million a year on training, paying full-time drivers (on average) more than $50,000 a year, and surveying its employees for suggestions. The company is virtually 100 percent employee owned.[5]

Too often, newly hired employees are often left to fend for themselves. A large percentage of consumer complaints about service focuses on the action or inaction of employees. Critics of service quality have focused on "robotic" responses by staff and on staff who have been trained in using the technology associated with the business but not in dealing with different types of customers. Experts in service quality believe that employees must also be trained in "soft" management skills such as reliability, responsiveness, empathy, assurance, and managing the tangibles that surround the service.

## CONSUMER MANAGEMENT

The problems created by inseparability can also be minimized through effective **consumer management.** Separating smokers from nonsmokers is an example of one way to minimize the impact of other customers. Sending a patient insurance forms and information about office procedures before the patient arrives may help control the length of the service encounter. Restaurant reservation systems may help smooth out demand created by traditional cycles. Providing delivery services may eliminate the need for many consumers to be physically present within a service factory, thereby increasing the firm's operating efficiencies. Finally, isolating the technical core of the business from the consumer allows for consumer involvement but limits the customer's direct impact on the firm's operations. For example, the typical dry cleaning firm is designed so that customers are attended to at the front counter; meanwhile, the core operation is located in an area of the building where customer contact is not permitted. The management of service consumers is discussed in much greater detail in Chapter 11.

## USE OF MULTISITE LOCATIONS

To offset the effects of inseparability on centralized mass production, service firms that mass produce do so by setting up multiple locations. Typical examples include H & R Block accounting services, Hyatt Legal Services, and LensCrafters (an eye-care service firm). **Multisite locations** serve at least two purposes. First, because the consumer is involved in the production process, multisite locations limit the distance the consumer must travel to purchase the service. Second, each multisite location is staffed by different service providers, each of whom can produce their own supply of services to serve their local market. Multisite locations

**selection and training**
A strategy that minimizes the impact of inseparability by hiring and educating employees in such a way that the customer's service experience is positive and the employees are properly equipped to handle customers and their needs.

**consumer management**
A strategy service personnel can implement that minimizes the impact of inseparability, such as separating smokers from nonsmokers in a restaurant.

**multisite locations**
A way service firms that mass produce combat inseparability, involving multiple locations to limit the distance the consumers have to travel and staffing each location differently to serve a local market.

Multisite locations such as this LensCrafters limit the distance the consumer has to travel to purchase the service and provide their own staff to serve the local market.

**factories in the field**
Another name for multisite locations.

act as **factories in the field.** Without them, every consumer who desired legal services would have to travel to a single location that housed all the lawyers in the country plus all their clients for that day. Obviously, this is not practical or realistic.

The use of multisite locations is not without its own set of special challenges. Each site is staffed by different service providers who have their own personalities and their own sets of skills. For example, every H & R Block representative does not have the same personality and same set of skills as the founder, Henry Block. The differences in personnel are particularly troublesome for service firms attempting to establish a consistent image by providing a standardized product. The variability in performance from one multisite location to another and even from one provider to another within a single location leads us to the next special characteristic of services—heterogeneity.

## HETEROGENEITY

One of the most frequently stressed differences between goods and services is the lack of ability to control service quality before it reaches the consumer. Service encounters occur in real time, and consumers are already involved in the factory, so if something goes wrong during the service process, it is too late to institute quality-control measures before the service reaches the customer. Indeed, the customer (or other customers who share the service experience with the primary customer) may be part of the quality problem. If, in a restaurant, something goes wrong during a meal, that service experience for a customer is bound to be affected; the manager cannot logically ask the customer to leave the restaurant, re-enter, and start the meal again.

**Heterogeneity,** almost by definition, makes it impossible for a service operation to achieve 100 percent perfect quality on an ongoing basis. Manufacturing operations may also have problems achieving this sort of target, but they can isolate mistakes and correct them over time, since mistakes tend to reoccur at the same points in the process. In contrast, many errors in service operations are one-time events; the waiter who drops a plate of food in a customer's lap creates a service failure that can be neither foreseen nor corrected ahead of time.[6]

Another challenge heterogeneity presents is that not only does the consistency of service vary from firm to firm and among personnel within a single firm, but it also varies when interacting with the same service provider on a daily basis. For example, some McDonald's franchises have helpful and smiling employees, whereas other franchises employ individuals who act like robots. Not only can this be said for different franchises, but the same is true within a single franchise on a daily basis because of the mood swings of individuals.

**heterogeneity**
A distinguishing characteristic of services that reflects the variation in consistency from one service transaction to the next.

## Marketing Problems Caused by Heterogeneity

The major obstacles presented by heterogeneity translate into the fact that service standardization and quality control are difficult to achieve. Why is this so? Because of the inseparability characteristic previously discussed, you now know that in many instances the service provider must be present to provide the service. Firms such as financial institutions employ a multitude of front-line service providers. As an individual, each employee has a different personality and interacts with customers differently. In addition, each employee may act differently from one day to the next as a result of mood changes as well as numerous other factors. As an example, many students who work as wait staff in restaurants frequently acknowledge that the quality of interaction between themselves and customers will vary even from table to table.

The marketing problems created by heterogeneity are particularly frustrating. A firm could produce the best product in the world, but if an employee is having a "bad day," a customer's perceptions may be adversely affected. The firm may never have another opportunity to serve that customer. Returning to our McDonald's example, the franchisee may pay $500,000 for the franchise and the right to sell a "proven product." However, the real secret to each individual franchise's success is the 16-year-old behind the counter who is interacting with customers and operating the cash register. Can you imagine the franchisee who has just spent $500,000 for the franchise trying to sleep at night while thinking that his or her livelihood depends on the "kid" behind the counter? It does!

## Possible Solutions to Heterogeneity Problems

### CUSTOMIZATION

One possible solution to the problems created by heterogeneity is to take advantage of the variation inherent in each service encounter and **customize** the service. Producers of goods typically manufacture the good in an environment that is isolated from the customer. As such, mass-produced goods do not meet individual

**customize**
Taking advantage of the variation inherent in each service encounter by developing services that meet each customer's exact specifications.

customer needs. However, because both the customer and the service provider are involved in the service delivery process, it is easier to customize the service based on the customer's specific instructions.

Note that there are tradeoffs associated with a customized service. On one hand, if everything is provided exactly to the customer's specifications, the customer ends up with a service that meets his or her specific needs; however, the service will take longer to produce. Consequently, the provider can obtain higher prices, which lead to higher profit margins for the provider. Providers pursuing a customization strategy focus on profit margins on a per-customer basis as opposed to achieving profits through a mass volume or turnover strategy.

The downside of providing customized services is threefold. First, customers may not be willing to pay the higher prices associated with customized services. Second, the speed of service delivery may be an issue. Customized services take extra time to provide and deliver, and the customer may not have the luxury of waiting for the final product . Finally, customers may not be willing to face the uncertainty associated with customized services. Each customized service is different, so the customer is never sure exactly what the final product will be until it is delivered. So, do customers prefer customized services over standardized services? Intuitively, most believe that customers would prefer customized products; however, the answer is, "It depends." If price, speed of delivery, and consistency of performance are issues, the customer will probably be happier with a standardized service.

## STANDARDIZATION

**standardizing**
Reducing variability in service production through intensive training of providers and/or replacing human labor with machines.

**Standardizing** the service is a second possible solution to the problems created by heterogeneity. Service firms can attempt to standardize their service through intensive training of their service providers. Training certainly helps reduce extreme variations in performance. However, despite all the training in the world, employees ultimately will continue to vary somewhat from one transaction to the next. One way to eliminate this variance is to replace human labor with machines.

An automatic teller machine (ATM) and an automated car wash are prime examples of standardized services that appeal to consumers' convenience-oriented needs. Taco Bell is now experimenting with a system that allows its customers to enter their own orders from one of several computer screens. This type of system minimizes the amount of customer contact and variations in quality during the ordering process.

On the positive side, standardization leads to lower consumer prices, consistency of performance, and faster service delivery. However, some consumer groups believe that standardization sends the message that the firm does not really care about individual consumer needs and is attempting to distance itself from the customer. Perceived distancing is particularly an issue as organizations are increasingly replacing human labor with machines such as automated phone services. In many instances, customers are becoming increasingly frustrated when forced to select from a menu of phone messages. Of course, standardization and customization do not have to be all-or-nothing propositions. Numerous companies, particularly in the travel and tourism arena, provide a standardized core product and allow consumers to select options to semi-customize their final outcome.

## PERISHABILITY

The fourth and final unique characteristic that distinguishes goods from services is perishability. **Perishability** also distinguishes goods from services and refers to the fact that services cannot be inventoried. Unlike goods that can be stored and sold at a later date, services that are not sold when they become available cease to exist. For example, hotel rooms that go unoccupied for the evening cannot be stored and used at a later date; airline seats that are not sold cannot be inventoried and added on to aircraft during the holiday season, when airlines seats are scarce; and service providers such as dentists, lawyers, and hairstylists cannot regain the time lost from an empty client appointment book.

Some service firms find it possible to inventory part of their service process. McDonald's, for example, can inventory hamburgers for a limited period; however, a McDonald's outlet cannot inventory the entire service experience. Spare capacity in the system on a Thursday evening cannot be saved for the Friday evening peak, nor can the hamburgers.

The inability to inventory creates profound difficulties for marketing services. When dealing with tangible goods, the ability to create an inventory means that production and consumption of the goods can be separated in time and space. In other words, a good can be produced in one locality in the United States and transported for sale in another. Similarly, a good can be produced in January and not released into the channels of distribution until June. In contrast, most services are consumed at the point of production. From a goods-marketing manager's point of view, concerns about when and where the customer consumes the product are important in understanding consumer behavior and motivation but are largely irrelevant in day-to-day operations.

The existence of inventory also greatly facilitates quality control in goods-producing organizations. Statistical sampling techniques can be used on ware house stock to select individual items for testing, to the point of destruction if necessary (e.g., automobile crash tests). The sampling process can be set up to ensure minimum variability in the quality of product released for distribution. Quality-control systems also provide numerical targets against which managers can work. It is thus possible for Procter & Gamble to produce tens of millions of packages of Tide laundry detergent that are essentially identical. In contrast, when you purchase a room at a hotel, you are likely to experience a wide range of factors that may influence your good night's sleep. Issues such as air conditioning, plumbing, and noisy neighbors factor into the hotel guest's experience.

Finally, in goods-producing businesses, inventory performs the function of separating the marketing and the production departments. In many organizations, stock is actually sold at a transfer price from one department to another. The two parts of the firm have what amounts to a contract for quality and volumes. Once this contract has been negotiated, each department is able to work relatively independently of the other. In service firms, however, marketing and operations constantly interact with each other—because of the inability to inventory the product.[7]

**perishability**
A distinguishing characteristic of services in that they cannot be saved, their unused capacity cannot be reserved, and they cannot be inventoried.

## Marketing Problems Caused by Perishability

Without the benefit of carrying an inventory, matching demand and supply within most services firms is a major challenge. In fact, because of the unpredictable nature of consumer demand for services, the only way that supply matches demand is by accident! For example, as a manager, try to imagine scheduling cashiers at a grocery store. Although we can estimate the times of the day that the store will experience increased demand, that demand may fluctuate widely within any 15-minute interval. Simply stated, consumer demand for many services at any given time is unpredictable. The lack of inventories and the need for the service provider to provide the service leads to several possible demand and supply scenarios. In contrast to their service-producing counterparts, manufacturers of goods could more easily adapt to these scenarios through selling or creating inventories.

### HIGHER DEMAND THAN MAXIMUM AVAILABLE SUPPLY

Within this scenario, consumer demand simply outpaces what the firm can supply, which results in long waiting periods and, in many cases, unhappy customers. Business may be lost to competitors as waiting times become too excessive for consumers to endure. Ironically, in cases of consistent excess consumer demand, consumers may continue to attempt to patronize a firm out of curiosity and/or the social status obtained by telling others of their experience: "We finally got in to see the show!"

### HIGHER DEMAND THAN OPTIMAL SUPPLY LEVEL

In many instances, the consequences associated with demand exceeding optimal supply may be worse than when demand exceeds maximum available capacity. By accepting the customer's business, the firm implicitly promises to provide the same level of service that it always provides, regardless of the quantity demanded. For example, it seems that airlines typically staff flights with the same number of flight attendants regardless of the number of tickets actually sold. However, when demand exceeds optimal levels, the service provided is generally at inferior levels. As a result, customer expectations are not met, and customer dissatisfaction and negative word-of-mouth publicity results.

When demand exceeds optimal supply levels, the temptation is to accept the additional business. However, in many instances the firm's personnel and operations are not up to the task of delivering service effectively beyond optimal demand levels. For example, suppose that a landscaper became very successful in a short time by providing high-quality services to upscale customers. As the word spread to other potential clients, demand for the landscaper's time dramatically increased. As the landscaper's firm expanded to serve new clients via the purchase of new equipment and the hiring of new personnel, the landscaper quickly found that he was losing control over the quality of service delivered by his firm. His new personnel simply did not provide the same level of service that his original customer base had grown accustomed to receiving. Over time the landscaper lost his new clients as well as his old clients, and he eventually filed for bankruptcy. In this case the service traits of perishability, inseparability, and heterogeneity all took their toll on the business.

## LOWER DEMAND THAN OPTIMAL SUPPLY LEVEL

As we discussed earlier, providing the exact number of grocery store cashiers needed at any given time is a challenge for most store managers. One solution would be to staff each line with a full-time cashier; however, this strategy would result in an inefficient deployment of the firm's resources. During times when demand is below optimal capacity, resources are underutilized (e.g., cashiers are standing around), and operating costs are needlessly increased.

## DEMAND AND SUPPLY AT OPTIMAL LEVELS

The optimal scenario is to have demand match supply. This scenario describes the situation in which customers do not wait in long lines and in which employees are utilized to their optimal capacity. Because services cannot be stored, a buffer to ease excess demand cannot be developed. Moreover, service providers are not machines and cannot produce a limitless supply. Consequently, service demand and supply rarely balance. Customers do at times experience lengthy waits, and service providers are sometimes faced with no one to serve.

## Possible Solutions to Perishability Problems

Because service demand and supply balance only by accident, service firms have developed strategies that attempt to adjust supply and demand to achieve a balance. The strategies presented below are possible solutions to overcome the difficulties associated with the perishability of services. The first group of strategies concerns the management of the firm's demand. This discussion is followed by a second group of strategies that focuses on managing supply.

## DEMAND STRATEGY: CREATIVE PRICING

**Creative pricing** strategies are often used by service firms to help smooth demand fluctuations. For example, offering price reductions in the form of "earlybird specials" and "matinees" have worked well for restaurants and movie theaters, respectively. Price-conscious target markets, such as families with children, are willing to alter their demand patterns for the cost savings. At the same time, service firms are willing to offer price reductions to attract customers during nonpeak hours, thereby making their operations more efficient. By shifting demand to other periods, the firm can accommodate more customers and provide better service during periods in which demand in the past has been (1) turned away because of limited supply, and (2) not served as well as usual because demand surpasses optimal supply levels.

**creative pricing**
Pricing strategies often used by service firms to help smooth demand fluctuations, such as offering "matinee" prices or "earlybird specials" to shift demand from peak to nonpeak periods.

Creative pricing has also been used to target specific groups such as senior citizens, children and their parents (families), and college students. This type of pricing strategy has not only helped smooth fluctuating demand but has also aided in separating diverse target markets from sharing the same consumption experience at the same time. For example, by providing family-type specials during late afternoon and early evening hours, a restaurant significantly reduces the amount of potential conflict between its "family customers" and its "adult customers," who generally dine later in the evening.

Price incentives have also been recently used to persuade customers to use the company's Web site. Customers who are willing to place their orders on the Internet may do so 24 hours a day, 7 days a week. Increasing Web site usage reduces demand for personal service during regular business hours.

## DEMAND STRATEGY: RESERVATION SYSTEMS

**reservation system**
A strategy to help smooth demand fluctuations in which consumers ultimately request a portion of the firm's services for a particular time slot.

Another common strategy used to reduce fluctuations in demand is to implement a **reservation system** by which consumers ultimately reserve a portion of the firm's services for a particular time slot. Typical service firms that use reservation systems include restaurants, doctors of all varieties, golf courses (tee times), and tanning salons. On the plus side, reservations reduce the customer's risk of not receiving the service and minimize the time spent waiting in line for the service to be available. Reservation systems also allow service firms to prepare in advance for a known quantity of demand. Consequently, the customer and the firm benefit from improved service.

Despite the advantages of a reservation system, a host of disadvantages also accompanies this strategy. First, someone must maintain the reservation system, which adds additional cost to the operation. Next, customers do not always show up on time or sometimes fail to show up at all. As a result, the operation ends up with unused services and lost revenues. For example, a common strategy for some golfers (particularly young and single) is to reserve a tee time at two or three different golf courses at two or three different times on the same day. Depending on their whims and which golf course they decide to play that particular day, the golfers choose which tee time to use, leaving the other two golf courses holding the tee for a foursome that is not going to show up. Given that the greens fee for an 18-hole round averages at least $25, the golf course has just lost $100 that it could have otherwise collected by filling the spot with another foursome.

Another drawback of reservation systems is that they offer to the customer an implied guarantee that the service will be available at a specified time, thereby increasing the customer's expectation. All too often, this implied guarantee is not met. For example, customers with early appointments may show up late, causing a chain reaction of delayed appointments for the rest of the day. Similarly, the rate at which restaurant tables turn over is difficult to determine and is further compounded by the size of the party sitting at a table compared with the size of the party waiting for a table. In addition, medical doctors schedule as many as four patients at the same appointment time in an attempt to serve patient demand. Despite the use of reservation systems, customers may still end up waiting and become even more unhappy (compared with a "first come, first serve" system) because of the implied promise made by the reservation system.

## DEMAND STRATEGY: DEVELOPMENT OF COMPLEMENTARY SERVICES

**complementary services**
Services provided for consumers to minimize their perceived waiting time, such as driving ranges at golf courses, arcades at movie theaters, or reading materials in doctors' offices.

The trials and tribulations associated with perishability can also be buffered by developing **complementary services** that directly relate to the core service offering. A lounge in a restaurant is a typical example of a complementary service that not only provides the space to store customers while they wait but also provides the restaurant with an additional source of revenue. Similarly, golf courses often provide putting greens for their customers as a form of complementary service. Although free of charge to customers, the putting green occupies the customer's time, thereby minimizing their perceived waiting time. The result is more satisfied customers. Other complementary services that have been developed to help manage demand include driving ranges at golf courses, arcades at movie theaters, reading materials in doctors' offices, and televisions in the waiting areas of hospital emergency rooms.

## DEMAND STRATEGY: DEVELOPMENT OF NONPEAK DEMAND

The effects of perishability can also be modified by developing **nonpeak demand**. This strategy can reduce the effects of perishability in two ways. First, the supply of service demanded during peak periods can be increased by utilizing nonpeak periods to prepare for high-demand periods. For example, employees can be cross-trained to perform a variety of other duties to assist fellow personnel (e.g., dishwashers may trained to set up and clear tables) during peak demand periods. In addition, although services cannot be stored, the tangibles associated with the service (such as salads at a restaurant) can be prepared and ready prior to the service encounter. Advance preparation activities such as these free personnel to perform other types of service when needed.

> **nonpeak demand**
> A strategy in which service providers use their downtime by marketing to a different segment that has a different demand pattern than the firm's traditional market segment.

Nonpeak demand can also be developed to generate additional revenues. Many fast-food restaurants such as McDonald's and Wendy's did not always serve breakfast. The restaurants were simply closed to the public while personnel prepared for the lunch and dinner crowds. By offering a breakfast menu, the fast-food industry significantly increased its revenues.

Nonpeak demand is generally generated by marketing to a market segment that has a different demand pattern than the firm's traditional segment. For example, golf courses have filled nonpeak demand by marketing to housewives, senior citizens, and shift workers (e.g., factory workers, nurses, students, and teachers) who use the golf course during the morning and afternoon hours, which are traditionally slow periods during weekdays. These groups exhibit different demand patterns than traditional golfers, who work from 8:00 to 5:00 and demand golf course services in the late afternoons, early evenings, and on weekends.

As another example of marketing to different market segments with different demand patterns, one golf course struggled for many years to find a league that was willing to play on Friday evenings and large enough (profitable enough) to justify reserving a space. After an examination of the problem, it became clear that many of the course's current customers spent Friday evenings with their significant others. As a result, a couples league was started and became so successful that a waiting list to join the league now exists. In fact, the couples league has become so popular that it holds parties during the off-season, when the golf course is closed due to inclement weather.

## SUPPLY STRATEGY: PART-TIME EMPLOYEE UTILIZATION

In addition to managing consumer demand, the effects of perishability can also be minimized through strategies that make additional supply available in times of need. One such supply strategy is the use of **part-time employees** to assist

> **part-time employees**
> Employees who typically assist during peak demand periods and who generally work fewer than 40 hours per week.

during peak demand periods. Retailers have successfully used part-time employees to increase their supply of service during the holidays for years.

The advantages of employing part-time workers as opposed to adding additional full-time staff include lower labor costs and a flexible labor force that can be employed when needed and released during nonpeak periods. On the negative side, using part-time employees sometimes causes consumers to associate the firm with lower job skills and lack of motivation and organizational commitment. Such traits subsequently lead to dissatisfied customers. However, these disadvantages appear most commonly in organizations who staff their operations with part-time workers on a full-time basis as opposed to employing part-time employees only during peak demand periods.

## SUPPLY STRATEGY: CAPACITY SHARING

**capacity sharing**
Strategy to increase the supply of service by forming a type of co-op among service providers that permits co-op members to expand their supply or service as a whole.

Another method of increasing the supply of service is **capacity sharing,** forming a type of service co-op with other service providers, which permits the co-op to expand its supply of service as a whole. For example, many professional service providers are combining their efforts by sharing the cost and storage of expensive diagnostic equipment. By sharing the cost, each service firm is able to supply forms of service it may not otherwise be able to provide because of the prohibitive costs associated with such equipment. In addition, the funds saved through cost sharing are freed to spend on additional resources such as equipment, supplies, and additional personnel, thereby expanding the supply of service to consumers even further.

## SUPPLY STRATEGY: ADVANCE PREPARATION FOR EXPANSION

**expansion preparation**
Planning for future expansion in advance and taking a long-term orientation to physical facilities and growth.

Although the strategy of **expansion preparation** does not provide a "quick fix" to the supply problems associated with perishability, it may save months in reacting to demand pressures, not to mention thousands of dollars in expansion costs. In the effort to prepare in advance for expansion, many service firms are taking a long-term orientation with regard to constructing their physical facilities.

For example, one local airport was built with future expansion in mind. This facility was built on a isolated portion of the airport property, where no adjoining structure would interfere with future growth. All plumbing and electrical lines were extended to the ends on both sides of the building and capped, making "hook-ups" easier when expansion becomes a reality. Even the road leading to the terminal was curved in the expectation that new terminal additions will follow along this predetermined pattern.

In contrast, one Lowe's hardware superstore apparently failed to keep expansion in mind. Only four and a half years after a new Lowe's was built, another Lowe's superstore was built directly next to the existing facility. However, the relatively new "old Lowe's" had to be torn down to provide adequate parking for the new store because of the proximity of other store locations. The Lowe's superstore turned out to be a great facility that supplies its customers with additional services despite the puzzling manner in which the new store was built. In fact, billboards advertising the new store, as you might expect, do not stress the vast amounts of lumber and hardware available. Instead, the billboards promote, "Lowe's...Check Out All of Our New Services."

## SUPPLY STRATEGY: UTILIZATION OF THIRD PARTIES

A service firm can also expand its supply of a service through use of **third parties**. Travel agencies are a typical example. Travel agents provide the same information to customers as an airline's own representatives. This third-party arrangement, however, enables the airline to reduce the number of personnel it employs to make flight reservations and lets it redirect the efforts of existing personnel to other service areas. The cost savings associated with using third parties is evidenced by the airlines' willingness to pay commissions to travel agencies for booking flights.

Note that although the use of third parties increases the supply of service, this type of arrangement may expose customers to competitive offerings as well. As a result, a tradeoff does exist. Many third parties, such as travel agents, represent a variety of suppliers. A customer who intended to book a flight on British Airways may end up taking a Lufthansa flight because of a more compatible flight schedule and/or a less expensive fare. This type of competitive information would not have been available if the customer had called British Airways directly to make the flight reservation.

**third parties**
A supply strategy in which a service firm uses an outside party to service customers and thereby save on costs, personnel, etc.

## SUPPLY STRATEGY: INCREASE IN CUSTOMER PARTICIPATION

Another method for increasing the supply of service available is to have the customer perform part of the service. For example, in many fast-food restaurants, **customer participation** means giving customers a cup and expecting them to fill their own drink orders. In other restaurants, customers make their own salads at a "salad bar," dress their own sandwiches at the "fixings bar," prepare plates of food at the "food bar," and make their own chocolate sundaes at the "dessert bar."

Without a doubt we are performing more and more of our own services every day. We pump our own gas, complete our own bank transactions at automatic teller machines, and bag our own groceries at wholesale supermarkets. In fact, one of the major advantages of a Web site is that it enables customers to help themselves, or at least be more prepared when they request help from service personnel. However, although self-service does free employees to provide other services, a number of advantages and disadvantages are associated with customer participation. The willingness of customers to provide their own service is generally a function of convenience, price, and customization. For example, automatic teller machines offer the customer the convenience of 24-hour banking, bagging groceries is generally accompanied by lower grocery prices, and Dell Computers provides customers the opportunity to configure their own personal computer order to their own individual specifications.

**customer participation**
A supply strategy that increases the supply of service by having the customer perform part of the service, such as providing a salad bar or dessert bar in a restaurant.

In contrast, customer participation may also be associated with a number of disadvantages that predominantly concern loss of control. In many instances, the more the customer becomes a major player in the production of the service, the less control the service firm is able to maintain over the quality of the service provided. For example, the physician who instructs a patient to administer his own medicine relinquishes control over the outcome of the prescribed care. Quality control may also suffer as a result of confused customers who decrease the efficiency of the operating system. Customer confusion in a self-service environment is likely to affect not only the outcome of the confused customer's service, but also the delivery process of other customers who are sharing that customer's experience. For example, customers who are standing in line behind a customer who is using an ATM for the first time experience the effects of the new customer's learning curve.

The loss of quality control may also be accompanied by the loss of control over operating costs. Self-service, particularly in the food industry, is associated with waste as a result of abuse of the system. Customers may take more food than they would normally order and then consume or share food with nonpaying friends.

Finally, increasing customer participation may be interpreted by some customers as the service firm's attempt to distance itself from the customer. As a result, the image of an uncaring, unresponsive, and out-of-touch firm may develop, driving many customers away to full-service competitors. Hence, the tradeoff is apparent. While increasing customer participation frees service providers to provide additional services and may provide the customer with increased convenience, opportunities for customization, and reduced prices, this strategy may also create unhappy customers who are forced to fend for themselves.

## The Role of Marketing in the Service Firm

This chapter has outlined some of the factors that characterize services marketing in general, and some of the problems that service marketers face. Because of the effects of intangibility, inseparability, heterogeneity, and perishability, marketing plays a very different role in service-oriented organizations than it does in pure goods organizations. As a result of the effects of intangibility, inseparability, heterogeneity, and perishability, this chapter has shown how closely the different components of the service organization are interwoven. The invisible and visible parts of the organization, the contact personnel and the physical environment, the organization and its customers, and indeed the customers themselves are all bound together by a complex series of relationships. Consequently the marketing department must maintain a much closer relationship with the rest of the service organization than is customary in many goods businesses. The concept of the operations department being responsible for producing the product and the marketing department being responsible for selling it cannot work in a service firm.

## SUMMARY

The major differences between the marketing of goods and the marketing of services are most commonly attributed to four distinguishing characteristics—intangibility, inseparability, heterogeneity, and perishability. This chapter has discussed the marketing challenges presented by these four characteristics and possible solutions that minimize their impact on service firms.

Intangibility means that services lack physical substance and therefore cannot be touched or evaluated like goods. The marketing challenges associated with intangibility include difficulties in communicating services to consumers, pricing decisions, patent protection, and storage of services for future use. Strategies developed to offset the challenges posed by intangibility include the use of tangible clues, organizational image development, and the development of personal sources of information that consumers access when selecting service providers.

Inseparability reflects the interconnection between service providers and their customers. Unlike the producers of goods, service providers engage in face-to-face interactions with their customers, who are directly involved in the service production process. Strategies developed to minimize the challenges of inseparability include the selective screening and thorough training of customer contact personnel, the implementation of strategies that attempt to manage customers throughout the service experience, and the use of multisite facilities to overcome the inseparability difficulties associated with centralized mass production.

Heterogeneity pertains to the variability inherent in the service delivery process. The primary marketing problem associated with heterogeneity is that standardization and quality control are difficult for a service firm to provide on a regular basis. Service firms typically react to heterogeneity in two diverse directions. Some firms try to standardize performance by replacing human labor with machines. In contrast, other firms take advantage of the variability by offering customized services that meet individual customer needs. Neither strategy is universally superior, because customer preference for customization versus standardization is dependent on price, speed of delivery, and consistency of performance.

Perishability refers to the service provider's inability to store or inventory services. Services that are not used at their appointed time cease to exist. Moreover, because services cannot be inventoried, the few times that supply matches demand often occur by accident. A variety of strategies have been developed to try to offset the potential problems created by perishability. Some strategies attack the problems by attempting to manage demand, while others attempt to manage supply. Demand management strategies include creative pricing strategies, reservation systems, staging demand through complementary services, and developing non-peak demand periods. Supply management strategies include using part-time employees, capacity sharing, third-party utilization, increasing customer participation in the production process, and preparing in advance for future expansion to reduce the response time in reaction to demand increases.

Because of the challenges posed by intangibility, inseparability, heterogeneity, and perishability, marketing plays a very different role in service-oriented organizations than it does in pure goods organizations. Traditional management practices, which work under the premises that the operations department is solely responsible for producing the product and that the marketing department is solely responsible for selling it, cannot work in a service firm. The four characteristics presented in this chapter that distinguish the marketing of goods from the marketing of services provide ample evidence that the invisible and visible parts of the organization, the contact personnel, the physical environment, and the organization and its customers are bound together by a complex set of relationships. As a result, marketing must maintain a much closer relationship with the rest of the service organization than is customary in a traditional goods manufacturing plant.

# Key Terms

| | |
|---|---|
| Capacity sharing | Multisite locations |
| Complementary services | Nonpeak demand |
| Consumer management | Nonpersonal sources |
| Creative pricing | Organizational image |
| Critical incident | Part-time employees |
| Customer participation | Perishability |
| Customize | Personal sources |
| Expansion preparation | Physical evidence/tangible clues |
| Factories in the field | Reservation system |
| Heterogeneity | Selection and training |
| Inseparability | Standardizing |
| Intangibility | Third parties |

# Discussion Questions

1. Discuss the ordering of the following terms as they relate to goods and services: consumption, production, and purchase.
2. Why is the pricing of services particularly difficult in comparison with the pricing of goods?
3. What strategies have the insurance industry utilized in its attempt to minimize the effects of intangibility?
4. Discuss the implications of having the customer involved in the production process.
5. Discuss the reasons that centralized mass production of services is limited.
6. Why are standardization and quality control difficult to maintain throughout the service delivery process?
7. Which is better for consumers: (1) a customized service or (2) a standardized service? Explain.
8. What are the limitations associated with a service firm's inability to maintain inventories?

# Notes

1. Leonard L. Berry and A. Parasuraman, "Building a New Academic Field—The Case of Services Marketing," *Journal of Retailing* 69 (Spring 1993), 1, 13.
2. The framework for this chapter was adapted from Figures 2 and 3 in Valerie A. Zeithaml, A. Parasuraman, and Leonard L. Berry, "Problems and Strategies in Services Marketing," *Journal of Marketing* 49 (Spring 1985), 33–46. For a more in-depth discussion of each of the problems and strategies associated with services marketing, consult Figures 2 and 3 in this article for the appropriate list of references.

3. Adapted from John E. G. Bateson, *Managing Services Marketing,* 3rd ed. (Fort Worth, Tex.: The Dryden Press, 1995), 9.

4. Ibid., 17.

5. Jim Kelley, "From Lip Service to Real Service: Reversing America's Downward Service Spiral," *Vital Speeches of the Day* 64, no. 10 (1998), 301–304.

6. Bateson, *Managing Services Marketing,* p. 18.

7. Ibid., 11–13.

8. The framework and materials for this section were adapted from W. Earl Sasser, "Match Supply and Demand in Service Industries," *Harvard Business Review* (November/December 1976), 133–140.

## chapter 3

# An Overview of the Services Sector

## CHAPTER OBJECTIVES

This chapter provides an overview of the service sector and focuses on the most substantial changes taking place within the sector. New concepts such as *e-services* and *supplemental services* are presented, and predicted keys to success within the service encounter are also discussed.

After reading this chapter, you should be able to:

- Understand how the "best practices" philosophy relates to service marketing classification schemes.
- Discuss the changes taking place within the most dynamic segments of the service sector.
- Appreciate how the millennial themes of technological advances (e.g., e-service), demographic changes, and competitive pressures continue to fuel the growth of the service sector.
- Discuss how e-services overcome many of problems traditionally caused by intangibility, inseparability, heterogeneity, and perishability.
- Describe the role of supplemental services as they relate to the "service imperative."
- Discuss the keys to success within the service sector.

"Okay, everyone knows that the Net is changing everything . . . that's old news. The savvy companies are already asking themselves: *what comes next?* Chapter Two of the Internet will be about the mass proliferation of e-services."

*An E-Services Strategy Book,*
The Hewlett-Packard Company

# Introduction

This chapter provides an overview of the service sector and highlights the similarities and differences among various service industries. The chapter promotes the stance that services industries should not be studied solely as separate entities. Clearly, many service industries share common service delivery challenges and therefore would benefit from sharing their knowledge with each other. Unfortunately, many service firms look only to firms within their own industry for guidance. For example, banks look to other banks, insurance companies to other insurance companies, and so on. This myopic approach slows the progress of truly unique service innovations within each of the respective industries. One needs only to consider the advances that hospitals could make if they borrowed concepts from restaurants and hotels instead of relying on other hospitals for innovative service ideas.

As we enter the new millennium, the service sector continues to thrive due in large part to technological developments, demographic changes, and competitive pressures. With respect to technological developments, we introduce the concept of e-services, which, in the opinion of many, represents the single most important change in how people will interact with the Internet in the immediate future. Demographic changes such as aging populations will also facilitate the growth of services into the foreseeable future. Finally, as competition continues to become more intense and firms lose their traditional differential advantages, the role of supplemental services in providing competitive advantages is becoming increasingly important. The chapter concludes with a summary of the predicted key factors that many believe lead to success within the service sector.

## WHAT CAN SERVICE FIRMS LEARN FROM EACH OTHER?

One of the major objectives of this text is to convey the message that fields of services marketing should not be studied as separate entities (such as banking, health care, and food service firms). Seemingly too often companies diminish their own chances to develop truly innovative ideas by only examining the practices of competitors within their own industries.

More successful companies have gone beyond standard competitive analysis by examining the "best practices" in the world.[1] **Best practices** represents a fundamental change in philosophy from focusing on "what gets done" to "how things get done." Thus far, best practices have taught corporations three lessons. First, other companies outside industry lines have much to teach each other. For example, Xerox has redesigned (1) its warehouse and software systems based on lessons learned from L.L. Bean; (2) its billing systems through the help of American Express; and (3) its production scheduling through benchmarking Cummins Engine. The second lesson is that of creating value. Often the biggest strides in creating value are the result of continuously improving processes, particularly in small ways, rather than in making large overall improvements. Finally, the best practices philosophy has taught us that someone needs to take ownership of the entire service delivery process and transcend traditional functional boundaries.

**best practices**
The philosophy of borrowing quality improvement ideas from outside traditional industry boundaries.

# TABLE 3.1

## Traditional Service Classifications

| Degree of Tangibility | Labor Intensiveness | Goal of the Service Provider |
|---|---|---|
| • Owned goods | • People-based | • Profit |
| • Rented goods | • Equipment-based | • Nonprofit |
| • Nongoods | | |

| Skill Level of the Service Provider | Degree of Customer Contact |
|---|---|
| • Professional | • High |
| • Nonprofessional | • Low |

# TABLE 3.2

## Understanding the Nature of the Service

| What Is the Nature of the Service Act? | Who or What Is the Direct Recipient of the Service? | |
|---|---|---|
| | **People** | **Things** |
| **Tangible Actions** | Services directed at people's bodies: <br> • Health care <br> • Passenger transportation <br> • Beauty salons <br> • Exercise clinics <br> • Restaurants <br> • Haircutting | Services directed at goods and other physical possessions: <br> • Freight transportation <br> • Industrial equipment repair and maintenance <br> • Janitorial services <br> • Laundry and dry cleaning <br> • Landscaping/lawn care <br> • Veterinary care |
| **Intangible Actions** | Services directed at people's minds: <br> • Education <br> • Broadcasting <br> • Information services <br> • Theaters <br> • Museums | Services directed at intangible assets: <br> • Banking <br> • Legal services <br> • Accounting <br> • Securities <br> • Insurance |

Source: Christopher H. Lovelock, "Classifying Services to Gain Strategic Marketing Insights" *Journal of Marketing* 47 (Summer 1983), pp. 9–20. Reprinted by permission of the American Marketing Association.

Consistent with the best practices philosophy of looking across industries for quality improvement ideas, individuals need to be able to look across their own organizations and integrate the processes produced by the various departments. The advances made by companies who practice benchmarking provide the proof that different industries really can learn from each other. One method of analyzing commonalities across industries is the development of classification schemes.

# TABLE 3.3

## Relationships with Customers

| Nature of Service Delivery | Type of Relationship between the Service Organization and Its Customers | |
|---|---|---|
| | "Membership" Relationship | No Formal Relationship |
| **Continuous Delivery of Service** | Insurance | Radio station |
| | Telephone subscription | Police protection |
| | College enrollment | Lighthouse |
| | Banking | Public highway |
| | American Automobile Association | |
| **Discrete Transactions** | Long-distance phone calls | Car rental |
| | Theater series subscriptions | Mail service |
| | Commuter ticket or transit pass | Toll highway |
| | | Pay phone |
| | | Movie theater |
| | | Public transportation |
| | | Restaurant |

Source: Christopher H. Lovelock, "Classifying Services to Gain Strategic Marketing Insights" *Journal of Marketing* 47 (Summer 1983), pp. 9–20. Reprinted by permission of the American Marketing Association.

## Service Classification Schemes

Marketing has traditionally developed classification schemes to facilitate an understanding of how different products share similar characteristics. For example, the product classification of convenience, shopping, and specialty products has aided in the understanding of how consumers spend their time shopping for various products and has led to the development of new types of retail stores. Convenience stores obviously sell convenience products. Shopping malls have been developed for those who like to compare prices and styles of shopping goods under one roof. In addition, category killers such as Toys R Us and Circuit City (which specializes in electronics) provide specialty products for consumers. Similarly, the classification of consumer and industrial products has led to numerous implications concerning promotion mix strategies, types of goods purchased, evaluation processes, usage behavior, and purchasing procedures, to name a few.

Classification schemes applied solely to services have also been developed to facilitate our understanding of what different types of service operations have in common. Typical classification categories include those presented in Table 3.1. Tables 3.2 through 3.6 expand on these categories and provide examples of service industries that fit within each scenario.[2] Services marketing classes may want to discuss each of these classification schemes and their marketing implications. For example, many service jobs such as a bank teller and an airline gate agent, who

## TABLE 3.4

**Customization and Judgment in Service Delivery**

| Extent to Which Customer Contact Personnel Exercise Judgment in Meeting Individual Customer Needs | Extent to Which Service Characteristics Are Customized | |
|---|---|---|
| | **High** | **Low** |
| **High** | Legal services | Education (large classes) |
| | Health care/surgery | Preventive health programs |
| | Architectural design | |
| | Executive search firm | |
| | Real-estate agency | |
| | Taxi service | |
| | Beautician | |
| | Plumber | |
| | Education (tutorials) | |
| **Low** | Telephone service | Public transportation |
| | Hotel services | Routine appliance repair |
| | Retail banking | Fast-food restaurant |
| | (excluding major loans) | Movie theater |
| | Good restaurant | Spectator sports |

Source: Christopher H. Lovelock, "Classifying Services to Gain Strategic Marketing Insights" *Journal of Marketing* 47 (Summer 1983), pp. 9–20. Reprinted by permission of the American Marketing Association.

## TABLE 3.5

**What Is the Nature of Demand for the Service Relative to Supply?**

| Extent to Which Supply Is Constrained | Extent of Demand Fluctuations over Time | |
|---|---|---|
| | **Wide** | **Narrow** |
| **Peak Demand Can Usually Be Met without a Major Delay** | Electricity | Insurance |
| | Natural gas | Legal services |
| | Telephone | Banking |
| | Hospital maternity unit | Laundry and dry cleaning |
| | Police and fire emergencies | |
| **Peak Demand Regularly Exceeds Capacity** | Accounting and tax preparation | Services similar to those |
| | Passenger transportation | above but that have |
| | Hotels and motels | insufficient capacity for |
| | Restaurants | their base level of |
| | Theaters | business |

Source: Christopher H. Lovelock, "Classifying Services to Gain Strategic Marketing Insights" *Journal of Marketing* 47 (Summer 1983), pp. 9–20. Reprinted by permission of the American Marketing Association.

## TABLE 3.6

**Method of Service Delivery**

| Nature of Interaction between Customer and Service Organization | Availability of Service Outlets | |
|---|---|---|
| | **Single Site** | **Multiple Site** |
| **Customer goes to service organization** | Theater<br>Barbershop | Bus service<br>Fast-food chain |
| **Service organization comes to customer** | Lawn care service<br>Pest control service<br>Taxi | Mail delivery<br>AAA emergency repairs |
| **Customer and service organization transact at arms length (mail or electronic communications)** | Credit card company<br>Local TV station | Broadcast network<br>Telephone company |

Source: Christopher H. Lovelock, "Classifying Services to Gain Strategic Marketing Insights" *Journal of Marketing* 47 (Summer 1983), pp. 9–20. Reprinted by permission of the American Marketing Association.

on the surface seem quite different, actually perform similar tasks and experience many of the same customer-related challenges throughout a typical day. Consequently, lessons that have been learned in the front-lines of banking operations may be of value to those who work the front-lines of the airline industry.

## AN OVERVIEW OF THE MOST DYNAMIC SERVICE INDUSTRIES[3]

Much of the service sector is continuing to grow at a steady rate. Sectors appearing to enjoy the greatest gains in growth and/or are undergoing the most substantial changes include business services, health care, professional services, and the hospitality industry.

### Business Services

Despite corporate claims that "employees are the firm's most important assets," when it comes to becoming cost efficient, "employees are the firm's most expendable asset." **Corporate downsizing** has led to a boom in the consulting area and to dramatic growth in **business services.** Ironically, because of downsizing, most new consultants' first clients are their former employers.[9] Business services is the fastest growing service sector in terms of sales and establishments. In particular, Las Vegas has seen the largest establishment increase in terms of new startups. Businesses relocating from California and the tremendous revenues generated from tourism have been noted as the sources of the growth. Throughout the country, business services experiencing the most dramatic increases in growth include:

**corporate downsizing** Reduction in the number of corporate workers in order for a corporation to become more cost efficient.

**business services** Service sector that provides "outsourced" services such as advertising, credit reporting and collection, and building maintenance to businesses.

- Advertising
- Credit reporting and collections
- Mail and copying
- Building maintenance
- Equipment rental
- Temporary help services
- Computer services
- Detective agencies
- Security guards

## Health Care

**health care services**
Services such as hospitals, physicians, group practices, and home health care that provide physical care to consumers.

Business services, along with **health care services** and professional services, account for two thirds of all service firms. The health care service sector is undergoing significant changes in terms of daily operation and the competitive structure of the sector. Independent hospitals are being swallowed by hospital systems that enjoy the cost savings of economies of scale. Likewise, independent physicians are moving into group practices, which allow them to share overhead costs with other physicians plus provide them the opportunity to have a more independent lifestyle. Group practices share on-call duties, allowing each individual physician more personal time.

Other physicians are leaving hospitals and focusing on niches within the health care sector. Independent surgery centers and corner "doc-in-a-box" diagnostic centers have created leaner and meaner niche players with whom traditional health care delivery systems must contend. Other health care services that are predicted to see dramatic growth include outpatient care and home health care. As a result of the aging population and an increase in insurance coverage for home health care services, its future growth is predicted to be particularly explosive. Health services expected to experience the most dramatic increases in growth include the following:

- Physicians
- Dentists
- Nursing and personal care homes
- Hospitals
- Medical laboratories
- Home health services
- Kidney dialysis centers
- Outpatient clinics

**professional services**
Services such as accounting, engineering, research, and management consulting provided by firms traditionally classified as "professional."

## Professional Services

Over the years, the competitive area of **professional services** has also experienced significant change. Court rulings and the use of marketing techniques have led to easier entry into some professions, more freedom to compete on price, the removal of geographic competitive restrictions, the incentive to differentiate services, and the ability to use mass media. Accounting, engineering, research, and management consulting firms alone have created an $18 billion-a-year industry. As is the case with health care services, many professional services are also finding profitable niches in the marketplace. Attorneys, for example, are creating "boutique firms" that specialize in areas of litigation such as intellectual property, labor law, and trusts and estates.

## The Hospitality Industry

The **hospitality industry** has experienced tremendous growth over the past several decades. In the past, many of the services offered by the industry were available only to the privileged few. Fortunately for the industry, times have changed. In many countries the standard of living is higher, consumers are living longer and have increased leisure time, education is improving, and opportunities for individuals to improve themselves and their standard of living are increasing as society continues to rapidly advance. In short, the hospitality industry has advanced with society.[11]

The hospitality industry comprises a variety of segments including food service, lodging, travel and tourism, and meeting and convention planning. The hospitality industry is the world's largest industry and largest generator of jobs, with an estimated 338 million people to be employed in 2005, up from 212 million in 1995. The industry generates more than $300 billion in revenues and employs 6 million people in the United States alone.

**hospitality industry**
The hospitality industry comprises a variety of segments including food service, lodging, travel and tourism, and meeting and convention planning.

### THE FOOD SERVICE INDUSTRY

The food service segment is the largest and most diverse segment of the hospitality industry. One out of every three meals is now eaten outside the home, and food service operations provide nearly half of all meals eaten in the United States today.

Competition in the $200 billion-a-year food industry is intense. In addition to traditional competitors, nontraditional competitors such as convenience stores and grocery stores have modified their product offerings to include meals that were at one time available only in restaurants. Meanwhile, traditional competitors are constantly altering their marketing strategies to adapt to changes in consumer demands. For example, some fast-food restaurants are now offering table service to compete with more traditional family restaurants, gourmet restaurants are now offering take-out services, and a great deal of product bundling is occurring to create "value meals" that are sold at discounted prices.

Other changes in the industry reflect consumers' changing tastes in what they want to eat and drink. Sales of ethnic foods, chicken, and turkey are up, whereas the consumption of beef is down. Additionally, coffee bars and wine have become increasingly popular as people have become more aware of the problems associated with drinking traditional alcoholic beverages. Moreover, despite claims that Americans are eating healthier, sales of gourmet ice cream, cookies, and pastries are increasing.

### THE LODGING INDUSTRY

The primary service offering of hotels and lodging facilities is overnight accommodations for guests. Similar to the food industry, consumers have a wide array of lodging choices that serve a variety of market segments, such as luxury hotels, bed and breakfast inns, and economy motels. Within the service industry as a whole, hotels and lodging facilities account for 3 percent of service establishments and 6 percent of sales.

The lodging industry has recently undergone significant change. In the early 1990s an oversupply of hotel rooms existed, and too few customers were available to fill them. Consumer demand had dropped off during the recession of the early 1990s, and many hotels were forced to close because of their debt load. In 1993 the average occupancy rate was barely above 60 percent. This means that four out of every ten rooms were vacant every evening. The oversupply of rooms forced many hotels to cut room rates to the point that the average daily rate is now between $55 and $60.

The success stories in the lodging industry today include those firms that are creative in how they conduct business. Marriott, for example, operates Marriott Hotels and Resorts, Courtyard by Marriott, Fairfield Inn, Residence Inn by Marriott, and Marriott Suites to appeal to a variety of market segments. Hence, the many corporations in the industry are competing not only against one another but also against themselves. Competition in the United States has also increased as a result of the rise in international hotel companies that now have properties in the United States. In turn, U.S.-based companies continue to expand overseas, with particular interest in the Pacific Rim and Eastern Europe. Finally, for some hotels and for some customers the room itself is only a small part of the lodging experience. Hotels such as the MGM Grand and the Mirage in Las Vegas and the Taj Mahal in Atlantic City provide an atmosphere that caters to the customer's entertainment as well as lodging needs.

## THE TRAVEL AND TOURISM INDUSTRY

Like many of the other hospitality industries, the specific components of travel and tourism are difficult to define, and they are often divided into the areas of travel and recreation. The travel segment of the industry involves the physical movement of people from one place to another and includes services associated with automobiles, airlines, bus lines, railroads, passenger ships, sightseeing companies, travel agencies, and tour companies.

In comparison, the recreation segment provides recreation and relaxation to the public and includes attractions, clubs, and public parks. More specifically, attractions include theme parks, sporting events, scenic attractions, and special activities such as the Olympics or Mardi Gras in New Orleans. Clubs include civic clubs, fraternal clubs, and country clubs to name a few. The first and best-known public park in the United States is Central Park in New York City.

The travel and tourism industry generates $2 trillion in worldwide revenues. In 1992, 476 million travelers generated 7 percent of world trade and 100 million jobs. In the United States, tourism ranks as the first, second, or third largest industry in 47 states and directly employs 4.7 million Americans, who receive more than $50 billion in wages and salaries. Tourism destinations such as Las Vegas and other gaming destinations are experiencing tremendous growth. In fact, the location experiencing the most recent growth in hotel and lodging facilities is Dubuque, Iowa, because of the introduction of riverboat gambling.

## MEETING AND CONVENTION PLANNING

A meeting planner must be well acquainted with all areas of the hospitality industry. Typically, the planner works with the convention group and the meeting site to coordinate all the activities involved, such as booking hotel rooms, arranging for meals, and securing travel arrangements. The meeting and convention industry in the United States generates approximately $56 billion annually and hosts meetings ranging in size from a few people to the 100,000 who regularly attend the Consumer Electronics Show usually held in Las Vegas.

# MILLENNIAL THEMES: TECHNOLOGICAL DEVELOPEMENTS, DEMOGRAPHIC CHANGES, COMPETITIVE PRESSURES AND SERVICE GROWTH

As we enter the new millennium, the service sector continues to thrive in large part as a result of technological developments, demographic changes, and competitive pressures.[4]

## Technology: The Emergence of E-Service[5]

One of the most profound changes driving the growth of the service economy has been the phenomenal advance in technology, in particular the Internet. Sometime around 1996 the obsession with the Internet began. Thousands of businesses, customers, employees, and partners got wired to one another and began conducting business processes online ("e-business"). Eventually, more and more customers (business-to-business and final) became wired and formed a critical mass. Through repeated usage, customer trust dramatically increased, and the Net became a viable means for revenue production and economic growth ("e-commerce"). Hewlett Packard (www.hp.com) refers to this period as "Chapter One of the Internet."

Chapter One of the Internet laid the foundation and provided the infrastructure so that the next evolutions of the Internet could follow. Chapter One required users to:

- do it yourself
- at your desk
- on a PC
- tapping into Web storefronts
- using monolithic applications
- where information technology (IT) is viewed as an asset

Chapter One is old news. Let's move on to Chapter Two. According to the experts, Chapter Two will be about the mass proliferation of e-services. In comparison to the Chapter One requirements listed above, which required users to work the Web, Chapter Two is about the Internet working for the user:

- do it for me
- while I am living my life
- on PCs, devices, and other things

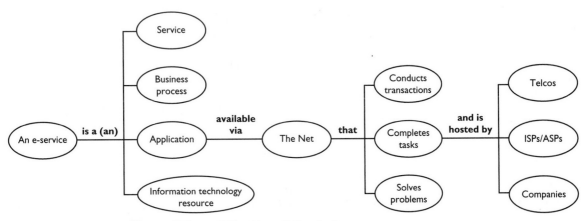

**Figure 3.1** **What Is an E-Service?**
Source: Adapted from http://e-services.hp.com/understanding/images/blkstrat_page3.gif

- through the use of automated e-services
- using modular e-services
- where IT is viewed as a service

## E-Service Defined

**e-service**
An electronic service available via the Net that completes tasks, solves problems, or conducts transactions.

What exactly is an **e-service?** According to Hewlett-Packard (www.e-service.hp .com), "Simply put, an e-service is an electronic service available via the Net that completes tasks, solves problems, or conducts transactions. E-services can be used by people, businesses, and other e-services and can be accessed via a wide range of information appliances." Figure 3.1 provides an overview of an e-service. E-services that are available today include your local bank's online account services, UPS package tracking service, and Schwab's stock trading services. A list of Hewlett-Packard's e-service mix is provided in Table 3.7. In essence, an e-service is any asset that is made available via the Net that creates new efficiencies and new revenue streams (see Services in Action 3.1). In an Internet context, the term asset can include any software application that is placed on the Net and made available as an **ap-on-tap.** "Applications-on-tap" refer to e-services that are available for rent on the Internet (Table 3.8). Those who provide aps-on-tap are known as **ASPs** (application service providers).

**ap-on-tap**
E-service that is available for rent on the Internet.

**ASPs**
Application service providers—those who provide aps-on-tap.

According to Sun Microsystems (www.sun.com), nobody had even heard of an ASP 12 to 18 months ago. "In the short space of a year and a half, the concept of leasing applications to businesses has grown from an interesting but unproven proposition to an industry that has generated its own subsets." In the beginning, the ASP model was championed by heavyweight corporations such as telecommunications companies (telcos), Internet service providers (ISPs), and enterprise resource planning (ERP) vendors. The early thinking was that these companies were going to develop and provide a host of e-services and virtually own the market space; however, it has not worked out that way. The heavyweights have backed

## TABLE 3.7

### HP's E-Service Mix

| Consumer Portals | Employee Portals | Trading Portals | Printing and Imaging | Publishing | IT Infrastructure | General Business | Vertical Industries |
|---|---|---|---|---|---|---|---|
| FusionOne Internet Sync™ Service | HP E-Services Portal | Ariba Network™ eCommerce Platform | Dazel | New-Media Publishing Services | Digital Safe™ | Corporate My Yahoo | HP Open Skies |
| Cartogra | | | Encryptix.com | | !job e-recruitment | My Yahoo | Impresse.com |
| | | | !IPS | | IP Messaging Services | Digital Safe™ | Vital Works |
| | | ATG Dynamo | InterNetShip | | | eDolphin | Custom!Content |
| | | Impresse.com™ e-service | ImageTag | | Messaging-On Tap | E-Learning on-Tap | SURF |
| | | ResourceLink | Impresse.com™ e-services | | Netsourcing | Enterprise Application Services for SAP | |
| | | Virtual Trading Communities | Mimeo.com | | PSINet Outsourced E-Mail | e-Vis.com | |
| | | Custom!Content | NewspaperDirect | | QuickStart™ | FusionOne Internet Sync™ Service | |
| | | | PrintCafe | | | Impresse.com™ e-services | |
| | | | Stamps.com | | | MyContracts.com | |
| | | | | | | Personal Analyst® | |
| | | | | | | Sales and Marketing Information Exchange | |
| | | | | | | E-Portal Suite™ | |

away, at least for the short-term, from the idea that they themselves would be ASPs. Instead, strategies are now being developed to attract ASPs.

The switch in approach reflects the successes in the marketplace. So-called ASP aggregators and distributors such as Corio, US Internetworking, and Interpath have been very successful pulling together applications from a variety of vendors; however, a new trend seems to be emerging. Application service developers are now creating applications specifically for ASP distribution. In the past, applications were often developed in-house and sold to corporate customers. This new approach, termed *dot-com ASPs*, develops apps (such as those offered by LivePerson.com) to be specifically sold over the Web on a lease or rental basis. Larger companies, such as Hewlett Packard, are now offering e-scholarships through their HP Garage Program, to attract developers of e-services in their early stages. Winners of the scholarships receive more than $1.5 million in products and services such as a

TABLE 3.8

### Examples of Possible E-Services

Opportunities abound in e-services as they replace and/or supplement traditional methods of commerce. Examples of possibilities include an e-service that:

| | |
|---|---|
| Translates voice to text | Rents out computing resources |
| Manages data security | Teaches languages |
| Plans delivery routes | Orders food |
| Automates auditing | Performs credit card transactions |
| Updates software automatically | Monitors health |
| Automates procurement | Provides distance learning |
| Builds Web sites | Processes orders |
| Facilitates voting | Conducts legal research |
| Processes taxes | Rates other e-services |
| Conducts spell-checks | Facilitates supply-chain management |
| Appraises valuables | Manages personal finances |

Source: Adapted from *An E-Services Strategy Book,* The Hewlett-Packard Company, Palo Alto, Calif. (1999).

comprehensive suite of hardware and software, integration and installation services, support, consulting, and training.

## How Does an E-Service Differ from Traditional E-Business and E-Commerce Systems?

*Web sites are not necessary to trigger e-services.* One of the drawbacks of using the Internet has been its lack of mobility. Until recently, if you wanted to use the Internet you were chained to your PC. In the future, e-services will be accessed by pushing a button in your automobile, speaking into a PDA or cell phone, or using the TV remote control (see Services in Action 3.2). It is even feasible that new refrigerators will be equipped with scanners that automatically reorder food supplies simply by running the item's UPC bar past a scanner. The purpose of e-services is to do the work for you, and some of it may be done automatically, such as turning on the lights when you enter your household, turning down the thermostat when you leave, or informing a driver of the nearest service station when the fuel gauge is low.

*E-services are modular, not monolithic.* E-services are purposely designed to function as building blocks. This enables e-services to be readily customizable. For example, an international travel service may bring together a variety of e-services from a number of different vendors such as an airline reservation e-service, a hotel reservation e-service, a translation e-service, a car rental e-service, and a weather e-service. Similarly, a manufacturer may employ the assistance of an e-service that streamlines its employees travel arrangements, another e-service that bills its

ERVICES 3.1

ACTION    **E-Services: Chapter Two of the Internet**

Hewlett-Packard believes that e-services could easily become the dominant entity on the Net. In fact, HP refers to e-services as "Chapter Two of the Internet." "Chapter One" was about building the infrastructure and providing access. "Chapter Two" is about what the Internet can do for you—the customer. HP forecasts that entire ecosystems or e-services will be built around specific industries (insurance, travel), specific types of customers (physicians, attorneys), specific processes (buying a house, procurement), specific problems (too few computers and too much demand for processing), and specific transaction chains (new product development).

Product lines in HP's current e-service product mix include: employee portals, trading portals, consumer portals, printing and imaging, general business, IT infrastructure, vertical industries, and publishing. As an example of what is available, e-service selections falling under the printing and imaging product category include the following:

- Dazel—An HP document router featuring Dazel technology that ensures delivery of important business documents.
- Encryptix.com—Turns your printer into a ticket office.
- IIPS—A print appliance that provides IT managers with a cost-effective way to manage print queues by using a browser. In addition, this category also includes a color pocket PC which can beam color images to color printers with the tap of a stylus.
- InterNetShip—Turns your printer into a personal shipping station.
- ImageTag—Stores, retrieves, and sends important documents using uniquely bar-coded labels called Post-it eFlags.
- Mimeo.com—Securely receives documents via the Internet to be printed, bound and sent overnight anywhere in the United States and Canada.
- NewspaperDirect—Prints international newspapers locally on demand.
- PrintCafe—E-procurement solutions for corporate print buyers and commercial printers.
- Stamps.com—Turns your printer into a post office.

Source: http://www.e-services.hp.com/solutions/ips_solutions.html.

customers, an e-service for procurement, and an e-service for ERP. Because of the modularity of e-services, security systems will need to be modified. "Security is no longer about building an impermeable firewall. In an e-service world, borders need to be much more fluid—it's data and transactions that must be secured" (www.sun.com).

*E-services can talk to one another.* Because they are modular by design, e-services that join together form a sort of ecosystem where individual e-services must be able to communicate with one another. HP has created a common services

SERVICES **3.2**
N
ACTION     **Meet Mya—The Virtual Service Provider**

In an attempt to expand sales, many of the traditional PC manufacturers are looking for new product development ideas that pertain to mobile methods of using the Net. For example, Motorola has recognized that many consumers are away from the computers when they would like to use it the most. The solution was found in the development of Mya—a mobile platform that integrates both voice and data. According to Motorola, Mya is essentially a voice-enabled browser that eliminates the middleman (the computer).

Mya has been purposely designed to act like a sort of digital secretary. Subscribers, who sign up for Mya's services, are provided with an 800 number and pin that provides 7-day, 24-hour access. Theoretically, a subscriber will be able call Mya and ask her for a list of Italian restaurants within a specified location. If the restaurant's Web site has been designed to take reservations, Mya can book the reservation. The limitation is that Mya can only access what is on the Internet. So, if the restaurant of choice does not have a Web site, then Mya has no way of knowing that it exists. Other services that Mya can provide include checking the subscriber's e-mail and providing a reminder service for upcoming appointments, birthdays, and anniversaries.

Although Mya is virtual, she has been given a human voice and physical appearance in order to assist in Motorola's marketing efforts. Mya's voice is that of Gabrielle Carteras, an actress who played Andrea on Fox television's *Beverly Hills 90210*. Mya's physical appearance is digitally animated—she is a tall, thin blonde, with spiked hair and a silver pantsuit. She was created by the same firm that conducted the special effects work for *Terminator 2* and *Titanic*. Mya is scheduled for release in December 2000 and her services will be available to BellSouth subscribers. Other networks have yet to be finalized.

Source: Tobey Grumet, "Mya Desires Your Attention," *Revolution* 1, no. 5 (July 2000), 25.

interface called e-speak technology that makes it easier and faster for e-services to connect with one another. Another way to think about this is to compare it with the variety of video and audio components that you may own. If they are all the same brand (common interface), they connect much easier to one another. For example, a Sony video camera easily attaches to a Sony VCR, which easily attaches to a Sony television. By speaking to one another, each e-service can clearly communicate its own capabilities to other e-services. For example, a translation e-service can communicate what languages it translates to a travel reservation e-service.

*Ecosystems of e-services will be dynamic.* Experts forecast that entire ecosystems or e-services will be built around specific industries (insurance, travel), specific types of customers (physicians, attorneys), specific processes (buying a house, procurement), specific problems (too few computers and too much demand for processing), and specific transaction chains (new product development). When forming ecosystem relationships, these relationships will not necessarily be permanent. For example, a travel e-service may submit a customer's travel request to four or five different airline reservation e-services who compete (or bid) for the customer's business. By providing a host of options as opposed to forming a single (more permanent) relationship, customers will have many more choices and e-service firms will be much more able to provide customized solutions to customer requests if the ecosystems of e-services remains dynamic.

*E-services will fuel the growth of new types of mediators and brokers.* As the number of ASPs continues to grow, new kinds of electronic brokers and mediators will be formed to serve as aggregators (collectors) of similar types of e-services. These new brokers and mediators will facilitate the transaction process. As noted earlier, the original ASP model was championed by heavyweight corporations such as telecommunications companies, ISPs, and ERP vendors. It was thought that these companies were going to develop and provide a multitude of their own e-service applications. This strategy has now changed to one in which these same corporations want to act as anchors for the location, aggregation, and mediation of e-service transactions.

All in all, it is an exciting time with respect to new technological developments. (Throughout this discussion, Hewlett Packard has been frequently mentioned, and rightly so. The HP Web site (www.hp.com) provides a wealth of information pertaining to concepts that surround e-services.) E-services are believed to be the next big thing on the Net. E-services will provide new revenue streams for providers and lower the operating costs of users. New e-service portals will be formed that provide collection points for e-services that cater to specific types of customers. Because of their modular design, dynamic ecosystems of e-services will be constructed that offer consumers more choices, and e-service firms will be able to provide much more customized solutions. Many in the industry believe that companies will continue to build their own most strategic applications but will "rent" virtually every other business process as an e-service on the Net.

## E-Services: Managing the Traditional Problems Faced by Service Marketers

One of the many intriguing aspects of e-services is that they apparently overcome many of the traditional challenges faced by service marketers—namely, intangibility, inseparability, heterogeneity, and perishability (as discussed in Chapter 2).[6]

### MANAGING INTANGIBILITY

Perhaps the main problem associated with intangibility is that service marketers have nothing to show the customer. E-services can overcome some of the challenges provided by intangibility by using the Web to provide evidence of service. For example, an innovative Ford Motor Company dealership is planning to install video cameras in its service bays to provide a live feed to the dealership's Web site. This strategy will enable customers to visit the service bay (without actually being there) and check on their vehicle's progress throughout the day. Other Web sites such as the Royal Automobile Club (RAC) in Europe provides tangible evidence by e-mailing new members who join online almost instantaneously with the new member's membership number and policy document. E-services also make tangible the intangible by providing additional evidence such as the appearance of the site, the frequency of information updates, the accuracy of information, the speed of the server, and ease of navigation. Customers are also able to sample e-services prior to purchase, which is not true of traditional services such as hairstyling, surgical procedures, and dental services.

## MANAGING INSEPARABILITY

Inseparability reflects the simultaneity of service production and consumption. Inseparability also describes services as a shared experience in which, in many cases, the producer and the consumer both have to be present in order for the transaction to be completed. In addition, other customers are often involved in the service delivery process. One of the possible solutions to minimize the challenges presented by customer involvement is to provide customized solutions. Because of the modularity of e-services, solutions to individual customer requests can be more easily customized. In addition, information that is requested on Web sites requires that consumers become active participants in the process to the point where the customers themselves are actually becoming "partial employees." For example, if a customer places an order over the phone, the service firm has a paid employee who answers that phone, records the order, and requests billing and shipping information. By providing an access portal on the Web, that same company can reduce its labor costs by having customers input that same information on the Web site. In essence, the customer is now working for the provider.

Another suggested method to reduce the negative affects of inseparability is to standardize (or industrialize) the service. Once again, e-services can be very effective. Because e-services are accessed at a distance (e.g., Web, cell phone, PDA), customer involvement in the actual production process is minimized. Customers are often purposely led step by step to control the flow of the process. Because one third of customer complaints are related to problems caused by the customers, a number of companies are instituting fail-safe procedures into their online operations. Examples include informing customers what information they are going to need prior to the encounter, providing online map services so that customers will not get lost driving to physical locations, requesting that customers enter e-mail addresses twice to cut down on data entry errors, and having customers "click" as opposed to type in choices and information whenever possible.

## MANAGING HETEROGENEITY

The characteristic of heterogeneity reflects the variability in quality of service provided from one transaction to the next. When services are provided by people, variations are going to occur and mistakes will happen in real time. Because e-services are electronically based, variations in quality provided from one customer to the next should be minimal. In addition, other e-services that perhaps monitor customer service conversations may assist future customer service training sessions as typical problems are identified, resolved, and appropriate responses to customer complaints are formalized.

## MANAGING PERISHABILITY

Perishability reflects the challenges faced by service marketers as a result of the inability to inventory services. Supply and demand problems are rampant. Services that are not consumed at their appointed time cease to exist. Hotel rooms that are not sold on Thursday night cannot be added to the supply of rooms available for occupancy on Friday night. E-services are not faced with these same problems. E-services are available 24 hours a day, 7 days a week. Applications not purchased one day are available for sale the next. E-services such as online auctions can help airlines fill unused capacity. On the demand side of the equation, if 10 customers want to rent the same e-service application on the same day, this is not a problem. Although not perfect, e-services can handle supply and demand fluctuations with much greater ease than most other types of services, such as restaurants, hospitals, and hotels.

E-services are able to overcome many of the traditional challenges faced by service marketers as a result of three main properties—**quantization,** the ability to **search,** and the ability to **automate.** Traditional service firms often bundle their offerings to the customer. For example, a hotel may bundle the room, breakfast and dinner, and a show for one price. Quantization (the breaking down of services [modularity] into component parts) allows opportunities for unparalleled mass customization. In addition, search facilitates ultra-efficient information markets. As such, supply and demand can be more carefully monitored and matched. Finally, by offering consumers choices on a 24/7 basis, automation overcomes the traditional limitations of time and space.

**quantization**
The breaking down of monolithic services into modular components.

**search**
The ability and ease in which information can be sought.

**automate**
Replacing tasks that required human labor with machines.

## Demographic Changes

The second millennial theme fueling the growth of services involves the many demographic changes that are taking place throughout the world.[7] In essence, a type of chain reaction is occurring that facilitates the growth of the service sector. Consumers have less time than ever to accomplish their various roles. The growth in the number of time-pressured consumers has led to an increase in time-saving services such as restaurants, housekeeping services, laundry services, hairstyling shops, and tax preparation services. The time saved through the use of these services is now being spent on entertainment, travel, and recreation services.[8]

The continued growth of the service sector throughout the world will be influenced by each area's demographic make-up. For example, on average the population of the United States is becoming older. By the year 2008 the median age of the U.S. labor force is projected to rise to nearly 41 years. This will exceed the previous high of 40.5 set in 1962.[9] In addition, advances in health care and more health-conscious consumers have led to a dramatic growth in "older" market segments. Although the immediate implication is an increase in demand for health care-related services, other service industries stand to benefit from an aging population. The over-50 age group controls 77 percent of the nation's assets and 50 percent of the country's discretionary income.[10] In fact, the term **woofs,** which stands for "well-off older folks," has been coined to represent this group's purchasing power. It has also been noted that this particular group is engaged in "down aging"—acting younger than one's years. As a result, amusement and recreation ser-

**woofs**
Stands for "well-off older folks," that segment of the population that controls 77 percent of the nation's assets and 50 percent of its discretionary income.

More services are being provided to older market segments as a result of the aging of the population. Entertainment and recreation services such as tennis, golf, and other activities are now being offered to older Americans.

vices are currently in a tie with business services for the fastest employment growth within the service sector. In addition, personal services that assist older age groups in accomplishing everyday activities are also experiencing increases in demand.

## Competitive Pressures: The Emergence of Supplemental Services as Differential Advantage

As we enter the new millennium, competitive pressures continue to grow.[11] The companies that remain are actively looking for strategies to differentiate themselves from each other. As we discussed in Chapter 1, the "service imperative" referred to the situation in which the intangible aspects of many products (consumer and business-to-business) are becoming the key features that differentiate products in the marketplace (see Services in Action 3.3). This is true not only of businesses that would be traditionally included as part of the service sector but also includes businesses that are in the manufacturing sector. One of the advantages of increased competition is that it generally leads to better quality products and better values for the customer. However, as time progresses, companies tend to lose their differential advantage from each other as the tangible product offering becomes similar from one producer to the next. Companies are now faced with fighting the commodity battle, in which customers believe that all products are the same and that it really doesn't matter from whom the product is purchased. In this situation, companies struggle with how to sustain a strategic competitive advantage over time. Many of these strategic opportunities exist today in the form of **supplemental services.** The eight categories of supplemental services listed on page 71 are described in detail in Table 3.9.

**supplemental services**
Peripheral services, which are outside the core, that assist firms in differentiating themselves from the competition.

## TABLE 3.9

## Eight Categories of Supplementary Services

### Information

To obtain full value from any good or service, customers need relevant information about it, ranging from schedules to operating instructions, and from user warnings to prices. Globalization affects the nature of that information (including the languages and format in which it is provided). New customers and prospects are especially information hungry and may need training in how to use an unfamiliar service.

### Consultation and Advice

Consultation and advice involve a dialogue to probe customer requirements and then develop a tailored solution. Customers' need for advice may vary widely around the world, reflecting such factors as level of economic development, nature of the local infrastructure, topography and climate, technical standards, and educational levels.

### Order-Taking

Once customers are ready to buy, suppliers need to make it easy for them to place orders or reservations in the language of their choice, through telecommunications and other channels, at times and in locations that are convenient to them.

### Hospitality: Taking Care of the Customer

Well-managed businesses try, at least in small ways, to treat customers as guests when they have to visit the supplier's facilities (especially when, as is true for many people-processing operations, the period extends over several hours or more). Cultural definitions of appropriate hospitality may differ widely from one country to another, such as the tolerable length of waiting time (much longer in Brazil than in Germany) and the degree of personal service expected (not much in Scandinavia but lavish in Indonesia).

### Safekeeping: Looking After the Customer's Possessions

When visiting a service site, customers often want assistance with their personal possessions, ranging from car parking to packaging and delivery of new purchases. Expectations may vary by country, reflecting culture and levels of affluence.

### Exceptions

Exceptions fall outside the routine of normal service delivery. They include special requests, problem solving, handling of complaints/suggestions/compliments, and restitution (compensating customers for performance failures). Special requests are particularly common in people-processing services, as in the travel and lodging industries and may be complicated by differing cultural norms. International airlines, for example, find it necessary to respond to an array of medical and dietary needs, sometimes reflecting religious and cultural values. Problem solving is often more difficult for people who are traveling overseas than it would be in the familiar environment of their native country.

### Billing

Customers need clear, timely bills that explain how charges are computed. With abolition of currency exchange restrictions in many countries, bills can be converted to the customer's home currency. Hence, currencies and conversion rates need to be clarified on billing statements. In some instances, prices may be displayed in several currencies even though this policy may require frequent adjustments in the light of currency fluctuations.

### Payment

Ease and convenience of payment (including credit) are increasingly expected by customers when purchasing a broad array of services. Major credit cards and travelers' checks solve the problem of paying in foreign funds for many retail purchases, but corporate purchasers may prefer to use electronic fund transfers in the currency of their choice.

SERVICES 3.3

ACTION

### Delighting the Global Customer: Managing Supplemental Services

When operating globally, the manner in which supplemental services are presented can make a world of difference. A few key areas to pay close attention to include the following:

## Ordering

Ordering should be made as easy as possible and forms should be adapted where necessary such as:

1. Name and address—plenty of room should be provided, since many addresses are much longer than U.S. addresses.
2. Instructions—clothing merchandisers should provide size conversion charts to increase customer confidence and reduce the number of returns.
3. Product descriptions—should be provided using the local language to reduce confusion.
4. Response channels—make sure that your provide customers with a variety of choices in which to place their orders including phone, mail, fax, and the Web. In America the vast majority of orders are taken over the phone. In Japan phone calls are expensive and most orders are taken by mail. The majority of business-to-business transactions are received by fax.
5. Fulfillment switch—if orders are collected by phone, language, culture, time, and costs are four good reasons why it makes sense to set up an overseas call center.
6. Payment options—preferred methods of payment often vary by country. For example, German customers are typically billed after their purchases are delivered. Options such as cash on delivery, check, payment by invoice, direct debit, credit card, and bank transfers should be considered.

## Fulfillment

Fulfillment pertains to the actual delivery of goods and services.

1. Distribution centers—establishing overseas distribution centers makes sense when overseas sales represent a high rate of return or when the company is fully vested in its global operations.
2. Delivery—cost savings are often offset by lengthy delivery timetables. Shipping from local warehouses obviously saves time. For example, if shipped from the United States, a package can take 10 days to reach its destination in Japan. If sent from a local warehouse, that same package can reach its destination in less than 24 hours.

---

**Returns and Refunds**

How are exchanges and refunds to be executed?

1.  Refunds—currency fluctuations should not impact a customer's refund. The customer should be reimbursed at the same rate as when the original payment was paid.
2.  Postage—postage is always to be refunded when specifically asked by the customer to do so. Otherwise, experts suggest that refunding postage is dependent on the profit margin of the sale. When affordable, postage should be refunded.

---

Source: Lisa A. Yorgey, "Delighting the Global Customer," *Target Marketing*, 23, no. 2, (February 2000), 104-106.

- Information
- Consultation and advice
- Order-taking
- Hospitality
- Safekeeping
- Handling exceptions
- Billing
- Payment

## Service Growth

Demand for services has grown tremendously as a result of technological advancements, demographic changes, and increases in competitive pressures.[12] According to the U.S. Bureau of Labor Statistics workforce projections for the years 1998 to 2008, the service sector is expected to account for more than 90 percent of all job growth.[13]

The service sector clearly dominates the economy in new and **emerging occupations.** Technically, emerging occupations are considered those that are new occupations created by changes in technology, society, markets, or regulations. In addition, emerging occupations may be existing occupations that have been substantially modified by these same changes and are increasing in employment. Some of the most recent emerging occupations include the following:[14]

**emerging occupations**
New occupations that are created by changes in technology, society, markets, or regulations.

- *Administrative assistants*—typically have more responsibilities than general secretaries and could be described as executive secretaries, providing high level support to executive staff. (Employers: a variety of industries.)
- *Convention managers*—coordinate activities of convention center/hotel/banquet personnel in order to make arrangements for group meetings and conventions. (Employers: membership organizations, business services, educational services, social services, health services, and hotels among others.)
- *Web masters*—design and maintain Internet Web sites. (Employers: printing and publishing, wholesale trade, retail trade, business services, and membership organizations.)

- *Environmental engineers*—may involve the disposal of hazardous materials, monitoring the emissions of pollutants, or safety of employees on the job. (Employers: business services, health services, and electric, gas, and sanitary services.)
- *Computer managers*—oversee the installation, configuration, and maintenance of both software and hardware in a local area network (LAN), wide area network (WAN), or Internet/Intranet system. (Employers: business services, health services, legal services, and social services industries.)
- *Bankruptcy specialists*—ensure that their employers receive the maximum revenue when a client or debtor declares bankruptcy; they can also represent the bankrupt party. (Employers: depository institutions, nondepository institutions, business services, and holding and other investment offices.)
- *Desktop publishing specialists*—produce various documents such as reports, proposals, benefit books, advertisements, brochures, flyers, and so on. (Employers: business services, among others.)
- *Utilization review coordinators*—nurses who review medical and hospital records to ensure that appropriate and cost-effective treatment was provided. (Employers: health services, insurance companies, business services, social services, and management services industries.)
- *Quality assurance (QA) directors*—administer quality assurance, total quality management, or statistical control programs, and formulate plans for quality improvement. (Employers: Many QA professionals work to ensure compliance with health, safety, and environmental regulations in a variety of industries.)
- *Consumer credit counselors*—provide advice on personal finance issues such as budgeting, money management, mortgages, and financial planning, often to persons with financial problems. (Employers: nonprofit social services industry.)
- *Resettlement coordinators*—provide aid in finding services related to immigrant employment, immigrant legal status and citizenship, learning English, health, or education. (Employers: social services industry.)
- *Bus aides*—assist drivers and passengers but do not drive the bus. (Employers: educational services, health services, auto repair services, and hotels and lodging places, among others.)
- *Volunteer coordinators*—recruit, train, schedule, and organize volunteers. (Employers: educational services, local government, health services, residential care, membership organizations, and social services industries.)
- *Credentiallers*—obtain and verify employment, education, or licensing credentials for physicians, professors, and other personnel being considered for employment. (Employers: health services, business services, educational services, engineering services.)
- *Job coaches*—provide job training and counseling to disabled individuals or persons going from welfare to work. (Employers: health services, educational services, and social services.)
- *Development directors*—Fundraising specialists and grant writers who generate revenue from donors for nonprofit organizations. (Employers: trusts, social services, and membership organizations.)

## CONCERNS ABOUT SERVICE GROWTH

Although the service economy is growing in leaps and bounds, not everyone is rejoicing about the transformation of the United States from an industrial economy to a service economy.[15] **Materialismo snobbery** reflects the attitude that only manufacturing can create real wealth and that all other sectors of the economy are parasitic and/or inconsequential. Materialismic individuals believe that without manufacturing, there will be little for people to service. As a result, more people will be available to do less work. Consequently, the abundance of labor will drive wages down and subsequently decrease the standard of living in the United States. Ultimately, these individuals believe that the shift to a service economy will jeopardize the American way of life.

**materialismo snobbery**
Belief that without manufacturing there will be less for people to service and so more people available to do less work.

Similar concerns were voiced in the United States more than 140 years ago, when the economy was shifting from agriculture to manufacturing. In 1850, 50 years after industrialization, 65 percent of the population was connected to farming. During this period, many experts voiced great concern over workers leaving the farms to work in the factories. The concerns centered on the same type of logic: If the vast majority of the population left the farms, what would the people eat? Today, 3 percent of the U.S. labor force is involved in farming operations. This 3 percent provides such a surplus of food that the federal government provides price supports and subsidies to keep the farms in business. Apparently, the concerns regarding the shift to manufacturing were unwarranted. In fact, the shift lead to economic growth.

Similarly, with advances in technology and new management practices, the need no longer exists to have as many people in manufacturing as we had in the mid 1900s. Manufacturing is not superior to services. The two are interdependent. In fact, half of all manufacturing workers perform service-type jobs.[16]

Another criticism of the service economy pertains to the **dichotomization of wealth** among service workers. In the United States, 60 percent of the population has experienced a decrease in real income over the past 15 years. In contrast, the wealthiest 5 percent has seen an increase of 50 percent, and the top 1 percent has seen a doubling in income.[17] Although experts disagree, some believe that because of the poor wages paid by some service industries, the shift of the economy away from manufacturing will lead to a further dichotomization of wealth. In other words, the rich will get richer and the poor will get poorer. Without a doubt, the service sector has a lot of low-paying jobs.[18] For individuals under the age of 30, service jobs pay 25 percent less than manufacturing jobs. Some experts believe that as the manufacturing sector continues to decline, the supply of labor available for service jobs will increase, driving wages even lower.

**dichotomization of wealth**
Theory that the service sector's low wages will lead to further polarization in the distribution of wealth.

However, not everyone in services is poorly paid. For example, in the finance and wholesale trade, salaries are much closer to manufacturing wages. Moreover, an increasing number of service personnel are highly skilled and employed in knowledge-based industries. In fact, more than half the U.S. labor force is currently employed in either the production, storage, retrieval, or dissemination of knowledge. Furthermore, the fastest-growing service sector employment opportunities are in finance, insurance, property, and business services, occupations that require educated personnel.[19] Overall, service wages seem to be catching up with wages obtained via manufacturing employment. According to one recent report, service worker pay has risen from a pay disadvantage of 18 percent below to 1 percent below the average of all private sector workers.[20]

The concern over wages associated with service employment is real, and continued acceptance of the industrial model within service industries will do nothing but perpetuate the problem. "Most service enterprises consist of a well-paid brain trust and poorly paid support staff—$500-an-hour lawyers and $5-an-hour secretaries."[21] As a result of the democratic election process in most service economies, a multitude of workers unable to feed and support their families could substantially alter the makeup and direction of future governments.

## PREDICTED KEYS TO SUCCESS WITHIN THE SERVICE SECTOR

Several guidelines to success become clear when examining the growth and dominance of the service sector. First, many of the successful firms excel at niche marketing. Niche marketing strategies include focusing on particular consumer groups and on filling voids in specific locations. For example, the areas currently experiencing the fastest service firm growth are the small Southern metro areas, where competition is scarce and the population base is rapidly expanding.

The second key to success seems to be directly related to the firm's ability to master technological change. Firms that view technology as a source of innovation as opposed to a "necessary evil" are particularly successful. Improvements in technology have enabled successful service firms to open new avenues of communication between them and their customers. Other technological innovations have led to improved services that permit more customer involvement in the service delivery process, offering the dual advantages of decreasing customer-handling costs while providing customers with convenient services. Automatic teller machines (ATMs) and a variety of online services are prime examples.

Another key to success is the firm's ability to blow away the competition when it comes to customer service. Because of the absence of a tangible product, successful service firms must look to their customer service delivery systems to differentiate themselves from competitors. In 1898, Caesar Ritz, the founder of Ritz Hotels, became the manager of the struggling Savoy Hotel in London. Ritz understood men and women and their desire for beautiful things, and he went to great lengths to achieve the atmosphere he desired. First, he turned the Savoy into a center of cultural activity by introducing an orchestra to the dining room and extending the dining period. Proper evening attire was made compulsory, and unescorted women were prohibited from the premises. Ritz also understood his guests' need for romance. For a time, the lower dining room of the Savoy was converted into a Venetian waterway, complete with gondolas and gondoliers who sang Italian love songs. So it seems that regardless of the industry involved, one common thread connects all service firms that are successful—service excellence, the ability to continuously provide courteous, professional, and caring service to customers.[22]

The final key to success, which also differentiates successful service firms from mediocre ones, is an understanding of the value of customer retention strategies. Businesses commonly lose 50 percent of their customers every 5 years.[23]

However, most companies have no idea how many customers are lost or the reasons for their defections. Consequently, companies that do not excel at customer retention are destined to make the same mistakes over and over.

The lack of attention paid to customer retention can be explained by the time-honored tradition of conquest marketing—the pursuit of new customers as opposed to the retention of existing ones. Successful service firms understand the value of retaining existing customers: (1) The marketing costs associated with retaining customers are much lower than the costs associated with acquiring new customers; (2) existing customers tend to purchase more services more frequently; (3) current customers are more familiar with the firm's personnel and procedures and are therefore more efficient in their service transactions; and (4) reducing customer defections by 5 percent in some industries can increase profits by as much as 50 percent.

## SUMMARY

This chapter has provided an overview of the service sector by discussing the following:

- The characteristics service firms share with one another
- The industries experiencing the most substantial changes
- The themes that appear to be driving the growth of the service sector into the new millennium
- The predicted keys to success with the service sector

Many service industries share common service delivery challenges and therefore would benefit from sharing their knowledge with each other. One method for analyzing commonalities across service firms is the use of classification schemes. Service classification schemes include (1) the degree of tangibility, which further classifies services as owned goods, rented goods, and nongoods; (2) the skill level of the provider, which includes professional and nonprofessional providers; (3) the amount of labor intensiveness, which pertains to people-based as opposed to equipment-based services; (4) the degree of customer contact, which varies from high to low; and (5) the goal of the service provider, be it profit or nonprofit. Additional methods for classifying services are presented in Tables 3.2 to 3.6.

Specific industries leading the growth of the service sector include business services, health care, professional services, and hospitality. The growth of the service sector has not received unanimous support. Broad criticisms have been voiced regarding the shifting the economy from an industrial base to a services base. These criticisms include materialismo snobbery—the belief than only manufacturing can create real wealth. In addition, there is some fear that because some service jobs tend to pay lower wages than their manufacturing counterparts it may adversely affect the standard of living in many countries. As time has passed, both these concerns appear to be unfounded.

As we enter the new millennium, the service sector continues to thrive due in large part to technological developments, demographic changes, and competitive pressures. With respect to technological developments, the concept of *e-services,* which in the opinion of many represents the single most important change in how people will interact with the Internet in the immediate future, was discussed. Demographic changes such as aging populations will also facilitate the growth of services into the foreseeable future. In addition, as competition continues to become more intense and firms lose their traditional differential advantages, the role of supplemental services in providing competitive advantages is becoming increasingly important. Supplemental services include information, consultation and advice, order-taking, hospitality, safekeeping, handling exceptions, billing, and payment.

Several guidelines to success become clear when examining the growth and dominance of the service sector across industries. These strategies include (1) excelling at niche marketing; (2) providing customer service far superior to that offered by competitors; (3) mastering technological change; and (4) excelling at customer retention.

## Key Terms

Ap-on-tap
ASPs
Automate
Best practices
Business services
Corporate downsizing
Dichotomization
Emerging occupations
E-service

Health care services
Hospitality industry
Materialismo snobbery
Professional services
Quantization
Search
Supplemental services
Woofs

## Discussion Questions

1. What role do supplemental services play and how do they relate to the concept of the "service imperative"?
2. What is an e-service?
3. How do e-services differ from traditional e-business and e-commerce systems?
4. Service firms can learn a great deal from other firms in other industries. What strategies appear to be linked with success across the service spectrum?
5. Discuss the marketing implications of Table 3.2, "Understanding the Nature of the Service Act."
6. Define the term *materialismo snobbery.*
7. Compare changing from an agricultural economy to an industrial economy with moving from an industrial economy to a service economy.
8. Discuss the possible political consequences associated with the dichotomization of wealth in the United States.

9. On paper, create an ecosystem of e-services that an aggregator could market to the public.
10. How can an e-service minimize the problems caused by inseparability that traditionally impact other types of traditional service firms?

# Notes

1. Sources: Thomas A. Stewart, "G.E. Keeps Those Ideas Coming," *Fortune,* August 12, 1991, pp. 41–49; Robert C. Camp, *Benchmarking: The Search for Industry-Best Practices That Lead to Superior Performance* (White Plains, NY: Quality Resources, 1989); Michael J. Spendolini, *The Benchmarking Book* (New York: AMACOM, 1992); Jeremy Main, "How to Steal the Best Ideas Around," *Fortune,* October 19, 1992; and A. Steven Walleck et al., "Benchmarking World Class Performance," *Mckinsey Quarterly* 1 (1990), pp.3–24.
2. Christopher H. Lovelock, "Classifying Services to Gain Strategic Marketing Insights," *Journal of Marketing* 47 (Summer 1983), 9–20.
3. Fanglan Du, Paula Mergenhagen, and Marlene Lee, "The Future of Services," *American Demographics* (November 1995). Web site: http://www.marketing tools.com. The hospitality industry section was developed from the following sources: Richard L. Brush and Teresa M. Schulz, "Pioneers and Leaders of the Hospitality Industry," pp. 24–34; Robert A. Brymer and Lynn M. Huffman, "Overview of the Hospitality Industry," pp. 3–15; Leland L. Nichols, "Introduction to Travel and Tourism Management," pp. 307–322; and Sheryl Fried, "Casino Hotel Operations and Management," pp. 370–385. In *Hospitality Management,* 7th ed., Robert A. Brymer, ed. (Dubuque, Iowa: Kendall/Hunt Publishing, 1995); and Rocco M. Angelo and Andrew N. Vladimir, *Hospitality Today* (East Lansing, Mich.: The Educational Institute of the American Hotel & Motel Association, 1991).
4. "Millennial themes: age, education, services," *MLR: The Editor's Desk,* http:// stats.bls.gov/opub/ted/1999/nov/wk5/art03.htm.
5. This section was developed from materials obtained from www.e-services .hp.com.
6. Leyland F. Pitt, Pierre Berthon, and Richard T. Watson, "Cyberservice: Taming service marketing problems with the World Wide Web," *Business Horizons* 42, no. 1 (1999), 11–18.
7. "Millennial themes: age, education, services," *MLR: The Editor's Desk,* http:// stats.bls.gov/opub/ted/1999/nov/wk5/art03.htm
8. Ibid.
9. Robert W. Van Geizen, "Occupational pay in private goods- and service-producing industries," *Compensation and Working Conditions Online* 1, no. 1 (June 1996).
10. Philip Kotler, *Marketing Management,* 8th ed. (New York: Prentice-Hall, 1995).
11. "Millennial themes: Age, education, services," *MLR: The Editor's Desk,* http://stats.bls.gov/opub/ted/1999/nov/wk5/art03.htm

12. Joseph R. Meisenheimer II, "The Service Industry in the 'Good' Versus 'Bad' Jobs Debate," *Monthly Labor Review Online* 121, no. 2 (February 1998).
13. http://stats.bls.gov/opub/fed/1999/nov/wk5/art03.htm
14. http://stats.bls.gov/new98.htm
15. Michael E. Raynor, "After Materialismo . . . ," *Across the Board* (July–August 1992), pp. 38–41.
16. "Wealth in Services," *The Economist,* February 20, 1993, p. 16.
17. Raynor, "After Materialismo . . . ," p. 41.
18. "The Manufacturing Myth," *The Economist,* March 19, 1994, p. 92.
19. "The Final Frontier," *The Economist,* February 20, 1993, p. 63.
20. Van Giezen, "Occupational Pay."
21. Raynor, "After Materialismo . . . ," p. 41.
22. Richard L. Brush and Teresa Schulz, "Pioneers and Leaders in the Hospitality Industry," in *Hospitality Management,* 7th ed., Robert A. Brymer, ed. (Dubuque, Iowa: Kendall/Hunt Publishing, 1995), 24–34.
23. Frederick F. Reichheld, "Learning from Customer Defections," *Harvard Business Review* (March–April 1996), 56–69.

# chapter 4

# Consumer Decision Process Issues in Services Marketing

## CHAPTER OBJECTIVES

In this chapter we discuss consumer decision process issues as they relate to the purchase of services.

After reading this chapter, you should be able to:

- Describe the steps involved in the consumer decision process model.
- Discuss the factors that influence the consumer decision-making process.
- Discuss the special considerations about services during the prepurchase stage.
- Discuss the special considerations about services during the consumption stage.
- Discuss the special considerations about services during the postpurchase stage.
- Describe models that attempt to explain the consumer's postpurchase evaluation.

"The consumer's mind is still closed to us; it is a 'black box' that remains sealed. We can observe inputs to the box and the decisions made as a result, but we can never know how the act of processing inputs (information) truly happens."

John E. G. Bateson

# Introduction

Consumer orientation lies at the heart of the marketing concept.[1] As marketers, we are required to understand our consumers and to build our organizations around them. This requirement is particularly important for services, which in many instances still tend to be operations dominated rather than customer oriented (Figure 4.1). Hence, today it is more important than ever to understand consumers, how they choose among alternative services offered to them, and how they evaluate these services once they have received them.

Throughout the three stages of *prepurchase, choice,* and *postpurchase evaluation,* the consumer must be using a process or model to make his or her decision. Although a variety of models have been developed and are discussed in this chapter, it is important to point out that no model is wholly accurate. The consumer's mind is still closed to us; it is a "black box" that remains sealed. We can observe inputs to the box and the decisions made as a result, but we can never know how the act of processing inputs (information) truly happens.

Why, then, bother with such models? Whether marketing managers like it or not, every time they make marketing decisions, they are basing their decisions on some model of how the consumer will behave. Quite often these models are implicit and seldom shared with others, representing, in effect, the marketing manager's own experience. However, every time a price is changed, a new product is launched, or advertising appears, some assumption has been made about how the consumer will react.

The purpose of this chapter is to discuss the consumer decision process as it relates to the purchase of services. Because of the unique characteristics of services, differences exist between the way consumers make decisions regarding services versus goods. This chapter has been constructed in two sections. The first section is an overview of the consumer decision-making process. It provides a summary of the process and its applications to marketing decisions. The second section of the chapter is dedicated to specific considerations about the consumer decision-making process as it relates to services.

## THE CONSUMER DECISION PROCESS: AN OVERVIEW

**consumer decision process**
The three-step process consumers use to make purchase decisions; includes the prepurchase stage, the consumption stage, and the postpurchase evaluation stage.

To market services effectively, marketing managers need to understand the thought processes used by consumers during each of the three stages of the **consumer decision process:** the prepurchase choice among alternatives, the consumer's reaction during consumption, and the postpurchase evaluation of satisfaction (Figure 4.2). Although we can never truly know the thought process used by the individual when making that choice, the consumer decision process helps to structure our thinking and to guide our marketing research regarding consumer behavior. Let's begin this discussion by focusing on the prepurchase stage.

1700 EASTWOOD RD
PO BOX 1110
WILMINGTON NC 28402

00011606  1 AC  0.230  00  **AUTOCR **C064
|..|.|||..|.|..|.|Ill..|.|...|.|.|.|..|.|.|||..||...|.|...||..|

# Customer Bill

page 1 of 2

| Account | 872 675 5229 |
|---|---|
| Date mailed | Oct 3, 1996 |
| Usage period | Sep 4 - Oct 2 |
| Payment received - Sep 30 | $197.22 |
| Total due | **$146.86** |
| Payment due | Oct 28 |

*Thank you for your last payment!*

Hurricane Fran has made things tough for many of us by bringing financial hardship and inconvenience. In addition to restoring your power, we are here to answer billing questions and to find a payment option that will work for you. If you have questions, or face a financial hardship due to Fran, please call 1-800-228-8485.

## Usage

| Meter number | | | | R71133 |
|---|---|---|---|---|
| Readings: Oct | 2 | | | 60947 |
| Sep | 4 | | | - 58872 |
| Kwh usage | | | | 2075 |

*Total Peak Registration*

| On-peak KW | Sep 11 at  8:15 pm | 13.35 |
|---|---|---|
| On-peak KW | Oct  1 at  8:00 am | 7.50 |
| Off-peak KW | Sep 29 at  7:30 pm | 13.72 |
| Off-peak KW | Oct  1 at 10:15 pm | 5.98 |

## Billing

**Residential-Time of Use Demand rate**

| | | | | 28 Days |
|---|---|---|---|---|
| Basic customer charge | | | | 9.85 |
| *Summer, September 04 - September 30* | | | | |
| On-peak KWH | 777 kwh | x | $0.04301 | 33.4188 |
| Off-peak KWH | 1,226 kwh | x | $0.02927 | 35.8850 |
| On-peak KW at .9361 proration | 13.35 kw | x | $5.02000 | 62.7346 |
| *Non-summer, October 1 - October 02* | | | | |
| On-peak KWH | 53 kwh | x | $0.04301 | 2.2795 |
| Off-peak KWH | 19 kwh | x | $0.02927 | 0.5561 |
| On-peak KW at .0639 proration | 7.50 kw | x | $3.73000 | 1.7876 |
| Energy conservation discount | | | | -6.8331 |
| | | | | |
| Total R-TOUD Rate Billing | | | | 139.68 |

*On-peak kw proration factor*

| Non-summer | on-peak kwh | 53 kwh / | 830 kwh | .0639 |
|---|---|---|---|---|
| Summer | on-peak kwh | 777 kwh / | 830 kwh | .9361 |
| Total on-peak kwh | | 830 | | |

**SLR rate**

| | | | | 28 Days |
|---|---|---|---|---|
| *Sodium vapor lights,    8 kwh,  9500 lumens, enclosed* | | | | |
| Residential lighting | 1 Light | x | $2.90 | 2.90 |
| 3% North Carolina sales tax | | | | 4.28 |
| Total due | | | | $146.86 |

**Figure 4.1    Example of Operations-Dominated Communications**
The first page of a typical electric bill is dominated by operations-oriented information. Company bills are often the only form of communication with customers, yet most fail to communicate with customers effectively.

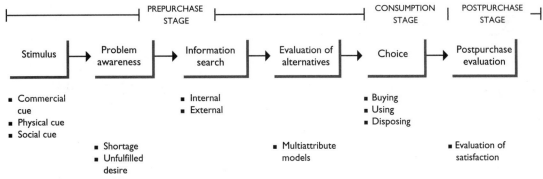

**Figure 4.2**     **Consumer Decision Process**

## The Prepurchase Stage

### THE STIMULUS

The **prepurchase stage** of the consumer decision process refers to all consumer activities occurring before the acquisition of the service. This stage begins when an individual receives a **stimulus** that may incite the person to consider a purchase.[2] The stimulus may be a commercial cue, a social cue, or a physical cue. **Commercial cues** are the result of promotional efforts. For example, a consumer may be exposed to a commercial about a local college. As a result, the individual may begin to assess his or her current situation and the possibility of enrolling at a university to pursue a degree. Similarly, **social cues** are obtained from the individual's peer group or from significant others. For example, watching friends leave for college in the fall may incite an individual to consider furthering his or her own education. The stimulus may also be the result of **physical cues** such as thirst, hunger, or various other biological cues.

### PROBLEM AWARENESS

Once the consumer has received the stimulus, the next phase of the process is **problem awareness.** During the problem awareness phase, the consumer examines whether a need or want truly exists for the product. The need may be based on a **shortage** (a need) or on an **unfulfilled desire** (a want). For example, if the consumer is incited by a commercial cue for a university and is not currently enrolled in any other university, then a shortage exists. In contrast, if the consumer is currently enrolled in a college but in one that he or she no longer values, then an unfulfilled desire exists. If the consumer does not recognize a shortage or unfulfilled desire the decision process stops at this point. Otherwise, the decision process continues on to the information search stage.

### INFORMATION SEARCH

The recognition of a problem demands a solution from the individual, and it usually implies that a potential purchase will ensue. The individual searches for alternatives during the **information search** phase of the prepurchase stage. As the name implies, during the information search phase, the consumer collects information regarding possible alternatives. It is clear that in all consumer decision

**prepurchase stage**
All consumer activities occurring before and leading up to the acquisition of the service.

**stimulus**
The thought, action, or motivation that incites a person to consider a purchase.

**commercial cues**
Events or motivations that provide stimulus to the consumer and are promotional efforts on the part of the company.

**social cues**
Events or motivations that provide stimulus to the consumer, obtained from the individual's peer group or from significant others.

**physical cues**
Motivation, such as thirst, hunger, or another biological cue that provides stimulus to the consumer.

making, consumers seldom consider all feasible alternatives. Instead, they have a limited list of options chosen on the basis of past experience, convenience, and knowledge. This list is often referred to by theorists as the **evoked set**—the set of "brands" that comes to the consumer's mind when thinking about a particular product category and from which the choice will be made.

Returning to our college selection example, when considering alternatives, the consumer may first engage in an **internal search.** An internal search accesses the consumer's own memories about possible alternative colleges. In this example, the previous knowledge may be based on the proximity to a local college, information obtained while watching local sporting events, or listening to older family members reminisce about their own college experiences. An internal search is a passive approach to gathering information.

The internal search may be followed by an **external search,** which would involve the collection of new information obtained via campus visits, talking to friends, and/or reading *U.S. News & World Report,* which rates universities on an annual basis.

## EVALUATION OF ALTERNATIVES

Once relevant information has been collected from both internal and external sources, the consumer arrives at a set of alternative solutions to the recognized problem. The possible solutions are considered in the **evaluation of alternatives** phase of the consumer decision process. This phase may consist of a **nonsystematic evaluation** of alternatives, such as the use of intuition—simply choosing an alternative by relying on a "gut-level feeling"—or it may involve a **systematic evaluation** technique, such as a multiattribute model. Such systematic models utilize a set of formalized steps to arrive at a decision.

Marketing theorists have made extensive use of multiattribute models to simulate the process of evaluating products.[3] According to these models, consumers employ a number of attributes or criteria as basic references when evaluating a service. For example, consumers may compare alternative colleges based on entrance requirements, tuition, academic reputation, and location. Consumers compute their preference for the service by combining the scores of the service on each individual attribute.

Within the evaluation of alternatives phase of the decision process, consumers are assumed to create a matrix similar to the one shown in Table 4.1 to compare alternatives. The example in the table is the choice of a college for an undergraduate degree. Across the top of the table are two types of variables. The first is the evoked set of brands to be evaluated. As previously mentioned, this evoked set will, for various reasons, be less than an exhaustive list of all possible choices; in this example it includes UNT, ETU, SCSU, and SCG. The second type of variable is the importance rating with which the consumer ranks the various attributes that constitute the vertical axis of the table. For example, in Table 4.1, the consumer rates location as the most important attribute, followed by tuition, and so on. To complete the table, the consumer rates each brand on each attribute based on his or her expectations of each attribute. For example, this particular consumer gives UNT top marks for location, tuition, and admission requirements but perceives the university to be not as strong on academic reputation.

**problem awareness**
The second phase of the prepurchase stage, in which the consumer determines whether a need exists for the product.

**shortage**
The need for a product or service as a result of the consumer's not having that particular product or service.

**unfulfilled desire**
The need for a product or service as a result of a consumer's dissatisfaction with a current product or service.

**information search**
The phase in the prepurchase stage in which the consumer collects information on possible alternatives.

**evoked set**
The limited set of "brands" that comes to the consumer's mind when thinking about a particular product category from which the purchase choice will be made.

**internal search**
A passive approach to gathering information in which the consumer's own memory is the main source of information about a product.

**external search**
A proactive approach to gathering information in which the consumer collects new information from sources outside the consumer's own experience.

TABLE 4.1
_____

## A Typical Multiattribute Choice Matrix

| | Evoked Sets of Brands | | | | |
|---|---|---|---|---|---|
| **Attributes** | **UNT** | **ETU** | **SCSU** | **SCG** | **Importance Weights** |
| Location | 10 | 10 | 10 | 9.9 | 10 |
| Tuition | 10 | 10 | 9 | 9 | 9 |
| Admission requirements | 10 | 10 | 10 | 10 | 8 |
| Academic reputation | 8 | 9 | 9 | 9 | 7 |
| Degree programs | 10 | 8 | 8 | 10 | 6 |

**evaluation of alternatives**
The phase of the pre-purchase stage in which the consumer places a value or "rank" on each alternative.

**nonsystematic evaluation**
Choosing among alternatives in a random fashion or by a "gut-level feeling" approach.

**systematic evaluation**
Choosing among alternatives by using a set of formalized steps to arrive at a decision.

**linear compensatory approach**
A systematic model that proposes that the consumer creates a global score for each brand by multiplying the rating of the brand on each attribute by the importance attached to the attribute and adding the scores together.

Given such a table, various choice processes have been suggested with which the consumer can use the table to make a decision. The **linear compensatory approach** proposes that the consumer creates a global score for each brand by multiplying the rating of the brand on each attribute by the importance attached to the attribute and adding the scores together. UNT would score $10 \times 10$ (location) plus $10 \times 9$ (tuition) plus $10 \times 8$ (admission requirements), and so on. The university with the highest score, in this example UNT, is then chosen.

Another type of multiattribute approach that has been suggested is the **lexicographic approach.** This approach describes so-called lazy decision makers who try to minimize the effort involved. They look at each attribute in turn, starting with the most important, and try to make a decision. The individual whose preferences are shown in Table 4.1 would look first at location and rule out SCG. Next, tuition would rule out SCSU. At this stage, the choice is reduced to UNT and ETU, but admission requirement produces a tie in the scoring. Finally, the choice would be made in favor of ETU based on the next attribute, academic reputation. Thus a different decision rule results in a different choice: ETU under the lexicographic model and UNT under the liner compensatory model.

Given the popularity of multiattribute models, it is no surprise that they have been used to describe and explain the consumer's service decision processes. The merit of these models lies in their simplicity and explicitness. The attributes identified cover a wide range of concerns related to the service experience, and they are easily understood by service managers. For example, analyzing consumer multi-attribute models provides:

- A list of alternatives that are included in the evoked set
- The list of criteria that consumers consider when making purchase decisions
- The importance weights attached to each criteria
- Performance beliefs associated with a particular firm
- Performance beliefs associated with the competition

The tasks for management when using these models are relatively straightforward. For example, advertising can be used to stress a particular attribute on which the firm's service appears to be weak in the mind of consumers. A college may have had a poor academic reputation in the past, but advertising may change consumer perceptions by featuring the school's accomplishments. If necessary, competitive advertising can also be used to try and reduce the attribute scores obtained by competitors. For example, many regional universities are attracting students by comparing the student/instructor ratio of large universities with their own ratios.

## The Consumption Stage

Thus far we have discussed the prepurchase stage of the consumer decision process, which described the stimulus, problem awareness, information search, and evaluation of alternatives phases. An important outcome of the prepurchase stage is a decision to buy a certain brand of the product category. During this **consumption stage,** the consumer may make a **store choice**—deciding to purchase from a particular outlet, or a **nonstore choice**—deciding to purchase from a catalog, the Internet, or a variety of mail-order possibilities. This decision is accompanied by a set of expectations about the performance of the product. In the case of goods, the consumer then uses the product and disposes of any solid waste remaining. The activities of buying, using, and disposing are grouped together and labeled the **consumption process.**[4]

## The Postpurchase Evaluation Stage

Once a choice has been made and as the product is being consumed, **postpurchase evaluation** takes place. During this stage, consumers may experience varying levels of **cognitive dissonance**—doubt that the correct purchase decision has been made. Marketers often attempt to minimize the consumer's cognitive dissonance by reassuring the customer that the correct decision has been made. Strategies to minimize cognitive dissonance include aftersale contact with the customer, providing a reassuring letter in the packaging of the product, providing warranties and guarantees, and reinforcing the consumer's decision through the firm's advertising. For example, learning through the college's advertising that the school has been nationally recognized by *U.S. News & World Report* would positively reinforce the consumer's enrollment decision. Simply stated, postpurchase evaluation is all about customer satisfaction, and customer satisfaction is the key outcome of the marketing process. Customer satisfaction is achieved when consumers' perceptions meet or exceed their expectations. Customer satisfaction is an end in itself but is also the source of word-of-mouth recommendations and can thus stimulate further purchases (see Services in Action 4.1).

During the evaluation process of the postpurchase stage, multiattribute models can once again be utilized. For this process, the choices of schools are replaced by two columns. The first is the score expected by the consumer on each attribute. The second is the perceived score on each attribute obtained by the consumer after enrollment. The satisfaction score is then derived by creating a global score of the comparisons between perceptions and expectations weighted by the importance of each attribute. This is shown in Table 4.2.

In this example, the customer chose UNT by using the multiattribute choice matrix shown in Table 4.1 and based on the linear compensatory approach. The

**lexicographic approach**
A systematic model that proposes that the consumer makes a decision by examining each attribute, starting with the most important, to rule out alternatives.

**consumption stage**
The stage of the consumer decision process in which the consumer purchases and uses the product.

**store choice**
The decision to purchase from a particular outlet or store.

**nonstore choice**
The decision to purchase from a catalog, the Internet, or through mail order.

**consumption process**
The activities of buying, using, and disposing of a product.

**postpurchase evaluation**
The stage of the consumer decision-making process during which the consumer determines whether the correct purchase decision was made.

**cognitive dissonance**
Doubt in the consumer's mind regarding the correctness of the purchase decision.

SERVICES 4.1
ACTION    **Cultural Perceptions**

Customer expectations and perceptions are psychological phenomena and are not necessarily based on reality. For example, individual customers can experience the same service situation and walk away with different impressions of the same event. This inherent variation in customer expectations and perceptions makes managing service operations particularly challenging.

According to a recent study, it appears that in addition to individual differences, cultural background also influences customer expectations and perceptions. A study of more than 10,000 Kaiser Permanente HMO patients, consisting of 7,747 Caucasians, 836 African Americans, 710 Latinos, and 1,007 Asians, requested information pertaining to health care-related outcomes such as overall satisfaction with the care provided; accessibility; willingness to recommend their physician to a friend; the technical competence of their health care provider; the physician's focus on health promotion; the physician's communication style; adequacy of explanations; time spent with patient; and concern, courtesy, and respect for patient.

In terms of what each cultural group found most important, all groups rated technical competence and adequacy of explanation as the most important outcomes. Higher proportions of non-Caucasian groups indicated that the physician's display of concern, courtesy, and respect were more important than anything else. Other interesting findings included that for 7 of the 10 performance measures, Asians rated overall physician performance lower than Caucasian groups. Within the Asian group, Chinese and Filipino patients were the least satisfied, and Japanese patients were least likely to recommend their doctor. African Americans rated technical competence and focus on health promotion higher than did Caucasians. Latinos and Caucasians reported the most comparable ratings; however, Latinos rated the accessibility of physicians significantly lower.

Source: Anonymous, "Ethnicity Defines Patient Satisfaction," *Trustee* 53, no. 5 (May 2000), 5.

expected levels on each attribute are, therefore, taken from that matrix. In reality, the tuition was increased, and the school did not live up to its academic reputation. The consumer, therefore, downgraded his evaluation on those attributes. The smaller the gap between expectations and perceptions, the more positive the postpurchase evaluation.

## SPECIAL CONSIDERATIONS PERTAINING TO SERVICES

Although the consumer decision process model applies to both goods and services, unique considerations arise with respect to services (see Services in Action 4.2). The considerations addressed in this part of the chapter help in developing a deeper understanding of the challenges faced when marketing services.

# TABLE 4.2

## College Selection: A Postpurchase Evaluation for UT

| Attributes | Expected Score (from Table 4.1) | Perceived Score | Importance Weights |
|---|---|---|---|
| Location | 10 | 10 | 10 |
| Tuition | 10 | 9.5 | 9 |
| Admission requirements | 10 | 10 | 8 |
| Academic reputation | 8 | 6 | 7 |
| Degree programs | 10 | 10 | 6 |

# SERVICES 4.2

## IN ACTION    The Consumer Decision Process as It Relates to E-Commerce

### Information Search

1. Ease of navigation—is it easy to move throughout the Web site?
2. Speed of page downloads—does each page load quickly enough?
3. Effectiveness of search features—are search features returning the information users are looking for?
4. Frequency of product updates—is product information updated often enough to meet user needs?

### Evaluation of Alternatives

1. Ease of product comparisons—is it easy to compare the different products the Web site offers?
2. Product descriptions—are product descriptions accurate, clear, and comprehensive enough to allow customers to make informed decisions?
3. Contacting customer service representatives—are customer service phone numbers easy to locate?
4. In-stock status—are out-of-stock products flagged before the customer proceeds to the checkout process?

### Purchase

1. Security and privacy issues—do users feel comfortable transmitting personal information?
2. Checkout process—are users able to move through the checkout process in a reasonable amount of time?
3. Payment options—are payment options offered that non-buyers desire?
4. Delivery options—are delivery options offered that non-buyers desire?
5. Ordering instructions—are ordering instructions easy to understand?

Source: Adapted from Jody Dodson, "What's Wrong with Your Web Site," *Target Marketing* 23, no. 2 (February 2000), 135–139.

SERVICES 4.3

ACTION    **Riverside Methodist Hospital**

Hospitals are unique among service providers in that they provide services that most people need but don't necessarily want. Relatively few people use the services of a hospital out of pure choice.

A number of factors set hospitals apart from other services. In the first place, hospitals' levels of risk are higher—a poor service can endanger health or life, not just create an unpleasant impression of the experience. Second, because many patients lack proper knowledge about how a hospital functions and the nature of the treatment they are receiving, even a merely unpleasant service experience can be genuinely frightening.

Riverside Methodist Hospital in Columbus, Ohio, is part of U.S. Health Corporation, a small for-profit hospital chain. A key aspect of Riverside's competitive strategy centers on changing the image of the hospital and the service experience in the eyes of patients and potential patients. Reducing patients' concerns can change the nature of the patients' evaluation of the service before, during, and after the hospital visit.

Understanding patient demands is an important part of this strategy, which recognizes that not all patients are the same and that the needs of different groups can become important points of differentiation. For example, the presence of a large Honda automobile plant nearby means that the hospital regularly serves Japanese-speaking patients and visitors. On a different note, Riverside Methodist has developed the Elizabeth Blackwell Center, a separate facility dealing specifically with women's needs for health care.

Once patients have been admitted to the hospital, the principal objective is to reduce patient anxiety and insecurity. The physical facilities of the hospital, the attitude and demeanor of the nursing and medical staff, and the perceived quality and frequency of care can all have an impact, as can more peripheral factors such as frequency and duration of family visits to patients. The question is not one of improving patient care but of improving patient perceptions of care by making an otherwise unpleasant experience as comfortable as possible.

One area where this policy has been put into practice is the hospital emergency ward. In most emergency wards, the patient is first met by an admitting clerk, whose primary function is to take information about the patient and get the patient to wait until a doctor is available. Riverside has put nursing staff directly into the emergency ward. First, the patient is met immediately by a senior nurse, who determines the severity of his or her condition; serious cases are taken immediately for treatment. Less serious cases are assigned a primary nurse, who looks after the patient until a doctor is available. Because patients receive at least basic attention immediately, patient uncertainty is reduced.

Source: John E. G. Bateson, *Managing Services Marketing: Text and Readings,* 2nd ed. (Fort Worth, Tex.: The Dryden Press, 1992), 103. ©1992 by The Dryden Press. Reprinted by permission of the publisher.

## Prepurchase Stage Considerations

### PERCEIVED RISK AND THE PURCHASE OF CONSUMER SERVICES

In comparison with goods consumers, consumers of services tend to perceive a higher level of risk during the prepurchase decision stage. The concept of perceived risk as an explanation for customer purchasing behavior was first suggested in the 1960s.[5] The central theory is that consumer behavior involves risk in the sense that any action taken by a consumer will produce consequences that he or she cannot anticipate with any certainty, and some of which are likely to be unpleasant (see Services in Action 4.3). Perceived risk is proposed to consist of two dimensions:

- **Consequence,** the degree of importance and/or danger of the outcomes derived from any consumer decision.
- **Uncertainty,** the subjective possibility of the occurrence of these outcomes.

Surgery provides an excellent example of how consequence and uncertainty play a major role in service purchases. With respect to uncertainty, the consumer may have never undergone surgery before. Moreover, even though the surgeon has performed the operation successfully in the past, the patient is not guaranteed that this particular surgery will end with the same successful outcome. In addition, uncertainty is likely to increase if the patient lacks sufficient knowledge prior to the operation concerning details of the surgery and its aftereffects. The consequences of a poor decision regarding surgery could be life threatening.

**TYPES OF RISK**   As the idea of consumer perceived risk developed, five types of perceived risk were identified, based on five different kinds of outcomes: financial, performance, physical, social, and psychological.[6] **Financial risk** assumes that financial loss could occur if the purchase goes wrong or fails to operate correctly. **Performance risk** relates to the idea that the item or service purchased will not perform the task for which it was purchased. The **physical risk** of a purchase can emerge if something does go wrong and injury is inflicted on the purchaser. **Social risk** suggests that there might be a loss of personal social status associated with a particular purchase (e.g., a fear that one's peer group will react negatively—"Who bought this?"). **Psychological risk** pertains to the influence of the purchase on the individual's self-esteem. For example, you will not consider wearing certain clothes or you will refuse to own certain cars because they are not consistent with your self-image.

**RISK AND STANDARDIZATION**   Much of the heightened level of perceived risk can be attributed to the difficulty in producing a standardized service product. In Chapter 2 we introduced the concept of heterogeneity. Because a service is an experience involving highly complex interactions, it is, not surprisingly, very difficult to replicate the experience from customer to customer or from day to day.[7] As a result, the customer may find it difficult to predict precisely the quality of service he or she will be buying. The fact that Brown's Auto Repair Shop did a good tune-up for your neighbor does not mean that it will perform on the same level for you. Perceived risk, therefore, tends to be higher for purchasing services in contrast to the purchase of goods.

**consequence**
The degree of importance and/or danger of the outcomes of any consumer decision.

**uncertainty**
The subjective possibility of occurrence of consequences.

**financial risk**
The possibility of a monetary loss if the purchase goes wrong or fails to operate correctly.

**performance risk**
The possibility that the item or service purchased will not perform the task for which it was purchased.

**physical risk**
The possibility that if something does go wrong, injury could be inflicted on the purchaser.

**social risk**
The possibility of a loss in personal social status associated with a particular purchase.

**psychological risk**
The possibility that a purchase will affect an individual's self-esteem.

**CO-PRODUCER RISK**    The involvement of the consumer in the "production process of services" is another source of increased perceived risk. Co-producer risk is directly related to the concept of inseparability. Once again, surgery is a good example of the consumer's involvement in the production process. Unlike goods, which can be purchased and taken away, services cannot be taken home and used in private, where the buyer's mistakes will not be visible. Instead, the consumer must take part in the ritual of the service itself. To be part of such a process and not to know exactly what is going on clearly increases the uncertainty about the consequences, particularly the physical consequences of being involved in a service encounter such as surgery, or the social consequences of doing the "wrong" thing, such as wearing the wrong type of clothing to an important dinner party in the presence of other guests.

**INFORMATION AND RISK**    Others have argued that the higher levels of risk associated with service purchases is due to the limited information that is readily available before the purchase decision is made. For example, the economics literature suggests that goods and services possess three different types of attributes:[8]

**search attributes**
Attributes that can be determined prior to purchase.

**experience attributes**
Attributes that can be evaluated only during and after the production process.

**credence attributes**
Attributes that cannot be evaluated confidently even immediately after receipt of the good or service.

- **Search attributes**—attributes that can be determined prior to purchase.
- **Experience attributes**—attributes that can be evaluated only during and after the production process.
- **Credence attributes**—attributes that cannot be evaluated confidently even immediately after receipt of the good or service.

Because of the intangible nature of services, it is often extremely difficult for consumers to objectively evaluate a service before it is bought. Services thus have very few search attributes. In contrast, goods can be touched, seen, smelled, heard, and, in some instances, tasted prior to purchase and are therefore predominantly characterized by search attributes.

A large proportion of the properties possessed by services (e.g., the friendliness of the flight attendants of a particular airline or the skill level of a hairstylist) can be discovered by consumers only during and after the consumption of the service; these are thus experience attributes. Moreover, some of the properties of many services (e.g., how well a car has been repaired by a body shop or how well your doctor performs services) cannot be assessed even after the service is completed; these are called credence attributes. All in all, because of the properties of intangibility (which limits search attributes), inseparability (which increases credence attributes), and the variation in quality provided by service personnel, services tend to be characterized by experience and credence attributes.

## BRAND LOYALTY AMONG SERVICE CONSUMERS

If we start with the premise that consumers do not like taking risks, then it would seem obvious that they will try, whenever possible, to reduce risk during the purchase process. One strategy is to build brand or store loyalty.[9] Brand loyalty is based on the degree to which the consumer has obtained satisfaction in the past. If consumers have been satisfied in the past with their supplier of service, they have little incentive to risk trying someone or something new.

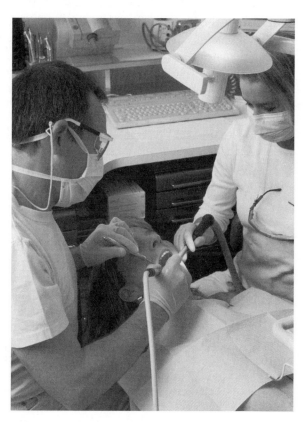

Maintaining a long-term relationship with the same service provider, such as going to the same dentist every time you need dental work, reduces the perceived risk associated with the purchase. In a sense, customers are "brand loyal" to their service providers as well as to the products they buy.

Having been satisfied with a high-risk purchase, a consumer is less likely to experiment with a different purchase. Maintaining a long-term relationship with the same service provider, in and of itself, helps to reduce the perceived risk associated with the purchase. This is why it is common to observe consumers acquiring services from the same physician, dentist, and hairstylist over long periods.

Brand loyalty may also be greater in purchasing services as a result of the limited number of alternative choices available. This is particularly true of professional services, where acceptable substitutes may not be available. In contrast, consumers of goods generally have more substitutes available in a given area. Moreover, purchasing alternative goods does not represent the same level of increased risk as purchasing alternative services.

Finally, brand loyalty may also be higher for services due to the **switching costs** that can accrue when changing from one service provider to another. An array of switching costs can be accrued, depending on the product involved. Consider, for example, the switching costs involved in changing from one brand of canned vegetables to another compared with the costs involved in changing banks. Typical switching costs include:

- **Search costs**—the time it takes to seek out new alternatives.
- **Transaction costs**—the costs associated with first-time visits, such as new x-rays when changing dentists.

**switching costs**
The costs that accrue when changing from one service provider to another.

**search costs**
The time it takes to seek out new alternatives.

**transaction costs**
The costs associated with first-time visits.

**learning costs**
The costs associated with learning new systems.

**loyal customer discounts**
Discounts that are given for maintaining the same service over time and that are lost when switching from one supplier to another.

**customer habit**
Costs associated with changing established behavior patterns.

**emotional costs**
Emotional turmoil that can be experienced when severing a long-term relationship with a provider.

**cognitive costs**
Costs associated with thinking about changing providers.

- **Learning costs**—costs such as time and money that are associated with learning new systems, such as new versions of software packages.
- **Loyal customer discounts**—discounts that are given for maintaining the same service over time, such as accident-free auto insurance rates. Such discounts are sacrificed when switching from one supplier to the next.
- **Customer habit**—costs associated with changing established behavior patterns.
- **Emotional costs**—emotional turmoil that one may experience when severing a long-term relationship with a provider. Emotional costs are particularly high when a personal relationship has developed between the client and the provider.
- **Cognitive costs**—costs in terms of the time spent simply thinking about making a change in service providers.

## THE IMPORTANCE OF PERSONAL SOURCES OF INFORMATION

Another special consideration during the prepurchase stage is the importance of personal sources of information. Research has shown that in the area of communications, personal forms such as word-of-mouth references and information from opinion leaders are often given more importance than company-controlled communications. A reference from a friend becomes more important when the purchase to be made has a greater risk. For example, a visit to a new hairdresser can be stressful because the outcome of the service will be highly visible. That stress can be reduced by a recommendation from someone whose judgment the consumer trusts. The consumer will then feel more confident about the outcome.

Similarly, evidence suggests that opinion leaders play an important role in the purchase of services. An opinion leader in a community is an individual who is looked to for advice. Within the perceived-risk framework, an opinion leader can be viewed as a source of reduced social risk. A woman who visits a hairdresser for the first time may feel uncertain about the quality of the outcome. However, she might be reassured by the fact that the friend who recommended the service is widely known to have good judgment in such matters and will convey this to others in their mutual social group. In this way, the opinion leader's judgment partially substitutes for the consumer's own.

In addition to reducing perceived risk, the importance of personal sources of information to service consumers is relevant for a number of other reasons. Because of the intangibility of services, mass media is not as effective in communicating the qualities of the service compared with personal sources of information. For example, would you feel comfortable purchasing services from a surgeon who is featured in television advertising? Moreover, would it be feasible for the physician to adequately describe the surgical procedure during a 30-second television spot? Overall, personal sources of information become more important as objective standards for evaluation decrease and as the complexity of the product being marketed increases.

Another reason that consumers rely to such a great extent on personal sources of information is that nonpersonal sources may simply not be available because of professional restrictions or negative attitudes regarding the use of advertising. Alternatively, many service providers are small and may lack the resources or knowledge to advertise. How many marketing or communications classes do you suppose your dentist or physician enrolled in while attending college? Most have no idea what a target market is, what a marketing mix is for, or what a marketing plan entails. Regardless of their training and subsequent status, professional service providers are operating businesses and must effectively compete in order to maintain their livelihoods. The bottom line is that many professional service providers either lack the knowledge or feel uncomfortable marketing their services.

## FEWER ALTERNATIVES TO CONSIDER

In comparison with goods, consumers of services tend to evaluate a smaller number of alternative sources of supply during the prepurchase stage for a variety of reasons. First, each service provider tends to offer only one brand. For example, State Farm Insurance sells only one brand of insurance—State Farm. Similarly, your dentist provides only one brand of dental care. In contrast, consumers shopping for a blender generally have many brands to consider at each retail location.

The second reason the evoked set tends to be smaller pertains to the number of establishments providing the same service. The tendency in services is to have a smaller number of outlets providing the same service. For example, a market area can support only so many psychologists, dentists, and medical doctors. In comparison, similar goods tend to be available in many locations. The difference between the distribution of goods and services relates directly to the diversification of the product mix. Retailers of goods sell many products under many brand names, thereby earning their revenues through many different sources. As a result of the diversified product mix, the same goods are available at many locations. In contrast, the survival of the service firm is dependent on selling only one brand of service.

A third reason consumers consider fewer service alternatives relates to the lack of available prepurchase information. Consumers of services simply are not aware of as many service substitutes and/or choose not to undertake the time-consuming task of obtaining information from competing service providers. In contrast, consumers of goods often simply look at what is on the store's shelves and are able to compare prices as well as a number of other factors such as ingredients, construction quality, feel, and scent.

## SELF-SERVICE AS A VIABLE ALTERNATIVE

Another difference between goods and services in the prepurchase choice stage of the consumer decision process is that self-provision often becomes a viable alternative for such services as lawn care, fence installation, housekeeping, painting, and a number of other services. In comparison, consumers rarely consider building a refrigerator over purchasing one from a local retailer. For obvious reasons, many professional service providers are not generally competing against the self-service alternative. However, some self-service solutions, such as homeopathic medicines, do exist.

## Consumption Stage Considerations

The consumption of goods can be divided into three activities: buying, using, and disposing. The three activities occur in a definite buy-use-dispose order and have clear boundaries between them. The customer buys a box of detergent at a supermarket, uses it at home in the washing machine, and disposes of the empty box after the detergent is used up.

This scenario does not apply to the consumption of services, however. First of all, no clear-cut boundary or definite sequence exists between the acquisition and the use of services because there is no transfer of ownership. Because of the prolonged interactions between the customer and the service provider, the production, acquisition, and use of services become entangled and appear to be a single process.[10] Furthermore, the concept of disposal is irrelevant because of the intangibility and experiential nature of services.

Without a doubt, the consumption stage is more complex for services in comparison with that of goods. The servuction system concept introduced in Chapter 1 suggests that the benefits bought by a customer consist of the experience that is delivered through an interactive process. Even when a service is rendered to something that the consumer owns, such as a car, rather than to the individual's person, the service production/consumption process often involves a sequence of personal interactions (face-to-face or by telephone) between the customer and the service provider.[11]

Interactions between the customer and the company's facilities and personnel are inevitable. It is from these interpersonal and human-environment interactions that the service experience is acquired.[12] Perhaps the most important outcome of these interactions is the contradiction of the idea that postchoice evaluation occurs only at a certain point in time after use.[13] The use of goods is essentially free from any kind of direct marketer influence. For example, the manufacturer of the breakfast cereal that you ate this morning had no interaction with you whatsoever. Hence, consumers of goods can choose when, where, and how they will use a good. On the other hand, service firms play an active role in customer consumption activities because services are produced and consumed simultaneously.

No service can be produced or used with either the consumer or the service firm absent. Because of the extended service delivery process, many believe that the consumer's postchoice evaluation occurs both during and after the use of services rather than only afterward. In other words, consumers evaluate the service while they are experiencing the service encounter during the consumption stage as well as during the postpurchase stage.

From a marketer's point of view, this opens up the prospect of being able to directly influence that evaluation. Hence, the restaurant manager who visits diners' tables and asks, "How is your dinner this evening?" is able to catch problems and change evaluations in a way that the manufacturer of a packaged good cannot.

## Postchoice Considerations

The postpurchase evaluation of services is a complex process. It begins soon after the customer makes the choice of the service firm he or she will be using and continues throughout the consumption and postconsumption stages. The evaluation is influenced by the unavoidable interaction of a substantial number of social, psychological, and situational variables. Service satisfaction relies not only on the properties of the four elements of the servuction system—contact personnel, inanimate environment, other customers, and internal organization systems—but also on the synchronization of these elements in the service production/consumption process.

The success or failure of a service firm can be at least partly attributed to management's ability or inability to manipulate the customer experience as the output of a collection of interpersonal interactions (client versus client, client versus employee) and human-environment interactions (employee versus working environment and supporting facilities, customer versus service environment and supporting facilities). A number of proposed models attempt to describe the process by which consumers evaluate their purchase decisions.

## THE EXPECTANCY DISCONFIRMATION MODEL

How does service satisfaction arise during the consumption and postpurchase stages? A number of approaches have been suggested, but perhaps the simplest and most powerful is the **expectancy disconfirmation model.** The concept of this model is straightforward. Consumers evaluate services by comparing expectations with perceptions. If the perceived service is better than or equal to the expected service, then consumers are satisfied. Hence, ultimately customer service is achieved through the effective management of customer perceptions and expectations (see Services in Action 4.4).

**expectancy disconfirmation model**
The model in which consumers evaluate services by comparing expectations with perceptions.

It is crucial to point out that this entire process of comparing expectations with perceptions takes place in the mind of the customer. It is the perceived service that matters, not the actual service. One of the best examples that reinforces this issue involves a high-rise hotel. The hotel was receiving numerous complaints concerning the time guests had to wait for elevator service in the lobby. Realizing that from an operational viewpoint, the speed of the elevators could not be increased, and that attempting to schedule the guests' elevator usage was futile, management installed mirrors in the lobby next to the elevator bays. Guest complaints were reduced immediately—the mirrors provided a means for the guests to occupy their waiting time. Guests were observed using the mirror to observe their own appearance and that of others around them. In reality, the speed of the elevators had not changed; however, the perception was that the waiting time was now acceptable.

It is also feasible to manage expectations in order to produce satisfaction without altering in any way the quality of the actual service delivered. Motel 6, for example, by downplaying its service offering in its cleverly contrived advertising, actually increases consumer satisfaction by lowering customer expectations prior to purchase. The firm's advertising effectively informs consumers of both what to expect and what not to expect: "A good clean room for $19.99 . . . a little more in some places . . . a little less in some others . . . and remember . . . we'll leave the light on for you." Many customers simply do not use services such as swimming pools, health clubs, and full-service restaurants, which are associated with the higher-priced hotels. Economy-minded hotels, such as Motel 6, are carving out a niche in the market by providing the basics. The result is that customers know exactly what they will get ahead of time and are happy not only with the quality of the service received but also with the cost savings.

SERVICES 4.4
IN
ACTION      **Managing Visitor Expectations:
Finland—What It Is Not**

One way to influence customer satisfaction is to effectively manage consumer expectations prior to arrival. For example, the market saturation rate for cell phones in Finland approaches 80 percent. Ironically, Finns are not known for making "small talk." In fact, Finnlandia Vodka publishes a variety of light-hearted scenarios titled "You know you have been in Finland too long when . . ." One such scenario read,

> You know you have been in Finland too long when you assume when someone smiles at you as they pass you on the street that:
> • they are drunk
> • they are insane
> • they are American

Finland actively attempts to manage visitor expectations. In one attempt to manage tourist expectations about the country and people of Finland, the *Helsinki Guide* published the following list in its visitor publications:

### Finland—What It Is Not!

1. Finland is not a small country, nor is it close to the North Pole.
2. Finland is not awfully cold all the time, and polar bears do not roam the streets of Helsinki.
3. Finnish is not a Slavic language, and only very few Finns speak Russian, which, of course, is a pity.
4. Finland did not suffer too badly from any wartime occupation.
5. Finns and Lapps are not the same thing.
6. Finland is not, and has never been, a member of the Eastern Bloc—if there is one any more.
7. Finns don't drink as much as the rumors say.
8. Finns don't eat just fish.
9. Finland is not the country of limitless sex that it is made out to be.
10. Finland is not in a very uncomfortable position between East and West.

> Visitors flying to Finland on Finnair receive an extra dose of "expectation management." During the last hour of flight, a 30-minute film titled *The Finnish Way* is shown to passengers.

Source: *Helsinki Guide* (2000), (January–February), 16.

**perceived-control perspective**
A model in which consumers evaluate services by the amount of control they have over the perceived situation.

## THE PERCEIVED-CONTROL PERSPECTIVE

Another model that assists in describing the postpurchase stage is the **perceived-control perspective.** The concept of control has drawn considerable attention from psychologists. They argue that in modern society, in which people no longer

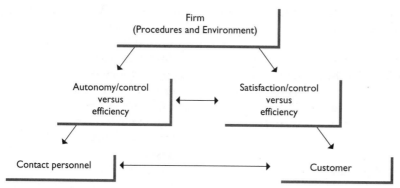

**Figure 4.3**    **The Perceived Behavioral Control Conflicts in the**
**Service Encounter**
Source: Adapted from John E. G. Bateson, "Perceived Control and the Service Encounter," in
John A. Czepiel, Michael R. Solomon, and Carol F. Suprenant, eds., *The Service Encounter*
(Lexington, Mass.: Heath, 1985), 67-82.

have to bother about the satisfaction of primary biological needs, the need for control over situations in which one finds oneself is a major force driving human behavior.[14] Rather than being treated as a service attribute, as implied by multi-attribute models, perceived control can be conceptualized as a superfactor—a global index that summarizes an individual's experience with a service. The basic premise of this perspective is that during the service experience, the higher the level of control over the situation perceived by consumers, the higher their satisfaction with the service will be. A similar positive relationship is proposed between service providers' experience of control and their job satisfaction.

In a slightly different way, it is equally important for the service firm itself to maintain control of the service experience. If the consumer gets too much control, the economic position of the firm may be affected as consumers tip the value equation in their favor, even to an extent that the firm may begin to lose money. On the other hand, if the service employees take complete control, consumers may become unhappy and leave. Even if this does not happen, the operational efficiency of the firm may be impaired. This three-cornered struggle among the service firm, its employees, and consumers is described in Figure 4.3.

Services can be thought of as a consumer's giving up cash and control in exchange for benefits, with each party seeking to gain as much advantage as possible. But it would appear that no one can truly win in such a "contest." In fact, the concept of control is much broader than implied. Behavioral control, the ability to control what is actually going on, is only part of the idea. Research shows that cognitive control is also important. Thus when consumers perceive that they are in control, or at least that what is happening to them is predictable, the effect can be the same as that achieved by behavioral control. In other words, it is the perception of control, not the reality, that is important.

Managerially, this concept raises a number of interesting ideas. The first idea raised is the value of the information given to consumers during the service experience in order to increase their sense that they are in control and that they know what will happen next. This is particularly important for professional service firms, which often assume that simply doing a good job will make their clients happy—they forget that their clients may not have heard from them for more than a month and might be frantic due to the lack of contact and little or no information. It is equally important to an airline that delays a flight after passengers have boarded but fails to let them know what is happening or how long the delay will be.

Similarly, if a firm is due to make changes in its operation that will have an impact on consumers, it is important that those consumers be forewarned. If they are not, they may perceive themselves to be "out of control" and become dissatisfied with the service received to the extent that they change suppliers.

The control perspective raises interesting issues about the trade-off between predictability and choice. Operationally, one of the most important strategic issues is the amount of choice to give the consumer. Because both choice and predictability (standardization) can contribute to a sense of control, it is crucial to determine which is the more powerful source of control for the consumer.

## THE SCRIPT PERSPECTIVE—ALL THE WORLD'S A STAGE AND ALL THE PEOPLE PLAYERS

A number of theories in psychology and sociology can be brought together in the ideas of a script and a **role**. A role is defined as "a set of behavior patterns learned through experience and communication, to be performed by an individual in certain social interaction in order to attain a maximum effectiveness in goal accomplishment."[15] The principal idea proposed is that in a service encounter, customers perform roles, and their satisfaction is a function of **role congruence**—whether the actual behaviors by customers and staff are consistent with the expected roles.

This role congruence thus focuses on the postpurchase phases of a service encounter. The described interaction is two-way, so role congruence is expected to exert an impact on the customer as well as on the service provider. In other words, satisfaction of both parties is likely when the customer and the service provider engage in behaviors that are consistent with each other's role expectation; otherwise, both performers may be upset by the interaction.

The key managerial tasks implied by role theory perspectives are (1) to design roles for the service encounter that are acceptable and capable of fulfilling the needs of both the customers and the service providers and (2) to communicate these roles to both customers and employees so that both have realistic perceptions of their roles as well as those of their partners in their interactions.

Role is assumed to be **extra-individual.** Hence, every individual is expected to display the same predetermined set of behaviors when he or she takes up a certain role, either as a customer or as a service provider. Because role theory originally was not directly concerned with the perception of participants in the service encounter, it is incompatible with the concepts of service evaluation and customer satisfaction. For example, consider that two customers, one an introvert and one an extrovert, may have completely different perceptions and evaluations of interactions with the same chatty service provider. In this case, **intra-individual** variables must be employed in order to explain the differences in customer evaluation and satisfaction.

The role idea can, however, be adapted for use in service situations. This adaptation draws on the psychological idea of a **script.** The script theory and role theory

### Margin glossary

**role**
Behavior patterns learned through experience and communication, to be performed in social interaction to attain a maximum effectiveness in goal accomplishment.

**role congruence**
The property of actual behaviors by customers and staff being consistent with their expected roles.

**extra-individual**
Term used to describe roles that theorizes that every individual is expected to display the same set of behaviors in certain roles.

**intra-individual**
Term used to describe scripts that are a function of an individual's experience and personality and that can therefore differ among individuals.

**script**
A learned sequence of behavior patterns that consumers and service providers follow during service transactions; can be modified via training and experience.

perspectives appear on the surface to be similar. Script theory argues that rules, mostly determined by social and cultural variables, exist to facilitate interactions in daily repetitive events, including a variety of service experiences.[16] These rules shape the participants' expectations in these types of interactions. Furthermore, the rules must be acknowledged and obeyed by all participants if satisfactory outcomes are to be generated. For example, patrons of a fine restaurant will have behavioral expectations of their waiter that are consistent with the service setting. Similarly, the waiter will have expectations of the patron's behavior as well. If one participant deviates from the rules, the other co-actors in the service setting will be uncomfortable. Therefore, a satisfied customer is unlikely given a dissatisfied service provider, and a dissatisfied customer is unlikely given a satisfied service provider.

Despite the similarity of the role theory and script theory perspectives, basic differences exist between them. First, the script theory perspective has a wider range of concerns (including the impact of the service setting) and hence is concerned with the whole service experience rather than with only the interpersonal service encounter. Second, scripts are by definition intra-individual and are a function of an individual's experience and personality. Finally, consumer scripts can be revised by service providers who educate consumers about the service process.

The expectancy disconfirmation model, the perceived-control perspective, and the script perspective may not totally reflect reality, but because they are the result of much research in marketing and psychology, they at least allow us to make logical deductions about consumer behavior when making marketing decisions. Moreover, because all the models to be described have both strengths and weaknesses, they should be considered complementary rather than mutually exclusive. Managerial insights can be developed more effectively through a combination of these various perspectives as we continue to learn about consumer decision processing.

## SUMMARY

This chapter has presented consumer decision process issues as they relate to service consumers. The consumer decision process model consists of three main stages: the prepurchase stage, the consumption stage, and the postpurchase stage. The prepurchase stage consists of the events that occur prior to the consumer's acquisition of the service and includes stimulus reception, problem awareness, information search, and evaluation of alternatives. The outcome of the prepurchase stage is a choice that takes place during the consumption stage. The consumption stage includes the activities of buying, using, and disposing of the product. The postpurchase stage refers to the process by which the consumer evaluates his or her level of satisfaction with the purchase.

Although the consumer decision process model applies to both goods and services, unique considerations arise with respect to services in each of the three stages. Compared with their considerations when purchasing goods, consumers of services during the prepurchase stage of the decision process (1) perceive higher levels of risk to be associated with the purchase; (2) tend to be more brand loyal;

(3) rely more on personal sources of information; (4) tend to have fewer alternatives to consider; and (5) often include self-provision as a viable alternative.

The consumption stage is more complex for services in comparison with that of goods as the production, acquisition, and use of services become entangled in a single process. Moreover, because of the extended service delivery process, many believe that the consumer's postchoice evaluation occurs both during and after, rather than only after, the use of services. From a marketer's point of view, this provides the opportunity to directly influence the consumer's evaluation during the service delivery process. Because of the client/company interface, the service provider is able to catch problems and change evaluations in a way that the manufacturer of a packaged good cannot.

Similarly, the postpurchase evaluation of services is also a complex process. The evaluation process begins soon after the customer makes the choice of the service firm he or she will be using and continues throughout the consumption and postconsumption stages. The evaluation is influenced by the unavoidable interaction of a substantial number of social, psychological, and situational variables. Service satisfaction relies not only on the technical quality of the service and the four elements of the servuction system (contact personnel, inanimate environment, other customers, and internal organizational systems), but also on the synchronization of these elements in the service production/consumption process.

Models that assist in our understanding of the consumer's postpurchase evaluation process include the expectancy disconfirmation model, the perceived control perspective, and the script perspective. In short, the expectancy disconfirmation model defines satisfaction as meeting or exceeding customer expectations. The perceived-control perspective proposes that during the service experience, the higher the level of control over the situation perceived by consumers, the stronger will be their satisfaction with the service. The script perspective proposes that in a service encounter, customers perform roles, and their satisfaction is a function of "role congruence"—whether or not the actual behaviors by customers and staff are consistent with the expected roles. Models such as these help us understand how consumer evaluations are processed and indicate areas where service marketers can focus their efforts in pursuit of the ultimate goal of providing customer satisfaction.

# Key Terms

Cognitive costs
Cognitive dissonance
Commercial cues
Consequence
Consumer decision process
Consumption process
Consumption stage
Credence attributes
Customer habit

Emotional costs
Evaluation of alternatives
Evoked set
Expectancy disconfirmation mode
Experience attributes
External search
Extra-individual
Financial risk
Information search

Internal search
Intra-individual
Learning costs
Lexicographic approach
Linear compensatory approach
Loyal customer discounts
Nonstore choice
Nonsystematic evaluation
Perceived-control perspective
Performance risk
Physical cues
Physical risk
Postpurchase evaluation
Prepurchase stage
Problem awareness
Psychological risk

Role
Role congruence
Script
Search attributes
Search costs
Shortage
Social cues
Social risk
Stimulus
Store choice
Switching costs
Systematic evaluation
Transaction costs
Uncertainty
Unfulfilled desire

# Discussion Questions

1. In general terms, discuss the value of consumer behavior models.
2. Why do consumers of services perceive higher levels of risk associated with their purchases?
3. Discuss the different types of risk.
4. Define and discuss the following terms: search attributes, experience attributes, and credence attributes. Which type(s) of attributes most accurately apply to services? Explain.
5. Regarding multiattribute models, what is the difference between the linear compensatory approach and the lexicographic approach?
6. Explain why consumers of services tend to be more brand loyal.
7. Why do personal sources of information tend to be more important for consumers of services?
8. Discuss the managerial implications of the client–company interface during the consumption stage.
9. What is the difference between a role and a script?
10. Explain the relevance of the perceived-control model as it relates to the post-consumption stage.

# Notes

1. John E. G. Bateson, *Managing Services Marketing: Text and Readings,* 2nd ed. (Fort Worth, Tex.: The Dryden Press, 1992), 93.
2. Adapted from Michael Levy and Barton A. Weitz, *Retailing Management* (Homewood, Ill.: Irwin, 1992), 117–154.

3. Adapted from Bateson, *Managing Services Marketing.*

4. Nicosia and R. N. Mayer, "Toward a Sociology of Consumption," *Journal of Consumer Research* 3, no. 2 (1976), 65–75.

5. D. Guseman, "Risk Perception and Risk Reduction in Consumer Services," in *Marketing of Services,* eds. J. Donnelly and William R. George (Chicago: American Marketing Association, 1981), 200–204; and R. A. Bauer, "Consumer Behavior as Risk Taking," in *Dynamic Marketing for a Changing World,* ed. R. S. Hancock (Chicago: American Marketing Association, 1960), 389–398.

6. L. Kaplan, G. J. Szybilo, and J. Jacoby, "Components of Perceived Risk in Product Purchase; A Cross-Validation," *Journal of Applied Psychology* 59 (1974), 287–291.

7. Guseman, "Risk Perception," 200–204.

8. Adapted from Bateson, *Managing Services Marketing.*

9. Valerie A. Zeithaml, "How Consumer Evaluation Processes Differ between Goods and Services," in *Marketing of Services,* eds. J. Donnelly and W. R. George (Chicago: American Marketing Association, 1981), 191–199.

10. Bernard Booms and Jody Nyquist, "Analyzing the Customer/Firm Communication Component of the Services Marketing Mix," in *Marketing of Services,* eds. J. Donnelly and W. R. George (Chicago: American Marketing Association, 1981), 172; and Raymond Fisk, "Toward a Consumption/Evaluation Process Model for Services," in *Marketing of Services,* eds. J. Donnelly and W. R. George (Chicago: American Marketing Association, 1981), 191.

11. Christopher H. Lovelock, "Classifying Services to Gain Strategic Marketing Insights," *Journal of Marketing,* (Summer 1983), 9–20.

12. Alan Andrasen, "Consumer Research in the Service Sector," in *Emerging Perspectives on Services Marketing,* eds. L. Berry, G. L. Shostack, and G. Upah (Chicago: American Marketing Association, 1982), 63–64.

13. Raymond Fisk, "Toward a Consumption/Evaluation Process Model for Services," in *Marketing of Services,* eds. J. Donnelly and W. R. George (Chicago: American Marketing Association, 1981), 191.

14. John E. G. Bateson, "Perceived Control and the Service Encounter," in *The Service Encounter,* eds. John A. Czepiel, Michael R. Solomon, and Carol F. Suprenant (Lexington, Mass.: Lexington Books, 1984), 67–82.

15. Michael R. Solomon, Carol F. Suprenant, John A. Czepiel, and Evelyn G. Gatman, "A Role Theory Perspective on Dyadic Interactions: The Service Encounter," *Journal of Marketing* 1, no. 49 (Winter 1985), 99–111.

16. Ruth A. Smith and Michael Houston, "Script-Based Evaluations of Satisfaction with Services," in *Emerging Perspectives in Services Marketing,* eds. L. Berry, G. L. Shostack, and G. Upah (Chicago: American Marketing Association, 1982), 59–62.

## chapter 5

# Ethical Issues in Services Marketing

## CHAPTER OBJECTIVES

The primary purpose of this chapter is to introduce students to a variety of ethical issues as they relate to services marketing.

After reading this chapter, you should be able to:

- Define the difference between ethical decisions and ordinary decisions.
- Discuss the reasons that consumers are particularly vulnerable to ethical misconduct within the service sector.
- Describe the moral philosophies on which individuals base their ethical decisions.
- Discuss the types of ethical issues that often arise in the business sector.
- Discuss factors, other than moral philosophies, that may influence ethical decision making.
- Describe the consequences of ethical misconduct.
- Discuss strategies that attempt to control ethical behavior.

"Always do right. This will gratify some people, and astonish the rest."

Mark Twain

# Introduction

Within the past decade, integrating ethics into the business curriculum has become a common topic of discussion among marketing educators and practitioners. Originally business ethics was generally taught as a single course; however, many business schools now believe that business ethics should be taught across the curriculum and that ethical issues as they relate to each topic area should be discussed.[1]

Because of the unique opportunities that exist for ethical misconduct in service fields, students of the services marketing course in particular should be made aware of the issues surrounding ethical decision making. Although the majority of service providers fulfill their duties ethically, infamous service providers such as Jim Bakker, Leona Helmsley, and Ivan Boesky have provided recent evidence that not all service providers may be trustworthy.

Unique circumstances occur in the service sector that create an ethical environment worth examination and discussion. This chapter presents a variety of ethics-related topics as they pertain to the service sector. More specifically, these topics include (1) methods of ethical decision making, (2) issues that create ethical conflict, (3) factors influencing ethical decision making, (4) the effects of ethical misconduct, and (5) strategies for controlling ethical behavior.

**ethical vigilance**
Paying close attention to whether one's actions are "right" or "wrong," and if ethically "wrong," asking why you are behaving in that manner.

This chapter is not intended to "preach" what the authors think is right or wrong. Such a decision is left to the discretion of the individual student. Unfortunately, as you will live to learn, the appropriateness and/or public acceptance of your decision is usually decided on syndicated talk shows such as *Oprah*, *Rosie O'Donnell*, or *Dr. Laura*. Our objective is primarily to provide you with food for thought, to encourage **ethical vigilance**, and to facilitate class discussions about an important subject that is often overlooked. Overall, we hope that the

---

## SERVICES IN ACTION 5.1

### College Student Faces Extortion Charges

According to court papers filed by the FBI, a university student has been charged with the attempted extortion of an online digital book company. The student claimed that he had found a flaw in the book company's delivery system and that books could be downloaded for free. In exchange for the information and his silence, the student requested money, a 2001 Volvo wagon, two digital audio players, and free downloads.

After contacting the FBI, the company agreed to all the demands with the exception of the money. The student then provided the company with his name, address, and work phone number. Bail has been set at $50,000, and the student has been barred from any Internet access and from disseminating information about the book company. If convicted of the single charge of using the Internet to send extortion threats, the student could face up to two years in prison and a $100,000 fine.

Source: wysiwyg://18/jtt[://seatlep-i.nw/source.com/business/xtrt26/shtml

information provided in this chapter will aid in your understanding of ethics and perhaps have an impact on the decisions with which you will be faced as you pursue your career (see Services in Action 5.1).

## WHAT ARE ETHICS?

In general, **ethics** are commonly defined as: (1) "a branch of philosophy dealing with what is good and bad and with moral duty and obligation"; and (2) "the principles of moral conduct governing an individual or group."[2] **Business ethics** comprises moral principles and standards that guide behavior in the world of business.[3] The distinction between an ordinary decision and an ethical one is that values and judgments play a critical role in ethical decisions. In contrast, ordinary decisions are generally decided utilizing a set of preordained acceptable rules.

The field of business ethics is particularly intriguing. On one hand, businesses must make a profit in order to survive. The survival of the firm provides employees salaries with which employees feed their families and educate their children, thereby leading to the betterment of society. In addition, company profits and employee salaries are taxed, the funds from which furnish the support for various governmental programs. On the other hand, business profits should not be obtained by any means necessary. A trade-off must exist between the firm's desire for profits and what is good for individuals and society.

**ethics**
A branch of philosophy dealing with what is good and bad and with moral duty and obligations; the principles of moral conduct governing an individual or group.

**business ethics**
The principles of moral conduct that guide behavior in the business world.

## ETHICS AND BUSINESS

How does the public feel about business when it comes to ethical behavior? Not very positive.[4] According to a Business Week/Harris poll, 46 percent of respondents believed that the ethical standards of businesspeople were only average. In addition, 90 percent of respondents believed that white-collar crime was somewhat or very common.

Another survey reported that the majority of Americans believe that many businesspeople regularly engage in ethical misconduct. In fact, 76 percent of respondents in yet another study believe that the decline in moral standards in the United States is a direct result of the lack of business ethics practiced daily. Perhaps even more damaging are the results of a survey of business practitioners themselves: 66 percent of executives surveyed believe that businesspeople will occasionally act unethically during business dealings, while another 15 percent believe that ethical misconduct occurs often in the business sector (see Services in Action 5.2).

## THE OPPORTUNITY FOR ETHICAL MISCONDUCT IN SERVICES MARKETING

Opportunities for ethical misconduct within the service sector can be attributed predominantly to the intangibility, heterogeneity, and inseparability dimensions inherent in the provision of services.[5] As introduced in Chapter 2, intangibility

SERVICES IN ACTION **5.2**

### Sears Auto Centers: Preventive Maintenance or Ethical Misconduct?

The marketing concept states that the goal of the organization is to recognize and satisfy customer needs while making a profit. Such was the goal of Edward Brennan, chairman of Sears, Roebuck and Company. Under his leadership, market research studies were conducted on customer automotive repair needs. Subsequently, Sears established a preventive maintenance program that instructed the auto repair centers to recommend repair/replacement of parts based on the mileage indicated on the odometer. Concurrently, sales quotas were established for Sears' 850 auto repair centers. Meeting or exceeding these quotas earned bonus money for the service personnel and provided management with an objective means of evaluating employee performance.

The new sales incentive program required the sale of a certain number of repairs or services, including alignments, springs, and brake jobs, every 8 hours. Service employees were also able to qualify for bonus money by selling a specified number of shock absorbers or struts for every hour worked. The objective of this program was to meet customer needs while increasing the profits of the auto service centers.

After the program was put into place, the automotive unit became the fastest growing and most profitable unit in recent Sears history; however, a growing number of consumer complaints were lodged against Sears. These complaints sparked investigations by the states of California, New Jersey, and Florida into practices at Sears auto service centers. The state of California alleged that Sears consistently overcharged its customers an average of $223 for unnecessary repairs or work that was never done. Sears contends that its auto centers were merely servicing vehicles based on the manufacturer's suggested maintenance schedule. Moreover, Sears maintains that its failure to make these suggestions for improvements would neglect the safety of the consumer.

Sources: Lawrence M. Fisher, "Sears Auto Centers Halt Commissions After Flap," *The New York Times,* 1992, pp. D1, D2; Gregory A. Patterson, "Sears' Brennan Accepts Blame for Auto Flap," *The Wall Street Journal,* 1992, p. B1; "Systematic Looting," *Time Magazine,* June 22, 1992, pp. 27, 30; and Tung Yin, "Sears Is Accused of Billing Fraud at Auto Centers," *The Wall Street Journal,* June 12, 1992, pp. B1, B5.

complicates the consumer's ability to objectively evaluate the quality of service provided; heterogeneity reflects the difficulty in standardization and quality control; and inseparability reflects the human element involved in the service delivery process. All three dimensions contribute to consumer vulnerability to and reliance on the service provider's ethical conduct during the service encounter.

Specialized services such as auto repair are difficult for consumers to evaluate intelligently.

In more specific terms, consumer vulnerability to ethical misconduct within the service sector can be attributed to several sources, including the following[6]:

- Services are characterized by few search attributes.
- Services are often specialized and/or technical.
- Some services have a significant time lapse between performance and evaluation.
- Many services are sold without guarantees and warranties.
- Services are often provided by boundary-spanning personnel.
- Variability in service performance is somewhat accepted.
- Reward systems are often outcome-based as opposed to behavior-based.
- Customers are active participants in the production process.

## Few Search Attributes

As discussed in Chapter 4, search attributes can be determined prior to purchase and include such attributes as touch, smell, visual cues, and taste. However, because of the intangibility of services, consumers lack the opportunity to physically examine a service before purchasing it. Consequently, consumers have little prepurchase information available to help them make an informed, intelligent decision. Hence, consumers of services often must base their purchase decisions on information provided by the service provider.

Using Sears Auto Centers (Services in Action 5.2) as an example, the dilemma a consumer faces as a result of the lack of search attributes is clear. The car may look fine on the outside, but the mechanic provides information about parts and systems that may not be visible to the consumer. The consumer now must rely on the advice of the mechanic. In addition, even though price is a search attribute that can be obtained prior to purchasing an auto repair service, the price is only an estimate. The final price is not calculated until after the service is performed.

SERVICES 5.3

IN ACTION    **Dot-Com Ethics**

In pursuit of venture capital and higher stock prices, many dot-com companies, including the most well-known, are engaging in accounting practices that have the Securities and Exchange Commission (SEC) clearly concerned. The issue of primary concern is that of revenue recognition. Below are listed some of the more controversial accounting practices that are, for now, legal. Whether they are ethical is another question. Practices such as those listed below have raised the eyebrows of the SEC and investment houses alike. Investors are now turning to measures other than earnings to determine the fair value of Internet companies.

### Net versus Gross

Some companies, such as Priceline.com, report the full price of the hotel rooms and airline tickets that its customers buy as reported revenues. However, much of that revenue goes directly back to the airlines and hotels, and Priceline.com only keeps the commissions on those sales. Priceline calls its commissions "gross profits" instead of "revenue." The difference is significant. For example, Priceline's reported revenue is $152.2 million. In contrast, its "gross profits" are $18.2 million.

### Barter

Barter exchanges involve exchanges of property other than cash. For example, Internet companies often exchange advertising space on its Web pages for ads on television and radio. Barter transactions are common in all kinds of media. However, what concerns the SEC is that these transactions are being recorded as earned revenues. In a recent press release, the StarMedia Network reported that its revenues were up 44% from the previous quarter. The press release failed to communicate that 26% of its increase did not represent real cash. Instead, it was barter revenue. In the world of the Internet, it is not unusual for startups to derive as much as half their revenues from barter.

### Coupons, Discounts, and Loss Leaders

Another way to pump up the top line is to record coupons, discounts, and loss leaders as marketing expenses and to record the original prices of products sold as reported revenues. For example, if a customer buys a $50 jacket using a 20 percent off coupon, the firm reports revenues earned as $50 and then takes a $10 charge under marketing expenses. Companies such as 1-880-flowers.com and Plow & Hearth engage in such practices.

## Fulfillment Costs

Fulfillment costs generally include costs such as warehousing, packaging, and shipping. Typically, offline companies record fulfillment costs as cost of sales. However, dot-com companies typically record these types of costs as marketing expenses so as to not reduce earned revenue figures.

## Auction Accounting

Auction companies earn revenues by charging listing fees to post items for bid and by collecting commissions on those items that sell. General accounting practices state that listing revenues should be recognized over the whole period that the item is up for bid and that commissions should only be reported once items are actually sold. Once again, dot-com companies bend accepted practices by recognizing full listing fees and commissions on items immediately. This practice once again inflates earned revenue figures and potentially misleads investors.

Source: Jeremy Kahn, "Presto Chango! Sales are Huge!" *Fortune* 141, no. 6 (March 20, 2000), 90–96.

## Technical and Specialized Services

Many services are not easily understood and/or evaluated; consequently, the opportunity exists to easily mislead consumers (see Services in Action 5.3). Evaluating the performance of professional service providers is particularly intriguing. As a consumer, how do you know whether your doctor, lawyer, broker, priest, or minister is competent at his or her job? Often, our evaluations of these people are based on their clothing, the furniture in their offices, and whether they have pleasant social skills. In other words, in the absence of information that they can understand, customers often resort to evaluating information that surrounds the service as opposed to the core service itself.

The auto repair industry is also characterized by services that are technical, specialized, and not easily understood or evaluated by the average consumer. Again, the consumer must rely on the service provider for guidance. As a result, unethical service providers can easily mislead consumers, perform unnecessary services, or charge for services that are never performed. Do you check your oil when it's changed? How do you know that the mechanic really did rotate and balance your tires?

## Time Lapse between Performance and Evaluation

The final evaluation of some services such as insurance and financial planning is often conducted only at a time in the distant future. For example, the success or failure of retirement planning may not be realized until 30 years after the original service transaction is conducted. Hence, service providers may not be held accountable for their actions in the short run. This could lead to a scenario where unethical service providers may maximize their short-term gains at the expense of consumers' long-term benefits.

Unethical auto mechanics may also benefit from the time lapse between service performance and service evaluation. The discovery of low-quality work may happen via mechanical problems 30 days after repairs have been made or by having a future mechanic question the previous mechanic's work. In either case, the consumer is left to deal with the situation and generally experiences little success in convincing the original mechanic that the inferiority of past efforts is at the root of present problems.

## Services Sold without Guarantees and Warranties

Another opportunity for ethical misconduct in the service sector results from few meaningful guarantees and warranties. Consequently, when the consumer experiences difficulties with an unscrupulous provider, there are few or no means of seeking quick retribution. For example, what are your options if you get a bad haircut—glue, a new hat?

Although the auto repair industry is famous for its 90-day guarantee on all parts, the guarantee generally fails to cover the labor required to reinstall the part that failed. Moreover, the 90-day guarantee does little to calm the consumer who experiences failure 120 days after the repair. One of the authors had the experience of paying more than $400 to replace the rear window motor of a Chrysler LeBaron twice within a 16-month period. The 90-day guarantee did little but indicate that the company that built the replacement motor had little faith in its product—and rightly so!

## Services Performed by Boundary-Spanning Personnel

Many service providers deliver their services outside their firm's physical facilities. In doing so, these types of service providers expand the boundary of a firm beyond the firm's main office. Service providers such as painters, lawn-care specialists, paramedics, and carpet cleaners are typical examples.

**boundary-spanning personnel**
Personnel who provide their services outside the firm's physical facilities.

Because of the physical distance from the main office inherent in the role of **boundary-spanning personnel**, these particular service providers often are not under direct supervision and may act in a manner inconsistent with organizational objectives. Hence, the opportunity to engage in ethical misconduct without repercussions from upper management increases.

## Accepted Variability in Performance

Another opportunity for ethical misconduct within the service sector is provided via the heterogeneity inherent in the provision of services. Because of heterogeneity, standardization and quality control are difficult to maintain throughout each individual service delivery transaction. Many services are customized, requiring different skills of the service provider, and often consumers are exposed to different providers within the same firm. The bottom line is that variability in performance is unavoidable.

Variability in performance is evident in the auto repair industry. Automobiles develop a variety of problems that require an array of skills from the service provider, who may not be equivalently skilled to undertake each task. Moreover, consumers often receive services from a number of different mechanics. Each mechanic's performance is likely to vary from the next. As a result of consumer acceptance of variability in service performance, unethical service providers may attempt to broaden the window of acceptable performance through slightly increasing gaps in performance quality.

## Outcome-Based Reward Systems

The reward system of an organization often dictates the behavior of its employees, and it does not take employees long to figure out the shortest route to the largest rewards. Hence, the reward system of an organization may encourage, albeit unintentionally, the unethical conduct of its employees.

Straight commissions and quotas reinforce activities that are directly linked to making the sale while discouraging nonselling activities such as maintaining the store, stocking shelves, and spending an inordinate amount of time fielding customer questions.

Looking at the reward structure at Sears Auto Centers, the impact that it likely had on employee behavior is clear. Employees were indeed rewarded for making repairs regardless of whether they were needed or not.

## Consumer Participation in Production

On the surface one would think that the more the consumer is involved in the service encounter, the less the opportunity exists for the service provider to engage in ethical misconduct. However, service exchanges may be jeopardized by coercive influence strategies used by the service provider.

The consumer's involvement in the service delivery process enables a service provider to try to influence the consumer through fear or guilt to agree to a purchase the consumer would otherwise decline. An auto mechanic who makes a statement such as, "I wouldn't want my family riding around in a car that has brakes like these," is a typical example of the type of influence a service provider can have on a customer. Moreover, because of the consumer's input into the production process, the consumer often accepts much of the responsibility for less-than-satisfactory service transactions. Consumers often feel that they didn't explain themselves clearly enough and will accept much of the blame to avoid a confrontation with the service provider. In fact, conflict avoidance is one of the major reasons customers do not complain to service providers. (For a more complete discussion of customer complaining behavior, see Chapter 13.) This situation further removes service providers from taking responsibility for their own actions and provides yet another opportunity to engage in unethical behavior.

## METHODS FOR ETHICAL DECISION MAKING

**moral philosophies**
The principles or rules service providers use when deciding what is right or wrong.

The behavior of service providers engaged in ethical decision making reflects the **moral philosophies** in which they believe.[7] Moral philosophies are the principles or rules service providers use when deciding what is right or wrong. For example, if for economic reasons a company is forced to lay off workers, does it notify the workers ahead of the actual layoff? On one hand, notifying employees provides them with time to seek other employment before they are out of a job. On the other hand, disgruntled employees, after learning of the layoff, may not work as hard, and the quality of subsequent service delivery suffers.

As you review Services in Action 5.2 regarding Sears Auto Centers, you should ponder the moral philosophies and decision-making processes embraced by the parties involved. Methods for ethical decision making include teleology, deontology, and relativism. Again, note that we are not proposing that one moral philosophy is better than another. We are merely providing you with alternative schools of thought regarding the way decisions are made.

### Teleology

**teleology**
A type of ethical decision making in which an act is deemed morally acceptable if it produces some desired result.

**consequentialism**
A type of ethical decision making that assesses the morality of decisions based on their consequences.

Followers of **teleology** believe an act is morally right or acceptable if the act produces some desired result. Teleology is referred to as a type of **consequentialism.** As such, teleologists assess the morality of their decisions based on the consequences. If the decision leads to some desired result, such as increased pay, promotion, or recognition, then the decision is acceptable.

As an example, consider the following. Most persons would agree that robbery is an unethical behavior. Let's say that a drug is available at the drugstore, and the pharmacist is charging $1000 for it. Meanwhile, you have a family member who

What if a family member desperately needed drugs such as these to survive, and the pharmacy refused to sell them to you? Would theft be a viable option? Would it be a morally correct option?

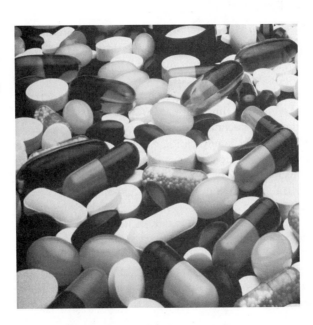

desperately needs the drug in order to survive. A problem arises when you have only $900 and the pharmacist refuses to sell you the drug. Would you steal from the drugstore in order to save a family member? If your answer is yes, then the consequences of your behavior are dictating the morality of your actions.

Teleology is further broken down into two subclasses, **egoism** and **utilitarianism**, which reflect the beneficiary of the decision's consequences. Egoists define acceptable actions as those that benefit an individual's self-interest as defined by that individual. Benefits can take the form of fame, personal wealth, recognition, and other self-gratifying consequences. Egoists believe that they should "do the act that promotes the greatest good for oneself."[8]

Returning to the example of Sears Auto Centers, employees who act as egoists may choose a number of alternative behaviors. First, if the employee wants to increase his own personal wealth, he may engage in activities that lead to greater commissions, such as suggesting repairs that do not need to be made. On the other hand, if the employee believes that reporting the unethical behavior of others would lead to a promotion, the egoist may notify upper management of a problem. Further, as another alternative, an egoist who notifies the press of the problem may be looking for personal recognition.

In contrast to the egoist, the utilitarianist defines acceptable behavior as that which maximizes the **principle of utility**—the greatest good for the greatest number of people. This philosophy of promoting "the needs of the many over the needs of the few" has led to some interesting decisions. Cuba, for example, isolated all its HIV-positive citizens from the general population. The decision was made to sacrifice the personal freedoms of these people for the health and well being of the remainder of the Cuban population. (Incidentally, reports tend to support the notion that this decision has led to control of the spread of AIDS in Cuba.)

Referring back to the Sears example, the mechanic who engages in ethical misconduct to make a sale in order to benefit the company so that all concerned can keep their jobs may be classified as a utilitarianist. The utilitarianist may also believe that although not every customer's car may need a specific type of repair, many will benefit from the repairs made over time.

## Deontology

In contrast to teleology, a deontologist believes that the inherent rightness or wrongness of an act should guide behavior regardless of the outcome. Hence, **deontology** is not a form of consequentialism, since it does not focus on the consequences of an action. In contrast, deontology focuses on individual rights and the intentions associated with a particular behavior. Deontologists believe that the rights of the individual should prevail over what is better for society as a whole, thereby differentiating itself from the utilitarian philosophy.

Deontologists believe that there are some things people should never do, regardless of the consequences. If recalling a product to save lives means bankrupting the company, then the company should go bankrupt. Deontologists further believe that moral standards are permanent. They do not alter over time and are based on the **categorical imperative**. "Simply put, if you feel comfortable allowing everyone in the world to see you commit an act and if your rationale for acting

**egoism**
A subclass of teleology in which acceptable actions are defined as those that benefit the individual's self-interest as defined by the individual.

**utilitarianism**
A subclass of teleology in which acceptable behavior is defined as that which maximizes total utility—the greatest good for the greatest number of people.

**principle of utility**
The behavior that produces the most good for the most people in a specific situation.

**deontology**
A type of ethical decision making in which the inherent rightness or wrongness of an act guides behavior, regardless of the outcome.

**categorical imperative**
Asks whether the proposed action would be right if everyone did it.

in a particular manner is suitable to become a universal principle guiding behavior, then committing that act is ethical."[9]

Returning again to the Sears example, a deontological mechanic would probably never make repairs that were not needed. Making an unnecessary repair would be a form of lying, and based on the deontological perspective, lying is inherently wrong. On the other hand, it could also be argued, based on the deontological perspective, that Sears felt it was inherently wrong not to do the preventive maintenance as suggested by manufacturers. The deontological mechanic might believe that not conducting the maintenance as suggested by the manufacturer could possibly lead to the harm of an individual customer.

## Relativism

**relativism**
A type of ethical decision making in which the correctness of ethical decisions is thought to change over time.

In contrast to deontology and teleology, people practicing **relativism** are prone to believe that the correctness of ethical decisions may change over time. Relativists evaluate ethical decisions subjectively on a case-by-case basis based on past individual or group experiences. As such, relativists observe the actions of their relevant group to determine the consensus of opinion concerning decisions. The consensus reflects whether the decision is "right" or "wrong."

Because relativists use themselves or the people around them to judge the ethicality of decisions, they may follow one set of ethical guidelines at work and a different set at home. Consequently, service providers, as relativists, working within an unethical work environment (from an outsider's viewpoint) may eventually come to adopt these behaviors as their own. Sears mechanics who made unnecessary repairs may have simply adopted the actions of their co-workers and supervisors. Co-worker and supervisor opinions can particularly influence the decisions made by new employees. An overview of methods for ethical decision making is presented in Table 5.1.

## TABLE 5.1

### Methods for Ethical Decision Making

| | |
|---|---|
| **Teleology** | Acts are morally right or acceptable if they provide some desired result. |
| **Egoism** | Acceptable actions are those that maximize a particular person's self-interest as defined by the individual. Egoism is a form of teleology. |
| **Utilitarianism** | Acceptable actions are those that maximize total utility—the greatest good for the greatest number of people. Utilitarianism is a form of teleology. |
| **Deontology** | Acceptable actions are those that focus on the preservation of individual rights and on the intentions associated with a particular behavior rather than on its consequences. |
| **Relativism** | Acceptable actions are determined by the actions of some relevant group. A relativist evaluates ethicalness on the basis of individual and group experiences. |

## ISSUES THAT CREATE ETHICAL CONFLICT

The types of ethical issues service providers encounter are not always unique to the service sector. This can be accounted for by the mix of products and customer service involved in a multitude of different businesses. Table 5.2 contains a sample of the many types of ethical issues that are encountered in the business world. Through surveying their personnel, individual companies can determine the specific ethical issues that pertain to their firm. The discussion below focuses on the most typical issues that managers and/or employees will face while conducting business.[10]

### Conflict of Interest

Service providers are often in close proximity to customers during the provision of services. Consequently, the service provider may experience a **conflict of interest** as the service provider/customer relationship develops and friendships

**conflict of interest**
The situation in which a service provider feels torn between the organization, the customer, and/or the service provider's own personal interest.

# TABLE 5.2

### Types of Ethical Issues Encountered by Businesses

| | |
|---|---|
| Honesty | Use of company proprietary information |
| Conflict of interest | Accuracy of books, records |
| Marketing, advertising issues | Privacy of employee records |
| Environmental issues | Political activities and contributions |
| Discrimination by age, race, or sex | Misuses of company assets |
| Product liability and safety | Corporate governance |
| Codes of ethics and self-governance | Issues |
| Relations with customers | Ethical theory |
| Bribery | Ethics in negotiation |
| Rights of and responsibilities to shareholders | Relations with local communities |
| Whistleblowing | Plant closing and layoffs |
| Kickbacks | Employee discipline |
| Insider trading | Use of others' proprietary information |
| Antitrust issues | Relations with U.S. government representatives |
| Issues facing multinationals | Relations with competitors |
| Relations with foreign governments | Employee benefits |
| Ethical foundations of capitalism | Mergers and acquisitions |
| Workplace health and safety | Drug and alcohol abuse |
| Managing an ethical environment | Drug and alcohol testing |
| Relations with suppliers and subcontractors | Intelligence gathering |
| | Leveraged buyouts |

Source: Adapted from Lynn Sharp Paine, "Report on Ethics Issues Covered in the Undergraduate Curriculum," in *Ethics Education in American Business Schools* (Washington, D.C.: Ethics Resource Center, Inc., 1988), 17. ©1988 Ethics Resource Center, Inc. All Rights Reserved. Reprinted with permission from Ethics Resource Center, Inc., Washington, D.C.

are formed. In such a situation, the service provider may feel torn between the organization, the customer, and/or the service provider's own personal interest.

For example, insurance personnel may coach friends and family members on how to complete the necessary forms in order to obtain a less expensive rate. In this situation, the customer benefits (via lower rates), the employee benefits (via "the sale"), but the organization suffers (by failing to obtain the proper premium amount). Likewise, Sears employees may have felt torn between what was best for the customer, what was best for the company, and what was best for their own personal finances.

## Organizational Relationships

**organizational relationships**
Working relationships formed between service providers and various role partners such as customers, suppliers, peers, subordinates, supervisors, and others.

Service providers form working **organizational relationships** with a variety of role partners, including customers, suppliers, peers, subordinates, supervisors, and others. The information gained via these relationships is often highly sensitive. For example, most people would not want their priest to reveal the contents of their confession or their doctor to tell others of their medical problems. Because of the sensitivity of information, ethical service providers are required to maintain confidentiality in relationships to meet their professional obligations and responsibilities (see Services in Action 5.4). In contrast, unethical service providers may use

---

### SERVICES 5.4
### ACTION — Protecting Confidential Information Online

Customers must have confidence in the transmission of sensitive financial and personal information to Web merchants. The challenge of operating a secure Web site is very real. The 1999 Information Security Industry Survey conducted by ICSA reports that the number of companies that have been attacked by hackers jumped 92 percent from 1997 to 1998. The losses from security breaches averaged $256,000 and a total of more than $23 million for the 91 businesses surveyed.

Netscape summarizes security threats as follows:

- Unauthorized access: accessing or misusing a computer system to intercept transmissions and steal sensitive information
- Data alteration: altering the content of a transaction—user names, credit card numbers, and dollar amounts—during transmission
- Monitoring: eavesdropping on confidential information
- Spoofing: a fake site pretending to be yours to steal data from unsuspecting customers or just disrupt your business
- Service denial: an attacker shuts down your site or denies access to visitors
- Repudiation: a party to an online purchase denies that the transaction occurred or was authorized

Source: www.ncsu.edu

the information acquired from organizational relationships for their own personal gain. Ivan Boesky, one of Wall Street's top arbitragers, was charged with insider trading activities by the Securities and Exchange Commission. Boesky allegedly made millions from obtaining information concerning company takeovers before the public announcements of the takeovers were made. Once Boesky learned of a takeover, he would purchase large blocks of stock that he later sold at huge profits. In exchange for the names of other inside traders, Boesky plead guilty to one charge of criminal activity and agreed to pay $100 million in penalties. He also served 3 years in jail. The old adage that "knowledge is power" is often embraced by those who engage in ethical misconduct.

The structure of the organizational relationship may also provide an opportunity for an unethical firm to place undue influence on its employees. In particular, the relationship between supervisor and subordinate comes to mind. Regarding the Sears example, the mechanics could argue that they felt they would lose their jobs or suffer large decreases in pay if they did not make the repairs required by the quota system that was put into place by upper management.

## Honesty

**Honesty** is a partner of truthfulness, integrity, and trustworthiness (see Services in Action 5.5). Examples of dishonesty in customer service include promising to do something for a customer but having no intention of delivering on the promise or stating that a service has been performed when, in fact, it has not. Honesty issues may also cover selected business strategies used by service firms to manage consumer expectations. For example, a typical practice at some restaurants today is to purposely estimate waiting times in excess of the actual expected waiting times. If customers are seated before expected, they feel they are getting better service. Do you think this practice is ethical?

**honesty**
The characteristics of truthfulness, integrity, and trustworthiness.

Other honesty issues involve (1) respecting the private property of clients when services are provided in the clients' homes and places of business; (2) performing services as promised at the designated time; (3) providing accurate billing for services delivered; and (4) providing clients accurate information even if it means the loss of a sale.

## Fairness

**Fairness** is an outcome of just treatment, equity, and impartiality. Clients should be treated equitably, and deals based on favoritism should be avoided. In addition, service discrimination issues should also be addressed. Do men receive better service compared with women, or vice-versa? Are well-dressed persons served better than blue jean–clad clients? Does a client's race or general appearance affect the level of service provided?

**fairness**
The characteristics of just treatment, equity, and impartiality.

## Communication

Ethical issues also arise through the communication that the service organization releases to the public. Communication may range from mass advertising to warranty

[SERVICES] **5.5**
[IN]
[ACTION]     **Who Needs the Lottery?**

Although Pat O'Neal doesn't understand what all the fuss is about, her boss thinks that she at least deserves some kind of recognition. Pat is the cash auditor at the Fresh Fish Company located in Denver, Colorado. One of her job responsibilities is to sign for cash that is delivered by armored vehicle. The way the system works is that once Pat signs the manifest, she and the armored car company agree that the correct amount of money has been sent.

Within a 6-month period, Pat had two opportunities to walk away with much more than she had signed for. In one incident, O'Neal had signed for $1,500 in $10 bills and actually received $15,000. Several months earlier she discovered an extra $35,000 in the money bag. "I said, 'Oh my God' . . . Then I started counting and I said, *Oh, my God!*" In both incidents, O'Neal immediately called the armored-car company to report the mistake. "The money wasn't mine. It wasn't the company's. It didn't belong to us." It didn't matter that that's the way the system works; no one would have ever found out if she had kept the money for herself.

Her reward from the armored car company for her honesty: zip, nada, nothing. O'Neal probably wouldn't have accepted a reward anyway. "You can't be paid for being honest. They were probably embarrassed. They probably just wanted to forget about it." O'Neal's boss, Don Cook, disagreed: "I thought about it more and more. The least reward she deserves is some kind of recognition. If people hear the story, [Pat] can serve as a model for those who are a little shakier than she is when it comes to dealing with moral dilemmas." What would you have done?

Source: "Honest Mistake Worth $35,000 Fails to Tempt Auditor," *Denver Rocky Mountain News,* February 28, 2000, p. 6A.

information to interpersonal communication between the service provider and the customer. Ethical misconduct stemming from communication may include making false claims about the superiority of the company's services, making false claims about competitive offerings, and/or making promises the company knows it cannot keep.

## FACTORS THAT INFLUENCE ETHICAL DECISION MAKING

Different people make different decisions in similar ethical situations. Some individuals make consistent ethical decisions over time, whereas others evaluate each ethical decision on a case-by-case basis. The reasons that we make different ethical decisions are functions of a variety of factors that may influence our judgments. Factors influencing ethical decision making include[11]:

- Stage of cognitive moral development
- Personal values
- Corporate culture

## TABLE 5.3

### Stages of Cognitive Moral Development

**Stage 1**  "Right" is based on rules and authority.
**Stage 2**  "Right" is based on one's own needs or another's in terms of what is fair.
**Stage 3**  The individual focuses more on others as opposed to personal gains.
**Stage 4**  "Right" is based on the individual's duty to society.
**Stage 5**  "Right" is based on basic rights, values, and legal contracts.
**Stage 6**  "Right" is a set of universal ethical principles that everyone should adhere to.

- Cultural differences
- Organizational structure
- Opportunity
- Reward systems
- Significant others
- Competitive environment
- Changes in technology

## Cognitive Moral Development

The model of **cognitive moral development** proposes that individuals progress through six stages of ethical development (Table 5.3). As the individual develops, ethical decisions are evaluated differently. In the first stage, the stage of punishment and obedience, a person defines what is right based on rules and authority. Consequently, when faced with an ethical decision, the individual bases it on a set of rules or instructions provided by an authority figure. In the second stage, the stage of individual instrumental purpose and exchange, decisions are based on fulfilling one's own needs or another's in terms of what is fair. During the third stage, the stage of mutual interpersonal expectations, relationships, and conformity, the individual focuses more on others as opposed to personal gains.

As the individual progresses to the fourth stage, the stage of social system and conscience maintenance, the individual defines what is right based on his or her duty to society. In the fifth stage, the stage of prior rights, social contract, or utility, the individual begins to more narrowly define what is right based on basic rights, values, and legal contracts. The sixth and final stage, the stage of universal ethical principles, reflects the individual's belief that right is determined by a set of universal ethical principles that everyone should adhere to when confronted with ethical decisions.

**cognitive moral development**
A model of ethical development that proposes individuals progress through six stages of ethical development.

## Personal Values

Ethical decisions are also influenced by an individual's **personal values**. In general, personal values are not necessarily static. Hence, as the person matures, personal values may change. Furthermore, individuals may apply one set of personal values to their personal life and another set to their business life. Incidentally, this explains why, when television tabloids interview the neighbors of an accused

**personal values**
The standards by which each person lives in both a personal and professional life.

embezzler, the neighbors always say, "He was just a regular guy, a good family man, and a great neighbor…we had no idea he was a crook!"

## Corporate Culture

**corporate culture**
The general philosophy of a company, which guides decisions, actions, and policies of the company.

Another factor that impacts individual ethical decision making is the **corporate culture** within the firm. Corporate cultures guide decisions, actions, and policies of organizations and are functions of (1) the personal values of those employed by the organization, (2) the procedures used to carry out the daily business, and (3) the policies that are put in place to guide decision making. Overall, procedures and policies play a more important role in corporate culture than do personal values.

## Cultural Differences

**cultural differences**
Differences in standards of behavior from one culture to another.

In addition to corporate cultures, service firms may have **cultural differences** because of their own nationality-based cultures.[12] For example, although considered unethical in the United States, bribes are common business practice in some countries. Some further argue that ethical behaviors should not be regionally generalized. Accordingly, Asian countries, such as Japan and South Korea, should not be viewed as a single, homogeneous entity with respect to business conduct.[13] Service firms that engage in international operations should consider developing policies that help guide ethical decision making in different cultural climates.

## Organizational Structure

**organizational structure**
The way an organization is set up regarding hierarchy of authority and decision making.

The **organizational structure** of a service firm may also impact the ethical decision making of its employees. Traditional organizational structures are characterized as centralized or decentralized. Service providers employed by decentralized firms, where authority is spread throughout the firm, have more latitude when making decisions. In contrast, centralized firms, where authority is concentrated in one area, tend to place stricter controls over employees. Past studies have proposed that centralized organizations tend to be more ethical because of the development and implementation of rigid controls such as codes of ethics and other similar corporate policies.[14] Service firms wishing to implement the concept of empowerment need to consider and discuss with front-line personnel the decentralizing effects of this philosophy because it may create new opportunities for ethical misconduct.

## Opportunity

**opportunity**
An occasion in which a chance for unethical behavior exists.

As discussed earlier in the chapter, service organizations often operate within a business environment, where ethical misconduct is not easily detected. Hence, the **opportunity** to engage and benefit from unethical behavior within the service sector is fairly prevalent. Opportunity acts as temptation and has been proposed to be a better predictor of behavior than an individual's own personal moral beliefs.[15] Moreover, opportunity is said to increase along with title and status. Recent history has taught us via savings and loan scandals, insider trading schemes, and corrupt governmental officials that professional service providers may be particularly tempted by the opportunities that arise with a higher title and status.

## Reward Systems

Ethical misconduct may further be encouraged if rewarded (or not punished) by a firm's **reward system**. As with many types of employees, service providers are often rewarded according to outcome-based control measures (e.g., sales, number of calls handled, etc.). The major problem associated with outcome-based control systems is that employees are evaluated and compensated based on results (outcomes) rather than on behaviors utilized to achieve results. In other words, what you accomplish is judged, and how you accomplished it is seldom examined. Under this system, if a behavior (ethical or unethical) leads to outcomes valued by the organization (sales), then the employee should be rewarded (salary plus commissions). Thus outcome-based control systems tend to focus employee efforts on activities with immediate payoffs rather than on behaviors that build long-term relationships between the service provider and the client. Service firms wishing to enhance the ethical behavior of their employees should consider implementing a behavior-based control system that monitors employees' activities and evaluates employees on the aspects of their jobs over which they exercise control.[16] Compared with outcome-based reward systems, behavior-based reward systems are more harmonious with a long-term relationship marketing approach.

**reward systems**
The methods used by an organization to evaluate and compensate employees.

## Significant Others

As proposed by the theory of **differential association**, ethical decision making is greatly influenced by **significant others** (e.g., supervisors, peers, subordinates, and customers) with whom the service provider interacts. The more frequent the contact with the significant other, the more likely the employee will adopt similar ethical (or unethical) beliefs. "Association with others who are unethical, combined with the opportunity to act unethically oneself, is a major influence on ethical decision making."[17]

**differential association**
A theory that proposes ethical decision making is greatly influenced by significant others.

**significant others**
Supervisors, peers, subordinates, customers, and others who influence a service provider's behavior.

## Competitive Environment

Past research also indicates that the competitive environment in which the individual operates has an impact on ethical behavior.[18] Pressures from business superiors and ethical climate in the industry are cited as reasons for ethical conflict. Furthermore, it has been suggested that when individuals feel the pressure to succeed and realize what must be done in order to compete, they tend to compromise their own personal standards to reach corporate goals.

## Changes in Technology

As science has advanced, many products and services have been developed that carry with them an array of ethical considerations (e.g., abortion, euthanasia, cloning, fertility clinics, etc.). And in handling consumer information, advances in direct marketing techniques (e.g., database technology that allows greater storage and access to consumer information and purchase histories) have given service marketers powerful tools to "identify" their optimal customer profiles and track customer purchase/service histories.[19] For example, when a customer calls Sears to check a catalog order, the service representative has instant access (via an order number) to the customer's previous sales/service transactions. This data can be used to sell other products and service warranties as well as enable more efficient order processing. However, the availability of this information and ease of access to it creates the opportunity to use the data in a unethical manner and may violate the customer's right to privacy.

### Factors Contributing to Sears Employee Behavior

Returning to the Sears example, factors contributing to the decisions made by Sears Auto Center employees may have included the following: (1) corporate culture—employees were apparently following company procedures and policies; (2) opportunity—because of the difficulty involved in consumer evaluation of service quality, the situation existed in which consumers could be easily misled; (3) reward systems—the quota/bonus system rewarded outcomes (sales) rather than ethical behavior; (4) significant others—supervisors and co-workers were engaging in and/or encouraging the method of operation; (5) competitive environment— employees may have felt the pressure to succeed and tended to compromise their own personal standards to reach corporate goals; and (6) technology—the technological advances in the production of automobiles makes it very difficult these days to be one's own mechanic. Hence, technology contributed to the consumer's vulnerability.

## THE EFFECTS OF ETHICAL MISCONDUCT

Service organizations should stress the importance of ethical conduct by employees for several reasons. First, in terms of social responsibility, service organizations should be required to act in a manner that is in the best interest of society. Second, employees forced to deal with ethical issues on a continuing basis frequently suffer from job-related tension, frustration, anxiety, ineffective performance (i.e., reduced sales and reduced profits), turnover intentions, and lower job satisfaction.[20] One only needs to witness Firestone's and Ford's dilemma regarding the recall of millions of tires to see firsthand the impact of covering up mistakes.

In addition to the personal effects of ethical misconduct, the organization as a whole suffers. Ethical improprieties have also been linked to customer dissatisfaction (loss of sales), unfavorable word-of-mouth publicity for the organization, and a negative public image for the entire industry.[21]

The effects of the Sears Auto Centers policies have been damaging. Some of the consequences have included loss of consumer trust, lost sales as a result of the publicity surrounding the charges, and an increase in legal actions filed against the company. It could be argued that employees suffered as well, via increased anxiety, job-related tensions, and low job satisfaction.

# CONTROLLING ETHICAL DECISION MAKING

The adverse effects of unethical decision making may lead service firms to try to control the ethical behavior of their employees in a number of ways. Suggestions for controlling and managing ethical behavior include[22]:

- Employee socialization
- Standards of conduct
- Corrective control
- Leadership training
- Service/product knowledge
- Monitoring of employee performance
- Building long-term customer relationships

## Employee Socialization

**Employee socialization** refers to the process through which an individual adapts and comes to appreciate the values, norms, and required behavior patterns of an organization. Ethical issues such as cheating, payment of bribes, and lying may be defined through socialization of organizational values and norms. These values and norms may be transmitted via new employee orientation sessions and subsequent formal meetings to address new issues and reinforce past lessons.

Service organizations can also convey organizational values and norms through communications such as company newsletters and advertising. For example, Delta Airlines has been commended for its advertising that depicts very helpful, friendly, and happy employees who exert discretionary effort to assist the airline's customers. The ads not only appeal to customers but also help define for Delta employees their role within the company and the types of behavior the company expects and rewards.

> **employee socialization**
> The process through which an individual adapts and comes to appreciate the values, norms, and required behavior patterns of an organization.

## Standards of Conduct

As part of the socialization process, formal standards of conduct can be presented to service employees through a **code of ethics**. Research indicates that employees desire codes of ethics to help them define proper behavior, thereby reducing role conflict and role ambiguity.[23] Although developing a code of ethics does not guarantee subsequent employee ethical behavior, it is an important early step in the process of controlling ethical decision making.

> **code of ethics**
> Formal standards of conduct that assist in defining proper organizational behavior.

## Corrective Control

For the service firm's code of ethics to be effective, the conditions set forth in it must be enforced. Enforcement of the code of ethics may be accomplished through **corrective control**, the use of rewards and punishments. Service providers who are rewarded (or not punished) for unethical behavior will continue practicing it. Interestingly, research indicates that employees of firms that have codes of ethics are more prone to believe that violators of ethical codes should be punished.

> **corrective control**
> The use of rewards and punishments to enforce a firm's code of ethics.

## Leadership Training

Because of the apparent effects of differential association on ethical decision making, service organizations need to stress to their leaders the importance of those leaders' own behavior and its influence on subordinates. Leaders must be examples of the standards of ethical conduct. They need to understand that employees faced with ethical decision making often emulate the behavior of their supervisors. This is particularly true of young employees, who tend to comply with their supervisors to demonstrate loyalty.

## Service/Product Knowledge

Service firms need to constantly train all employees concerning the details of what the service product can and cannot provide. Because of the complex nature of many service offerings and an ever-changing business environment, service firms cannot afford to assume that employees completely understand the ramifications of new service/product developments. A few service industries understand the social responsibility of keeping employees informed. For example, the insurance industry now requires continuing education of its sales agents.[24]

## Monitoring of Employee Performance

Another possible method of controlling ethical decision making is the measurement of employee ethical performance. This approach involves comparing behaviors used in obtaining performance levels against organizational ethical standards. Service firms may monitor employee performance by either observing employees in action or by using employee questionnaires regarding ethical behavior. Results obtained from monitoring should be discussed with the employees to alleviate any ambiguities in the employees' minds about the appropriate actions to take when questionable situations arise.

## Stress Building Long-term Customer Relationships

Service providers must build trusting relationships between themselves and their customers to promote long-term, mutually beneficial relationships.[25] Ethical marketing practices provide the basis from which such trust-based relationships are formed. Many unethical decisions that are made emphasize the short-run benefits that the decision provides. For example, a service provider may mislead a customer in order to make a quick sale. Service firms that properly socialize their employees should stress the importance of building long-term relationships. Service firms whose employees are oriented toward a long-term customer relationship should be able to minimize the frequency of unethical decision-making.

## Strategies for Controlling the Ethical Behavior at Sears Auto Centers

Strategies for controlling the future ethical behavior of Sears Auto Centers employees might include the following: (1) employee socialization—orientation sessions regarding ethics for new employees; (2) standards of conduct—a code of ethics needs to be developed or reviewed; (3) corrective control—violations of the code of ethics need to be enforced; (4) leadership training—supervisors need to understand that subordinates emulate their behavior and that they are role models, particularly to new employees; (5) service/product training—all employees must be required to have adequate skills so that mechanical problems are not misdiagnosed or unnecessary repairs made; (6) monitor employee performance—assess and discuss behavior used to obtain results as well as the results themselves; (7) stress long-term customer relationships—emphasize that long-term satisfaction is more important than meeting the company's short-term (monthly) sales quota.

## SUMMARY

This chapter has presented an overview of ethics as they apply to the service sector. Service consumers are particularly vulnerable to ethical misconduct for a variety of reasons. For example, services possess few search attributes and therefore are difficult to evaluate before the purchase decision has been made; services are often technical and/or specialized, making evaluation by the common consumer even more difficult; many services are sold without warranties and/or guarantees and are often provided by unsupervised boundary-spanning personnel. In addition, reward systems that compensate service personnel are often based on results as opposed to the behaviors utilized to achieve those results. Other factors contributing to consumer vulnerability include the time lapse that occurs for some services between service performance and customer evaluation (e.g., financial planning, life insurance), the inherent variation in service performance, and the consumer's willingness to accept the blame for failing to effectively communicate his or her wishes to the service provider.

The most common ethical issues involve conflict of interest, confidentiality in organizational relationships, honesty, fairness, and the integrity of the firm's communications efforts. The behavior of service providers engaged in ethical decision-making reflects the moral philosophies in which they believe. Moral philosophies are the principles or rules service providers use when deciding what is right or wrong and include philosophies such as teleology, deontology, and relativism.

Different service personnel may make different decisions under similar ethical situations because of their cognitive moral development and a variety of other factors, including personal values, cultural differences, corporate culture, organizational structure, opportunity, reward systems, significant others, and the pressures of conducting business in a competitive environment.

Employees forced to deal with ethical issues on a continuous basis frequently suffer from job-related tension, frustration, anxiety, ineffective performance, turnover intention, and low job satisfaction.

In addition to the personal effects of ethical misconduct, the organization as a whole is likely to suffer as well. Ethical improprieties have been linked to customer dissatisfaction, unfavorable word-of-mouth publicity, and negative public images for an entire industry.

Organizations have utilized a number of strategies that attempt to control the ethical behavior of employees, including employee socialization, the development and enforcement of codes of ethics, leadership training, service/product knowledge training, monitoring employee performance, and education of employees regarding the benefits of long-term customer relationships.

## Key Terms

Boundary-spanning personnel
Business ethics
Categorical imperative
Code of ethics
Cognitive moral development
Conflict of interest
Consequentialism
Corporate culture
Corrective control
Cultural differences
Deontology
Differential association
Egoism
Employee socialization
Ethical vigilance

Ethics
Fairness
Honesty
Moral philosophies
Opportunity
Organizational relationships
Organizational structure
Personal values
Principle of utility
Relativism
Reward systems
Significant others
Teleology
Utilitarianism

## Review Questions

1. Discuss the difference between ethics and social responsibility.
2. How does the public feel about the ethical behaviors of businesspeople?
3. What are boundary-spanning personnel? What provides these employees with the opportunity to engage in ethical misconduct?
4. Does consumer participation in the service delivery process increase or decrease the service provider's opportunity to engage in unethical behavior? Explain.
5. Which moral philosophies best describe your own personal ethical behavior? Explain.
6. Discuss the difference between an egoist and a utilitarianist.
7. Discuss the primary difference between a teleologist and a deontologist.
8. Discuss the theory of differential association.

# Notes

1. Mary L. Nicastro, "Infuse Business Ethics into Marketing Curriculum," *Marketing Educator* 11, no. 1 (1992), 1.
2. *Webster's New Ideal Dictionary* (Springfield, Mass.: G. & C. Merriam Co., 1973), 171.
3. O. C. Ferrell and John Fraedrich, *Business Ethics* (Boston: Houghton Mifflin, 1991), 5.
4. Gene R. Laczniak and Patrick E. Murphy, *Ethical Marketing Decisions* (Needham Heights, Mass.: Allyn and Bacon, 1993), 3.
5. Valerie A. Zeithaml, A. Parasuraman, and Leonard L. Berry, "Problems and Strategies in Services Marketing," *Journal of Marketing* 49, no. 2 (1985), 33–46.
6. K. Douglas Hoffman and Judy A. Siguaw, "Incorporating Ethics into the Services Marketing Course: The Case of the Sears Auto Centers," *Marketing Education Review* 3, no. 3 (1993), 26–32.
7. Ferrell and Fraedrich, *Business Ethics*, 40–48.
8. Ibid., 42.
9. Ibid., 45.
10. Ibid., 22–29.
11. Ibid., 68–133.
12. David J. Fritzsche and Helmet Becker, "Linking Management Behavior to Ethical Philosophy: An Empirical Investigation," *Academy of Management Journal* 27 (March 1984), 166–175.
13. Alan J. Dubinsky, Marvin A. Jolson, Masaaki Kotabe, and Chae Un Lim, "A Cross-National Investigation of Industrial Salespeople's Ethical Perceptions," *Journal of International Business Studies* 22, no. 4 (1990), 651–671.
14. Sandra Pelfrey and Eileen Peacock, "Ethical Codes of Conduct Are Improving," *Business Horizons* (Spring 1991), 14–17.
15. O. C. Ferrell and Larry G. Gresham, "A Contingency Framework for Understanding Ethical Decision Making in Marketing," *Journal of Marketing* (Summer 1985), 87–96.
16. Gilbert A. Churchill, Jr., Neil M. Ford, Steven W. Hartley, and Orville C. Walker, Jr., "The Determinants of Salesperson Performance: A Meta-Analysis," *Journal of Marketing Research* 22, no. 2 (1985), 103–118.
17. Ferrell and Fraedrich, *Business Ethics*, 110.
18. K. Douglas Hoffman, Vince Howe, and Don Hardigree, "Selling of Complex Others and Competitive Pressures," *Journal of Personal Selling and Sales Management* 11, no. 4 (1991), 13–25.
19. David Shepard, *The New Direct Marketing: How to Implement a Profit-Driven Database Marketing Strategy* (Homewood, Ill.: Business One Irwin, 1990).
20. Orville C. Walker, Gilbert A. Churchill, and Neil M. Ford, "Where Do We Go from Here: Selected Conceptual and Empirical Issues Concerning the Motivation and Performance of the Industrial Sales Force," in *Critical Issues in Sales Management: State-of-the-Art and Future Research Needs*, G. Albaum and

G. A. Churchill, eds. (Eugene, Ore.: College of Business Administration, University of Oregon, 1979).

21. Ronald W. Vinson, "Industry Image Stuck in Downcycle," *National Underwriter Property & Casualty-Risk & Benefits Management,* January 7, 1991, pp. 25–29.

22. Ferrell and Fraedrich, *Business Ethics,* 137–150.

23. Sandra Pelfrey and Eileen Peacock, "Ethical Codes of Conduct are Improving," *Business Horizons* (Spring 1991), 14–17.

24. C. King, "Prof. Challenges Industry to Face Ethical Issues," *National Underwriter Life & Health-Financial Services,* August 16, 1990, pp. 15–16.

25. Lawrence A. Crosby, Kenneth R. Evans, and Deborah Cowles, "Relationship Quality in Services Selling: An Interpersonal Influence Perspective," *Journal of Marketing* (July 1990), 68–81.

# part 2

# SERVICE STRATEGY: MANAGING THE SERVICE ENCOUNTER

Part II is dedicated to topics that pertain to managing the service encounter. As a result of consumer involvement in the production of services, many challenges for management occur that rarely, if ever, need to be considered in the production of goods. In this part, you will learn about the strategic issues that affect both the marketing mix and the components of the servuction model, including process, pricing, promotion, physical evidence, and people (employee and customer) issues.

## chapter 6

# Service Delivery Process

## CHAPTER OBJECTIVES

The main objective in this chapter is to familiarize you with operations concepts and explain the importance of balancing operations and marketing functions in service operations.

After reading this chapter, you should be able to:

- Discuss the relationship between operations and marketing as it pertains to developing service delivery systems.
- Discuss the type of operation that would typify peak efficiency.
- Describe the difficulties associated with applying efficiency models to service organizations.
- Describe alternative strategies available to facilitate the balance of supply and demand.
- Discuss the fundamental components of a service blueprint.
- Understand the necessary calculations for determining the service cost per output.
- Discuss the strategies available for new service development.

"Customers cannot be satisfied until after they are not dissatisfied. Your first service priority should be to eliminate all the opportunities for dissatisfying customers, because they are what cause customers to leave. Then you can invest in satisfying and delighting them."

Jim Donnelly, Jr.

# Introduction

The operations of a service firm are the heart of the "product." Throughout the last two decades, the distribution center of L.L. Bean was a required stop for companies engaging in benchmarking exercises. Many companies, including Nike, Disney, Gillette, and Chrysler, came to see how Bean could fill orders so effectively. In fact, the center they visited is no more; it has been replaced by a completely new approach. The new approach was driven by an ever-increasing volume of orders, an increasingly global reach, and a growing variety of customized products. The old system would build orders from the telephone operations and then issue them every 12 hours to pickers. The pickers would assemble the orders from around the center and then deliver them to packers, who prepared the orders for shipment.

The new system, Wave Pick Technology, operates differently. Orders come straight from the telephones and are allocated immediately to pickers with available capacity. Moreover, the orders are broken down by item and assigned to different pickers, who themselves are assigned to different parts of the warehouse. The items are placed on a conveyor belt and bar coded. Scanners then automatically assemble the orders for packing. As a result, 100 percent of orders can be serviced within 24 hours; from order to delivery to the on-site Federal Express depot only takes 2 hours.

Without a successful operation, the firm is out of business, because it will have nothing to offer to the customer. However, firms setting out to construct a service operation can choose from a large range of operational options. Strategically, the service firm can choose to use its operations as the key component of its competitive strategy. The manner in which "operational competitiveness" is embraced by various service firms can be described by four stages.[1]

## Stage 1: Available for Service

Operations for a firm with this level of competitiveness are viewed as a "necessary evil." Operations are, at best, reactive to the needs of the rest of the organization and deliver the service as specified. As its mission, the operations department attempts primarily to avoid mistakes. Back office support is minimized to keep costs down. Technological investment is also minimized, as is investment in training for front-line personnel. Management designs skill out of the work done by these personnel and pays them the minimum wage whenever possible.

## Stage 2: Journeyman

This level of competitiveness is often provided by the arrival of competition. It is no longer enough just to have an operation that works. The firm must now seek feedback from its customers on the relative costs and perceived qualities of the service. At this point, the operations department becomes much more outward looking and often becomes interested in benchmarking.

Technology for firms at this stage tends to be justified based on the cost savings possible. The back office is now seen as a contributor to the service but tends to be treated as an internal service function. In the management of front-line employees, the emphasis shifts from controlling workers to managing processes. Employees are often given procedures to follow, and management consists of ensuring that these procedures are followed.

## Stage 3: Distinctive Competence Achieved

By this stage, operations have reached a point where they continually excel, reinforced by the personnel management function and systems that support the customer focus. By this time, the firm has mastered the core service and understands the complexity of changing such operations. The back office is now seen to be as valuable as the front-of-house personnel. Technology is no longer seen as a source of cost advantage alone, but also as a way of enhancing the service to customers.

Perhaps the biggest changes come about in the workforce and in the nature of front-line management. Front-line workers are allowed to select from alternative procedures and are not tied down in the same way. The role of front-line management is to listen to customers and become coaches to the front-line workers.

## Stage 4: World-Class Service Delivery

To sustain this level of performance, operations not only have to continually excel but also become a fast learner and innovator. The back office, once seen as a second-class citizen, now must be proactive, develop its own capabilities, and generate opportunities. Technology is seen as a way to break the paradigm—to do things competitors cannot do.

The workforce itself must be a source of innovators, not just operators. To achieve this, the front-line supervisors must go beyond coaching to mentoring. As mentors, they need to be accountable for the personal development of the workforce so that employees can develop the skills necessary for them to innovate for the firm.

Overall, the purpose of this chapter is to highlight the fact that operations management problems in services cannot be solved by the operations function alone. As pointed out by the four stages noted above, the search for operations efficiency can be crucial to long-term competitiveness. However, efficiency must be balanced against the effectiveness of the system from the customer's point of view. Table 6.1 provides a quick glimpse into the major trade-offs between efficiency and customer service when developing operations for low-customer-contact versus high-customer-contact services.

Frequently, it is too easy to view the customer as a constraint: "If we could get rid of all these customers, we could run a good service operation!" Such a negative perspective ignores a golden opportunity. Customers in a service operation can be used to help operations. Such a positive view does, however, require that operations personnel recognize the importance of their marketing counterparts.

More importantly, such a view also requires that marketing personnel have an intimate knowledge of the operations system and its problems. It is not enough to propose new products that can be delivered through the system. The impact of such products on the whole system must be considered.[2]

# TABLE 6.1

## Major Design Trade-offs in High- and Low-Contact Systems

| Decision | High-Contact System | Low-Contact System |
|---|---|---|
| Facility location | Operations must be near the customer. | Operations may be placed near supply, transportation, or labor. |
| Facility layout | Facility should accomodate the customer's physical and psychological needs and expectations. | Facility should enhance production. |
| Product design | Environment as well as the physical product define the nature of the service. | Customer is not in the service environment so the product can be defined by fewer attributes. |
| Process design | Stages of production process have a direct immediate effect on the customer. | Customer is not involved in the majority of processing steps. |
| Scheduling | Customer is in the production schedule and must be accommodated. | Customer is concerned mainly with completion dates. |
| Production planning | Orders cannot be stored, so smoothing production flow will result in loss of business. | Both backlogging and production smoothing are possible. |
| Worker skills | Direct workforce makes up a major part of the service product and so must be able to interact well with the public. | Direct workforce need have only technical skills. |
| Quality control | Quality standards are often in the eye of the beholder and, hence, variable. | Quality standards are generally measurable and, hence, fixed. |
| Time standards | Service time depends on customer needs, so time standards are inherently loose. | Work is performed on customer surrogates (e.g., forms), and time standards can be tight. |
| Wage payments | Variable output requires time-based wage systems. | "Fixable" outputs permits output-based wage systems. |
| Capacity planning | To avoid lost sales, capacity must be set to match peak demand. | Storable output permits setting capacity at some average demand level. |
| Forecasting | Forecasts are short term, time oriented. | Forecasts are long term, output oriented. |

Source: Richard C. Chase, "Where Does the Customer Fit in a Service Operation?" *Harvard Business Review* (November–December 1978), pp. 137–142. Reprinted by permission of *Harvard Business Review*. Copyright © 1978 by the President and Fellows of Harvard College.

## THE CUSTOMER'S INVOLVEMENT IN THE PRODUCTION PROCESS

The servuction model presented in Chapter 1 clearly demonstrates that consumers are an integral part of the service process. Their participation may be active or passive, but they are always there. If the consumer is in the factory, it is clear that if the factory is changed, consumer behavior will have to be changed. Clearly, changes to the visible part of the service firm will be apparent to the consumer. Moreover, the changes frequently demand that the consumer change his or her behavior to adapt to the new procedures.

SERVICES 6.1
IN ACTION

### Sometimes It's What They Can't See That Drives Customers Away

When moving to North Carolina several years ago, I rented the largest moving truck that U-Haul offered, which cost approximately $1,200. I also purchased several U-Haul boxes, some masking tape, and other moving accessories. With the help of many friends, I loaded the truck and began the 600-mile trip to the East Coast. The truck worked like a charm. It was clean, the air conditioning and radio worked, the cab of the truck was immaculate, and, all in all, it was relatively easy to handle on the highway.

Everything was great until I went to return the truck after I reached my destination. The peculiar thing is that the problem did not have anything to do with the truck. The problem occurred when I wanted to return a $3.95 dish box. It seemed that U-Haul had implemented a new inventory control system that required customers to provide receipts with any items they wished to return. The objective of the new system was to identify any box's original place of purchase so that it could be taken out of inventory at that location and then re-entered into inventory where the return was taking place.

Unfortunately, I had not kept the receipt for the $3.95 dish box. Why keep it? The box had the "U-Haul" logo plastered all over its outside, so it was fairly obvious from whom the box had been purchased. Secondly, I knew exactly which U-Haul distribution center from which I had purchased the box. I offered that information to the U-Haul representative, but she informed me of the new inventory control system and insisted that I needed the receipt in order for her to process the refund.

My next problem was that I was not able to get upset with the U-Haul representative. She was obviously doing what she was told to do. In fact, when I reminded her that I had just spent $1,200.00 on one of her company's trucks and yet it was refusing my return of a $3.95 dish box, she responded with, "Yeah, it's just crazy, isn't it!" The funny thing was that she really meant it—she offered to give me the "1-800" number for U-Haul customer service so that I could complain.

The lesson learned from this experience is that someone, somewhere within the confines of U-Haul's headquarters, who probably has little, if any, contact with customers, developed what he or she thought was an efficient method of monitoring inventory levels throughout the company. However, U-Haul failed to recognize how this change, which took place in the invisible organization and systems component of the servuction model, would affect the customer, not to mention U-Haul's own representatives, who would now have to field customer complaints about the new procedures. It was ludicrous to turn away a customer who just spent more than $1,200 for a $3.95 return. However, the new "process" had accomplished exactly that.

Source: Adapted from K. Douglas Hoffman, co-author, *Essentials of Services Marketing: Concepts, Strategies and Cases.*

Pumping your own gasoline at a convenience station is a commonly accepted practice today. The change in operations also required a change in consumer behavior.

For example, when convenience stores first opened, gasoline was not part of the product offering. The introduction of gasoline to the product mix presented two new challenges to consumers. First, from a psychological standpoint, the initial thought of buying gasoline at the same location as food products was resisted. Gasoline stations at the time were generally dirty, grimy places staffed by burly men who had years of grit built up under their fingernails. A gasoline station was hardly the place one wanted to buy food. The second challenge, having customers pump their own gas, created a change in operations that required a change in consumer behavior. Consumers had to learn how to work a gas pump, and the convenience store and gasoline pump manufacturers had to develop gas pumps and monitoring procedures for this new type of self-service operation.

It can be argued that a decision to change the benefit concept developed for the consumer, such as providing self-service operations, has a far greater impact on a service firm than on a goods firm. Both types of firms will probably have to change their factory procedures. However, many of the changes made in the service firm will be directly visible to the consumer, including the customer service disasters that are likely to occur during the startup of the operation.

Managers of service firms must understand the interactive nature of services and the involvement of the consumer in the production process. As we discussed in Chapter 4, consumers appear to develop a script for frequently used services. This script is similar to a theatrical script in that it helps guide the consumer through the service experience. Changes in the service factory process will imply changes in the consumer script—the way in which the consumer participates in the process.

New developments coming from either the service factory or the consumer imply major changes in the consumer script as well as changes in the scripts of contact personnel. This chapter highlights the trade-offs between the search for operational efficiency and the need to create marketing effectiveness. In the service factory, many of the traditional methods for increasing operational effectiveness cannot be implemented behind closed doors. In fact, changes made to increase the service operation's efficiency can often downgrade the final service product, as was the customer's experience with U-Haul (see Services in Action 6.1). This chapter focuses on the positive things marketing can achieve to help improve the efficiency of the servuction system.

## MARKETING AND OPERATIONS: BALANCE IS CRITICAL

In a broad sense, one way of viewing the task of marketing is to think of it as the marrying of consumers' needs with the technology and manufacturing capabilities of the firm. Such a marriage will obviously involve compromises, since the consumers' needs can seldom be met completely and economically. In a goods firm, this marriage requires marketing's understanding of the capabilities of manufacturing and of research and development. The task of marketing goods is made somewhat easier because the different functions can be separated by means of an inventory.

In a service firm, this marketing problem is magnified. Significant aspects of the operation are the product, since they create the interactive experience that delivers the bundle of benefits to the consumer. For example, a restaurant experience is not based solely on the quality of the food. The physical environment and interactions with contact personnel throughout the experience also affect consumer perceptions of the quality of service delivered. A successful compromise between operations efficiency and marketing effectiveness is, therefore, that much more difficult to achieve. Success in services marketing demands a much greater understanding of the constraints and opportunities posed by operations.

To introduce these complexities, in this chapter we first adopt the perspective of an operations manager and ask, "What would be the ideal way to run the system from an operations perspective?" The impact on marketing and the opportunities for marketing to assist in the creation of this ideal are then developed.

As pointed out in Chapter 1, the key distinctive characteristic of services is that the product is an experience. That experience is created by the operating system of the firm's interaction with the customer. Thus the operating system of the firm, in all its complexity, is the product. For a marketing manager, this imposes constraints on the strategies that can be employed, but it also presents new and challenging opportunities for improving the profitability of the firm.

Chapter 4 provided one base on which to build an understanding of the product design problem for services. An understanding of consumer behavior has always been a necessary condition for successful marketing. One way of viewing the product design process is to think of it as the process of combining such an understanding with the technological and manufacturing skills of the organization. To be an effective services marketer, a knowledge of consumer behavior is not sufficient in itself to produce economically successful products. Successful managers require a keen understanding of operations and human resource concepts and strategies as well.

As we discussed in Chapter 2, it is possible for goods producers to separate the problems of manufacturing and marketing by the use of inventory. Even so, there are many areas of potential conflict, as can be viewed in Table 6.2. Although the issues are characterized as conflicts, they can be reconceptualized as opportunities. In each area it is clear that a better integration of marketing and manufacturing plans could yield a more efficient and profitable organization. For example, the determination of the extent of the product line should be seen as a compromise between the heterogeneous demands of consumers and the manufacturing demand of homogeneity. If marketing managers have their way, too many products will probably be developed, and the operation will become inefficient. As long as

## TABLE 6.2

**Sources of Cooperation/Conflict Between Marketing and Operations**

| Problem Area | Typical Marketing Comment | Typical Manufacturing Comment |
|---|---|---|
| 1. Capacity planning and long-range sales forecasting | "Why don't we have enough capacity?" | "Why didn't we have accurate sales forecasts?" |
| 2. Production scheduling and short-range sales forecasting | "We need faster response. Our lead times are ridiculous." | "We need realistic customer commitments and sales forecasts that don't change like wind direction." |
| 3. Delivery and physical distribution | "Why don't we ever have the right merchandise in inventory?" | "We can't keep everything in inventory." |
| 4. Quality assurance | "Why can't we have reasonable quality at reasonable costs?" | "Why must we always offer options that are too hard to manufacture and that offer little customer utility?" |
| 5. Breadth of product line | "Our customers demand variety." | "The product line is too broad—all we get are short, uneconomical runs." |
| 6. Cost control | "Our costs are so high that we are not competitive in the marketplace." | "We can't provide fast delivery, broad variety, rapid response to change, and high quality at low cost." |
| 7. New product introduction | "New products are our lifeblood." | "Unnecessary design changes are prohibitively expensive." |
| 8. Adjunct services such as spare parts, inventory support, installation, and repair | "Field service costs are too high." | "Products are being used in ways for which they weren't designed." |

Source: Reprinted by permission of *Harvard Business Review.* An exhibit from "Can Marketing and Manufacturing Coexist?" by Benson P. Shapiro (September/October 1977), p. 105. Copyright © 1977 by the President and Fellows of Harvard College; all rights reserved.

this is compensated for by higher prices, a successful strategy can be implemented. In contrast, if the operations people have their way, everyone would be driving the same model of car, painted the same color, which is less attractive for consumers. As long as this is compensated for by lower costs and hence lower prices, a successful strategy can emerge.

Marketing and operations are in a tug-of-war that should be resolved by compromise. In the service sector, the possible areas of conflict or compromise are much broader because the operation itself is the product. Again, there is no single solution, since operational efficiency and marketing effectiveness may push in opposite directions.

By its very nature, this chapter is meant to be operations oriented rather than marketing oriented. To polarize the issues, the perspective adopted in this chapter is that of the operations manager, just as in Chapter 4 the consumer's position was presented. The focus is on the requirements for operational efficiency and the ways that marketing can help achieve those requirements. We stress that in the drive for competitive advantage in the marketplace, marketing demand may in the end mean less operational efficiency. As the amount of customer contact increases, the likelihood that the service firm will operate efficiently decreases. Customers ultimately determine:

- the type of demand
- the cycle of demand
- the length of the service experience

Meanwhile, the service firm loses more and more control over its daily operations. It's the nature of the service business.

## IN A PERFECT WORLD, SERVICE FIRMS WOULD BE EFFICIENT

### Thompson's Perfect-World Model

**technical core**
The place within an organization where its primary operations are conducted.

**perfect-world model**
J. D. Thompson's model of organizations proposing that operations' "perfect" efficiency is possible only if inputs, outputs, and quality happen at a constant rate and remain known and certain.

The starting point for this discussion is the work of J. D. Thompson.[3] Thompson, who started from an organizational perspective, introduced the idea of a **technical core**—the place within the organization where its primary operations are conducted. In the service sector, the technical core consists of kitchens in restaurants, garages in auto service stations, work areas at dry cleaners, and surgical suites in a hospital. Thompson proposed in his **perfect-world model** that to operate efficiently, a firm must be able to operate "as if the market will absorb the single kind of product at a continuous rate and as if the inputs flowed continuously at a steady rate and with specified quality." At the center of his argument was the idea that uncertainty creates inefficiency. In the ideal situation, the technical core is able to operate without uncertainty on both the input and output side, thereby creating many advantages for management.

The absence of uncertainty means that decisions within the core can become programmed and that individual discretion can be replaced by rules; the removal of individual discretion means that jobs are "de-skilled" and that a lower quality of labor can be used. Alternatively, the rules can be programmed into machines and labor replaced with capital. Because output and input are fixed, it is simple to plan production and to run at the high levels of utilization needed to generate the most efficient operations performance.

All in all, a system without uncertainty is easy to control and manage. Performance can be measured using objective standards. And because the system is not subject to disturbances from the outside, the causes of any problems are also easy to diagnose.

## The Focused Factory Concept

Obviously, such an ideal world as proposed by Thompson is virtually impossible to create, and even in goods companies the demands of purchasing the inputs and marketing's management of the outputs have to be traded off against the ideal operations demands. In goods manufacturing, this trade-off has been accomplished through the **focused factory**.[4] The focused factory focuses on a particular job; once this focus is achieved, the factory does a better job because repetition and concentration in one area allow the workforce and managers to become effective and experienced in the task required for success. The focused factory broadens Thompson's perfect-world model in that it argues that focus generates effectiveness as well as efficiency. In other words, the focused factory can meet the demands of the market better whether the demand is low cost through efficiency, high quality, or any other criterion.

## Plant Within a Plant Concept

The idea of a focused factory can be extended in another direction by introducing the **plant-within-a-plant (PWP)** concept. Because there are advantages to having production capability at a single site, the plant within a plant strategy introduces the concept of breaking up large, unfocused plants into smaller units buffered from one another so that they can each be focused separately.

In goods manufacturing, the concept of **buffering** is a powerful one. "Organizations seek to buffer environmental influences by surrounding their technical core with input and output components."[5] A PWP can thus be operated in a manner close to Thompson's perfect-world model if buffer inventories are created on the input and output sides. On the input side, the components needed in a plant can be inventoried and their quality controlled before they are needed; in this way, it can appear to the PWP that the quality and flow of the inputs into the system are constant. In a similar way, the PWP can be separated from downstream plants or from the market by creating finished goods inventories. Automobile manufacturers are good examples. Finished goods are absorbed downstream by an established retail dealership system that purchases and holds the manufacturer's inventory in regional markets until sold to the final consumer.

The alternatives proposed by Thompson to buffering are smoothing, anticipating, and rationing. Smoothing and anticipating focus on the uncertainty introduced into the system by the flow of work; **smoothing** involves managing the environment to reduce fluctuations in supply and/or demand, and **anticipating**

**focused factory**
An operation that concentrates on performing one particular task in one particular part of the plant; used for promoting experience and effectiveness through repetition and concentration on one task necessary for success.

**plant within a plant**
The strategy of breaking up large, unfocused plants into smaller units buffered from each other so that each can be focused separately.

**buffering**
Surrounding the technical core with input and output components to buffer environmental influences.

**smoothing**
Managing the environment to reduce fluctuations in supply and/or demand.

**anticipating**
Mitigating the worst effects of supply and demand fluctuations by planning for them.

**rationing**
Direct allocations of inputs and outputs when the demands placed on a system by the environment exceed the system's ability to handle them

involves mitigating the worst effects of those fluctuations by planning for them. Finally, **rationing** involves resorting to triage when the demands placed on the system by the environment exceed its ability to handle them. Successful firms pre-plan smoothing, anticipating, and rationing strategies so that they can be more efficiently implemented in times of need.

## APPLYING THE EFFICIENCY MODELS TO SERVICES

The application of operations concepts to services is fraught with difficulty. The problem can be easily understood by thinking about the servuction model presented in Chapter 1. From an operational point of view, the key characteristics of the model are that the customer is an integral part of the process and that the system operates in real time. Because the system is interactive, it can be (and often is) used to customize the service for each individual.

To put it bluntly, the servuction system itself is an operations nightmare. In most cases it is impossible to use inventories and impossible to decouple production from the customer. Instead of receiving demand at a constant rate, the system is linked directly to a market that frequently varies from day to day, hour to hour, and even minute to minute. This creates massive problems in capacity planning and utilization. In fact, in many instances supply and demand match up purely by accident.

It is clear from this simplified model that services by their very nature do not meet the requirements of the perfect-world model. The closest the servuction model comes to this ideal state is the part of the system that is invisible to the customer. Even here, however, the customization taking place may introduce uncertainty into the system. Provided that all customization can take place within the servuction system itself, then the part invisible to the customer can be run separately. It can often be located in a place different from the customer contact portion of the model.[6] However, when customization cannot be done within the servuction system, uncertainty can be introduced into the back office.

Instead of "the single kind of product" desired by the perfect-world model, the service system can be called on to make a different "product" for each customer. Indeed, one could argue that because each customer is different and is an integral part of the process, and because each experience or product is unique, the uncertainty about the next task to be performed is massive.

The Thompson model requires inputs that flow continuously, at a steady rate, and at a specified quality. Consider the inputs to the servuction system: the physical environment, contact personnel, other customers, and the individual customer. The environment may remain constant in many service encounters, but the other three inputs are totally variable, not only in their quality, but also in their rate of arrival into the process.

Moreover, contact personnel are individuals, not inanimate objects. They have emotions and feelings and, like all people, are affected by things happening in their lives outside the work environment. If they arrive in a bad mood, this can influence their performance throughout the day. And that bad mood directly affects the customer, since the service worker is a visible part of the experience being purchased.

Customers can also be subject to moods that can affect their behavior toward the service firm and toward each other. Some moods are predictable, like the mood when a home team wins and the crowds hit the local bars. Other moods are individual, specific, and totally unpredictable until after the consumer is already part of the servuction system.

Finally, customers arrive at the service firm at unpredictable rates, making smoothing and anticipation of incoming demand difficult. One minute a restaurant can be empty, and in the next few minutes, it can be full. One need only consider the variability of demand for cashiers in a grocery store to understand the basics of this problem. Analysis of demand can often show predictable peaks that can be planned for in advance; but even this precaution introduces inefficiency into the firm, since the firm would ideally prefer the customers to arrive in a steady stream. Worse still are the unpredictable peaks. Planning for these peaks would produce large amounts of excess capacity at most times. The excess would strain the entire system, undermining the experience for customer and contact personnel alike.

## POTENTIAL SOLUTIONS TO SERVICE OPERATIONS PROBLEMS

Within the operations management and marketing literatures of the past decade, a growing body of ideas has emerged regarding overcoming some of the problems of service operations. These ideas can be classified into six broad areas:

* Isolating the technical core
* Minimizing the servuction system
* Production-lining the whole system (including the servuction system)
* Creating flexible capacity
* Increasing customer participation
* Moving the time of demand

### Isolating the Technical Core and Minimizing the Servuction System

Isolating the technical core of the service firm and minimizing the servuction system have been combined because they are closely related from an operations viewpoint and because their marketing implications are similar. This approach proposes the clear separation of the servuction system, which is characterized by a high degree of customer contact, from the technical core. Once separation is achieved, different management philosophies should be adopted for each separate unit of operation. In other words, let's divide the service firm into two distinct areas—high customer contact and no/low customer contact—and operate each area differently.

In the servuction system, management should focus on optimizing the experience for the consumer. Conversely, once the technical core (no/low contact area) has been isolated, it should be subjected to traditional production-lining approaches.[7] In sum, high-contact systems should sacrifice efficiency in the interest of the customer, but low-contact systems need not do so.[8]

Unpredictable arrivals of customers can make it difficult to match consumer demand with the supply of service available.

Isolating the technical core argues for minimizing the amount of customer contact with the system. "Clients . . . pose problems for organizations . . . by disrupting their routines, ignoring their offers for service, failing to comply with their procedures, making exaggerated demands and so forth."[9] Operating efficiency is thus reduced by the uncertainty introduced into the system by the customer.[10]

**decoupling**
Disassociating the technical core from the servuction system.

Examples of **decoupling** the technical core from high contact areas of the servuction system include suggestions from operations experts such as handling only exceptions on a face-to-face basis, with routine transactions as much as possible being handled by telephone or, even better, by mail—mail transactions have the great advantage of being able to be inventoried.[11] In addition, the degree of customer contact should be matched to customer requirements, and the amount of high-contact service offered should be the minimum acceptable to the customer.[12] Overall, operational efficiency always favors low-contact systems, but effectiveness from the customer's point of view may be something completely different.

## THE MARKETING PERSPECTIVE

At this point, the need for marketing involvement in the approach becomes clear, since a decision about the extent of customer contact favored by the customer is clearly a marketing issue (see Services in Action 6.2). In some cases, a high degree of customer contact can be used to differentiate the service from its competitors; in such cases, the operational costs must be weighed against the competitive benefits. Consider the competitive advantages that a five-star restaurant has over a fast-food franchise.

Conversely, in some situations, the segment of the firm that the operations group views as the back office is not actually invisible to the customer. For example, in some financial services, the teller operation takes place in the administrative

S E R V I C E S 6.2
I N
A C T I O N

**For Innovative Service Processes,
Run for the Border**

While the vast majority of other food franchises have remained in the traditional management mode by focusing on more advertising, more promotions, more new products, and more new locations, Taco Bell has been focusing on the customer. Taco Bell believes that the company should be organized to support what the customer truly values ... the food and the service delivery system.

Unlike other food franchises, Taco Bell has shifted its operation from manufacturing to assembly. Backroom tasks such as cleaning heads of lettuce, slicing tomatoes, shredding cheese, and making taco shells [have] been outsourced to other operations. As a result, labor's primary focus is now on serving customers as opposed to preparing food. In contrast, much of the remainder of the industry is expanding its on-site food manufacturing operations by offering products such as freshly baked biscuits and pizzas. Firms pursuing this strategy have complicated their operations and have placed their emphasis on production as opposed to service delivery.

Other changes within Taco Bell's operations have included a total revamping of the firm's managerial hierarchy. This change has translated into managers who coach and counsel rather than direct and control. In addition, a renewed emphasis on selecting and training public contact personnel has also occurred. An investment in advanced technology has also helped move Taco Bell and its employees to the forefront. Unlike other companies that utilize technology to monitor, control, and sometimes replace their employees, Taco Bell provides technology to employees as a resource to assist them in their duties.

Taco Bell has also recognized the importance of employee morale and loyalty to customer perceptions of service quality. To enhance employee morale, Taco Bell offers front-line employees higher-than-average wages compared with those throughout the rest of the industry. Moreover, because of a generous bonus system, managers are able to make 225 percent more than their competitive counterparts. Such actions have not only improved employee morale but have also resulted in lower employee turnover rates and an improved caliber of recruits.

Taco Bell's training efforts are also unique. Managers are encouraged to spend half their time on developing employees in areas such as communication, empowerment, and performance management. As a result, the majority of Taco Bell employees now feel they have more freedom, more authority to make decisions, and more responsibility for their own actions.

Overall, the consequences of Taco Bell's restructuring efforts to improve its service delivery systems have been overwhelmingly positive. In times of stagnant market growth for the rest of the industry, sales growth at company-owned Taco Bells has exceeded 60 percent, and profits have increased by more than 25 percent per year. In comparison, McDonald's U.S. franchises have increased their profitability during this same period at a rate of 6 percent. What makes the 25 percent increase in profits even more amazing is that Taco Bell has decreased the price on most menu items by 25 percent! Strategies such as these have led to value-oriented perceptions of Taco Bell that surpass competitive offerings.

Source: Leonard A. Schlesinger and James L. Heskett, "The Service-Driven Service Company," *Harvard Business Review* (September–October 1991), 71–81. Reprinted by permission of Harvard Business Review. Copyright © 1991 by the President and Fellows of Harvard College.

offices. Operationally, this means that staff members can leave their paperwork to serve customers only when needed. Unfortunately, customers view this operationally efficient system negatively. A customer waiting to be served can see a closed teller window and observe staff who apparently do not care because they sit at their desks without offering to assist the customer. However, the reality is that these tellers may be very busy, but the nature of the administrative work is such that they may not give this impression to customers.

Even if it is decided that part of the system can be decoupled, marketing has a major role in evaluating and implementing alternative approaches. Any change in the way in which the servuction system works implies a change in the behavior of the customer. A switch from a personal service to a combined mail and telephone system clearly requires a massive change in the way the customer behaves in the system.

Sometimes decoupling the system to become more efficient does not go over well with customers. For example, in its effort to make its tellers use their time more efficiently, First National Bank of Chicago made national news when it started charging customers with certain types of accounts a $3 fee for speaking with a bank teller. The bank's Chicago competition quickly developed promotions, featuring "live tellers" and giving away "free" money at their teller windows. Even Jay Leno from NBC's *The Tonight Show* got in on the act: "Nice day isn't it? . . . That'll be $3.00 please. Huh? What? Who?. . .That'll be another $9.00 please."[13]

**production line approach**
The application of hard and soft technologies to a service operation in order to produce a standardized service product.

## Production-Lining the Whole System

The **production line approach** involves the application of hard and soft technologies to both the "front" and "back" of the service operation.[14] **Hard technologies** involve hardware to facilitate the production of a standardized product. Similarly, **soft technologies** refer to rules, regulations, and procedures that should be followed to produce the same result. This kind of approach to increasing operational efficiency is relatively rare, and, indeed, fast-food firms provide a classic example in which customization is minimal, volume is large, and customer participation in the process is high.

**hard technologies**
Hardware that facilitates the production of a standardized product.

**soft technologies**
Rules, regulations, and procedures that facilitate the production of a standardized product.

Generating any kind of operational efficiency in such a high contact system implies a limited product line. In the case of fast food, the product line is the menu.

Moreover, customization must be kept to a minimum, since the whole operating system is linked straight through to the consumer. The primary problem is how to provide efficient, standardized service at some acceptable level of quality while simultaneously treating each customer as unique.[15] Past attempts to solve this problem illustrate its complexity. Attempts at forms of routine personalization such as the "have-a-nice-day" syndrome have had positive effects on the perceived friendliness of the service provider but have had adverse effects on perceived competence. Consequently, an apparently simple operations decision can have complex effects on customer perceptions.

The servuction system applied to fast food also depends for its success on a large volume of customers being available to take the standardized food that is produced. Because the invisible component is not decoupled and food cannot be prepared to order, the operating system has to run independently of individual demand and assume that, in the end, aggregate demand will absorb the food produced. This is why pre-made sandwiches are stacked in bins as they wait to be absorbed by future demand in the marketplace.

Such an operating system is extremely demanding of its customers. They must preselect what they want to eat. They are expected to have their order ready when they reach the order point. They must leave the order point quickly and carry their food to the table. Finally, in many cases, these same customers are expected to bus their own tables.

## Creating Flexible Capacity

As pointed out in Chapter 2, the few times that supply matches demand during service encounters occur primarily by accident. One method used to minimize the effects of variable demand is to create flexible capacity (supply).[16] However, even in this area, strategies that start as common-sense operational solutions have far-reaching marketing implications as these new initiatives come face-to-face with the service firm's customer base. For example, a few of the strategies to create flexible capacity mentioned in Chapter 2 included (1) using part-time employees; (2) cross-training employees so that the majority of employee efforts focus on customer contact jobs during peak hours; and (3) sharing capacity with other firms.

Although these strategies are fairly straightforward from an operational point of view, consider their marketing implications. Part-time employees appear to be a useful strategy because they can be used to provide extra capacity in peak times without increasing the costs in off-peak times. There are, however, a number of marketing implications. For example, part-time employees may deliver a lower-quality service than full-time workers; their dedication to quality may be less, as will their training probably be. They are used at times when the operation is at its busiest, such as Christmas or during tourist seasons, when demand is fast and furious, and this may be reflected in their attitudes of frustration, which can be highly visible to customers and negatively influence customer perceptions of the quality of service delivered.[17]

In a similar way, the other two possible solutions for creating flexible capacity also have major marketing implications. First, focusing on customer contact jobs during peak demand presupposes that it is possible to identify the key part of the service from the customer's point of view. Secondly, the dangers of sharing capacity are numerous. The television show *Cheers* provided ample examples of the problems associated with the upscale and upstairs customers of Melville's Restaurant as they mixed with Cheers' everyday clientele such as Norm and Cliff. Confusion may be produced in the customer's mind over exactly what the service facility is doing, and this could be particularly critical during changeover times when customers from two different firms are in the same facility, each group with different priorities and different scripts.

## Increasing Customer Participation

The essence of increasing customer participation is to replace the work done by the employees of the firm with work done by the customer.[18] Unlike the other strategies discussed, which focus on improving the efficiency of the operation, this approach primarily focuses on reducing the costs associated with providing the service to the customer. This strategy, too, has its trade-offs.

Consider for a moment our earlier discussions about consumer scripts. Increasing consumer participation in the service encounter requires a substantial modification of the consumer's script. Moreover, the customers are called on to take greater responsibility for the service they receive. For example, the automatic teller machine (ATM) is seen by many operations personnel as a way of saving labor. In fact, the substitution of human labor with machines is a classic operations approach, and the ATM can definitely be viewed in that light. From a customer's point of view, such ATMs provide added convenience in terms of the hours during which the bank is accessible. However, it has been shown that for some customers, an ATM represents increased risk, less control of the situation, and a loss of human contact.[19]

Such a switching of activities to the customer clearly has major market implications, since the whole nature of the product received is changing. Such changes in the customer's script, therefore, require much customer research and detailed planning.

## Moving the Time of Demand to Fit Capacity

Finally, yet another strategy used to optimize the efficiency of service operations is the attempt to shift the time of demand to smooth the peaks and valleys associated with many services. Perhaps the classic example of this problem is the mass transit system that needs to create capacity to deal with the rush hour and, as a consequence, has much of its fleet and labor idle during non–rush hours. Many mass transit authorities have attempted to reduce the severity of the problem by inducing customers through discounts and giveaways to travel during off-peak periods. Once again, operations and marketing become intertwined. Smoothing demand is a useful strategy from an operations point of view; however, this strategy fails to recognize the change in consumer behavior needed to make the strategy effective. Unfortunately, because much of the travel on the mass transit system is derived from demand based on consumer work schedules, little success in the effort to reallocate demand can be expected.[20]

# THE ART OF BLUEPRINTING

One of the most common techniques used to analyze and manage complex production processes in pursuit of operational efficiency is flowcharting. Flowcharts identify:

*   the time it takes to move from one process to the next
*   the costs involved with each process step
*   the amount of inventory build-up at each step
*   the bottlenecks in the system

The flowcharting of a service operation, commonly referred to as **blueprinting,** is a useful tool not only for the operations manager but for the marketing manager as well.[21]

**blueprinting**
The flowcharting of a service operation.

Because services are delivered by an interactive process involving the consumer, the marketing manager in a service firm needs to have a detailed knowledge of the operation. Blueprinting provides a useful systematic method for acquiring that knowledge. Blueprints enable the marketing manager to understand which parts in the operating system are visible to the consumer and hence part of the servuction system—the fundamental building blocks of consumer perceptions.

Identifying the components of an individual firm's servuction system turns out to be more difficult than it first appears. Many firms, for example, underestimate the number of points of contact between them and their customers (see Services in Action 6.3). Many forget or underestimate the importance of telephone operators, secretarial and janitorial staff, and accounting personnel. The material that follows describes the simple process of flowcharting these numerous points of contact. Service flowcharts, in addition to being useful to the operations managers, allow marketing managers to better understand the servuction process.

The heart of the service product is the experience of the consumer, which takes place in real time. This interaction can occur in a building or in an environment created by the service firm, such as the complex environments that are created at Disney World, Epcot Center, and Universal Studios. In some instances, such as lawn care, the service interaction takes place in a natural setting. It is the interactive process itself that creates the benefits desired by the consumer. Designing that process, therefore, becomes key to the product design for a service firm.

The interactive process that is visible to consumers develops consumers' perceptions of reality and defines the final service product. However, as the servuction model discussed in Chapter 1 demonstrated, the visible part of the operations process, with which the consumer interacts, must be supported by an invisible process.

The search for operational efficiency is not unique to service firms, but it does pose some interesting problems. A change in the service operation may be more efficient, but it may also change the quality of interaction with the consumer. For example, students at many universities are now able to register for classes through automated telephone services. This type of operation offers increased efficiency but sometimes minimizes the quality of the student/advisor interaction. A detailed blueprint provides a means of communications between operations and marketing and can highlight potential problems on paper before they occur in real time.

SERVICES 6.3

ACTION     **Virtual Processes: The Moment of Truth**

Service blueprints can be constructed for Web sites as well as for brick-and-mortar firms. "In the brick-and-mortar world, [the experience] is everything from the layout of the store, the signposting and lighting, to the smiles on the faces of the shop assistants. Online, the essential ingredients of the shopping experience have to do with Web site navigation, ease of finding what you are looking for, the clarity of reassurance that your personal and credit card details are secure, how well the business handles queries or unusual requests, and other related issues." The bottom line is that many of these essential ingredients are customer service process issues that can make or break the online component of a firm's marketing efforts.

For example, some of the Internet's top Web sites were recently put to the test. In terms of user experience, the following process concerns were noted:

- *eBay*—Huge number of concurrent auctions makes navigation a nightmare. A personalized MY eBay Page is necessary for tracking multiple auctions.
- Priceline—*First-time grocery buyers must compile their list, make their bids, pay up-front via credit card, and then wait for a WebHouse Club card to arrive in the mail before traveling to a participating store.*
- *Buy.com*—Buy.com doesn't offer the depth of product descriptions users of other sites take for granted.
- Egghead.com—*Not easy to get a clear sense of what's available on the site.*
- *Travelocity*—Users wanted to "Find/Reserve a Hotel" in Virginia Beach, Virginia (a popular tourist destination). Travelocity did not recognize Virginia Beach as a destination even after the city's zip code was entered.
- *TOYSRUS.com*—During initial attempts to shop the site, the screen froze several times during the shipping and billing process. The site's technical support personnel blamed the problem on Netscape. Later attempts using Internet Explorer were trouble free.
- *CDNOW*—Product availability is not listed until after the user places an order. In addition, unless the user calls the helpline, the customer has no information concerning when the product will be delivered.

Source: David Ward, "10 Top Stores Put to the Test," *Revolution* 1, no. 5 (July 2000), 66–74.

## An Example of a Simple Blueprint[22]

Figure 6.1 shows a simple process in which, for now, it is assumed that the entire operation is visible to the customer. It represents the blueprint of a cafeteria-style restaurant and specifies the steps involved in getting a meal. In this example, each process activity is represented by a box. In contrast to a goods manufacturer, the "raw materials" flowing through the process are the customers. Because of the intangibility of services, there are no inventories in the process, but clearly inventories of customers form at each step in the process while they wait their turn to proceed to the next counter. A restaurant run in this manner would be a single long chain of counters with customers progressing along the chain and emerging after paying, such as a Western Sizzlin' or Golden Corral. In Figure 6.1, the cost figure by each stage represents the cost of providing personnel to service each counter.

To calculate the **service cost per meal,** or the labor costs associated with providing the meal on a per-meal basis, the following calculations are made. First, the **process time** is calculated by dividing the **activity time** (the time required to perform the activity) by the number of **stations,** or locations performing the activity. In our example, the process and activity times are the same because only one station is available for each activity.

Second, the **maximum output per hour** for each location is calculated based on the process time. Simply stated, the maximum output per hour is the number of people that can be served at each station in an hour's time. For example, the process time at the salad counter is 30 seconds. This means that two people can be processed in a minute, or 120 people (2 people × 60 minutes) in an hour. Another easy way to calculate the maximum output per hour is to use the formula: 60(60/process time). In our example, the salad counter calculation would be 60(60/30) = 120.

Finally, to calculate the service cost per meal, total labor costs per hour of the entire system are divided by the maximum output per hour for the system (total labor costs/maximum output per hour). Total labor costs per hour are calculated by simply adding the hourly wages of personnel stationed at each counter. In our example, total labor cost per hour equals $50 (8 + 8 + 8 + 8 + 8 + 10). Maximum

**service cost per meal**
The labor costs associated with providing a meal on a per-meal basis (total labor costs/maximum output per hour).

**process time**
Calculated by dividing the activity time by the number of locations at which the activity is performed.

**activity time**
The time required to perform one activity at one station.

**stations**
A location at which an activity is performed.

**maximum output per hour**
The number of people that can be processed at each station in one hour.

| | Appetizer counter | Salad counter | Hot-food counter | Dessert counter | Drinks counter | Cashier |
|---|---|---|---|---|---|---|
| | $8/hr | $8/hr | $8/hr | $8/hr | $8/hr | $10/hr |
| Number of stations | 1 | 1 | 1 | 1 | 1 | 1 |
| Activity time | 15 sec | 30 sec | 60 sec | 40 sec | 20 sec | 30 sec |
| Process time | 15 sec | 30 sec | 60 sec | 40 sec | 20 sec | 30 sec |
| Maximum output/hr | 240 | 120 | 60* | 90 | 180 | 120 |

*Bottleneck    Service cost per meal = $\frac{50}{60}$ = $0.83

**Figure 6.1    Blueprint for Cafeteria-Style Restaurant**

output per hour is determined by selecting the lowest maximum output calculated in the second step. Hence, the service cost per meal in our example is $50/60 customers, or $0.83 per meal.

Why would you use the lowest maximum output per hour? This step is particularly confusing for some students. The lowest maximum output in the system is the maximum number of people who can be processed through the entire system in a hour's time. In our example, 240 customers can be processed through the appetizer counter in an hour; however, only 120 customers can be processed through the salad counter in the same amount of time. This means that after the first hour, 120 customers (240 − 120) are still waiting to be processed through the salad counter. Similarly, only 60 customers can be processed through the hot-food counter in an hour's time. Because 60 is the lowest maximum output per hour for any counter in the system, only 60 customers can actually complete the entire system in an hour.

### The Service Operations Manager's Perspective

The first thing the blueprint does is provide a check on the logical flow of the whole process. Clearly, a service blueprint makes it immediately apparent if a task is being performed out of sequence. At this point, we shall place a constraint on our example system that the cashier's station is fixed and cannot be moved to another point in the process. All other stations can be moved and resequenced.

**bottlenecks**
Points in the system at which consumers wait the longest periods of time.

Once the different steps have been identified, it is relatively easy to identify the potential **bottlenecks** in the system. Bottlenecks represent points in the system where consumers wait the longest periods of time. In Figure 6.1 the hot-food

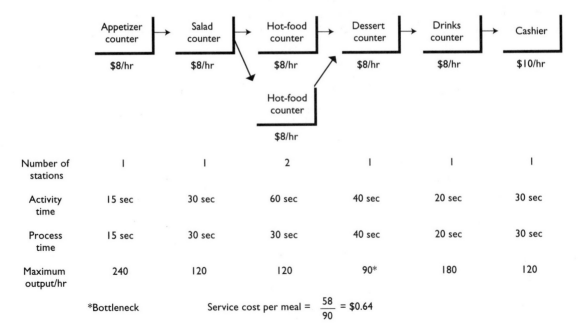

**Figure 6.2**     **Modified Blueprint for Cafeteria-Style Restaurant**

counter is an obvious bottleneck because it represents the longest process time—the time to process one individual through that stage. A balanced production line is one in which the process times of all the steps are the same and inventories or, in our case, consumers flow smoothly through the system without waiting for the next process.

To solve this particular bottleneck problem, we could consider adding one extra station, in this case an extra counter, to the hot-food stage. The process time would drop to 30 seconds (60 seconds divided by 2). The bottleneck would then become the dessert counter, which has a process time of 40 seconds and a maximum turnover rate of 90 persons per hour. Costs would go up by $8 per hour; however, the service cost per meal would go down to $0.64 per meal. These changes are illustrated in Figure 6.2.

The creative use of additional counters and staff may produce a model such as that shown in Figure 6.3, which combines certain activities and uses multiple stations. This particular layout is capable of handling 120 customers per hour, compared with the original layout presented in Figure 6.1. Although labor costs rise,

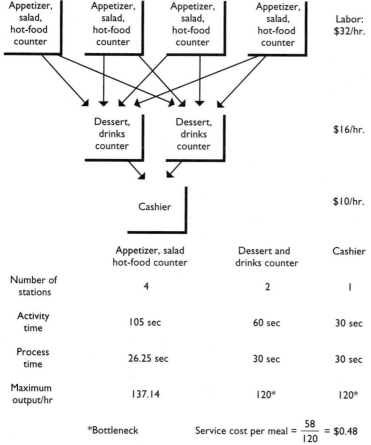

| | Appetizer, salad hot-food counter | Dessert and drinks counter | Cashier |
|---|---|---|---|
| Number of stations | 4 | 2 | 1 |
| Activity time | 105 sec | 60 sec | 30 sec |
| Process time | 26.25 sec | 30 sec | 30 sec |
| Maximum output/hr | 137.14 | 120* | 120* |

*Bottleneck       Service cost per meal $= \dfrac{58}{120} = \$0.48$

**Figure 6.3**    **Alternate Blueprint for Cafeteria-Style Restaurant**

the service cost per meal falls because of the increase in number of consumers that are processed through the system in a shorter time. Further changes to this particular setup would be fruitless. Adding counters at the bottlenecks created by both the dessert/drinks and cashier counters would actually increase the service cost per meal from $0.48 ($58/120 meals) to $0.50 ($68/137.14 meals).

## The Service Marketing Manager's Perspective

A marketing manager dealing with the process illustrated in Figure 6.1 has some of the same problems as the operations manager. The process as defined is designed to operate at certain production levels, and these are the service standards that customers should perceive. But if the process is capable of processing only 60 customer per hour, there may be a problem. For example, lunch customers who need to return to work quickly might purchase their lunches at a competing restaurant that serves its customers more efficiently. Also, it is clear that the bottleneck at the hot-food counter will produce lengthy, possibly frustrating waits within the line.

The marketing manager should immediately recognize the benefits of changing the system to process customers more effectively. However, the blueprint also shows the change in consumer behavior that would be required in order for the new system to operate. In Figure 6.1 the consumer goes from counter to counter, has only one choice at each counter, will probably have to wait in line at each counter, and will definitely have to wait longer at the hot-food counter. Moreover, the wait at each stage will certainly exceed the time spent in each activity. In the process proposed in Figure 6.3 the consumer visits fewer stations but is frequently faced with a choice between different stations. Clearly, depending on the format chosen, the script to be followed by consumers will be different. In addition, the restaurant itself will look completely different.

The use of the blueprinting approach allows the marketing and operations personnel to analyze in detail the process that they are jointly trying to create and manage (see Services in Action 6.4). It can easily highlight the types of conflict between operations and marketing managers and provide a common framework for their discussion and a basis for the resolution of their problems.

## Using Service Blueprints to Identify the Servuction Process

Blueprints may also be used for a different purpose. Consider Figure 6.4, which shows a much more detailed blueprint for the production of a discount brokerage service. This chart is designed to identify the points of contact between the service firm and the customer. The points above the line are visible to the consumer and those below are invisible. In assessing the quality of service received, according to the servuction model, the customer refers to the points of contact when developing perceptions regarding the value of service quality received.

To illustrate, consider the customers to be proactive rather than reactive. Consider them as worried individuals looking for clues that they have made the right decision rather than as inanimate raw materials to which things are done. The points of contact are the clues that develop the servuction process.

SERVICES **6.4**
IN

ACTION     **Electronic Wallets: Reducing Processing Time**

Given the recent number of dot-com companies that are performing at lower-than-expected levels, it has become apparent that the basics of business strategy and technology cannot be viewed as two separate entities. E-services such as those that offer consumers time-saving features may be critical to the ultimate success of e-commerce. Case in point: the virtual checkout counter. Douglas F. Aldrick, author of *Mastering the Digital Marketplace,* reports that "more than two-thirds of Internet shopping carts are left at the virtual checkout counter." The virtual checkout counter is where consumers are required to type in credit card numbers, shipping addresses, and phone numbers. They must also select desired shipping options and answer follow-up questions. This is very time-consuming for something that is suppose to save time.

One possible solution to speed up the ordering process is the development of "electronic wallets," which store the customer's credit card information and desired shipping preferences. This would allow persons who are repeat customers of a site to move through the ordering process much faster. Consequently, the number of abandoned shopping carts should be reduced. The problem with this approach is that the customer's personal information now lives on the company's server. Customers concerned about confidentiality issues may be wary of the electronic wallet concept.

Youpowered.com is currently beta testing software that provides the consumer control over their own personal information. The idea is that the customer would download a universal application from youpowered.com that is accepted at participating Web sites. The customer's personal information is then stored on the customer's desktop and not a variety of company servers. Sixteen high-powered e-commerce sites are currently involved in the beta test.

Sources: C. Brune, "E-business Misses the Mark on Customer Service," *Internal Auditor* 57, no. 3 (June 2000), 13–15; "The Cookies Are Crumbling," *Revolution* 1, no. 5 (July 2000), 14.

Besides illustrating a more complicated process, Figure 6.4 has a number of added features. First, each of the main features is linked to a target time. In the top right corner, for example, the time to mail a statement is targeted as 5 days after the month's end. In designing a service, these target times should initially be set by marketing, and they should be based on the consumers' expected level of service. If the service is to be offered in a competitive marketplace, it may be necessary to set standards higher than those of services currently available. Once the standards have been set, however, the probability of achieving them must be assessed. If the firm is prepared to invest enough, it may be feasible to meet all the standards developed by marketing; doing so, however, affects the costs and therefore the subsequent price of the service. The process should, then, be an interactive one.

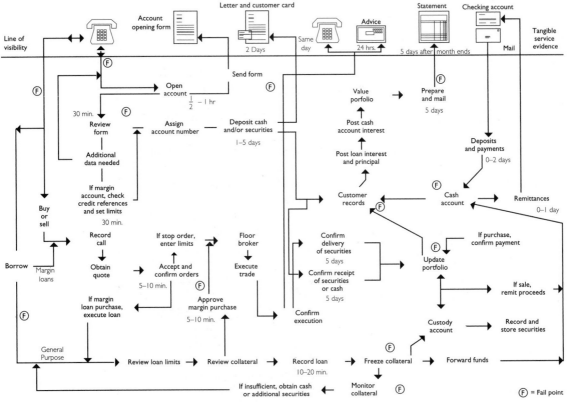

**Figure 6.4**    **Flowchart of a Discount Brokerage Service**

Source: G. Lynn Shostack, "Service Design in the Operating Environment," in *Developing New Services,* William R. George and Claudia Marshall, eds. (Chicago: American Marketing Association, 1984), 27–43. Reprinted with permission.

**fail points**

Points in the system at which the potential for malfunction is high and at which a failure would be visible to the customer and regarded as significant.

Figure 6.4 also highlights the potential **fail points**, "F." Fail points have three characteristics:

- The potential for operations to malfunction is high.
- The result of the malfunction is visible to consumers.
- A system malfunction is regarded by consumers as particularly significant.

## A Marketing or an Operations Blueprint?

Although the idea of a blueprint is attractive to both marketing and operations, it may well be that a marketing blueprint should be prepared in a different way. The blueprints we have discussed so far have an internal focus—although they identify clearly the tangible points of contact with the client, they start from the organization and look outward.

An alternative way to develop a blueprint would be to start from consumer scripts. Consumers, individually or in groups, would be asked to describe the process or steps they follow in using a service. Obviously, such an approach cannot cover the invisible part of the service firm, but it can provide a much better understanding of the points of contact. The process as described by the consumer may differ greatly from that perceived by the firm.

Consumers asked to describe a flight on USAir, for example, might start with their experience with the travel agent. They might then describe the process of getting to the airport, parking, and entering the terminal. If the signs for USAir and the entrance to its specific terminal are confusing, this will be reflected in consumers' perceptions of the airline. A parking lot that is littered, poorly lit, and inhabited by vagrants will also deter customers. Although the airline may not have direct control over these points of contact, it could be a wise investment for the airline to use its own staff to improve the parking lot. McDonald's long ago learned the value of removing the litter not only from its own property but also from the adjoining roadways. McDonald's recognized that their customers' experiences began long before they entered the actual restaurant.

## Constructing the Service Blueprint[23]

The first step in the design of a service blueprint is to elicit scripts from both employees and consumers. The primary objective of this task is to break down the service system into a sequence of events followed by both parties. Too often, management makes the mistake of developing a **one-sided blueprint** based on its own perception of how the sequence of events should occur. This one-sided approach fails to recognize that consumer perceptions, not management's, define the realities of the encounter. Similarly, employee scripts are equally important in identifying those parts of the service system not observable to the consumer. Hence, both scripts are necessary to develop a successful blueprint.

Script theory suggests that consumers possess purchasing scripts that guide their thinking and behavior during service encounters. The scripts contain the sequence of actions that consumers follow when entering a service interaction. Experts believe that "these action sequences, or cognitive scripts, guide the interpretation of information, the development of expectations, and the enactment of appropriate behavior routines."[24]

Similarly, service employees also have scripts that dictate their own behavior during interactions with the customer. **Convergent scripts,** those that are mutually agreeable, enhance the probability of customer satisfaction and the quality of the relationship between the customer and the service operation. **Divergent scripts** point to areas that need to be examined and corrected because consumer expectations are not being met and evaluations of service quality could decline.

Obtaining consumer and employee scripts is a potentially powerful technique for analyzing the service encounter. Scripts provide the dialogue from which consumer and employee perceptions of the encounter can be analyzed and potential or existing problems identified. Overall, scripts provide:

*   the basis for planning service encounters
*   setting of goals and objectives
*   developing of behavioral routines that maximize the opportunities for a successful exchange
*   evaluation of the effectiveness of current service delivery systems

**one-sided blueprint**
An unbalanced blueprint based on management's perception of how the sequence of events *should* occur.

**convergent scripts**
Employee/consumer scripts that are mutually agreeable and enhance the probability of customer satisfaction.

**divergent scripts**
Employee/consumer scripts that "mismatch" and point to areas in which consumer expectations are not being met.

**two-sided blueprint**
A blueprint that takes into account both employee and customer perceptions of how the sequence of events actually occurs.

**script norms**
Proposed scripts developed by grouping together events commonly mentioned by both employees and customers and then ordering those events in their sequence of occurrence.

The procedure used to develop **two-sided blueprints** is to present employees and customers with a script-relevant situation, such as the steps taken to proceed through an airline boarding experience. Respondents are requested to note specific events or activities expected in their involvement in the situation. In particular, employees and consumers are asked to pay special attention to those contact activities that elicit strong positive or negative reactions during the service encounter. **Script norms** are then constructed by grouping together commonly mentioned events and ordering the events in their sequence of occurrence.

To facilitate the process of identifying script norms, the blueprint designer can compare the frequency of specific events mentioned by each of the groups. The value of this process is the potential recognition of gaps or discrepancies existing between employee and consumer perceptions. For example, consumers may mention the difficulties associated with parking, which employees may not mention because many report to work before the operation is open to customers.

The second step of the blueprint development process is to identify steps in the process at which the system can go awry. By asking employees and customers to further focus on events that are important in conveying service dis/satisfaction, fail points can be isolated. The consequences of service failures can be greatly reduced by analyzing fail points and instructing employees on the appropriate response or action when the inevitable failure occurs.

After the sequence of events/activities and potential fail points have been identified, the third step in the process involves specifying the timeframe of service execution. The major cost component of most service systems relates to the time required to complete the service; consequently, standard execution time norms must be established.

Once the standard execution times of the events that make up the service encounter have been specified, the manager can analyze the profitability of the system, given the costs of inputs needed for the system to operate. The resulting blueprint allows the planner to determine the profitability of the existing service delivery system as well as to speculate on the effects on profitability when changing one or more system components. Consequently, the service blueprint allows a company to test its assumptions on paper and to minimize the system's shortcomings before the system is imposed on customers and employees. The service manager can test a prototype of the delivery system with potential customers and use the feedback to modify the blueprint before testing the procedure again.

## Blueprinting and New-Product Development: The Roles of Complexity and Divergence

Blueprints may also be used in new-product development. Once the process has been documented and a blueprint has been drawn, choices can be made that will produce "new" products. Although the processes in Figures 6.1, 6.2, and 6.3 are for the same task, from the consumer's point of view they are very different. The two blueprints define alternatives that are operationally feasible; the choice between which of the two to implement is for marketing.

Strategically, the decision may be to move the line separating visibility and invisibility. Operationally, arguments have been made for minimizing the visible component by isolating the technical core of the process. From a marketing point of view, however, more visibility may create more differentiation in the mind of the consumer. For example, a restaurant can make its kitchen into a distinctive feature by making it visible to restaurant patrons. This poses constraints on the operational personnel, but it may add value in the mind of the consumer.

New-product development within service firms can be implemented through the introduction of complexity and divergence.[25] **Complexity** is a measure of the number and intricacy of the steps and sequences that constitute the process—the more steps, the more complex the process. **Divergence** is defined as the degrees of freedom service personnel are allowed when providing the service. As an example, Figures 6.5 and 6.6 illustrate the blueprints for two florists who differ dramatically in their complexity and divergence. Although they perform equivalent tasks from an operations viewpoint, they can be very different from a marketing viewpoint and therefore constitute new products.

Figure 6.5 presents a traditional florist. The process, as in our restaurant example in Figure 6.1, is linear and involves a limited number of steps and so is low in complexity. However, the generation of flower arrangements under such a system calls for considerable discretion or degrees of freedom to be allowed the florist at each stage—in the choice of vase, flowers, and display—and produces a heterogeneous final product. The system is therefore high in divergence.

Figure 6.6 provides the blueprint for a second florist that has attempted to standardize its final product. Because the objective of this system is to de-skill the job, the system is designed to generate a limited number of standardized arrangements. The divergence of the system is therefore reduced, but to achieve this, the complexity of the process is increased significantly.

In developing products in the service sector, the amount of manipulation of the operation's complexity and divergence are the two key choices. Reducing

**complexity**
A measure of the number and intricacy of the steps and sequences that constitute a process.

**divergence**
A measure of the degrees of freedom service personnel are allowed when providing a service.

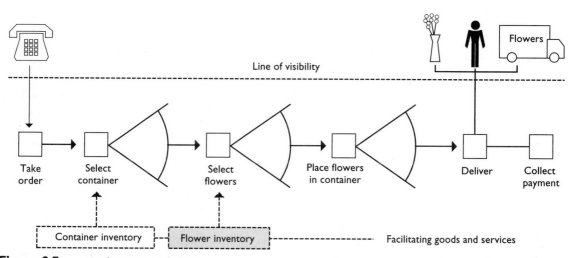

**Figure 6.5**   **Park Avenue Florist**

Source: G. Lynn Shostack, "Service Positioning Through Structural Change," *Journal of Marketing* 51 (January 1987), 34–43. Reprinted by permission of the American Marketing Association.

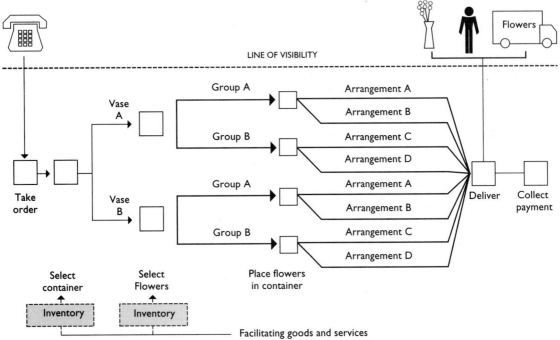

**Figure 6.6     Florist Services: Alternative Design**
Source: G. Lynn Shostack, "Service Positioning Through Structural Change," *Journal of Marketing* 51 (January 1987), 34–43. Reprinted by permission of the American Marketing Association.

**volume-oriented positioning strategy**
A positioning strategy that reduces divergence to create product uniformity and reduce costs.

divergence creates the uniformity that can reduce costs, but it does so at the expense of creativity and flexibility in the system. Companies that wish to pursue a **volume-oriented positioning strategy** often do so by reducing divergence. For example, a builder of swimming pools who focuses on the installation of prefabricated vinyl pools has greatly reduced the divergence of his operations. In addition to lowering production costs, reducing divergence increases productivity and facilitates distribution of the standardized service. From the customer's perspective, reducing divergence is associated with improved reliability, availability, and uniform service quality. However, the downside of reduced divergence is the lack of customization that can be provided individual customers.

On the other hand, increasing divergence creates flexibility in tailoring the experience to each customer, but it does so at increased expense, and consumer prices are subsequently higher. Companies wishing to pursue a **niche positioning strategy** do so through increasing the divergence in their operations. For example, our pool builder may increase the divergence of his operation by specializing in the design and construction of customized pools and spas that can be built to resemble anything from a classical guitar to an exclamation point! Profits, under this scenario, depend less on volume and more on margins on each individual purchase. The downside of increasing divergence is that the service operation becomes more difficult to manage, control, and distribute. Moreover, customers may not be willing to pay the higher prices associated with a customized service.

**niche positioning strategy**
A positioning strategy that increases divergence in an operation to tailor the service experience to each customer.

Reducing complexity is a **specialization positioning strategy** often involving the **unbundling** of the different services offered. Hence, our hypothetical pool builder may restrict himself to the installation of a single type of prefabricated pool and divest operations that were focused on supplemental services such as maintenance and repair as well as the design of pools and spas. The advantages associated with reduced complexity include improved control over the final product and improved distribution. However, risks are involved if full-service competitors, offering one-stop convenience, continue to operate. The full-service competitor appeals to consumers wishing to work with a provider that offers a number of choices.

Increasing complexity is utilized by companies that pursue a mass market or **penetration strategy.** Increasing complexity translates into the addition of more services to the firm's offering as well as the enhancement of current ones. Within this scenario, our pool builder would offer customized pools and spas and a wide variety of prefabricated vinyl pools. In addition to installation, other services such as general pool maintenance and repair would be offered. Firms pursuing a penetration strategy often try to be everything to everybody and often gloss over individual consumer needs. Moreover, when providing such a broad range of services, the quality of the provider's skills are bound to vary depending on the task being performed, leaving some customers less than satisfied. Hence, firms that increase complexity of their operations by offering enhanced and/or additional services run the risk of becoming vulnerable to companies that pursue more specialized types of operations.

**specialization positioning strategy**
A positioning strategy that reduces complexity by unbundling the different services offered.

**unbundling**
Divesting an operation of different services and concentrating on providing only one or a few services in order to pursue a specialization positioning strategy.

**penetration strategy**
A positioning strategy that increases complexity by adding more services and/or enhancing current services to capture more of a market.

## SUMMARY

The primary objective of this chapter was to highlight the idea that for a service firm to be successful, its marketing and operations departments must work together. In a broad sense, one could view the functions of marketing and operations as the marriage of consumers' needs with the technology and manufacturing capabilities of the firm. This marriage entails many compromises that attempt to balance operational efficiency with the effectiveness of the system from the consumer's point of view. To be effective, operations personnel must recognize the importance of their marketing counterparts, and vice-versa.

Firms operating at peak efficiency are free from outside influences and operate as if the market will consume the firm's production at a continuous rate. Uncertainty creates inefficiency. Hence, in an ideal situation, the technical core of the firm is able to operate without uncertainty on either the input or output side.

Although the attempt to operate at peak efficiency is a worthy goal, it likely represents an unrealistic objective for most service firms. The production of most services is an operations nightmare. Instead of receiving demand at a constant rate, service firms are often linked directly to a market that frequently varies from day to day, hour to hour, and even minute to minute. Service customers frequently affect the time of demand, the cycle of demand, the type of demand, and the duration of many service transactions.

Plans to operate at peak efficiency must be altered to cope with the uncertainties inherent in service operations. Strategies that attempt to increase the efficiency of the service operation by facilitating the balance of supply and demand include minimizing the servuction system by isolating the technical core; production-lining the whole system using hard and soft technologies; creating flexible capacity; increasing customer participation; and moving the time of demand to fit capacity. In addition, service blueprints can be developed that identify the directions in which processes flow and parts of a process that may both increase operational efficiency and enhance the customer's service experience.

Operational changes made to the service blueprint often require changes in consumer behavior and in some instances lead to new service products. New service development is achieved through the introduction of complexity and divergence. Reducing divergence standardizes the service product and reduces production costs, whereas increasing divergence enables service providers to tailor their products to individual customers. Similarly, reducing complexity is consistent with a specialization positioning strategy, whereas increasing complexity is appropriate for firms pursuing a penetration strategy.

# Key Terms

| | |
|---|---|
| Activity time | Penetration strategy |
| Anticipating | Perfect-world model |
| Blueprinting | Plant within a plant (PWP) |
| Bottlenecks | Process time |
| Buffering | Production line approach |
| Complexity | Rationing |
| Convergent scripts | Script norms |
| Decoupling | Service cost per meal |
| Divergence | Smoothing |
| Divergent scripts | Soft technologies |
| Fail points | Specialization positioning strategy |
| Focused factory | Stations |
| Hard technologies | Technical core |
| Maximum output per hour | Two-sided blueprint |
| Niche positioning strategy | Unbundling |
| One-sided blueprint | Volume-oriented positioning |

# Discussion Questions

1. Explain how the inability to inventory services affects the operational efficiency of most service firms.
2. Compare Thompson's perfect-world model with the focused factory and plant within a plant concepts.
3. What is buffering? How do the strategies of anticipating, smoothing, and rationing relate to buffering?

4. Discuss some specific examples of how the customer's involvement in the service encounter influences the operational efficiency of the average service firm.
5. What does it mean to isolate the technical core of a business?
6. Provide examples of hard and soft technologies and explain their relevance to this chapter.
7. Discuss the steps for developing a meaningful blueprint.
8. What are the trade-offs associated with increasing/decreasing divergence and increasing/decreasing complexity?

# Notes

1. Richard B. Chase and Robert H. Hayes, "Beefing Up Operations in Service Firms," *Sloan Management Review* (Fall 1991), 15–26.
2. Much of this chapter is adapted from Chapters 3 and 4 of John E. G. Bateson, *Managing Services Marketing*, 2nd ed. (Fort Worth, Tex.: The Dryden Press, 1992), 156–169, 200–207.
3. J. D. Thompson, *Organizations in Action* (New York: McGraw-Hill, 1967).
4. W. Skinner, "The Focused Factory," *Harvard Business Review* 52, no. 3 (May–June 1974), 113–121.
5. Thompson, *Organizations in Action*, 69.
6. R. J. Matteis, "The New Back Office Focuses on Customer Service," *Harvard Business Review* 57, no. 2 (1979), 146–159.
7. Matteis, "The New Back Office."
8. These extensions of the customer contact model are developed in Richard B. Chase, "The Customer Contact Approach to Services: Theoretical Base and Practical Extensions," Operations Research 29, no. 4 (July–August 1981), 698–706; and Richard B. Chase and David A. Tansik, "The Customer Contact Model for Organization Design," *Management Service* 29, no. 9 (1983), 1037–1050.
9. B. Danet, "Client-Organization Interfaces," in *Handbook of Organization Design*, 2nd ed., P. C. Nystrom and W. N. Starbuck, eds. (New York: Oxford University Press, 1984), 384.
10. These studies employed the critical incident technique to look at service encounters that fail. See Mary J. Bitner, Jody D. Nyquist, and Bernard H. Booms, "The Critical Incident Technique for Analyzing the Service Encounter," in *Service Marketing in a Changing Environment*, Thomas M. Block, Gregory D. Upah, and Valerie A. Zeithaml, eds. (Chicago: American Marketing Association, 1985), 48–51.
11. Chase, "The Customer Contact Approach."
12. For a detailed description, see Richard B. Chase and Gerrit Wolf, "Designing High Contact Systems: Applications to Branches of Savings and Loans," working paper, Department of Management, College of Business and Public Administration, University of Arizona.
13. Chad Rubel, "Banks Should Show that They Care for Customers," *Marketing News,* July 3, 1995, p. 4.

14. T. Levitt, "Production-line Approach to Services," Harvard Business Review 50, no. 5 (September–October 1972), 41–52.

15. Carol F. Suprenant and Michael Solomon, "Predictability and Personalization in the Service Encounter," *Journal of Marketing* 51 (April 1987), 86–96.

16. W. Earl Sasser, "Match Supply and Demand in Service Industries," *Harvard Business Review* 54, no. 5 (November–December 1976), 61–65.

17. Benjamin Schneider, "The Service Organization: Climate Is Crucial," *Organizational Dynamics* (Autumn 1980), 52–65.

18. See also J. E. G. Bateson, "Self-Service Consumer: An Exploratory Study," *Journal of Retailing* 61, no. 3 (Fall 1986), 49–79.

19. Ibid.

20. Christopher H. Lovelock and Robert F. Young, "Look to Consumers to Increase Productivity," *Harvard Business Review* (May–June 1979), 168–178.

21. G. Lynn Shostack, "Service Positioning Through Structural Change," *Journal of Marketing* 51 (January 1987), 34–43.

22. Bateson, *Managing Services,* 200–207.

23. K. Douglas Hoffman and Vince Howe, "Developing the Micro Service Audit via Script Theoretic and Blueprinting Procedures," in *Marketing Toward the Twenty-First Century*, Robert L. King, ed. (Richmond, Va.: Southern Marketing Association, 1991), 379–383.

24. Thomas W. Leigh and Arno J. Rethans, "Experience with Script Elicitation Within Consumer Making Contexts," in *Advances in Consumer Research,* vol. 10, Alice Tybout and Richard Bagozzi, eds. (Ann Arbor, Mich.: Association for Consumer Research, 1983), 667–672.

25. Shostack, "Service Positioning," 34–43.

# chapter 7

# The Pricing of Services

## CHAPTER OBJECTIVES

The purpose of this chapter is to familiarize you with the special considerations needed when pricing services.

After reading this chapter, you should be able to:

- Discuss how consumers relate value and price.
- Discuss the special considerations of service pricing as they relate to demand, cost, customer, competitor, profit, product, and legal considerations.
- Discuss the circumstances under which price segmentation is most effective.
- Discuss typical price segmentation approaches.
- Discuss satisfaction-based, relationship, and efficiency approaches to pricing.

"The real price of anything is the toil and the trouble of acquiring it."

Adam Smith

# Introduction

Of the traditional marketing mix variables that are used to influence customer purchase decisions, the development of effective pricing strategies perhaps remains the most elusive. Pricing is often a perplexing issue for practitioners and researchers alike. Consider the following sample of opinions regarding pricing practices over the last 50 years, which reflect both the confusion and frustration associated with pricing decisions:

> . . . Pricing policy is the last stronghold of medievalism in modern management. [Pricing] is still largely intuitive and even mystical in the sense that the intuition is often the province of the big boss.[1]

> [P]erhaps few ideas have wider currency than the mistaken impression that prices are or should be determined by costs of production.[2]

> For marketers of industrial goods and construction companies, pricing is the single judgment that translates potential business into reality. Yet pricing is the least rational of all decisions made in this specialised field.[3]

> Many managing directors do not concern themselves with pricing details; some are not even aware of how their products are priced.[4]

> Pricing is approached in Britain like Russian roulette—to be indulged in mainly by those contemplating suicide.[5]

> Perhaps it is reasonable that marketers have only recently begun to focus seriously on effective pricing. Only after managers have mastered the techniques of creating value do the techniques of capturing value become important.[6]

Today, price remains one of the least researched and mastered areas of marketing. Research and expertise pertaining to the pricing of services is particularly lacking. Many of the concepts developed for goods apply equally to services. This chapter focuses on how the pricing approaches apply and how, to a greater or lesser extent, service pricing policies differ from those of goods.

## PERCEPTIONS OF VALUE

Buyers' perceptions of value represent a trade-off between the perceived benefits of the service to be purchased and the perceived sacrifice in terms of the costs to be paid (Figure 7.1). Total customer costs include more than simply the **monetary price** paid for the service. Other costs include **time costs, energy costs,** and **psychic costs,** which reflect the time and trouble the customer has to endure to acquire the service. Similarly, total customer value extends beyond **product value** and includes **service value, personnel value,** and **image value.**[7]

For example, a customer who wishes to purchase an 18-inch satellite dish system must pay the monetary price for the dish and receiver plus the monthly charges for the video services received. In this example, the customer chose a Sony system because of its hardware and software advantages (product value) and the

**monetary price**
The actual dollar price paid by the consumer for a product.

**time costs**
The time the customer has to spend to acquire the service.

**energy costs**
The physical energy spent by the customer to acquire the service.

**psychic costs**
The mental energy spent by the customer to acquire the service.

**product value**
The worth assigned to the product by the customer.

**service value**
The worth assigned to the service by the customer.

**personnel value**
The worth assigned to the service-providing personnel by the customer.

**image value**
The worth assigned to the image of the service or service provider by the customer.

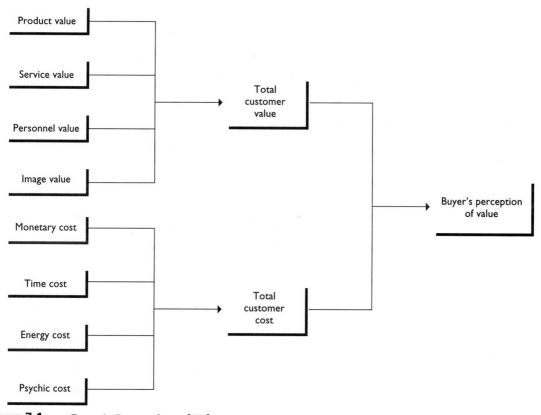

**Figure 7.1**    **Buyer's Perception of Value**
Source: Philip Kotler, *Marketing Management,* 9th ed. (Englewood Cliffs, N.J.: Prentice-Hall, 1997), 37.

quality associated with the Sony name (image value) over those of competitors. In addition, Sony's warranty (service value) was competitive with leading alternatives. The customer bought the system at Sears Department Store because of the sales representative's superior product knowledge (personnel value) compared with the dismal quality of information received at alternative purchase locations.

In addition to the monetary cost, the customer incurred time and energy costs while shopping at various locations and questioning sales representatives about the various brands of satellite systems. Additional time costs were incurred waiting for the installer to actually install the system. The installation, which should have taken 2 hours, took 6 hours. In addition, the installer's truck leaked vast amounts of oil onto the customer's driveway, the installer's ladder scraped paint off the outside of the house, and the installer accidentally dropped the satellite receiver from the large screen TV onto the floor. Each of these events added to the psychic cost (e.g., worrying, aggravation, etc.) of the whole experience.

Overall, if the signal sent by total customer cost is an indicator of sacrifice relative to value, then price will have a negative or repelling effect and may reduce demand. If the signal sent by the price is an indicator of benefit or value, then price will be an attractor and may increase demand. Because of the perceived connection between cost and benefit, buyers have both lower and upper price thresholds. For example, buyers might be discouraged from buying when the price is perceived to be too low simply because they see a low price as an indicator of inferior quality.

Consumers exchange their money, time, and effort for the bundle of benefits the service provider offers. Economic theory suggests that consumers will have a reservation price that captures the value they place on these benefits. As long as the total cost to the consumer is less than the reservation price, he or she will be prepared to buy. If the consumer can purchase the service for less than the reservation price, a consumer's surplus will exist. The eight dimensions of value described above provide direction for how service firms can differentiate themselves from competitors.

# SPECIAL CONSIDERATIONS OF SERVICE PRICING

The ultimate pricing challenge faced by most firms is determining a price that sells the services while at the same time offering a profitable return. When pricing retail services, many of the same factors that are considered for pricing goods should be examined. The literature suggests that retail price determination should be based on demand, cost, customer, competitive, profit, product, and legal considerations.[8] Although the considerations are the same for goods and services, the content of the considerations differ. The discussion that follows highlights these key differences (Table 7.1).

## Demand Considerations

### DEMAND FOR SERVICES TENDS TO BE MORE INELASTIC

In general, consumers of services are more willing to pay higher prices if doing so reduces their level of perceived risk. Perceived risk is a function of consequence (the degree of importance and/or danger associated with the purchase) and uncertainty (the variability in service performance from customer to customer or from day to day). The service characteristics of intangibility, inseparability, heterogeneity, and perishability contribute greatly to heightened levels of perceived risk.

Experts in the field suggest 10 factors that influence customer price sensitivity (Table 7.2). In short, price sensitivity decreases as[9]:

- the perceived number of substitutes decrease
- the perceived unique value of the service increases
- switching costs increase
- the difficulty in comparing substitutes increases
- the extent to which price is used as a quality cue increases
- the expenditure is relatively small in terms of dollars or as a percentage of household income
- the less price sensitive consumers are to the end-benefit
- the shared costs for the expenditure increase
- the price is perceived as fair compared with similar services purchased under similar circumstances
- the customer's ability to build an inventory decreases

# TABLE 7.1

## Unique Differences Associated With Service Prices

**Demand Considerations**

D1:     The demand for services tends to be more inelastic than the demand for goods.

D2:     Because of the implicit bundling of services by consumers, cross-price elasticity considerations need to be examined.

D3:     Price discrimination is a viable practice to manage demand and supply challenges.

**Cost Considerations**

D4:     With many professional services (and some others), the consumer may not know the actual price they will pay for the service until the service is completed.

D5:     Cost-oriented pricing is more difficult for services.

D6:     Services tend to be characterized by a high fixed cost to variable cost ratio.

D7:     Economies of scale tend to be limited.

**Customer Considerations**

D8:     Price tends to be one of the few cues available to consumers during prepurchase.

D9:     Service consumers are more likely to use price as a cue to quality.

D10:    Service consumers tend to be less certain about reservation prices.

**Competitive Considerations**

D11:    Comparing prices of competitors is more difficult for service consumers.

D12:    Self-service is a viable competitive alternative.

**Profit Considerations**

D13:    Price bundling makes the determination of individual prices in the bundle of services more complicated.

D14:    Price bundling is more effective in a services context

**Product Considerations**

D15:    Compared with the goods sector, there tend to be many different names for price in the service sector.

D16:    Consumers are less able to stockpile services by taking advantage of discount prices.

D17:    Product-line pricing tends to be more complicated.

**Legal Considerations**

D18:    The opportunity for illegal pricing practices to go undetected is greater for services than goods.

---

Clearly, price sensitivities will vary across different types of services, but in general the demand for services tends to be **inelastic.** Different groups of consumers will likely weigh the importance of each price sensitivity factor differently. Service firms must assess which of the factors are more salient to their target market's purchasing decisions.

**inelastic**
The type of market demand when a change in price of service is greater than a change in quantity demanded.

TABLE 7.2

## Factors Influencing Customers' Price Sensitivity

| Price Sensitivity Factors | Proposed Relationship |
| --- | --- |
| Perceived substitute effect | Price sensitivity increases when the price for service A is higher than the price of perceived substitutes. |
| Unique value effect | Price sensitivity increases as the unique value of service A is perceived to be equal or less than the unique value of perceived substitutes. |
| Switching costs effect | Price sensitivity increases as switching costs decrease. |
| Difficult comparison effect | Price sensitivity increases as the difficulty in comparing substitutes decreases. |
| Price-quality effect | Price sensitivity increases to the extent that price is not used as a quality cue. |
| Expenditure effect | Price sensitivity increases when the expenditure is large in terms of dollars or as a percentage of household income. |
| End-benefit effect | The more price sensitive consumers are to the end-benefit, the more price sensitive they will be to services that contribute to the end-benefit. |
| Shared-cost effect | Price sensitivity increases as the shared costs with third parties decrease. |
| Fairness effect | Price sensitivity increases when the price paid for similar services under similar circumstances is lower. |
| Inventory effect | Price sensitivity increases as the customer's ability to hold an inventory increases. |

**cross-price elasticity**
A measure of the responsiveness of demand for a service relative to a change in price for another service.

**complementary**
The effect of cross-price elasticity in which the consumption of one service is unlikely to affect the consumption of the other.

**substitutes**
The effect of cross-price elasticity in which the consumption of one service is likely to be at the expense of consumption of another service.

## CROSS-PRICE ELASTICITY CONSIDERATIONS NEED TO BE EXAMINED

Consumers of services often implicitly bundle prices. In other words, consumers may figure that the total cost of going to the movies includes the tickets and refreshments. Therefore, total revenues may be maximized by carefully considering the cross-price elasticities of the total product offering. This is particularly true in cases where the price of the core service offering influences the demand of supplemental services. **Cross-price elasticity** of demand measures the responsiveness of demand for a service relative to a change in price for another service. If this relationship is negative, the two services are said to be **complementary,** and the consumption of one is unlikely to affect the consumption of the other, such as lawn care and housekeeping. If the relationship is positive, however, then the two services may be **substitutes,** and consumption of one is at the expense of the consumption of the other. For example, new parents may give up their housekeeping and lawn services to help pay for child-care services.

Multiproduct considerations dominate many service industries such as business services, personal services, professional services, and the hospitality industry. The golf industry provides a prime example of the effects of cross-price elasticities. Consumers have different price sensitivities for greens fees, cart fees, range fees, and food and beverage expenses. If consumers perceive the price of admission (greens fees) as a good value, they are likely to purchase additional revenue-generating products in the form of riding carts, practice range balls, and food and beverages. In contrast, if the price of admission is perceived as low in value, consumer price sensitivities for supplemental services are likely to increase. In other words, consumers may forgo some or all of these additional services in order to keep their total expenses in line. In effect, the higher price of admission often leads to overall lower consumer expenditures and reduces the revenue stream for the firm.

## PRICE DISCRIMINATION IS A VIABLE PRACTICE TO MANAGE DEMAND AND SUPPLY CHALLENGES

**Price discrimination** involves charging customers different prices for essentially the same service. This unique aspect of service pricing relates to both the perishability and simultaneous production and consumption of services. Price discrimination is a viable practice in service industries due in part to differences in the demand elasticities held by customers and the need of the organization to balance demand and supply for its service products.

**price discrimination**
The practice of charging different customers different prices for similar services.

The viability of price discrimination is enhanced by the fact that in some services customers readily accept that prices often drop significantly before the opportunity to sell the service passes completely (e.g., Y2K New Year's Eve concert tickets). In other service settings, consumers have become quite accustomed to different customers paying different amounts for the same service (e.g., airfares). In addition, online services such as Priceline.com have now emerged that allow consumers to name their own price for airline tickets and car rentals (see Services in Action 7.1). Service providers accept these proposals in order to cover at least some portion of their fixed costs. Some revenue is deemed better than no revenue in these situations.

Effective price segmentation benefits consumers and providers alike. Consumers often benefit from options that offer lower prices, and providers are often able to manage demand and increase capacity utilization. The interaction that creates the service experience, which is what the consumer buys, takes place in real time. Because consumers must, in most cases, come to the service setting to be part of the experience, capacity utilization depends on when they arrive. For most services, consumers tend to arrive unevenly and unpredictably, such as at a grocery store or restaurant. The result is often periods of low utilization of capacity because of the impossibility of matching capacity to demand.

Capacity, in turn, represents the bulk of the costs for a service. The restaurant has to be open, staffed, and resourced even at times when it has no customers. The result is a very low level of variable costs for services and a high value attributable to incremental customers, even at discount prices. As a result, pricing is called on to try to smooth demand in two ways:

1.  Creating new demand in off-peak, low-capacity utilization periods
2.  Flattening peaks by moving existing customers from peaks to less busy times

## SERVICES 7.1

### ACTION    Reverse Auctions: Empowering Consumers to Name Their Own Prices

A number of new e-services are emerging whose value proposition is to save consumers money. Priceline.com is a reverse auction where consumers name their own price for various goods and services, and suppliers select whether or not they want to sell. According to Priceline.com's founder, Jay Walker, "Buyers would like lower prices, and are willing to trade some flexibility to get them. Sellers would like incremental sales and want to do so without disrupting their retail prices." In essence, services such as Pricline.com facilitate the selling of excess supply without alienating the company's traditional customer base.

Priceline.com is termed a reverse auction because of the way bidding is conducted. During a traditional auction, items are first presented and consumers then bid on those items. In a reverse auction the customers name what price they are willing to pay first, then suppliers of desired goods or services decide whether or not they would like to accept the bidder's price.

Since its introduction the company has experienced phenomenal growth. Customers are able to name their own prices on airline tickets, hotel rooms, rental cars, mortgages, new cars, long distance phone service, groceries, and gasoline. During the first quarter of 2000 the company added 1.5 million new customers, bringing its total customer base to 5.3 million. The company now claims to be the largest seller of leisure air tickets in America. Users appear to be happy with the service, since 830,000 of customers during the first quarter of 2000 were repeat customers.

Financial analysts are enthusiastic about Priceline.com's potential. According to a PaineWebber analyst, "We believe Priceline is truly revolutionizing commerce as we know it, providing a way for sellers to dispose of unwanted product while maintaining the integrity of their existing price structures." Analysts from Prudential agree but note, "We also believe that the 'name-your-price' concept is such a radical shift from consumer buying patterns that the ultimate success or failure of the business resides with market forces outside of the management's ability to control them."

Source: Adapted from Mike Troy, "Priceline.com: An On-line Auction Where the Price is Always Right," *Retailing Today* 39, no. 9 (May 8, 2000), 93–94.

## Criteria for Effective Price Segmentation[10]

### DIFFERENT GROUPS OF CONSUMERS MUST HAVE DIFFERENT RESPONSES TO PRICE

If different groups of consumers have the same response to price changes, price segmentation becomes counterproductive. For example, for years movie theaters have offered afternoon matinees at a reduced fee. This strategy helped the theater

Due to the flexibility of their lifestyles, senior citizens are often the beneficiaries of price segmentation schemes.

create demand for unused capacity during the day and also helped to smooth demand during the evening shows. Moreover, this approach has attracted market segments such as families with children and individuals on fixed incomes, who may not otherwise attend the higher-priced evening shows. This strategy has been effective because the price change did not create the same response for everyone. If most consumers had shifted their demand to the afternoon shows at lower rates, the movie theater would have overutilized capacity in the afternoons and would be generating lower total revenues for the firm.

## THE DIFFERENT SEGMENTS MUST BE IDENTIFIABLE, AND A MECHANISM MUST EXIST TO PRICE THEM DIFFERENTLY

Effective price segmentation requires that consumer segments with different demand patterns be identifiable based on some readily apparent common characteristic such as age, family life cycle stage, gender, and/or educational status. Discriminating based on a convoluted segmentation scheme confuses customers and service providers, who must implement the strategy. Common forms of segmentation identification include college ID card holders, AARP card holders, and drivers' licensees.

SERVICES 7.2

IN ACTION     **The Next New Big Thing: Aggregated Demand Buying Services**

Online auctions are already facing a new competitive threat in the form of online group buying services. The basic premise for this type of service is that as the number of buyers increases, the price of the item goes down. "If 20 people buy something you might save 5 percent. But if 2000 people buy, the savings becomes significant," according to Carrie Johnson, an analyst for Forrester Research in Cambridge, Massachusetts.

Currently, the two most established group buying sites are Accompany and Mercata, which have both been around since late 1998. AOL and Yahoo! are expected to launch their own group buying services the second half of 2000. The growth of Accompany and Mercata has been brisk. Mercata's largest buying group to date for a single item exceeded 10,000 participants. Accompany has experienced similar growth. Accompany's vice president of corporate development, Salim Teja, states, "When we launched, we would have 25 to 50 buyers for a given product . . . now we have up to more than 500 buyers consistently."

Group buying services are not for everyone. Buyers who are in a hurry to get what they want are unlikely to use the service and will most likely opt for a price search mechanism. Less technically sophisticated buyers are least likely to get involved, since group buying represents a radical behavior change to many. In addition, Mercata and Accompany customers can only buy what is being offered. On the flip side, Generation Y consumers are price sensitive and tech savvy. One report indicates that 45 percent of consumers age 16 to 22 have visited sites such as Mercata and Accompany. Group buying also has another advantage over online auctions. According to Accompany's Teja, "[Group buying] takes advantage of the web, which is to connect people. With group buying, it's to your advantage to encourage friends to come to the site to buy. With an auction site, it isn't, because they might outbid you."

Source: Adapted from Mara Janis, "Good Buys," *Adweek* 41, no. 10 (March 6, 2000), 58–64.

## NO OPPORTUNITY SHOULD EXIST FOR INDIVIDUALS IN ONE SEGMENT WHO HAVE PAID A LOW PRICE TO SELL THEIR TICKETS TO THOSE IN OTHER SEGMENTS

For example, it does the movie theater little good to sell reduced-price seats in the afternoon to buyers who can turn around and sell those tickets that evening in the parking lot to full-paying customers. Sometimes you just can't win! A local municipal golf course was trying to do "the right thing" by offering its senior citizen customers coupon books for rounds of golf priced at a reduced rate. Soon after the promotion began, some senior citizen customers were seen in the parking lot selling their coupons at a profit to the golf course's full-price customers.

## THE SEGMENT SHOULD BE LARGE ENOUGH
## TO MAKE THE EXERCISE WORTHWHILE

The time and effort involved in offering a price segmentation scheme should be justified based on the return it brings to the business (see Services in Action 7.2). Having little or no response to the firm's effort signals that either consumers are uninterested, eligible customers are few, or the firm's price segmentation offer is off its mark.

## THE COST OF RUNNING THE PRICE SEGMENTATION STRATEGY
## SHOULD NOT EXCEED THE INCREMENTAL REVENUES OBTAINED

The objectives of engaging in price segmentation efforts may be to reduce peak demand, fill periods of underutilized capacity, increase overall revenues, or achieve nonprofit issues, such as making your service available to individuals who otherwise may not be able to take advantage of the services the firm offers. If the cost of running the price segmentation strategy exceeds the returns produced, management needs to reconsider the offering.

## THE CUSTOMERS SHOULD NOT BE CONFUSED BY
## THE USE OF DIFFERENT PRICES

Phone companies and electric utilities often offer customers reduced rates that are based on the time of usage. Frequently, however, these time-related discounts change as new promotions arise. Customers caught unaware of the change often end up paying higher rates than expected, which negatively impacts customer satisfaction. Recently, phone companies such as AT&T have attempted to utilize "simple pricing" as a point of differentiation in their advertising. Other firms are offering higher-priced "peak rates" and lower-priced "nonpeak" rates that vary throughout the day, and customers must be aware at all times which rate they will be paying in order to take advantage of this particular type of pricing strategy.

## Cost Considerations

### CONSUMERS MAY NOT KNOW THE ACTUAL PRICE THEY WILL
### PAY FOR A SERVICE UNTIL AFTER THE SERVICE IS COMPLETED

Although consumers can usually find a base price to use as a comparison during prepurchase evaluation, many services are customized during delivery. Consumers may not know the exact amount they will be charged until after the service is performed. For example, a patient may know what a doctor's office visit costs but may not know what she charges for lab work or an x-ray. Similarly, a client may know how much an attorney charges for an hour of work but may not know how many hours it will take to finalize a will. In contrast to goods, which are produced, purchased, and consumed, services are purchased (implied), produced, and consumed simultaneously, and then actually paid for when the final bill is presented. The final price is sometimes the last piece of information revealed to the customer.

### COST-ORIENTED PRICING IS MORE DIFFICULT FOR SERVICES

Many service managers experience difficulties accurately estimating their costs of doing business. This difficulty arises for several reasons. First, when producing an

For many professional services (such as healthcare), the consumer may not know the actual price they will pay for the service until the service is completed.

intangible product, cost of goods sold is either a small or nonexistent portion of the total cost. Second, labor needs are difficult to accurately forecast in many service settings in part because of fluctuating demand. Third, workforce turnover is typically high in many service industries. This, coupled with the fact that finding good personnel is an ongoing challenge, leads to further difficulty in estimating the costs associated with a particular service encounter. These factors make what is often considered the most common approach to pricing, cost-oriented pricing, difficult at best for service firms. Consequently, the difficulties associated with controlling and forecasting costs are a fundamental difference between goods and services pricing.

Unfortunately, traditional cost accounting practices, which were designed to monitor raw material consumption, depreciation, and labor, offer little to help service managers understand their own cost structures. A more useful approach, **activity-based costing (ABC),** focuses on the resources consumed in developing the final product.[11] Traditionally, overhead in most service firms has been allocated to projects based on the amount of direct labor charged to complete the customer's requirements. However, this method of charging overhead has frustrated managers of specific projects for years. Consider the following example:

Let's say that ABC Company charges $2 for overhead for every dollar of direct labor charged to customers. As the manager of ABC Company, you have just negotiated with a customer to provide architectural drawings of a deck for $1,000. The customer wants the drawing in 3 days. Realizing that using your best architect, whom you pay $20 an hour, will result in a loss for the project, you assign the architect's apprentice, who makes $7 an hour. The results of the project are as follows:

**activity-based costing (ABC)**
Costing method that breaks down the organization into a set of activities, and activities into tasks, which convert materials, labor, and technology into outputs.

| Time Required | 40 hours | |
|---|---|---|
| Apprentice's Rate | $7 per hour | |
| Direct Labor | $280 | |
| Overhead @ $2 | $560 | |
| Project Cost | | $840 |
| Revenue | $1,000 | |
| Profit | $160 | |

If the firm's best architect had completed the job, the following results would have been submitted:

| Time Required | 20 hours | |
|---|---|---|
| Architect's Rate | $20 per hour | |
| Direct Labor | $400 | |
| Overhead @ $2 | $800 | |
| Project Cost | | $1,200 |
| Revenue | $1,000 | |
| Profit | ($200) | |

This traditional approach used in service firms makes little sense. Intuitively, it does not make sense that a job that took a shorter period of time should be charged more overhead. Moreover, this type of system encourages the firm to use less-skilled labor, who produce an inferior product in an unacceptable period of time as specified by the customer. The firm produces a profit on paper but will most likely never have the opportunity to work for this customer again (or his or her friends, for that matter). Even more confusing is that raises and promotions are based on profits generated, so the manager is rewarded for using inferior labor. Something is definitely wrong with this picture!

Activity-based costing focuses on the cost of activities by breaking down the organization into a set of activities and activities into tasks, which convert materials, labor, and technology into outputs. The tasks are thought of as "users" of overhead and identified as **cost drivers.** The firm's past records are used to arrive at cost-per-task figures that are then allocated to each project based on the activities required to complete the project. In addition, by breaking the overall overhead figure into a set of activities that are driven by cost drivers, the firm can now concentrate its efforts on reducing costs and increasing profitability.

**cost drivers**
The tasks in activity-based costing that are considered to be the "users" of overhead.

For example, one activity in the firm's overall overhead figure is ordering materials. Ordering materials is driven by the number of purchase orders submitted. Company records indicate that overhead associated with ordering materials cost the firm $10,400 during the period. During this same period, 325 purchase orders were submitted. Hence, the activity cost associated with each purchase order is $32. Similar calculations are made for other overhead items. Overhead is then allocated to each project based on the activities undertaken to complete the project. Table 7.3 presents examples of overhead items and their cost drivers.

## SERVICES ARE TYPICALLY CHARACTERIZED BY A HIGH FIXED TO VARIABLE COST RATIO

United Parcel Service (UPS) is a prime example. UPS maintains a vehicle fleet of more than 157,000 trucks and an air fleet of more than 500 planes. The company

## TABLE 7.3

### Activity-Based Costing

| Activity Pools | Cost Driver |
|---|---|
| General administration | Direct Labor $ |
| Project costing | No. of timesheet entries |
| Accounts payable/receiving | No. of vendor invoices |
| Accounts receivable | No. of client invoices |
| Payroll/mail sorting and delivery | No. of employees |
| Recruiting personnel | No. of new hires |
| Employee insurance processing | Insurance claims processed |
| Proposals/RFPs | No. of proposals |
| Client sales meeting/sales aids | Sales $ |
| Shipping | No. of project numbers |
| Ordering | No. of purchase orders |
| Copying | No. of copies |
| Blueprinting | No. of blueprints |

| Cost Driver | Fixed Overhead Cost | Total Base | Cost per Driver |
|---|---|---|---|
| Direct labor $ | 73 | 1,016,687 | 0.07 |
| No. of time entries | 10 | 13,300 | 0.78 |
| No. of vendor invoices | 29 | 2,270 | 12.60 |
| No. of client invoices | 10 | 1,128 | 9.22 |
| No. of employees | 18 | 67 | 271.64 |
| No. of new hires | 8 | 19 | 410.53 |
| Insurance claims filed | 3 | 670 | 3.88 |
| No. of proposals | 29 | 510 | 56.08 |
| Sales $ | 42 | 3,795,264 | 0.01 |
| No. of project numbers | 5 | 253 | 20.55 |
| No. of purchase orders | 10 | 325 | 32.00 |
| No. of copies | 16 | 373,750 | 0.04 |
| No. of blueprint sq. ft. | 8 | 86,200 | 0.09 |
| | 260 | | |

Source: Adapted from Beth M. Chapman and John Talbott, "Activity-Based Costing in a Service Organization," *CMA Magazine* (December 1990/January 1991), 15–18.

**fixed costs**
Costs that are planned and accrued during the operating period regardless of the level of production and sales.

**variable costs**
Costs that are directly associated with increases in production and sales.

also owns 12 mainframes, 90,000 PCs, 80,000 handheld computers, the nation's largest cellular network, and the world's largest DB-2 database. As a result of this infrastructure, the company handles more than 3 billion packages and 5.5% of the United States' GDP annually.[12]

In comparison with UPS' massive **fixed costs,** the **variable costs** associated with handling one more package are practically nil. The challenges faced by businesses that have a high fixed cost to variable cost ratio are numerous. First, what prices should be charged to individual customers? How should the firm sell off unused capacity? For example, should an airline sell 20 unsold seats at a reduced rate to customers who are willing to accept the risk of not reserving a seat on the plane prior to the day of departure? Does selling unused capacity at discounted rates alienate full-fare paying customers? How can companies offer reduced prices to sell off unused capacity without full-fare paying customers shifting their buying patterns?

## SERVICE ECONOMIES OF SCALE TEND TO BE LIMITED

Because of inseparability and perishability, the consumption of services is not separated by time and space. Inventory cannot be used to buffer demand, and the physical presence of customers and providers is frequently necessary for a transaction to take place. Consequently, service providers often produce services on demand rather than in advance. Therefore, it is difficult for service providers to achieve the cost advantages traditionally associated with economies of scale. Some services are also more likely than goods to be customized to each customer's specifications and/or needs. Customization limits the amount of work that can be done in advance of a customer's request for service.

## Customer Considerations

### PRICE TENDS TO BE ONE OF THE FEW CUES AVAILABLE TO CONSUMERS DURING PREPURCHASE

Because of the intangible nature of services, they are characterized by few search attributes. Search attributes are informational cues that can be determined prior to purchase. In contrast, the tangibility of goods dramatically increases the number of search attributes available for consumers to consider. For example, the style and fit of a suit can be determined prior to purchase. In contrast, the enjoyment of a dinner is not known until after the experience is complete.

Pricing research has noted that the informational value of price decreases as the number of other informational cues increase. Similarly, others have found consumer reliance on price to be U-shaped. In other words, price is heavily used if few cues are present, loses value as more cues become present, and then increases in value if consumers are overwhelmed with information.[13]

### SERVICE CONSUMERS ARE MORE LIKELY TO USE PRICE AS A CUE TO QUALITY

Service providers must also consider the message the service price sends to customers. Much work has been devoted to understanding whether price can be an indicator of quality. Some studies seem to imply that consumers can use price to infer the quality of the product they are considering. Conflicting studies seem to indicated that they cannot. For example, classic studies in the field have presented customers with identical products, such as pieces of carpet, priced at different levels. The respondents' judgment of quality seemed to indicate that quality followed price. However, very similar studies later found little relationship between price and perceived quality.[14]

Price plays a key informational role in service consumer decision processes. Decision theory suggests that consumers will use those cues that are most readily available in the alternative evaluation process to assess product quality. Because of the importance of its role, price should be a dominant cue for consumers attempting to evaluate service quality prior to purchase. Studies suggest that price is more likely to be used as a cue to quality under the following conditions:

- When price is the primary differential information available
- When alternatives are heterogeneous
- When comparative price differences are relatively large

Clearly, these conditions exist in many service purchase scenarios.

### SERVICE CONSUMERS TEND TO BE LESS CERTAIN ABOUT RESERVATION PRICES

**reservation price**
The price a consumer considers to capture the value he or she places on the benefits.

A consumer's **reservation price** is the maximum amount that the consumer is willing to pay for a product. Ultimately, a consumer's reservation price for a service determines whether a purchase or no purchase decision is made. If the reservation price exceeds the price charged for the service, the consumer is more inclined to purchase that particular service. However, if the reservation price is lower than the actual price charged, the consumer is precluded from purchasing that particular service offering.

Research has noted the lack of service consumer certainty regarding reservation prices. Consumers' reservation prices are determined in part by their awareness of competitive prices in the market. For some services, the lack of pricing information available and the lack of purchasing frequency may lead to less certainty regarding the reservation price of the service under consideration.[15]

## Competitive Considerations

### COMPARING PRICES OF COMPETITORS IS MORE DIFFICULT FOR SERVICE CONSUMERS

Actual price information for services tends to be more difficult for consumers to acquire than it is for goods. Further, when service price information is available to consumers, it also tends to be more difficult to make meaningful comparisons between services. For example, although base service prices can sometimes be determined in advance, competing services are not sold together in retail stores the way that many competing goods are in supermarkets and discount or department stores. Consumers have to either individually visit geographically separated service firms or contact them to compare prices. As a result, comparative shopping requires much more time and effort.

### SELF-SERVICE IS A VIABLE COMPETITIVE ALTERNATIVE

One result of the inseparability of production and consumption for services is the possibility of the customer actively participating in the service delivery process, commonly referred to as self-service options. The availability of self-service options has an effect on customer perceptions of the service. Initially, self-service options invariably provided the service customer with some form of price reduction (e.g., self-service gasoline). Today, the literature suggests that service customers often are seeking other benefits besides lower prices when purchasing self-service options. These benefits might include greater convenience, more control, less human contact, faster service time, greater efficiency, and greater independence. Self-service options must be considered in the formation of pricing strategy.

## Profit Considerations

### PRICE BUNDLING MAKES THE DETERMINATION OF INDIVIDUAL PRICES IN THE BUNDLE OF SERVICES MORE COMPLICATED

Bundling, the practice of marketing two or more goods and/or services for a single price, is a useful strategic pricing tool that can help services marketers achieve several different strategic objectives; however, it also complicates the alternative evaluation process for consumers. Consumers experience difficulty when attempting to calculate how much each component of the bundle is contributing to the total cost. For example, a consumer evaluating available alternatives for a trip to Jamaica might have a hard time comparing the costs associated with an all-inclusive hotel package bundled with airfare and transfers with a traditional pay-as-you-go vacation alternative.

### PRICE BUNDLING IS MORE EFFECTIVE IN A SERVICE CONTEXT

A wide variety of services make use of price bundling as a strategic approach to pricing. Many service organizations bundle their own service offerings together, as when a doctor combines diagnostic tests with physical examinations. Other service organizations choose to form strategic alliances with other firms and bundle services that each provides. For example, the travel industry bundles hotel charges, airline tickets and transfer services into a single price. Regardless of the form or type of bundling, this strategy essentially creates a new service that can be used to either attract new customers, cross-sell existing customers, or retain current customers. Bundling has proliferated in the service sector primarily because of high fixed/variable cost ratios, the degree of cost sharing, and the high levels of interdependent demand. For example, the demand for a hotel restaurant is directly related to the demand for hotel rooms.

## Product Considerations

### COMPARED WITH THE GOODS SECTOR, THERE TEND TO BE MANY DIFFERENT NAMES FOR PRICE IN THE SERVICE SECTOR

One of the interesting aspects of pricing in a service context involves the many different names that are used to express price in different service industries. For example, in the financial services industry the term *price* is rarely if ever used. Instead, customers pay service charges, points, and commissions. Similarly, travelers pay airfares or bus fares, apartment dwellers pay rent, hotel occupants are charged a room rate, and the list goes on and on.

Upon further examination, many of the terms used for price in the service sector incorporate the benefits customers receive. For instance, customers pay fares for the benefit of transportation, rents and room rates for occupancy, and service charges for processing requests. Is price by any other name still a price, or does incorporating the benefit into the term used for price alter consumer perceptions and affect price sensitivities?

### CONSUMERS ARE LESS ABLE TO STOCKPILE SERVICES BY TAKING ADVANTAGE OF DISCOUNT PRICES

Retail pricing researchers note that pricing policies and strategies can have a direct impact on inventory decisions and planning.[16] Goods are often discounted to reduce over-abundant inventories. Consumers take advantage of the discounts

S E R V I C E S  **7.3**
N

A C T I O N    **Ethnic Pricing . . . Is This Ethical?**

The practice of ethnic pricing, giving discounts to people of certain nation-
alities, has long been routine in countries such as India, China, and Russia.
Other countries also offer ethnic pricing but are not public about it because
of ethical and legal ramifications. According to a recent *Wall Street Journal*
article, airline passengers throughout Europe can obtain discount fares on
airline tickets based on the origin of their passport or those of their employers. Brenden McInerney, a passenger attempting to book a Lufthansa flight
to Japan, accidentally learned of the practice and was not too happy about
it. His wife could fly to Japan for 1,700 marks; however, Mr. McInerney's ticket
was priced at 2,700 marks! The reason given by the airline: Mr. McInerney is
an American, whereas his wife is Japanese. The airline eventually capitulated, and Mr. McInerney was given the same fare after he complained.

## Examples of Some Ethnic Discounts

| Airline | Route | Normal Price | "Ethnic Price" |
|---|---|---|---|
| Lufthansa | Frankfurt-Tokyo | $1,524 | $960 |
| Lufthansa | Frankfurt-Seoul | 1,524 | 903 |
| British Airways | Istanbul-London | 385 | 199 |

Note: Taxes, landing fees not included                    Source: Travel agents

Lufthansa does not deny its involvement with ethnic pricing. Dagmar
Rotter, a spokesperson for the airline, states that the airline is only reacting
to the competition from the national carrier of Japan that also flies out of
Germany. "The others started it . . . we only offer it [ethnic pricing] after the
market forced us to do so."

Other European airlines such as Swissair and Air France also practice
ethnic pricing. Swissair offers "guest-worker" fares to passengers from
Turkey, Portugal, Spain, Greece, and Morocco flying to these same destinations; however, it does not offer discount fares to Japanese flying to Japan.
A Swissair spokesperson argues that if the discounts were not provided to
the "guest-workers" from Southern Europe and the Mediterranean rim, they
would never be able to afford to go home to visit their families. Similarly, Air
France offers discounted rates to citizens of Vietnam, China, South Korea,
and Japan, but only for its flights that are departing from Germany. An Air
France spokesperson notes, "In Germany everybody seems to be doing
it . . . it seems to be something very specific to the German market."

British Airways' involvement was readily apparent when it offered its
travel package "Ho, Ho, Ho" for British citizens in Turkey. "Short of stuffing,
need some pork sausages, fretting about Christmas pud? Not to worry—
show your British passport and you can take 48% of normal fares to Britain."

> U.S. airlines were quietly involved in ethnic pricing until the practice was barred in 1998. A spokesperson for Lufthansa in New York noted that ethnic pricing could not occur in the U.S. "because it is discriminatory."

Source: Adapted from "Ethnic Pricing Means Unfair Air Fares," *Wall Street Journal*, December 5, 1997, pp. B1, B14.

and often engage in forward buying. **Forward buying** enables consumers to build their own inventories of goods and reduces the amount of defections to competitive brands. In contrast, services cannot be stored. Consequently, service consumers cannot stockpile service offerings. When consumers need or want a service, they must pay the prevailing price.

**forward buying**
When retailers purchase enough product on deal to carry over until the product is being sold on deal again.

## PRODUCT-LINE PRICING TENDS TO BE MORE COMPLICATED

Product-line pricing, the practice of pricing multiple versions of the same product or grouping similar products together, is widely used in goods marketing. For example, beginner, intermediate, and expert level tennis racquets are generally priced at different price points to reflect the different levels of quality construction. Consumers of goods can more easily evaluate the differences among the multiple versions offered, since tangibility provides search attributes. Search attributes assist consumers in making objective evaluations. In contrast, consider the difficulty of real estate consumers when faced with the choices offered by Century 21 Real Estate. The company offers home sellers three levels of service that are priced at increasing commission rates of 6, 7, and 8 percent. Customers, particularly those who sell their homes infrequently, lack the expertise to make an informed decision. The performance levels associated with the three levels of service offered cannot be assessed until after the contract with the real estate agent has been signed and the customer has committed to the commission rate.

Traditionally, product-line pricing provides customers with choices and gives managers an opportunity to maximize total revenues. However, the product-line pricing of services more often than not generates customer confusion and alienation. Industries struggling with the price lining of their services include telecommunications (e.g., AT&T, MCI, and Sprint calling plans), health care (e.g., multiple versions of Blue Cross/Blue Shield plans, HMOs, etc.), and financial services (e.g., multiple types of checking and savings accounts, investment options, etc.).

## Legal Considerations

### THE OPPORTUNITY FOR ILLEGAL PRICING PRACTICES TO GO UNDETECTED IS GREATER FOR SERVICES THAN GOODS

Is it legal for a physician to charge excessive prices for vaccinations during an influenza epidemic, or for repair services to triple their hourly rate to repair homes in neighborhoods damaged by severe weather? In some states there are gouging laws to protect consumers from such practices during special circumstances; however, the special circumstances (e.g., epidemics and severe weather) draw attention to such practices. In contrast, identifying excessive service pricing practices is not as clear for "everyday" types of purchase occasions (see Services in Action 7.3).

In general, the opportunity to engage in and benefit from illegal pricing practices in the service sector is predominantly attributed to intangibility and inseparability. As discussed in Chapter 5, intangibility decreases the consumer's ability to objectively evaluate purchases, whereas inseparability reflects the human element of the service encounter, which can potentially expose the customer to coercive influence techniques.

The pricing implications of service consumer vulnerability are twofold. First, consumer vulnerability and perceived risk are directly related. Consumers feeling particularly vulnerable are willing to pay higher prices for a service if it lowers their perceived risk. Second, dubious service providers that abuse the customer's trust by taking advantage of vulnerable consumers through excessive prices may benefit in the short term, but once they are discovered, the long-term success of their firms is doubtful. To consumers the issue is one of fairness and **dual entitlement.** Cost-driven price changes are perceived as fair because they allow sellers to maintain their profit entitlement. In contrast, demand-driven prices are often perceived as unfair. They allow the sellers to increase their profit margins purely at the expense of the increasing consumer demand.[17]

**dual entitlement**
Cost-driven price increases are perceived as fair, whereas demand-driven price increases are viewed as unfair.

## Emerging Service Pricing Strategies

Traditional pricing strategies such as penetration pricing, competitive pricing, and premium pricing offer little benefit to service customers or service providers. For example, competitive pricing has led to disappearing profit margins in industries such as car rental and health insurance and to customer confusion and mistrust in industries such as long distance telephone service. At the core of the pricing problem is a lack of understanding of the special considerations in the pricing of intangibles and how consumers use and benefit from the services they are purchasing. Service marketers should create pricing strategies that offer a compromise between the overly complex (Table 7.4) and the too simplistic, both of which neglect the variations in consumer needs.[18]

To effectively price services, the service firm must first understand what its target market truly values. Three alternative pricing strategies that convey value to the customer include satisfaction-based, relationship, and efficiency pricing (Table 7.5)[19]

### SATISFACTION-BASED PRICING

**satisfaction-based pricing**
Pricing strategies that are designed to reduce the amount of perceived risk associated with a purchase.

The primary goal of **satisfaction-based pricing** is to reduce the amount of perceived risk associated with the service purchase and appeal to target markets that value certainty. Satisfaction-based pricing can be achieved through offering guarantees, benefit-driven pricing, and flat-rate pricing.

Service guarantees are quickly becoming a popular way of attracting customers.[20] The guarantee assures customers that if they are less than satisfied with their purchase, they can invoke the guarantee, and a partial or full refund will occur. Offering guarantees signals to customers that the firm is committed to delivering quality services and confident in its ability to do so. In instances where competing services are priced similarly, the service guarantee offers a differential advantage.

**benefit-driven pricing**
A pricing strategy that charges customers for services actually used as opposed to overall "membership" fees.

**Benefit-driven pricing** focuses on the aspects of the service that customers actually use. The objective of this approach is to develop a direct association

# TABLE 7.4

## Reach Out and Confuse Someone . . . Remember These?

**AT&T's "True USA Savings" Program**
10 percent discount to customers spending $10 to $24.99
20 percent discount to customers spending $25 to $74.99
30 percent discount to customers spending $75 or more

**AT&T's "True Rewards" Program**
Allows frequent callers to accumulate points, which can be exchanged for frequent flyer
  miles, savings bonds, free calling time, and a variety of other products.

**MCI's "Friends & Family" Program**
20 percent discount to preset group of MCI customers

**MCI's "Friends & Family II/Sure Savings" Program**
40 percent discount to MCI customers
20 percent discount to non-MCI customers

**MCI's "Personal Thanks" Program**
Similar program to AT&T's "True Rewards" program

**Sprint's "The Most" Program**
20 percent discount on calls made to the most-called number, as well as to other Sprint
  customers
36 percent discount if the most-called number is a Sprint customer.

**Sprint's "The Most II" Program**
Tiered discounts based on level of long-distance calling

**Sprint's "Priority Rewards" Program**
Similar to AT&T's "True Rewards" and MCI's "Personal Thanks" programs

Source: Adapted from "Reach Out and Confuse Someone," *Services Marketing Today* (June 1995), 4.

---

between the price of the service and the components of the service that customers value. For example, online computer services typically do not use benefit-driven pricing strategies. This is evident by their practice of charging customers for the amount of time spent online as opposed to billing for services they actually use. Innovative online services, such as ESA-IRS and its "pricing for information" program, have introduced benefit-driven pricing and have shifted their marketing focus from keeping customers online to marketing information that is beneficial to their customers.

The concept of **flat-rate pricing** is fairly straightforward. Its primary objective is to decrease consumer uncertainty about the final price of the service by agreeing to a fixed price before the service transaction occurs. With flat-rate pricing, the provider assumes the risk of price increases and overruns. Flat-rate pricing makes the most sense when:

**flat-rate pricing**
A pricing strategy in which the customer pays a fixed price and the provider assumes the risk of price increases and cost overruns.

## TABLE 7.5

### Satisfaction-Based, Relationship, and Efficiency Pricing Strategies

| Pricing Strategy | Provides Value by . . . | Implemented as . . . |
|---|---|---|
| Satisfaction-based pricing | Recognizing and reducing customers' perceptions of uncertainty, which the intangible nature of service magnifies. | Service guarantees<br>Benefit-driven pricing<br>Flat-rate pricing |
| Relationship pricing | Encouraging long-term relationships with the company that customers view as beneficial. | Long-term contracts<br>Price bundling |
| Efficiency pricing | Sharing with customers the cost saving that the company has achieved by understanding, managing, and reducing the costs of providing the service. | Cost-leader pricing |

Source: Leonard L. Berry and Manjit S. Yadav, "Capture and Communicate Value in the Pricing of Services," *Sloan Management Review* (Summer 1996), 41–51.

- The price is competitive
- The firm offering the flat rate has its costs under control and operates an efficient operation
- The opportunities to engage in a long-term relationship and to generate additional revenues with the customer are possible

## RELATIONSHIP PRICING

**relationship pricing**
Pricing strategies that encourage the customer to expand his or her dealings with the service provider.

The primary objective of **relationship pricing** is to enhance the firm's relationship with its targeted consumers. For example, in the banking industry, relationship pricing strategies can be used to further nurture the relationship between the bank and its existing checking account customers by offering special savings accounts, deals on safe-deposit boxes, and special rates on certificates of deposit. Two types of relationship pricing techniques include long-term contracts and price bundling.

Long-term contracts offer prospective customers price and nonprice incentives for dealing with the same provider over a number of years. UPS recently entered into long-term shipping contracts with Lands' End and Ford Motor Company. Because of its customers' long-term commitments, UPS has been able to transform its business with these clients from discrete to continuous transactions. UPS now has operations and personnel dedicated solely to providing services to these specific customers. Because transactions are now continuous, economies of scale have developed, and cost savings that can be passed to the customer plus opportunities for improving the firm's profit performance have emerged.

**price bundling**
The practice of marketing two or more products and/or services in a single package at a single price.

Because most service organizations provide more than one service, the practice of bundling services has become more common.[21] **Price bundling,** broadly defined, is the practice of marketing two or more products and/or services in a single package at a single price. Common examples include hotels putting to-gether weekend packages that include lodging, meals, and sometimes entertain-ment at an inclusive rate. Airlines routinely price vacation packages that include air travel, car rental, and hotel accommodations.

Price bundling flows logically from the issues discussed earlier in the chapter. Individual services have low marginal costs and high shared costs. Moreover, the services offered by most businesses are generally interdependent in terms of demand. For example, the demand for the hotel's food service is directly related to the demand for hotel rooms.

Generally, services are concerned with **mixed bundling,** which enables consumers to either buy service A and service B together or purchase one service separately. The simplest argument for bundling is based on the idea of consumer surplus: Bundling makes it possible to shift the consumer surplus from one service to another service that otherwise would have a negative surplus (i.e., would not be purchased). Thus the combined value of the two services is less than the combined price, even though separately only one service would be purchased.

Three reasons have been suggested for why the sum of the parts would have less value than the whole. First, information theory would argue that the consumer finds value in easy access to information. Consumers of one financial service insti-tution have a lower information cost when buying another service from the same institution than when buying that service from a different institution. A second case argues that the bundling of service B with service A can enhance a con-sumer's satisfaction with service A, such as a ski resort that offers a ski rental and lessons package. The reservation price for the lessons is likely to be the same whether or not the skis are rented because the value of the lessons depends on the skills and needs of the skier. However, the reservation price of the ski rental will be enhanced, at least for novices, by lessons. The final argument is that the addition of service B to service A can enhance the total image of the firm. A financial-planning service offering both investment advice and tax advice enhances its credibility in both services.

**mixed bundling**
Price-bundling technique that allows consumers to either buy Service A and Service B together or purchase one service separately.

## EFFICIENCY PRICING

The primary goal of **efficiency pricing** is to appeal to economically minded con-sumers who are looking for the best price. "Efficiency pricers almost always are industry heretics, shunning traditional operating practices in search of sustainable cost advantages."[22] Southwest Airlines and its relentless efforts to reduce costs is one such example. Southwest reduces costs by flying shorter, more-direct routes to less congested, less expensive airports. No meals are served, passengers are seated on a first-come, first-served basis, and the airline was the first to offer "ticket-less" travel on all flights.

Efficiency pricing is focused on delivering the best and most cost-effective ser-vice available for the price. Operations are streamlined, and innovations that enable further cost reduction become part of the operation's culture. The leaner the cost structure, the more difficult it is for new competitors to imitate Southwest's success. Understanding and managing costs are the fundamental building blocks of efficiency pricing.

**efficiency pricing**
Pricing strategies that appeal to economically minded consumers by delivering the best and most cost-effective service for the price.

## SOME FINAL THOUGHTS ON PRICING SERVICES

Pricing services is a difficult task. Consumers are purchasing an experience and often feel uneasy about or do not understand what they are paying for. Similarly, service providers do not have a cost of goods sold figure on which to base their prices. Confused and bewildered, many providers simply look to what the competition is charging, regardless of their own cost structures and competitive advantage. In contrast, successful service providers tend to abide by the following pricing guidelines: [23]

- The price should be easy for customers to understand.
- The price should represent value to the customer.
- The price should encourage customer retention and facilitate the customer's relationship with the providing firm.
- The price should reinforce customer trust.
- The price should reduce customer uncertainty.

## SUMMARY

Successful service pricing depends on recognizing the value that a customer places on a service and pricing that service accordingly. Customer perceptions of value represent a trade-off between the perceived benefits obtained from purchasing the product and the perceived sacrifice in terms of cost to be paid. Total customer costs extend beyond monetary costs and include time, energy, and psychic costs. Similarly, total customer value extends beyond product value and includes service, personnel, and image value.

When developing service pricing strategies, managers should take into account a number of considerations including demand, cost, customer, competitive, profit, product, and legal considerations. Table 7.1 provides a summary of each of these considerations.

Overall, traditional pricing strategies and cost accounting approaches offer little benefit to either service consumers or service providers. Three alternative pricing strategies that convey value to the customer include satisfaction-based, relationship, and efficiency pricing. The primary goal of satisfaction-based pricing is to reduce the perceived risk associated with the purchase of services and to appeal to target markets that value certainty. Satisfaction-based pricing strategies include offering guarantees, benefit-driven pricing, and flat-rate pricing. The goal of relationship pricing is to enhance the firm's relationship with its targeted consumers. Relationship pricing techniques include offering long-term contracts and price bundling. In comparison, efficiency pricing appeals to economically minded consumers and focuses on delivering the best and most cost-effective service for the price. Understanding and managing costs are the fundamental building blocks of efficiency pricing.

# Key Terms

Activity-based costing (ABC)
Benefit-driven pricing
Complementary
Cost drivers
Cross-price elasticity
Dual entitlement
Efficiency pricing
Energy costs
Fixed costs
Flat-rate pricing
Forward buying
Image value
Inelastic demand
Mixed bundling

Monetary price
Personnel value
Price bundling
Price discrimination
Product value
Psychic costs
Relationship pricing
Reservation price
Satisfaction-based pricing
Service value
Substitutes
Time costs
Variable costs

# Discussion Questions

1. What factors comprise consumer perceptions of value?
2. Discuss the role of price as an indicator of quality to consumers.
3. Describe the trade-offs associated with taking hotel reservations from customers who pay lower rates than same-day customers.
4. Discuss the differences between traditional methods of allocating overhead expenses and activity-based costing.
5. Should self-service always be rewarded with lower prices? Please explain.
6. Under what conditions is price segmentation most effective?
7. Discuss the basic concepts behind satisfaction-based, relationship, and efficiency pricing.

# Notes

1. J. Dean, "Research Approach to Pricing," in *Planning the Price Structure,* Marketing Series No. 67 (Chicago: American Marketing Association, 1947).
2. J. Backman, *Price Practices and Price Policies* (New York: Ronald Press, 1953).
3. A. W. Walker, "How to Price Industrial Products," *Harvard Business Review* 45 (1967), 38–45.
4. A. Marshall, *More Profitable Pricing* (London: McGraw-Hill, 1979).
5. "Finding the Right Price is No Easy Game to Play," *Chief Executive* (September 1981), 16–18.
6. Thomas T. Nagle and Reed K. Holden, *The Strategy and Tactics of Pricing* (Englewood Cliffs, N.J.: Prentice Hall, 1995).

7. Philip Kotler, *Marketing Management,* 8th ed. (Englewood Cliffs, N.J.: Prentice-Hall, 1994), 38.

8. Dale Lewison, *Retailing*, 6th ed. (Upper Saddle River, NJ: Prentice Hall, 1997).

9. K. Douglas Hoffman and L. W. Turley, "Toward an Understanding of Consumer Price Sensitivity for Professional Services," in *Developments in Marketing Science,* Charles H. Noble, ed. (Miami: Academy of Marketing Science, 1999), 169–173.

10. Adapted from John E. G. Bateson, *Managing Services Marketing,* 2nd ed. (Fort Worth, Tex.: The Dryden Press, 1992), 357–365.

11. Beth M. Chaffman and John Talbott, "Activity-Based Costing in a Service Organization," *CMA Magazine* (December 1990/January 1991), 15–18.

12. John Alden, "What in the World Drives UPS?" *International Business* 11, no. 2 (1998), 6–7; and Jim Kelley, "From Lip Service to Real Service: Reversing America's Downward Service Spiral," *Vital Speeches of the Day* 64, no. 10 (1998), 301–304.

13. Kent B. Monroe, "Buyers Subjective Perceptions of Price," *Journal of Marketing Research* 10 (February 1973), 70–80.

14. Bateson, *Managing Services Marketing.*

15. Joseph P. Guiltinan, "The Price Bundling of Services: A Normative Framework," *Journal of Marketing* 51, no. 2 (1987), 74–85.

16. Saroja Subrahmanyan and Robert Shoemaker, "Developing Optimal Pricing and Inventory Policies for Retailers Who Face Uncertain Demand," *Journal of Retailing* 72, no. 1, (1996), 7–30.

17. Michael R. Czinkota, ed.: *Marketing: Best Practices* (Fort Worth, Tex.: The Dryden Press, 2000).

18. Leonard L. Berry and Manjit S. Yadav, "Capture and Communicate Value in the Pricing of Services," *Sloan Management Review* (Summer 1996), 41–51.

19. Ibid.

20. Christopher W. L. Hart, Leonard A. Schlesinger, and Dan Maher, "Guarantees Come to Professional Service Firms," *Sloan Management Review* (Spring 1992), 19–29.

21. Joseph P. Guiltinan, "The Price Bundling of Services: A Normative Framework," *Journal of Marketing* (April 1987), 51, 74–85.

22. Berry and Manjit, "Capture and Communicate Value," p. 49.

23. Ibid.

# chapter 8

B L U E P R I N T S
A
T C
E C O N C E P T
S M U S I
O U T O H O F F M A N
N M T

# Developing the Service Communication Mix

## CHAPTER OBJECTIVES

The purpose of this chapter is to provide an overview of communication mix strategies as they apply to the marketing of services.

After reading this chapter, you should be able to:

- Discuss factors that influence the development of the firm's communication mix.
- Discuss the goals of the communication mix during prepurchase, consumption, and postpurchase stages.
- Describe the special problems associated with developing the service communication mix.
- Discuss the basic guidelines for advertising services.
- Describe the special problems encountered by professional service providers.

"It is what you say and how you say it!"

Service Providers Who
Stay in Business

*Introduction*

Communications strategy is one of the key components of the service marketing mix.[1] In general, the primary role of a service firm's communication strategy is to inform, persuade, or remind consumers about the service being offered. Consumers cannot be expected to use a service they do not know about; therefore, a primary objective of communication strategy is to create consumer awareness and position the firm's service offering in the consumer's evoked set of alternatives. Moreover, even when awareness of the service product exists, consumers may need additional encouragement to try it and information about how to obtain and use the service. Finally, people forget. Just because they have been told something once does not mean that they will necessarily remember it over time.

**nonpersonal sources**
Communication channels that are considered impersonal, such as television advertising or printed information.

Communicating the firm's service offering may be accomplished through **nonpersonal sources,** such as television advertising or printed information in magazines and newspapers, or through **personal sources** on a face-to-face basis through all the individuals who come into contact with the consumer in the prepurchase, consumption, and postpurchase stages. In addition, the communications mix can be designed to influence customer expectations and perceptions of the service.

**personal sources**
Communication channels that are considered personal, such as a face-to-face encounter.

Communications objectives and strategies vary depending on the nature of the target audience (see Services in Action 8.1). Separate communications strategies are necessary for current users of a service in order to influence or change their patterns of service use, and for nonusers in order to attract them to the service.

## DEVELOPING A COMMUNICATIONS STRATEGY: THE BASICS

### Selecting Target Markets

Developing a communications strategy follows a common pattern whether the firm is producing goods or services. The service firm must first analyze the needs of consumers and then categorize consumers with similar needs into market segments. Each market segment should then be considered based on profit and growth potential and the segment's compatibility with organizational resources and objectives. Segments that become the focus of the firm's marketing efforts become **target markets.**

**target markets**
The segments of potential customers that become the focus of a firm's marketing efforts.

### Developing the Firm's Positioning Strategy

**positioning strategy**
The plan for differentiating the firm from its competitors in consumers' eyes.

Once the target market is selected, successful service firms establish a **positioning strategy,** which differentiates them from competitors in consumers' eyes. Effective positioning is particularly critical for service firms where intangibility clouds the consumer's ability to differentiate one service provider's offering from the next. For example, competing airlines that fly the same routes may stress operational elements such as the percentage of on-time arrivals, whereas others stress service elements such as the friendliness and helpfulness of the flight crew and the quality of the food served.

SERVICES **8.1**

IN ACTION    **Advertising Via Wireless Networks**

If services marketing advertising wasn't already a challenge for service firms, now marketers have the opportunity to promote their services on the many wireless devices that have recently appeared in today's consumer markets (e.g., cell phones, pagers, and PDAs). According to Mark Dolley, a writer for *Revolution* magazine, "Wireless advertising is like sex at high school: everybody talks about it, but who is actually doing it?" Recommended do's and don'ts for wireless advertising are listed below.

| Do's | Don'ts |
|------|--------|
| Do make sure your ads appear above the fold. | Don't interrupt users on their way to information they really need right now, such as traffic reports or flight status. |
| Do target ads using location where possible. | Don't use location information without permission of the user. |
| Do buy some ad space to try a wireless campaign. | Don't treat it as just another test: The wrong approach could do irreparable damage to your relationship with consumers. |
| Do make your ads useful and simple. | Don't demand any user input that you haven't tried to tap out yourself. Don't be cryptic. |
| Do make your ads actionable. | Don't make it hard for users to return to the place where they saw your ad. |
| Do rewrite your home page in Wireless Markup Language, ready for WAP browsers | Don't try to include pictures of your cat. |

By 2005, wireless advertising is expected to account for 20 percent of all online advertising; however, to date, service marketer expenditures for online advertising have been dwarfed by traditional goods manufacturers. For example, food and beverages account for 31 percent of online advertising, followed by personal care products and print media (both at 21 percent), and apparel at 9 percent.

Source: Adapted from Mark Dolley, "Moving Targets," *Revolution* 1, no. 5 (July 2000), 14, 62–64.

TABLE *8.1*

## Differentiation Approaches for Effective Positioning

| **Product Differentiation** | **Personnel Differentiation** |
|---|---|
| Features | Competence |
| Performance | Courtesy |
| Conformance | Credibility |
| Durability | Reliability |
| Reliability | Responsiveness |
| Repairability | Communication |
| Style | |
| Design (integrates the above) | |

| **Image Differentiation** | **Service Differentiation** |
|---|---|
| Symbols | Delivery (speed, accuracy) |
| Written, audio/visual media | Installation |
| Atmosphere | Customer training |
| Events | Consulting service |
| | Repair |
| | Miscellaneous service |

Source: Adapted from Philip Kotler, *Marketing Management,* 9th ed. (Englewood Cliffs, NJ: Prentice-Hall, 1997), p. 283.

**communications mix**
The array of communications tools available to marketers.

**personal selling**
The two-way element of the communications mix in which the service provider influences a consumer via direct interaction.

**media advertising**
A one-way communications tool that utilizes such media as television and radio to reach a broadly defined audience.

**publicity and public relations**
A one-way communications tool between an organization and its customers, vendors, news media, employees, stockholders, the government, and the general public.

**sales promotions**
A one-way communications tool that utilizes promotional or informational activities at the point of sale.

Ultimately, positioning involves a strategic manipulation of the firm's marketing mix variables: product, price, promotion, place, physical facilities, people, and processes. Each of these marketing mix variables is controllable. When effectively combined, the marketing mix can offset the effects of the uncontrollable factors that exist in every firm's operating environment such as technological advances, consumer needs, new and existing competitors, governmental regulations, economic conditions, and the effects of seasonality, which are constantly changing the environment in which the firm operates. Firms that fail to alter their positioning strategy to reflect environmental changes in order to differentiate themselves from competitors often falter in the long run (Table 8.1).[2]

## Developing the Communications Budget and Mix

The firm's promotion, or **communications mix,** communicates the firm's positioning strategy to its relevant markets, including consumers, employees, stockholders, and suppliers. The term *communications mix* describes the array of communications tools available to marketers. Just as marketers need to combine the elements of the marketing mix (including communications) to produce a marketing program, they must also select the most appropriate communication vehicles to convey their message.

The elements of the communications mix fall into four broad categories: **personal selling, media advertising, publicity and public relations,** and **sales promotions**—promotional or informational activities at the point of sale. Only

ERVICES 8.2

N

ACTION    **Unique Communication Strategy:**
**Taco Bell "Cracks" a Joke that Fools the Country**

In an effort to help the U.S. government reduce the federal budget deficit, Taco Bell announced that its corporation had purchased the Liberty Bell. The announcement was made in seven major newspapers in New York, Chicago, Los Angeles, Washington, D.C., Philadelphia, Dallas, and in *USA Today.* The announcement further explained that the bell would be renamed the "Taco Liberty Bell" and be rotated between the bell's traditional home of Philadelphia and Taco Bell's home headquarters in Irvine, California. Concerned citizens who were fed up with corporate sponsorship of anything and everything lit up phones across the country. Taco Bell's service hotline received 2,000 calls alone, and radio talk shows were overrun with upset listeners. However, what most of these people overlooked was the day the announcement was made: April 1— April Fools Day!

In an era of dull corporate pronouncements, Taco Bell made a bold move that caught the country's attention. Later in the day, Taco Bell issued a press release confessing to the carefully contrived and professionally executed communications gag and announced a $50,000 contribution to the fund to assist in the restoration of the aging national treasure. The final result was a publicity gold mine for Taco Bell.

The cost of the communication campaign was approximately $300,000; however, the value of the publicity generated by the campaign far exceeded Taco Bell's out-of-pocket costs. The company believes that the ploy generated more than 400 TV mentions, thousands of newspaper stories and radio mentions, and perhaps the crowning glory, a full news story by Tom Brokaw of *NBC Nightly News* that evening. Experts figure that the total exposure for Taco Bell was worth several million dollars.

Source: Adapted from Bob Lamons, "Taco Bell Rings in New Age of Publicity Stunts," *Marketing News* 30, no. 11 (1996), 15. Reprinted by permission of the American Marketing Association.

personal selling is a two-way form of communication. The remainder are one-way communications, going only from the marketer to the customer. Using more than one communications tool or using any one tool repeatedly increases the chances that existing and potential customers will be exposed to the firm's message, associate it with the firm, and remember it. By reinforcing its message, the firm can ensure that existing customers as well as potential ones become more aware of "who" the firm is and what it has to offer. The firm's communications mix often lays the foundation for subsequent contact with potential consumers, making discussions with consumers easier for the provider and more comfortable for consumers.

It is important at this stage of developing the firm's communications mix to determine the communications budget. Budget-setting techniques typically covered in most introductory marketing classes include the percentage-of-sales technique, the incremental technique, the all-you-can-afford approach, competitive parity, and the objective-and-task method.[3] After the budget has been established, the target audience or audiences, objectives, and budgets are divided among the different areas of the communications mix. Each area does not have to be assigned the same task or audience as long as together they meet the overall objectives of the firm's communications strategy. Once they do, information delivery can be planned and executed and the results monitored. Consider, for example, the objective and results of Taco Bell's campaign described in Services in Action 8.2.

## DEFINING COMMUNICATIONS OBJECTIVES

The objectives of a firm's communications mix often relate directly to the service offering's stage within the product life cycle (PLC) (Table 8.2). In general, the major communication objectives within the introduction and growth stages of the PLC are to inform the customer. Informational communications introduce the service offering and create brand awareness for the firm. Informational communications also encourage trial and often prepare the way for personal selling efforts to be conducted later.

As professional service providers slowly begin to advertise, informational communications objectives tend to be the first step. Informational communications tend to be less obtrusive than other forms of communication, and in many ways the information being conveyed often provides a public service to consumers who otherwise might not have access to or knowledge of the range of services available. Legal and medical referral services that advertise are typical examples. Although many of us poke fun at the ads that lawyers place on the airways, they do serve their purpose. Many of the clients who contact these services are lower-income, lower-educated clients who have stated that if it were not for the advertisements, they would not have known where to turn.[4] Information-based

## TABLE 8.2

### Communication Content and Objectives

| Product Life Cycle Stage | Communication Content | Communication Objectives |
|---|---|---|
| Introduction | Informational | Introduce the service offering<br>Create brand awareness<br>Prepare the way for personal selling efforts<br>Encourage trial |
| Growth and maturity | Informational and persuasive | Create a positive attitude relative to competitive offerings<br>Provoke an immediate buying action<br>Enhance the firm's image |
| Maturity and decline | Persuasive and reminder | Encourage repeat purchases<br>Provide ongoing contact<br>Express gratitude to existing customer base<br>Confirm past purchase decisions |

ERVICES 8.3
N

ACTION   **Informational Role of Web Outpaces
Online Spending**

According to a recent study conducted by Jupiter Communications, "skeptical retailers eyeing fluctuations in the financial market and the increasing failure rates of Internet companies are often blind to the most important issue—specifically, the degree to which online efforts will affect their offline business." Jupiter predicts that by 2005, U.S. online consumers will spend more than $632 billion in offline channels because of information that is obtained through Web sites. In comparison, actual online purchases are forecasted to be $199 billion. Hence, web-impacted spending, which includes online spending and web-influenced offline purchases, are forecasted to reach $831 billion by 2005. As of 2000, web-impacted spending is estimated to reach $235 billion.

This report and numerous others like it point once again to the advantages that traditional brick-and-mortar firms gain by expanding their communication channels into the Internet. When it comes to selecting channels for purchasing, online users are much more agnostic—they are willing to conduct business across multiple channels. A recent study of online purchasers indicated that 68 percent researched their selections online and then purchased them from physical stores. Another 47 percent indicated that purchases were made via the telephone after conducting searches on the Web.

Consumer use of the Web for reasons other than making online purchases includes:

- Identifying price                          75 percent
- Selecting products                         63 percent
- Selecting brand/manufacturer               50 percent
- Selecting offline store                    25 percent
- Finding store location                     25 percent
- Learn about sales/promos                   23 percent
- Collect coupons online to redeem offline   18 percent

Clearly the Web is as much an informational channel as it is a distribution channel.

Source: Adapted from Adam Katz-Stone, "Web-Influenced Offline Sales Dwarf E-commerce," *Revolution* 1, no. 5 (July 2000), 8–9.

communications are also ruling the Web. By 2005 it is predicted that U.S. online consumers will spend more than $632 billion in offline channels due to information that is obtained through Web sites. In comparison, actual online purchases are forecasted to be $199 billion (see Services in Action 8.3)

Communications objectives during the growth and maturity stages of the PLC tend to lean toward informational and persuasive content. Objectives during this stage include creating a positive attitude toward the service offering relative to competitive alternatives, attempting to provoke an immediate purchase action, and enhancing the firm's image. Professional service organizations often discourage the use of persuasive advertising among their members because it pits one professional member of the organization against another. Many in professional organizations believe that members engaged in persuasive communications ultimately cheapen the image of the entire industry. As a result, promotional messages that are primarily information based are viewed as a more acceptable and tasteful method of promotion.

Finally, communications objectives during the maturity and decline stages of the PLC tend to utilize persuasive and reminder communications. The communications objectives during this phase of the PLC are to influence existing customers to purchase again, to provide ongoing contact with the existing client base in order to remind clients that the firm still values their relationship, and to confirm clients' past purchase decisions, thereby minimizing levels of felt cognitive dissonance. As with informational communications, reminder communications tend to be less obtrusive and more acceptable to professional organizations than persuasive communications.

## DIVIDING THE COMMUNICATIONS OBJECTIVES AND TARGET AUDIENCES

Once the overall objectives and target audiences for the entire communications mix have been set, it is necessary to divide the tasks among advertising, selling, publicity and public relations, and sales promotions. This is a process of matching the tasks to the capabilities of the different communications channels.

### Targeting Nonusers

If the objective is to reach nonusers of the service, then the choice of communications channel is reduced to media advertising, selling performed by a sales force rather than a service provider, and publicity and public relations.

One way of assigning tasks across the array of communications channels is to consider the degree to which the message can be targeted at specific audiences. Media advertising itself varies along this dimension. At the broadcast, "shotgun" level, television can reach a wide audience but is not especially selective except in the variation of audiences across channels by time of day. National print media such as newspapers and magazines offer more selective focus because they themselves tend to be targeted at more specific segments of consumers. Trade magazines are even more specific in their readership. Direct mail offers the most focused of the impersonal media. The choice among these media must be based on the cost per thousand members of the target audience and the risk and cost of reaching the wrong segments.

When the service provider has a broadly defined audience and little to lose in reaching the wrong segments, television advertising may work out to be the least expensive vehicle on a cost-per-person basis. However, television and other forms of mass media are unlikely to be efficient for a specialty service such as an upscale restaurant with a tightly defined target audience and a high cost associated with attracting the wrong segment.

Public relations and publicity can be either broad or tightly focused, depending on how they are used. Editorial comment can be solicited in broad or narrow media. Public relations carries with it the advantages and disadvantages of not being paid advertising. On the positive side, it is given more credence by the consumer; on the negative side, it is much more difficult to control. The content may not be designed, or the coverage may be limited.

Both media advertising and public relations and publicity are one-way forms of communication. They cannot respond to consumers' inquiries or tailor the message to the particular characteristics of the receiver. Personal or telemarketing is far more expensive per member of the target audience, but it does offer the flexibility of altering the message during the presentation. If the message is difficult to communicate or a great deal of persuasion is needed, personal communication may be most appropriate. A sales force can be highly targeted and trained to make complex arguments interactively, responding to the inputs of consumers during the process.

## Targeting Users

Users can be reached through all the channels discussed above, and they can be further reached by communications through the service provider. The role of the service provider is multifaceted. Different providers are called on to perform different communication functions. These providers and functions have been classified along the following lines[5]:

**Type 1 service staff** are required to deal with customers quickly and effectively in "once only" situations where large numbers of customers are present. The exchanges consist of simple information and limited responses to customer requests. Effective communication requires the ability to establish customer relationships quickly, deal efficiently with customer problems, and convey short, rapid messages that customers can easily understand. Typical examples include front-line personnel at fast-food restaurants or dry cleaners and patient representatives whose job is to obtain and process insurance information.

**Type 2 service staff** deal with numerous, often repeat customers in restricted interactions of somewhat longer duration. The information provided is mixed—partly simple and partly more complex—and requires some independent decision making on the part of the staff member. Communication in this category requires effective listening skills, the ability to establish trust, interpretation of customer information, and making decisions in customer relationships that are often ongoing. Communications are generally more intense than in Type 1 situations. Typical examples include relationships with suppliers or customer relationships such as with a customer who requests floral designs from a florist on a regular basis, a loyal customer of a seamstress/tailor, or an effective wait staff person at a fine dining establishment.

**Type 3 service staff** are required to have more complex communication skills. Interactions with consumers are repeated over time, extensive flow of

**type 1 service staff**
Service staff that are required to deal with customers quickly and effectively in "once only" situations where large numbers of customers are present.

**type 2 service staff**
Service staff that deal with numerous, often repeat customers in restricted interactions of somewhat longer duration.

**type 3 service staff**
Service staff required to have more highly developed communication skills because of more extended and complex interactions with customers.

FedEx improved its communications mix when it centralized its telephone customer contact system. Now employees can interact with customers and accomplish mailouts without having to worry about answering the phone during peak periods.

communication is required, and communication tasks are complicated and often nonrepeatable. Effective communication requires the ability to listen and process complicated information, to think creatively in face-to-face interactions with consumers, and to provide information in a clear and understandable manner. Typical examples include staff members who are likely to be qualified as professionals.

Any service organization may have employees in one, two, or all three of the above categories. Thus a bank may have tellers performing type 1 communications, a loan officer engaged in type 2, and a commercial loan officer engaged in type 3. A travel company may have an agent engaged in both type 2 (when writing tickets and booking arrangements) and type 3 communications (when planning trips) and a receptionist handling type 1 communications.

Each type of communication requires a different set of skills from the providers and places different levels of stress on them. It is clearly important that the correct communications role be assigned to the correct person within the organization. Type 1 is predominantly an operations role, whereas type 3 is a mixed selling and operations role.

When a communications mix that includes the service provider is developed, the final objectives for the staff will probably fall within one of the above categories; however, it is important to recall the position of the employee providing the service. The service provider is not simply a salesperson; he or she is an integral part of the operations process and a part of the experience purchased by the customer. An apparently simple decision—for example, to have a bank teller sell services—can have profound negative consequences. It could well be that the decision produces role conflict for the teller. Role/self-conflict could be caused by the tellers' wanting to see themselves not as salespeople but as bankers. Direct conflict between the two roles can arise when the operations role demands fast service and minimization of the time spent with each customer but the selling role demands the opposite. In addition, the script may break down for both the service provider and the customer as the teller tries to do something new. The customer may be expecting a brisk, businesslike transaction when suddenly the teller wants to build rapport by talking about the weather (before starting the sell).

Potentially, such a decision can also diminish operational efficiency as the transaction time per customer rises. This problem is illustrated by the experiences of FedEx before it centralized its telephone customer contact system. In times of peak demand, especially if those times were unpredicted, everyone in the FedEx depots answered telephones, including the field salespersons based at the depots. The result was that the various depot employees changed the service communication from type 1 to type 3. It also meant that calls took much longer than usual, and the telephone bottleneck consequently worsened.

## THE COMMUNICATIONS MIX AS IT RELATES TO CONSUMER BEHAVIOR CONSIDERATIONS[6]

Consumer behavior is important because it imposes constraints on the objectives set for services. It is perhaps best to consider behavior during the three phases discussed in Chapter 4—prepurchase, consumption, and postpurchase.

### The Preconsumption Choice Stage

Consumers will try to minimize risk taken in the purchase phase. Risk is some combination of consequences and uncertainty, so these are the two dimensions that the firm's communication objectives can attempt to minimize. In each case, the objective must be to ensure that the company's service is the one perceived to be the least risky alternative. For example, an Internet company can reduce consumer fears of ordering by taking the lead and communicating customer-friendly return policies. However, in a recent survey of dot-com sites, two out of three do not explicitly state whether it's the seller or the buyer who is responsible for shipping costs associated with returned items (see Services in Action 8.4).

Communication can obviously impart information that is a key factor in reducing the uncertainty in all risky decisions. It can also offer reassurance. Consequences are generally of three basic types: **financial consequences, social consequences,** and **performance consequences.** Financial consequences can be reduced by communications that ensure that consumers correctly understand the likely financial consequences of a purchase, particularly if a money-back guarantee is offered. Concerns about social consequences can be reduced by highlighting for consumers that other people are using the service and that it would not be embarrassing for them to use it. Performance consequences need to be made explicit and clearly communicated to ensure that consumers understand what would happen if the performance were not 100 percent successful. Clearly, most services are perceived as more risky on the

**financial consequences**
The perceived monetary consequences of a purchase decision by a consumer.

**social consequences**
The perceived consequences of a consumer's purchase decision among the consumer's peers or the public in general.

**performance consequences**
The perceived consequences of a consumer's purchase decision should the service perform less than 100 percent effectively.

SERVICES 8.4

ACTION    **Communicating Return Policies:**
**The Real Y2K Nightmare—E-Turns**

There is little doubt that the Internet is here to stay and that many opportunities in the field of e-service lay ahead. However, as more consumers order products on the Web, more problems for e-tailers emerge. One of those problems pertains to the customer service issue of processing exchanges and returns. Termed "The Season of E-Returns," ordering online during the 1999 holiday season turned out to be the real Y2K nightmare.

Extraprise, an e-business market research firm located in Boston, notes that of the 50 sites it researched, the vast majority had polices that penalized the customer for returns and exchanges. The company's most notable findings included the following:

- Few standard practices exist for returning purchases that were made online.
- It's the customer's responsibility to sift through the fine print to determine how exchanges and returns are to be conducted.
- In most cases the consumer has to pay the shipping cost of the returned item.
- In some cases, consumers must pay the shipping cost even if the item is delivered broken or in error.
- Many sites hide return-related expenses via hidden fees that are charged to customers.
- Dot-coms, as opposed to "click-and-mortar stores," are three times more likely to charge a restocking fee (Buy.com charges a $35 "reboxing fee") if the returned item's packaging is damaged.
- Two out of three dot-coms do not explicitly state whether the seller or buyer is responsible for the shipping costs associated with returned items.

Overall, "click-and-mortar" stores far outperformed dot-coms when it came to stating return policies and providing the customer with more friendly policies regarding exchanges and returns. Extraprise noted, "Retail brands with a reputation for providing excellent service tend to carry this trait over to their Web sites."

Source: Adapted from Becky Ebenkamp, "E-turns: Caveat Emptor," *Brandweek* 41, no. 2 (January 10, 2000), 25.

social and performance dimensions, and communications have a key role to play in reassuring customers.

The communications mix can, for example, be based on generating positive word-of-mouth references. This key communications area for services can be managed using public relations and publicity. It has also been shown to be a key method in reducing consumers' perceived risk.

The **rational mathematician model** assumes that consumers are rational decision makers using a choice matrix of attributes, brand or company scores, and importance weights like those described in the college selection example presented in chapter 4. Services in the evoked set are scored using the matrix, and the one with the highest score is chosen. Communications can be used to try to influence the choice in the following ways:

- To ensure that firm's service offering is in the evoked set
- To alter the weights consumers attach to different attributes to favor those in which the company is strong
- To alter the score on a given attribute for the company, particularly if a gap exists between performance and consumer's perceptions
- To alter the score on a given attribute given to a competitor again, particularly if a gap exists between performance and consumers' perceptions
- If the company is not in the evoked set, to build enough awareness of the offering to stimulate inclusion

It is important to remember the difference between tangible performance and perceived performance. If actual performance is higher than perceived performance, communications may be more effective than if the reverse were the case. Alternatively, advertising can be used to maintain a situation that is favorable to the firm. Consumers need to be reminded that a firm does well on particular attributes and that those attributes are important.

**rational mathematician model**
A model that assumes consumers are rational decision makers using a choice matrix of attributes, brand or company scores, and importance weights.

## The Consumption Stage

During the consumption stage, the service consumer is more or less an active participant in the production process. It is important that consumers perform that production role successfully. From the firm's point of view, successful performance will improve the efficiency of the operation and the satisfaction of other customers. From the consumer's point of view, successful performance will ensure a high level of perceived control and, in all probability, a high level of satisfaction in the postconsumption phase.

Communications, in the broadest sense, can be used to ensure successful performance by giving the consumer a clear script (Figure 8.1). Although this can be done through advertising, the presence of the consumer in the actual service setting gives the opportunity for a much broader range of communications channels. Point-of-purchase signs, service providers, and the environment itself can all be used to teach the consumer the script.

In times of operational change, managing the consumer's script takes on even more importance. An example can be seen in a bank that is changing from multiple-line queuing to single-line queuing. No longer may consumers wait in front of a specific teller window. Instead, they must form a single line and go to the first free window available to them when they arrive at the head of the line. Operationally, this offers shorter and more predictable waiting times; however, such a shift requires a script change. Arriving at the bank without prior warning of the change, the consumer finds a new experience, one that no longer conforms to

**Your recipe for a great Hamburger.**

At Wendy Restaurants we don't tell you how to have your hamburger. You tell us.

The order-taker will want to know what size hamburger you'd like. A glance at the menu will help you to make up your mind. With cheese or without?

Then you've a choice of what goes on top. Mayonnaise, Ketchup, Pickle, Fresh Onion, Juicy Tomato, Crisp Lettuce, Mustard. Choose as many as you like - or have the lot - all at no extra charge.

The rest is up to us. In no time at all you'll have a pure beef hamburger that's hot, fresh and juicy - and made just the way you like it.

**Figure 8.1   Teaching the Consumer the Script: Wendy's Hamburgers**
Source: Bateson and Hoffman, *Managing Services Marketing*, 4th ed. (Fort Worth, TX: Harcourt College Publishers, 1999), 170.

the existing script. Because it is not immediately obvious how the new system works, the customer may feel a loss of control. The line seems to be extremely long, and worse still, it is no longer possible to choose a specific, favorite teller. Clearly, the script needs to be modified.

It is fairly obvious how elements of the communications mix can be used to achieve script modification. The bank can use media advertising or leaflets to describe the new process. Contact personnel outside the bank can explain the new system to customers before they enter. Public relations can be used to generate consumer comment about the benefits of the new system. Inside the building, the layout and signs displayed can clearly signal the desired customer behavior. Finally, service providers can personally reassure customers and reinforce the new script.

## The Postconsumption Evaluation Stage

Chapter 4 also introduced the disconfirmation model of consumer satisfaction. This model hypothesizes that consumers determine satisfaction by comparing their prior expectations of performance with the perceived actual performance.

Consumer expectations come from a number of sources, some within the control of the service firm and some beyond its control. Expectations arise either from previous experience with the firm and/or its competitors or from some form of communication. The latter can encompass all aspects of the communications mix. Advertising, designed to influence prepurchase choice behavior, can set expectations in the customer's mind about the quality of service that will be received. Indeed, setting such expectations may be a key aspect of a firm's advertising strategy.

In chapter 4 you learned that, based on studies of consumer behavior, word-of-mouth communication can be expected to have an increased role in the service industry because of the high levels of perceived risk associated with the purchase of many services. Such word-of-mouth communication can be random, or it can be orchestrated through the public relations component of the communications mix. Service firms often strategically place customer testimonials in their promotional campaigns for this very reason.

# SPECIAL PROBLEMS OF THE SERVICE COMMUNICATIONS MIX[7]

## Mistargeted Communications

Segmentation is one of the basic concepts of marketing. In essence, it suggests that a firm's marketing efficiency can be improved by targeting marketing activities at discrete groups of consumers who behave differently in some way toward the firm. Although segmentation is applied in both goods and service companies, the consequences of reaching an inappropriate segment with a part of the communication mix are far less serious for goods companies than for services. If the wrong group of consumers buys a particular brand of detergent, for example, it does not really affect the company making the detergent; sales are still being generated. Or a product may have been developed for the youth market, but through some quirk of the advertising execution, the product has attracted some senior citizens. For example, take the Pepsi advertisement that portrayed the youthful effects of Pepsi being delivered to a senior citizens' home by error instead of to the college fraternity house. Let's say that the ad is interpreted by senior citizens as indicating that Pepsi will make them feel young again. Clearly, this was not Pepsi's (which targets the younger generation) original intent. Members of this group that misinterpreted the message visit the supermarket, buy the product, and use it in their homes. The negative consequences associated with the elder segment's use of the product are few.

Suppose, however, that some of the wrong segment decides to buy the services of a restaurant. An upscale concept has been developed, but to launch the restaurant, management decides to have a price promotion, and the advertising agency develops inappropriate advertising. Or, through poor management, publicity activity is unfocused and produces feature articles in the wrong media. The result is that the restaurant gets two types of customers: upscale, middle-aged couples and price-conscious groups of students. The former were the original target, and the latter were attracted by inappropriate marketing tactics. Unfortunately for the restaurant and for many other services, the other customers are part of the product. The result is that neither segment enjoys the experience because of the

**mistargeted communications**
Communications methods that affect an inappropriate segment of the market.

presence of the other, and neither type of customer returns. Hence, the consequences of **mistargeted communications** for service firms, because of the shared consumption experience, are clearly more significant than the consequences experienced by traditional goods-producing firms.

## Managing Expectations[8]

The service firm can play a key role in formulating customer expectations about its services. These are real-time expectations created during the service experience itself. Firms may reinforce pre-existing ideas or they may dramatically alter those ideas. Expectations can be set by something as explicit as a promise ("Your food will be ready in 5 minutes") or as implicit as a behavior pattern that sets a tone. Often such expectations are created unwittingly, as when a server promises to "be right back." Such a statement can be viewed both as a binding contract by a customer and as a farewell salutation by the service provider.

**technical service quality**
An objective, measurable level of performance produced by the operating system of the firm.

Perceived service also has many service sources. **Technical service quality** is an objective level of performance produced by the operating system of the firm. It is measurable with a stopwatch, temperature gauge, or other measuring instrument. Unfortunately, this is not the level of performance the customer perceives. Perception acts as a filter that moves the perceived service level up or down.

Perception is itself influenced by the same factors that dictate expectations. For example, communications can create warm feelings toward the organization that raises perceived service levels. Inappropriately dressed and ill-behaving staff can deliver high levels of technical service quality but be poorly perceived by the consumer, who will downgrade the perceived service level.

Many sources of expectations are under the direct control of the firm. Only past experience and competitors' activities cannot be directly influenced in one way or the other. Given such control, the firm must determine what the objectives of the communications mix should be.

In the absence of competition, reduced expectations will result in higher satisfaction levels, provided that levels of perceived service are maintained. One strategy would therefore be to reduce expectations as much as possible. Regardless of the service actually delivered, the customer would then be satisfied. Unfortunately, communications must also play the more traditional role of stimulating demand. It is inconsistent to think of achieving this by promising average service, even if doing so might minimize customers' expectations (for the few customers who use the service!).

In competitive terms, firms make promises and strive to build expectations that will differentiate them in the marketplace and cause customers to come to them and not to their competitors. The temptation is therefore to promise too much and to raise expectations to an unrealistic level. It is perhaps fortunate that the variability in services is well known to most consumers and that they therefore discount many of the promises made by service firms. When the promises are taken seriously, however, the result is often dissatisfied customers.

It is probably more effective to attempt to match customers' expectations to the performance characteristics of the service delivery system. In such a scenario, the behavior of the customer is most likely to conform to the script required by the operating system. There is little point, for example, in encouraging McDonald's customers to specify how well they want their hamburgers done. Not only would the customers be disappointed, but any attempt to meet their demands would destroy the efficiency of the operating system.

## Advertising to Employees

The staff of service firms frequently forms a secondary audience for any firm's advertising campaign. Clearly, communications seen by the staff, if they empathize with it, can be highly motivating. However, if communications are developed without a clear understanding of the operational problems, it can imply service performance levels that are technically or bureaucratically impossible; that is, it can set expectation levels unrealistically high. This has a doubly detrimental effect on the staff because (1) it shows that people who developed the communications (the marketing department) did not understand the business and (2) it raises the prospects that customers will actually expect the service to operate that way, and the staff will have to tell them that the reality differs from the level of service portrayed in the firm's communications. In both cases, the impact will be a negative influence on staff motivation, which will, in turn, negatively influence customer satisfaction. A classic example involved American Airlines. The company ran an ad that featured a flight attendant reading a young child a story during the flight. As a result, passengers expected the flight attendants to tend to their children, and flight attendants were miffed by the implication that they were suppose to be baby sitters in addition to all of their other duties.

The bottom line is that in order for service firms to succeed, they must first sell the service job to the employee before they sell the service to the customer.[9] For years, communications from Southwest Airlines have shown smiling employees going to great lengths to please the customer. Although the communications are clearly targeted toward customers, they also send a message to employees regarding appropriate role behavior. In the end, service communications not only provide a means of communicating with customers, but also serve as a vehicle to communicate, motivate, and educate employees.[10]

## Selling/Operation Conflicts

Another consideration unique to the service sector is that the individuals who sell the service are often the same people who provide the service. In many instances, the service provider is much more comfortable providing the service than marketing his or her own abilities. However, in some cases, providers become so involved in the communications aspects of their firm that they no longer actively participate in the operations end of the business.

The conflicts associated with selling versus operations are at least twofold. First are the economic considerations. Typically, service providers are paid for providing services and are not paid for time spent on communications activities. Clearly the provider must engage in marketing activities in order to generate future customers, but the time spent on marketing does not generate revenues for the provider at that particular moment. Moreover, the time spent on communications activities is often while an ongoing project is being conducted. This means that the time dedicated to communications activities must be considered when estimating completion dates to customers. Often the firm's communications efforts must occur while previously sold services are being processed in order to avoid shutdown periods between customer orders.

The second conflict that arises is often role related. Many professional service providers believe that communications activities such as personal selling are not within their areas of expertise. Consequently, some providers feel uncomfortable with communications activities, and, even more disturbing, some providers feel that this type of activity is beneath them. The health care field in particular has been plagued by this problem through the years; however, increased competition in the health care arena has lead to a recognition of the need for marketing training directed at technical specialists. Many health care institutions, particularly the good ones, now embrace the importance of the firm's communication efforts.

## GENERAL GUIDELINES FOR DEVELOPING SERVICE COMMUNICATIONS

After a review of the literature that directly examines the specifics of advertising services, several common themes emerge that create guidelines for advertising services. Many of these guidelines have developed directly as a result of the intangibility, inseparability, heterogeneity, and perishability inherent in service products.

### Develop a Word-of-Mouth Communications Network

Consumers of services often rely on personal sources of information more than nonpersonal sources to reduce the risk associated with a purchase. Given the importance of nonpersonal sources, communications should be developed that facilitate the creation of a word-of-mouth network. Advertising that features satisfied customers and promotional strategies that encourage current customers to recruit their friends are typical. Other communication strategies such as presentations for community and professional groups and sponsorship of community and professional activities have also been effective in stimulating word-of-mouth communications.

### Promise What Is Possible

In its most basic form, customer satisfaction is developed by customers' comparing their expectations with their perceptions of the actual service delivery process. In times of increasing competitive pressures, firms may be tempted to overpromise. Making promises the firm cannot keep initially increases customer expectations and then subsequently lowers customer satisfaction as those promises are not met.

Two problems are associated with overpromising. First, customers leave disappointed, and a significant loss of trust occurs between the firm and its customers. Moreover, disappointed customers are sure to tell others of their experience, which increases the fallout from the experience. The second problem directly affects the service firm's employees. Working for firms that make false promises places employees in compromising and often confrontational positions. Front-line personnel are left to repeatedly explain to customers why the company cannot keep its promises. Given the link between employee satisfaction and customer satisfaction, creating expectations that cannot be met can have devastating long-term effects.

## Tangibilize the Intangible[11]

In Chapter 1 we discussed that the distinction between goods and services is unclear and presented the scale of market entities—a continuum that assesses the tangible properties of the market entity, ranging from tangible dominant to intangible dominant. Interestingly, tangible dominant market entities such as perfume use image development in their advertising schemes. From a basic viewpoint, perfume is simply liquid scent in a bottle. The customer can pick it up, try it on, and smell the perfume's fragrance. Hence, the perfume is tangible dominant. As with many tangible dominant products, the advertising tends to make them more abstract in order to differentiate one product from another. For example, when you think of the fragrance Calvin Klein, what images come to mind? The company uses these images to differentiate its product from competitive offerings.

In contrast, services are already abstract. Hence, one of the principal guidelines for advertising a service is to make it more concrete. This explains why insurance companies use tangible symbols to represent their companies. For example, Merrill Lynch has the "bull," Prudential uses "the rock," and Traveler's Insurance promotes "the power of the pyramid." Insurance products are already abstract, so it becomes the advertisement's objective to explain the service in simple and concrete terms. In addition to tangible symbols, other firms have tangibilized their service offerings by using numbers in their advertisements, such as, "We've been in

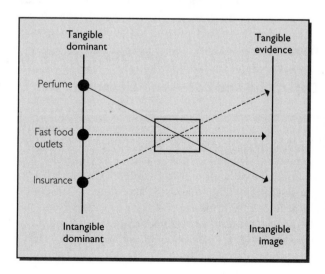

**Figure 8.2**
**The Impact of Intangibility: Different Communication Strategies for Different Products**
Source: Adapted from G. Lynn Shostack, "Breaking Free from Product Marketing," *The Journal of Marketing* (April 1977).

business since 1925," or "Nine out of ten customers would recommend us to a friend."

In tangiblizing the intangible, the scale of market entities should be turned on its ends (Figure 8.2). The advertising of tangible dominant products tends to make them more abstract in order to differentiate them from one another. In contrast, the advertising of intangible dominant products should concentrate on making them more concrete through the use of physical cues and tangible evidence. The advertising of products in the middle of the continuum often uses both approaches. McDonald's, for example, promotes "food, folks, and fun" in its advertisement. Food and folks are concrete and fun is abstract.

## Feature the Working Relationship between Customer and Provider

As you should well understand by now, service delivery is an interactive process between the service provider and the customer. Because of inseparability, it is appropriate in the firm's advertising to feature a company representative and a customer working together to achieve a desired outcome. H&R Block advertising commonly shows a company representative and a customer interacting in a friendly and reassuring manner. Many financial institutions, legal firms, and insurance companies also follow this same model. The advertising of services in particular must concentrate not only on encouraging customers to buy, but also on encouraging employees to perform. Clearly, advertising that illustrates the inseparability of the service delivery process should target both the customer and the firm's service providers.

## Reduce Consumer Fears about Variations in Performance

The firm's advertising can also minimize the pitfalls of heterogeneity in the customer's mind. To enhance the perception of consistent quality, the firm's advertising should provide some form of documentation that reassures the customer. Typical examples include stating the firm's performance record through numbers as opposed to qualitative testimonials. The use of "hard" numbers in advertisements reduces the consumer's fear of variability and also tangibilizes the service, as mentioned earlier.

## Determine and Focus on Relevant Service Quality Dimensions

The reasons customers choose among competing services are often closely related to the five dimensions of service quality—reliability, responsiveness, assurance, empathy, and the quality of the tangibles associated with the service; however, it is common that some features are more important to customers than others. For example, 30 percent of today's airline customers list "safety" as one of their top five considerations when choosing an airline.[12] Consequently, it would be appropriate for airlines to emphasize the assurance dimension of service quality by featuring the airline's safety record, maintenance and training programs, and any certified aspects of their particular airline operation. One advertising campaign that backfired promoted a hotel as one of the tallest hotels in the world. Although this reinforced the tangible dimension of service quality, this particular tangible component was not very important to customers in choosing hotels. In fact, many customers who had even the slightest fear of heights avoided the hotel for fear of being placed on an upper floor.

## Differentiate the Service Product Via the Service Delivery Process

A dramatic difference exists between what the service provides and how it is provided. Identifying the various inputs into the process that contribute to a competitive or quality advantage and stressing these inputs in the firm's advertising is likely to be a successful approach. On the surface, it appears somewhat difficult to differentiate one tax accountant from the next. However, if we consider the process of obtaining a consultation, which consists of calling to make an appointment, interacting with staff at the front desk, the appearance of the office in the reception area where the client is waiting, the appearance of the accountant's office, the interaction between the client and the accountant, and the payment procedures, several potential areas for differentiation arise. Outlining the various inputs within the service delivery process may indicate key competitive and/or quality advantages that traditionally have been overlooked.

## Make the Service More Easily Understood

Services can be more fully explained to potential customers via the communications mix by presenting the service as a series of events. When questioned, consumers often break down the service experience into a series of sequential events. Understanding the sequence permits the service provider to view the service from the customer's perspective. For example, bank customers may first view the external building, parking facilities, landscaping, and cleanliness of the grounds. When entering the bank, customers notice the interior furnishings, odors, music, temperature, and service personnel. While conducting bank transactions, the appearance and demeanor of specific contact personnel become additional quality cues. Hence, perceptions of quality are assessed at each stage of the service encounter. Advertising developed from the sequence-of-events perspective considers the customer throughout the process and highlights the firm's strengths in each area.

## SPECIAL CONSIDERATIONS OF PROFESSIONAL SERVICE PROVIDERS

Professional service providers often experience distinct challenges that may be tempered by the development of an effective communications program.[12] Specifically, the 10 most frequent problems encountered include the following:

   **1.** *Third-Party Accountability.* Investors, insurance companies, banks, governmental agencies, and even members of their own professions often hold professional service providers accountable for their actions or at least monitor those actions. Creating credibility and projecting the image of a quality firm to third parties can be accomplished through the firm's communications mix, thereby minimizing excessive scrutiny by outside parties. Communication strategies that come to mind include conducting business seminars, giving speeches, and writing trade articles.[13]

Business seminars in the professional's area of specialization demonstrate the provider's expertise not only to potential and existing clients, but also to interested third parties, particularly other industry members. Speeches to local civic organizations as well as national conventions spotlight the firm's talents and further enhance the firm's image. Reprints of articles should be included in company newsletters and sent to appropriate audiences.

**2.** *Client Uncertainty.* Many professional services are costly, are associated with danger or importance, and are, in some cases, technical and specialized, making them difficult for the customer/client to understand. Effective communications can describe the procedures involved, show the likely outcomes (which manages consumer expectations), answer consumers' common questions, and/or minimize consumers' areas of concern. For example, many surgical centers send patients informational pamphlets that describe surgical procedures prior to the patient's scheduled appointment.

**3.** *Experience Is Essential.* Communications must be effective in attracting and maintaining the customer base. The opening of a new doctor's office is not greeted with nearly the enthusiasm as that of a new restaurant. Once again, offering seminars, becoming a member of local organizations, speaking at civic functions or on talk-radio programs, and writing articles for local consumption are great ice breakers.

**4.** *Limited Differentiability.* As the level of competition increases among professional service providers, differentiation among providers decreases as they match one another's offerings with comparable alternatives. Communications that differentiate the provider on factors beyond the mere service product itself, such as personnel, customer service, and image, must be communicated to the marketplace to set the provider apart from the crowd (see Table 8.1)

**5.** *Maintaining Quality Control.* Because the consumer is part of the service production process, he or she ultimately has a large amount of control over the quality of the final outcome. Communications that stress the importance of following the professional's advice and its relationship to positive outcomes educates the consumer about the importance of his or her own role in the service delivery system.

**6.** *Turning Doers into Sellers.* In many instances the employment of outside sales representatives to market professional services to clientele is inappropriate and ineffective. Client uncertainty dictates that the professional provider herself must become actively involved in the sales process to reassure clients and minimize their fears. Ultimately, no one should be able to sell the available service better than the provider. However, whereas some providers thrive on making sales, many other providers feel uncomfortable when thrust into the sales spotlight.

**7.** *The Challenge of Dividing the Professional's Time between Marketing and Providing Services.* Directly related to the previous point are the problems associated with the professional's becoming too involved in the personal selling component of the firm's communications mix. Professionals generate revenues by billing for the time that they are servicing existing customers. Marketing activities not only consume a portion of the professional's billable hours, but the professional does not get paid directly for the time spent conducting marketing efforts. As a result, the professional must make decisions about how much personal time to allocate to marketing activities and also how to divide that time among cultivating new prospects, maintaining relationships with existing clients, and becoming involved in more general public relations work.

**8.** *Tendencies To Be Reactive Rather than Proactive.* The pressure of everyday business cuts into the amount of time the professional can devote to marketing activities. Existing customers demand the attention of the provider in the short run by expecting services to be delivered in an expedient manner. As a result, many professionals find themselves in a reactive mode as they search out new business while existing business transactions end. This creates the unenviable position of attempting to run a business while moving from one client to the next. Often, slack time develops between clients, which negatively affects the cash flow of the operation, not to mention placing increased pressure on the desperate provider looking for new clients.

The communications mix should not be based solely on the professional's personal selling efforts. Ongoing communications must work for the provider in a proactive manner while the provider performs everyday activities with existing clientele. The professional can make better use of the time devoted to marketing efforts by focusing on closing the sale, not starting from scratch.

**9.** *The Effects of Advertising Are Unknown.* In the not-so-distant past, many professional organizations such as those for U.S. lawyers forbade their members to engage in marketing communication activities. However, in 1978 the courts ruled that the ban on marketing communications was unconstitutional (*Bates* v. *The State Bar of Arizona*). Despite the ruling, some members of professional societies still frown upon the use of certain communication methods such as traditional advertising.

Consumer groups are particularly advocating that professional service providers engage in active marketing communications. Consumer advocates believe that an increase in communication efforts will provide consumers with much-needed information and increase the level of competition among providers. They also believe that as a result of the increase in competition, prices will fall and the quality of service will improve. However, service providers such as those in the health care arena do not agree. Health care providers quickly point to the legal profession and state that increasing communications will likely have a negative impact on their profession's image, credibility, and dignity. In addition, health care professionals believe that customer benefits created by increased communications efforts are unlikely. In fact, some state that if consumers believe that health care is expensive now, just wait until the profession has to start covering the costs of its communications efforts. Needless to say, the jury is still out on who is correct. However, as time has passed and as competitive pressures among professional service providers have mounted, the use of marketing communications seems to be becoming more acceptable in general.

**10.** *Professional Providers Have a Limited Marketing Knowledge Base.* As business students, many of the terms you take for granted, such as market segments, target markets, marketing mix variables, and differentiation and positioning strategies, are totally foreign terms to many service providers. Professional service providers are trained to effectively perform their technical duties. For example, lawyers attend law schools, physicians attend medical schools, dentists attend dental schools, and veterinarians attend veterinary schools. What do all these professional providers have in common when they go into practice for themselves? They all run businesses yet have no formal business educational backgrounds.

As a result of a limited marketing knowledge base, their temptation is to develop the firm's communications mix in isolation, without regard to the firm's overall marketing strategy. Ultimately, the firm's communications mix should be consistent with targeted consumer expectations and synergistic with other elements in the marketing mix.

## Communications Tips for Professionals[14]

### TURNING CURRENT CLIENTS INTO COMPANY SPOKESPERSONS

Too often, service firms lose sight of their existing clients as they develop a communications mix with the sole purpose of attracting new business. A firm's existing client base is the heart of its business and represents a vast potential for additional revenue. Existing clients are a rich resource of further revenue and offer opportunities for business that can be generated without substantial promotional expenditures, without additional overhead, and frequently without hiring additional personnel. By being constantly on the alert for suggestions and ideas and by discovering the clients' needs and responding to them in a professional and timely manner, professional service providers essentially win over clients, who, in turn, become a perpetual advertisement for the firm. Given the importance of personal sources of information in choosing among service alternatives, having existing clients who sing the praises of your firm to others is an invaluable resource.

### FIRST IMPRESSIONS ARE EVERYTHING

**halo effect**
An overall favorable or unfavorable impression based on early stages of the service encounter.

Because of the **halo effect,** early stages of the service encounter often set the tone for consumer evaluations made throughout the service experience. As a result, providers must pay special attention to the initial interactions in the encounter because they are often the most important. First impressions are believed to often establish or deny relationships within the first four minutes of contact.[15] For example, telephone calls need to be answered promptly and politely. During a speech about service excellence, Tom Peters of *In Search of Excellence* fame reported his personal experience with telephone contact personnel at FedEx. Mr. Peters reported that in 27 of 28 cases, FedEx operators answered the phone on or before the first ring. In fact, Mr. Peters admitted that FedEx may be 28 for 28, since he assumes that he misdialed and hung up the phone on the twenty-eighth event. Peters then redialed the number, and the phone was answered before the first ring.

Communication cues on which consumers base initial impressions include Yellow Pages advertisements, signage, and an easily accessible place of business. Once the client actually arrives, the firm's reception area should be a showplace, complete with tangible clues that reinforce the firm's quality image. Possible

Printed materials such as a company's logo create a visual pathway through which the professional image of the firm can be consistently transmitted.

tangible clues in the reception area include the names of the firm and its service providers prominently displayed, furnishings that reflect the personality of the business, fresh flowers, a "brag book" that includes letters from happy customers, past company newsletters, provider profiles, and indications of the firm's involvement in the community. Finally, the reception area should be staffed by professional and pleasant customer contact personnel. Despite the importance of first impressions, many firms simply view their reception areas as waiting rooms, making little effort to enhance the esthetics of these areas. In many cases, these areas are equipped with uncomfortable and unappealing furnishings and staffed by low-paid, poorly trained personnel.

## CREATE VISUAL PATHWAYS THAT REFLECT THE FIRM'S QUALITY

The firm's printed image includes all printed communication to clients such as correspondence, annual reports, newsletters, and billings. It also includes printed material of general use, such as firm brochures, letterhead, envelopes, and business cards, as well as internal communications—from agendas to checklists, from memos to manuals. Printed materials create a **visual pathway** through which the professional image of the firm can be consistently transmitted.

From the first time the firm's business card is put into a prospective client's hand, through the first letter the client receives, and on through finished reports delivered to the client and final billings, the presentation of printed material is making an impression. With every piece of material the client receives, he or she subconsciously reacts to the quality of paper, reproduction, and binding with which the firm has produced it. And most of all, he or she is responding to the visual images the professional provider has chosen to represent the firm, starting with the logo.

**visual pathway**
Printed materials through which the professional image of the firm can be consistently transmitted, including firm brochures, letterhead, envelopes, and business cards.

Effective communication of the firm's logo assists the firm in establishing familiarity throughout the region in which it operates. In addition to identifying the firm, other primary goals of logo development are to simplify and explain the purpose of the organization. In essence, logo development can be viewed as creating a form of hieroglyphic symbol that enables others to quickly identify the professional firm. The logo is the service firm's brand.

Given the lack of a substantial marketing knowledge base, professional service providers should seriously consider engaging the advice of a communications professional. Graphic artists, ad agencies, and public relations firms are typical examples of communications specialists who work with a client to produce the kind of image that will give the firm the an individual yet professional identity that successfully positions it in the marketplace. When a logo is designed, it can be printed in various sizes and in reverse. The various forms of the logo can then be easily applied to all manner and style of printed materials. Finally, the firm's choice of stock (paper), typeface, and kind of printing (engraving, offset, or thermograph) will complete the highly professional image of its printed material and create a visual pathway that consistently communicates quality to the client.

## ESTABLISH REGULAR COMMUNICATIONS WITH CLIENTS

Every letter sent to a client or a colleague is a potential promotional opportunity. Experts suggest taking advantage of this potential from the very beginning of the relationship with the client. Every new client should receive a special letter of welcome to the firm and a sample newsletter that conveys the firm's service concept. The use of standardized letters embossed with the firm's logo, which can be adapted for different circumstances such as welcome letters, thank yous for referrals, and reminder letters of upcoming appointments, is also effective. Better yet, handwritten, personalized messages on the firm's note cards provide a personal touch.

The most important piece of regular communication with clients should be the firm newsletter. It can be as simple as an $8\frac{1}{2}$-by-11 sheet, typed at the office and photocopied, or as elaborate as a small booklet, typeset and printed in color on quality stock. Some firms choose to make their newsletters informal bulletins; others prefer to make them polished publications. Regardless of the technique, the newsletter should always have a clean, professional appearance and be filled with information valuable to the clientele.

## DEVELOP A FIRM BROCHURE

The firm's brochure is a menu of the firm's service offerings and should be the written showpiece. In addition to providing an overview of available services, firm brochures typically include the firm's history, philosophy, and profiles of personnel. To add to its flexibility, the brochure may be developed with flaps on the inside front and/or back covers for holding supplemental materials or other information that changes from time to time. Personnel profiles featuring printed photographs and biographies are likely candidates for materials that frequently change as employees move from firm to firm. The flaps for supplemental materials also provide the option to customize each brochure for particular clients who desire specific services and who will be dealing with specific personnel. The firm brochure is a prime opportunity for the professional service firm to project its uniqueness.

Ultimately, the firm brochure should be the kind of product the firm can enthusiastically present to existing and prospective clients.

## AN INFORMED OFFICE STAFF IS VITAL

Last, but definitely not least, engendering respect and pride in the firm's capability does not stop with external promotion. In fact, it starts internally, and generating a professional image for the benefit of firm staff can be as important as promoting that image to clients. Remember, the staff is in constant, direct contact with clients. Failure to effectively communicate with the firm's staff is readily apparent and quickly erases all other communication efforts to project a quality program.

## SUMMARY

This chapter has provided an overview of communications mix strategies as they apply to the marketing of services. Communication strategy is one of the key components of a firm's overall marketing mix. Its role is to inform, persuade, and remind consumers about the services being offered. The components of the communications mix include personal selling, media advertising, publicity and public relations, and sales promotion. The service firm's budget is allocated among each component of the communications mix. Depending on the target audience and the firm's objectives, some components of the mix will be utilized more often than others.

The objectives of a firm's communications mix often relate directly to the service offering's stage within the product life cycle. For instance, the content of communications during the introduction stage tends to be informational to create consumer awareness. As the service moves into the growth and maturity stages of its life cycle, the content of the communication tends to be informational and persuasive to help position the service among competing alternatives. The content of the communication mix switches to persuasive and reminder as the firm progresses through the maturity stage and into the decline stage.

A variety of special considerations that pertain to services must be addressed when developing the communication mix. These issues include mistargeted communications, the role of communications in managing consumer expectations, the effects of the communications mix on employees, and the conflicts many professional service providers face when attempting to allocate their time to marketing activities while being directly involved in the day-to-day operations of the firm.

## Key Terms

| | |
|---|---|
| Communications mix | Mistargeted communications |
| Financial consequences | Nonpersonal sources |
| Halo effect | Performance consequences |
| Media advertising | Personal selling |

Personal sources
Positioning strategy
Publicity and public relations
Rational mathematician model
Sales promotions
Social consequences

Target markets
Technical service quality
Type 1 service staff
Type 2 service staff
Type 3 service staff
Visual pathway

# Discussion Questions

1. Discuss the options available for positioning and differentiating service firms.
2. Describe the strategic differences among the four elements of the communications mix.
3. Compare the communication skills necessary to conduct Type 1, Type 2, and Type 3 transactions.
4. What is the relevance of the rational mathematician model as it relates to developing communications strategy?
5. What problems are associated with mistargeted communications? Why do they occur?
6. Why should service employees be considered when developing communications materials?
7. Discuss how insurance companies make their services more easily understood.
8. What problems arise in turning professional service providers into proactive marketing personnel?
9. Discuss the concept of visual pathways.

# Notes

1. This section is adapted from John E. G. Bateson, *Managing Services Marketing,* 2nd ed. (Fort Worth, Tex.: The Dryden Press, 1992), pp. 393–401.
2. Adapted from Philip Kotler, *Marketing Management,* 9th ed. (Englewood Cliffs, N.J.: Prentice Hall, 1997), pp. 279–305.
3. See, for instance, Louis E. Boone and David L. Kurtz, *Contemporary Marketing,* 8th ed. (Fort Worth, Tex.: The Dryden Press, 1995).
4. Based on a customer satisfaction study conducted by K. Douglas Hoffman for Rainmaker Marketing's North Carolina Lawyer Referral Service.
5. Bernard H. Booms and Jody L. Nyquist, "Analyzing the Customer/Firm Communication Component of the Services Marketing Mix," in *Marketing of Services,* James H. Donnelly and William R. George, eds. (Chicago: American Marketing Association, 1981), pp. 172–177.
6. This section is adapted from Bateson, *Managing Services Marketing,* 3rd ed., pp. 338–341.

7. This section has been modified from William R. George and Leonard L. Berry, "Guidelines for the Advertising of Services," *Business Horizons* 24, no. 4 (July–August 1981), 52–56.
8. This section is adapted from Bateson, *Managing Services Marketing*, 2nd ed., pp. 397–399.
9. W. Earl Sasser and Stephen P. Albeit, "Selling Jobs in the Service Sector," *Business Horizons* (June 1976), 64.
10. George and Berry, "Guidelines for the Advertising of Services."
11. Donna H. Hill and Nimish Gandhi, "Service Advertising: A Framework to Its Effectiveness," *The Journal of Services Marketing* 6, no. 4 (Fall 1992), 63–77.
12. This section adapted from Philip Kotler and Paul N. Bloom, *Marketing Professional Services* (Englewood Cliffs, N.J.: Prentice-Hall, 1984), pp. 9–13.
13. Cyndee Miller, "Airline Safety Seen as New Marketing Issue," Marketing News, July 8, 1991, pp. 1, 11.
14. This section adapted from Jack Fox, *Starting and Building Your Own Accounting Business* (New York: John Wiley & Sons, 1994).
15. Leonard Zunin and Natalie Zunin, *Contact: The First Four Minutes* (Los Angeles: Nash Publishing, 1972).

## chapter 9

# Managing the Firm's Physical Evidence

## CHAPTER OBJECTIVES

This chapter's purpose is to provide you with an understanding of the importance of the service firm's physical evidence regarding customer perceptions of the quality of services provided.

After reading this chapter, you should be able to:

- Define the various elements that make up the firm's physical evidence.
- Discuss the strategic role of physical evidence as it relates to the marketing of service firms.
- Explain the stimulus-organism-response (SOR) model.
- Discuss the major components of the servicescapes model.
- Discuss the use of sensory cues when developing tactical design strategies.
- Discuss design considerations for low-contact versus high-contact firms.

"From the customer's point of view, if they can see it, walk on it, hold it, step in it, smell it, carry it, step over it, touch it, use it, even taste it, if they can feel it or sense it, it's customer service."

Kristen Anderson
& Ron Zemke
"Delivering Knock Your
Socks Off Service"

# Introduction

Managing the firm's physical evidence includes everything tangible, from the firm's physical facilities to brochures and business cards to personnel. A firm's physical evidence affects the consumer's experience throughout the duration of the service encounter. Consider the average consumer's restaurant experience.[1]

Before entering the restaurant, customers begin to evaluate it based on advertising they may have seen on television or in the phone book. As the consumer drives to the restaurant, the location, the ease with which the location can be found, the restaurant's sign, and the building itself all enter into the consumer's evaluation process. Similarly, the availability of parking spaces, the cleanliness of the parking lot, and the smells that fill the air once the customer steps out of the car affect consumer expectations and perceptions.

Upon entering, the restaurant's furnishings, cleanliness, and overall ambience provide further evidence regarding the quality of the ensuing experience. The appearance and friendliness of the firm's personnel and the ease with which customers can move about and find telephones and restrooms without asking also enters into the consumer's mind.

When seated at a table, the customer notices the stability and quality of the table and chairs and the cleanliness of napkins, silverware, and the table itself. Additional evaluations occur as well: is the menu attractive? Is it readable or crumbled and spotted with food stains from past customers? How are the waitstaff interacting with other customers? What do the other customers look like?

Once the meal is served, the presentation of the food is yet another indicator of the restaurant's quality. Consumers will make comparisons of the food's actual appearance and the way it is pictured in advertisements and menus. Of course, how the food tastes also enters into the customer's evaluation.

Upon completing the meal, the bill itself becomes a tangible clue. Is it correct? Are charges clearly written? Is the bill clean, or is it sopping wet with spaghetti sauce? Are the restrooms clean? Did the waitstaff say thank you and really mean it?

## THE STRATEGIC ROLE OF PHYSICAL EVIDENCE

Because of the intangibility of services, service quality is difficult for consumers to objectively evaluate. As a result, consumers often rely on the tangible evidence that surrounds the service to help them form their evaluations. The role of physical evidence in the marketing of intangibles is multifaceted (see Services in Action 9.1). Physical evidence can fall into three broad categories: (1) facility exterior, (2) facility interior, and (3) other tangibles. Examples of the elements that compose the **facility exterior** include the exterior design, signage, parking, landscaping, and the surrounding environment. For example, the facility may be built on a mountainside, overlooking a lake. The **facility interior** includes elements such as the interior design, equipment used to serve the customer directly or used to run the business, signage, layout, air quality, and temperature. Other **tangibles** that are part of the firm's physical evidence include such items as business cards, stationery, billing statements, reports, employee appearance, uniforms, and brochures.[2]

**facility exterior**
The physical exterior of the service facility; includes the exterior design, signage, parking, landscaping, and surrounding environment.

**facility interior**
The physical interior of the service facility; includes the interior design, equipment used to serve customers, signage, layout, air quality, and temperature.

**tangibles**
Other items that are part of the firm's physical evidence, such as business cards, stationery, billing statements, reports, employee appearance, uniforms, and brochures.

SERVICES *9.1*

IN ACTION     **The Maintenance of Physical Evidence**

The role of physical evidence in the marketing of intangibles is multifaceted. The firm's exterior, interior design, and other tangibles create a package that surrounds the service. In a study of 1,540 hospitality-related service failures, 123 of the failures were attributed to problems associated with the hospitality firms' physical facilities. Typical facility problems include the following:

## Mechanical Problems

- *Core Mechanical Problems* (e.g., core service is not available due to catastrophic mechanical problems such as airline engine problems)
- *Mechanical Problems Relating to the Core* (e.g., core service is available; however, inoperative equipment relating to the core inconvenienced the customer, such as computers, shower heads, toilets, heating and cooling equipment)

## Cleanliness Issues

- *Foreign Object (nonliving/nonhuman-related)* (e.g., foreign objects such as plastic, wood, and glass found in food, bedding)
- *Foreign Object (human-related)* (e.g., foreign objects such as hair, blood, fingernails, and used Band-aids found in food, bedding)
- *Foreign Object (insect/animal-related)* (e.g., foreign objects such as ants, flies, mice, and worms found in food, bedding, hotel room).
- *General Cleanliness Issues* (e.g., hotel room or plane not cleaned, deteriorating conditions)
- *Smells* (e.g., strange and/or offensive odors)

## Design Issues

- *Poor Facility Planning* (e.g., undesirable view from room, sleeping quarters located next to hotel ballrooms and/or elevators, slippery walkways, dangerous conditions)

After examining the results, a number of interesting observations can be made. First, based on our study of 1,540 service failures that have occurred in the hospitality sector, 123 (8 percent) are attributed to facility-based failures. The types of facility-based failures that are most likely to occur, in order of frequency of occurrence, include cleanliness issues, mechanical problems, and facility design issues. When asked to evaluate the magnitude of these three main failure types, respondents indicated that cleanliness issues were the most serious, followed by mechanical problems and facility design issues.

Respondents also reported that the offending firms were able to recover more effectively from design issues than mechanical problems and cleanliness issues. Perhaps the most striking finding from this study is that the vast majority of service failures attributed to facilities do not apply to facility design factors directly. In fact, only 4 percent of the failures mentioned dealt specifically with facility design issues. However, nearly 96 percent of failures dealt with the maintenance of these same facilities, with 39 percent pertaining to mechanical problems and approximately 57 percent relating directly to cleanliness issues.

The importance of facility maintenance is reinforced when we consider the customer retention rates associated with each type of failure. Although the overall retention rate for facility-based failures is 60.2 percent, the recovery rate for facility design issues is 80 percent. In comparison, mechanical problems and cleanliness issues reported much lower customer retention rates of 64.6 percent and 55.7 percent respectively. In other words, the lack of proper facility maintenance is driving customers away, who experience facility-based failures at a rate of one third to nearly one half. Clearly, the design of facilities is important, but their impact on customers is only as good as how well these facilities are maintained.

Source: K. Douglas Hoffman, Scott W. Kelley and Beth C. Chung, "Facility-based Failures and Recovery Strategies," *Working Paper* (Fall 2000).

The extensive use of physical evidence varies by the type of service firm (Figure 9.1). Service firms such as hospitals, resorts, and child care facilities often make extensive use of physical evidence in facility design and other tangibles associated with the service. In contrast, service firms such as insurance and express mail drop-off locations use limited physical evidence. Regardless of the variation in usage, all service firms need to recognize the importance of managing their physical evidence in its roles of:

- packaging the service
- facilitating the flow of the service delivery process

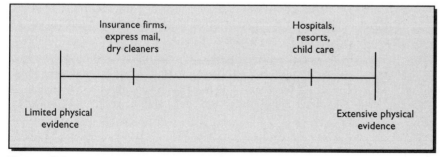

**Figure 9.1**    The Use of Physical Evidence

- socializing customers and employees alike in terms of their respective roles, behaviors, and relationships
- differentiating the firm from its competitors[3]

For example, the Rainforest Cafe and other restaurants that are sometimes described as "museums with food" offer food as an interactive experience with the carefully managed physical evidence that comprises the dining environment (see Services in Action 9.2).

## SERVICES 9.2

### ACTION    Rainforest Cafe

The Rainforest Cafe is one of a new genre of restaurants in the United States. Building on earlier concepts such as the Hard Rock Cafe and the Fashion Café, sometimes described as "museums with food," the Rainforest Cafe and similar venues offer food as part of an interactive experience.

With an average floor space of 23,000 square feet, Rainforest Cafe venues feature aquariums, live parrots, a waterfall, a mechanical crocodile, fiberglass monkeys, a video screen, a talking tree, and a regularly timed thunderstorm, complete with lightning. The concept began in the Midwest and has since spread to locations in Florida, Virginia, and Las Vegas.

The environment theme features strongly in the chain's décor and products. The restaurants make a point of not serving beef from deforested land or fish caught in nets. The talking trees give messages about the environment to customers waiting in line. However, the restaurants place a great deal of focus on their core business, the food, and work to ensure quality in this area. Management believes that no matter how strong the themes are, if the food is not good, the customers will not come back. Currently the estimate is that about 68 percent of customers are repeat visits, meaning the firm has been successful in this area.

So far, Rainforest Cafes have been located in centers where they are available to large crowds, primarily as attachments to large shopping centers. These high-volume traffic areas are able to generate the traffic the cafes need, in terms not only of numbers but also of demographic profile.

One important aspect of the Rainforest Cafe concept is that not all its turnover is generated by food sales. Each site also contains a 5,000 square foot retail space selling merchandise ranging from private-label merchandise such as T-shirts and embroidery to the spices and sauces featured in items on the restaurant menu. About 25 percent of annual sales currently come from these retail units, and that percentage is expected to grow.

Source: Adapted from John E. G. Bateson and K. Douglas Hoffman, *Managing Services Marketing,* 4th ed. (Fort Worth, Tex., Harcourt, 1999), 13.

## Packaging

The firm's physical evidence plays a major role in packaging the service. The service itself is intangible and therefore does not require a package for purely functional reasons. However, utilizing the firm's physical evidence to package the service does send quality cues to consumers and adds value to the service in terms of image development. Image development, in turn, improves consumer perceptions of service while reducing both levels of perceived risk associated with the purchase and levels of cognitive dissonance after the purchase.

The firm's exterior, interior elements, and other tangibles create the package that surrounds the service. The firm's physical facility forms the customer's initial impression concerning the type and quality of service provided. For example, Mexican and Chinese restaurants often utilize specific types of architectural designs that communicate to customers their firms' offerings. The firm's physical evidence also conveys expectations to consumers. Consumers will have one set of expectations for a restaurant with dimly lit dining rooms, soft music, and linen tablecloths and napkins and a different set of expectations for a restaurant that has cement floors, picnic tables, and peanut shells strewn about the floor.

## Facilitating the Service Process

Another use of the firm's physical evidence is to facilitate the flow of activities that produce the service. Physical evidence can provide information to customers on how the service production process works. Examples include signage that specifically instructs customers; menus and brochures that explain the firm's offerings and facilitate the ordering process for consumers and providers; physical structures that direct the flow of consumers while waiting; and barriers, such as counters at a dry cleaners, that separate the technical core of the business from the part of the business in which customers are involved in the production process.

## Socializing Employees and Customers

Organizational **socialization** is the process by which an individual adapts to and comes to appreciate the values, norms, and required behavior patterns of an organization.[4] The firm's physical evidence plays an important part in the socialization process by conveying expected roles, behaviors, and relationships among employees and between employees and customers. The purpose of the socialization process is to project a positive and consistent image to the public. However, the service firm's image is only as good as the image each employee conveys when interacting with the public.[5]

**socialization**
The process by which an individual adapts to the values, norms, and required behavior patterns of an organization.

Physical evidence, such as the use of uniforms, facilitates the socialization of employees toward accepting organizational goals and affects consumer perceptions of the caliber of service provided. Studies have shown that the use of uniforms:

* aids in identifying the firm's personnel
* presents a physical symbol that embodies the group's ideals and attributes
* implies a coherent group structure
* facilitates the perceived consistency of performance

- provides a tangible symbol of an employee's change in status (e.g., military uniforms change as personnel move through the ranks)
- assists in controlling the behavior of errant employees[6]

One classic example of how tangible evidence affects the socialization process of employees involves women in the military. Pregnant military personnel were originally permitted to wear civilian clothing when pregnant in lieu of their traditional military uniforms. However, the military soon noticed discipline and morale problems with these servicewomen as they began to lose their identification with their roles as soldiers. "Maternity uniforms are now standard issue in the Air Force, Army, and Navy, as well as at US Air, Hertz, Safeway, McDonald's, and the National Park Service."[7]

## A Means for Differentiation

The effective management of the physical evidence can also be a source of differentiation. For example, several airlines are now expanding the amount leg room available for passengers (see Services in Action 9.3). In addition, the appearance of personnel and facilities often have a direct impact on how consumers perceive that the firm will handle the service aspects of its business. Numerous studies have shown that well-dressed individuals are perceived as more intelligent, better workers, and more pleasant to engage in interactions.[8] Similarly, nicely designed facilities are going to be perceived as having an advantage over poorly designed alternatives.

Differentiation can also be achieved by using physical evidence to reposition the service firm in the eyes of its customers. Upgrading the firm's facilities often upgrades the image of the firm in the minds of consumers and may also attract more desirable market segments, which further aids in differentiating the firm from its competitors. On the other hand, a facility upgrade that is too elaborate

SERVICES 9.3
IN ACTION
**Airlines Attempting to Get a "Leg Up" on the Competition**

In their biggest move since the introduction of business class more than two decades ago, major airline carriers are now considering offering consumers more legroom. Airlines who are offering more legroom are hoping that this added perk will provide a differential advantage that is valued by consumers and subsequently will lead to higher profits. Consumers like Harry Dodge, a retired oil services company owner, agrees: "I have taken some transcontinental flights and developed some painful cramps in my legs. I swore I would never fly again. This extra room in coach will make a big difference for me."

Two of the major corporations leading the charge are United Airlines and American Airlines; however, their mutual goal of increasing profits is obtained through different routes.

## United's Strategy

United is dividing its coach section of airplanes into two classes—premium (referred to as economy plus) and economy. Passengers wanting the extra legroom will have to pay for it. For example, a United flight from New York to Chicago would cost $1602 for first class, $1094 for economy plus, and $324 for the cheapest economy fare. However, even passengers who do not want to pay for the extra legroom may be affected. By increasing the amount of space between the rows of seats, planes will now have fewer rows and fewer seats. Consequently, fewer economy seats will be available (best estimates are that United will reduce its economy seating by 5 percent), and customers will have to pay an additional 20 percent for the next available discount fare. In addition, some airlines are considering increasing the baggage weight limit for higher-paying passengers, thereby reducing the limits for baggage and carry-ons for budget passengers.

## American's Strategy

American Airlines is currently implementing a $70 million plan that refurbishes its fleet by providing "economy passengers more legroom than they have had on any domestic carrier in 20 years." American's strategy is to remove two rows of seats in coach cabins (each row takes up 37 inches) and provide each of the remaining 21 rows in a typical Boeing 737 with 3 extra inches. The extra room is provided at no additional charge. Samuel Buttrick, an airline analyst at Paine Webber, calls this approach "a big win for consumers . . . but it's not a way to increase profitability. What's good for the customer is not always good for the airline industry." Upon completion of the refurbishment project, American Airlines will have 6.4 percent fewer economy seats.

American believes that by offering the additional room at no cost its airline will become the number one choice for budget-minded consumers. According to American's Mike Gunn, executive vice president for marketing and planning, "By having a better product throughout coach, we think that we will be the first call that discount travelers make. We also expect to attract more business travelers who are willing to pay a higher-yielding fare."

Continental Airlines has characterized the latest moves as "fads." According to Gordon M. Bethune, CEO of Continental Airlines, "We believe at Continental in giving people what they will pay for . . . and at the end of the day, many passengers want to pay the cheapest air fare. There's more to a good product than a few inches of extra legroom. That's a dumb approach by a bunch of mediocre airlines."

Source: "Plane Seats Get Bigger, Cost More: Airlines Betting Fliers Will Pay Extra for Added Legroom," *Denver Rocky Mountain News,* February 28, 2000, pp. 2A, 31A.

may alienate some customers who believe that the firm may be passing on the costs of the upgrade to consumers through higher prices. This is precisely why many offices are decorated professionally but not lavishly.

In other instances, service firms such as Prodigy are using people in their marketing communications as physical evidence. By using carefully selected celebrities, it is hoped that consumers transfer the image of the celebrity onto the firm's brand name. In Prodigy's case, the use of people as physical evidence has been met with mixed results (see Services in Action 9.4).

## SERVICES 9.4
## IN ACTION

### People as Physical Evidence: Prodigy Misses Making the Connection

The use of physical evidence provides potential customers of intangible services an objective basis to make evaluations. Prodigy, an Internet service provider (ISP) with about 2.5 million users developed in 1984, recently enlisted the help of Aretha Franklin and Larry Bird to appear in its commercials. In the first ad, Ms. Franklin plays a nurse who is trying to page a doctor. The doctor does not respond, so Ms. Franklin grabs the microphone at the nurse's station and starts singing the doctor's name: "Paging Dr. Garetti." In the second ad, Mr. Bird plays a dorky hardware store clerk. Bored with his job, he wads up a cleaning towel and shoots it in a garbage can. The tag line "Everyone has potential. . . . Have you realized yours? . . . Are you a prodigy?" follows each commercial.

The problem with both these ads is that the customer, who has no knowledge of Prodigy, has no idea what prodigy does. There is no association with the product or mention of the product other than that Larry Bird and Aretha Franklin are prodigies. Many in the advertising industry feel that this 20 million dollar campaign is missing the connection. Says Bob Garfield, ad critic for Advertising Age International, "For people who knew what Prodigy was years ago, there is no new information about what the product is now. For people who don't know what Prodigy is now, there is no way to even know it's an ISP."

Neil Powell, creative director and president of Duffy, a branding and identity shop located in New York, also feels that the ads fall short of their potential objective. He says that the ads are a poor use of celebrity. The celebrities never discuss, refer to, or mention Internet services. Powell feels that the use of Bird and Franklin in these ads is nothing more than "gratuitous celebrity placement."

The problem with using Larry Bird and Aretha Franklin as physical evidence in this case is that no one would naturally link these two's talents with an Internet service provider. In contrast, MVP.com's use of John Elway, Wayne Gretsky, and Michael Jordan relates directly to the site. All three are legendary figures in their respective sports, and the site itself is a sports

> e-tailer. In general, celebrity endorsements of Web sites have failed to ensure a company's success. Celebrities such as William Shatner (Captain Kirk of Star Trek) and Cindy Crawford (supermodel/actress) have helped build awareness for Priceline.com and babystyle.com, but overall results remain inconclusive. Donald Trump's pitch for cozone.com did little for a company that closed its doors in less than a year. The bottom line is that the celebrity and product must fit well together to make sense.

Sources: Beth Snyder Bulik, "Most Visible Players," *Business* 2.0, September 12, 2000), p. 114; Bulik, "ADNAUSEUM," *Business* 2.0, September 12, 2000, p. 111.

## A Framework for Understanding the Use of Physical Evidence in Creating Service Environments

The use of physical evidence to create service environments and its influence on the perceptions and behaviors of individuals is referred to as **environmental psychology.** The **stimulus-organism-response (SOR) model** presented in Figure 9.2 was developed by environmental psychologists to help explain the effects of the service environment on consumer behavior.[9] The SOR model consists of three components:

1. A set of **stimuli**
2. An **organism** component
3. A set of **responses** or **outcomes**

In a service context, the different elements of the firm's physical evidence, such as exterior, interior design, lighting, and so on, compose the set of stimuli. The organism component, which describes the recipients of the set of stimuli within the service encounter, includes employees and customers. The responses of employees and customers to the set of stimuli are influenced by three basic emotional states: pleasure-displeasure, arousal-nonarousal, and dominance-submissiveness. The **pleasure-displeasure** emotional state reflects the degree to

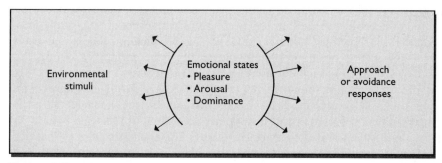

**Figure 9.2    Three Components of the SOR Model**
Source: Adapted from Robert J. Donovan and John R. Rossiter, "Store Atmosphere: An Environmental Psychology Approach," *Journal of Retailing* 58 (Spring 1982), 42.

---

**environmental psychology**
The use of physical evidence to create service environments and its influence on the perceptions and behaviors of individuals.

**stimulus-organism-response (SOR) model**
A model developed by environmental psychologists to help explain the effects of the service environment on consumer behavior; describes environmental stimuli, emotional states, and responses to those states.

**stimuli**
The various elements of the firm's physical evidence.

**organism**
The recipients of the set of stimuli in the service encounter; includes employees and customers.

**responses (outcomes)**
Consumer and/or employer reaction or behavior in response to stimuli.

**pleasure-displeasure**
The emotional state that reflects the degree to which consumers and employees feel satisfied with the service experience.

**arousal-nonarousal**
The emotional state that reflects the degree to which consumers and employees feel excited and stimulated.

**dominance-submissiveness**
The emotional state that reflects the degree to which consumers and employees feel in control and able to act freely within the service environment.

**approach/avoidance behaviors**
Consumer responses to the set of environmental stimuli that are characterized by a desire to stay or leave an establishment, explore/interact with the service environment or ignore it, or feel satisfaction or disappointment with the service experience.

**servicescapes**
The use of physical evidence to design service environments.

**remote services**
Services in which employees are physically present while customer involvement in the service production process is at arm's length.

**self-services**
Service environments that are dominated by the customer's physical presence, such as ATMs or postal kiosks.

**interpersonal services**
Service environments in which customers and providers interact.

which consumers and employees feel satisfied with the service experience. The **arousal-nonarousal** state reflects the degree to which consumers and employees feel excited and stimulated. The third emotional state, **dominance-submissiveness**, reflects feelings of control and the ability to act freely within the service environment. Ideally, service firms should use physical evidence to build environments that appeal to pleasure and arousal states and avoid creating atmospheres that create submissiveness.

Consumer and employee responses to the set of environmental stimuli are characterized as **approach behaviors** or **avoidance behaviors.** Consumer approach and avoidance behaviors and outcomes can be demonstrated in any combination of four ways (employees exhibit similar behaviors):[10]

1. A desire to stay (approach) or leave (avoid) the service establishment
2. A desire to further explore and interact with the service environment (approach) or a tendency to ignore it (avoidance)
3. A desire to communicate with others (approach) or to ignore the attempts of service providers to communicate with customers (avoid)
4. Feelings of satisfaction (approach) or disappointment (avoidance) with the service experience

## THE DEVELOPMENT OF SERVICESCAPES[11]

The framework presented in Figure 9.3 is a more comprehensive SOR model that directly applies to the influence of the service firm's physical evidence on consumers' and employees subsequent behaviors. The term **servicescapes** refers to the use of physical evidence to design service environments. Because of inseparability, the model recognizes that the firm's environment is likely to affect consumers and employees alike. However, the facility should be designed to meet the needs of those individuals who spend the most time within the confines of the facility.

### Remote, Self-Service, and Interpersonal Services

Figure 9.4 presents a continuum of facility usage by service type. Some services, such as mail order, coupon-sorting houses, and telephone and utility services are described as **remote services.** In remote services, employees are physically present, whereas customer involvement in the service production process is at arm's length. Consequently, facility design should facilitate the employees' efforts and enhance motivation, productivity, and employee satisfaction.

At the other end of the spectrum are services that customers can acquire on their own—**self-services.** Self-service environments are dominated by the customer's physical presence and include services such as ATMs, miniature golf courses, postal kiosks, and self-service car washes. The environment of self-service establishments should be constructed to enhance customer attraction and satisfaction.

In contrast to remote and self-service environments, many services such as restaurants, hospitals, hotels, banks, and airlines are **interpersonal services,**

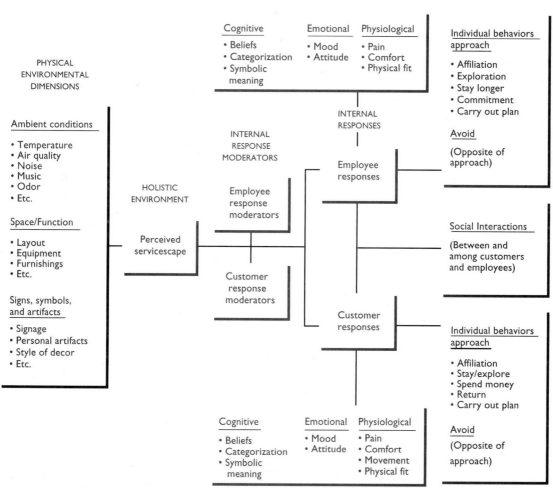

**Figure 9.3**    **The Servicescapes Model**
A framework for understanding environment-user relationships in service organizations.
Source: Mary J. Bitner, "Servicescapes: The Impact of Physical Surroundings on Customers and Employees," *Journal of Marketing* 56, no. 2 (April 1992), 60. Reprinted with permission of the American Marketing Association.

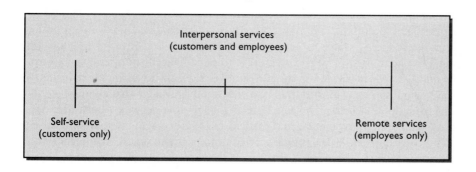

**Figure 9.4**
**Facility Usage**

**ambient conditions**
The distinctive atmosphere of the service setting, which includes lighting, air quality, noise, music, and so on.

**space/function**
Environmental dimensions that include the layout of the facility, the equipment, and the firm's furnishings.

**signs, symbols, artifacts**
Environmental physical evidence that includes signage to direct the flow of the service process, personal artifacts to personalize the facility, and the style of decor.

**holistic environment**
Overall perceptions of the servicescape formed by employees and customers based on the physical environmental dimensions.

**perceived servicescape**
A composite of mental images of the service firm's physical facilities.

**economic customers**
Consumers who make purchase decisions based primarily on price.

**personalized customers**
Consumers who desire to be pampered and attended to and who are much less price sensitive.

**apathetic customers**
Consumers who seek convenience over price and personal attention.

**ethical customers**
Consumers who support smaller or local firms as opposed to larger or national service providers.

where the physical space is shared jointly by consumers and employees. The environments of interpersonal services should be developed with the needs of both parties in mind and should facilitate the social interaction between and among customers and employees.

## Physical Environmental Dimensions

The servicescapes model depicted in Figure 9.3 begins by recognizing the set of stimuli that are commonly used when developing service environments. In broad terms, the set of stimuli include **ambient conditions, space/function,** and **signs, symbols,** and **artifacts.** Ambient conditions reflect the distinctive atmosphere of the service setting and include elements such as lighting, air quality, noise, and music. Environmental dimensions that pertain to the use of space/function include elements such as the layout of the facility, equipment, and the firm's furnishings. Signs, symbols, and artifacts include signage that directs the flow of the service process; personal artifacts, which lend character and individuality that personalize the facility; and the style of decor, such as Southwestern, contemporary, or traditional, to name a few.

## Holistic Environment

The **holistic environment** portion of the servicescapes model pertains to the perceptions of the servicescape that employees and customers form based on the physical environmental dimensions. In other words, the holistic environment is a perceived overview or image of the firm based on the physical evidence, which is referred to in the model as the **perceived servicescape.** The perceived servicescape is difficult to precisely define, and perceptions of the same establishment will vary among individuals. Essentially, the perceived servicescape is a composite of mental images of the service firm's physical facilities.

Strategically managing the perceived servicescape aids in establishing a positioning strategy that differentiates the firm from competitors and ultimately influences the customer decision process when choosing among competing alternatives. The firm should develop the servicescape with its target market in mind. Economic customers, who make purchase decisions based on price, will avoid service establishments that appear too fancy or plush, based on the perception that such an establishment will be a high-priced provider. **Economic customers** tend to be attracted to environments that are simple yet reflect quality and those that are clean and modern. Oil-change specialists such as the Jiffy Lube franchise use this type of environment. In contrast, **personalized customers** desire to be pampered and attended to and are much less price sensitive when choosing among alternative providers. Firms catering to personalized shoppers create environments that reflect the status their customers seek by investing more in items such as marble foyers, glass and brass fixtures, and furnishings that encourage customers to shop at a leisurely pace. Similarly, firms that service **apathetic customers,** who seek convenience, and **ethical customers,** who support smaller or local as opposed to larger or national service providers, should create their servicescapes accordingly.

## Internal Response Moderators

The **internal response moderators** of the servicescapes model simply pertain to the three basic emotional states of the SOR model discussed earlier: pleasure-displeasure, arousal-nonarousal, and dominance-submissiveness. The three response moderators mediate the reaction between the perceived servicescape and customers' and employees' responses to the service environment. For example, if a customer desires to remain in a state of nonarousal and spend a nice, quiet evening with someone special, that customer will avoid bright, loud, and crowded service establishments and will be attracted to environments that are more peaceful and conducive to conducting conversation. Similarly, the employees' responses to the firm's environment will also be affected by their own emotional states. Sometimes employees look forward to engaging in conversations with customers. Other days, employees would just as soon minimize conversations and process customers as raw materials on a production line. Response moderators help explain why services are characterized by heterogeneity as the service varies from provider to provider, and even from day to day with the same provider.

**internal response moderators**
The three basic emotional states of the SOR model that mediate the reaction between the perceived servicescape and customers' and employees' responses to the service environment.

## Internal Responses to the Environment

Theory asserts that customers and employees are exposed to the set of stimuli that make up the firm's perceived servicescape and the responses to these stimuli are moderated by emotional states. Customers and employees internally respond to the firm's environment at different levels—cognitively, emotionally, and physiologically.

### COGNITIVE RESPONSES

**Cognitive responses** are the thought processes of individuals and, according to the model, include beliefs, categorization, and symbolic meaning. In the formation of **beliefs,** the firm's environment acts as a form of nonverbal communication and influences a consumer's beliefs about the provider's ability to perform the service. For example, if a professor's lectures are difficult to follow in class, a student may attribute this difficulty to the professor's inability to teach or may blame himself or herself for an inability to learn the subject. Studies have shown that faced with this type of scenario, the physical environment influences consumers when they are attributing blame.[12] If the provider's office is in disarray, students are more likely to attribute poor service to the provider. Hence, physical evidence assists customers with beliefs about the provider's success, price for services, and competence. Employees form similar types of beliefs about the firm based on the overall perceived servicescape.

**cognitive responses**
The thought processes of individuals that lead them to form beliefs, categorize, and assign symbolic meanings to elements of their physical environment.

**beliefs**
Consumers' opinions about the provider's ability to perform the service.

**Categorization** is the second type of cognitive response. Bars and nightclubs operate within a number of environments. Some are high-class establishments, and others cater strictly to local clientele or specific market segments. The process of categorization facilitates human understanding at a quicker pace. Consumers assess the physical evidence and often quickly categorize new service establishments with existing types of operations. They then access the appropriate behavior script for the type of operation and act accordingly.

**categorization**
Consumer assessment of the physical evidence and a quick mental assignment of a firm to a known group of styles or types.

**symbolic meaning**
Meaning inferred from the firm's use of physical evidence.

Individuals also infer **symbolic meaning** from the firm's use of physical evidence. For example, if a nightclub features portraits of James Dean, Jimi Hendrix, Janice Joplin, Kurt Cobain, and others who have followed similar paths, the club evokes a symbolic meaning to its employees and customers. In this instance, the physical evidence may translate into a number of symbols, such as individuality, youthful success, shattered dreams, or other meanings, depending on individual interpretation. Symbolic meaning through the use of physical evidence aids in differentiation and positioning.

## EMOTIONAL RESPONSES

**emotional responses**
Responses to the firm's physical environment on an emotional level instead of an intellectual or social level.

In addition to forming beliefs, individuals will also respond to the firm's physical environment on an emotional level. **Emotional responses** do not involve thinking; they simply happen, often unexplainably and suddenly. Specific songs, for example, may make individuals feel happy, feel sad, or recreate other past feelings that were associated with the particular piece of music. Scents have similar effects on individuals. Obviously the goal of effective physical evidence management is to stimulate positive emotions that create atmospheres in which employees love to work and customers want to spend their time and money.

## PHYSIOLOGICAL RESPONSES

**physiological responses**
Responses to the firm's physical environment based on pain or comfort.

In contrast to cognitive and emotional responses, **physiological responses** are often described in terms of physical pleasure or discomfort. Typical physiological responses involve pain and comfort. Environments in which music is played very loudly may lead to employee and customer discomfort and movement away from the source of the noise. The lack of a nonsmoking section may cause some customers difficulty in breathing and further discomfort. Instead of being arousing, environments that are brightly lit may cause eye discomfort. In contrast, a dimly lit restaurant may cause eye strain as customers struggle to read their menus. All these responses determine whether a customer will approach and explore the firm's offerings or avoid and leave the premises to minimize the amount of physiological discomfort. Because of the duration of time spent in the firm's facility, employees might find the physical environment particularly harmful if mismanaged. Adequate work space, proper equipment to get the job done, and appropriate ambient conditions such as temperature and air quality are directly related to employees' willingness to continue to work, their productivity while at work, their job satisfaction, and their positive interactions with co-workers.

## Behavioral Responses to the Environment

### INDIVIDUAL BEHAVIORS

As stated in the section on the fundamentals of the SOR model, individual responses to environmental stimuli are characterized as approach and avoidance behaviors. In retail settings, the store's environment influences approach behaviors such as the following:

- shopping enjoyment
- repeat visits

- favorable impressions of the store
- money spent
- time spent shopping
- willingness of consumers to stay and explore the store

In other instances, environmental stimuli have been purposely managed to discourage unwelcome market segments. For example, some U.S. convenience stores have cleverly used "elevator music" (e.g., Muzak—boring music) outside their stores to repel unwelcome neighborhood gangs that hang out in the store's parking lot and who deter desired clientele from entering the store.

## SOCIAL INTERACTIONS

Because of the inseparability inherent in interpersonal services, the firm's servicescape should encourage interactions between employees and customers, among customers, and among employees. The challenge in creating such an environment is that often what the customer desires employees would prefer to forego so that they can complete their tasks with a minimum of customer involvement. Environmental variables such as physical proximity, seating arrangements, facility size, and flexibility in changing the configuration of the servicescape define the possibilities and place limits on the amount of social interaction possible.[13]

Consider the seating arrangements of a Japanese steakhouse, which combines different groups of customers at one table as opposed to traditional seating arrangements in which each party has its own table. Obviously, for better or worse, "community seating" at a Japanese steakhouse encourages interaction among customers. In addition, each table is assigned its own chef who interacts with the customers during the production process. Similar strides have been made in increasing consumer interaction at Max's and Erma's restaurants. Tables are numbered overhead and equipped with phones that enable customers to call one another. Oversized booths at Outback Steakhouse permit the waitstaff to actually sit at the customer's table while explaining the menu and taking dinner orders. This type of approach, while initially awkward to some customers who are not familiar with the practice (a modification to the traditional restaurant script), facilitates the amount of interaction between the waitstaff and their customers and yet permits them to stay within the traditional boundary of simply taking and delivering orders.

## SPECIFIC TACTICS FOR CREATING SERVICE ATMOSPHERES

When developing the facility's atmosphere, the service firm must consider the physical and psychological impact of the atmosphere on customers, employees, and the firm's operations. Just as the firm cannot be all things to all people, the atmosphere developed will likely not appeal to all consumers. Therefore, firms should develop facilities with a particular target market in mind. Experts suggest answering the following questions before implementing an atmosphere development plan:[14]

1. Who is the firm's target market?
2. What does the target market seek from the service experience?

3. What atmospheric elements can reinforce the beliefs and emotional reactions that buyers seek?
4. How do these same atmospheric elements affect employee satisfaction and the firm's operations?
5. Does the suggested atmosphere development plan compete effectively with competitors' atmospheres?

Ultimately, individuals base their perceptions of a firm's facilities on their interpretation of sensory cues. The following section discusses how firms can utilize the senses of sight, sound, scent, touch, and taste in creating sensory appeals that enhance customer and employee attraction responses.[15]

## Sight Appeals

**sight appeals**
Stimuli that result in perceived visual relationships.

**size, shape, colors**
The three primary visual stimuli that appeal to consumers on a basic level.

**harmony**
Visual agreement associated with quieter, plusher, and more formal business settings.

**contrast/clash**
Visual effects associated with exciting, cheerful, and informal business settings.

The sense of sight conveys more information to consumers than any other sense and therefore should be considered the most important means available to service firms when developing the firm's atmosphere. **Sight appeals** can be defined as the process of interpreting stimuli, resulting in perceived visual relationships.[16] On a basic level, the three primary visual stimuli that appeal to consumers are **size, shape,** and **colors.** Consumers interpret visual stimuli in terms of visual relationships, consisting of perceptions of harmony, contrast, and clash. **Harmony** refers to visual agreement and is associated with quieter, plusher, and more formal business settings. In comparison, **contrast** and **clash** are associated with exciting, cheerful, and informal business settings. Hence, based on the size, shape, and colors of the visual stimuli used and the way consumers interpret the various visual relationships, extremely differing perceptions of the firm emerge. For example, consider how different target markets might respond to entering a Chuck E. Cheese restaurant for the first time. Some segments would find the environment inviting, whereas others might be completely overwhelmed by too much stimuli.

### SIZE PERCEPTIONS
The actual size of the firm's facility, signs, and departments conveys different meanings to different markets. In general, the larger the size of the firm and its corresponding physical evidence, the more consumers associate the firm with importance, power, success, security, and stability. For many consumers, the larger the firm, the lower the perceived risk associated with the service purchase. Such consumers believe that larger firms are more competent and more likely to engage in service recovery efforts when problems do arise. Still other customers enjoy the prestige often associated with conducting business with a larger, well-known firm. On the flip side, other customers may view large firms as impersonal and uncaring and seek out smaller niche firms that they view as more personal, intimate, and friendly. Hence, depending on the needs of the firm's target market, size appeals differently to different segments.

### SHAPE
Shape perceptions of a service firm are created from a variety of sources, such as the use and placement of shelves, mirrors, and windows, and even the design of

wallpaper if applicable. Studies show that different shapes arouse different emotions in consumers. Vertical shapes or vertical lines are perceived as "rigid, severe, and lend[ing] a masculine quality to an area. It expresses strength and stability . . . gives the viewer an up-and-down eye movement…tends to heighten an area, gives the illusion of increased space in this direction."[17] In contrast, horizontal shapes or lines evoke perceptions of relaxation and restfulness. Diagonal shapes and lines evoke perceptions of progressiveness, proactiveness, and movement. Curved shapes and lines are perceived as feminine and flowing. Utilizing similar and/or dissimilar shapes in facility design will create the desired visual relationship of harmony, contrast, or clash. For example, the use of several different shapes in one area might be used to distinguish an area of emphasis.[18]

## COLOR PERCEPTIONS

The color of the firm's physical evidence often makes the first impression, whether seen in the firm's brochure, the business cards of its personnel, or the exterior or interior of the facility itself. The psychological impact of color on individuals is the result of three properties: hue, value, and intensity. **Hue** refers to the actual family of the color, such as red, blue, yellow, or green. **Value** defines the lightness and darkness of the colors. Darker values are called **shades,** and lighter values are called **tints. Intensity** defines the brightness or the dullness of the hue.

Hues are classified into warm and cool colors. Warm colors include red, yellow, and orange hues, whereas cool colors include blue, green, and violet hues. Warm and cool colors symbolize different things to different consumer groups, as presented in Table 9.1. In general, warm colors tend to evoke consumer feelings of

**hue**
The actual color, such as red, blue, yellow, or green.

**value**
The lightness and darkness of the colors.

**shades**
Darker values.

**tints**
Lighter values.

**intensity**
The brightness or the dullness of the colors.

## TABLE 9.1

### Perceptions of Colors

|  | Warm Colors |  |  | Cool Colors |  |
|---|---|---|---|---|---|
| **Red** | **Yellow** | **Orange** | **Blue** | **Green** | **Violet** |
| Love | Sunlight | Sunlight | Coolness | Coolness | Coolness |
| Romance | Warmth | Warmth | Aloofness | Restfulness | Shyness |
| Sex | Cowardice | Openness | Fidelity | Peace | Dignity |
| Courage | Openness | Friendliness | Calmness | Freshness | Wealth |
| Danger | Friendliness | Gaiety | Piety | Growth |  |
| Fire | Gaiety | Glory | Masculinity | Softness |  |
| Sin | Glory |  | Assurance | Richness |  |
| Warmth | Brightness |  | Sadness | Go |  |
| Excitement | Caution |  |  |  |  |
| Vigor |  |  |  |  |  |
| Cheerfulness |  |  |  |  |  |
| Enthusiasm |  |  |  |  |  |
| Stop |  |  |  |  |  |

Source: Dale M. Lewison, *Retailing*, 4th ed. (New York: Macmillan, 1991), p. 277.

comfort and informality. For example, red commonly evokes feelings of love and romance, yellow evokes feelings of sunlight and warmth, and orange evokes feelings of openness and friendliness. Studies have shown that warm colors, particularly red and yellow, are a better choice than cool colors for attracting customers in retail settings. Warm colors are also said to encourage quick decisions and work best for businesses where low-involvement purchase decisions are made.

In contrast to warm colors, cool colors are perceived as aloof, icy, and formal. For example, the use of too much violet may dampen consumer spirits and depress employees who have to continuously work in the violet environment. Although cool colors do not initially attract customers as well as warm colors, cool colors are favored when the customer needs to take time to make decisions, such as the time needed for high-involvement purchases. Despite their different psychological effects, when used together properly, combinations of warm and cool colors can create relaxing, yet stimulating atmospheres.

The value of hues also psychologically affects the firm's customers. Offices painted in lighter colors tend to look larger, whereas darker colors may make large, empty spaces look smaller. Lighter hues are also popular for fixtures such as electrical face plates, air conditioning vents, and overhead speaker systems. The lighter colors help the fixtures blend in with the firm's environment. On the other hand, darker colors can be used to grab consumers' attention. Retailers are often faced with the problem that only 25 percent of their customers ever make it more than halfway into the store. Some retailers have had some success in attracting more customers farther into the store by painting the back wall a darker color that attracts the customer's attention.

The intensity of the color also affects perceptions of the service firm's atmosphere. For example, bright colors make objects appear larger than duller colors; however, bright colors are perceived as harsher and "harder," whereas duller colors are perceived as "softer." In general, children appear to favor brighter colors, and adults tend to favor softer tones.

## THE LOCATION OF THE FIRM

The firm's location is dependent on the amount of customer involvement necessary to produce the service. Whereas low-contact services should consider locating in remote sites that are less expensive and closer to sources of supply, transportation, and labor, high-contact services have other concerns. Typically, when evaluating locations for the firm, three questions need to addressed.

First, how visible is the firm? Customers tend to shop at places of which they are aware. The firm's visibility is essential in creating awareness. Ideally, firms should be visible from major traffic arteries and can enhance their visibility by facing the direction of traffic that maximizes visibility. If available, sites that are set back from the street (which permit customers to gain a broad perspective) while still remaining close enough to permit customers to read the firm's signs are preferable.

The second question about a location under consideration pertains to the compatibility of the site being evaluated with its surrounding environment. Is the size of the site suitable for the size of the building being planned? More importantly, what other types of businesses are in the area? For example, it would make sense for a law office specializing in health care matters to locate close to a major hospital, which is generally surrounded by a number of private medical practices as well.

The third question concerns whether the site is suited for customer convenience. Is the site accessible? Does it have ample parking or alternative parking options nearby? Do customers who use mass transit systems have reasonable access to the firm?

## THE FIRM'S ARCHITECTURE

The architecture of the firm's physical facility is often a three-way trade-off among the type of design that will attract the firm's intended target market, the type of design that maximizes the efficiency of the service production process, and the type of design that is affordable. The firm's architecture conveys a number of impressions as well as communicates information to its customers, such as the nature of the firm's business, the firm's strength and stability, and the price of the firm's services.

## THE FIRM'S SIGN

The firm's sign has two major purposes: to identify the firm and to attract attention. The firm's sign is often the first "mark" of the firm the customer notices. All logos on the firm's remaining physical evidence, such as letterhead, business cards, and note cards, should be consistent with the firm's sign to reinforce the firm's image. Ideally, signs should indicate to consumers the who, what, where, and when of the service offering. The sign's size, shape, coloring, and lighting all contribute to the firm's projected image.

## THE FIRM'S ENTRANCE

The firm's entrance and foyer areas can dramatically influence customer perceptions about the firm's activities. Worn carpet, scuffed walls, unprofessional artwork, torn and outdated reading materials, and unskilled and unkempt personnel form one impression. In contrast, neatly appointed reception areas, the creative use of colors, distinctive furnishings, and friendly and professional staff create a much different, more positive impression. Other tactical considerations include lighting that clearly identifies the entrance, doors that are easy to open, flat entryways that minimize the number of customers who might trip, nonskid floor materials for rainy days, and doors that are wide enough to accommodate customers with disabilities as well as large materials being transported in and out of the firm.

## LIGHTING

The psychological effects of lighting on consumer behavior are particularly intriguing. Our response to light may have started when our parents put us to bed, turned out the lights, and told us to be quiet and go to sleep. Through repetitive conditioning, most individuals' response to dimly lit rooms is that of a calming effect. Lighting can set the mood, tone, and pace of the service encounter. Consumers talk more softly when the lights are low, the service environment is perceived as more formal, and the pace of the encounter slows. In contrast, brightly lit service environments are louder, communication exchanges among customers and between customers and employees are more frequent, and the overall environment is perceived as more informal, exciting, and cheerful.

## TABLE 9.2

### The Impact of Background Music on Restaurant Patrons

| Variables | Slow Music | Fast Music |
|---|---|---|
| Service time | 29 min. | 27 min. |
| Customer time at table | 56 min. | 45 min. |
| Customer groups leaving before seated | 10.5% | 12% |
| Amount of food purchased | $55.81 | $55.12 |
| Amount of bar purchases | $30.47 | $21.62 |
| Estimated gross margin | $55.82 | $48.62 |

Source: R. E. Milliman, "The Influences of Background Music on the Behavior of Restaurant Patrons," *Journal of Consumer Research* 13 (September 1986), 288; see also R. E. Milliman, "Using Background Music to Affect the Behavior of Supermarket Shoppers," *Journal of Marketing* (Summer 1982), 86–91.

## Sound Appeals

**sound appeals**
Appeals associated with certain sounds, such as music or announcements.

**Sound appeals** have three major roles: mood setter, attention grabber, and informer.

### MUSIC

Studies have shown that background music affects sales in at least two ways. First, background music enhances the customer's perception of the store's atmosphere, which in turn influences the consumer's mood. Second, music often influences the amount of time spent in stores.[19] In one study, firms that played background music in their facilities were thought to care more about their customers.[20]

Studies have shown that in addition to creating a positive attitude, music directly influences consumer buying behavior. Playing faster music increases the pace of consumer transactions. Slowing down the tempo of the music encourages customers to stay longer. Still other studies have indicated that consumers find music distracting when considering high-involvement purchases but that listening to music during low-involvement purchases made the choice process easier. Moreover, employees tend to be happier and more productive when listening to background music, which in turn leads to a more positive experience for customers.

Table 9.2 displays the impact of background music on consumer and provider behavior in a restaurant setting. As can be concluded by the figures, the pace of service delivered and the pace of consumer consumption is affected by the tempo of the music. Although the estimated gross margin was higher when the restaurant played slow music, the restaurant should also consider the additional number of tables that would turn if faster-paced music were played throughout the day.

### ANNOUNCEMENTS

Another common sound in service establishments is the announcements made over intercom systems, such as to alert restaurant patrons when their tables are ready, to inform airline passengers of their current location, and to page specific employees within the firm. The professionalism with which announcements are made directly influences consumer perceptions of the firm. An example of a bizarre announcement made in a grocery store setting involved a male who over the inter-com requested, "Red, what's the price on a box of so and so?" A female then responded for everyone in the store to hear, "Red, my ass!" If this type of announce-ment had been made in a doctor's or lawyer's office, consider how it would have reflected on the competence of the firm. Speaking of such incidents, now is prob-ably a good time to discuss sound avoidance.

### SOUND AVOIDANCE

When planning the firm's facilities, it is as important to understand the avoidance of undesirable sounds as it is to understand the creation of desirable sounds. Desirable sounds attract customers, and undesirable sounds distract from the firm's overall atmosphere. Within a restaurant setting, sounds that should be strate-gically masked include those emanating from kitchen, dish room, and restroom areas. Obviously, listening to a toilet flush throughout dinner does little to add to the enjoyment of the customer's dining experience. Other tactics for eliminating unwanted noise include installing durable hallway carpets to eliminate the dis-tracting sounds of clicking heels, strategically placing loud central air conditioning units in areas away from those where the firm conducts the majority of its busi-ness, and installing lower ceilings and sound-absorbing partitions so that unwanted sounds can be reduced even further.

## Scent Appeals

The atmosphere of the firm can be strongly affected by scents, and the service manager should be aware of this fact. When considering **scent appeals**, as was the case with sound appeals, service managers should pay as much attention to scent avoidance as to scent creation. Stale, musty, foul odors affect everyone and are sure to create negative impressions about the firm. Poor ventilation systems that fail to remove odors and poorly located trash receptacles are common contributors to potential odor problems.

**scent appeals**
Appeals associated with certain scents.

     On the other hand, pleasurable scents often induce customers to make pur-chases and can affect the perception of products that don't naturally have their own scent. For example, in one study conducted by Nike, customers examined pairs of gym shoes in two different rooms. One room was completely odor free, and the other was artificially permeated with a floral scent. Results of the study indicated that the floral scent had a direct positive effect on the desirability of the sneakers to 84 percent of the participants.[21] Although this particular example is related to a tangible product, it does seem to indicate that scents influence consumer percep-tions regarding products such as services that do not naturally smell on their own. Experts in scent creation note that a firm should smell like it's supposed to, accord-ing to target market expectations. Hospitals should smell clean and antiseptic, and perhaps older, established law firms should even smell a little musty.

## Touch Appeals

The chances of a product's selling increases substantially when the consumer han-dles the product. But how does one touch an intangible product? Service firms such as mail order retailers have a tangible component that can be shipped to customers. One of the reasons that nonstore retailing now accounts for 10 percent of all retail sales and is increasing is the liberal return policies that were implemented to increase **touch appeals.** Spiegel, for example, will send the customer the merchandise for inspection, and if the customer does not want it, the customer simply picks up the phone, notifies Spiegel, and places the returning product outside the door. Spiegel notifies UPS to pick up the package and pays for all costs associated with the return.

**touch appeals**
Appeals associated with being able to touch a tangible product or physical evidence of a service, such as shaking hands with service providers.

For purer services with a smaller tangible component, touch appeals can be developed through the use of "open houses" where the public has a chance to meet the people providing the service. Shaking hands and engaging in face-to-face communications with potential and existing customers is definitely a form of touch appeal. Clearly, firms engaged in creating touch appeals are perceived as more caring, closer to their customers, and genuinely concerned and interested in their customers' welfare.

## Taste Appeals

**taste appeals**
The equivalent of providing the customer with free samples.

**Taste appeals,** the final sensory cue, are the equivalent of providing the customer with samples. Within the service sector, the usefulness of taste appeals when developing service atmospheres is dependent on the tangibility of the service. Service firms such as car washes, dry cleaners, and restaurants may use taste appeals to initially attract customers. While sampling the firm's services, the customer will have the opportunity to observe the firm's physical evidence and form perceptions regarding the firm and its performance capabilities. Consequently, firms that use samples should view this process as an opportunity rather than as catering to a bunch of customers who want something for free.

# DESIGN CONSIDERATIONS FOR HIGH-CONTACT VERSUS LOW-CONTACT SERVICE FIRMS[22]

One final topic that deserves special attention is the design considerations for low-contact versus high-contact firms. High-customer-contact firms include self-service and interpersonal services; low-contact firms include remote services. Depending on the level of contact, strategic differences exist regarding facility location, facility design, product design, and process design.

## Facility Location

The choice location for the firm's service operation depends on the amount of customer contact that is necessary during the production process. If customers are an integral part of the process, convenient locations located near customers' homes or workplaces will offer the firm a differential advantage over competitors. For example, with all other things being equal, the most conveniently located car washes, dry cleaners, and hairstylists are likely to obtain the most business.

In contrast, low-contact businesses should consider locations that may be more convenient for labor and sources of supply and closer to major transportation routes. For example, mail-order facilities have little or no customer contact and can actually increase the efficiencies of their operations by locating closer to sources of supply and major transportation alternatives, such as interstate highways for trucking purposes or airports for overnight airline shipments. In many cases, these types of locations are less expensive to purchase or rent because they are generally in remote areas, where the cost of land and construction is not as expensive as it is inside city limits, where other businesses are trying to locate close to their customers.

## Facility Layout

In regard to the layout of the service operation, high-contact service firms should take the customers' physical and psychological needs and expectations into consideration. When a customer enters a high-contact service operation, that customer expects the facility to look like something other than a dusty, musty, old warehouse. Attractive personnel, clearly marked signs explaining the process, enough room to comfortably move about the facility, and a facility suited to bringing friends and family to are among consumer expectations. In contrast, low-contact facility layouts should be designed to maximize employee expectations and production requirements. Clearly, designing facilities for high-contact services is often more expensive than designing for their low-contact counterparts.

## Product Design

Because the customer is involved in the production process of high-contact services, the customer will ultimately define the product differently from one produced by a low-contact service. In services such as restaurants, which have a tangible product associated with their service offering, the customer will define the product by the physical product itself as well as by the physical evidence that surrounds the product in the service environment. High-contact services that produce purely intangible products such as education and insurance are defined almost solely by the physical evidence that surrounds the service and by the thoughts and opinions of others.

In low-contact services, the customer is not directly involved in the production process, so the product is defined by fewer attributes. Consider a mail-order operation in which the customer never physically enters the facility. The customer will define the end product by the physical product itself (a pair of boots), the conversation that took place with personnel when ordering the boots, the quality of the mail-order catalog that featured the boots, the box in which the boots were packaged, and the billing materials that request payment.

## Process Design

In high-contact operations, the physical presence of the customer in the process itself must also be considered. Each stage in the process will have a direct and immediate effect on the customer. Consequently, a set of mini-service encounters and the physical evidence present at each encounter will contribute to the customer's overall evaluation of the service process. For example, a hotel guest is directly involved in the reservation process, the check-in process, the consumption process associated with the use of the hotel room itself, the consumption processes associated with the use of hotel amenities such as the restaurant, pool, and health club, and the check-out process. In contrast, because the customer is not involved with many of the production steps in low-contact services, their evaluation is based primarily on the outcome itself.

## SUMMARY

The effective management of physical evidence is particularly important to service firms. Because of the intangibility of services, consumers lack objective sources of information when forming evaluations. As a result, customers often look to the physical evidence that surrounds the service when forming evaluations.

A firm's physical evidence includes, but is not limited to, facility exterior design elements such as the architecture of the building, the firm's sign, parking, landscaping, and the surrounding environment of the firm's location; interior design elements such as size, shape, and colors, the firm's entrance and foyer areas, equipment used to operate the business, interior signage, layout, air quality, and temperature; and other physical evidence that forms customer perceptions, including business cards, stationery, billing statements, reports, the appearance of personnel, and the firm's brochures.

From a strategic perspective, the importance of managing the firm's physical evidence stems from the firm's ability to (1) package the service; (2) facilitate the flow of the service delivery process; (3) socialize customers and employees in terms of their respective roles, behaviors, and relationships; and (4) differentiate the firm from its competitors.

From a theoretical perspective, the firm's environment influences the behavior of consumers and employees alike because of the inseparability of many services. When designing the firm's facilities, consideration needs to be given to whether the firm is a remote service, an interpersonal service, or a self-service. The subsequent design should reflect the needs of the parties who are dominating the service production process. Decisions about facility location, layout, product design, and process design in particular may result in different outcomes depending on whether the customer is actively involved in the production process or not. Figure 9.3 illustrates the theoretical framework that helps us to further understand how individuals are affected by the firm's environmental dimensions, which ultimately leads to approach and avoidance behaviors.

Finally, numerous tactical decisions must be made when designing the firm's environment. Individuals base perceptions of the firm's services on sensory cues that exist in the firm's environment. Specific tactical decisions must be made about the creation and sometimes the avoidance of scent appeals, sight appeals, sound appeals, touch appeals, and taste appeals. The design and management of the firm's sensory cues are critical to the firm's long-term success.

# Key Terms

Apathetic customers
Approach behaviors
Ambient conditions
Arousal-nonarousal
Avoidance behaviors
Beliefs
Categorization
Clash
Cognitive responses
Contrast
Dominance-submissiveness
Emotional responses
Environmental psychology
Ethical customers
Facility exterior
Facility interior
Harmony
Hue
Intensity
Interpersonal services
Internal response moderators
Organism

Personalized customers
Physiological responses
Pleasure-displeasure
Responses (outcomes)
Scent appeals
Self-services
Shades
Sight appeals
Signs, symbols, artifacts
Size, shape, colors
Socialization
Sound appeals
Stimulus-organism-response
  (SOR) model
Stimuli
Symbolic meaning
Tangibles
Taste appeals
Tints
Touch appeals
Value

# Discussion Questions

1. Discuss the strategic role of physical evidence.
2. Discuss the relevance of remote, self-service, and interpersonal services to facility design.
3. How should the servicescape of a firm that targets ethical shoppers be designed?
4. Discuss how internal response moderators relate to the characteristic of heterogeneity.
5. Discuss internal responses to the firm's environment.
6. What is the impact of music on customer and employee behavior?
7. Develop strategies for a service firm that would enhance the firm's touch and taste appeals.
8. Discuss the use of employee uniforms as physical evidence.
9. What are the major design differences between high-customer-contact and low-customer-contact services?

# *Notes*

1. Kristen Anderson and Ron Zemke, *Delivering Knock Your Socks Off Service* (New York: AMACOM, 1991), 27–30.
2. Mary Jo Bitner, "Servicescapes: The Impact of Physical Surroundings on Customers and Employees," *Journal of Marketing* 56 (April 1992), 57–71.
3. Ibid.
4. Edgar Schein, "Organizational Socialization and the Profession of Management," *Industrial Management Review* 9 (Winter 1968), 1–16.
5. Michael R. Solomon, "Packaging the Service Provider," in Christopher H. Lovelock, *Managing Services Marketing, Operations, and Human Resources* (Englewood Cliffs, N.J.: Prentice-Hall, 1988), 318–324.
6. Ibid.
7. Ibid.
8. Ibid.
9. Avijit Ghosh, *Retail Management,* 2nd ed. (Fort Worth, Tex.: The Dryden Press, 1994), 522–523.
10. Ibid.
11. Valerie A. Zeithaml and Mary Jo Bitner, *Services Marketing* (New York: McGraw Hill, 1996), 528.
12. Ibid, 531.
13. Ibid.
14. Philip Kotler, "Atmospherics as a Marketing Tool," *Journal of Retailing* (Winter 1973–1974), 48.
15. Dale M. Lewison, *Retailing*, 4th ed. (New York: MacMillan, 1991), 273–283.
16. Ibid.
17. Kenneth H. Mills and Judith E. Paul, *Applied Visual Merchandising* (Englewood Cliffs, N.J.: Prentice-Hall, 1982), 47.
18. Kenneth H. Mills and Judith E. Paul, *Create Distinctive Displays* (Englewood Cliffs, N.J.: Prentice-Hall, 1974), 61.
19. J. Barry Mason, Morris L. Mayer, and J. B. Wilkinson, *Modern Retailing: Theory and Practice,* 6th ed. (Homewood, Ill.: Irwin, 1993), 642–643.
20. Ronald E. Milliman, "Using Background Music to Affect the Behavior of Supermarket Shoppers," *Journal of Marketing* 46, no. 3 (Summer 1982), pp. 86–91; see also Douglas K. Hawse and Hugh McGinley, "Music for the Eyes, Color for the Ears: An Overview," in *Proceedings of the Society for Consumer Psychology,* David W. Schumann, ed. (Washington, D.C.: Society for Consumer Psychology, 1988), 145–152.
21. J. Barry Mason, Morris L. Mayer, and Hazel F. Ezell, *Retailing*, 5th ed. (Homewood, Ill.: Irwin, 1994).
22. Richard B. Chase, "Where Does the Customer Fit in a Service Operation?" *Harvard Business Review* (November–December 1978), 137–142.

# chapter 10

# People Issues: Managing Service Employees

## CHAPTER OBJECTIVES

The purpose of this chapter is to discuss the key issues that will help you understand the many challenges associated with managing employees within the service experience. Service business, by its very definition, is a people business and requires talented managers who can navigate the thin line between the needs of the organization, its employees, and its customers.

After reading this chapter, you should be able to:

- Discuss the importance of contact personnel as boundary spanners.
- Describe sources of conflict in boundary-spanning roles.
- Explain the consequences of role stress.
- Discuss methods for reducing role stress through marketing activities.
- Describe the concepts of empowerment and enfranchisement.
- Explain the contingency approach to empowerment.
- Discuss the relevance of employee satisfaction as it relates to the service-profit chain.

"Here's your food, and I hope you choke on it!"

Fast-food server to a customer who complained about waiting 10 minutes for his food

# Introduction

Employee satisfaction and customer satisfaction are clearly related. Let's say it again another way: If you want to satisfy your customers, employee satisfaction is critical! The public face of a service firm is its contact personnel. Part factory workers, part administrators, part servants, service personnel often perform a complex and difficult job.[1] Despite their importance and the complexity of their activities, service personnel are often the lowest paid and least respected individuals in most companies, and often in society. For example, in the health care community the individuals most responsible for patient care and patient perceptions of service quality received are the nurses. Who are the lowest paid and least respected individuals in the health care community? The nurses. In the education system, who is most responsible for the day-to-day education of and interaction with students? The classroom teachers. Who in the education system are the least paid and least respected individuals? The classroom teachers. The list goes on and on. Consider any service industry, and look to the individuals who are the most responsible for customer interactions and customer perceptions of quality delivered, and you will most likely see the lowest paid and least respected individuals in the company. It makes no sense!

It is little wonder, therefore, that service jobs often have extremely high levels of staff turnover. In one year, 119,000 sales jobs turned over within the retail network of the Sears Merchandise Group. The cost of hiring and training each new sales assistant was $900, or more than $110 million in total, a sum that represented 17 percent of Sears' annual income.[2]

Today more than 45 million people representing 42 percent of the U.S. workforce are employed in selling food; selling merchandise in retail stores; performing clerical work in service industries; cleaning hospitals, schools, and offices; or providing some other form of personal service. These are occupations that accounted for most of the U.S. job growth over the last two decades. Yet, for the most part, these jobs are poorly paid, lead nowhere, and provide little, if anything, in the way of health, pension, and other benefits.[3] It's no wonder why *Business Week* recently investigated the question "Why Service Stinks."[4]

## THE IMPORTANCE OF CONTACT PERSONNEL

**boundary-spanning roles**
The various parts played by contact personnel who perform dual functions of interacting with the firm's external environment and internal organization.

This chapter highlights the importance of contact personnel to the firm and explains their particular role in creating customer satisfaction. The importance of marketing personnel is especially being felt by today's Internet companies. Technological and financial smarts are still important, but not as important as personnel with a strong background in marketing (see Services in Action 10.1). This chapter also attempts to explain the pressures and tensions on service workers as they perform their **boundary-spanning roles**. As boundary spanners, service personnel perform the dual functions of interacting with both the firm's external environment and its internal organization and structure.

ERVICES *10.1*
N

ACTION    **Marketers: The New "It" People in Silicon Valley**

In the fast-paced business world of the Internet, technological and financial smarts are still important, but not as important as a strong background in marketing. According to a recent cover story in *USA Today,* "Pocket protectors are out, [and] marketing skills are in at tech start-ups." Labeled as the new rock stars of the Internet, marketers are in great demand at Internet firms. "This is absolutely a great time for people who have a real interest in marketing," says Paul Ray of Ray and Berenson Recruiting. Other recruiters agree. Powell Recruiting notes that in the early days of the internet, the big recruiting efforts were geared toward those who understood the infrastructure of the systems. "The pipeline had to get laid." Now, "emerging e-commerce companies [are] looking for CEOs or vice presidents of marketing." The former CEO of MVP.com, John Costello, agrees: "Technology is important, but it is a means to an end. The key to success is building a brand that meets customer needs better than anybody else."

Examples of the power of marketing as it relates to the Internet are numerous. Bob Pittman, who previously helped launch MTV and is the former CEO of Century 21, is now co-COO of the combined AOL Time Warner. Pittman was able to use his marketing savvy to make AOL one of the most valuable brands in the world. Similarly, William Razzouck, CEO of PlanetRx, recognizes the value of bringing marketers to his company. "The CEO knows how to run a business. But somewhere in the organization you need to have someone who knows marketing." Marketing jobs on the Internet are not just for Fortune 500 refugees. Karen Edwards, a 32-year-old Harvard MBA, became employee number 17 at Yahoo! Karen was one of the early marketing pioneers of the Internet and firmly established the importance of marketing by creating one of the most recognized names on the Internet.

One of the most attractive aspects of marketing on the Internet is the e-commerce attitude toward marketing. Traditionally, marketing has been looked at as a cost—a necessary evil. Within the world of the Internet, marketing is viewed as an investment, and marketers do not have to fight to obtain increases in the marketing budget to get the job done.

Source: "Sales Smarts Rule Internet," *USA Today* (January 19, 2000), pp. 1B, 2B.

Strategically, service personnel are an important source of product differentiation. It is often challenging for a service organization to differentiate itself from other similar organizations in the benefit bundle it offers or its delivery system. For example, one extreme view is that many airlines offer similar bundles of benefits and fly the same types of aircraft from the same airports to the same destinations. Their only hope of a competitive advantage is, therefore, from the service level— the way things are done. Some of this differentiation can come from staffing levels or the physical systems designed to support the staff. Often, however, the deciding factor that distinguishes one airline from another is the poise and attitude of the service providers.[5] Singapore Airlines, for example, enjoys an excellent reputation due in large part to the beauty and grace of their flight attendants. Other firms that hold a differential advantage over competitors based on personnel include the Ritz Carlton, IBM, and Disney.[6]

## THE BOUNDARY-SPANNING ROLE

The boundary-spanning role has been defined as one that links an organization with the outside world.[7] Employees in boundary-spanning roles create these links for the organization by interacting with nonmembers of the organization. Boundary-spanning personnel have two main purposes:

- Information transfer
- Representation

Boundary spanners collect information from the environment and feed it back into the organization, and they communicate with the environment on behalf of the organization. Boundary-spanning personnel are also the organization's personal representatives.

**subordinate service roles**
The parts played by personnel who work in firms where customers' purchase decisions are entirely discretionary, such as waitresses, bellmen, and drivers.

Individuals who occupy boundary-spanning roles can be classified along a continuum that ranges from **subordinate service roles** to **professional service roles** (Figure 10.1).[8] At one end of the continuum are the subordinate service roles that traditionally exist at the bottom of an organization. People who work in these roles work for service firms where the customers' purchase decision is entirely discretionary. They are subordinate to the organization and to the customer. Examples of subordinate service roles include waiters, bellmen, drivers, and others who operate at the very base of the organization and yet are the organization's primary contact personnel with the outside world.

**professional service roles**
The parts played by personnel who have a status independent of their place in an organization because of their professional qualifications.

Professional service roles occupy the position at the other end of the continuum. Professionals are also boundary spanners; however, their status is quite different from that of the subordinate provider. Because of their professional qualifications, professional service providers have a status that is independent of their place in the organization. Customers, or as they are more often called, clients, are not superior to professionals because clients acknowledge the professionals' expertise on which they wish to draw.

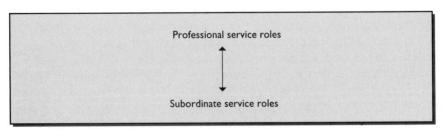

**Figure 10.1    Range of Boundary-Spanning Roles**

## Sources of Conflict in Boundary-Spanning Roles

Employees who occupy boundary-spanning roles are often placed in situations that produce conflict and stress. Consider, for example, the types of stress encountered by cashiers when performing as boundary spanners, which is described in Services in Action 10.2.

### PERSON/ROLE CONFLICTS

For services to operate successfully, both customers and contact personnel must conform to a script or role. Each must play his or her part. **Person/role conflicts** indicate that playing such a role may be inconsistent with an individual's self-perception. Some customers may wish boundary spanners to be subservient, a role that an employee normally would not desire to play, especially with certain types of customers. Boundary-spanning personnel often are called on to suppress their personal feelings and are asked to smile and be helpful while feeling miserable and

**person/role conflicts**
A bad fit between an individual's self-perception and the specific role the person must play in an organization.

ERVICES **10.2**

ACTION  **Role Stress in Boundary-Spanning Roles**

Customers have a major affect on supermarket cashiers because their influence is instantaneous, continuous, and simultaneous with the performance of the job. The manager, by comparison, who holds the legitimate influence, can only create the environment and set the stage for employee performance. It is the customers who directly create the stress in this role.

Observational research suggests that there are four main sources of cashier stress:

- An inability of contact personnel to develop a strong social network among co-workers because of a discipline imposed by the customers, who do not want the staff to be too "chatty" while they are working. This is obviously an idiosyncrasy of the supermarket situation but occurs to a greater or lesser extent in other settings as well.
- The constrained nature of the customer-cashier relationship means that cashiers often are denied the freedom to engage in normal social interaction with customers. This, combined with the inability to socialize with other staff, makes this particular contact role a lonely one.
- Role conflict and ambiguity are just as prevalent within this boundary-spanning role as in any other. Conflict and ambiguity are organizational behavior concepts that have been discussed at considerable length in the literature on this field.
- The fight for control. Everyone needs to believe that they are in control, and in service settings this is a source of much tension.

Source: John E. G. Bateson and K. Douglas Hoffman, *Managing Services Marketing*, 4th ed. (Fort Worth, Tex.: Harcourt, 1999).

aggressive; this is particularly the case for low-level staff.[9] Professionals are much more likely to be able to operate within their own self-image and to feel less obligated to maintain a pleasant "bedside manner." Person/role conflicts can be categorized into three types:

1. Inequality dilemmas. Although it is important to put the customer first, this can sometimes result in service personnel feeling belittled or demeaned. These feelings can be magnified if customers make a point of establishing their personal superiority over the server.

2. Feelings versus behavior. Contact personnel are required to hide their true feelings and present a "front" or "face" to the customer. This can result in role stress because the server does not identify with the role he or she is acting out.

3. Territorial conflict. Contact personnel will often try to establish their own personal space, which they can defend against clients and other servers. Trespassing on this space can lead to reactions that conflict with the server's own role.

## ORGANIZATION/CLIENT CONFLICTS

Contact personnel can sometimes receive conflicting instructions, one set from the client who wants a service performed in a particular way, the other from the organization, which wants the service performed in a different way. This three-cornered fight between the customer, service, and organization must essentially be resolved by compromise. However, such compromise can, if mishandled, leave the server feeling badly treated. Conflicts between the demands of the organization and those of the client are the most common source of conflict for boundary-spanning personnel. Conflicts of this type arise when the client or customer requests services that violate the rules of the organization. Such a violation can be as simple as a request for a second bread roll in a restaurant or as complex as a request that a bus driver leave the established route to drop off a passenger at home.[10]

The reaction to **organization/client conflicts** is often related to the employee's role within the organization. Subordinate service personnel are often unable to change the rules and regulations of the company. Moreover, they are

**organization/client conflicts**
Disagreements that arise when a customer requests services that violate the rules of the organization.

Some service roles, such as that of a taxi driver, may operate at the base of the organization but are its contact point with the outside world and, thus, are instrumental in maintaining a positive relationship with the consumer in the service experience.

unable to explain why the rules and regulations exist in the first place. However, subordinate service personnel appear to be well aware of the rules and regulations that prevent them from giving good service. In many cases, when faced with an organization/client conflict, subordinate service personnel will side with the client and away from the organization to resolve the conflict. In contrast, professional service personnel, with their higher status and clearer understanding of the purpose of specific rules and regulations, are more able to control what happens.

## INTERCLIENT CONFLICTS

Conflicts between clients, or **interclient conflicts,** arise because many service delivery systems have a number of clients who influence one another's experiences. Because different clients are likely to have different needs, they tend to have completely different scripts for themselves, the contact personnel, and other customers. When customers do experience conflict, it is usually the boundary-spanning personnel who are asked to resolve the confrontation. For example, it is the waiter who is generally requested to ask another patron not to smoke in a non-smoking section. Attempts to satisfy all the clients all the time can escalate the conflict or bring the boundary-spanning personnel into the battle. For example, a restaurant customer requesting speedy service and receiving it can cause complaints from other tables about the inequitable levels of service.

**interclient conflicts**
Disagreements between clients that arise because of the number of clients who influence each other's experience.

Employee reaction and effectiveness in resolving interclient conflicts appear to be once again related to the employee's role within the organization. Employees in subordinate roles start from the weakest position because they have low status with clients. Clients may simply disregard responses made by subordinate service providers. Professionals may face the same problems; for example, consider the patient in the hospital waiting room, demanding preferential treatment. In a case such as this, however, the professional can invoke his or her status and expertise to resolve the situation.

## The Implications of Role Stress for Boundary-Spanning Personnel

The consequences of conflict and stress produce dissatisfaction, frustration, and turnover intention in personnel. When faced with potential conflict and stress in their jobs, employees attempt a variety of strategies to shield themselves. The simplest way of avoiding conflict is to avoid the customers. This is exemplified by the waiter who refuses to notice a customer who wishes to place an order. This strategy allows the employee to increase his or her personal sense of control over the encounter. An alternative strategy is to move into a people-processing mode, where customers are treated as inanimate objects to be processed rather than as individuals.[11] This reduces the requirement of the boundary-spanning personnel to associate or empathize with an individual.

Boundary-spanning personnel also employ other strategies to maintain a sense of control of the encounter. Physical symbols and furniture are often used to boost the employee's status and hence his or her sense of control.[12] In an extreme case, the employee may overact the role and force the customer into a subservient role, as is the case with some waiters and waitresses. Interestingly, a restaurant franchise called Dick's Last Resort encourages employees to be overly demanding as part of

S̲E̲R̲V̲I̲C̲E̲S̲ **10.3**

A̲C̲T̲I̲O̲N̲    **Service Providers from You-Know-Where**

Within the service experience, it often seems that customers and providers are in pursuit of different goals. Inevitably, clashes occur that have profound long-term effects on how customers view the organization and how the service providers view customers in subsequent transactions. It is a self-perpetuating nightmare. Cynical service providers turn their clientele into "customers from hell," and nightmarish customers return the favor by eventually wearing down even the best service providers.

In a recent *Wall Street Journal* survey, approximately 1,000 customers were asked what irritated them the most about service personnel. Answers most frequently mentioned on customer lists included:

1. Service personnel who say that they will show up at a particular time and fail to show up at all (40 percent)
2. Poorly informed personnel (37 percent)
3. Contact personnel who continue their personal phone calls while they wait on the customer (25 percent)
4. Personnel who pass customers off by saying "It's not my department" (25 percent)
5. Personnel who talk down to the customer (21 percent)
6. Personnel who can't explain how products work (16 percent)

Similarly, in the book *At America's Service,* service personnel behaviors that irk customers the most have been classified into seven categories:

1. *Apathy:* What comedian George Carlin refers to as DILLIGAD—"Do I look like I give a damn?"
2. *Brush-off:* Attempts to get rid of the customer by dismissing the customer completely—the "I want you to go away" syndrome.
3. *Coldness:* Indifferent service providers who could not care less what the customer really wants.
4. *Condescension:* The "You are the client/patient, so you must be stupid" approach.
5. *Robotism:* When customers are treated simply as inputs into a system that must be processed.
6. *Rulebook:* Providers who live by the rules of the organization even when those rules do not make good sense.
7. *Runaround:* Passing the customer off to another provider, who will simply pass them off to yet another provider.

Unfortunately, customers experience service providers from you-know-where almost everyday, and anecdotal evidence continues to mount indicating that dramatic improvements in the customer/provider relationship are slow in coming. For example, a colleague recently relayed the story of his attempt to order a ham and cheese sandwich with mayonnaise from the deli department of a local grocery store. The employee informed him that she could not fulfill his request because the deli was out of mayonnaise. (Gee whiz, lady, do you think you could get a new jar on aisle 2?)

Source: Adapted from Ron Zemke and Kristen Anderson, "Customers from Hell," *Training* (February 1990), 25–29.

their overall theme. In fact the restaurant's theme could easily be: "Dick's Last Resort . . . Where the Customer Is Always Wrong!"

An alternative strategy employees use to reduce organization/client conflict is to side completely with the customer. When forced to obey a rule with which they disagree, boundary-spanning personnel will proceed to list for the customer all the other things about the organization with which they disagree. In this way, employees attempt to reduce stress by seeking sympathy from the customer.

## Reducing Role Stress with Marketing

Traditionally, marketing can either cause or reduce role stress. Marketing can, without making major strategic changes, help to reduce service employee stress levels, and it's in the firm's best interest to do so. Clearly, unhappy, frustrated, and disagreeing contact personnel are visible to customers and will ultimately affect consumer perceptions of service quality.[13] Strategies such as ignoring the customer or simply processing the customer as a raw material through the service delivery system will most likely generate negative customer perceptions (see Services in Action 10.3). Customers obviously do not like being ignored by waiters or treated as if they were inanimate objects. If contact personnel attempt to maximize their sense of control over their encounters, it will most likely be at the expense of the amount of control felt by customers. In addition, although customers may sympathize with a service provider's explanation that the organization stops them from providing excellent service, customers will still develop negative perceptions about the organization.

### REDUCING PERSON/ROLE CONFLICTS

Marketing can reduce the conflict between the individual and the assigned role by simply being sensitive and by actively seeking input from employees about the issue. A promotional gimmick dreamed up at the head office may look great on paper. For example, a medieval-theme day in the hotel almost certainly will have great public relations value, but how will the staff feel when they are called upon to wear strange and awkward (not to mention uncomfortable) costumes? How will these costumes affect the employees' relationships with customers during the service encounter?

To improve the quality of service, a change in operating procedure may be needed; however, it is important to ensure that service providers are well trained in the new script. Should they not be, they may well become extremely embarrassed in the presence of customers. This situation can be aggravated if the new service is advertised in such a way that the customers are more aware of the new script than the staff.

## REDUCING ORGANIZATION/CLIENT CONFLICTS

Similarly, marketing can help reduce conflicts between the organization and its clients. It is crucial, for example, that customer expectations be consistent with the capabilities of the service system. Customers should not ask for services the system cannot provide. Advertising is one of the main causes of inflated expectations, since the temptation is to exaggerate claims in advertising to maximize the impact. Consider, for example, the advertisement that depicted a flight attendant reading a young child a story while the plane was in flight. A number of passengers took the advertisement literally, either because they believed it or because they could not resist the temptation, and called on the flight attendants to read stories to their children.

## REDUCING INTERCLIENT CONFLICTS

Conflicts between clients can be avoided if the clients are relatively homogeneous in their expectations. Because of the inseparability of services, customers often share their service experiences with other customers. Hence, successful service firms recognize the importance of effective segmentation, which minimizes the chances that two or more divergent groups will share the encounter simultaneously. As long as all the clients share the same script and expect the same standard of service, the chances of interclient conflicts are much reduced.

## TABLE 10.1

### Descriptions of Staffing Issues in Firms with a High, Moderate, and Low Passion for Service

**High Passion for Service**
There is not enough staff to whom we can delegate responsibilities.
Management is running lean at the top.
There aren't enough people for cross-training.

**Moderate Passion for Service**
There is nobody to replace someone who takes a vacation.
We have been reduced to a skeleton staff, but the work must still go out.
Unusually heavy workloads are our biggest problem.

**Low Passion for Service**
When people leave, they are not replaced.
Every day there is another staffing problem.
Our receptionist has so many duties she can't even answer the phone sometimes.

Source: Benjamin Schneider and David E. Bowen, *Winning the Service Game* (Boston, Mass.: Harvard Business School Press, 1995), 130.

# THE IMPORTANCE OF HUMAN RESOURCES FOR SERVICE FIRMS

Personnel constitutes the bulk of the product of most service firms. However, marketing theory is ill equipped to provide insights into the problem of where contact personnel fit in to the hierarchy of the service firm. Human resources, by comparison, is a field of study focused on this and similar problems. Human resource policies are associated with the outcomes experienced by customers and the culture created within the service firm.[14]

Because service firms often involve the customer as a co-producer, they operate open systems, where the effects of human resource practices and policies as well as the organization's climate are visible to customers. **Climate** is defined as employee perceptions of one or more strategic imperatives. For example, a passion for service within the organization would lead to a climate that sets service as the key strategic imperative (Tables 10.1 and 10.2). When service commitment is high, the service firm displays a passion for doing things directly related to the provision of service. Consider, for example, employee comments from The Container Store, recently chosen as the number one best place to work by *Fortune* magazine.[15]

**climate**
Employee perceptions of their employer's passion for service.

*   "I love this company because 'Customer Service is #1'!! ... All customers can use our phones at any time."

# T·A·B·L·E 10.2

## Descriptions of Training in Firms with a High, Moderate, and Low Passion for Service

**High Passion for Service**
There is cross-training in operations to improve service.
Seminars are held for both in-house personnel and customers.

**Moderate Passion for Service**
We can't learn other jobs because there is nobody here to relieve us while we are being trained.
Some people get terrific training; others get none.
We need more sales training.

**Low Passion for Service**
We have to go through hell to get permission to attend a training seminar.
No one is being trained to use the PCs; automation is occurring without the necessary training.
I'm taking a real estate course, and my company won't pay for it even though we are a mortgage bank.

Source: Benjamin Schneider and David E. Bowen, *Winning the Service Game* (Boston, Mass.: Harvard Business School Press, 1995), 135.

- "We grew up with 'family values' and it's rare to find a company with the same values, philosophy, and foundation principles. Going to work is like going to a family reunion everyday."
- "Working for this company has made me a better person and certainly made the world a better, more organized place."
- "I miss everyone when I go on vacation."
- "I will never leave."

Employees speak often and favorably about the service delivery process and the product offered to consumers, as well as about the concern for and/or responsiveness of the firm to customer opinions. In addition, when service passion is strong, employees speak favorably about performance feedback, internal equity of compensation, training, and staff quality, which is communicated to customers throughout the service delivery process.

## Creating the Right Type of Organization

Human resource management practices are the key drivers available to senior management for creating the type of organization that can be a source of sustainable competitive advantage. Often, however, front-line customer contact jobs are designed to be as simple and narrow as possible so that they can be filled by anyone—in other words, "idiot-proof" jobs. Employers place few demands on employees, selection criteria are minimal, and wages are low.

The result is the classic cycle of failure of the industrial model as discussed in Chapter 1. Fewer and less knowledgeable contact personnel are available, and hence the customer gets less and lower-quality help (Table 10.3). Customers vent their feelings of impatience and dissatisfaction on the staff, which, in turn, demotivates the employees, especially the most conscientious ones, since they are already aware of the poor service they are being forced to give. The best staff leave and are replaced with poorly trained recruits, and the cycle continues. Current human resource theory is looking for ways to break out of the industrial model mindset and, in particular, how to use empowerment and enfranchisement to break the cycle of failure.

## TABLE 10.3

### Temp Worker Facts (United States)

- Temps earn an average of 40 percent less per hour than full-time workers.
- 55 percent do not have health insurance.
- 80 percent work 35 hours a week.
- 25 percent are under age 25.
- 53 percent are women; in the total workforce, 47 percent are women.
- 60 percent of the women have children under 18.
- 22 percent of the temp workforce is African-American; 11% of the total workforce is African-American.

Source: "Temporary Workers Getting Short Shrift," *USA Today*, April 11, 1997, p. B1.

ERVICES 10.4
N

ACTION    **Rewards That Encourage Service Excellence:
The Seven Tests of Reward Effectiveness**

Rewarding employees is the most powerful way to encourage customer-oriented behaviors. Rewards can be extrinsic (e.g., pay) or intrinsic, such as enjoying the job itself, receiving recognition from coworkers and supervisors, and/or accomplishing challenging and meaningful goals. Effective reward systems pass the seven tests listed below. In many instances, pay does not pass these effectiveness tests.

- **Availability:** Rewards must available and substantial. Not having enough rewards or large enough rewards is likely to discourage desired behaviors rather than encourage them.
- **Flexibility:** Rewards should be flexible enough that they can be given to anyone at any time.
- **Reversibility:** If rewards are given to the wrong people for the wrong reasons, they should not be lifelong. Bonuses are better than pay increases that become lifetime annuities.
- **Contingent:** Rewards should be directly tied to desired performance criteria.
- **Visibility:** Rewards should be visible, and their value should be understood by all employees. For example, pay is not visible and is often shrouded in secrecy.
- **Timeliness:** Not to say that employees are rats, but rats are trained to receive food pellets immediately following the execution of a desired behavior (e.g., pushing a bar). In this instance, employees are not that much different. Rewards should be given immediately following desired behaviors.
- **Durability:** The motivating effects of a reward should last for a long time. The motivational effects of plaques and medallions last longer than the short-term effects of pay.

Source: Adapted from Benjamin Schneider and David E. Bowen, *Winning the Service Game* (Boston, Mass: Harvard Business School Press, 1995).

## Empowerment and Enfranchisement

One of the most powerful tools for breaking free of the old logic is the use of employee empowerment and enfranchisement. **Empowerment** means giving discretion to contact personnel to "turn the front-line loose." Empowerment is the reverse of "doing things by the book." **Enfranchisement** carries this logic even further by first empowering individuals and then coupling this with a compensation method that pays people for their performance (Services in Action 10.4).

The most significant and successful enfranchisement programs have occurred in the field of retailing. Here, advocates argue that it can improve sales and earnings

**empowerment**
Giving discretion to front-line personnel to meet the needs of consumers creatively.

**enfranchisement**
Empowerment coupled with a performance-based compensation method.

dramatically while at the same time requiring less supervision from corporate management. Perhaps the most commonly used example is Nordstrom, which pays salespeople a commission not only on what they sell but also on the extent to which they can exceed their superior's projected sales forecasts. At the same time, Nordstrom's management frees salespeople of normal constraints and publicly celebrates associates' outstanding service accomplishments.

## When to Empower and Enfranchise

No single solution exists to the problems encountered in managing contact personnel. Empowerment and enfranchisement do not always win out over the industrial-based models of management. Consider the examples of FedEx and UPS.

FedEx was the first service organization to win the coveted Malcolm Baldrige National Quality Award. Behind the blue, white, and red planes and uniforms are self-managed work teams, garnishing plans, and empowered employees seemingly concerned with providing flexible and creative service to customers with varying needs. In contrast, at UPS we find turned-on people and profits, but we do not find empowerment. Instead we find controls, rules, a detailed union contract, and carefully studied work methods. UPS makes no promises that its employees will bend over backward to meet individual customer needs. However, what we do find are rigid operational guidelines, which help guarantee the customer reliable, low-cost service.[16]

### THE BENEFITS

Empowerment clearly brings benefits. Empowered employees are more customer focused and are much quicker in responding to customer needs. They will customize the product or remix it in real time.[17] Empowered employees are more likely to respond in a positive manner to service failures and to engage in effective service recovery strategies.

Employees who are empowered tend to feel better about their jobs and themselves. This is automatically reflected in the way they interact with customers. They will be genuinely warmer and friendlier. Empowerment, therefore, not only can reduce unnecessary service recovery costs but also can improve the quality of the product.

If close to the front line, an empowered employee is in a position continuously exposed to both the good and the bad aspects of the service delivery system. This employee can be the key to new service ideas and often be a cheaper source of market research than going to the customer directly.

### THE COSTS

Unfortunately, empowerment and enfranchisement do carry costs. The balance between benefits and costs determines the appropriateness of the approach. Empowerment increases the costs of the organization. A greater investment is needed in remuneration and recruitment to ensure that the right people are empowered. A low-cost model of using inexpensive and/or part-time labor cannot cope with empowerment, so the basic labor costs of the organization will be higher.

If costs are higher, marketing implications also arise. By definition, an empowered employee will customize the product. This means that the service received will vary from one encounter to the next, depending on the employee. The delivery is also likely to be slower because the service is customized. Moreover, because customers are treated differently, other customers may perceive that some customers are receiving preferential treatment. Finally, empowered employees, when attempting to satisfy customers, sometimes give away too much and make bad decisions. For example, a bellman who notices that a businessman forgot his briefcase at the front desk should make every attempt to return the briefcase to its owner. However, tracking the owner to the airport and hopping on the next available flight to the owner's destination is far beyond the call of duty and worlds beyond what is economically feasible.

The balance of empowerment and enfranchisement, therefore, comes down to the benefit concept of the organization. A branded organization that guarantees consistency of product and service dare not empower for fear of the inconsistency that doing so would produce. For example, McDonald's would lose one of its key differential advantages if it empowered its employees.

An organization that competes on the basis of value driven by a low cost base cannot afford to empower because of the costs involved. Equally, a high-cost service organization using a nonroutine and complex technology almost certainly has to empower because its ability to use an industrial approach is severely limited.

## Levels of Empowerment

As evidenced by the UPS and FedEx examples, empowerment is not for every firm. Firms can indeed be successful without fully empowering their employees. However, empowerment approaches vary by degree and include suggestion involvement, job involvement, and high involvement. Each of the three levels of empowerment fall along a continuum that ranges from control-oriented to involvement-oriented approaches (Figure 10.2).

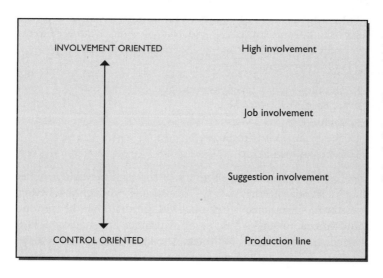

**Figure 10.2**
**Levels of Empowerment**
Source: Adapted from David E. Bowen and Edward E. Lawler III, "The Empowerment of Service Workers: What, Why, How, and When," *Sloan Management Review* (Spring 1992), 31–39.

**suggestion involvement**
Low-level empowerment that allows employees to recommend suggestions for improvement of the firm's operations.

**quality circles**
Empowerment involving small groups of employees from various departments in the firm who use brainstorming sessions to generate additional improvement suggestions.

**job involvement**
Allows employees to examine the content of their own jobs and to define their role within the organization.

**high involvement**
Allows employees to eventually learn to manage themselves, utilizing extensive training and employee control of the reward allocation decisions.

**basic business strategy**
A firm's fundamental approach regarding whether it produces a standardized, low-cost, high-volume product or a differentiated, customized, personalized product.

**Suggestion involvement** falls near the control-oriented point of the empowerment continuum. Suggestion involvement empowers employees to recommend suggestions for improving the firm's operations. Employees are not empowered to implement suggestions themselves but are encouraged to suggest improvements for formal review. Firms that use suggestion involvement typically maintain formal suggestion programs that proactively solicit employee suggestions. **Quality circles**, which often involve small groups of employees from various departments in the firm, are also utilized as brainstorming sessions to generate additional suggestions. Typical success stories of suggestion involvement programs include McDonald's, whose employees recommended the development of products such as the Big Mac, Egg McMuffin, and McDLT.

**Job involvement** typically falls in the middle of the empowerment continuum between control-oriented and involvement-oriented approaches. Job involvement allows employees to examine the content of their own jobs and to define their role within the organization. Firms engaged in job involvement use teams of employees extensively for the betterment of the firm's service delivery system. In contrast to suggestion involvement, employees engaged in job involvement use a variety of skills, have considerably more freedom, and receive extensive feedback from management, employees, and customers. However, higher-level decisions and reward allocation decisions remain the responsibility of the firm's upper management.

**High involvement** falls at the involvement-oriented end of the empowerment continuum. Essentially, the goal of high involvement is to train people to manage themselves. Extensive training is used to develop skills in teamwork, problem solving, and business operations. Moreover, employees control the majority of the reward allocation decisions through profit sharing and employee ownership of the firm. In sum, virtually every aspect of a high-involvement firm is different from those of a control-oriented firm.

## How Much to Empower: A Contingency Approach

When deciding among suggestion involvement, job involvement, and high involvement empowerment strategies, the firm must consider several factors in order to select the correct strategy. Table 10.4 provides a rating system to help managers assess their particular situations. According to the table, managers should rate their firms on five contingencies:

1. The firm's basic business strategy
2. Its tie to the customer
3. Technology
4. The business environment
5. Types of leadership

The **basic business strategy** of the firm pertains to whether the firm produces a standardized, low-cost, high-volume product or whether it produces a differentiated, customized, personalized product. As the product becomes more standardized, lower levels of empowerment are suggested. Production-lining the service delivery system will make the system more efficient, thereby controlling costs and increasing the standardization of product produced.

## TABLE 10.4

### The Contingencies of Empowerment

| Contingency | Production-Line Approach | | Empowerment |
|---|---|---|---|
| Basic business strategy | Low cost, high volume | 1 2 3 4 5 | Differentiation, customized, personalized |
| Tie to the customer | Transaction, short time period | 1 2 3 4 5 | Relationship, long time period |
| Technology | Routine, simple | 1 2 3 4 5 | Nonroutine, complex |
| Business environment | Predictable, few surprises | 1 2 3 4 5 | Unpredictable, many surprises |
| Types of people | Theory X managers, employees with low growth needs, low social needs, and weak interpersonal skills | 1 2 3 4 5 | Theory Y managers, employees with high growth needs, high social needs, and strong interpersonal skills |

Source: David E. Bowen and Edward E. Lawler III, "The Empowerment of Service Workers: What, Why, How, and When," *Sloan Management Review* (Spring 1992), 31–39.

The firm's **tie to the customer** refers to the type of relationship the firm has with its customers. If the relationship involves discrete transactions that occur over a short time, control-oriented approaches should dominate. In contrast, if the customer-client relationship is long-term, such as that with an insurance agent, broker, or CPA, employees should be empowered to meet the individual needs of clients.

Similarly, if the **technology** used to carry out the firm's operations is simple and routine and the **business environment** within which the firm operates is predictable, then the costs associated with empowered employees outweigh the benefits. If, on the other hand, the technology is nonroutine and complex and the business environment is volatile, empowered employees are necessary for coping with client concerns and the constantly changing environment.

Finally, empowered employees need different kinds of leadership. Theory Y managers, who coach and facilitate rather than control and manipulate, are needed to work with employees who have high growth needs and strong interpersonal skills—the needs and skills of empowered employees. In contrast, firms governed by Theory X managers believe that employees are working primarily to collect a paycheck. Theory X managers work best with employees who have low growth needs, low social needs, and weak interpersonal skills. Theory X managers fit best with control-oriented organizations.

The contingency approach presented in Table 10.4 rates each of the five factors (basic business strategy, tie to the customer, technology, business environment, and types of people) on a scale from 1 to 5, where lower numbers favor a control-oriented approach and higher numbers favor an empowerment approach. Upon adding the scores of the five factors together, firms scoring in the 5 to 10 range are recommended to pursue a very control-oriented, production-line approach. Firms scoring 11 to 15 are recommended to implement a suggestion involvement strategy. Firms rating 16 to 20 are urged to utilize a job involvement approach, and

**tie to the customer**
The degrees of involvement the firm has with its customers.

**technology**
The level of automation a firm utilizes.

**business environment**
The social, technological, and financial environment in which a firm operates and markets.

firms that score 21 to 25 are suggested to implement a high-involvement empowerment approach. The selection of empowerment strategy should be dependent on the firm and the market in which it operates. Different types of firms have different needs.

## PULLING IT ALL TOGETHER

Ultimately, the use of empowerment and enfranchisement is to break free from the shackles imposed by the industrial management model and move to values embraced by the market-focused management approach. As we introduced in Chapter 1, the market-focused management model champions the notion that the purpose of the firm is to service its customers. By following this approach, the service delivery process becomes the focus of the organization and the overall key to successfully differentiating the firm from its competition. People become the key to success.

The market-focused management approach recognizes that employee turnover and customer satisfaction are clearly related. As a result, the recruitment and training of front-line personnel is emphasized. Pay is directly tied to performance throughout every level of the organization. Companies that compensate employees better than competitors often find that as a percentage of sales, their labor costs are actually lower than industry averages (Table 10.5). The benefits of superior training and education programs are clear. Better-trained and better-paid employees provide better service, need less supervision, and are more likely to stay on the job. High employee retention rates reflect well on the image of the company, as illustrated in Figure 10.3. In turn, customers are more satisfied, return to make purchases more often, purchase more when they do return, and tell their friends of the positive experience.

## TABLE 10.5

### Best Perks to Employees of the 100 Best Companies

| Perks | Number of Companies | Perks | Number of Companies |
|---|---|---|---|
| Overnight dependent child care | 7 | Subsidized cafeterias | 64 |
| Free lunch (or other meals) | 15 | On-site ATM or banking service | 64 |
| Personal concierge service | 15 | Personal travel services | 68 |
| On-site child care | 31 | Elder-care resource and referral | 73 |
| Dry-cleaning service | 40 | Casual dress every day | 75 |
| Home-purchasing service | 44 | Relocation services | 83 |
| Adoption aid | 60 | Child care resource and referral | 83 |

Source: "The 100 Best Companies to Work for in America," *Fortune* 137, no. 1 (January 12, 1998), 88.

**Figure 10.3**   **Bragging Rights Belong to Companies with High Employee Retention Rates**

## THE SERVICE-PROFIT CHAIN

The benefits of the market-focused management model are illustrated in the **service-profit chain** presented in Figure 10.4.[18] The links in the chain reveal that employee satisfaction and customer satisfaction are directly related. Employee satisfaction is derived from a workplace and job design that facilitate internal service quality. Hiring, training, and rewarding effective personnel are also major contributors to internal service quality.

    Satisfied employees remain with the firm and improve their individual productivity. Hence, employee satisfaction is linked with increases in the firm's overall productivity and decreases in recruitment and training costs. Moreover, the increase in productivity coupled with a sincere desire to assist customers results in external service value. Employee attitudes and beliefs about the organization are often reflected in their behaviors. Given the customer's involvement in the production process, these behaviors are visible to the customer and ultimately influence the customer's satisfaction.

    Customer satisfaction is directly related to customer loyalty, which is demonstrated through repeat purchases and positive word-of-mouth referrals to other

**service-profit chain**
A model that depicts the relationship between employee satisfaction and customer satisfaction.

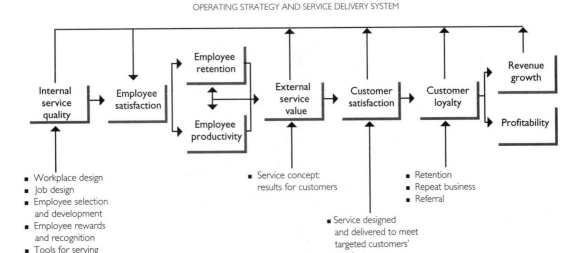

**Figure 10.4    The Service-Profit Chain**
Source: James L. Heskett, Thomas O. Jones, Gary W. Loveman, W. Earl Sasser, Jr., and Leonard A. Schlesinger, "Putting the Service-Profit Chain to Work," *Harvard Business Review* (March–April 1994), 164–174. Reprinted by permission of *Harvard Business Review*. Copyright © 1994 by the President and Fellows of Harvard College.

customers. The net effects of customer retention are increased revenues and profitability for the firm.

Simultaneously, employees are also rewarded for their efforts. The outcomes associated with employee satisfaction—external service values, customer satisfaction, customer loyalty, revenue growth, and increased profitability—reinforce the company's commitment for continually improving internal service quality. As the recipients of internal quality improvements and positive customer responses, employees directly experience the fruits of their efforts. Employee satisfaction is subsequently reinforced and the integrity of the service-profit chain is maintained.

The service-profit chain provides the logic behind the change in perspective that has led to the new services model. The major lessons to be learned by the chain are twofold. First, a firm must satisfy its employees in order for customer satisfaction to become a consistent reality. Second, the chain proclaims the simple fact that service and quality pay!

## SUMMARY

Successful service firms develop a seamless relationship between marketing, operations, and human resources. This chapter has focused on some of the human resource issues that must be considered when marketing services. Much has been written about the fact that, for many service firms, personnel constitute the bulk of their product. It is thus important that the place of personnel within the organization be understood. By drawing on the concepts of organizational behavior and, in particular, the concepts of boundary-spanning roles, empowerment, and enfranchisement, this chapter has provided a solid framework on which to develop the marketing implications of personnel as a key component of the firm's overall product offering.

As boundary spanners, service personnel perform the dual functions of interacting with both the firm's external environment and its internal organization and structure. Employees who occupy boundary-spanning roles are often placed in situations that produce conflict and stress. Five common types of stress include inequality dilemmas, feelings versus behavior, territorial conflict, organization/ client conflicts, and interclient conflicts.

Because service firms often involve the customer as a co-producer, they operate open systems in which the effects of human resource practices and policies as well as the organization's climate are visible to customers. Current human resource theory is looking for ways to break out of the industrial model mindset and, in particular, how to use empowerment and enfranchisement to break the cycle of failure. When deciding among empowerment strategies, the firm must consider the following:

- The firm's basic business strategy
- Its tie to the customer
- Technology
- The business environment
- Types of leadership

The selection of empowerment strategy should be dependent on the firm and the market in which it operates. Different types of firms have different needs. Ultimately the use of empowerment and enfranchisement is to break free from the shackles imposed by the industrial management model and move to values embraced by the market-focused management approach. The benefits of the market-focused management model are illustrated in the service-profit chain. The major lessons to be learned by the chain are twofold. First, a firm must satisfy its employees in order for customer satisfaction to become a consistent reality. Second, the chain proclaims the simple fact that service and quality pay!

# Key Terms

| | |
|---|---|
| Basic business strategy | Organization/client conflicts |
| Boundary-spanning roles | Person/role conflicts |
| Business environment | Professional service roles |
| Climate | Quality circles |
| Empowerment | Service-profit chain |
| Enfranchisement | Subordinate service roles |
| High involvement | Suggestion involvement |
| Interclient conflicts | Technology |
| Job involvement | Tie to the customer |

## Discussion Questions

1. Relate the concepts of intangibility, inseparability, heterogeneity, and perishability to the importance of personnel in the service firm.
2. What are boundary-spanning personnel? Discuss the five types of conflict that they generally encounter.
3. How can marketing be utilized to reduce the amount of stress and conflict experienced by boundary-spanning personnel?
4. In what types of organizations would it be best to avoid empowerment approaches?
5. In what type of organization would it be best to implement a job involvement empowerment approach?
6. Discuss the benefits and costs associated with empowerment and enfranchisement.
7. Discuss the relevance of employee satisfaction as it relates to the service-profit chain.
8. What is climate? Why is organizational climate of particular importance to service firms?
9. Define enfranchisement. Summarize the seven tests of reward effectiveness.

## Notes

1. The first section of this chapter is based on chapters 4 and 6 of John E. G. Bateson, *Managing of Services Marketing,* 3rd ed. (Fort Worth, Tex.: The Dryden Press, 1995).
2. Dave Ulrich et al, "Employee and Customer Attachment: Synergies for Competitive Advantage," *Human Resource Planning* 14, no. 3 (1991), 89.
3. Leonard A. Schlesinger and James L Heskett, "The Service-Driven Service Company," *Harvard Business Review* (September–October, 1991), 71–81.
4. Daine Brady, "Why Service Stinks," *Business Week* (October 23, 2000), 118–128.
5. This idea was originally suggested in a slightly different form in W. Earl Sasser, P. Olsen, and D. Daryl Wycoff, *Management of Service Operations: Text, Cases, and Readings* (Boston: Allyn and Bacon, 1978).
6. Philip Kotler, *Marketing Management,* 8th ed. (Englewood Cliffs, N.J.: Prentice-Hall, 1994), 303.
7. J. D. Thompson, "Organization and Output Transactions," *American Journal of Sociology* 68 (1967), 309–324.
8. Boas Shamir, "Between Service and Servility: Role Conflict in Subordinate Service Roles," *Human Relations* 33, no. 10 (1980), 741–756.
9. See Arlie Hochshild, *The Managed Heart* (Berkeley, Calif.: University of California Press, 1983).
10. For example, see Jody D. Nyquist, Mary Jo Bitner, and Bernard Booms, "Identifying Difficulties in the Service Encounter: A Critical Incident

Approach," in John Czepiel, Michael R. Solomon, and Carol F. Suprenant, eds., *The Service Encounter* (Lexington, Mass.: Heath, 1985), 195–212.

11. Peter Klaus, "The Quality Epiphenomenon," in John Czepiel, Michael R. Solomon, and Carol F. Suprenant, eds., *The Service Encounter* (Lexington, Mass.: Heath, 1985), 15.

12. Charles T. Goodsell, "Bureaucratic Manipulation of Physical Symbols: An Empirical Investigation," *American Journal of Political Science* XXI (February 1977), 79–91.

13. Benjamin Schneider, Jill K. Wheeler, and Jonathan F. Cox, "A Passion for Service: Using Content Analysis to Explicate Service Climate Themes," *Journal of Applied Psychology* 77, no. 5 (1992), 705–716.

14. See Benjamin Schneider, "The Service Organization: Climate Is Crucial," *Organizational Dynamics* (Autumn 1980), 52–65; and Benjamin Schneider and David E. Bowen, "The Service Organization: Human Resource Management Is Crucial," *Organizational Dynamics* (Spring 1993), 39–52.

15. Daniel Roth, "My Job at the Container Store," *Fortune* 141, no. 1 (January 10, 2000), 74–78.

16. David E. Bowen and Edward E. Lawler III, "The Empowerment of Service Workers: What, Why, How, and When," *Sloan Management Review* (Spring 1992), 31–39.

17. Martin L. Bell, "Tactical Services Marketing and the Process of Remixing," in *Marketing of Services,* W. R. George and J. M. Donnelly, eds. (Chicago: American Marketing Association, 1986), 162–165.

18. James L. Heskett, Thomas O. Jones, Gary W. Loveman, W. Earl Sasser, Jr., and Leonard A. Schlesinger, "Putting the Service-Profit Chain to Work," *Harvard Business Review* (March–April 1994), 164–174.

# chapter 11

# People Issues: Managing Service Consumers

## CHAPTER OBJECTIVES

The purpose of this chapter is to explore the special role of the service consumer. The consumer's role in service production can both facilitate and hinder the exchange process. Hence, developing a strategic understanding of how the consumer can be effectively managed within the service encounter is critical.

After reading this chapter, you should be able to:

- Discuss strategies for managing consumer participation within the service encounter.
- Describe approaches that manage consumer waits.
- Explain appropriate methods for dealing with difficult customers.
- Understand the fundamental concepts behind customer relationship management (CRM).

"They put their two year old on your register, let her crawl around, and get #$#@!! when you try to prevent the snotfaced little tot from spitting up all over your scanner."

www.customerssuck.com

# Introduction

Ultimately, the success of many service encounters depends on how effectively the service firm manages its clientele. As mentioned in previous chapters, the service encounter can be viewed as a three-way fight for control between the customer, the employee, and the organization itself.[1] The procedures and systems established by the organization to balance this arrangement are not created to simply add to the bureaucracy of the encounter but are primarily put into place for economic reasons to ensure profitability.

Unlike the goods manufacturer, who may seldom see an actual customer while producing the good in a secluded factory, service providers are often in constant contact with their customers and must construct their service operations with the customer's physical presence in mind. This interaction between customer and service provider defines a critical incident. Critical incidents represent the greatest opportunity for both gains and losses in regard to customer satisfaction and customer retention.

During the customer's interaction with the service provider, the customer provides inputs into the service production process. As such, the customer often plays a key role in the successful completion of the service encounter. The customer's involvement in the production process may vary from (1) a requirement that the customer be physically present to receive the service, such as in dental services, a haircut, or surgery; (2) a need for the customer to be present only to start and stop the service, such as in dry cleaning and auto repair; and (3) a need for the customer to be only mentally present, such as in participation in college courses that are transmitted via the Internet. Each scenario reflects different levels of customer contact, and as a result each service delivery system should be designed differently.

The focus of this chapter is on four consumer management areas of particular importance:

- The management of consumer participation in the service process
- The management of consumer waiting periods
- Dealing with difficult customers—managing to keep your cool while those around you are losing theirs
- An introduction to customer relationship management

## MANAGING CUSTOMER PARTICIPATION

Overall, as customer participation increases, the efficiency of the operation decreases. The customer's involvement in the production process creates uncertainties in the scheduling of production. For example, the customer has a direct impact on the type of service desired, the length of the service delivery process, and the cycle of service demand. Attempting to manage consumer participation in the production process with efficient operating procedures is a delicate art.

Increasing consumer participation in the service delivery process has become a popular strategy to increase the supply of service available to the firm and to provide a form of service differentiation (see Services in Action 11.1). By allowing

SERVICES **11.1**

ACTION    **Customer Inputs into the Service Game**

### Focus or Falter in the Marketplace

Customers in different market segments have different expectations. Once expectations are identified, all the policies and practices of the business from human resources to operations and from financing to marketing must fit the market segment—or the business will falter.

### Recognize That Quality Starts with Needs

Customers are driven to satisfy their needs at a more fundamental level than at which they are driven to satisfy their expectations. Be in the business of gratifying, not violating, customer needs.

### Recognize That Violating Needs Means Losing a Customer

If you dissatisfy a customer by not meeting their expectations, you can still recover. If you dissatisfy customers by violating their basic needs, you will lose them.

### Respect Customers' Need for Security

Service business must (1) present cues that customers will be safe; (2) ensure stability and predictability in the service offering; (3) prepare for crises that might threaten customers; and (4) find ways to tell customers that they [the customer] may not be right about how to best satisfy their own security needs.

### Respect Customers' Need for Justice

The core service, procedures, and the interpersonal way in which customers are handled must leave them feel justly treated.

### Clarify the Customer's Co-production Role

Service firms must define what role they want their customers to play. Providing customers with realistic service previews (RSPs) can help customers make more informed decisions about their own co-production role.

### Improve Customer Ability through Selection and Training

A job analysis of the partial employee's role will reveal the abilities required to play that role. Those abilities must either come with the customer you choose to service or provided to them through training. Training is often the only alternative. Designing training and information programs is an investment in service quality.

## Motivate Customers to Participate

Customers must clearly see the connection between their co-production efforts and obtaining available valued rewards. Rewards should be desired by customers, and customers should understand the required behaviors that are necessary to obtain rewards.

## Conduct Customer Performance Appraisals

Tracking customer errors provides the firm with an opportunity to take corrective action to improve customers' role clarity, ability, and motivation.

## Watch for Clues That Customers Could Do More

There are many indicators of possibilities for increasing the customer's involvement in the service production process—customers idly standing around while waiting, peaks and valleys in customer requests for service, and customers not utilizing available service personnel.

## Rely on Customers as Substitutes for Leadership

Employees use customers as a source of good feeling, and customers provide a source of guidance for employees. Research shows that employees do indeed derive good feelings from customers—but guidance provided by customers may generate employee dissatisfaction. Customers can be trained as a source of good feelings for employees and socialized to limit task direction to employees.

## Draw in Customers as Co-designers of the Service Delivery System

Customers can serve as designers of policies and procedures as well as producers of their own services. Customers can also be involved in decisions regarding staffing, marketing, and operations. Involving customers in such ways can deepen the relationship between service businesses and customers and make both more effective.

Source: Adapted from David E. Bowen and Benjamin Schneider, *Winning the Service Game* (Boston, Mass.: Harvard Business School Press, 1995).

**co-produce**
When service is produced via a cooperative effort between customers and service providers

consumers to **co-produce** at least part of their own service, contact personnel are freed to perform other duties, such as serving other customers or engaging in non-customer-related activities (such as completing paperwork). Increasing customer participation is associated with a number of advantages and disadvantages. The primary advantage to the customer and the service firm is that customers can customize their own service and produce it faster and less expensively than if the firm had produced it. Customers who pump their own gas, make their own salads, and pick their own strawberries are classic examples. On the other hand, increased levels of customer participation are also associated with the firm's losing control of quality; increased waste, which increases operating costs; and customer perceptions that the firm may be attempting to distance itself from its customers.

When making the transition from a full-service to a self-service operation, the firm needs to be sensitive to the reasons the customer may prefer one format over another. Guidelines have evolved that help facilitate this transition and avoid insensitivity.[2]

## Develop Customer Trust

Efforts to increase customer participation throughout the production process should not be interpreted as the firm's way of distancing itself from the customer. The firm should provide information to the customer that explains why self-service opportunities are being provided and the potential customer benefits. When it is readily apparent that the only reason the firm is offering self-service options is to benefit the firm, customers will quickly flock to full-service competitors.

## Promote the Benefits and Stimulate Trial

The typical benefits associated with self-service are convenience, customization, and cost savings to the customer. Self-service gas stations provide a cost savings, self-service salad and dessert bars allow customers to customize their own salads and ice cream sundaes, and automatic teller machines (ATM) provide 24-hour service and extend the bank's services to hundreds of convenient locations.

To promote new self-service options, customers may need an incentive to stimulate trial. For example, one bank purposely rigged its new automatic teller machine to sporadically distribute more cash than its customers requested to stimulate trial of the machine. The cash was used as a promotional tool and was free to the customer. The strategy was originally intended to make customers aware of the new ATM's location and to encourage older clientele, who traditionally resist change, to use the ATM. Soon after the promotion started, clever college students began withdrawing and redepositing their money over and over again to increase their chances to win extra cash. The grand prize of $500 was eventually awarded to an elderly gentleman, who believed the ATM had made a mistake and attempted to return the money to the bank. Ironically, it took bank employees several attempts to convince the man that this was his money to take and that it had not been withdrawn from his account.

An automatic teller machine enables a bank to provide 24-hour service to its customers and extend the bank's services to hundreds of convenient locations. What is another advantage of providing an ATM?

## Understand Customer Habits

Part of the problem when transferring from full-service to self-service is that we tend to forget why customers might prefer using full-service options in the first place. Despite the convenience of ATMs, many customers like the personalization of dealing with a particular teller. Friendships and trust develop that cannot be replaced by machinery. In addition, many bank customers will use an ATM for withdrawals but refuse to make deposits through the same ATM. The thought of handing over checks and cash to a machine seems to be too much of a risk for some customers.

## Pretest New Procedures

All new self-service options should be thoroughly pretested, not only by the firm's employees but particularly by customers who do not have the advantage of full information. For example, the British postal system attempted to enlist the help of its customers by requesting them to use extremely long zip codes when addressing envelopes. The plan was a disaster. The zip codes were far too long to remember, and the public basically vetoed any further development of the project by simply refusing to participate.

Pretesting helps in identifying and correcting potential problems before new procedures are fully introduced. In many instances, the company may have only one or two chances to prove to customers the benefits of self-service alternatives. However, if the procedures themselves are flawed and/or difficult to understand, the firm may lose its chance to convince customers of the advantages. For example, more customers might use ATMs if the screens did not face the sun and were easier to read, if initially the machines had not frequently "eaten" the customer's ATM cards, and if customers did not have to be gymnasts to use drive-through ATMs from their vehicles.

## Understand the Determinants of Consumer Behavior

When considering consumer benefits of self-service alternatives, firms should understand the determinants of consumer behavior. Why would a customer use an ATM instead of a bank teller? Or why would customers like to select and cook their own steaks in a fine dining restaurant? The consumer benefits promoted by the firm should be defined by the customer. For example, customers who work shifts other than the traditional 8-to-5 slot enjoy the 24-hour accessibility of ATMs. Other customers may simply be in a hurry, and the ATM provides a faster means of service. At self-service cookeries, the experience of selection and preparation may facilitate social interaction and/or be ego driven.

## Teach Consumers How To Use Service Innovations

Many of today's self-service options are technology driven, and in many cases customers are left to fend for themselves in attempts to use these new alternatives. An "on your own" approach does not exactly encourage customers to try new self-service methods. For customers to be taught, employees must first know how to use the technology themselves. Nothing will turn off customers faster than employees who have no idea how to use the new systems themselves.

## Monitor and Evaluate Performance

Finally, if a firm's self-service option enjoys an initial success, it should be continuously monitored and evaluated throughout the year. Does demand fluctuate? What are the possible causes? Has demand increased, decreased, or leveled off? What other services do consumers want self-service access to? Customer surveys and focus groups will not only define satisfaction with today's services but also will provide insight pertaining to the needs of tomorrow.

# MANAGING CONSUMER WAITS

In addition to managing consumer participation, service managers are often faced with managing other customer-related challenges as well. Because production and consumption occur simultaneously, several customers often share a common service experience. As a result, demand often outpaces supply and queues develop that must be effectively managed to minimize customer dissatisfaction. Because of the unpredictability of consumer demand inherent in many service operations, the only cases in which the supply of available services and consumer demand balance exactly are by accident. As a result, consumers of services often find themselves waiting for service.

Effectively managing consumer waits is particularly crucial because of the importance of first impressions on consumer perceptions of the service experience. First impressions are often long lasting and can dramatically affect customer evaluations of the total experience, regardless of how good the service was after the wait. A dental patient waiting until 4:00 P.M. for an appointment that was supposed to begin at 2:00 P.M. will most likely care little about how friendly the staff and the dentist are by the time the appointment actually begins.

Over the years, through trial and error, eight principles of waiting have developed to help service firms effectively manage consumer waits.[3] Service firms sensitive to these principles have developed strategies to deal with consumer waits and to minimize the negative affects associated with delays. In fact, in some instances, effective management of consumer waits has actually led to increased profit opportunities.

## Principle #1: Unoccupied Waits Feel Longer Than Occupied Waits

Waiting around with nothing to do makes every minute seem so much longer. Successful service firms have learned to manage consumer waits by occupying the consumer's time. Restaurants can occupy consumer waits by offering to let the consumer wait in the lounge area, which also increases the profit-making opportunity for the firm. Similarly, golf courses offer driving ranges, and the medical community tends to offer reading materials. Ideally, tactics used to occupy consumers should be related to the ensuing service encounter. Trivial attempts to occupy consumer waits, such as forcing the customer to listen to Muzak when placed on hold during a phone call, are sometimes met with customer resistance and frustration.

## Principle #2: Preprocess Waits Feel Longer than In-process Waits—Postprocess Waits Feel Longest of All

The waiting period before the service starts feels longer to customers than waiting while the service is in process. For example, doctors often move waiting patients into empty examining rooms to convey the sense that the service has started. Realistically, the physician has simply changed the location of the wait. Effective techniques to manage preprocess waits include simply acknowledging the customer. For example, wait staff are often too busy to serve customers as soon as they are seated. Phrases such as "I'll be with you as soon as I can" acknowledge the customer's presence and conveys the message that the service has started. Other phrases such as "Your order is being processed" are also effective in keeping the customer informed of the status of the order.

Postprocess waits feel the longest of all. In many instances the service has been delivered, and the customer is simply waiting for the check or bill. It's baffling to customers to be subjected to delays when the customer simply wants to give the service establishment money. Another example of customer impatience regarding postprocess waits can be experienced during deplaning procedures at the airport. On your next flight, listen to the sounds of passengers releasing their seatbelts as soon as (or before) the plane comes to a full stop. The door to the plane is not open, no one is leaving the plane, yet people are literally fighting for positions to get themselves off the plane as quickly as possible.

## Principle #3: Anxiety Makes the Wait Seem Longer

Have you ever noticed how much longer traffic lights take to change when you are in a hurry? This is because anxiety expands consumer perceptions of time. Effective service firms manage the anxiety levels of their customers by attempting to identify and then removing anxiety-producing components of the service encounter. The use of focus groups is particularly helpful in effectively identifying anxiety producers because many consumer fears may be irrational and/or over-looked by providers who fully understand the service delivery process. Often, information is one of the most effective tools in relieving consumer anxiety. For example, informing delayed airline passengers that connecting flights are being held for them, notifying waiting moviegoers that seats are available, and assisting new students in finding the right lines during registration will remove much of the anxiety felt by these consumer groups.

## Principle #4: Uncertain Waits Are Longer Than Known, Finite Waits

While waiting in a doctor's office, the wait before the stated appointment time passes much more quickly than the time spent waiting beyond the appointment time. Restaurants have learned this lesson the hard way. In the not-so-distant-past, it seemed that restaurants would purposely underestimate their wait times to encourage patrons not to leave the restaurant to dine at a competitor's establish-ment. This strategy resulted in angry, frustrated customers who felt they had been purposely misled and lied to for the sake of greed. By the time the customers were seated, they were so consumed with anger that the food, service, and atmosphere of the encounter became irrelevant, regardless of their quality. Moreover, many of these patrons would vow never to return. Today it seems that restaurants overesti-mate their waits to provide consumers with a realistic time frame from which to develop expectations. Other service providers simply make and keep appoint-ments, which eliminates the customer's wait altogether. Even other providers, such as Disney, provide finite waiting times stated on signage that is strategically placed at certain points along the line (e.g., 10 minutes from this point).

## Principle #5: Unexplained Waits Are Longer Than Explained Waits

It is human nature to want an explanation. You can almost see the disappointment in people's faces when the slow speed during a traffic jam on the highway resumes its normal pace without an explanation. Customers want to know why they have to wait, and the earlier the information is provided, the more under-standing the consumer becomes, and the shorter the wait seems to take.

Because of the inseparability of services, customers sometimes have a diffi-cult time understanding why all the service providers in the factory are not serv-ing customers. Banks are a good example. Bank tellers must sometimes perform operational duties, such as balancing the cash drawer, which prohibits them from serving customers. However, because all bank teller stations are visible to the customers, customers often question why all the bank tellers are not actively serving the bank's customers.

Effective management may try to minimize this problem in one of two ways. First, management may consider educating consumers about the realities of the bank teller's duties, which extend beyond interactions with customers. Second, management may consider developing a physical facility where the teller is out of sight when performing non-customer-related duties. This type of problem extends beyond the banking industry. Airlines, grocery stores, and other businesses that grant their employees rest breaks that are visible to the customer face similar challenges.

## Principle #6: Unfair Waits Are Longer Than Equitable Waits

Effective consumer management should strive to provide a level playing field that is fair for all consumers. The majority of consumers are not unreasonable. Most restaurant consumers understand that larger parties will wait longer than smaller parties and that parties with reservations will be seated sooner than those who arrive unannounced. However, probably nothing will ignite a serious confrontation faster than consumers who feel they have been passed over by other customers who entered the service experience at a later time under the same set of circumstances.

Lines such as those found at McDonald's, supermarkets, and drive-through banks are classic examples of why consumers become frustrated. In each instance the customer must pick the line he or she thinks will move fastest. Inevitably the other lines move faster, and customers who entered the lines at a later time are served first, out of order. From a fairness perspective, methods that form a single line, such as those used at Wendy's, Burger King, and many banks, are preferable. Customers are served in the order in which they enter the service process.

Another classic example of unfair service is the priority that telephone calls receive over customers who are physically standing in line. The person on the telephone usually takes priority. This is the equivalent of that person walking up to the front of the line and bypassing all the other customer who have been patiently waiting for their turn. Management needs to consider the costs of having employees return phone calls at a more appropriate time versus the cost of alienating existing customers and placing employees in an awkward and often indefensible position.

## Principle #7: The More Valuable the Service, the Longer the Customer Will Wait

Why else would you wait in a doctor's office for two hours? Is it any wonder that the word *patient* is a form of the word *patience?* The amount of time customers are willing to wait is often situational. When the service is considered valuable and few competitive alternatives exist, customers will be willing to wait much longer than if the reverse were true.

Perceived value of the service tends to increase with the title and status of the provider. Students will tend to wait longer for a full professor who is late for class than they will for an assistant professor, and they will wait for a dean or chancellor of the university even longer. Similarly, customers are willing to wait much longer for their meals at upscale restaurants than at fast-food establishments. When managing consumer waits, the firm must understand the value its customers place on its services and the time they consider to be a reasonable wait, because it does vary from sector to sector and within sectors.

### Principle #8: Solo Waits Are Longer Than Group Waits

It is amusing to consider the amount of customer interaction typically displayed in a grocery store line. Generally, there is none at all, even though we are standing within inches of one another. However, note what happens when a delay occurs, such as a price check on an item or a customer who takes too long to fill out a check—the rest of the line quickly bonds like old friends! Group waits serve the function of occupying customers' time and reduces the perceived wait. When managing consumer waits, the practicality of actively encouraging consumers to interact may be considered.

## MANAGING UNCOOPERATIVE CUSTOMERS

Because services are often a "shared experience," one of the primary challenges is to manage different market segments with different needs within a single service environment. Customers are not always saints, and disruptive behavior impacts not only other customers but service personnel as well. For further insight into the realities of dealing with customers see Services in Action 11.2 and visit customerssuck.com for a variety of providers' stories about their customers.

Few companies ever sit down with employees to discuss how to deal with difficult customers. The lack of discussion about dealing with difficult customers may be a result of the lack of attention paid to the subject in institutions of higher learning. Despite the importance of the customer as the central theme that runs throughout the field of marketing, little discussion, if any, occurs on how to interact with a real, live customer in most colleges and universities. Here's your chance to be part of the cutting edge.

Five customer profiles have been developed, representing the worst that customers have to offer.[4] By categorizing unreasonable customers into one of the five profiles, contact personnel are more easily able to depersonalize the conflict and handle customer complaints more objectively. In reality, the worst customer of all is a little of all five types. The characteristics of each of the five "customers from hell" and suggestions for ways to deal with them are discussed below.

**Egocentric Edgar**
The type of customer who places his or her needs above all other customers and service personnel.

### Egocentric Edgar

**Egocentric Edgar** is the guy Carly Simon had in mind when she wrote the song "You're So Vain." Edgar doesn't believe he should stand in line for any reason. He'll

Source: Ron Zemke and Kristin Anderson, "Customers from Hell," *Training* 26 (February 1990), 25–31. Reprinted with permission from TRAINING Magazine. ©1990, Lakewood Publications, Minneapolis, MN. All rights reserved. Not for Resale.

SERVICES **11.2**
IN ACTION

### All Is Fair in Love and War: www.customerssuck.com

Despite the old adage that the customer is never wrong, www.customers suck.com gives employees the chance to vent their frustrations with customers. To date, approximately 500,000 people have visited the site. Visitors can subscribe to The Customers Suck! newsletter, chat with fellow customer service reps on the site's message boards, and contribute to moderated sites such as the following:

- At the Movies: Stories from the film industry
- Customer Service Definitions: Terms that should be used for customers that do certain things
- Coffee Shop Blues: Stories about dealing with customers before they get their daily dose of caffeine
- The Real Cellular Craze: Stories from those in the cellular/digital phone industry
- Loving the Library: Stories from librarians
- Sick of Seniors: The idea of a second childhood is apparently true
- Dealing with Drunks: Customers are bad enough sober, but add a little alcohol . . .
- Customers Coming Clean: Stories from customers that knew they screwed up
- Customers Being Bad to Other Customers: When customers decided that for some reason they are the only customers that deserve respect in the store
- Disgruntled Employees Union!: Other sites that deal with employees, customer service, etc.

Source: http://www.customerssuck.com/main.html (June 25, 2000).

Source: Ron Zemke and Kristin Anderson, "Customers from Hell," *Training* 26 (February 1990), 25–31. Reprinted with permission from TRAINING Magazine. ©1990, Lakewood Publications, Minneapolis, MN. All rights reserved. Not for Resale.

push his way to the front and demand service on a variety of things that demand little immediate attention. If your company's credo is "We Are Here To Serve," Edgar interprets that message as, "Your Company Exists To Serve My Needs and My Needs Alone, and Right Now!"

Another of Edgar's nasty characteristics is that he will walk over front-line employees to get to who he'll call "the man in charge." Edgar treats front-line employees as well-worn speed bumps that deserve just that much consideration. Once he gets to the top, Edgar uses the chance to belittle upper management and prove he knows how things should be done.

Dealing with Edgar is particularly troublesome for providers who are new on the job, unsure of their own abilities, and easily pushed around. The key to dealing with Edgar is to not let his ego destroy yours, while at the same time appealing to his ego. Because Edgar believes you are incapable of performing any function, take action that demonstrates your ability to solve his problem. This will surprise Edgar. In addition, never talk policy to Edgar. Edgar thinks he is special and that the rules that apply to everyone else should not apply to him. Policy should still apply to Edgar, but just don't let him know that you are restating policy. Phrases such as, "For you, Edgar, I can do the following…" where "the following" is simply policy will appeal to Edgar's ego while still managing him within the policies of the organization.

## Bad-Mouth Betty

**Bad-Mouth Betty**
The type of customer who becomes loud, crude, and abusive to service personnel and other customers alike.

**Bad-Mouth Betty** lets you know in no uncertain terms exactly what she thinks of you, your organization, and the heritage of both. If she cannot be right, she will be loud, vulgar, and insensitive. She is crude not only to service employees but also to other customers who are sharing her unpleasant experience.

Dealing with Betty consists of at least four options. First, because Betty is polluting the service environment with her foul mouth, attempt to move her "offstage" so as to not further contaminate the service environment of your other customers. Once isolated, one option is to ignore her foul language and listen to determine the core of the problem and take appropriate action. This is a difficult option to undertake, particularly if her language is excessively abusive and

personal in nature. A second option is to use selective agreement in an attempt to show Betty that you are listening and are possibly on her side. **Selective agreement** involves agreeing with Betty on minor issues, such as, "You're right, waiting 10 minutes for your Egg McMuffin is a long time." However, agreeing with Betty that your boss really is an "SOB" is not advisable, since Betty is likely to use this to her advantage at a later date. The last option that every good service firm should seriously consider is to "force the issue." In other words, let Betty know that you would be more than willing to help her solve her problem but that you don't have to listen to her abusive language. If Betty continues to be crude, hang up, walk away, or do whatever is necessary to let her know she is on her own. In most cases, she will return the call, or walk over and apologize, and let you get on with your job.

**selective agreement**
A method of dealing with a dissatisfied customer by agreeing on minor issues in order to show that the customer is being heard.

## Hysterical Harold

**Hysterical Harold** is a screamer. If he doesn't get his way, his face will turn colors and veins will literally pop out from his neck. "Harold demonstrates the dark side . . . of the child inside all of us. He is the classic tantrum thrower, the adult embodiment of the terrible twos. Only louder. Much louder."[5]

Dealing with Harold is much like dealing with Betty in many ways. These two occupy the "other customers" slot of the servuction model and negatively affect everyone else's service experience. Consequently, move Harold offstage and give your other customers a chance to enjoy the remainder of their encounter. When Harold has a problem, Harold has to vent. When offstage, let him vent and get it off his chest. This is when you can finally get to the heart of the matter and begin to take action. Finally, take responsibility for the problem. Do not blame the problem on fellow employees, upper management, or others who may ultimately be responsible. Offer an apology for what has occurred and, more importantly, a solution to Harold's problem.

**Hysterical Harold**
The type of customer who reverts to screaming and tantrums to make his or her point.

## Dictatorial Dick

**Dictatorial Dick**
The type of customer who assumes superiority over all personnel and management.

**Dictatorial Dick** is claimed to be Egocentric Edgar's evil twin. Dick likes to tell everyone exactly how they are supposed to do their jobs because he has done it all before. Just so you don't get confused, Dick will provide you a written copy of his instructions, which is copied to your boss, your boss's boss, and his lawyer. Dick will most likely make you sign for your copy.

If his brilliant instructions do not produce the desired outcome, then it's your company's fault, or, more likely, your fault because you were too incompetent to fully understand Dick's brilliance. Or perhaps Dick's paranoia will set in, which makes him believe that you deliberately sabotaged his plan to make him look bad.

Dealing with Dick would test anyone's patience. The main key is to not let him push you around. Employees should stick to their game plans and provide service in the manner they know is appropriate and equitable for all concerned. Because other customers are likely to be present, employees need to be consistent in how they deal with individual customers. Dick should not be treated as the "squeaky wheel" who always gets the grease. The best strategy for dealing with Dick is to tell him in a straightforward fashion exactly what you can do for him. If reasonable to do so, fulfilling his request will break up Dick's game plan and resolve the conflict.

## Freeloading Freda

**Freeloading Freda**
The type of customer who uses "tricks" or verbal abuse to acquire services without paying.

**Freeloading Freda** wants it all for free. Give her an inch and she'll take the plates, the silverware, and everything else that's not nailed down. Freda will push your return policy to the limits. If her kid's shoes begin to wear out in a year or two, she'll return them for new ones. Question her credibility, and Freda will scream

Source: Ron Zemke and Kristin Anderson, "Customers from Hell," *Training* 26 (February 1990), 25–31. Reprinted with permission from TRAINING Magazine. ©1990, Lakewood Publications, Minneapolis, MN. All rights reserved. Not for Resale.

bloody murder to anyone and everyone who will listen, including the news media and the Better Business Bureau.

Dealing with Freda in many cases involves biting your tongue and giving her what she wants. Despite popular beliefs, the Fredas of the world probably represent only 1 to 2 percent of your customers, if that. Most customers are honest and believe that they should pay for the goods and services they consume. Another possibility is to track Freda's actions and suggest possible legal action to persuade her to take her business elsewhere. Managers of competing firms often share information regarding the Fredas of the world to avoid their excessive abuses. Finally, recognize that Freda is the exception and not the common customer. Too often, new policies are developed for the sole purpose of defeating Freda and her comrades. These new policies add to the bureaucratization of the organization and penalize the customers who follow the rules. The filing of lengthy forms to return merchandise or invoke service guarantees is a common example of penalizing the majority of customers by treating them as suspected criminals rather than as valued customers.

## Hellish Thoughts

When dealing with "customers from hell," it is difficult for employees not to take these sorts of confrontations personally. The consumer profiles introduced above should help employees prepare for the various types of difficult customers and provide strategies for minimizing the amount of conflict that actually occurs. Viewing customers as distinct profile types helps depersonalize the situation for the employee: "Oh, it's just Edgar again." This is not to say that each customer shouldn't be treated as an individual, but simply that customer complaints and behavior shouldn't be taken overly personally. In closing, one word of warning: Employees who truly master the art of dealing with difficult customers are rewarded by becoming these customers' favorite provider, the one they request by name time after time. No good deed goes unpunished!

## CUSTOMER RELATIONHIP MANAGEMENT: AN INTRODUCTION

In addition to managing customer participation, customer waiting times, and handling disruptive customers, advances in technology have now enabled service firms to manage customers based on their profitability via customer relationship management (CRM) systems. The last section of this chapter introduces CRM and discusses the pros and cons of this practice as it relates to coding, routing, targeting, and sharing.

**customer relationship management**
The process of identifying, attracting, differentiating, and retaining customers.

**Customer relationship management** (CRM) is the process of identifying, attracting, differentiating, and retaining customers. CRM allows the firm to focus its efforts disproportionately on its most lucrative clients. CRM is based on the old adage that 80 percent of a company's profits come from 20 percent of its customers; therefore, the 20 percent should receive better service than the 80 percent. For example, when a plastics manufacturer focused on its most profitable customers, it cut the company's customer base from 800 to 90 and increased revenue by 400 percent.[6,7]

The increased usage of CRM practices, in which high-value customers are treated as superior to low-value customers, can be attributed to several trends.[8] First, some believe that customers have done it to themselves by opting for price, choice, and convenience over high-quality service. However, there are tradeoffs. For example, although Priceline.com offers discounted tickets to customers at significant savings, customers often miss the tradeoffs such as forfeiting the right to any refund, flying on whatever brand of airline is available, and being forced on to connecting flights in many instances. In addition, according to one state investigation, another tradeoff is that Priceline is inappropriately prepared to handle customer complaints.

**coding**
Categorizing customers based on how profitable their business is.

**routing**
A process of directing incoming customer calls to customer service representatives in which more profitable customers are more likely to receive faster and better customer service.

Another reason CRM is currently fashionable is that labor costs have risen, yet competitive pressures have kept prices low. The end result is that gross margins have been reduced to 5 to 10 percent in many industries. With these kinds of margins, companies simply cannot afford to treat of all its customers equally. Consider the plight of Fidelity Investments. Ten years ago the company received 97,000 calls a day. Half those calls were handled by an automated telephone system. Today, Fidelity receives 700,000 calls and 550,000 Web site visits a day. Three-quarters of the calls are now handled by automated systems (telephone and Web site), which cost the company less than a dollar per call. The remaining calls are handled by live customer service personnel at $13 per call. This is just one of the reasons the company contacted 25,000 of its customers to request that they use its Web site or automated phone system.

**targeting**
Offering the firm's most profitable customers special deals and incentives.

Finally, CRM is being increasingly implemented because markets are increasingly fragmented and promotional costs are on the rise. Bass Hotels & Resorts, the owners of Holiday Inn and Inter-Continental Hotels, have recently learned a valuable lesson by not treating customers equally. The company now only sends its promotional mailings to those who "bit" on earlier mailings. The end result is that company has reduced mailing costs by 50 percent; meanwhile, response rates have increased by 20 percent.

**sharing**
Making key customer information accessible to all parts of the organization and in some cases selling that information to other firms.

## CRM Outcomes

Typical outcomes of CRM practices include **coding, routing, targeting,** and **sharing.** Each is described on the following pages and is typically associated with both positive and negative consequences for customers.[9]

## CODING

Customers are graded based on how profitable their business is. Service staff are instructed to handle customers differently based on their category code. For example:

- A New York customer travels to New Jersey to buy a table from an Ikea store. After returning home, he discovers that the table is missing necessary brackets and screws. Based on his customer code, the store refuses to mail him the missing parts and insists that he must return to the store. The customer does not own a car. In comparison . . .
- A "platinum" customer of Starwood Hotels & Resorts Worldwide wants to propose to his girlfriend in India. Starwood arranges entry to the Taj Mahal after hours so that he can propose in private. Starwood also provides a horse-driven carriage, flowers, a special meal, an upgraded suite, and a reception led by the hotel's general manager.
- Sears, Roebuck & Co.'s most profitable credit card customers get to choose a preferred two-hour time window for repair appointments. Regular customers are given a four-hour time window.

## ROUTING

Call centers route incoming calls based on the customer's code. Customers in profitable code categories get to speak to live customer service representatives. Less profitable customers are inventoried in automated telephone queues. For example:

- Call this particular electric utility company and, depending on your status, you may have to stay on the line for quite awhile. The top 350 business clients are served by six people. The next tier, consisting of the next 700 most profitable customers, are handled by six more people. The next 30,000 customers are served by two customer service representatives. The final group, consisting of 300,000 customers, are routed to an automated telephone system.
- Charles Schwab Corporation's top-rated "Signature" clients, consisting of customers who maintain $100,000 in assets or trade at least 12 times a year, never wait more than 15 seconds to have their calls personally answered by a customer service representative. Regular customers can wait up to 10 minutes or more.

## TARGETING

Profitable customers have fees waived and are targeted for special promotions. Less profitable customers may never hear of the special deals. Examples include:

- Centura Bank Inc. of Raleigh, North Carolina, ranks its two million customers on a profitability scale from one to five. The most profitable customers are called several times a year for what the bank calls "friendly chats," and the CEO calls once a year to wish these same customers a happy holiday. Since the program was implemented, the retention rate of the most profitable group has increased by 50 percent. In comparison, the most unprofitable group has decreased from 27 percent to 21 percent.

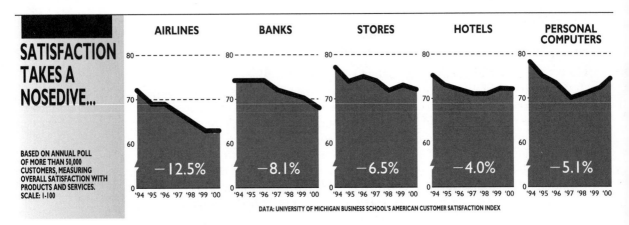

**Figure 11.1**     **Satisfaction Takes a Nosedive . . .**
Source: Diane Brady, "Why Service Stinks," *Business Week* (October 23, 2000), 120–121.

- First Bank in Baltimore, Maryland, provides its most profitable customers a Web option that its regular customers never see. The option allows its preferred customer to click a special icon that connects customers with live service agents for phone conversations.
- First Union codes its credit card customers with colored squares that flash on customer service representatives' screens. "Green squares" means the customer is profitable and should be granted fee waivers and given the "white glove" treatment.

## SHARING

Customer information is shared with other parts of the organization, and information is sold to other companies. Although the customer may be new to the organization, their purchase history and buying potential are well-known to insiders. For example:

- A United Airlines passenger was shocked when a ticketing agent told him, "Wow, somebody doesn't like you." Apparently the passenger was involved in an argument with another United employee several months earlier. The argument became part of the passenger's permanent record, which follows him wherever he flies with United. The passenger, who is a Premier Executive accountholder, feels that the airline has been less than accommodating following the incident.
- Continental Airlines has introduced a customer information system in which every one of Continental's 43,000 gate, reservation, and service employees has access to the history and value of each customer. The system also suggests specific service recovery remedies and perks such as coupons for delays and automatic upgrades. The system is expected to provide more consistent staff behavior and service delivery.

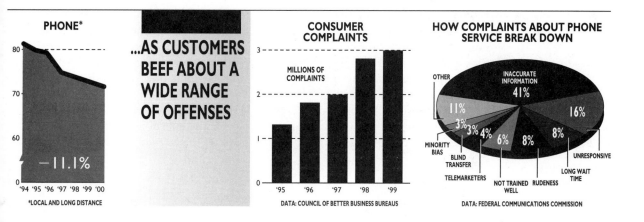

## PHONE*

−11.1%

*LOCAL AND LONG DISTANCE

## ...AS CUSTOMERS BEEF ABOUT A WIDE RANGE OF OFFENSES

## CONSUMER COMPLAINTS

MILLIONS OF COMPLAINTS

DATA: COUNCIL OF BETTER BUSINESS BUREAUS

## HOW COMPLAINTS ABOUT PHONE SERVICE BREAK DOWN

INACCURATE INFORMATION 41%

OTHER 11%

16%

MINORITY BIAS 3%

BLIND TRANSFER 3%

TELEMARKETERS 4%

NOT TRAINED WELL 6%

RUDENESS 8%

LONG WAIT TIME 8%

UNRESPONSIVE

DATA: FEDERAL COMMUNICATIONS COMMISSION

## Limitations of CRM Practices

Technology greatly enhances CRM processes by identifying current and potential customers, differentiating among high-value and low-value customers, and customizing offers to meet the needs of individual high-value customers; however, there are limitations. First, customers do not like hearing that some customers are valued more than others, especially where they are not the ones receiving the "white glove" treatment. Many companies are well aware of potential customer ill will and are fairly protective about discussing the outcomes of their respective CRM practices. In a recent *Business Week* story pertaining to CRM issues, companies such as GE Capital, Sprint, and WorldCom declined repeated requests to speak about their service discrimination practices.[10] Meanwhile, in service operations where service discrimination is common, such as airlines, banks, retail stores, hotels, and telecommunication companies, customer satisfaction is taking a nosedive and customer complaints are on the rise (Figure 11.1).

Another concern relating to CRM practices involves privacy issues. How much should a company really know about its customers? When discussing its new customer information system, the vice president of Continental Airlines recently boasted, "We even know if they [the customers] put their eyeshades on and go to sleep." Ironically, in this day and age of high-tech CRM systems, experts are now suggesting that if customers want better service, they should protect their privacy. In doing so, it is recommended that customers avoid filling out surveys and be protective about credit card and social security information. The less companies know about customers, the less likely they will be able to categorize them, and the less likely customers will be treated as low-value customers.

CRM is also limited by its focus on past purchase patterns. In reality, what someone spends today is not necessarily a good predictor of what their behavior will be tomorrow. Questions are being asked such as, How many potential profitable customers are being eliminated today because their current purchasing behavior has them slotted and treated as "commoners"? Spurned by such treatment, how many of these customers defect to another provider that appreciates their potential and treats them appropriately? Life situations and spending habits do change over time. The question is how CRM systems track these changes in behavior.

Service discrimination also leads to some interesting ethical questions. Should only the wealthy be recipients of quality service? Is this a form of **red-lining**—the practice of identifying and avoiding unprofitable types of neighborhoods or types of people?

**red-lining**
The practice of identifying and avoiding unprofitable types of neighborhoods or people.

## SUMMARY

The consumer's role in service production can both facilitate and hinder the exchange process. Hence, developing a strategic understanding of how the consumer can be effectively managed within the service encounter is critical. The focus of this chapter has been on four consumer management areas of particular importance:

1. The management of consumer participation in the service process
2. The management of consumer waiting periods
3. Dealing with difficult customers—managing to keep your cool while those around you are losing theirs
4. An introduction to an electronic customer relationship management system

Increasing consumer participation in the service delivery process has become a popular strategy to increase the supply of service available to the firm and to provide a form of service differentiation. Increasing customer participation is associated with a number of advantages and disadvantages. The primary advantage to the customer and the service firm is that customers can customize their own service and produce it faster and less expensively than if the firm had produced it. On the other hand, increased levels of customer participation are also associated with the firm's losing control of quality; increased waste, which increases operating costs; and customer perceptions that the firm may be attempting to distance itself from its customers. When making the transition from a full-service to a self-service operation, the firm needs to be sensitive to the reasons the customer may prefer one format over another. Guidelines were presented within this chapter to help facilitate this transition and avoid insensitivity to customers' underlying needs.

In addition to managing consumer participation, service managers are often faced with managing other customer-related challenges as well. Because production and consumption occur simultaneously, several customers often share a common service experience. As a result, demand often outpaces supply and queues develop that must be effectively managed to minimize customer dissatisfaction. Eight "principles of waiting" were presented in the chapter that are designed to help service managers minimize customer frustrations associated with waiting for service.

Because services are often a shared experience, one of the primary challenges is to manage different market segments with different needs within a single service environment. Customers are not always saints, and disruptive behavior impacts not only other customers but service personnel as well. Five customer profiles were presented, representing the worst that customers have to offer. By categorizing unreasonable customers into one of the five profiles, contact personnel are more easily able to depersonalize the conflict and handle customer complaints more objectively.

Finally, given the dynamic growth of e-services, a number of electronic mechanisms exist that comprise customer relationship management systems. The last section of this chapter was dedicated to explaining the pros and cons of CRM systems as they relate to coding, routing, targeting, and sharing.

# Key Terms

Bad-Mouth Betty
Coding
Co-produce
Dictatorial Dick
Egocentric Edgar
Freeloading Freda

Hysterical Harold
Routing
Selective agreement
Sharing
Targeting

# Discussion Questions

1. Discuss the pros and cons of increasing customer participation in the service delivery process.
2. When transitioning from a full-service to a self-service operation, this chapter has offered a number of guidelines to facilitate the change. Select four of these guidelines and discuss their importance as it pertains to increasing customer participation.
3. Despite the best attempts of many service firms to balance supply and demand, the only time the balance truly occurs may be by accident. Explain why this is so.
4. Select four of the eight principles of waiting and discuss their significance to managing the consumer's experience.
5. How does profiling disruptive customers assist customer contact personnel in dealing with "customers from hell"?
6. From a managerial perspective, what is the usefulness of Web sites such as www.customerssuck.com?
7. Why is the management of consumer waits and customer participation particularly important for service firms?
8. Select one of the profiles of "customers from hell." Describe the profile of this customer and offer suggested methods for dealing with this type of individual.

# Notes

1. John E. G. Bateson, "Perceived Control and the Service Encounter," in John Czepiel, Michael R. Solomon, and Carol F. Suprenant, eds., *The Service Encounter* (Lexington, Mass.: Heath, 1985), 67–82.

2. Christopher Lovelock and Robert F. Young, "Look to Consumers to Increase Productivity in Services," *Harvard Business Review* (May-June 1979), 168–178.

3. D. H. Maister, *The Psychology of Waiting in Lines* (Boston: Harvard Business School Note 9-684-064, Rev. May 1984), 2–3.

4. Ron Zemke and Kristen Anderson, "Customers from Hell," *Training* 26 (February 1990), 25–31.

5. John E. G. Bateson, *Managing Services Marketing,* ed. 4 (Fort Worth, Tex.: The Dryden Press, 1999), 121.

6. Jeremy Galbreath and K. Douglas Hoffman, "An Introduction to E-Services: The ABCs of an E-CRM Ecosystem (working paper).

7. Diane Brady, "Why Service Stinks," *Business Week* (October 23, 2000), 118–128.

8. Ibid., 122.

9. Ibid., 124.

10. Brady, "Why Service Stinks," 122.

# part three

## ASSESSING AND IMPROVING SERVICE DELIVERY

Part III, Assessing and Improving Service Delivery, focuses on customer satisfaction and service quality issues. Methods for tracking service failures and employee recovery efforts as well as customer retention strategies are presented. Ideally, assessing and improving the service delivery system will lead to "seamless" service provided without interruption, confusion, or hassle to the customer.

# chapter 12

# Defining and Measuring Customer Satisfaction

## CHAPTER OBJECTIVES

The major objectives of this chapter are to introduce you to the importance and benefits of customer satisfaction and the special factors to consider in measuring customer satisfaction.

After reading this chapter, you should be able to:

- Define customer satisfaction.
- Discuss the benefits associated with satisfied customers.
- Discuss various methods for measuring customer satisfaction.
- Discuss the limitations of customer satisfaction measurements.
- Discuss factors to consider when investing in customer satisfaction improvements.
- Discuss the three types of expectations and their relationships to customer satisfaction and service quality measurement.
- Discuss the factors that influence customer expectations.

"If you can't measure it, goes the old cliché, you can't manage it. In fact, if you can't measure it, managers seem unable to pay attention to it."

*Fortune* Magazine

# *Introduction*

Customer satisfaction is one of the most studied areas in marketing. Over the past 20 years, more than 15,000 academic and trade articles have been published on the topic.[1] In fact, *The Journal of Advertising Research* has suggested that customer satisfaction surveys may be the fastest growing area of market research. Such devotion to the subject is certainly understandable given that satisfaction is a central theme of the marketing concept and is frequently included in the mission statements and promotional campaigns of American corporations.

From a historical perspective, a great deal of the work in the customer satisfaction area began in the 1970s, when consumerism was on the rise. The rise of the consumer movement was directly related to the decline in service felt by many consumers. The decline in customer service and resulting customer dissatisfaction can be attributed to a number of sources. First, skyrocketing inflation during this period forced many firms to slash service in the effort to keep prices down. In some industries, deregulation led to fierce competition among firms who had never had to compete before. Price competition became the attempted means of differentiation, and price wars quickly broke out. Firms once again slashed costs associated with customer service to cut operating expenses.

As time went on, labor shortages also contributed to the decline in customer service. Service workers who were motivated were difficult to find, and who could blame them? The typical service job included low pay, no career path, no sense of pride, and no training in customer relations. Automation also contributed to the problem. Replacing human labor with machines indeed increased the efficiency of many operating systems, but often at the expense of distancing customers from the firm and leaving customers to fend for themselves. Finally, over the years customers have become tougher to please. They are more informed than ever, their expectations have increased, and they are more particular about where they spend their discretionary dollars.

Researchers in the field of consumer satisfaction clearly recognized the connection between the study of satisfaction and the consumer movement. The connection between the marketing concept, satisfaction, and consumerism continues to be one of the driving forces behind the study of consumer satisfaction (see Services in Action 12.1).

## THE IMPORTANCE OF CUSTOMER SATISFACTION

The importance of customer satisfaction cannot be overstated. Without customers the service firm has no reason to exist. Every service business needs to proactively define and measure customer satisfaction. Waiting for customers to complain in order to identify problems in the service delivery system or gauging the firm's progress in customer satisfaction based on the number of complaints received is naive. Consider the following figures gathered by the Technical Assistance Research Program (TARP)[2]:

SERVICES *12.1*

ACTION   **Tracking Consumer Satisfaction in the United States**

Tracking customer satisfaction in the United States is a highly complex task that has recently been undertaken through the joint efforts of the American Society for Quality Control and the University of Michigan's business school. The two groups have developed the American Customer Satisfaction Index (ACSI), which is based on 3,900 products representing more than two dozen manufacturing and services industries. Companies included in the study are selected based on size and U.S. market share and together represent about 40 percent of the United States' gross domestic product. Government services are also included in the index.

The ACSI consists of 17 questions rated on a scale from 1 to 10, regarding issues such as consumer perceptions of service, quality, value, the performance of the product compared with expectations, how the product compares with an ideal product, and how willing consumers would be to pay more for the product. Consumer responses are gathered via telephone surveys of approximately 30,000 people. The products of each company included in the survey are assessed roughly 250 times. Results from the latest ACSI indicate that, as a whole, customer satisfaction in the United States is headed slightly downward over the last seven years (see Figure 12.1).

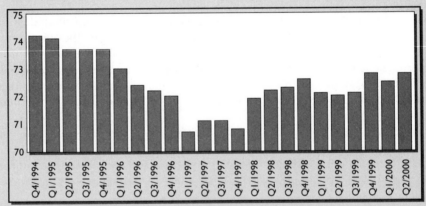

**Figure 12.1**   **American Customer Satisfaction Index: National Scores 1994–2000**

Source: Data Source: www.bus.umich.edu/researchnqre/natscores.html

Based on an analysis of ACSI results, businesses often make three common mistakes that lead to lower levels of customer satisfaction. First, many firms continue to view customer service as a cost rather than as an investment. Second, firms tend to forget that customer satisfaction is a constantly rising bar. During the 1980s, automobile consumers demanded technical excellence from manufacturers. Now consumers are looking beyond

> technical excellence and demanding better ways to purchase and service
> their vehicles. These areas are the new battlefields on which fights for future
> customer satisfaction will be won or lost. Finally, the third most common
> mistake is a firm's inability to link customer satisfaction to its bottom line.
> Some firms still do not see (or fail to appreciate) the connection. However,
> others, like those in the advertising industry, realize that a 5 percent increase
> in customer retention rate translates into a 95 percent increase in customer
> net present value.

Source: Thomas A. Stewart, "After All You've Done for Your Customers, Why Are They Still
NOT HAPPY," *Fortune* (December 11, 1995), 178–181; and Jacklyn Fierman, "Americans Can't
Get No Satisfaction," *Fortune* (December 11, 1995), 186–194.

- The average business does not hear from 96 percent of its unhappy customers.
- For every complaint received, 26 customers actually have the same problem.
- The average person with a problem tells 9 or 10 people. Thirteen percent will tell more than 20.
- Customers who have their complaints satisfactorily resolved tell an average of five people about the treatment they received.
- Complainers are more likely to do business with you again than noncomplainers: 54 to 70 percent if resolved at all, and 95 percent if handled quickly.

The TARP figures demonstrate that customers do not actively complain to service firms themselves. Instead, consumers voice their dissatisfaction with their feet, by defecting to competitors, and with their mouths, by telling your existing and potential customers exactly how they were mistreated by your firm. Based on the figures, a firm that serves 100 customers per week and boasts a 90 percent customer satisfaction rating will be the object of thousands of negative stories by the end of a year. For example, if 10 dissatisfied customers per week tell 10 of their friends of the poor service received, by the end of the year (52 weeks) 5,200 negative word-of-mouth communications will have been generated.

The TARP figures are not all bad news. Firms that effectively respond to customer complaints are the objects of positive word-of-mouth communications. Although positive news travels at half the rate of negative news, the positive stories can ultimately translate into customer loyalty and new customers. A firm should also learn from the TARP figures that complainers are the firm's friends. Complainers are a free source of market information, and the complaints themselves should be viewed as opportunities for the firm to improve its delivery systems, not as a source of irritation.

TABLE *12.1*

## Alternative Satisfaction Definitions

| | |
|---|---|
| Normative deficit definition | Compares actual outcomes to those that are culturally acceptable. |
| Equity definition | Compares gains in a social exchange—if the gains are inequal, the loser is dissatisfied. |
| Normative standard definition | Expectations are based on what the consumer believes he/she *should* receive—dissatisfaction occurs when the actual outcome is different from the standard expectation. |
| Procedural fairness definition | Satisfaction is a function of the consumer's belief that he/she was treated fairly. |

Source: Keith Hunt, "Consumer Satisfaction, Dissatisfaction, and Complaining Behavior." *Journal of Social Issues* 47, no. 1 (1991), 109–110.

**expectancy disconfirmation model**
Model proposing that comparing customer expectations with their perceptions leads customers to have their expectations confirmed or disconfirmed.

**confirmed expectations**
Customer expectations that match customer perceptions.

**disconfirmed expectations**
Customer expectations that do not match customer perceptions.

**negative disconfirmation**
Customer perceptions are lower than customer expectations.

**positive disconfirmation**
Customer perceptions exceed customer expectations.

## WHAT IS CUSTOMER SATISFACTION/DISSATISFACTION?

Although a variety of alternative definitions exist, the most popular definition of customer satisfaction/dissatisfaction is that it is a comparison of customer expectations with perceptions regarding the actual service encounter (alternative definitions are provided in Table 12.1).[3] Comparing customer expectations with their perceptions is based on what marketers refer to as the **expectancy disconfirmation model.** Simply stated, if customer perceptions meet expectations, the expectations are said to be **confirmed,** and the customer is satisfied. If perceptions and expectations are not equal, the expectation is said to be **disconfirmed.**

Although the term *disconfirmation* sounds like a negative experience, it is not necessarily so. There are two types of disconfirmations. If actual perceptions were less than what was expected, the result is a **negative disconfirmation,** which results in customer dissatisfaction and may lead to negative word-of-mouth publicity and/or customer defection. In contrast, a **positive disconfirmation** exists when perceptions exceed expectations, thereby resulting in customer satisfaction, positive word-of-mouth publicity, and customer retention.

Every day consumers use the disconfirmation paradigm by comparing their expectations with perceptions. While dining at a resort restaurant on the west coast of florida, our waiter not only provided everything we requested but also was very good at anticipating needs. My three-year-old niece had had enough fun and sun for the day and was very tired. She crawled up into a vacant booth located directly behind our table and went to sleep. The waiter, noticing her absence from our table, and on his own initiative, placed a white tablecloth over her to use as a blanket. This particular incident combined with other incidents throughout the evening lead to a positive disconfirmation of our expectations. That evening's great service reinforced the notion that with so much poor service all around, customers really do notice when the service is excellent.

# T A B L E  *12.2*

## America's Most Admired Companies

| The Top Ten | The Bottom Ten |
|---|---|
| 1. General Electric | 495. Humana |
| 2. Microsoft | 496. Revlon |
| 3. Dell Computer | 497. Trans World Airlines |
| 4. Cisco Systems | 498. CKE Restaurants |
| 5. Wal-Mart Stores | 499. CHS Electronics |
| 6. Southwest Airlines | 500. Rite Aid |
| 7. Berkshire Hathaway | 501. Trump Resorts |
| 8. Intel | 502. Fruit of the Loom |
| 9. Home Depot | 503. Amereco |
| 10. LucentTechnologies | 504. Caremark Rx |

Source: Geoffrey Colvin,"America's Most Admired Companies,*Fortune,* 141,no. 4 (February 21, 2000), 108.

## THE BENEFITS OF CUSTOMER SATISFACTION

Although some may argue that customers are unreasonable at times, little evidence can be found of extravagant customer expectations.[4] Consequently, satisfying customers is not an impossible task. In fact, meeting and exceeding customer expectations may reap several valuable benefits for the firm. Positive word-of-mouth generated from existing customers often translates into more new customers. For example, consider the positive publicity generated for the firms listed in the top 10 most admired companies listed in Table 12.2. In comparison, as a potential employee, would you have any reservations about working for the bottom 10? Satisfied current customers often purchase more products more frequently and are less likely to be lost to competitors than are dissatisfied customers.

Companies who command high customer satisfaction ratings also seem to have the ability to insulate themselves from competitive pressures, particularly price competition. Customers are often willing to pay more and stay with a firm that meets their needs than to take the risk associated with moving to a lower-priced service offering. Finally, firms that pride themselves on their customer satisfaction efforts generally provide better environments in which to work. Within these positive work environments, organizational cultures develop in which employees are challenged to perform and rewarded for their efforts. Table 12.3 provides an example of the types of attributes that are key in building great corporate reputations and lists companies that excel at particular key attributes.

In and of themselves, customer satisfaction surveys also provide several worthwhile benefits. Such surveys provide a formal means of customer feedback to the firm, which may identify existing and potential problems. Satisfaction surveys also convey the message to customers that the firm cares about their well-being and values customer input concerning its operations.[5] However, the placement of

## TABLE 12.3

### Eight Key Attributes of Reputation

| Attributes | Most Admired Companies |
|---|---|
| 1. Innovativeness | Enron, Charles Schwab, Herman Miler |
| 2. Quality of management | Enron, General Electric, Omnicom Corp. |
| 3. Employee talent | Goldman Sachs, Enron, Cisco Systems |
| 4. Financial soundness | Microsoft, Intel, Cisco Systems |
| 5. Use of corp. assets | Berkshire Hathaway, Cisco, General Electric |
| 6. Long-term investment value | Microsoft, Home Depot, Cisco Systems |
| 7. Social responsibility | McDonald's, Du Pont, Herman Miler |
| 8. Quality of products/services | Omnicom Group, Philip Morris, UPS |

Source: Geoffrey Colvin, "America's Most Admired Companies," *Fortune,* 141, no. 4 (February 21, 2000), 110.

## SERVICES 12.2

### IN ACTION  They're Listening . . . But Do They Really Want To Hear It?

According to the "We're Listening" section of Delta's in-flight magazine, *SKY,* "becoming No. 1 in the eyes of our customers is the top priority in our goal to be the world's greatest airline." However, the "We're Listening" section and the customer feedback card (below) are printed on pages 128 and 129 of the 150-page magazine. What are your impressions of the comment card? Why do you think there is a separate box to be checked (lower right-hand corner) to indicate whether the respondent is an airline employee or a travel agent?

**▲ Delta Air Lines**        Also available at www.delta-air.com/trip_a2z/faqs/ser_csmf.htm

First  Business  Coach  Date
Flight No.   Flight Class (circle)   Month  Day  Year   Departure City   Destination City   SkyMiles#

Comments/Suggestions: _____

Would you like to be contacted about your experience?   No ☐   Yes ☐   If yes, be sure to include your daytime phone or email address below.
Check the nature of your comments:   Service ☐   Amenities ☐   Delay/ Cancellation ☐   Other ☐

☐ Mr.  ☐ Ms.   First Name _____  Last Name _____  MI

Street Address _____

City _____

State/Province   Postal Code   Country

E-Mail Address _____   Daytime Phone Number

Please rate your experience on this flight:   Excellent ☐   Very Good ☐   Good ☐   Fair ☐   Poor ☐   ☐ I am an airline employee
Would you purchase your next flight on Delta?   Yes ☐   Maybe ☐   No ☐   ☐ I am a travel agent

Source: Vicki Escarra, "We're Listening," *SKY* (February 2000), 128–129.

customer feedback forms by some companies makes customers wonder if they really want the feedback (see Services in Action 12.2).

Other benefits are derived directly from the results of the satisfaction surveys. Satisfaction results are often used in evaluating employee performance for merit and compensation reviews and for sales management purposes, such as the development of sales training programs. Survey results are also useful for comparison purposes to determine how the firm stacks up against the competition. When ratings are favorable, many firms use the results in their corporate advertising.[6]

# MEASURING CUSTOMER SATISFACTION

Measures of customer satisfaction are derived via indirect and direct measures. **Indirect measures** of customer satisfaction include tracking and monitoring sales records, profits, and customer complaints. Firms that rely solely on indirect measures are taking a passive approach to determining whether customer perceptions are meeting or exceeding customer expectations. Moreover, if the average firm does not hear from 96 percent of its unhappy customers, it is losing a great many customers while waiting for the other 4 percent to speak their minds.

**Direct measures** of satisfaction are generally obtained via customer satisfaction surveys. However, to say the least, customer satisfaction surveys are not standardized among firms. For example, the scales used to collect the data vary (e.g., 5-point to 100-point scales), questions asked of respondents vary (e.g., general to specific questions), and data collection methods vary (e.g., personal interviews to self-administered questionnaires). The following section focuses on the use of various scales.

**indirect measures**
Tracking customer satisfaction through changes in sales, profits, and number of customer complaints registered.

**direct measures**
The proactive collection of customer satisfaction data through customer satisfaction surveys.

## The Scale of 100 Approach

Some firms request customers to rate the firm's performance on a scale of 100. In essence the firm is asking customers to give the firm a grade. However, the problems with this approach are readily apparent. Let's say that the firm scores an average of 83. What does the 83 mean—the firm received a B-? Does an 83 mean the same thing to all customers? Not likely. More importantly, what should the firm do to improve its satisfaction rating? The 83 does not provide specific suggestions for improvements that would lead to an increased customer satisfaction rating.

## The "Very Dissatisfied/Very Satisfied" Approach

Other firms present customers with a 5-point scale, which is typically labeled using the following format:

1. Very dissatisfied
2. Somewhat dissatisfied
3. Neutral
4. Somewhat satisfied
5. Very satisfied

TABLE 12.4
_____

**FedEx's "Hierarchy of Horrors"**

1. Wrong day delivery (packaged delivered a day later than promised)
2. Right day late delivery (packaged delivered on the promised day, but after the promised deadline)
3. Pick-up not made (failure to make a pick-up on the day requested)
4. Lost package
5. Customer misinformed by Federal Express (mistaken or inaccurate information on rates, schedules, etc.)
6. Billing and paperwork mistakes (invoice errors, overcharges, missing proof-of-delivery documents)
7. Employee performance failures (courtesy, responsiveness, etc.)
8. Damaged packages

Source: AMA Management Briefing, *Blueprints for Service Quality: The Federal Express Approach* (New York: AMA Membership Publications Division, 1991).

_____

Firms using this format generally combine the percentage of "somewhat satisfied" and "very satisfied" responses to arrive at a satisfaction rating. Similarly, firms that use a 10-point scale with anchor points of "very dissatisfied" and "very satisfied" define customer satisfaction as the percentage of customers rating their satisfaction higher than 6. Although this approach provides more meaning to the satisfaction rating itself, it still lacks the diagnostic power to indicate specific areas of improvement. In other words, regardless of whether a firm uses a 100-point, 10-point, or 5-point scale, the interpretive value of the information is restricted by its quantitative nature. Qualitative information is needed to highlight specific areas of improvement. This is exactly the problem Federal Express encountered when it set up its first customer satisfaction measurement program. Initially, customer satisfaction was measured on a 100-point scale, and transaction success was defined as whether or not the package actually arrived the next day. Upon further qualitative examination, Federal Express determined that transaction success as defined by the customer was a much broader concept (Table 12.4). The company now proactively improves its customer satisfaction ratings by continually improving on those activities that were identified by its customer base—termed "the hierarchy of horrors."

## The Combined Approach

The combined approach uses the quantitative scores obtained by the "very dissatisfied/very satisfied" approach and adds a qualitative analysis of feedback obtained from respondents who indicated that they were less than "very satisfied." Customers who indicate that they are less than "very satisfied" are informing the firm that the delivery system is performing at levels lower than expected. By prompting customers to suggest how the firm could perform better, the firm can then categorize and prioritize the suggestions for continuous improvement efforts.

The combined approach provides two valuable pieces of information. The quantitative satisfaction rating provides a benchmark against which future satisfaction surveys should be compared. In addition, the quantitative rating provides the means of comparing the firm's performance against its competition. Complementing the quantitative rating, the qualitative data provides diagnostic information and pinpoints areas for improvement. Combining the qualitative and quantitative data outperforms either approach used alone.

## UNDERSTANDING CUSTOMER SATISFACTION RATINGS

After a consultant conducted a customer satisfaction survey for a regional engineering firm, the results were revealed to upper management that the firm commanded an 85 percent customer satisfaction rating. Immediately, upper management wanted to know whether 85 percent was a "good" satisfaction rating or not. To effectively utilize customer satisfaction ratings, it is necessary to understand the factors that may influence customer responses.

Despite the lack of standardization among satisfaction studies, they share one common characteristic. "Virtually all self-reports of customer satisfaction possess a distribution in which a majority of the responses indicate that customers are satisfied and the distribution itself is negatively skewed."[7] Figure 12.2 depicts the negatively skewed distribution of customer satisfaction results.

Typically, customer satisfaction ratings are fairly high. Table 12.5 displays a sample of customer satisfaction results across various industries. As can be viewed from the table, it is not unusual to see results in the 80 to 90 percent range. Repeated findings such as these have led some researchers to conclude that to feel above average is normal.

The truth of the matter is that satisfaction ratings may be influenced by numerous confounding factors that occur during the data collection process. The following section provides explanations for inflated satisfaction results and reinforces the notion that obtaining accurate measures of customer satisfaction is not an easily accomplished task.

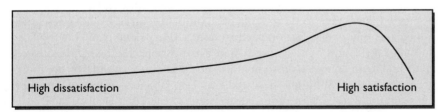

High dissatisfaction                                    High satisfaction

**Figure 12.2**     **Conceptual Distribution of Satisfaction Measurements**
Source: Robert A. Peterson and William R. Wilson, "Measuring Customer Satisfaction: Fact and Artifact," *Journal of the Academy of Marketing Science* 20, no. 1 (1992), 61.

## TABLE 12.5

### Sampling of Satisfaction Results

| Sample | Percentage Satisfied |
| --- | --- |
| British Airways customers | 85 |
| HMO enrollees | 92 |
| Sears' customers | 84 |
| Children's instructional Programs/parents | 82 |
| Medical care | 84 |
| Clothing/and white Goods/adults | 82 |
| Shoes/students | 83 |

Source: Robert A. Peterson and William R. Wilson, "Measuring Customer Satisfaction: Fact and Artifact," *Journal of the Academy of Marketing Science* 20, no. 1 (1992), 61.

## Factors Influencing Customer Satisfaction Ratings

### CUSTOMERS ARE GENUINELY SATISFIED

One possible reason for high satisfaction scores is simply that customers are satisfied with the goods and services they typically purchase and consume—that's why they buy these products from the firm in the first place! Intuitively, this makes good sense. If the majority of customers were neutral or dissatisfied, they would most likely defect to competitive offerings of goods and services. Of course, this explanation assumes that competitors in the market are better at providing goods and services than the original supplier.

### RESPONSE BIAS

**response bias**
A bias in survey results because of responses being received from only a limited group among the total survey participants.

Another possible explanation for inflated satisfaction results may be **response bias.** Some experts argue that the reason ratings are so high is that companies hear from only satisfied customers. In contrast, dissatisfied customers do not believe that the firm's survey will do them any good; therefore, the questionnaire is discarded.

Other experts discount this explanation. Their argument is that it makes more sense for highly dissatisfied customers to express their opinion than it does for highly satisfied customers to do so. This position is supported by prior research, which indicates that dissatisfaction itself is more action oriented and emotionally intense than satisfaction.[8] Others argue that it is possible that highly dissatisfied customers and highly satisfied customers are more likely to respond than are those who are more neutral. Although these additional explanations are intriguing, they fail to explain the traditional response distribution depicted in Figure 12.2.

### DATA COLLECTION METHOD

**data collection method**
The method used to collect information, such as questionnaires, surveys, and personal interviews.

A third explanation for inflated satisfaction scores is the **data collection method** used to obtain results. Prior research suggests that higher levels of satisfaction are

Customers differ . . . and so do their expectations and perceptions of service.

obtained via personal interviews and phone surveys compared with results from mail questionnaires and self-administered interviews. In fact, studies indicate that as much as a 10 percent difference exists between questionnaires administered orally and self-administered questionnaires. The reason is that respondents to personal interviews and phone surveys may feel awkward expressing negative statements to other "live" individuals as opposed to expressing them anonymously on a self-administered questionnaire.

Research on data collection modes' effects on satisfaction ratings has produced some interesting results. The data collection mode does indeed appear to influence the level of reported satisfaction; however, the negatively skewed distribution of the satisfaction ratings remains unchanged regardless of the data collection mode.

## QUESTION FORM

The way the question is asked on the questionnaire, or the **question form,** has also been posited as a possible explanation for inflated satisfaction ratings. It does appear that the question's being asked in positive form ("How satisfied are you?"), as opposed to in a negative form ("How dissatisfied are you?"), has an impact on satisfaction ratings. Asking a question in the positive form appears to lead to greater reported levels of satisfaction than does posing the question in a negative form.

**question form**
The way a question is phrased, i.e., positively or negatively.

## TABLE 12.6

### Responses by Question Form

| Response Category | Question Form | |
|---|---|---|
| | "Satisfied" | "Dissatisfied" |
| Very satisfied | 57.4% | 53.4% |
| Somewhat satisfied | 33.6% | 28.7% |
| Somewhat dissatisfied | 5.0% | 8.5% |
| Very dissatisfied | 4.0% | 9.4% |

Source: Robert A. Peterson and William R. Wilson, "Measuring Customer Satisfaction: Fact and Artifact," *Journal of the Academy of Marketing Science* 20, no. 1 (1992), 65.

Table 12.6 presents results from a study about the effects of stating the same question in two forms. In one version the question asked respondents "how satisfied" they were, and in the other version the question asked "how dissatisfied" they were. Results reveal that 91 percent of respondents reported feeling "very" or "somewhat satisfied" when the question was stated in its positive form but only 82 percent when stated in the negative form. Similarly, 9 percent of respondents expressed that they were somewhat or very dissatisfied when asked in the positive form, compared with nearly 18 percent when asked in the negative form.

### CONTEXT OF THE QUESTION

**question context**
The placement and tone of a question relative to the other questions asked.

The **question context** may also affect the satisfaction rating. Question context effects pertain to the ordering of questions and whether questions asked earlier in a questionnaire influence answers to subsequent questions. For example, in a study concerning satisfaction with vehicles, asking a general satisfaction question (e.g., "In general, how satisfied are you with the products in your house?") prior to a specific vehicle satisfaction question (e.g., "How satisfied are you with your Saturn?") increased the tendency toward a "very satisfied" response for the specific question.

### TIMING OF THE QUESTION

**timing of the question**
The length of time after the date of purchase that questions are asked.

Satisfaction ratings may also be influenced by the **timing of the question** relative to the date of purchase. Customer satisfaction appears to be highest immediately after a purchase and then begins to decrease over time. Again, regarding automobile purchases, researchers have noted a 20 percent decline in satisfaction ratings over a 60-day period. It's not clear whether the initial ratings are inflated to compensate for feelings of cognitive dissonance or the latter ratings are deflated. Some consideration has been given that there may be different types of satisfaction measured at different points in time.

Another possible explanation is that satisfaction rates may decay over time as customers reflect on their purchase decision. Prior research indicates that the influence of negative events, which are more memorable than positive events, carries more weight in satisfaction evaluations over time. Consequently, satisfaction surveys distributed longer after purchases provide respondents the opportunity to take retribution as they recall such negative events.

## SOCIAL DESIRABILITY BIAS

**Social desirability** bias describes a respondent's tendency to provide information that the respondent believes is socially appropriate. In satisfaction surveys, some researchers argue that respondents tend to withhold critical judgment because to do otherwise would be socially inappropriate. This would explain high satisfaction ratings and the shape of the distribution of results. Although the explanation is intriguing, widespread empirical support is lacking.

## MOOD

One more factor that could possibly influence customer satisfaction ratings is the mood of the customer while completing the survey. An abundance of research demonstrates the influence of positive mood states toward prosocial behaviors.[9] More specifically, prior research has shown that respondents in positive mood states make more positive judgments, rate products they own more favorably, tend to see the brighter side of things, and are more likely to rate strangers favorably. Hence, consumers in positive moods should give higher marks to service personnel and service firms than their neutral- or negative-mood counterparts.

## ARE CUSTOMER SATISFACTION SURVEYS WORTH IT?

Given the number of factors that may distort the "true" customer satisfaction ratings, one may wonder whether it's worth spending the time and money to measure satisfaction at all. Customer satisfaction ratings may fall under the category of the Hawthorne effect; that is, in and of themselves, satisfaction surveys might increase customer satisfaction regardless of the good or service being evaluated. Furthermore, because of the high levels of customer satisfaction that already exist for most firms, it may not make sense to attempt to increase satisfaction levels across the board. However, two areas of satisfaction that do deserve special attention are (1) company attempts to maintain satisfaction over time to counter the decay effect, and (2) concentration on the tail of the satisfaction distribution—those customers who are dissatisfied. Without context, satisfaction ratings cannot be interpreted with much meaning. Consequently, **benchmarking** with past satisfaction measures and comparisons with competition provides more meaningful feedback to companies.

All in all, despite all the possible complications and given the benefits derived from customer satisfaction, when firms use satisfaction surveys in conjunction with other measures, such as those described later in this chapter, the information provided is invaluable.

## CUSTOMER SATISFACTION: HOW GOOD IS GOOD ENOUGH?

How much satisfaction is enough? At 98 percent, a company that completes 1,000 transactions per week upsets 20 customers per week, who tell 9 or 10 of their friends. Given this scenario, the bottom line translates into 200 negative stories per

**social desirability bias**
A bias in survey results because of respondents' tendencies to provide information they believe is socially appropriate.

**benchmarking**
Setting standards against which to compare future data collected.

week and 10,400 negative stories per year. Although these numbers provide support for continuous improvements that enhance customer satisfaction ratings, we tend to forget that for every percentage of satisfaction improvement, very real investment costs are involved.

For example, if a firm currently boasts a 95 percent customer satisfaction rating, is it worth a $100,000 investment to improve satisfaction to 98 percent?[10] It depends. Pete Babich, the quality manager for the San Diego division of Hewlett-Packard, was faced with this exact question. Hewlett-Packard defines customer satisfaction as the customer's willingness to refer Hewlett-Packard products to friends. Hewlett-Packard has found that 70 percent of its purchases are made because of previous positive experiences with the product or referrals from others.

Although Babich found an abundance of anecdotal evidence that retaining customers was much less expensive than seeking out new customers, this information failed to answer his original question: Is it worth a $100,000 investment to improve satisfaction to 98 percent? As a result, Babich proceeded to develop a **customer satisfaction model** that would predict market share changes over time as they related to customer satisfaction ratings.

The model is based on an algorithm that can easily be converted into a spreadsheet and that is built on a number of assumptions. First, in this particular example, the model assumes a closed market of three firms that begin at period "zero" with equal market shares (i.e., 33.3 percent). The three firms offer comparable products and prices and compete for a growing customer base. Next, the model assumes that satisfied consumers will continue to buy from the same firm and that dissatisfied customers will defect to other firms in the market. For example, dissatisfied customers of firm A will buy from firm B or firm C during the next time period. The length of the time period varies depending on the product (e.g., eye exam versus lawn care).

The direction of customer defection depends on the firm's market share. In other words, if Firm C's market share is higher than Firm B's market share, Firm C will obtain a higher share of Firm A's dissatisfied customers. This logic is based on the premise that dissatisfied customers will be more particular the next time around and will conduct more research and seek out referrals from others. In this case, because of Firm C's higher market share, Firm C would be the beneficiary of more positive referrals.

Results generated from the customer satisfaction model when given three different scenarios are presented in Figure 12.3. *Panel a* illustrates the scenario of how a firm with a 95 percent customer satisfaction rating would stack up against firms commanding 90 percent and 91 percent customer satisfaction ratings. Clearly the firm with 95 percent satisfaction dominates the market after 12 time periods. *Panel b* illustrates how that same firm with a 95 percent satisfaction rating would compete with firms commanding 98 percent and 99 percent ratings. In this scenario the 95 percent firm controls less than 10 percent of the market after 24 time periods. This scenario dramatically illustrates the impact of the competition's satisfaction ratings.

Finally, *Panel c* illustrates the effect of customer satisfaction on market share at lower customer satisfaction levels. In this scenario, Firms A, B, and C command

**customer satisfaction model**
A model that predicts market share changes over time as they relate to customer satisfaction ratings; developed by Peter Babich.

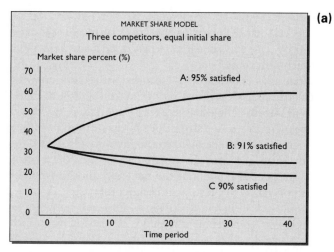

**(a)**

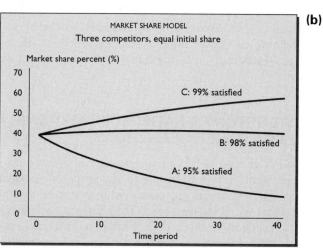

**(b)**

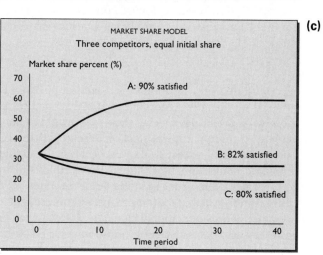

**(c)**

**Figure 12.3**
**Customer**
**Satisfaction Model:**
**Three Scenarios**

Source: Adapted
from Peter Babich,
"Customer
Satisfaction: How
Good Is Good
Enough," Quality
Progress (December
1992), 65–67.

satisfaction ratings of 90 percent, 82 percent, and 80 percent, respectively. In essence, this panel illustrates the effect of increasing the dissatisfaction levels of *Panel a* by 2. In this scenario, Firm A once again achieves market dominance, but at a much faster rate.

What does Peter Babich's customer satisfaction model tell us? First, firms with higher customer satisfaction ratings make the firm more resistant to competitors' efforts to improve their market share. Secondly, if the firm knows what a 1-percent improvement in market share does for its bottom line, then comparing the 1 percent increase in market share to the investment needed to improve customer satisfaction gives the firm the necessary information to make a business decision. Finally, the model points out the necessity of knowing not only your own firm's satisfaction rating but also your competitors'.

Should a firm invest $100,000 to improve customer satisfaction ratings from 95 percent to 98 percent? It depends on the following factors:

- The satisfaction ratings of the firm's competitors
- The dollar investment necessary to increase customer satisfaction relative to the impact of increasing the firm's market share
- The number of time periods required to recoup the investment
- The opportunity costs associated with other uses of the $100,000

## DOES CUSTOMER SATISFACTION TRANSLATE INTO CUSTOMER RETENTION?

High satisfaction ratings do not necessarily mean that a firm is going to retain a customer forever.[11] In fact, according to one group of consultants, on average, 65 percent to 85 percent of customers who defect to competitors say they were "satisfied" or "very satisfied" with their former providers. Five criticisms of customer satisfaction research as they relate to customer retention provide insights into why firms with high satisfaction ratings may potentially lose customers.

First, satisfaction research focuses on whether current needs are being met but customers' future needs are not being investigated. As customers' needs change, they will seek out a firm that best satisfies this new set of needs. Consequently the progressive service firm must proactively engage in assessing its customers' future needs.

A second criticism of customer satisfaction research is that it tends to focus on registered complaints. According to the TARP figures presented earlier, many customers who defect never relay their complaints to an employee or the firm's management. Consequently, satisfaction research that examines only registered complaints overlooks a great deal of information. In addition, limiting research to only registered complaints most likely also overlooks many of the problems that need to be remedied in order to lower defection rates.

A third criticism is that customer satisfaction research tends to focus on global attributes and ignores operational elements. For example, firms often phrase questions in their customer satisfaction questionnaires using broad, global statements such as, "The firm provides good service" and "The firm has good employees." Global statements such as these overlook the operational elements that make up these statements. Examples of operational elements that measure employee performance may include such items as eye contact, product knowledge, courteous actions, and credibility. Operational elements pertaining to good service might include the amount of time it takes to check in and check out at a hotel, the cleanliness of the facility, and the hours of operation. Using global attributes instead of operational elements in surveys fails to provide the company with the information it needs for developing effective solutions to problems. Consider, for example, the operational usefulness of the Sheraton Hotels and Resorts guest satisfaction survey conducted by J.D. Powers and Associates presented in Figure 12.4.

A fourth criticism of customer satisfaction research is that it often excludes the firm's employees from the survey process. Employee satisfaction drives customer loyalty. Employees' perceptions of the service delivery system need to be compared with customers' perceptions. This process provides feedback to employees about the firm's performance and assists in ensuring that employees and customers are on the same wavelength. As internal customers, employees often contribute valuable suggestions for improving the firm's operations.

Finally, a fifth criticism is that some firms are convinced that customers may not know what they want and that sometimes ignoring the customer is the best strategy to follow, particularly when it comes to new product innovation.[12] Some believe that firms can go overboard listening to customers, thereby becoming slaves to demographics, market research, and focus groups. In fact, listening to customers often does discourage truly innovative products. As evidence, 90 percent of so-called new products are simply line extensions of existing products.

Listening to customers does have its faults. Customers often focus on current needs and have a difficult time projecting their needs into the future. In addition, consumers sometimes pick up cues from the person asking questions and attempt to answer questions in a direction that will please the interviewer. Other problems include the consumer's being in a hurry, not fully understanding what is being asked, not wanting to be rude and so cheerfully agreeing with whatever is being asked, and most importantly, not making decisions using real money.

The list of products consumers initially rejected that went on to be huge successes is impressive. Products such as the Chrysler minivan, fax machines, VCRs, FedEx, CNN, Compaq PC servers, cellular phones, personal digital assistants, microwave ovens, and even Birdseye frozen foods were all rejected by customers during initial survey attempts. In contrast, products that surveyed customers indicated would be great successes, such as McDonald's McLean Deluxe, KFC's skinless fried chicken, Pizza Hut's low-calorie pizza, and New Coke, among others, turned out to be flops.

The problem is not so much listening to what customers have to say as it is companies' feeling paralyzed to make strategic moves without strong consumer support. Of course, customers should not be completely ignored. However, some marketers argue that the best consumer information is obtained through detached observation instead of through traditional survey techniques. "Ignore what your customers say; pay attention to what they do."[13]

# SHERATON HOTELS & RESORTS GUEST SATISFACTION SURVEY

MAKE YOUR ANSWERS COUNT!    Correct Mark ☒ ☑

| | Very Likely | Somewhat Likely | Somewhat Unlikely | Very Unlikely |
|---|---|---|---|---|
| **1. How likely are you to...** | | | | |
| Return to this hotel if you are in the same area again? | ☐ | ☐ | ☐ | ☐ |
| Recommend this hotel to a friend or colleague planning to visit the area? | ☐ | ☐ | ☐ | ☐ |
| Stay at a Sheraton hotel again? | ☐ | ☐ | ☐ | ☐ |

**2. How satisfied were you with...**    Outstanding ◄————————————————► Unacceptable

| | | | | | | | | | | | |
|---|---|---|---|---|---|---|---|---|---|---|---|
| Your overall experience as a guest in this hotel | ☐ | ☐ | ☐ | ☐ | ☐ | ☐ | ☐ | ☐ | ☐ | ☐ | |
| The value for the price paid | ☐ | ☐ | ☐ | ☐ | ☐ | ☐ | ☐ | ☐ | ☐ | ☐ | |
| Cleanliness and maintenance of hotel | ☐ | ☐ | ☐ | ☐ | ☐ | ☐ | ☐ | ☐ | ☐ | ☐ | |
| Responsiveness of staff to your needs | ☐ | ☐ | ☐ | ☐ | ☐ | ☐ | ☐ | ☐ | ☐ | ☐ | |
| Knowledge of staff | ☐ | ☐ | ☐ | ☐ | ☐ | ☐ | ☐ | ☐ | ☐ | ☐ | |
| **Check-In** | | | | | | | | | | | |
| Accuracy of reservation | ☐ | ☐ | ☐ | ☐ | ☐ | ☐ | ☐ | ☐ | ☐ | ☐ | |
| Speed/efficiency of check-in | ☐ | ☐ | ☐ | ☐ | ☐ | ☐ | ☐ | ☐ | ☐ | ☐ | |
| Staff friendliness at check-in | ☐ | ☐ | ☐ | ☐ | ☐ | ☐ | ☐ | ☐ | ☐ | ☐ | |
| **Guest Room** | | | | | | | | | | | |
| Size of room | ☐ | ☐ | ☐ | ☐ | ☐ | ☐ | ☐ | ☐ | ☐ | ☐ | |
| Comfort of bed | ☐ | ☐ | ☐ | ☐ | ☐ | ☐ | ☐ | ☐ | ☐ | ☐ | |
| Room décor/furnishings | ☐ | ☐ | ☐ | ☐ | ☐ | ☐ | ☐ | ☐ | ☐ | ☐ | |
| Ability to work in guest room | ☐ | ☐ | ☐ | ☐ | ☐ | ☐ | ☐ | ☐ | ☐ | ☐ | |
| Cleanliness of guest room | ☐ | ☐ | ☐ | ☐ | ☐ | ☐ | ☐ | ☐ | ☐ | ☐ | |
| Maintenance of guest room | ☐ | ☐ | ☐ | ☐ | ☐ | ☐ | ☐ | ☐ | ☐ | ☐ | |
| Cleanliness of bathroom | ☐ | ☐ | ☐ | ☐ | ☐ | ☐ | ☐ | ☐ | ☐ | ☐ | |
| Bath/shower water pressure | ☐ | ☐ | ☐ | ☐ | ☐ | ☐ | ☐ | ☐ | ☐ | ☐ | |
| **Hotel Services (If Used)** | | | | | | | | | | | |
| Helpfulness of bell staff | ☐ | ☐ | ☐ | ☐ | ☐ | ☐ | ☐ | ☐ | ☐ | ☐ | ☐ N/A |
| Hotel safety/security | ☐ | ☐ | ☐ | ☐ | ☐ | ☐ | ☐ | ☐ | ☐ | ☐ | ☐ N/A |
| **Food and Dining (If Used)** | | | | | | | | | | | |
| Food quality | ☐ | ☐ | ☐ | ☐ | ☐ | ☐ | ☐ | ☐ | ☐ | ☐ | ☐ N/A |
| Speed/efficiency of service | ☐ | ☐ | ☐ | ☐ | ☐ | ☐ | ☐ | ☐ | ☐ | ☐ | ☐ N/A |
| Room service speed/efficiency | ☐ | ☐ | ☐ | ☐ | ☐ | ☐ | ☐ | ☐ | ☐ | ☐ | ☐ N/A |
| **Check-Out** | | | | | | | | | | | |
| Speed/efficiency of check-out process | ☐ | ☐ | ☐ | ☐ | ☐ | ☐ | ☐ | ☐ | ☐ | ☐ | |
| Accuracy of billing | ☐ | ☐ | ☐ | ☐ | ☐ | ☐ | ☐ | ☐ | ☐ | ☐ | |

**3. Please rate...**

| | | | | | | | | | | | |
|---|---|---|---|---|---|---|---|---|---|---|---|
| Delivery of Sheraton promise "I'll take care of you" | ☐ | ☐ | ☐ | ☐ | ☐ | ☐ | ☐ | ☐ | ☐ | ☐ | |
| This experience compared to other Sheraton hotels | ☐ | ☐ | ☐ | ☐ | ☐ | ☐ | ☐ | ☐ | ☐ | ☐ | |

**4. Are you a member of the Starwood Preferred Guest Program?**    ☐ Yes    ☐ No

**5. If you are a member of the Starwood Preferred Guest Program, how satisfied were you with the benefits you received during your stay?**    ☐ ☐ ☐ ☐ ☐ ☐ ☐ ☐ ☐ ☐    ☐ N/A

**6. Please mark any problem you experienced during your stay. (MARK ALL THAT APPLY)**

| | | | |
|---|---|---|---|
| ☐ Air conditioner/heater | ☐ Hotel maintenance | ☐ Reservation date | ☐ Room maintenance |
| ☐ Bathroom cleanliness | ☐ Noise | ☐ Reservation rate | ☐ Room readiness |
| ☐ Check-in | ☐ No reservation | ☐ Responsiveness of staff | ☐ Sink/tub/toilet |
| ☐ Guest room cleanliness | ☐ Number of towels | ☐ Room assignment | ☐ Other |

**7. Did you contact anyone in the hotel to resolve the problem?**    ☐ Yes    ☐ No

**8. Was the problem resolved to your satisfaction?**    ☐ Yes    ☐ No

**9. Which of the following best describes the reason for your stay?**    ☐ Business    ☐ Both Business/Leisure    ☐ Leisure    ☐ Meeting/Conference

**10. Your gender:**    ☐ Female    ☐ Male

Please write in your e-mail address: |_|_|_|_|_|_|_|_|_|_|_|_|_|_|_|_|_|_|_|_|_|_|_|_|_|_|_|_|_|

Additional comments: _____

Please return in the enclosed envelope to: J.D. Power and Associates, 30401 Agoura Road, Suite 200, Agoura Hills, CA 91301

**Figure 12.4    Sheraton Hotels and Resorts Guest Satisfaction Survey**

J.D. Power and Associates, Agoura Hills, CA 91301.

# CUSTOMER SATISFACTION: A CLOSER LOOK

So far this chapter has provided a broad overview of customer satisfaction. The following section takes a closer look at customer expectations and how they relate to customer satisfaction and service quality assessments. This section further defines customer satisfaction and provides the transition into the next chapter, which focuses solely on service quality issues.

## Types of Customer Expectations

At first glance, comparing expectations with perceptions when developing customer satisfaction evaluations sounds fairly straightforward. Expectations serve as benchmarks against which present and future service encounters are compared. However, this relatively simple scenario becomes a bit more confusing when you realize that there exist at least three different types of expectations.[14]

**Predicted service** is a **probability expectation** that reflects the level of service customers believe is likely to occur. For example, bank customers tend to conduct their banking business at the same location. Customers become accustomed to dealing with the same bank personnel and begin to anticipate certain performance levels. It is generally agreed that customer satisfaction evaluations are developed by comparing predicted service with perceived service received (Figure 12.5).

**Desired service** is an **ideal expectation** that reflects what customers actually want compared with predicted service, which is what is likely to occur. Hence, in most instances, desired service reflects a higher expectation than predicted service.

**predicted service**
The level of service quality a consumer believes is likely to occur.

**probability expectation**
A customer expectation based on the customer's opinion of what will be most likely when dealing with service personnel.

**desired service**
The level of service quality a customer actually wants from a service encounter.

**ideal expectation**
A customer's expectation of what a "perfect" service encounter would be.

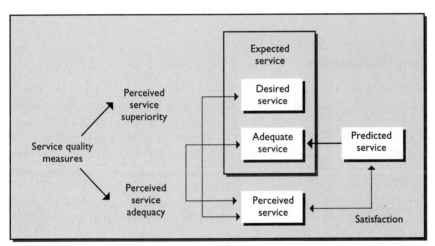

**Figure 12.5**     **Comparison between Customer Evaluation of Service Quality and Customer Satisfaction**

Source: Adapted from Valerie A. Zeithaml, Leonard L. Berry, and A. Parasuraman, "The Nature and Determinants of Customer Expectations of Service," *Journal of the Academy of Marketing Science* 21, no. 1 (1993), 1–12.

**Figure 12.6**

**The Zone of Tolerance**

Source: Valerie A. Zeithaml, Leonard L. Berry, and A. Parasuraman, "The Nature and Determinants of Customer Expectations of Service," *Journal of the Academy of Marketing Science* 21, no. 1 (1993), 1–12.

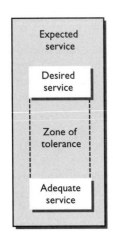

**perceived service superiority**
Measure of service quality derived by comparing desired service expectations and perceived service received.

**adequate service**
The level of service quality a customer is willing to accept.

**minimum tolerable expectation**
A customer expectation based on the absolute minimum acceptable outcome.

**zone of tolerance**
Level of quality ranging from high to low and reflecting the difference between desired service and adequate service; expands and contracts across customers and within the same customer, depending on the service and the conditions under which it is provided.

For example, our bank customer's desired service is that he not only receive his predicted service but that the tellers call him by his first name and enthusiastically greet him as he enters the bank. Comparing desired service expectations to perceived service received results in a measure of **perceived service superiority** (see Figure 12.6).

In contrast, **adequate service** is a **minimum tolerable expectation** and reflects the level of service the customer is willing to accept. Adequate service is based on experiences or norms that develop over time. For example, most adult consumers have dined at hundreds, if not thousands, of restaurants. Through these experiences, consumers develop expected norms. Hence, one factor that influences adequate service is predicted service. Encounters that fall below expected norms fall below adequate service expectations. Comparing adequate service with perceived service produces a measure of **perceived service adequacy** (see Figure 12.6).

## The Zone of Tolerance

Because services are characterized by heterogeneity, consumers learn to expect variation in service delivery from one location to the next and even in the same provider from one day to the next. Consumers who accept this variation develop a **zone of tolerance**, which reflects the difference between desired service and adequate service (Figure 12.6). The zone of tolerance expands and contracts across customers and within the same customer depending on the service and the conditions under which the service is provided. Other factors, such as price, may influence the zone of tolerance. Typically, as the price increases, the customer's zone of tolerance decreases as desired service needs begin to dominate and the customer becomes less forgiving for sloppy service.

Another interesting characteristic of the zone of tolerance is that desired service is less subject to change than adequate service. One way to picture the zone of tolerance is to compare it with a projector screen located at the top of a blackboard. The metal canister bolted to the wall that holds the screen represents the desired service level. The desired service level represents what the customer believes the ideal service firm should provide to its customers. Its movement is less subject to change than the rest of the screen. The screen itself represents the zone of tolerance, and the metal piece with the handle at the bottom of the screen represents the adequate service level. Adequate service fluctuates based on circumstances surrounding the service delivery process and changes the size of the zone of tolerance accordingly.

## Factors Influencing Service Expectations: Desired Service

Desired service expectations are developed as a result of six different sources (Figure 12.7). The first source, **enduring service intensifiers,** are personal factors that are stable over time and that increase a customer's sensitivity to how the service should be best provided. Two types of enduring service intensifiers include the customer's **derived expectations** and **personal service philosophies.** Derived expectations are created from the expectations of others. For example, if your boss requests that you find someone to pressure-wash the office building, your expectations of the provider performing the job will most likely be higher than if you had hired the provider on your own initiative. In the attempt to satisfy your boss's expectations, your sensitivity to the caliber of service significantly increases.

Similarly, the customer's personal service philosophies, or personal views of the meaning of service and the manner in which service providers should conduct themselves, will also heighten his or her sensitivities. Customers who work in the service sector are particularly sensitive to the caliber of service provided. These customers hold their own views regarding exactly how service should be provided—they want to be treated the way they believe they treat their customers.

The second factor influencing desired service expectations is the customer's own **personal needs,** including physical, social, and psychological needs. Simply stated, some customers have more needs than others. Some customers are very particular about where they are seated in a restaurant, whereas others are happy to sit nearly anywhere. In a hotel, some customers are very interested in the hotel's amenities, such as the pool, sauna, dining room, and other forms of available entertainment, whereas others are simply looking for a clean room. This is one of the reasons that managing a service firm is particularly challenging. Customers have a variety of needs, and no two customers are alike in every way.

## Factors Influencing Service Expectations: Desired Service and Predicted Service

The other four factors that influence desired service expectations also influence predicted service expectations and include (1) explicit service promises, (2) implicit service promises, (3) word-of-mouth communications, and (4) past experience (see Figure 12.7).

**enduring service intensifiers**
Personal factors that are stable over time and increase a customer's sensitivity to how a service should be best provided.

**derived expectations**
Expectations appropriated from and based on the expectations of others.

**personal service philosophies**
A customer's own internal views of the meaning of service and the manner in which service providers should conduct themselves.

**personal needs**
A customer's physical, social, and psychological needs.

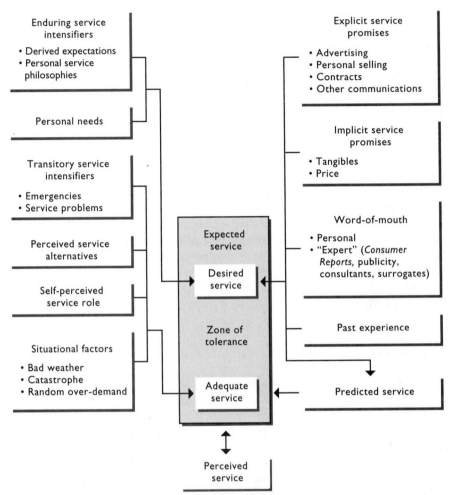

**Figure 12.7**    **Factors Influencing Expected Service**

Source: Adapted from Valerie A. Zeithaml, Leonard L. Berry, and A. Parasuraman, "The Nature and Determinants of Customer Expectations of Service," *Journal of the Academy of Marketing Science* 21, no. 1 (1993), 1–12.

**explicit service promises**

Obligations to which the firm commits itself via its advertising, personal selling, contracts, and other forms of communication.

**Explicit service promises** encompass the firm's advertising, personal selling, contracts, and other forms of communication. Because of the lack of a tangible product, consumers of services base their evaluations of the service on various forms of information available. The more ambiguous the service, the more customers rely on the firm's advertising when forming expectations. If a hotel stresses modern and clean rooms, customers expect the rooms to be exactly the way they were pictured in the advertisement. Similarly, if a builder states that a customer's new house will be completed in December, the customer takes this as the builder's promise, and the standard is established on which the customer will base subsequent evaluations.

Some guests like the amenities of a hotel to include a private beach or a swimming pool, while others simply want a clean room and a quiet place to rest. This is why managing a service firm is particularly challenging—consumers have different expectations.

**Implicit service promises** also influence desired service and predicted service. The tangibles surrounding the service and the price of the service are common types of implicit service promises. As the price increases, customers expect the firm to deliver higher-quality services. In the absence of a tangible product, the price becomes an indicator of quality to most consumers. For example, customers would probably have higher expectations for service at a higher-priced hair salon than they would for "Cheap Charley's Barber Shop." Similarly, if the tangibles surrounding a service are plush, customers interpret those tangibles as a sign of quality. In general, the nicer the furnishings of the service establishment, the higher customer expectations become.

**implicit service promises**
Obligations to which the firm commits itself via the tangibles surrounding the service and the price of the service.

**Word-of-mouth communications** also play an important role in forming customer expectations. As discussed in Chapter 4, customers tend to rely more on personal sources of information than on nonpersonal ones when choosing among service alternatives. Because services cannot be evaluated fully before purchase, customers view word-of-mouth information as unbiased information from someone who has been through the service experience. Sources of word-of-mouth information range from friends and family to consultants to product review publications such as *Consumer Reports.*

**word-of-mouth communications**
Unbiased information from someone who has been through the service experience, such as friends, family, or consultants.

Finally, **past experience** also contributes to customer expectations of desired and predicted service. Service evaluations are often based on a comparison of the current service encounter to other encounters with the same provider, other providers in the industry, and other providers in other industries. In the education system, students' desired and predicted service expectations of instructors are

**past experience**
The previous service encounters a consumer has had with a service provider.

likely to be based on past experiences in other classes with the same instructor and on other classes with other instructors.

## Factors Influencing Service Expectations: Adequate Service

Adequate service reflects the level of service the consumer is willing to accept and is influenced by five factors: (1) transitory service intensifiers, (2) perceived service alternatives, (3) customer self-perceived service roles, (4) situation factors, and (5) predicted service (see Figure 12.7).

### TRANSITORY SERVICE INTENSIFIERS

**transitory service intensifiers**
Personal, short-term factors that heighten a customer's sensitivity to service.

In contrast to enduring service intensifiers, **transitory service intensifiers** are individualized, short-term factors that heighten the customer's sensitivity to service. For example, customers who have had service problems in the past with specific types of providers are more sensitive to the quality of service delivered during subsequent encounters. Another example is the need for service under personal emergency situations. Typically, consumers are willing to wait their turn to see a physician. However, under personal emergency conditions, consumers are less willing to be patient and expect a higher level of service in a shorter period of time. Hence, the level of adequate service increases, and the zone of tolerance becomes more narrow.

### PERCEIVED SERVICE ALTERNATIVES

**perceived service alternatives**
Comparable services customers believe they can obtain elsewhere and/or produce themselves.

The level of adequate service is also affected by the customer's **perceived service alternatives.** The larger the number of perceived service alternatives, the higher the level of adequate service expectations, and the more narrow the zone of tolerance. Customers who believe that they can obtain comparable services elsewhere or that they can produce the service themselves expect higher levels of adequate service than those customers who believe they are not able to receive sufficiently better service from another provider.

### SELF-PERCEIVED SERVICE ROLE

**self-perceived service role**
The input a customer believes he or she is required to present in order to produce a satisfactory service encounter.

As has been discussed on numerous occasions, the service customer is often involved in the production process and can directly influence the outcome of the service delivery system. When customers have a strong **self-perceived service role**—that is, when they believe that they are doing their part—their adequate service expectations are increased. However, if customers willingly admit that they have failed to complete forms or provide the necessary information to produce a superior service outcome, then their adequate service expectations decrease and the zone of tolerance increases.

### SITUATIONAL FACTORS

**situational factors**
Circumstances that lower the service quality but that are beyond the control of the service provider.

As a group, customers are not unreasonable. They understand that from time to time **situational factors** beyond the control of the service provider will lower the quality of service. If the power goes out in one part of town around dinner time, restaurants in other parts of town will be overrun by hungry patrons. As a result, lengthy waits will develop as the service delivery system becomes backed up. Similarly, after a hurricane, tornado, or other natural disaster occurs, the customer's insurance agent may not be as responsive as under normal circumstances. When circumstances occur beyond the control of the provider and the customer has knowledge of those circumstances, adequate service expectations are lowered and the zone of tolerance becomes wider.

## PREDICTED SERVICE

The level of service consumers believe is likely to occur is the fifth and final factor that influences adequate service expectations. Predicted service is a function of the firm's explicit and implicit service promises, word-of-mouth communications, and the customer's own past experiences. Taking these factors into consideration, customers form judgments regarding the predicted service that is likely to occur and set adequate service expectations simultaneously.

## The Link between Expectations, Customer Satisfaction, and Service

Now that we have introduced the concepts of predicted, adequate, and desired service, you may wonder what all the fuss is about. It is actually simple and straightforward. When evaluating the service experience, consumers compare the three types of expectations (predicted service, adequate service, and desired service) with the perceived service delivered. Customer satisfaction is calculated by comparing predicted service and perceived service. Perceived service adequacy, which compares adequate service and perceived service, and perceived service superiority, which compares desired service and perceived service, are measures of service quality (see Figure 12.5). Other major differences between service quality and customer satisfaction as well as issues related to service quality measurement are discussed in greater detail in Chapter 13.

## SUMMARY

Customer satisfaction research is one of the fastest growing areas in market research today. Defined as a comparison of perceptions and predicted service expectations, customer satisfaction has been associated with such benefits as repeat sales, more frequent sales, increased sales per transaction, positive word-of-mouth communications, insulation from price competition, and pleasant work environments for employees. Customer satisfaction questionnaires send the signal to consumers that the firm cares about its customers and wants their input. In addition, data collected from questionnaires facilitates the development of employee training programs, identifies strengths and weaknesses in the firm's service delivery process, and provides information to be used in employee performance reviews and compensation decisions.

Firms use a variety of methods to track customer satisfaction. Moreover, a number of factors can dramatically increase or decrease the firm's satisfaction ratings. The main lessons to be learned are that (1) customer satisfaction surveys that collect qualitative and quantitative data are better than those that collect either qualitative or quantitative data alone; and (2) regardless of the methods used, such as the timing of the questions, the context of the questions, the data collection method, and a variety of other research issues, the firm must be consistent in its approach in order to make comparisons over time meaningful. Overall, customer satisfaction ratings tend to be negatively skewed, and responses indicating above-average performance tend to be the norm.

Despite its problems, customer satisfaction assessment is a valuable management exercise. However, firms should not attempt to increase their satisfaction ratings without carefully considering (1) the satisfaction ratings of competing firms; (2) the cost of an investment in increasing market share relative to the impact on the firm's bottom line; (3) the number of time periods it takes to recoup such an investment; and (4) the opportunity costs associated with the use of the firm's funds. Finally, one of the driving forces behind customer satisfaction is the customer's expectations. Three types of expectations and the factors influencing each type were presented. The three types of expectations form the bases for both customer satisfaction and service quality assessments, which are discussed in Chapter 13.

# Key Terms

| | |
|---|---|
| Adequate service | Perceived service adequacy |
| Benchmarking | Perceived service alternatives |
| Confirmed expectations | Perceived service superiority |
| Customer satisfaction model | Personal needs |
| Data collection method | Personal service philosophies |
| Derived expectations | Positive disconfirmation |
| Desired service | Predicted service |
| Direct measures | Probability expectation |
| Disconfirmed expectations | Question context |
| Enduring service intensifiers | Question form |
| Expectancy disconfirmation model | Response bias |
| Explicit service promises | Self-perceived service role |
| Ideal expectation | Situational factors |
| Implicit service promises | Social desirability bias |
| Indirect measures | Timing of the question |
| Minimum tolerable expectation | Transitory service intensifiers |
| Negative disconfirmation | Word-of-mouth communications |
| Past experience | Zone of tolerance |

# Discussion Questions

1. Discuss the differences among a confirmation, a positive disconfirmation, and a negative disconfirmation.
2. What is meant by the description that most satisfaction scores are negatively skewed? Why does this score distribution occur?
3. Discuss how the form of a question can influence satisfaction scores.
4. Should a company always attempt to achieve 100 percent customer satisfaction?
5. Discuss the relationship between customer satisfaction and customer retention.
6. What are the drawbacks of listening to customers and assessing customer satisfaction?
7. Define and explain the relevance of the terms *predicted service, desired service,* and *adequate service* as they pertain to customer satisfaction and service quality.
8. What are the factors that influence customer expectations?

# Notes

1. Robert A. Peterson and William R. Wilson, "Measuring Customer Satisfaction: Fact and Artifact," *Journal of the Academy of Marketing Science* 20, no. 1 (1992), 61.
2. Karl Albrecht and Ron Zemke, *Service America! Doing Business in the New Economy* (Homewood, Ill.: Business One Irwin, 1985), 6.
3. Keith Hunt, "Consumer Satisfaction, Dissatisfaction, and Complaining Behavior," *Journal of Social Issues* 47, no. 1 (1991), 109–110.
4. Leonard L. Berry, A. Parasuraman, and Valerie A. Zeithaml, "Improving Service Quality in America: Lessons Learned," *Academy of Management Executive* 8, no. 2 (1994), 36.
5. Peterson and Wilson, "Measuring Customer Satisfaction," 61.
6. Ibid.
7. Ibid., 62.
8. Marsha L. Richins, "Negative Word-of-Mouth by Dissatisfied Consumers: A Pilot Study," *Journal of Marketing* 47 (Winter 1983), 68–78.
9. K. Douglas Hoffman, "A Conceptual Framework of the Influence of Positive Mood States on Service Exchange Relationships," in *Marketing Theory and Applications,* Chris T. Allen, et al, eds. (San Antonio, Tex.: American Marketing Association Winter Educator's Conference), 147.
10. Adapted from Peter Babich, "Customer Satisfaction: How Good is Good Enough," *Quality Progress* (December 1992), 65–67.
11. Adapted from Michael W. Lowenstein, "The Voice of the Customer," *Small Business Reports* (December 1993), 57–61.

12. Justin Martin, "Ignore Your Customer," *Fortune* (May 1, 1995), 121–126.

13. Ibid., 126.

14. This section adapted from Valerie A. Zeithaml, Leonard L. Berry, and A. Parasuraman, "The Nature and Determinants of Customer Expectations of Service," *Journal of the Academy of Marketing Science* 21, no. 1 (1993), 1–12.

## chapter 13

# Defining and Measuring Service Quality

## CHAPTER OBJECTIVES

The major objectives of this chapter are to introduce you to the concepts of service quality, service quality measurement, and service quality information systems.

After completing this chapter, you should be able to:

- Define service quality as it relates to customer satisfaction.
- Identify and discuss the gaps that influence consumer perceptions of service quality.
- Discuss factors that influence the size of each of the service quality gaps.
- Discuss the basic concepts of SERVQUAL.
- Describe the components of a service quality information system.

"It's just the little touches after the average man would quit that makes the master's fame."

Orison Swett Marden, founder, *Success* magazine

# Introduction

One of the few issues on which service quality researchers agree is that service quality is an elusive and abstract concept that is difficult to define and measure.[1] This particular problem is challenging for academicians and practitioners alike. For example, traditional measures of productivity such as gross domestic product (GDP) do not account for increases in service quality delivered. In fact, providing poor quality can actually increase the country's GDP.[2] If a mail-order company sends you the wrong product, the dollars spent on phone calls and return mailings to correct the mistake will add to the GDP.

Other governmental institutions, such as the Bureau of Labor Statistics (BLS), have attempted to account for increases in quality by adjusting the consumer price index. For example, if a car costs more this year than last but includes quality improvements such as an air bag, better gas mileage, and cleaner emissions, the BLS will subtract the estimated retail value of the improvements before calculating the consumer price index. However, the BLS does this for only a few industries and without the help of customers—the true evaluators of quality improvements. Efficiency measures are also of no help. A retail store that stocks lots of merchandise may please more customers and make more money while decreasing the firm's efficiency rating.

The productivity of education and government services is notoriously difficult to measure. Increases in quality, such as improving the quality of education and training governmental employees to be more pleasant throughout their daily interactions with the pubic, do not show up in productivity measures. However, it is readily apparent that increases in quality can have a dramatic impact on a firm's or industry's survival. As evidence, Japan did not simply bulldoze its way into U.S. markets by offering lower prices alone—superior quality relative to the competition at that time ultimately won customers over.

## WHAT IS SERVICE QUALITY?

**service quality**
An attitude formed by a long-term, overall evaluation of a firm's performance.

Perhaps the best way to begin a discussion of service quality is to first attempt to distinguish **service quality** measurement from customer satisfaction measurement. Most experts agree that customer satisfaction is a short-term, transaction-specific measure, whereas service quality is an attitude formed by a long-term, overall evaluation of a performance.

Without a doubt, the two concepts of customer satisfaction and service quality are intertwined. However, the relationship between these two concepts is unclear. Some believe that customer satisfaction leads to perceived service quality, whereas others believe that service quality leads to customer satisfaction. In addition, the relationship between customer satisfaction and service quality and the way these two concepts relate to purchasing behavior remains largely unexplained.[3]

One plausible explanation is that satisfaction assists consumers in revising service quality perceptions.[4] The logic for this position consists of the following:

- Consumer perceptions of the service quality of a firm with which he or she has no prior experience is based on the consumer's expectations.
- Subsequent encounters with the firm lead the consumer through the disconfirmation process and revise perceptions of service quality.
- Each additional encounter with the firm further revises or reinforces service quality perceptions; revised service quality perceptions modify future consumer purchase intentions toward the firm.

To deliver a consistent set of satisfying experiences that can build into an evaluation of high quality requires the entire organization to be focused on the task. The needs of the consumer must be understood in detail, as must the operational constraints under which the firm operates. Service providers must be focused on quality, and the system must be designed to support that mission by being controlled correctly and delivering as it was designed to do.

## THE DIFFERENCE IN QUALITY PERSPECTIVES BETWEEN GOODS AND SERVICES

Service quality offers a way of achieving success among competing services.[5] Particularly when a small number of firms that offer nearly identical services are competing within a small area, such as banks might do, establishing service quality may be the only way of differentiating oneself. Service quality differentiation can generate increased market share and ultimately mean the difference between financial success and failure.

Ample evidence suggests that the provision of quality can deliver repeat purchases as well as new customers. The value of retaining existing customers is discussed in much greater detail in Chapter 15. Briefly, repeat customers yield many benefits to the service organization. The cost of marketing to them is lower than that of marketing to new customers. Once customers have become regulars of the service, they know the script and are efficient users of the servuction system. As they gain trust in the organization, the level of risk for them is reduced, and they are more likely to consolidate their business with the firm. For example, insurance customers tend to move current policies to and purchase new policies from the one provider they feel serves their needs the best.

Goods manufacturers have already learned this lesson over the past decade and have made producing quality goods a priority issue. Improving the quality of manufactured goods has become a major strategy for both establishing efficient, smoothly running operations and increasing consumer market share in an atmosphere in which customers are consistently demanding higher and higher quality. Goods quality improvement measures have focused largely on the quality of the products themselves, and specifically on eliminating product failure. Initially these measures were based on rigorous checking of all finished products before they came into contact with the customer. More recently, quality control has focused on the principle of ensuring quality during the manufacturing process, on "getting it right the first time," and on reducing end-of-production-line failures to zero. The final evolution in goods manufacturing has been to define quality as delivering the right product to the right customer at the right time, thus extending quality beyond the good itself and using external as well as internal measures to assess overall quality.

However, service quality cannot be understood in quite the same way. The servuction system depends on the customer as a participant in the production process, and normal quality control measures that depend on eliminating defects before the consumer sees the product are not available. Consequently, service quality is not a specific goal or program that can be achieved or completed but must be an ongoing part of all management and service production on a daily basis.

## DIAGNOSING FAILURE GAPS IN SERVICE QUALITY

**service gap**
The distance between a customer's expectation of a service and perception of the service actually delivered.

**knowledge gap**
The difference between what consumers expect of a service and what management perceives the consumers to expect.

**standards gap**
The difference between what management perceives consumers to expect and the quality specifications set for service delivery.

**delivery gap**
The difference between the quality standards set for service delivery and the actual quality of service delivery.

**communications gap**
The difference between the actual quality of service delivered and the quality of service described in the firm's external communications.

Many difficulties are inherent in implementing and evaluating service quality. In the first place, perceptions of quality tend to rely on a repeated comparison of the customer's expectation about a particular service. If a service, no matter how good, fails repeatedly to meet a customer's expectations, the customer will perceive the service to be of poor quality. Second, unlike goods marketing, where customers evaluate the finished product alone, with services the customer evaluates the process of the service as well as its outcome. A customer visiting an accountant, for example, will evaluate service not only on the basis of whether he or she likes the outcome, but also on the accountant's appearance and interpersonal skills.

Conceptually the service quality process can be examined in terms of gaps between expectations and perceptions on the part of management, employees, and customers (Figure 13.1).[6] The most important gap, the **service gap,** is between customers' expectations of service and their perceptions of the service actually delivered. Ultimately the goal of the service firm is to close the service gap or at least narrow it as far as possible. Consequently, examining service quality gaps is much like the disconfirmation of expectations model discussed in Chapter 12. However, remember that service quality focuses on the customer's cumulative attitude toward the firm, which is collected by the consumer from a number of successful or unsuccessful service experiences.

Before the firm can close the service gap, it must close or attempt to narrow four other gaps:

The **knowledge gap,** or the difference between what consumers expect of a service and what management perceives the consumers to expect.

The **standards gap,** or the difference between what management perceives consumers to expect and the quality specifications set for service delivery.

The **delivery gap,** or the difference between the quality specifications set for service delivery and the actual quality of service delivery. For example, do employees perform the service as they were trained?

The **communications gap,** or the difference between the actual quality of service delivered and the quality of service described in the firm's external communications such as brochures and mass media advertising.

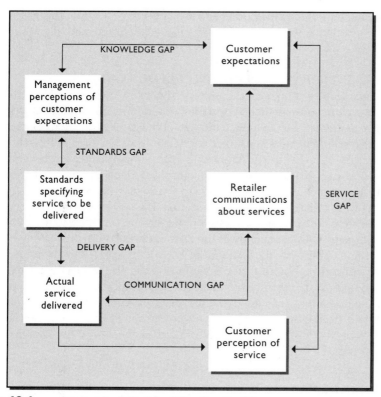

**Figure 13.1**     **Conceptual Model of Service Quality**

Source: Adapted from A. Parasuraman, Valerie Zeithaml, and Leonard Berry, "A Conceptual Model of Service Quality and Its Implications for Future Research," *Journal of Marketing* 49 (Fall 1985), 41–50.

Ultimately, the service gap is a function of the knowledge gap, the standards gap, the delivery gap, and the communications gap. As each of these gaps increases or decreases, the service gap responds in a similar manner.

## The Knowledge Gap

The most immediate and obvious gap is usually between what customers want and what managers think customers want. Many managers think they know what their customers want but are, in fact, mistaken. Banking customers may prefer security to a good interest rate. Some restaurant customers may prefer quality and taste of food over an attractive arrangement of the tables or a good view from the window. A hotel may feel that its customers prefer comfortable rooms, when, in fact, the majority of them spend little time in their rooms and are more interested in on-site amenities.

When a knowledge gap occurs, a variety of other mistakes tend to follow. The wrong facilities may be provided, the wrong staff may be hired, and the wrong training may be undertaken. Services may be provided that customers have no use for, whereas the services they do desire are not offered. Closing this gap requires minutely detailed knowledge of what customers desire and then building a response into the service operating system.

### FACTORS INFLUENCING THE KNOWLEDGE GAP

Three main factors influence the size of the knowledge gap. First, the firm's **research orientation,** which reflects its attitude toward conducting consumer research, can dramatically influence the size of the gap. Information obtained from consumer research defines consumer expectations. As the firm's research orientation increases, the size of the knowledge gap should decrease. The amount of **upward communication** is a second factor that influences the size of the knowledge gap. Upward communication refers to the flow of information from front-line personnel to upper levels of the organization. Front-line personnel interact with customers frequently, so they are often more in touch with customer needs than is top management. Consequently, as the flow of upward communication increases through the organization, the smaller the knowledge gap should become. Finally, the **levels of management** in the organization can also influence the size of the knowledge gap. As the organizational hierarchy becomes more complex and more levels of management are added, higher levels of management tend to become more distant from customers and the day-to-day activities of the organization. As a result, when the levels of management increase, the size of the knowledge gap tends to increase.

## The Standards Gap

Even if customer expectations have been accurately determined, the standards gap may open between management's perception of customer expectations and the actual standards set for service delivery, such as order processing speed, the way cloth napkins are to be folded, or the way customers are to be greeted. When

**research orientation**
A firm's attitude toward conducting consumer research.

**upward communication**
The flow of information from front-line personnel to upper levels of the organization.

**levels of management**
The complexity of the organizational hierarchy and the number of levels between top management and the customers.

Every service firm must maintain certain standards in order to give customers a pleasant experience. For hotel employees, it may be acknowledging the customer on arrival, establishing eye contact, smiling, answering questions, and providing keys to the hotel room.

developing standards, the firm should use a flowchart of its operations to identify all points of contact between it and its customers. Detailed standards can be written for (1) the way the system should operate, and (2) the behavior of contact personnel at each point in the system. Hotel front-desk personnel, for example, may be trained to perform to specification in such areas as acknowledging the customer upon arrival, establishing eye contact, smiling, completing the proper paperwork, reviewing with the customer the available amenities, and providing the customer with keys to the room.

## FACTORS INFLUENCING THE STANDARDS GAP

In many cases, management does not believe it can or should meet customer requirements for service. For example, overnight delivery of mail used to be thought of as an absurd possibility before Fred Smith and FedEx proved that, in fact, it could be done (see Services in Action 13.1).

Sometimes management has no commitment to the delivery of service quality. Corporate leadership may set other priorities that interfere with setting standards that lead to good service. For example, a company's orientation toward implementing cost-reduction strategies that maximize short-term profits is often cited as a misguided priority that impedes the firm's progress in delivering quality services. Personal computer companies whose automated service hotlines reduce the number of customer service representatives employed are typical examples. In some instances, customers in need of service have been forced to remain on hold for hours before they could actually speak to a "real person." Hotlines were originally named to reflect the speed with which the customer could talk to the manufacturer. Now the name more appropriately reflects the customer's temper by the time he or she talks to someone who can actually help.

Sometimes there is simply no culture of service quality, and management genuinely fails to understand the issues involved. In other cases, management may

S E R V I C E S **13.1**
IN

A C T I O N    **Measuring Service Quality: The FedEx Approach**

When Federal Express (known today as FedEx) first opened its doors on April 17, 1973, it shipped eight packages, seven of which were trial runs addressed from one FedEx employee to another. No one had any idea that this event marked the birth of an entire industry—overnight mail or parcel delivery. Particularly inspiring to college students is that Fred Smith, the CEO of FedEx, had sketched out the early details of the operation in an undergraduate paper at Yale University. The paper was given a grade of "C." By 1990 the company was generating $7 billion in annual sales revenue and controlled 43 percent of the air express market.

FedEx has two ambitious goals: 100 percent customer satisfaction with every interaction and transaction, and 100 percent performance on every package handled. In its early days, FedEx defined service quality as the percentage of packages delivered on time. After cataloging complaints for many years, it became apparent that percentage of on-time delivery was an internal measure of service quality and did not necessarily reflect absolute service quality by customer standards.

The customer's definition of service quality, which included eight service failures to be avoided, became known as the "hierarchy of horrors" and included (1) wrong-day delivery; (2) right day, late delivery; (3) pick-up not made; (4) lost package; (5) customer misinformed by FedEx; (6) billing and paperwork mistakes; (7) employee performance failures; and (8) damaged packages. Based on these categories generated by customer complaints, it was readily apparent that on-time delivery was not the only measure important to FedEx customers.

In addition to categorizing customer complaints, FedEx measures service quality by tracking 12 service quality indicators every day, both individually and in total. Moreover, the firm conducts numerous customer research studies each year in five major categories. (1) Service quality studies, conducted quarterly, of four market segments: base business that is phoned to FedEx, U.S. export customers, manned-center customers, and drop-box customers; (2) 10 targeted customer studies, conducted semiannually, that contact customers who have had an experience with one of 10 specific FedEx processes such as customer service, billing, and invoice adjustments; (3) FedEx center comment cards, which are collected and tabulated twice a year and used as feedback to the managers of each center; (4) customer automation studies of FedEx's 7,600 largest customers, representing 30 percent of the company's total package volume, who are equipped with automated systems that permit package tracking and a variety of other self-service activities; and (5) the Canadian customer study conducted yearly, which is the single most frequent point of destination for FedEx packages shipped outside the United States.

How successful is FedEx? In monetary terms, its success has been history making. FedEx was the first company in U.S. history to top $1 billion in revenues within its first 10 years of existence. Customer satisfaction ratings at FedEx are also legendary. The highest quarterly rating of customer satisfaction achieved thus far has been a 94 percent "completely satisfied" rating from customers on a five-point scale that ranges from "completely dissatisfied" to "completely satisfied." Most firms combine "somewhat satisfied" and "completely satisfied" responses when calculating customer satisfaction ratings, but not FedEx. As a result of achievements such as these and many others, FedEx is a recipient of the Malcolm Baldrige National Quality Award.

wish to meet customer requirements but feel hampered by insufficient methods of measuring quality or by converting those measurements into standards. Because of the difficulties in attempting to write specifications for particular employee behaviors, some managers feel that quality measurement is not worth the effort.

## The Delivery Gap

The delivery gap occurs between the actual performance of a service and the standards set by management. The existence of the delivery gap depends on both the willingness and the ability of employees to provide the service according to specification. For example, do employees wear their name tags, do they establish eye contact, and do they thank the customer when the transaction is completed?

### FACTORS INFLUENCING THE DELIVERY GAP

One factor that influences the size of the delivery gap is the employee's **willingness to perform** the service. Obviously, employees' willingness to provide a service can vary greatly from employee to employee and in the same employee over time. Many employees who start off working to their full potential often become less willing to do so over time because of frustration and dissatisfaction with the organization. Furthermore, a considerable range exists between what the employee is actually capable of accomplishing and the minimum the employee must do in order to keep his or her job. Most service managers find it difficult to keep employees working at their full potential all the time.

**willingness to perform**
An employee's desire to perform to his/her full potential in a service encounter.

Other employees, no matter how willing, may simply not be able to perform the service to specification. Hence, a second factor that influences the size of the delivery gap is the **employee-job fit.** Individuals may have been hired for jobs they are not qualified to handle or to which they are temperamentally unsuited, or they may not have been provided with sufficient training for the roles expected of them. Generally, employees who are not capable of performing assigned roles are less willing to keep trying.

**employee-job fit**
The degree to which employees are able to perform a service to specifications.

Another common factor influencing the size of the delivery gap is **role conflict.** Whether or not the knowledge gap has been closed, service providers may still see an inconsistency between what the service manager expects employees to provide and the service their customers actually want. A waiter who is expected to promote various items on the menu may alienate some customers who prefer to make their own choices undisturbed. For example, how long does it take a McDonald's employee to finally realize that most customers really don't want an apple pie with their meal and are annoyed by the constant prompting? In some instances, customers even finish relaying their order by saying, "And no, I don't want an apple pie with that."

**role conflict**
An inconsistency in service providers' minds between what the service manager expects them to provide and the service they think their customers actually want.

In more formal settings, persistent waiters may find customers retaliating by not leaving a tip. In other cases, the service provider may be expected to do too many kinds of work, such as simultaneously answering telephones and dealing with customers face to face in a busy office. If this kind of conflict continues to occur, employees become frustrated, gradually lose their commitment to providing the best service they can, and/or simply quit altogether.

**role ambiguity**
Uncertainty of employees' roles in their jobs and poor understanding of the purpose of their jobs.

**dispersion of control**
The situation in which control over the nature of the service being provided is removed from employees' hands.

**learned helplessness**
The condition of employees who, through repeated dispersion of control, feel themselves unable to perform a service adequately.

**inadequate support**
Management's failure to give employees personal training and/or technological and other resources necessary for them to perform their jobs in the best possible manner.

Another cause of the delivery gap is **role ambiguity.** Role ambiguity results when employees, because of poor employee-job fit or inadequate training, do not understand the roles of their jobs or what their jobs are intended to accomplish. Sometimes, too, they are even unfamiliar with the service firm and its goals. Consequently, as role ambiguity increases, the delivery gap widens.

A further complication for employees is the **dispersion of control,** the situation in which control over the nature of the service being provided is removed from employees' hands. When employees are not allowed to make independent decisions about individual cases without first conferring with a manager, they may feel alienated from the service and less a part of their job. Furthermore, when control over certain aspects of the service is moved to a different location, such as control over credit being removed from individual bank branches, employee alienation is bound to increase. Employees experience **learned helplessness** and feel unable to respond to customer requests for help. Consequently, as the dispersion of control increases, the delivery gap becomes wider.

Finally, the delivery gap may also suffer as a result of **inadequate support,** such as not receiving personal training and/or technological and other resources necessary for employees to perform their jobs in the best possible manner. Even the best employees can be discouraged if they are forced to work with out-of-date or faulty equipment, especially if the employees of competing firms have superior resources and are able to provide the same or superior levels of service with far less effort. Failure to properly support employees leads to a lot of wasted effort, poor employee productivity, unsatisfied customers, and an increase in the size of the delivery gap.

## The Communications Gap

The communications gap is the difference between the service the firm promises it will deliver through its external communications and the service it actually delivers to its customers (see Services in Action 13.2). If advertising or sales promotions promise one kind of service and the consumer receives a different kind of service, the communications gap becomes wider. External communicators are essentially promises the firm makes to its customers. When the communications gap is wide, the firm has broken its promises, resulting in a lack of future customer trust. A customer who orders a bottle of wine from a menu only to be told it is out of stock may feel that the offer held out on the menu has not been fulfilled. A customer who is promised delivery in three days but who then has to wait a week will perceive service quality to be lower than expected.

**overpromise**
A firm's promise of more than it can deliver.

**horizontal communication**
The flow of internal communication between a firm's headquarters and its service firms in the field.

### FACTORS INFLUENCING THE COMMUNICATIONS GAP

The communications gap is influenced primarily by two factors. The first, the propensity of the firm to **overpromise** often occurs in highly competitive business environments as firms try to outdo one another in the name of recruiting new customers. The second factor pertains to the flow of **horizontal communication** within the firm. In other words, does the left hand know what the right hand is doing? All too often, communications are developed at the firm's headquarters without conferring with service firms in the field. In some instances, new service

ⒺⓇⓋⒾⒸⒺⓈ 13.2
Ⓝ

ⒶⒸⓉⒾⓄⓃ    **The Communication Gap Comes to E-Services**

Findings from a recent study conducted by the International Customer Service Association and e-Satisfy.com indicate that only 36 percent of the 50,000 e-shoppers who were surveyed report that they were satisfied with electronic commerce service. One of the primary service gaps appears to be in the area of communications. Customers report that they typically expect a reply to their e-mail requests within one hour; however, only 12 percent receive such a response, and only 42% of respondents were replied to within 24 hours.

A Rainer-Web index study of the Fortune 100 and FTSE 100 found that more than two in five U.S. and U.K. companies failed to reply to e-mail requests promptly. In fact, 29 FTSE companies and 21 Fortune 100 companies could not be contacted at all from their Web sites. These companies included Marks & Spencer, Thames Water, GTE, and Intel. Of the companies contacted by e-mail, 15 FTSE and 20 Fortune 100 never replied. These types of results led the chairman of Rainer to comment, "All too often, companies focus on the content and look and feel of the site without considering its integration with existing customer contact systems. The result is [that these types of Web sites end up being] little more than corporate wallpaper."

Despite high levels of customer dissatisfaction with the quality of e-services offered by online firms, the number of offline businesses that will offer online shopping will double from last year. Customer participation in making online purchases is also continuing to grow at a rapid rate. Apparently, the zone of tolerance for acceptable service is wider for e-purchases than brick-and-mortar purchases. Customers realize that purchasing on the Web is new and that the ordering and delivery processes may not be perfect. Consequently, many online customers are willing to accept a certain amount of risk in exchange for potential cost savings (money, time, etc.) and appear more forgiving when perceptions fall short of expectations . . . at least for now.

Part of the problem in delivering quality e-services appears to be setting priorities. According to a recent study conducted by Retail Info Systems and Computer Sciences Corporation, order fulfillment was the most pressing issue for 40 percent of business respondents who participated in the study. Disturbingly, 35 percent of business respondents indicated that attracting visitors to their Web sites was top priority. These companies might eventually find that failing to provide quality e-services will sacrifice customer loyalty and long-term profitability. Internet analysts agree: "Companies need more than just a pretty Web site and e-mail address URLs. People who use this technology expect it to work, and if it doesn't it's frustrating."

Source: C. Brune, "E-business Misses the Mark on Customer Service," *Internal Auditor* 57, no. 3 (June 2000), 13–15; "Rainer: Top Companies Lax in Replying to Email," http://www.nua.ie/surveys, August 3, 2000.

programs are announced to the public by corporate headquarters before the local service firms are aware that the new programs exist. A lack of horizontal communication places an unsuspecting service provider in an awkward position when a customer requests the service promised and the provider has no idea what the customer is talking about.

## MEASURING SERVICE QUALITY: SERVQUAL

Although measurements of customer satisfaction and service quality are both obtained by comparing perceptions with expectations, subtle differences between the two concepts are seen in their operational definitions. Whereas satisfaction compares consumer perceptions with what consumers would normally expect, service quality compares perceptions with what a consumer should expect from a firm that delivers high-quality services. Given these definitions, service quality appears to measure a higher standard of service delivery.

**SERVQUAL**
A 44-item scale that measures customer expectations and perceptions regarding five service quality dimensions.

A frequently used and highly debated measure of service quality is the **SERVQUAL** scale.[7] According to its developers, SERVQUAL is a diagnostic tool that uncovers a firm's broad weaknesses and strengths in the area of service quality. The SERVQUAL instrument is based on five service quality dimensions that were obtained through extensive focus group interviews with consumers. The five dimensions include tangibles, reliability, responsiveness, assurance, and empathy, and they provide the basic "skeleton" underlying service quality.

The SERVQUAL instrument consists of two sections: a 22-item section that records customer expectations of excellent firms in the specific service industry, and a second 22-item section that measures consumer perceptions of a particular company in that service industry (i.e., the firm being evaluated). Results from the two sections are then compared to arrive at "gap scores" for each of the five dimensions. The larger the gap, the further consumer perceptions are from expectations and the lower the service quality evaluation. In contrast, the smaller the gap, the higher the service quality evaluation. Customer expectations are measured on a seven-point scale with the anchor labels of "not at all essential" and "absolutely essential."[8] Similarly, customer perceptions are measured on another seven-point scale with anchor labels of "strongly agree" and "strongly disagree." Hence, SERVQUAL is a 44-item scale that measures customer expectations and perceptions regarding five service quality dimensions.

### The Tangibles Dimension

**tangibles dimension**
The SERVQUAL assessment of a firm's ability to manage its tangibles.

Because of the absence of a physical product, consumers often rely on the tangible evidence that surrounds the service in forming evaluations. The **tangibles dimension** of SERVQUAL compares consumer expectations with the firm's performance regarding the firm's ability to manage its tangibles. A firm's tangibles consist of a variety of objects such as carpeting, desks, lighting, wall colors, brochures, daily correspondence, and the appearance of the firm's personnel. Consequently, the tangibles component in SERVQUAL is two-dimensional—one focusing on equipment and facilities, the other focusing on personnel and communications materials.

The tangibles component of SERVQUAL is obtained via four expectations questions (E1 to E4) and four perception questions (P1 to P4). Keep in mind that the expectations questions apply to excellent firms within a particular industry, whereas the perception questions apply to the specific firm under investigation. Comparing the perception scores with the expectation scores provides a numerical variable that indicates the tangibles gap. The smaller the number, the smaller the gap, and the closer consumers' perceptions are to their expectations. The items that pertain to the tangibles dimension are as follows[9]:

## TANGIBLES EXPECTATIONS

**E1.** Excellent companines will have modern-looking equipment.
**E2.** The physical facilities at excellent companies will be visually appealing.
**E3.** Employees of excellent companies will be neat in appearance.
**E4.** Materials associated with the service (such as pamphlets or statements) will be visually appealing in an excellent company.

## TANGIBLES PERCEPTIONS

**P1.** XYZ has modern-looking equipment
**P2.** XYZ's physical facilities are visually appealing.
**P3.** XYZ's employees are neat in appearance.
**P4.** Materials associated with the service (such as pamphlets or statements) are visually appealing at XYZ.

## The Reliability Dimension

In general, the **reliability dimension** reflects the consistency and dependability of a firm's performance. Does the firm provide the same level of service time after time, or does quality dramatically vary with each encounter? Does the firm keep its promises, bill its customers accurately, keep accurate records, and perform the service correctly the first time? Nothing can be more frustrating for customers than unreliable service providers.

**reliability dimension**
The SERVQUAL assessment of a firm's consistency and dependability in service performance.

A constantly amazing observation is the number of businesses that fail to keep their promises. In many instances the consumer is ready to spend money if only the service provider will show up and conduct the transaction as promised. As students, you may have experienced the reliability gap while attempting to have the local cable company install its services in your new apartment. Typically the cable company will approximate the time at which the installer will come to your apartment in four-hour increments (e.g., morning or afternoon). In many cases, you may miss class or work waiting for the cable installer to arrive. All too often, the installer fails to show up during this time period and you must reschedule, missing yet more classes and/or time at work. Further aggravating this process is that you, the customer, must initiate the rescheduling process. Often the cable company offers no apology and provides little explanation other than, "Our installers are very busy."

Consumers perceive the reliability dimension to be the most important of the five SERVQUAL dimensions. Consequently, failure to provide reliable service generally translates into an unsuccessful firm. SERVQUAL assesses the reliability gap as follows:

## RELIABILITY EXPECTATIONS

**E5.** When excellent companies promise to do something by a certain time, they will do so.

**E6.** When customers have a problem, excellent companies will show a sincere interest in solving it.

**E7.** Excellent companies will perform the service right the first time.

**E8.** Excellent companies will provide their services at the time they promise to do so.

**E9.** Excellent companies will insist on error-free records.

## RELIABILITY PERCEPTIONS

**P5.** When XYZ promises to do something by a certain time, it does so.

**P6.** When you have a problem, XYZ shows a sincere interest in solving it.

**P7.** XYZ performs the service right the first time.

**P8.** XYZ provides its services at the time it promises to do so.

**P9.** XYZ insists on error-free records.

### The Responsiveness Dimension

**responsiveness dimension**
The SERVQUAL assessment of a firm's commitment to providing its services in a timely manner.

Responsiveness reflects a service firm's commitment to provide its services in a timely manner. As such, the **responsiveness dimension** of SERVQUAL concerns the willingness and/or readiness of employees to provide a service. Occasionally, customers may encounter a situation in which employees are engaged in their own conversations with one another while ignoring the needs of the customer. Obviously, this is an example of unresponsiveness.

Responsiveness also reflects the preparedness of the firm to provide the service. Typically, new restaurants do not advertise their "opening night" so that the service delivery system can be fine-tuned and prepared to handle larger crowds, thereby minimizing service failures and subsequent customer complaints. The SERVQUAL expectation and perception items that address the responsiveness gap are as follows:

## RESPONSIVENESS EXPECTATIONS

**E10.** Employees of excellent companies will tell customers exactly when services will be performed.

**E11.** Employees of excellent companies will give prompt service to customers.

**E12.** Employees of excellent companies will always be willing to help customers.

**E13.** Employees of excellent companies will never be too busy to respond to customer requests.

## RESPONSIVENESS PERCEPTIONS

**P10.** Employees of XYZ tell you exactly when service will be performed.

**P11.** Employees of XYZ give you prompt service.

**P12.** Employees of XYZ are always willing to help you.

**P13.** Employees of XYZ are never too busy to respond to your requests.

## The Assurance Dimension

SERVQUAL's **assurance dimension** addresses the competence of the firm, the courtesy it extends its customers, and the security of its operations. Competence pertains to the firm's knowledge and skill in performing its service. Does the firm possess the required skills to complete the service on a professional basis?

Courtesy refers to how the firm's personnel interact with the customer and the customer's possessions. As such, courtesy reflects politeness, friendliness, and consideration for the customer's property (e.g., a mechanic who places paper floor mats in a customer's car so as to not soil the car's carpet).

Security is also an important component of the assurance dimension. Security reflects a customer's feelings that he or she is free from danger, risk, and doubt. Recent robberies at ATM locations provide ample evidence of the possible harm that may arise at service locations. In addition to physical danger, the security component of the assurance dimension also reflects financial risk issues (e.g., Will the bank fail?) and confidentiality issues (e.g., Are my medical records at the school's health center kept private?). The SERVQUAL items utilized to address the assurance gap are as follows:

**assurance dimension**
The SERVQUAL assessment of a firm's competence, courtesy to its customers, and security of its operations.

### ASSURANCE EXPECTATIONS

**E14.** The behavior of employees of excellent companies will instill confidence in customers.

**E15.** Customers of excellent companies will feel safe in their transactions.

**E16.** Employees of excellent companies will be consistently courteous to customers.

**E17.** Employees of excellent companies will have the knowledge to answer customer questions.

### ASSURANCE PERCEPTIONS

**P14.** The behavior of employees of XYZ instills confidence in customers.

**P15.** You feel safe in your transactions with XYZ.

**P16.** Employees of XYZ are consistently courteous to you.

**P17.** Employees of XYZ have the knowledge to answer your questions.

## The Empathy Dimension

Empathy is the ability to experience another's feelings as one's own. Empathetic firms have not lost touch with what it is like to be a customer of their own firm. As such, empathetic firms understand their customer needs and make their services accessible to their customers. In contrast, firms that do not provide their customers individualized attention when requested and that offer operating hours convenient to the firm and not its customers fail to demonstrate empathetic behaviors.

The SERVQUAL **empathy dimension** addresses the empathy gap as follows:

**empathy dimension**
The SERVQUAL assessment of a firm's ability to put itself in its customers' place.

### EMPATHY EXPECTATIONS

**E18.** Excellent companies will give customers individual attention.

**E19.** Excellent companies will have operating hours convenient to all their customers.

**E20.** Excellent companies will have employees who give customers personal attention.

**E21.** Excellent companies will have the customer's best interest at heart.

**E22.** The employees of excellent companies will understand the specific needs of their customers.

## EMPATHY PERCEPTIONS

**P18.** XYZ gives you individual attention.

**P19.** XYZ has operating hours convenient to all its customers.

**P20.** XYZ has employees who give you personal attention.

**P21.** XYZ has your best interests at heart.

**P22.** Employees of XYZ understand your specific needs.

## Criticisms of SERVQUAL

Since the development of the SERVQUAL instrument, it has received its share of criticism.[10] The major criticisms of the instrument involve the length of the questionnaire, the validity of the five service quality dimensions, and the predictive power of the instrument in regard to subsequent consumer purchases. The following section focuses on each of these issues and their respective importance to interpreting SERVQUAL results.

### LENGTH OF THE QUESTIONNAIRE

Combining the expectation and perception items of SERVQUAL results in a 44-item survey instrument. Opponents of the SERVQUAL instrument argue that the 44 items are highly repetitive and unnecessarily increase the questionnaire's length. Opponents further argue that the expectations section of the instrument is of no real value and that the perceptions (actual performance) section should be utilized alone to assess service quality.[11]

In response, the developers of SERVQUAL effectively argue that including the expectations section enhances the managerial usefulness of the scale as a diagnostic tool because of the gap scores developed for each dimension. Perception scores alone merely rate whether the respondent agrees or disagrees with each question. For example, Table 13.1 provides a set of perception scores and SERVQUAL scores for a hypothetical firm. Utilizing this information for diagnostic purposes, perception

## TABLE 13.1

### The Diagnostic Advantage of SERVQUAL Scores

| Dimension | Perception Scores | SERVQUAL Scores |
|---|---|---|
| Tangibles | 5.3 | 0.0 |
| Reliability | 4.8 | −1.7 |
| Responsiveness | 5.1 | −1.0 |
| Assurance | 5.4 | −1.5 |
| Empathy | 4.8 | −1.1 |

scores alone would suggest placing an equal emphasis on improving the reliability and empathy dimensions. Incorporating expectations into the SERVQUAL score indicates that improving the reliability dimension should be the firm's top priority. Given that implementing service quality improvements requires a financial investment from the firm, maintaining the expectation section becomes valuable.

Creative suggestions have been made for maintaining the expectations component while at the same time reducing the questionnaire's length by 22 questions. Three approaches have been suggested: (1) On a single scale, ask respondents where they would rate a high-quality company and then where they would rate the firm under investigation; (2) use the scale's midpoint as the expected level of service from a high-quality company, and then rate the specific firm in relation to the midpoint—above expectation or below; and (3) use the end point (e.g., seven on a seven-point scale) as the expected level of a high-quality company, and rate the specific company relative to the high-quality company on the same scale. All three approaches provide alternatives for assessing customer perceptions and expectations while reducing the questionnaire's length.

## THE VALIDITY OF THE FIVE DIMENSIONS

Another frequent criticism of the SERVQUAL instrument is that the five proposed dimensions of service quality—reliability, responsiveness, assurance, empathy, and tangibles—do not hold up under statistical scrutiny. Consequently, opponents of SERVQUAL question the validity of the specific dimensions in the measurement instrument.

SERVQUAL's developers argue that although the five dimensions represent conceptually distinct facets of service quality, they are interrelated. Hence, some overlap may exist (as measured by correlations) among items that measure specific dimensions. In particular, the distinction among the responsiveness, assurance, and reliability dimensions tends to blur under statistical scrutiny. However, when respondents are asked to assign importance weights to each dimension, results indicate that consumers do indeed distinguish among the five dimensions, as exhibited in Table 13.2.

### TABLE 13.2

**Relative Importance of SERVQUAL Dimensions as Reported by Consumers**

| SERVQUAL Dimension Importance* | |
|---|---|
| Reliability | 32% |
| Responsiveness | 22% |
| Assurance | 19% |
| Empathy | 16% |
| Tangibles | 11% |

Source: Leonard L. Berry, A. Parasuraman, and Valerie A. Zeithaml, "Improving Service Quality in America: Lessons Learned," *Academy of Management Executive* 8, no. 2 (1994), 32–52.

*Consumers were asked to allocate 100 points among the five dimensions. The importance percentage reflects the mean point allocation for each dimension.

According to the developers of SERVQUAL, this ranking provides additional evidence of the dimensions' distinctiveness. For the statistical enthusiast, a variety of articles offering additional evidence and rationale supporting the viability of the five-dimensional framework is cited in the notes at the end of the chapter.[12]

## THE PREDICIVE POWER OF SERVQUAL

The third major criticism of SERVQUAL pertains to the instrument's ability to predict consumer purchase intentions. Research has indicated that the performance (perceptions) section alone of the SERVQUAL scale is a better predictor of purchase intentions than the combined expectations-minus-perception instrument. As such, opponents of the SERVQUAL instrument conclude that satisfaction has a more significant effect on purchase intentions than does service quality. Consequently, they assert that managers need to emphasize customer satisfaction programs over strategies focusing solely on service quality.

The developers of SERVQUAL once again take issue with the preceding objections based on a variety of conceptual, methodological, analytical, and practical issues. Consequently, the jury is still out regarding this particular objection. From a managerial standpoint, perhaps the SERVQUAL proponents' most important counterpoint is the diagnostic value of the expectations-minus-perceptions approach. Based on information provided earlier, the developers of SERVQUAL make a convincing argument that incorporating customer expectations provides richer information than does examining the perceptions scores alone.

## SERVQUAL: Some Final Thoughts

### THE IMPORTANCE OF CONTACT PERSONNEL

The SERVQUAL instrument highlights several points that service providers should consider when examining service quality. First, customer perceptions of service are heavily dependent on the attitudes and performance of contact personnel. Of the five dimensions measured, responsiveness, empathy, and assurance directly reflect the interaction between customers and staff. Even tangibles depend partly on the appearance, dress, and hygiene of the service staff.

### PROCESS IS AS IMPORTANT AS OUTCOME

The manner in which customers judge a service depends as much on the service process as on the outcome. How the service is delivered is as important as the frequency and nature of the service. Consequently, customer satisfaction depends on the production of services as well as their consumption.

Viewing services as a process raises considerable difficulties for management when trying to write service quality standards. Standards can be examined either from the perspective of the consumer or from that of the operating system. Thus a specification can be written based on consumers' ratings of the responsiveness of the organization. Unfortunately, although this is a quantitative measure, it does little to guide the behavior of operations managers and contact personnel.

### CONSUMER PERCEPTIONS ARE UNPREDICTABLE

Ratings of service quality dimensions may be influenced by factors outside the control of the organization that may not be readily apparent to managers. For example, consumer moods and attitudes may influence ratings. Studies have shown that when rating services, consumers use a diverse variety of clues. A recent study shows that even if a service firm generates a negative disconfirmation for a consumer, it may not be judged as delivering a poor level of satisfaction. Because they are part of the process, consumers may attribute failures to themselves or to factors outside the control of the firm. Such attributions are shown to depend on the physical characteristics of the service firm. For example, a tidy office setting leads negative attributions away from the firm, whereas a messy office generates attributions of dissatisfaction toward the firm.[13]

## ASSESSING THE CRITICISMS OF SERVQUAL

Finally, the criticisms of SERVQUAL should not be taken lightly. As is the case with most measurement scales, constructive criticisms assist in the further development of improved measurement instruments. Moreover, concerns regarding measurement instruments should remind practitioners that firms should not "live or die" and make drastic decisions based solely on one measurement instrument's results. The value of measurement tools is that they provide management the opportunity to make more informed decisions.

Despite its opponents, SERVQUAL remains a frequently used instrument to assess service quality and is currently being modified to address service quality issues in e-business (see Services in Action 13.3). From the beginning its developers have claimed that SERVQUAL is a useful starting point for measuring service quality and was never presented as "the final answer." The developers of SERVQUAL further contend that when used in conjunction with other forms of measurement, both quantitative and qualitative, SERVQUAL provides a valuable diagnostic tool for evaluating the firm's service quality performance. Overall, as was the case with

---

SERVICES IN ACTION 13.3

### The Seven Dimensions of E-QUAL

The importance of service quality in improving customer satisfaction and loyalty in traditional business settings has been established via SERVQUAL. Recommendations are given below for how consumers might evaluate online business via E-QUAL.

* *Accessibility*—Is the site easily found? The number of search engines and directories that a site is registered on and links to related sites.
* *Navigation*—How easy is it to move around the site? A good rule of thumb is to be within three clicks of the information that is most desired by customers.
* *Design and Presentation*—What is the image projected from the site? Design elements include colors, layout, clarity, and originality.
* *Content and Purpose*—The substance (breadth) and richness (depth) of the site. Currency and accuracy are important aspects of the "content"

dimension. The strategic purpose of the site includes sites that are developed for an internet presence (informational purpose) and online storefronts (revenue-producing purpose).

- *Responsiveness*—The company's propensity to respond to e-mail messages. The collection of visitor information (i.e., cookies, guest book, contests, chat rooms, clubs, storybooks, auto e-mail, and options to speak to customer representatives), and what the company does with this information.
- *Interactivity, Customization, and Personalization*—The level of service provided. Interactivity, customization, and personalization relate to the empathy dimension of service quality. Amazon.com, for example, provides a quality of interaction and personalization that rivals traditional brick-and-mortar businesses.
- *Reputation and Security*—Related to the assurance dimension of service quality, reputation and security pertain to consumer confidence issues. Consumer confidence is being built via proven encryption technologies.

Source: Shohreh A. Kaynama, "A Conceptual Model to Measure Service Quality of Online Companies: E-qual, in Developments in Marketing Science," in Harlan E. Spotts and H. Lee Meadow, eds., Proceedings of the Academy of Marketing Science, vol. 22 (Montreal, Quebec, Canada, 2000), 46–51.

satisfaction measures, SERVQUAL is most valuable when compared with a firm's own past service quality trends and when compared with measures of competitive service quality performance.

## SERVICE QUALITY INFORMATION SYSTEMS

**service quality information system**
An ongoing research process that provides relevant data on a timely basis to managers, who use the data in decision making.

A **service quality information system** is an ongoing research process that provides relevant data on a timely basis to managers, who utilize the data for decision-making purposes.[14] More specifically, service quality information systems use service quality and customer satisfaction measures in conjunction with other measures obtained at various points to assess the firm's overall performance. Components of a service quality information system include:

- Reports on solicitation of customer complaints
- After-sales surveys
- Customer focus group interviews
- Mystery shopping results
- Employee surveys
- Total market service quality surveys

**customer research**
Research that examines the customer's perspective of a firm's strengths and weaknesses.

In general, service quality information systems focus on two types of research: customer research and noncustomer research. **Customer research** examines the customer's perceptions of a firm's strengths and weaknesses and includes such measures as customer complaints, after-sales surveys, focus group interviews, and service quality surveys. In contrast, **noncustomer research** focuses on employee perceptions of the firm's strengths and weaknesses and employee performance (e.g., employee surveys and mystery shopping). In addition, noncustomer research examines how competitors perform on service (via total market service quality surveys) and serves as a basis for comparison.

**noncustomer research**
Research that examines how competitors perform on service and how employees view the firm's strengths and weaknesses.

## Solicitation of Customer Complaints

The primary objectives of soliciting customer complaints are twofold. First, customer complaints identify unhappy customers. The firm's follow-up efforts may enable it to retain many of these customers before they defect to competitors. The second objective of soliciting customer complaints is to identify weaknesses in the firm's service delivery system and take the corrective actions necessary to minimize future occurrences of the same problem. Customer complaints should be solicited on a continuous basis.

The value of continuous customer feedback cannot be understated. Unfortunately, many firms address one complaint at a time and fail to analyze the content of the complaints as a group. The Chicago Marriott took 15 years to figure out that 66 percent of the calls to its customer service line concerned requests for an iron or ironing board.[15] As a result of learning this, the hotel redesignated $20,000 that had been earmarked for color televisions in guest bathrooms to purchase irons and ironing boards for the hotel. Interestingly, few, if any, customers had ever complained about the black-and-white televisions in the bathrooms. If the color televisions had been installed, we would have seen a classic example of a firm defining service quality on its own as opposed to listening to the voice of the customer. Chapter 14 takes an in-depth look at analyzing customer complaints and developing effective recovery strategies for use when service failures do occur.

## After-Sales Surveys

As part of the service quality information system, **after-sales surveys** should also be conducted on a continuous basis. Because after-sales surveys pertain to discrete transactions, they are a type of satisfaction survey and, as such, are subject to the advantages and disadvantages of all customer satisfaction surveys, as discussed in Chapter 12. For example, after-sales surveys address customer satisfaction while the service encounter is still fresh in the customer's mind. Consequently, the information reflects the firm's recent performance but may be biased by the customer's inadvertent attempt to minimize cognitive dissonance.

**after-sales surveys**
A type of satisfaction survey that addresses customer satisfaction while the service encounter is still fresh in the customer's mind.

Although after-sales surveys can also identify areas for improvement, after-sales surveys are a more proactive approach to assessing customer satisfaction than soliciting customer complaints. Many firms wait for customers to complain and then take action based on those complaints. Given the average customer's reluctance to complain, waiting for customer complaints does not provide the firm a "true" picture of its performance. The after-sale survey attempts to contact every customer and take corrective action if a customer is less than satisfied with his or her purchase decision.

Focus groups can provide invaluable feedback to service firms. A roundtable format with participants and a facilitator helps identify areas that need to be improved, ways the service firm best meets the customers' needs, and other valuable information.

## Customer Focus Group Interviews

**focus group interviews**
Informal discussions with eight to twelve customers that are usually guided by a trained moderator; used to identify areas of information to be collected in subsequent survey research.

Another important component of the service quality information system involves customer **focus group interviews.**[16] Focus group interviews are informal discussions with eight to twelve customers that are usually guided by a trained moderator. Participants in the group are encouraged to express their views and to comment on the suggestions made by others in the group. Because of the group interaction, customers tend to feel more comfortable, which motivates them to talk more openly and honestly. Consequently, researchers feel that the information obtained via focus group interviews is richer than data that reflects the opinions of a single individual.

Focus groups are probably the most widely used market research method. However, their primary purpose is to identify areas of information to be collected in subsequent survey research. Although the information provided by the group is considered valuable, other forms of research are generally necessary to confirm that the group's ideas reflect the feelings of the broader segment of customers. Advocates of service quality information systems believe that customer focus groups should be conducted on a monthly basis.

## Mystery Shopping

**mystery shopping**
A form of noncustomer research that consists of trained personnel who pose as customers, shop at the firm unannounced, and evaluate employees.

**Mystery shopping** is a form of noncustomer research that measures individual employee service behavior. As the name indicates, mystery shoppers are generally trained personnel who pose as customers and who shop at the firm unannounced. The idea is to evaluate an individual employee during an actual service encounter.

Mystery shoppers evaluate employees on a number of characteristics, such as the time it takes for the employee to acknowledge the customer, eye contact, appearance, and numerous other specific customer service and sales techniques promoted by the firm.

Mystery shopping is a form of observation research and is recommended to be conducted on a quarterly basis. Results obtained from mystery shoppers are used as constructive employee feedback. Consequently, mystery shopping aids the firm in coaching, training, evaluating, and formally recognizing its employees.

## Employee Surveys

Another vital component of the service quality information system is employee research. When the product is a performance, it is essential that the company listen to the performers. Too often, employees are forgotten in the quest for customer satisfaction. However, the reality is that employee satisfaction with the firm directly corresponds with customer satisfaction. Hence, the lesson to be learned by service firms is that if they want the needs of their customers to come first, they cannot place the needs of their employees last.

Conducted quarterly, **employee surveys** provide an internal measure of service quality concerning employee morale, attitudes, and perceived obstacles to the provision of quality services. Often employees would like to provide a higher level of quality service but feel that their hands are tied by internal regulations and policies. Employee surveys provide the means to uncover these obstacles so that they can be removed when appropriate. Moreover, employees are customers of internal service and assess internal service quality. Because of their direct involvement in providing service delivery, employee complaints serve as an early warning system; that is, employees often see the system breaking down before customers do.

**employee surveys** Internal measures of service quality concerning employee morale, attitudes, and perceived obstacles to the provision of quality services.

## Total Market Service Quality Surveys

**Total market service quality surveys** not only measure the service quality of the firm sponsoring the survey but also assess the perceived service quality of the firm's competitors. When service quality measures such as SERVQUAL are used in conjunction with other measures, a firm can evaluate its own performance compared with previous time periods and with its competitors. Service quality surveys provide a firm with information about needed improvements in the service delivery system, plus they measure the progress in making needed improvements that have been previously identified.

**total market service quality surveys** Surveys that measure the service quality of the firm sponsoring the survey and the service quality of the firm's competitors.

Advocates of the service quality information system recommend that total market service quality surveys be conducted three times a year. However, as is the case with all the components of the service quality information system, the recommended frequencies are dependent on the size of the customer base. Too frequent contact with the same customers can be an annoyance to them. On the other hand, conducting surveys too infrequently may ultimately cost the business its existence.

Overall, the service quality information system provides a comprehensive look at the firm's performance and overcomes many of the shortcomings of individual measures used in isolation. As with all measures, the information system's true value lies in the information it gives managers to help in their decision making. The measures should serve as a support system for decisions but not be the only inputs into the decision process. Managerial expertise and intuition remain critical components of every business decision. Ultimately, the key components that need to be built in to every service quality system include the following[17]:

- *Listening:* Quality is defined by the customer. Conformance to company specifications is not quality; conformance to customers' specifications is. Spending wisely to improve service comes from continuous learning about expectations and perceptions of customers and manufacturers (see Services in Action 13.4).
- *Reliability:* Reliability is the core of service quality. Little else matters to a customer when the service is unreliable.
- *Basic Service:* Forget the frills if you cannot deliver the basics. Service customers want the basics. They expect fundamentals, not fanciness; performance, not empty promises.
- *Service Design:* Reliably delivering the basic service that customers expect depends, in part, on how well various elements function together in a service system. Design flaws in any part of a service system can reduce the perception of quality.
- *Recovery:* Research shows that companies consistently receive the most unfavorable service quality scores from customers whose problems were not resolved satisfactorily. In effect, companies that do not respond effectively to customer complaints compound the service failure, thereby failing twice.
- *Surprising Customers:* Exceeding customers' expectations requires the element of surprise. If service organizations can not only be reliable in output but also surprise the customer in the way the service is delivered, then they are truly excellent.
- *Fair Play:* Customers expect service companies to treat them fairly and become resentful and mistrustful when they perceive they are being treated otherwise.
- *Teamwork:* The presence of "teammates" is an important dynamic in sustaining a server's motivation to serve. Service team building should not be left to chance.
- *Employee Research:* Employee research is as important to service improvement as customer research.
- *Servant Leadership:* Delivering excellent service requires a special form of leadership. Leadership must serve the servers, inspiring and enabling them to achieve.

## SUMMARY

This chapter has focused on defining and measuring service quality. The concepts of service quality and customer satisfaction, discussed in Chapter 12, are intertwined. In general, customer satisfaction can be defined as a short-term, transaction-specific measure. In turn, service quality is a long-term, overall measure. Another

**ERVICES 13.4**

**ACTION    Quality Improvements Need Focus, Not Just $$$**

Although adequate resource support is directly related to the successful implementation of service delivery systems, providing support without direction can be a huge waste of resources. For example, the United States leads the world in health care expenditures per capita, yet ranks thirty-seventh in terms of the quality of care provided to its citizens. The United States devotes 10 to 14 percent of national income to health care, with an average per-capita expenditure of $3,724; meanwhile, England spends 6 percent and is ranked eighteenth in the world.

## The most doesn't mean the best

A study of world health systems has found that the United States spends the most per person but ranked 37th for quality of service. Here are the top rankings for overall performance and spending.

**\* Indicates G-7 country, the seven richest countries in the world**

| Overall performance | Total spending, per capita | |
|---|---|---|
| 1. France* | 1. **United States*** | $3,724 |
| 2. Italy* | 2. Switzerland | $2,644 |
| 3. San Marino | 3. Germany* | $2,365 |
| 4. Andorra | 4. France* | $2,125 |
| 5. Malta | 5. Luxembourg | $1,985 |
| 6. Singapore | 6. Austria | $1,960 |
| 7. Spain | 7. Sweden | $1,943 |
| 8. Oman | 8. Denmark | $1,940 |
| 9. Austria | 9. Netherlands | $1,911 |
| 10. Japan* | 10. Canada* | $1,836 |
| 18. United Kingdom* | 11. Italy* | $1,824 |
| 25. Germany* | 13. Japan* | $1,759 |
| 30. Canada* | 26. United Kingdom* | $1,193 |
| 37. **United States*** | | |

*Source: World Health Report 2000*                                    AP

Source: Robert Cooke, "U.S. Leads in Health-Care Spending, but Not Quality," *Fort Collins Coloradoan*, June 21, 2000, p. B1.

difference is that satisfaction compares perceptions with what customers would normally expect. Service quality compares perceptions with what customers should expect from a high-quality firm. Customer satisfaction and service quality assessments complement each other. Satisfaction evaluations made after each service transaction help revise customers' overall service quality evaluations of the firm's performance.

Firms that excel in service quality do so by avoiding potential quality gaps in their delivery systems. Service quality gaps discussed in this chapter include knowledge, standards, delivery, and communication. Numerous managerial, marketing, and operational factors influence the size of each of these gaps. Ultimately the goal of every firm is to minimize the service gap—the difference between customer perceptions and expectations. The service gap is a function of the knowledge, standards, delivery, and communication gaps and responds accordingly in the combined direction of the four gaps.

One popular method for assessing service quality is the SERVQUAL scale. The original SERVQUAL survey instrument consists of 44 questions that compare consumers' expectations with perceptions along five service quality dimensions—tangibles, responsiveness, reliability, assurance, and empathy. Gap scores for each of the five dimensions can be calculated by comparing consumer expectation with perception ratings. The SERVQUAL gaps indicate specific areas in need of improvement and assist the service firm in its continuous improvement efforts.

SERVQUAL is only one method to assess a firm's service quality. A service quality information system uses a variety of continuous measures to assess the firm's overall performance. The major components of such a system collect information about both customer and noncustomer research. Customer research methods include analyzing customer complaints, after-sales surveys, focus group interviews, and service quality surveys. Noncustomer research methods include employee surveys and mystery shopping.

In sum, service quality offers a means of achieving success among competing firms that offer similar products. The benefits associated with service quality include increases in market share and repeat purchases. Ultimately the keys to delivering service quality are a detailed understanding of the needs of the consumer, service providers who are focused on providing quality, and service delivery systems that are designed to support the firm's overall quality mission.

# Key Terms

| | |
|---|---|
| After-sales surveys | Noncustomer research |
| Assurance dimension | Overpromise |
| Communications gap | Reliability dimension |
| Customer research | Research orientation |
| Delivery gap | Responsiveness dimension |
| Dispersion of control | Role ambiguity |
| Empathy dimension | Role conflict |
| Employee surveys | Service gap |
| Employee-job fit | Service quality |
| Focus group interviews | Service quality information system |
| Horizontal communication | SERVQUAL |
| Inadequate support | Standards gap |
| Knowledge gap | Tangibles dimension |
| Learned helplessness | Total market service quality surveys |
| Levels of management | Upward communication |
| Mystery shopping | Willingness to perform |

# Discussion Questions

1. What are the basic differences between customer satisfaction and service quality?
2. Explain how a manager might use the conceptual model of service quality to improve the quality of his or her own firm.
3. What factors contribute to the size of the knowledge gap?
4. How does the communication gap relate to success in e-business (see Services in Action 13.2)?
5. Discuss the basics of the SERVQUAL measurement instrument.
6. Develop specifications for the role of a "good student."
7. What are the criticisms of SERVQUAL? What are its developers' responses to these criticisms?
8. You have been hired by a firm to develop the firm's service quality information system. What are the components of this system?

# Notes

1. J. Joseph Cronin, Jr., and Steven A. Taylor, "Measuring Service Quality: A Re-examination and Extension," *Journal of Marketing* 56 (July 1992), 55.
2. Thomas A. Stewart, "After All You've Done for Your Customers, Why Are They Still NOT HAPPY," *Fortune* (December 11, 1995), 178–182.
3. Cronin and Taylor, "Measuring Service Quality," 60–63.
4. Ibid.
5. This section was adapted from John E. G. Bateson, *Managing Services Marketing,* 3rd ed. (Fort Worth, Tex.: The Dryden Press, 1995), 558–565.
6. A. Parasuraman, Valerie A. Zeithaml, and Leonard L. Berry, "A Conceptual Model of Service Quality and Its Implications for Future Research," *Journal of Marketing* 49 (Fall 1985), 41–50.
7. A. Parasuraman, Leonard L. Berry, and Valerie A. Zeithaml, "SERVQUAL: A Multiple-Item Scale for Measuring Customer Perceptions of Service Quality," *Journal of Retailing* 64, no. 1 (1988), 12–40.
8. Parasuraman, Zeithaml, and Berry, "A Conceptual Model."
9. Scale items from A. Parasuraman, Leonard L. Berry, and Valerie A. Zeithaml, "Refinement and Reassessment of the SERVQUAL Scale," *Journal of Retailing* 67 (Winter 1991), 420–450.
10. Cronin and Taylor, "Measuring Service Quality," 60–63.
11. A. Parasuraman, Valerie A. Zeithaml, and Leonard L. Berry, "Reassessment of Expectations as a Comparison Standard in Measuring Service Quality: Implications for Future Research," *Journal of Marketing* 58 (January 1994), 111–124.
12. See Parasuraman, Berry, and Zeithaml, "Refinement and Reassessment"; A. Parasuraman, Leonard L. Berry, and Valerie A. Zeithaml, "More On Improving

Service Quality Measurement," *Journal of Retailing* 69, no. 1 (Spring 1993), 1401; and Parasuraman, Zeithaml, and Berry, "Reassessment of Expectations."

13. Mary Jo Bitner, "Evaluating Service Encounters: The Effects of Physical Surroundings and Employee Responses," *Journal of Marketing* (April 1990), 42–50.

14. Leonard L. Berry, A. Parasuraman, and Valerie A. Zeithaml, "Improving Service Quality in America: Lessons Learned," *Academy of Management Executive* 8, no. 2 (1994), 32-52.

15. Ibid., 33.

16. Adapted from Henry Assael, *Marketing Principles & Strategy,* 2nd ed. (Fort Worth, Tex.: The Dryden Press, 1993), 226; and Michael Levy and Barton Weitz, *Retailing Management,* (Homewood, Ill.: Irwin, 1992), 149.

17. Berry, Parasuraman, and Zeithaml, "Improving Service Quality."

## chapter 14

# Service Failures and Recovery Strategies

## CHAPTER OBJECTIVES

The major objectives of this chapter are to introduce the concepts of service failures, consumer complaint behavior, service recovery strategies, and procedures for tracking and monitoring service failures and employee recovery efforts.

After reading this chapter, you should be able to:

- Specify the different categories of service failures.
- Discuss the reasons customers complain.
- Discuss the reasons customers do not complain.
- Describe how consumers evaluate service recovery efforts.
- Discuss the value of tracking and monitoring service failures and employee recovery efforts.

"Don't fight a battle if you don't gain anything by winning."

General George S. Patton, Jr.

## Introduction

Despite the service firm's best efforts, service failures are inevitable. Planes are late, employees are rude or inattentive, and the maintenance of the tangibles surrounding the service is not always perfect. Don't give up! Developing an indifferent attitude or accepting service failures as a part of everyday business can be "the kiss of death." The secrets to success are to take a proactive stance to reduce the occurrence of **service failures** and to equip employees with a set of effective recovery tools to repair the service experience when failures do occur.

The reasons failures are inherent events in the service encounter are directly related to the unique characteristics that distinguish services from goods. Because of intangibility, customer comparison of perceptions to expectations is a highly subjective evaluation; consequently, not all customers are going to be satisfied. Because of heterogeneity, variations in the service delivery process are going to occur, and not every service encounter is going to be identical. Because of perishability, supply and demand match each other only by accident. Hence, service customers will experience delays from time to time, and service workers will occasionally lose their patience while attempting to appease an overabundance of anxious customers. Finally, inseparability places the service provider face to face with the customer, which provides a Pandora's box of failure possibilities.

**service failures**
Breakdowns in the delivery of service; service that does not meet customer expectations.

## CRITICAL INCIDENTS

**critical incidents**
The moments of actual interaction between the customer and the firm.

Service failures occur at **critical incidents** in the service encounter. Every service encounter is made up of numerous critical incidents, or "moments of truth," the moments of interaction between the customer and the firm. Consider the number of critical incidents described in Services in Action 14.1. Critical incidents that resulted in service failures include poor food preparation, mishandled luggage, overworked flight attendants, out-of-stock conditions concerning a variety of items, slow service, poorly managed physical facilities, unannounced flight schedule changes, and an unsympathetic and uncooperative company representative. Services in Action 14.1 provides an excellent example of the variety of "moments of truth" a successful firm needs to effectively manage.

## TYPES OF SERVICE FAILURES

Employee responses to service failures are related directly to customer satisfaction and dissatisfaction. Service failures are generally categorized into one of three main categories: (1) responses to service delivery system failures; (2) responses to customer needs and requests; and (3) unprompted and unsolicited employee actions (Figure 14.1).[1]

**system failures**
Failures in the core service offering of the firm.

Service delivery **system failures** are failures in the core service offering of the firm. In the airline horror story presented in Services in Action 14.1, service delivery system failures included providing spoiled food and warm beer;

*Text continued on page 357*

SERVICES 14.1

IN ACTION    **Is This Any Way to Run an Airline?**

The following letters are detailed accounts of an actual service encounter and the company's response to the service failures.

July 23, 200x

Dear Customer Service Manager:

Through the Carolina Motor Club my wife and I booked round-trip first-class and clipper-class seats on the following World Airlines flights on the dates indicated:

> 1 July World Airlines 3072 Charlotte to Kennedy
> 1 July World Airlines 86 Kennedy to Munich
> 21 July World Airlines 87 Munich to Kennedy
> 21 July World Airlines 3073 Kennedy to Charlotte

We additionally booked connecting flights to and from Wilmington and Charlotte on Trans Air flights 263 (on 1 July) and 2208 (on 21 July).

The outbound flights 3072 and 86 seemed pleasant enough, especially since World Airlines had upgraded our clipper-class seats on flight 86 to first class. However, midflight on 86 we discovered that we had been food poisoned on flight 3072, apparently by the seafood salad that was served in first class that day (it seemed warm to us and we hesitated to eat it but unfortunately did so anyway). My wife was so ill that, trying to get to the restroom to throw up, she passed out cold, hitting her head and, we discovered over the next few days, apparently damaging her back. The flight attendants were very concerned and immediately tried to help her, but there was nothing they could do except help her clean herself up and get the food off her from the food trays she hit. In addition to the nausea and diarrhea, she had a large knot on her head and headaches for several days. Her lower back has been in constant pain ever since. I, too, was very ill for several days. A nice start for a vacation! But it gets worse.

During the long layover between flights at Kennedy, there was a tremendous rainstorm, and our baggage apparently was left out in it, a situation that we discovered when we arrived at our first night's lodging and discovered ALL of our clothing was literally wringing wet. In addition, four art prints we were bringing as gifts for friends were ruined.

The return flights were better only in that we did not get poisoned; instead we did not get fed! Flight 87 out of Munich was apparently short-handed and, due to our seating location, the flight attendant who had to do double duty always got to us last. We had to ask for drinks; there were no hot towels left for us; the meals ran out and we were given no choice but an overdone piece of gray meat with tomato sauce on it—we tasted it, but it was odd tasting and, given our experience on flight 3072, we were afraid to eat it.

Flight 87 was delayed in boarding due to the slowness in cleaning the aircraft (according to an announcement made) and also due to the late arrival of the crew. In addition, the flight was further delayed due to a heavy rainstorm, which backed up traffic for takeoff. However, had the flight boarded on time it would have not lost its takeoff priority and could likely have taken off two hours sooner than it did. We might have been able to make our connection in Charlotte. Onboard the flight, the plane was the dirtiest and in the most disrepair of any aircraft I have ever flown on—peeling wall coverings, litter on floor, overhead bins taped shut with duct tape, etc. As a first-class passenger I asked for some cold beer while we were waiting for the rest of the passengers to board; it was warm. We were quite hungry, having not eaten much in the past 12 hours, and asked for some peanuts; there were none; the plane had not been stocked. I asked for a pillow and blanket for my wife; there was none. What a great first-class section! There were only three flight attendants for the whole plane, and I felt sorry for the pregnant one who had to do double duty in first class and the rear cabin. She was very sympathetic to the poor conditions; I don't see how you keep employees when they are treated like that.

Due to the excess delay at Kennedy, flight 87 was very late and we could not make our connection from Charlotte to Wilmington. As it turned out, we would have barely been able to make it if the flight had been on time because World Airlines had changed not only the flight numbers but also the flight times on the Kennedy-Charlotte leg of our journey—AND WE WERE NEVER NOTIFIED OF THIS CHANGE UNTIL WE ARRIVED AT THE AIRPORT! I deplaned in Raleigh to try to alert the people meeting us in Wilmington that we would not be in that night; however, it was too late and they had already gone to the airport. The gate attendant at Raleigh assured me that World Airlines would put us up for the night in Charlotte, so I returned to the plane. However, when we arrived in Charlotte, the World Airlines representative refused to take care of us, stating that, since we had not booked the Wilmington-Charlotte portion of our trip through World Airlines, "it is not our problem." Furthermore, he tried to wash his hands of it, saying we had an "illegal connection" due to the times between flights and that he wouldn't provide lodging and meals. After I pointed out to him at least three times that the connection was not illegal when booked and World Airlines changed its flight times without notifying us, and further made it clear that not only was I not going to go away, but that there was going to be a lot more said about the matter, he finally capitulated and gave us a voucher.

After traveling for 24 hours, receiving lousy service, poor food, no amenities, it is a real pleasure to run into an argumentative SOB like your agent in Charlotte. He should be fired!!! As first-class passengers we have been treated like cattle! But it does not end here.

Upon arriving in Wilmington the next morning, only two of our four bags arrived with us. We had to initiate a baggage trace action. Our missing bags were finally delivered to our house around 3:00 p.m. on 23 July. And SURPRISE, they were left out in the rain at Kennedy again and EVERYTHING was so wet that water poured out of the pockets. I poured water out of the hairdryer. All of our paper purchases, maps, guide books, photos, souvenir brochures, etc. are ruined. I don't know yet if the dryer, radio, electric toothbrush, voltage converters, etc., will work—they are drying out as this is being written. In addition, my brand new bag now has a hole in the bottom of a corner where it was obvious that World Airline baggage handlers dragged it on the tarmac (obviously a water-logged duffel bag-size piece of luggage is too heavy to lift).

As near as I can figure, we have lost at least a roll of color prints (irreplaceable); approximately $100.00 in travel guides and tour books, many souvenir booklets, brochures, menus, etc.; $100.00 in art prints; $50.00 in damage to luggage; an unknown amount in electronics that may not work; a lot of enjoyment due to pain and suffering resulting from illness and injury (bill for x-rays enclosed); and all sense of humor and patience for such inexcusable treatment by an airline.

If there is to be any compensation for what we have suffered, it should be in monetary form. There is no recapturing the lost time and pleasure on the vacation. The art, books, etc. (except for the photos) can be replaced . . . assuming we should make such a trip again. But if we do, you can be assured we would not choose World Airlines.

In closing, I am particularly angry and adamant about this whole fiasco as we wanted this vacation to be special and treated ourselves to the luxury of first-class treatment . . . which we got everywhere except on World Airlines . . . it is almost unbelievable how poorly we were treated by your airline, almost a perfect negative case study in customer service. I have purposely tried to mention every little nit-picky thing I can recall because I want you to realize just how totally bad this whole experience has been!

In disgust,

J. Q. Customer

## World Airlines' Recovery Strategy

The following is World Airlines' actual responses, which occurred approximately two and three months following the customer's letter. The first letter was written by the claims manager and the second by the customer relations manager.

September 25, 200x

Dear Mr. and Mrs. Customer:

This letter confirms the settlement agreed upon during our phone conversation just concluded.

Accordingly, we have prepared and enclosed (in duplicate) a general release for $2,000.00. Both you and your wife should sign in the presence of a notary public, have your signatures notarized, and return the original to this office, keeping the copy for your records.

As soon as we receive the notarized release, we will forward our draft for $2000.00.

Again, our sincerest apologies to Mrs. Customer. It will be most helpful for our customer relations staff if you included with the release copies of all available travel documents.

Very truly yours,

Manager, Claims

\* \* \*

October 12, 200x

Dear Mr. Customer:

Let me begin by apologizing for this delayed response and all the unfortunate incidents that you described in your letter. Although we try to make our flights as enjoyable as possible, we obviously failed on this occasion.

Our claims manager informs me that you have worked out a potential settlement for the matter regarding the food poisoning. We regret you were not able to enjoy the food service on the other flights on your itinerary because of it. I assure you that such incidents are a rare occurrence and that much time and effort is expended to ensure that our catering is of the finest quality.

Fewer things can be more irritating than faulty baggage handling. Only in an ideal world could we say that baggage will never again be damaged. Still, we are striving to ensure baggage is handled in such a way that if damage should occur, it will be minimized.

Flight disruptions caused by weather conditions can be particularly frustrating since, despite advanced technology, accurate forecasts for resumption of full operations cannot always be obtained as rapidly as one would wish. These disruptions are, of course, beyond the airlines' control. Safety is paramount in such situations, and we sincerely regret the inconvenience caused.

We make every reasonable effort to lessen the inconvenience to passengers who are affected by schedule changes. Our practice is, in fact, to advise passengers of such changes when we have a local contact for them and time permits. We also try to obtain satisfactory alternative reservations. We are reviewing our schedule change requirements with all personnel concerned and will take whatever corrective measures are necessary to ensure that a similar problem does not arise in the future.

You made it clear in your letter that the interior of our aircraft was not attractive. We know that aircraft appearance is a reflection of our professionalism. We regret that our airplane did not measure up to our standards, since we place great emphasis on cabin maintenance and cleanliness. Please be assured that this particular matter is being investigated by the responsible management and corrective action will be taken.

As tangible evidence of our concern over your unpleasant trip, I have enclosed two travel vouchers, which may be exchanged for two first-class tickets anywhere that World Airlines flies. Once again, please accept our humble apology. We hope for the opportunity to restore your faith in World Airlines by providing you with completely carefree travel.

Sincerely,

Customer Relations Manager

## Epilogue

World Airlines filed for bankruptcy within 24 months of this incident.

Source: Richard A. Engdahl and K. Douglas Hoffman, "World Airlines: A Customer Service Air Disaster," in Carol A. Anderson, *Retailing: Concepts, Strategy, and Information* (Minneapolis/St. Paul: West, 1993), 215–218.

mishandling baggage; unannounced changes in flight schedules; poor condition of the plane; inadequate stocks of food supplies, blankets, and pillows; and a shortage in the number of flight attendants adequate to meet the needs of passengers. All these activities are directly tied to the core service of the airline.

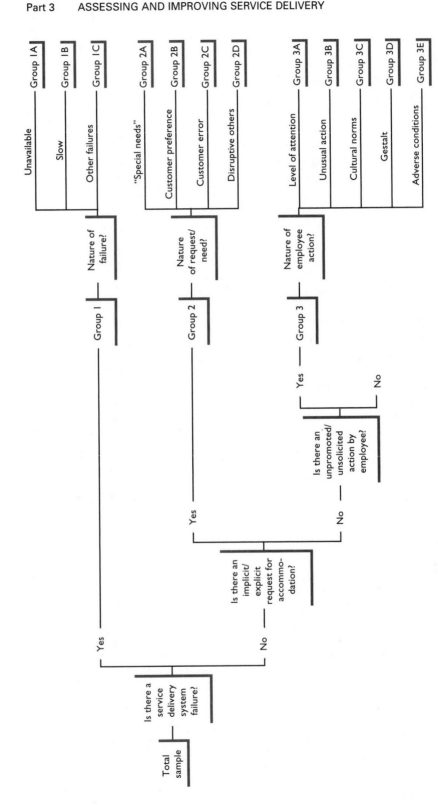

**Figure 14.1   Incident Sorting Process**

Source: Mary Jo Bitner, Bernard H. Booms, and Mary Stanfield Tetreault, "The Service Encounter: Diagnosing Favorable and Unfavorable Incidents," *Journal of Marketing* (January 1990), 71–84.

In general, service delivery system failures consist of employee responses to three types of failures: (1) unavailable service, (2) unreasonably slow service, and (3) other core service failures. **Unavailable service** refers to services normally available that are lacking or absent. **Unreasonably slow service** concerns services or employees that customers perceive as being extraordinary slow in fulfilling their function. **Other core service failures** encompasses all other core service failures. This category is deliberately broad to reflect the various core services offered by different industries (e.g., the food was cold, the plane was dirty, and the baggage was mishandled).

The second type of service failure, responses to **customer needs and requests,** pertains to employee responses to individual consumer needs and special requests. Consumer needs can be implicit or explicit. **Implicit needs** are not requested. For example, in Services in Action 14.1, when the wife of the airline customer became sick and fainted, her implicit needs were readily apparent. The flight attendants immediately came to her aid to help her clean up and expressed genuine concern for her health. Despite all the failures that occurred, the customer noted and appreciated the employees' response to this particular failure. The airline also failed to meet an implicit need when the flight schedule was changed and the airline failed to notify its customers so that alternative connecting flights could be arranged. In contrast, **explicit requests** are overtly requested. The airline employee in Charlotte who initially refused to provide the couple with vouchers for a night's lodging failed to accommodate the passengers' explicit request.

In general, customer needs and requests consist of employee responses to four types of possible failures: (1) special needs; (2) customer preferences; (3) customer errors; and (4) disruptive others. Employee responses to **special needs** involve complying with requests based on a customer's special medical, dietary, psychological, language, or sociological difficulties. Preparing a meal for a vegetarian would fulfill a "special needs request." Employee responses to **customer preferences** require the employee to modify the service delivery system in some way that meets the preferred needs of the customer. A customer request for a substitution at a restaurant is a typical example of a customer preference. An employee response to a **customer error** involves a scenario in which the failure is initiated by an admitted customer mistake (e.g., lost tickets, lost hotel key, forgot to tell the waitress to "hold the mustard"). Finally, employee responses to **disruptive others** require employees to settle disputes between customers, such as requesting patrons to be quiet in movie theaters or requesting that customers not smoke in nonsmoking sections of a restaurant.

The third type of service failure, **unprompted and unsolicited employee actions,** pertains to events and employee behaviors—both good and bad—that are totally unexpected by the customer. These actions are not initiated by the customer via a request, nor are they part of the core delivery system. Subcategories in this group include (1) level of attention, (2) unusual action, (3) cultural norms, (4) gestalt, and (5) adverse condition. In the airline example from Services in Action 14.1, the customer did not note unprompted or unsolicited employee actions as failures. However, if a flight attendant had become abusive or began jumping up and down while singing "My Way" in the aisle, such actions would have qualified as unprompted or unsolicited employee actions.

---

**unavailable service**
Services normally available that are lacking or absent.

**unreasonably slow service**
Services or employees that customers perceive as being extraordinarily slow in fulfilling their function.

**other core service failures**
All remaining core service breakdowns or actions that do not live up to customer expectations.

**customer needs and requests**
The individual needs and special requests of customers.

**implicit needs**
Customer needs that are not requested but that should be obvious to service providers.

**explicit requests**
Customer needs that are overtly requested.

**special needs**
Requests based on a customer's special medical, psychological, language, or sociological difficulties.

**customer preferences**
The needs of a customer that are not due to medical, dietary, psychological, language, or sociological difficulties.

**customer errors**
Service failures caused by admitted customer mistakes.

**disruptive others**
Customers who negatively influence the service experience of other customers.

**unprompted and unsolicited actions**
Events and employee behaviors, both good and bad, totally unexpected by the customer.

**level of attention**
Positive *and/or* negative regard given a customer by an employee.

**unusual action**
Both positive and negative events in which an employee responds with something out of the ordinary.

Within the failure group of unprompted or unsolicited employee action, the subcategory of **level of attention** refers to both positive and negative events. Positive levels of attention occur when an employee goes out of his or her way to pamper a customer and anticipate the customer's needs. Negative levels of attention pertain to employees who have poor attitudes, employees who ignore a customer, and employees who exhibit behaviors consistent with an indifferent attitude.

The **unusual action** subcategory can also reflect positive and negative events. For example, a Domino's Pizza employee happened to see a family searching through the burnt-out remains of their house while making a delivery to another customer in the area. The employee reported the event to the manager, and the two immediately prepared and delivered pizzas for the family free of charge. The family was stunned by the action and never forgot the kindness that was extended toward them during their time of need. Unfortunately, an unusual action can also be a negative event. Employee actions such as rudeness, abusiveness, and inappropriate touching would also qualify as unusual actions.

The **cultural norms** subcategory refers to actions that either positively reinforce cultural norms, such as equality, fairness, and honesty, or violate the cultural norms of society. Violations would include discriminatory behavior, acts of dishonesty such as lying, cheating, and stealing, and other activities considered unfair by customers.

The **gestalt** subcategory refers to customer evaluations that are made holistically; that is, the customer does not describe the service encounter as discrete events but uses overall terms such as "pleasant" or "terrible." In our airline example, if the customer had not specified the individual failure events but had commented

Domino's Pizza provides not only a service, but also goodwill, such as the time a delivery person observed a family searching through the burned remains of their house. The local pizza provider prepared pizzas for the family free of charge, making this unusual action one of social responsibility.

only, "It is almost unbelievable how poorly we were treated by the employees of your airline, almost a perfect negative case study in customer service," the complaint would be categorized as a gestalt evaluation.

Finally, the **adverse conditions** subcategory covers positive and negative employee actions under stressful conditions. If an employee takes effective control of a situation when all others around him or her are "losing their heads," customers are impressed by the employee's performance under those adverse conditions. In contrast, if the captain and crew of a sinking ship board the lifeboats before the passengers, this would obviously be remembered as a negative action under adverse conditions.

## CUSTOMER COMPLAINING BEHAVIOR

In a striking example of the impact of service failures, consumers were asked, "Have you ever gotten so upset at a store (or manufacturer) that you said, 'I'll never go into that store or buy that brand again,' and you haven't?" Researchers found that they had to limit respondents to relating only three incidents to keep the interview time reasonable. The oldest incident had happened more than 25 years ago, and 86 percent of the incidents were more than 5 years old. Apparently customers are not prone to "forgive and forget" when it comes to customer service failures!

The consequences of service failures can be dramatic (see Services in Action 14.2). The vast majority of respondents in the survey (87 percent) indicated that they were still somewhat or very emotionally upset and were more upset about the treatment they received from employees than at the store or product performance. More than three-quarters of respondents indicated that they had engaged in negative word-of-mouth communications regarding the incident (46 percent claimed that they had told "lots of people"). Finally, true to form in what is typical consumer complaint behavior today, only 53 percent had voiced their complaint to the store, even though 100 percent defected to other firms.[2]

Most companies cringe at the thought of customers who complain, whereas other companies look at complaints as a necessary evil in conducting business. The truth of the matter is that every company should encourage its customers to complain. Complainers are telling the firm that it has some operational or managerial problems that need to be corrected. Hence, complainers are offering the company a free gift; that is, they act as consultants and diagnose the firm's problems—at no fee. Moreover, complainers provide the firm with the chance to reestablish a customer's satisfaction. Complainers are more likely to do business with the firm again than are noncomplainers. Consequently, successful firms view complaints as an opportunity to satisfy unhappy customers and prevent defections and unfavorable word-of-mouth communications.[3]

It's not the complainers the company should worry about, it's the noncomplainers. Customers who do not express their complaints are already gone or ready to leave for the competition at any moment. In fact, 63 percent of dissatisfied customers who do not complain and who have purchased goods or services costing $1 to $5 will defect to a competitor. Even more disturbing is that as purchases exceed $100, the defection rate approaches 91 percent.[4]

**cultural norms**
Service personnel actions that either positively reinforce or violate the cultural norms of society.

**gestalt**
Customer evaluations that are made holistically and given in overall terms rather than in descriptions of discrete events.

**adverse conditions**
Positive and negative employee actions under stressful conditions.

SERVICES IN ACTION  **14.2**

### E-Failures

According to research from Anderson Consulting, 40 percent of Internet shoppers in the U.S. experienced problems with online stores during the 1999 Christmas season. Of that 40 percent,

- 64 percent experienced stock shortages
- 38 percent felt the delivery charge was too high
- 36 percent experienced difficulty connecting to/downloading from a Web site
- 35 percent who experienced difficulty left one site for another

Despite the problems, 73 percent of customers shopping online reported that they were satisfied with their experience. This compares to a 60 percent satisfaction rate for brick-and-mortar stores and a 56 percent rate for catalog shopping. Even with the relatively high satisfaction rates, a partner at Anderson Consulting commented, "E-tailers can't continue to lose one of every three consumers and expect to survive."

Source: John Sterlicchi and Barbara Gengler, "E-tailers Costly Lessons," *Upside* 12, no. 6 (June 2000), 195–200.

## Types of Complaints

*Complaining* is defined in Webster's Third International Dictionary as "expressing discontent, dissatisfaction, protest, resentment, or regret."[5] Complaining is different from criticism. Complaining expresses a dissatisfaction within the complainer, whereas criticism may be an objective and dispassionate observation about a person or object.

**instrumental complaints**
Complaints expressed for the purpose of altering an undesirable state of affairs.

Based on past research in consumer psychology, complaints can be instrumental or noninstrumental.[6] **Instrumental complaints** are expressed for the purpose of altering an undesirable state of affairs. For example, complaining to a waiter about an undercooked steak is an instrumental complaint. In such a case, the complainer fully expects the waiter to correct the situation. Interestingly, research indicates that instrumental complaints make up only a very small number of the complaints that are voiced every day.

**noninstrumental complaints**
Complaints expressed without expectation that an undesirable state will be altered.

In contrast, **noninstrumental complaints** are voiced without any expectation that the undesirable state will be altered. These kinds of complaints are voiced much more often than are instrumental complaints. For example, complaints about the weather such as "It's too hot!" are voiced without any real expectation that conditions will change. Another type of noninstrumental complaint is an instrumental complaint that is voiced to a second party and not to the offending source. For example, complaining to a friend about your roommate being a slob is a noninstrumental complaint.

**ostensive complaints**
Complaints directed at someone or something outside the realm of the complainer.

Complaints are also categorized as ostensive or reflexive. **Ostensive complaints** are directed at someone or something outside the realm of the complainer.

SERVICES 14.3

IN ACTION    **Sorry Seems To Be the Hardest Word**

Apologies alone are sometimes not enough to retain unhappy customers. This is particularly true when the apology seems to be standard operating procedure and nothing is being done to keep the service failure from happening again. Employees at the Alternative Federal Credit Union of Ithaca, New York, want to make sure that when mistakes are made, "sorry" is indeed sincere and that mistakes and suggestions are taken seriously. One customer who lodged a complaint noted that he received a letter of apology from a bank teller and that the word "sorry" was emblazoned with chocolate. Now, when the customer speaks of the credit union, it's not of the mistake but how he was responded to by the credit union's employees. Other recovery ideas that the credit union has implemented include:

- Sending a follow-up letter to each member who conveys a complaint
- Providing discounts such as $5 off share drafts
- Giving members a "go to the head of the line on a busy day" card
- Handing out a fortune cookie with "we're sorry" inside
- Stocking "goof gifts" such as pens, pocket planners, and appointment books that are sent with letters of apology

The bottom line is that complaints should be viewed as an opportunity to show the member that the credit union truly cares and is listening. "Complaints can give businesses a wake-up call when they are not achieving their fundamental purpose of meeting customer needs. Complaints provide a feedback mechanism that can help organizations rapidly and inexpensively shift products, service style, and market focus."

Source: Bill Merrick, "Make Mistakes Easier to Swallow," *Credit Union Magazine* 66, no. 4 (June 2000), 14.

are great at delivering service until something goes wrong, other companies thrive on recovering from service failures and impressing customers in the process (see Services in Action 14.3). Customers of service organizations often allow the firm one mistake.[12] Consequently, when a failure occurs, the customer generally provides the business with an opportunity to make amends. Unfortunately, many companies still drop the ball and further aggravate the customer by failing to take the opportunity to recover.

When the service delivery system fails, it is the responsibility of contact personnel to react to the complaint. The content and form of the contact personnel's response determines the customer's perceived satisfaction or dissatisfaction with the service encounter.[13] Ironically, customers will remember a service encounter favorably if the contact personnel respond in a positive manner to the service failure. Hence, even though the service encounter included a service failure, the customer recalls the encounter as a positive event. In fact, a customer may rate

**service recovery paradox**
Situation in which the customer rates performance higher if a failure occurs and the contact personnel successfully recover from it than if the service had been delivered correctly the first time.

performance higher if a failure occurs and the contact personnel successfully recover from the failure than if the service had been delivered correctly the first time. This phenomena has been termed the **service recovery paradox.**

Experts in the area of service recovery recommend that in establishing service recovery as a priority and developing recovery skills, firms should consider the following issues.

## Measure the Costs

The costs of losing and the benefits of keeping existing customers as opposed to chasing new customers are substantial. In short, the costs of obtaining new customers are three to five times greater than those of keeping existing customers. Current customers are more receptive to the firm's marketing efforts and are, therefore, an important source of profit for the firm. In addition, existing customers ask fewer questions, are more familiar with the firm's procedures and employees, and are willing to pay more for services.

## Actively Encourage Complaints

Experts assert that actively encouraging complaints is a good way to "break the silence." Remember that complainers who actually voice their complaints to the source of the problem are the exception—most customers don't speak up. In fact, research indicates that the average company does not hear from 96 percent of its unhappy customers.[14] This doesn't mean that customers don't complain, only that they complain to friends and family rather than to the offending firm. The average unhappy customer voices displeasure with a firm to 11 other people. If these 11 tell 5 other people, the firm has potentially lost 67 customers.[15] Strategies to encourage complaints include customer surveys, focus groups, and active monitoring of the service delivery process to ensure customer satisfaction throughout the encounter, before a customer leaves the premises.

## Anticipate Needs for Recovery

Every service encounter is made up of a series of critical incidents, the points in the system where the customer and the firm interact. Firms that are effective in service recovery anticipate in advance the areas in their service delivery process where failures are most likely to occur. Of course, these firms take every step possible to minimize the occurrence of the failure in the first place, but they are prepared for recovery if delivery goes awry. Experts believe that firms should pay special attention to areas in which employee turnover is high. Many high-turnover positions are low-paying customer contact positions, and employees often lack motivation and/or are inexperienced in effective recovery techniques. A good example of failing to anticipate a need for recovery was provided in Services in Action 14.1. World Airlines had changed its flight schedule without notifying passengers. The airline should have anticipated that this change would cause passengers problems with connecting flights. The problem was further aggravated by the employee in Charlotte who initially would not provide the passenger and his wife a voucher for a night's lodging. Had World Airlines anticipated the events caused by its flight schedule change and made alternative arrangements for passengers or provided hassle-free vouchers for the night's lodging, the magnitude of the failure would have been minimized.

## Respond Quickly

When a service failure does occur, the faster the company responds, the more likely that the recovery effort will result in a successful outcome (see Services in Action 14.4). In fact, past studies have indicated that if the complaint is handled

SERVICES *14.4*

ACTION    **The Snowball Effects of Not Dealing with Consumer Complaints**

Complaint recognition and service recovery are important customer service issues for any type of firm regardless of whether it's a traditional goods manufacturer or a high-tech service operation. Failing to respond to customer complaints can become disastrous. Case in point, Mitsubishi Motors. For decades, Mitsubishi employees have apparently been going to great lengths to hide consumer complaints. Letters have been hidden in boxes, in changing rooms, behind lockers, and stashed in secret computer files. The primary reason for the cover-up appears to be cultural. On August 22, 2000, the company's president stood before the world press, took a deep sigh and an even deeper bow of apology, and confessed to the company's systematic and deliberate attempts to avoid the recall of more than 800,000 of its defective vehicles. "We were ashamed of reporting recalls," said the company's president, Katsuhiko Kawasoe.

The cost of the recall to the company is estimated to be in the tens of millions; however, the damage to its reputation and brand name may be much worse. DaimlerChrysler Corporation, which recently agreed to a 34 percent stake in Mitsubishi, is carefully watching how the company responds to its admission of guilt.

Analysts blame the problem on the company's corporate culture of arrogance. Others note that Japan's reputation for excellence is quickly eroding because of its political leadership and that the country is losing its confidence, strength, and momentum. Several other Japanese companies have also recently experienced difficulties with the quality of their products, including Japan's Bridgestone Corp. and its subsidiary Firestone, which produced defective tires in the United States; Snow Brand milk, which poisoned more than 15,000 of its customers; Kirin Beverage Company, which recently recalled more than 600,000 cans of tomato juice; and the Tokiamura nuclear reactor, at which careless accidents occurred.

Source: Mark Magnier and John O'Dell, "Mitsubishi Admits to Complaint Cover-up," *Coloradoan* (August 23, 2000), pp. A1–A2.

promptly, the company will retain 95 percent of its unhappy customers. In contrast, if the complaint is resolved at all, the firm retains only 64 percent of unhappy customers.[16] Time is of the essence. The faster the firm responds to the problem, the better the message the firm sends to customers about the value it places on pleasing its customers. It took World Airlines two to three months to respond to our unhappy passenger. What kind of message does that send? In addition, the severity of the failure regarding the voucher for the night's lodging was magnified tremendously by the delay in response. Why not give customers what they want, when they want it? Is it really worth it to the firm for employees to actively argue with customers?

Another firm that learned this lesson the hard way is a bank in Spokane, Washington. A customer who had millions of dollars in the bank's checking, investment, and trust accounts was denied having his parking validated because he "only" cashed a check as opposed to making a deposit. The customer was at a branch bank that was not his normal bank. After explaining the situation to the teller, who was unimpressed, and more loudly voicing his opinion to the branch manager, the customer drove to his usual bank and threatened to close his accounts if he did not receive a response from the bank's upper management by the end of the day. As incredible as it may seem, the call never came, and the customer withdrew $1 million the first thing next morning. This action did get the bank's attention, and the bank has been trying to recover ever since.[17]

## Train Employees

Expecting employees to be naturals at service recovery is unrealistic. Most employees don't know what to do when a failure occurs, and many others find making on-the-spot decisions a difficult task. Employee training in service recovery should take place on two levels. First, the firm must work at creating in the employee an awareness of customer concerns. Placing an employee in the shoes of the customer is often enlightening for an employee who has forgotten what it's like to be a customer of his or her own firm. For example, hospitals have made interns and staff dress in hospital gowns and had them rolled around on gurneys to experience some of the hospitals' processes firsthand.

The second level of employee training, beyond developing an appreciation for customer needs, is defining management's expectation toward recovery efforts. What are acceptable recovery strategies from management's perspective? Effective recovery often means that management has to let go and allow employees to take risks, a transition that often leads to the empowerment of front-line employees.

## Empower the Front Line

Effective recovery often means that the employee has to bend the firm's rules and regulations—the exact type of activity that employees are trained not to do at any cost. Often the rules and regulations of the firm tie the hands of employees when it comes to effective recovery efforts, particularly in the area of prompt response. In many instances, firms require managerial approval before any effort to compensate a customer is undertaken. However, the manager is often engaged in other

Employees such as this bank teller make up the "front line" in a service encounter. If empowered, these employees can make the appropriate decisions in order to recover effectively from any lapse in the service experience.

duties, which delays the response and adds to the frustration for both customer and employee.

## Close the Loop

One of the most important activities in service recovery is providing feedback to the customer about how that customer's complaint made a difference. Referring again to Services in Action 14.1, the airline's response letters fail to mention how any of the events that befell the customer will be prevented in the future. The letters express why the events occur but do not really say what the company is doing to correct the situations. Statements such as, "We will take whatever corrective measures are necessary to ensure that a similar problem does not arise in the future" fail to close the loop and convey the impression that the firm is attempting to push the whole matter aside.

# EVALUATING RECOVERY EFFORTS: PERCEIVED JUSTICE

Throughout the service recovery process, customers weigh their inputs against their outputs when forming recovery evaluations.[18] Inputs could be described by the costs associated with the service failure, including economic, time, energy, and psychic (cognitive) costs. The sum of the inputs is compared with the sum of the outputs, which includes the specific recovery tactic (e.g., cash refund, apology, replacement, etc.), the manner of personnel, the service policies developed to handle such situations, and the image associated with responsive organizations.

**perceived justice**
The process where customers weigh their inputs against their outputs when forming recovery evaluations.

**distributive justice**
A component of perceived justice that refers to the outcomes (e.g., compensation) associated with the service recovery process.

**procedural justice**
A component of perceived justice that refers to the process (e.g., time) the customer endures during the service recovery process.

**interactional justice**
A component of perceived justice that refers to human content (e.g., empathy, friendliness) that is demonstrated by service personnel during the service recovery process.

The customer's perception of whether the recovery strategy is just includes evaluations of the recovery process itself, the outcomes connected to the recovery strategy, and the interpersonal behaviors enacted during the recovery process. Accordingly, **perceived justice** consists of three components: distributive justice, procedural justice, and interactional justice.

**Distributive justice** focuses on the specific outcome of the firm's recovery effort. In other words, what specifically did the offending firm offer the customer to recover from the service failure, and did this outcome (output) offset the costs (inputs) of the service failure? Typical distributive outcomes include compensation (e.g., gratis, discounts, coupons, free upgrades, and free ancillary services), offers to mend or totally replace/re-perform, and apologies.

The second component of perceived justice, **procedural justice,** examines the process that is undertaken to arrive at the final outcome. Hence, even though a customer may be satisfied with the type of recovery strategy offered, recovery evaluation may be poor as a result of the process endured to obtain the recovery outcome. For example, research has indicated that when implementing identical recovery strategies, those that are implemented "promptly" are much more likely to be associated with higher consumer effectiveness ratings and retention rates than their "delayed" counterparts.

**Interactional justice** refers to the manner in which the service recovery process is implemented and how recovery outcomes are presented. In other words, interactional justice involves the courtesy and politeness exhibited by personnel, empathy, effort observed in resolving the situation, and the firm's willingness to provide an explanation of why the situation occurred.

A limited amount of research exists that specifically examines the influence of perceived justice on recovery strategy effectiveness. However, the bottom line is that the three components of perceived justice must be taken into consideration when formulating effective service recovery strategies. Deploying recovery efforts that satisfy distributive justice without consideration of customer procedural and interactional justice needs may still result in customer defections. If service firms are truly committed to the recovery process and retaining customers for life, all three aspects of perceived justice must be integrated into the service recovery process.

## SERVICE FAILURE AND RECOVERY ANALYSIS: AN EMPIRICAL EXAMPLE IN THE RESTAURANT INDUSTRY[19]

The obvious benefit of service failure and recovery analysis is that management can identify common failure situations, minimize their occurrence, and train employees to recover from failures when they do occur. The example that follows is an actual study of service failures and recovery strategies in the restaurant industry.

### The Value of Tracking Service Failures

As is the case in most service industries today, restaurant managers and service personnel are facing intensive customer service pressures now more than ever.[20] When a service failure does occur, the service provider's reaction can either reinforce a

strong customer bond or change a seemingly minor distraction into a major incident. For example, an employee's indifferent reaction to a customer's complaint
about cold french fries can cost a restaurant years of that particular customer's business and an abundance of negative word-of-mouth publicity. Consequently, it is
imperative that managers have an established service recovery plan to overcome
possible service failures.

Analyzing service failures and service recovery strategies is an extremely useful management tool.[21] In general, service failure analysis provides the type, frequency, and magnitude of various failures. By systematically categorizing consumer
complaints, a hierarchy of criteria evolves that reflect the consumer's perspective
of effective performance. This is a very important point. Typically, firms using measures such as FedEx's initial approach to measuring customer satisfaction have
defined performance based on measures developed internally.[22] However, performance should be measured based on what the customer, not upper management, perceives as important.

## The Value of Analyzing Service Recovery Strategies

In addition to tracking service failures, analyzing service recovery strategies is
equally enlightening. Service recovery analysis provides a sometimes frightful
insight into the following:

- How personnel react to service failures
- How consumers rate the effectiveness of the employee's recovery efforts
- The relationship between recovery strategies and customer retention rates

Recent studies suggest that nearly half the responses to customer complaints actually reinforce a customer's negative feeling toward a firm.[23] Effective recovery
strategies often require contact personnel to make decisions and to occasionally
break company rules—the types of behaviors that many firms prohibit their
employees from initiating. Contact personnel are often frustrated by rules and regulations that tie their hands and prevent them from assisting a customer when
needed. Furthermore, because of the lack of training in recovery efforts exhibited
by most firms, many employees simply do not know how to recover from service
failures. The result is a poor response or no response to customer complaints.

## The Restaurant Study

The study was conducted by services marketing students and is a great example
of the valuable managerial information that can be obtained by monitoring and
tracking service failures. The example is presented in a series of steps that can be
easily duplicated. We highly recommend this exercise to services marketing classes
as a group project. Different groups may investigate different industries or specific
businesses.

### STEP 1: DEVELOPING THE QUESTIONNAIRE
An example of the questionnaire used to collect the data for this study is provided
in the appendix to this chapter. The main objective of the questionnaire is to

- Assess customer perceptions of the magnitude of each failure
- Identify and classify recovery strategies used by restaurants to correct failures
- Assess customer perceptions of the effectiveness of each type of recovery
- Assess subsequent patronage behaviors that reflect restaurants' customer retention rates
- Provide demographic information about respondents

## STEP 2: DATA COLLECTION

**critical incident technique**
A method of studying service failures by analyzing critical incidents described in story form by respondents.

**THE CRITICAL INCIDENT TECHNIQUE**   The study used a data collection method referred to as the **critical incident technique** (CIT). The purpose of CIT in this study is to examine the sources of customer satisfaction and dissatisfaction regarding restaurant services. In essence, CIT is a qualitative approach to analyzing and categorizing critical incidents. CIT analyzes the content of the critical incidents described by respondents in story form.

The actual critical incidents (or stories) for this study were recorded by students. Respondents were asked to report a restaurant service failure that was associated with a positive service recovery as well as a service failure that was associated with a negative service recovery. Both scenarios were requested in order to identify recovery strategies that were effective as well as responses that were inadequate. Incidents associated with positive recovery strategies accounted for 49.6 percent of the sample, whereas 50.4 percent of the sample was associated with poor recoveries.

In addition, respondents were asked to do the following:

- Rate the magnitude of the failure on a scale from 1 through 10, which ranges from trivial to serious
- Rate the effectiveness of the recovery strategy on a scale from 1 through 10, which ranges from poor to good
- Report changes in shopping behavior subsequent to the service failure attributed to the encounter
- Provide demographic information on gender, education, and age

The data collection efforts resulted in the accumulation of 373 critical incidents.

## STEP 3: DATA ANALYSIS

The critical incident technique is a qualitative approach to analyzing and categorizing critical incidents. More specifically, the CIT used in this study involved three steps:

1. *Identify the Failure Incident.* Initially, each of the 373 critical incidents was systematically categorized through a deductive sorting process into one of the three major failure groups discussed earlier in the chapter: (1) employee responses to service delivery system failures, (2) employee responses to implicit/explicit customer requests, and (3) unprompted and unsolicited employee actions.

2. *Identify Failure Subgroups within the Three Major Groups.* This step involved classifying failures into subgroups within each of the three major failure

groups noted above. This process resulted in the identification of 11 unique failure subgroups (five in Group 1; two in Group 2; and four in Group 3).

3. *Classify Recovery Strategies*. This step involved classifying the service recovery strategies within each failure subgroup. This process resulted in eight
final service recovery strategies that are applicable to a variety of food service
operations.

## STEP 4: ESTABLISHING THE RELIABILITY OF THE CATEGORIES

An important procedure when categorizing data is to determine the reliability of
the categories. Reliability simply refers to the issue of whether other researchers,
given the same set of data, would assign each of the critical incidents to the same
set of categories. To assess the reliability of the 11 failure subgroups and eight
recovery strategies established through the sorting process in the study, an independent judge (such as a group member not involved in the original categorization) categorized each of the incidents included in the sample.

As a starting point to test for reliability, the critical incidents were presorted
into the three main failure categories: (1) employee responses to service delivery
system failures, (2) employee responses to implicit/explicit customer requests, and
(3) unprompted and unsolicited employee actions. The independent judge was
then presented with the 11 previously identified failure subgroups and asked to
independently sort each failure incident into one of the 11 categories. In this
example, the task resulted in agreement rates of 92 percent, 90 percent, and 90
percent. Typically, agreement rates of 70 percent or higher are regarded as acceptable for establishing reliability.

After establishing the reliability of the service failure categories, the independent judge's next task is to verify the reliability of the service recovery categories. Following a procedure similar to the one described above, the independent
judge is given the stack of recovery strategies and the names of the eight categories of recovery strategies previously identified. The independent judge then
compares his or her categorization efforts with the original results. For this study
the recovery agreement rate was 93 percent, and reliability was established for the
recovery categories as well as for the failure categories.

## STEP 5: PRESENTING THE RESULTS

**DEMOGRAPHIC RESULTS**    Sample demographics revealed that 42.5 percent of
the respondents were male and 57.5 percent were female. Regarding education,
68.2 percent of the respondents did not have college degrees, 21.7 percent had
undergraduate degrees, and 10.1 percent had "some" or had completed graduate
school. Results concerning the age of respondents revealed that 67.5 percent were
25 years old or younger, 14.1 percent were from 26 to 35, and 18.4 percent were
36 years of age or older.

Statistical tests were used in examining the relationships between demographics and restaurant type, failure type, recovery strategies, failure ratings, recovery ratings, and retention rates. Results revealed no statistically significant findings.
These tests provide evidence that the findings, reported across different types of
customers and across restaurant types, can be safely generalized.

**THE FAILURE CATEGORIES: FREQUENCY AND DEFINITION**    After carefully sorting the 373 critical incidents, the following restaurant service failure categories were developed and their reliability established. As described earlier in step 3, the incidents were first sorted into three main failure groups and then into subclass failures within each main failure group.

Group 1, "Employee Responses to Core Service Failures," accounted for 44.4 percent of all critical incidents. Core service failures included the following subclass categories (the frequency of occurrence expressed as a percentage of the total critical incidents is reported in parentheses):

*Product Defects* (20.9 percent): Food that was described as cold, soggy, raw, burnt, spoiled, or containing inanimate objects such as hair, glass, bandages, bag ties, and cardboard.

*Slow/Unavailable Service* (17.9 percent): Waiting an excessive amount of time and/or not being able to find assistance.

*Facility Problems* (3.2 percent): Cleanliness issues such as bad smells, dirty utensils, and animate objects found in food or crawling across the table (e.g., insects).

*Unclear Policies* (1.6 percent): Restaurant policies that were perceived as unfair by the customer (e.g., coupon redemption, form of payment).

*Out-of-Stock Conditions* (0.8 percent): An inadequate supply of menu items.

Group 2, "Employee Responses to Implicit/Explicit Customer Requests," accounted for 18.4 percent of the critical incidents. Implicit/explicit customer requests included the following subclass categories (the frequency of occurrence expressed as a percentage of the total critical incidents is reported in parentheses):

*Food Not Cooked to Order* (15 percent): The scenario in which the customer explicitly asks for the food to be prepared in a specific manner (e.g., medium rare, no mustard) and the request is not honored.

*Seating Problems* (3.4 percent): Involved seating smokers in nonsmoking sections and vice-versa, lost or disregarded reservations, denial of request for special tables, and seating among unruly customers.

Group 3, "Unprompted/Unsolicited Employee Actions," accounted for 37.2 percent of the total critical incidents. Unprompted/unsolicited employee actions included the following subclass categories (the frequency of occurrence expressed as a percentage of the total critical incidents is reported in parentheses):

*Inappropriate Employee Behavior* (15.2 percent): Rudeness, inappropriate verbal exchanges, and poor attitudes that were associated with unpleasant behaviors.

*Wrong Orders* (12.6 percent): The delivery of an incorrect food item to the table, or in the case of fast food, packaging an incorrect food item that was not discovered until the customer was no longer on the restaurant premises.

*Lost Orders* (7.5 percent): Situations in which the customer's order was apparently misplaced and never fulfilled.

*Mischarged* (1.9 percent): Being charged for items that were never ordered, charging incorrect prices for items that were ordered, and providing incorrect change.

**THE FAILURE CATEGORIES: MAGNITUDE AND RECOVERY**   In addition to developing the failure categories, we also recorded each respondent's perception of the magnitude of the failure. Respondents rated the magnitude of the failure on a scale from 1 (minor mistake) through 10 (major mistake). In addition, the average effectiveness of recovery for each failure was calculated on a scale from 1 (poor recovery) through 10 (good recovery). Magnitude and recovery rankings presented according to the failures' perceived severity are as follows:

| Failure Category | Magnitude | Recovery |
|---|---|---|
| 1.  Seating Problems | 8.00 | 5.61 |
| 2.  Out of Stock | 7.33 | 6.00 |
| 3.  Facility Problems | 7.25 | 3.92 |
| 4.  Inappropriate Employee Behavior | 7.12 | 3.71 |
| 5.  Slow/Unavailable Service | 7.05 | 5.38 |
| 6.  Lost Orders | 6.71 | 5.82 |
| 7.  Product Defects | 6.69 | 6.21 |
| 8.  Wrong Orders | 6.25 | 6.44 |
| 9.  Unclear Policy | 6.16 | 6.33 |
| 10. Food Not Cooked to Order | 6.02 | 5.80 |
| 11. Mischarged | 5.86 | 7.71 |

**THE RECOVERY CATEGORIES: FREQUENCY AND DEFINITION**   In addition to categorizing the primary service failures in the restaurant industry, a second objective of this study was to use the critical incident technique to categorize employee response (recovery strategies) to the various service failures. The service recovery strategies resulting from the CIT approach are defined below (the frequency of occurrence expressed as a percentage of the total critical incidents is reported in parentheses):

*Replacement* (33.4 percent): Replacing the defective order with a new order.

*Free Food* (23.5 percent): Providing the meal, desserts, and/or drinks on a complimentary basis.

*Nothing* (21.3 percent): No action was taken to correct the failure.

*Apology* (7.8 percent): The employee apologized for the failure.

*Correction* (5.7 percent): Fixing the existing defective order as opposed to replacing the order with a new one as in Replacement.

*Discount* (4.3 percent): Discounts were provided to customers for food items at the time of the incident.

*Managerial Intervention* (2.7 percent): Management in some way became involved and helped resolve the problem.

*Coupon* (1.3 percent): Discounts for food items purchased at the restaurant were provided to customers for use on their next visit.

**THE RECOVERY CATEGORIES: PERCEIVED EFFECTIVENESS AND CORRE-SPONDING CUSTOMER RETENTION RATES**    Respondents rated the effectiveness of each recovery on a scale from 1 (very poor) through 10 (very good). Recoveries ranked in declining order of effectiveness and their corresponding customer retention rates are as follows:

| Recovery Strategy | Effectiveness | Retention Rate (%) |
| --- | --- | --- |
| 1. Free Food | 8.05 | 89.0 |
| 2. Discount | 7.75 | 87.5 |
| 3. Coupon | 7.00 | 80.0 |
| 4. Managerial Intervention | 7.00 | 88.8 |
| 5. Replacement | 6.35 | 80.2 |
| 6. Correction | 5.14 | 80.0 |
| 7. Apology | 3.72 | 71.4 |
| 8. Nothing | 1.71 | 51.3 |

The customer retention rates revealed in this study suggest that it is possible to recover from failures regardless of the type. Overall, customer retention for the incidents considered was above 75 percent. Even customers experiencing less-than-acceptable recoveries were still retained at a rate approaching 60 percent. However, in general, the statistical relationship between failure rating and recovery rating does indicate that as the magnitude of the seriousness of the failure increases, so does the difficulty in executing an effective recovery.

## STEP 6: DEVELOPING MANAGERIAL IMPLICATIONS BASED ON RESULTS

This research provides restaurant managers and employees with a list of service failures that are likely to occur in the restaurant industry as well as methods for effectively (and ineffectively) recovering from these failures when they occur. Managers should use this type of information when designing service delivery systems and procedures, establishing policies regarding service recovery, and selecting and training service personnel. Remarkably, approximately one out of every four service failures (23.5 percent) was met with no response by the offending firm. Unfortunately, other research has indicated that this "no response" rate is typical.[24]

The findings also suggest that it is difficult to recover from two failure types in particular. On a 10-point scale, failures associated with facility problems (failure 3) and employee behavior (failure 8) had mean recovery ratings of only 3.92 and 3.71, respectively. This amplifies the importance of providing the basics of service delivery well, since recovery from facility problems are particularly difficult. In addition, these findings provide evidence indicating the importance of employee training in the restaurant industry, since employee failures were difficult to effectively recover from as well. The mean recovery ratings of all other failure types exceeded the midpoint on the 10-point scale.

The recovery findings provide information concerning the desirability of specific recovery strategies. For example, recoveries involving some form of compensation were rated most favorably. Compensation took the form of free food (recovery 1), discounts (recovery 2), and coupons (recovery 3). On a 10-point scale, these three recovery strategies had mean recovery ratings of 8.05, 7.75, and 7.00, respectively.

Several less effective recovery strategies were also identified. Based on recovery ratings, simply correcting a failure (recovery 6), apologizing (recovery 7), and doing nothing (recovery 8) seem to be less effective; these recovery strategies had ratings of 5.14, 3.72, and 1.71, respectively.

As a result of this study and others like it that track service failure and recovery strategies, the categorization process reveals enlightening information about the particular industry's "hierarchy of horrors" and its sometimes feeble, sometimes admirable attempts to recover from its failures. Managing service firms is a highly complex task. Exercises like this make this point abundantly clear.

## SUMMARY

The benefit of service failure and recovery analysis is that service managers can identify common failure situations, minimize their occurrence, and train employees to recover from them when they do occur. The value associated with developing effective service recovery skills is clear. Two-thirds of lost customers do not defect to competitors because of poor product quality but because of the poor customer service they receive when problems arise.

Many of today's service firms are great as long as the service delivery system is operating smoothly. However, once kinks develop in the system, many firms are unprepared to face unhappy customers who are looking for solutions to their problems. As evidence, nearly half the responses to customer complaints reinforce customers' negative feelings toward a firm. Consequently, firms that truly excel in customer service equip employees with a set of recovery tools to repair the service encounter when failures occur and customer complaints are voiced.

Customer complaints should be viewed as opportunities to improve the service delivery system and to ensure that the customer is satisfied before the service encounter ends. Customers voice complaints for a number of reasons, including the following: to have the problem resolved, to gain an emotional release from frustration, to regain some measure of control by influencing other people's evaluation of the source of the complaint, to solicit sympathy or test the consensus of the complaint, or to create an impression.

However, it's not the complainers who service firms should worry about, it's the people who leave without saying a word, who never intend on returning, and who inform others, thereby generating negative word-of-mouth information. A number of reasons explain why many consumers do not complain. Most simply, customers of services often do not know who to complain to and/or do not think complaining will do any good. Other reasons consumers fail to complain are that (1) consumer evaluation of services is highly subjective; (2) consumers tend to shift some of the blame to themselves for not clearly specifying to the service provider their exact needs; (3) since many services are technical and specialized, many consumers do not feel qualified to voice their complaints; and (4) because of the inseparability of services, consumers may feel that a complaint is too confrontational.

Service failures generally fall into one of three main categories: (1) employee responses to core service failures such as slow service, unavailable service, and others; (2) employee responses to implicit/explicit customer requests such as special needs, customer preferences, customer error, and disruptive others; and (3) unprompted/unsolicited employee actions, which include level of attention, unusual actions, cultural norms, gestalt evaluations, and employee actions under adverse conditions.

Service recovery strategies are often industry specific, such as the restaurant example provided in this chapter. However, in general, responses to service failures can be categorized as two types: (1) responses to service failures that are attributed to the firm, and (2) responses to service failures that are attributed to customer error. Successful tactics for recovery from failures attributed to the firm include acknowledging the problem, making the customer feel unique or special, apologizing when appropriate, explaining what happened, and offering to compensate the customer. Successful responses to service failures attributed to customer error include acknowledging the problem, taking responsibility for the problem, and assisting in solving the problem without embarrassing the customer. Successful service recovery efforts such as these play an important role in customer retention.

# Key Terms

| | |
|---|---|
| Adverse conditions | Ostensive complaints |
| Critical incident technique | Other core service failures |
| Critical incidents | Perceived justice |
| Cultural norms | Procedural justice |
| Customer errors | Reflexive complaints |
| Customer needs and requests | Retaliation |
| Customer preferences | Service failures |
| Disruptive others | Service recovery |
| Distributive justice | Service recovery paradox |
| Exit | Special needs |
| Explicit requests | System failures |
| Gestalt | Unavailable service |
| Implicit needs | Unprompted and unsolicited actions |
| Instrumental complaints | Unreasonably slow service |
| Interactional justice | Unusual action |
| Level of attention | Voice |
| Noninstrumental complaints | |

# Discussion Questions

1. Define and discuss the subclass failures associated with the implicit/explicit request failure category.
2. Discuss the following types of complaints: instrumental, noninstrumental, ostensive, and reflexive.
3. What is the service recovery paradox? Provide an example based on your own personal experience.
4. Discuss the following types of failure outcomes: voice, exit, and retaliation.
5. What are the pros and cons of complaining customers?
6. Discuss how consumers evaluate a firm's service recovery efforts.
7. Give an overview of the steps described in the chapter necessary to track and monitor employee service failures and recovery efforts.

# Notes

1. Mary Jo Bitner, Bernard H. Booms, and Mary Stanfield Tetreault, "The Service Encounter: Diagnosing Favorable and Unfavorable Incidents," *Journal of Marketing* (January 1990), 71–84.
2. H. Keith Hunt, "Consumer Satisfaction, Dissatisfaction, and Complaining Behavior," *Journal of Social Issues* 47, no. 1 (1991), 116.
3. Mary C. Gilly, William B. Stevenson, and Laura J. Yale, "Dynamics of Complaint Management in the Service Organization," *The Journal of Consumer Affairs* 25, no. 2 (1991), 296.
4. Oren Harari, "Thank Heaven for Complainers," *Management Review* (January 1992), 60.
5. Mark D. Alicke et al, "Complaining Behavior in Social Interaction," *Personality and Social Psychology Bulletin* (June 1992), 286.
6. Ibid., 287.
7. T. M. Amabile, "Brilliant but Cruel: Perceptions of Negative Evaluators," *Journal of Experimental Social Psychology* 19 (1983), 146–156.
8. Gilly, Stevenson, and Yale, "Dynamics of Complaint Management," 297.
9. Hunt, "Consumer Satisfaction," 114.
10. Ibid., 115.
11. Adapted from Christopher W. L. Hart, James L. Heskett, and W. Earl Sasser, "The Profitable Art of Service Recovery," *Harvard Business Review* (July–August 1990), 148–156.
12. James L. Heskett et al, "Putting the Service-Profit Chain to Work," *Harvard Business Review* (March-April 1994), 172.
13. Bitner, Booms, and Tetreault, "The Service Encounter," 321.
14. Karl Albrecht and Ron Zemke, *Services America* (Homewood, Ill.: Dow-Jones Irwin, 1985), 6.
15. Donna Partow, "Turn Gripes into Gold," *Home Office Computing* (September 1993), 24.

16. Albrecht and Zemke, *Services America,* 6.

17. Hart, Heskett, and Sasser, "The Profitable Art," 150.

18. This section adapted from K. Douglas Hoffman and Scott W. Kelley, "Perceived Justice Needs and Recovery Evaluation: A Contingency Approach," *European Journal of Marketing,* 34, no. 3/4 (2000), 418–432.

19. Adapted from K. Douglas Hoffman, Scott W. Kelley, and Holly M. Rotalsky, "Tracking Service Failures and Employee Recovery Efforts," *Journal of Services Marketing* 9, no. 2 (1995), 49–61.

20. Eleena De Lisser, "Today's Specials Include Customer Satisfaction," *The Wall Street Journal* (June 7, 1993), p. B1.

21. Terry Vavra, "Learning from Your Losses," *Brandweek* 33, no. 46 (December 7, 1992), 20(2).

22. American Management Association, *Blueprints for Service Quality: The Federal Express Approach,* (New York: AMA Membership Publication Division, 1991).

23. Hart, Heskett, and Sasser, "The Profitable Art," 150.

24. See Scott W. Kelley, K. Douglas Hoffman, and Mark A. Davis, "A Typology of Retail Failures and Recoveries," *Journal of Retailing* (Winter 1993), 429–445; and K. Douglas Hoffman, Scott W. Kelley, and Laure M. Soulage, "Customer Defection Analysis: A Critical Incident Approach" (1994), working paper.

# Appendix A

## SAMPLE OF CRITICAL INCIDENT FORM

### I. Introduction/Purpose of Study

Have you ever been at a restaurant and received poor service?

We are conducting a study on service mistakes or failures made by restaurants and how restaurants recover when a service failure occurs. Would you be willing to participate in this study?

### II. Think of a time when you had an experience at a restaurant where a mistake was made and the restaurant tried to correct that mistake but did a POOR job of recovering. Please describe the nature of this service failure.

Where? _____

When? _____

What happened? _____

_____

_____

_____

_____

What did the restaurant do to correct the failure? _____

_____

_____

_____

_____

_____

On a scale of 1 to 10, 1 being a MINOR MISTAKE and 10 being a MAJOR MISTAKE, how would you rate the severity of the mistake?

| Minor Mistake | | | | | | | | Major Mistake | |
|---|---|---|---|---|---|---|---|---|---|
| 1 | 2 | 3 | 4 | 5 | 6 | 7 | 8 | 9 | 10 |

On a scale of 1 to 10, 1 being VERY POOR and 10 being VERY GOOD, how would you rate the efforts of the restaurant regarding the correction of the mistake?

| Very Poor | | | | | | | | Very Good | |
|---|---|---|---|---|---|---|---|---|---|
| 1 | 2 | 3 | 4 | 5 | 6 | 7 | 8 | 9 | 10 |

Do you still patronize this restaurant?

_____ No, due to the service failure

_____ No, due to other reasons

_____ Yes

**III. Think of a time when you had an experience at a restaurant where a mistake was made and the restaurant tried to correct that mistake and did a GOOD job of recovering. Please describe the nature of this service failure.**

Where? _____

When? _____

What happened? _____

_____

_____

_____

What did the restaurant do to correct the failure? _____

_____

_____

_____

_____

On a scale of 1 to 10, 1 being a MINOR MISTAKE and 10 being a MAJOR MISTAKE, how would you rate the severity of the mistake?

| Minor Mistake | | | | | | | | Major Mistake | |
|---|---|---|---|---|---|---|---|---|---|
| 1 | 2 | 3 | 4 | 5 | 6 | 7 | 8 | 9 | 10 |

On a scale of 1 to 10, 1 being VERY POOR and 10 being VERY GOOD, how would you rate the efforts of the restaurant regarding the correction of the mistake?

| Very Poor | | | | | | | | Very Good | |
|---|---|---|---|---|---|---|---|---|---|
| 1 | 2 | 3 | 4 | 5 | 6 | 7 | 8 | 9 | 10 |

Do you still patronize this restaurant?

_____ No, due to the service failure

_____ No, due to other reasons

_____ Yes

**IV. Demographics**

Sex (Categorical choices)

Education (Categorical choices)

Age (Categorical choices)

## chapter 15

# Customer Retention

## CHAPTER OBJECTIVES

The major objective of this chapter is to introduce you to the concept of customer retention.

After reading this chapter, you should be able to:

- Define customer retention.
- Discuss why the concept of customer retention has become increasingly important.
- Discuss the benefits of retaining existing customers.
- Explain defection management.
- Describe successful tactics for retaining existing customers.
- Discuss the trade-offs associated with unconditional service guarantees.

"Who will testify to your existence during the last twelve months?"

Tom Peters

## Introduction

Depending on who you ask within a service operation, you will likely discover that the various managers within the firm evaluate the firm's value differently. The chief financial officer might spout a variety of impressive financial ratios that are great to use at cocktail parties; the operations manager will speak in terms of inventory and equipment; and the human relations manager will focus on the strengths of the firm's employees.[1] Although all these measures are crucial to the firm's success, they all ignore the value of the customer.

This chapter focuses on the important concept of customer retention (Figure 15.1). Customer retention is a key strategy in today's leading-edge service firms and reflects a more futuristic outlook than does the concept of customer satisfaction. As discussed in Chapter 12, satisfaction measures assess the customer's current state of evaluation but fail to tap into the customer's set of changing needs.

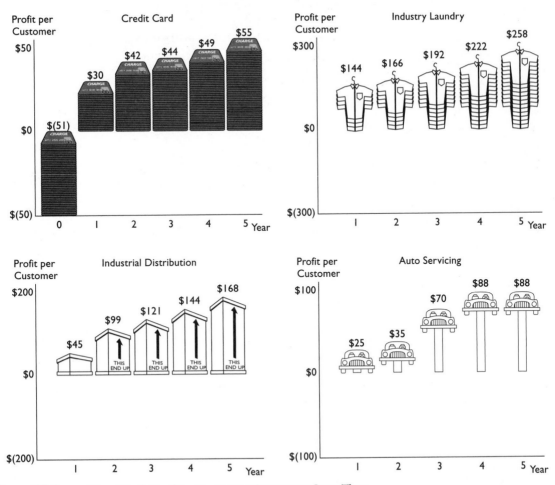

**Figure 15.1     How Much Profit a Customer Generates Over Time**

Source: Adapted from Frederick F. Reichheld and W. Earl Sasser, Jr., "Zero Defections: Quality Comes to Services," *Harvard Business Review* (September–October 1990), 106–07.

Consequently, additional measures that assess evolving customer expectations, the probability of future purchases with the firm, and the customer's willingness to conduct business with competitive firms are necessary in order to truly assess the firm's customer retention efforts.

## WHAT IS CUSTOMER RETENTION?

Simply stated, **customer retention** refers to focusing the firm's marketing efforts toward the existing customer base. More specifically, in contrast to seeking new customers, firms engaged in customer retention efforts work to satisfy existing customers with the intent of developing long-term relationships between the firm and its current clientele (see Services in Action 15.1).

**customer retention**
Focusing the firm's marketing efforts toward the existing customer base.

ERVICES **15.1**
IN
ACTION    **Cost of New versus Old Customers: The Leaky Bucket**

The leaky bucket depicted below portrays two companies. Each company is working hard to generate new customers each year and has managed to generate 10 percent more new customers per year, perhaps by developing new services or targeting new segments. However, not all of the customers acquired by the firm in a given year stay with the firm. The retention rate is not 100 percent; there is a "hole in the bucket." For company A, the "hole" is small, and the company loses only 5 percent of its customers each year. As a result, after 14 years company A has doubled the number of its customers. Company B has a bigger problem, because retention is 90 percent and the "hole in the bucket" is 10 percent. As a result, company B loses and gains customers at the same rate.

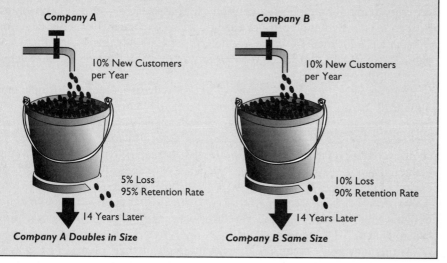

Source: John E. G. Bateson and K. Douglas Hoffman, *Managing Services Marketing,* 4th ed. (Fort Worth, Tex.: The Dryden Press, 1999).

Many examples of successful customer retention efforts are based on the firm's ability to redefine its existing business. Companies are challenging themselves, now more than ever before, to look at what the product really provides to their customers. Understanding consumer uses of the product and the steps required by consumers to obtain the product often leads to ideas that assist the firm in differentiating itself from its competition. Providing value-added services to the consumer reshapes the traditional and often confrontational supplier-customer relationship into more of a partnership.

After rethinking its business, British Airways no longer viewed itself solely as a provider of air transportation.[2] As a result, the airline has revised its focus on first-class transatlantic customers to include improved services on the ground as well as in the air. Realizing that many of its customers would like to sleep through the night rather than eat huge meals followed by lavish desserts, accompanied with an endless supply of alcohol and bad movies, British Airways now provides its first-class passengers with the option of having dinner on the ground in its first-class lounge. Once on board, passengers are provided British Airway pajamas, real pillows, and a duvet to curl up in.

Once the plane has landed and after a good night's sleep, passengers are provided with breakfast on the ground as well as a shower and dressing room so that they can be fresh for the day's events. British Airways will even have passengers' clothes pressed while they are enjoying their breakfasts. With value-added services such as these, it is not surprising to learn that British Airways' profits have steadily increased.

## THE TREND TOWARD CUSTOMER RETENTION

Today's market is totally different than the ones U.S. marketers have experienced in the past. Competition is intense, and service and goods differentiation among competitors is minimal.[3] Let's face it—there is no great difference today among products, be they insurance companies, banks, or eye exams. Because of the relative parity among brand choices, consumer risk associated with switching brands has been drastically minimized. For example, consumers may be indifferent about the firm that holds their car insurance policy. Consequently, many consumers have forgone brand loyalty and selected the product that offers the best value—the best product at the best price.

**conquest marketing**
A marketing strategy for constantly seeking new customers by offering discounts and markdowns and developing promotions that encourage new business.

Unfortunately, the majority of marketers today have reacted to this new environment of "brand parity" and "nonbrand loyalty" by constantly chasing new customers. Firms that are constantly seeking new customers are engaged in **conquest marketing.** Typical conquest marketing techniques include offering discounts and markdowns and developing promotions that encourage new business. Results obtained from conquest marketing are generally successful in the short run because of customers' lack of brand loyalty. The firm engaged in conquest marketing may even get a repeat purchase or two. However, as soon as the competition offers another "discount special," the firm loses many of the customers it previously obtained.

To this day, many companies spend the bulk of their marketing efforts on attracting new customers instead of on keeping the customers they already have.

However, the long-term profitability of firms that use conquest marketing techniques is highly questionable. When one considers the cost of a sales promotion to attract customers, followed by sales at a discounted price, profits are minimal.

Even when conquest marketing techniques are successful, they sometimes lead to the demise of the firm. All too often, businesses are tempted to grow as fast as they can in order to increase their sales volume. However, because of the inseparability inherent in services, extensive growth of many service firms is commonly associated with a decrease in the quality of service provided.

As the firm continues to grow, the owner/provider will likely take on more of an administrative role, providing estimates, handling customer complaints, and managing employees. These additional duties result in the owner spending less time in the field attending to the original customer base. Consequently, the owner/provider might have to hire additional help, who may not provide the same level of service as the owner once delivered. Subsequently, customers may become disgruntled about the poor service and begin to look for other alternatives.

Considering the costs associated with winning new customers, the only way to make a profit and avoid the continuous cycle of price discounts is to increase the lifetime spending of existing customers. "Customer retention is, therefore, far more important than customer attraction."[4] Given today's marketing environment, coddling existing clients makes good economic sense (see Services in Action 15.2).

SERVICES IN ACTION **15.2**

### The Profitability of Customer Retention Efforts at MBNA

MBNA America, a Delaware-based credit card company, has improved its industry ranking from 38 to 4 and increased its profits sixteenfold. How did MBNA do it? Profitability in the credit card industry is directly linked to customer retention.

In general, credit card companies lose money during the first year of a new account because the fees obtained by establishments that honor credit cards do not offset the costs of advertising, setting up new accounts, and printing. Consequently, retaining customers beyond that first year is critical to the profitability of the credit card industry.

The key to developing customer loyalty is to employ measures that monitor the firm's customer retention efforts. If you can measure it, you can manage it! Specific measures provide managers concrete targets on which to focus their efforts. In MBNA's case, the company tracks the average balance per card plus 15 measures of customer satisfaction daily.

MBNA further reinforces to employees the importance of customer retention through its reward structure. MBNA's employees earn up to 20 percent of their salaries in bonuses associated with customer retention efforts. MBNA employees talk with every customer who wishes to drop its services, and by doing so, they retain 50 percent of these customers.

How do MBNA's customer retention efforts affect the bottom line? MBNA's overall customer retention rate is 95 percent, and MBNA keeps its customers twice as long as industry average. In fact, MBNA's retention rate of profitable customers, those who revolve their balances, is 98 percent. In addition, MBNA's credit losses due to bad debt are one third to one half lower than those of other companies. Moreover, MBNA customers use their cards more often and maintain higher balances—$2,500 compared with the industry average of $1,600.

Source: Adapted from Larry Armstrong, "Beyond May I Help You?" *Business Week/Quality* (1991), 100–103; Ron Zemke, "The Emerging Art of Service Management," *Training* (January 1992), 37(42; Frederick F. Reichheld and W. Earl Sasser, Jr., "Zero Defections: Quality Comes to Services," *Harvard Business Review* (September–October 1990), 105–111; and Rahul Jacob, "Why Some Customers Are More Equal Than Others," *Fortune* (September 19, 1994), 218.

## THE IMPORTANCE OF CUSTOMER RETENTION

Customer retention has become increasingly important because of several changes in the marketing environment.[5] First, in the United States, consumer markets are stagnant. The U.S. population for the next 50 years is predicted to grow at half the rate of the period from 1965 to 1990. As a result, there are fewer new customers to go around. Concurrent with the decrease in population growth, the once vibrant economic growth rate has suddenly begun to decline. In sum, there are not as many new customers as there once were, and those customers who exist are spending less.

Another reason customer retention has become important to today's marketers is the increase in competition (see Services in Action 15.3). Factors contributing to increased competition include the relative parity and lack of differential advantage of goods and services on the market, deregulated industries that now must compete for customers in an open market, the growth of online alternatives, and accessible market information that is available to more firms, thereby minimizing informational advantages among competing firms. As a result of the increase in competition and the predominant use of conquest marketing techniques, firms are finding that retaining their current customer base is now more challenging than ever.

Customer retention is also becoming increasingly important because of the rising costs of marketing. In particular, the cost of mass marketing, the primary tool of conquest marketers, has substantially increased. For example, the cost of a 30-second television spot in 1965 was $19,700. In contrast, a 1991 30-second spot sold for $106,400.

Coupled with the increased cost of advertising has been the loss of the advertiser's "share of voice." As a result of the shorter time now allotted for individual commercials (the average length of commercials has decreased from 60 seconds to 30 seconds to 15 seconds), the number of commercials has increased by approximately 25 percent over the past 10 years. Hence, firms are competing for attention in a medium that is constantly expanding. In addition, new forms of advertising have

ERVICES 15.3

## ACTION    **Customer Retention: Offline versus Online**

There is little doubt that online service firms such as Geico (insurance products) and E*TRADE (brokerage services) have cut into the market shares of the traditional offline firms. However, in terms of customer retention, it's the brick-and-mortar firms with an online presence that are beating their pure online counterparts. Termed "bricks-and-clicks," firms that pursue a multi-channel strategy appear to be winning the customer retention battle.

A recently published survey conducted by the Boston Consulting Group revealed that although "brick-and-click" sites were more likely to have a greater number of shopping carts abandoned (76 percent), 45 percent of their online revenues come from regulars. One explanation for the high abandonment rate is that users are simply collecting information before they trek off to a brick location. Hence, although the purchases were not made on the Web, they were Web-influenced—adding additional value to the firm's Web site. In comparison, pure online firms report that 30 percent of their revenues are from repeat purchasers. More impressive is the cost savings in acquiring customers. Many of the "brick-and-click" firms already have established brands. As a result, the average cost of acquiring an online customer is $31 compared with $82 for a pure online firm.

Why does it matter? When the financial markets began to reevaluate Internet stocks, stock prices became much more oriented toward bottom-line profits than reported revenues. This sent the dot-coms into a frenzy as they attempted to reorganize their budgets so that profits could be shown sooner than previously anticipated. Ad campaigns, customer service, and customer acquisition costs were reduced in the attempt to cut expenses. Getting the most out of the customers they have, as opposed to trying to recruit as many customers as possible, has become a much higher priority. For example, CD-NOW has 3.5 million customers, but it is still spending cash faster than it is able to return profits.

Source: Adapted from David Butcher, "You've Got Your Customers, Now Milk 'em," *Revolution* 1, no. 5 (July 2000), 76–77.

evolved, and consumer markets have become more fragmented, which further dilutes the chances of an advertiser's message reaching its intended target audience.

Interestingly, the growth of direct mail marketing in the 1980s is directly attributed to the high costs of mass marketing and subsequent heightened importance of customer retention efforts. Marketers became more selective about how and where their advertising dollars were spent. As a result, the databases built for direct marketing provided the means to identify current customers and track purchases. Subsequently, advertising to current customers became much more efficient than mass marketing in reaching the firm's target market.

The use of marketing intermediaries, such as a travel agent who sells an airline's service, has its advantages and disadvantages. The intermediary can become a surrogate provider and, as such, represent the original firm that produces the product or service.

Changes in the channels of distribution used in today's markets are also having an impact on customer retention. In many cases, the physical distance between producer and consumer is increasing. The growth of nonstore retailing is a prime illustration of how the physical distance between the provider of products and the customer is changing. Transactions can be conducted by phone, mail order, or over the Internet, thereby limiting the physical contact between the provider and the customer. Firms engaged in customer retention efforts should beware of the old saying, "Out of sight, out of mind," and realize that separation from the customer does not diminish their obligation to the customer.

Another change in the channel of distribution is the increasing use of market intermediaries, or "third parties," that assist in the transaction between provider and customer. In this scenario, the marketing intermediary becomes a surrogate provider and, as such, represents the firm that produces the product. Although the use of third parties and other market intermediaries increases the firm's market coverage, it can also adversely affect customer retention rates. For example, a travel agent who sells an airline's service may misrepresent the airline (e.g., flight times, seating arrangements, etc.) and damage the relationship between the customer and the airline. Again, firms engaged in customer retention efforts must recognize that the physical distance between themselves and their customers does not minimize their responsibility.

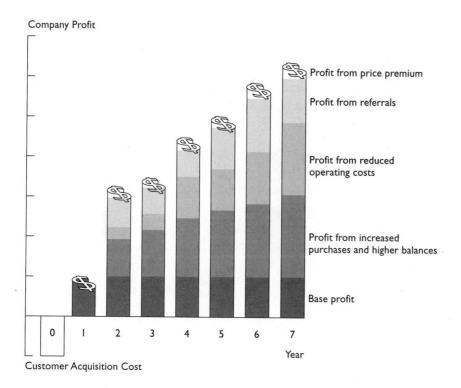

Company Profit

Profit from price premium

Profit from referrals

Profit from reduced
operating costs

Profit from increased
purchases and higher balances

Base profit

0    1    2    3    4    5    6    7

Year

Customer Acquisition Cost

**Figure 15.2**
**Why Customers
Are More
Profitable over
Time**
Source: Adapted from
Frederick F. Reichheld
and W. Earl Sasser,
Jr., "Zero Defections:
Quality Comes to
Services," *Harvard
Business Review*
(September–October
1990), 108.

Customer retention has also become increasingly important to firms because today's customers have changed. Typical consumers today compared with past generations are more informed about purchasing decisions, command more discretionary income, and are increasingly skeptical about the average firm's concern for their business. Consequently, firms that engage in customer retention practices are usually noticed by today's consumers and rewarded for their efforts via repeat sales.

## THE BENEFITS OF CUSTOMER RETENTION

Some experts believe that customer retention has a more powerful effect on profits than market share, scale economies, and other variables commonly associated with competitive advantage. In fact, studies have indicated that as much as 95 percent of profits come from long-term customers via profits derived from sales, referrals, and reduced operating costs (Figure 15.2).[6]

### Profits Derived from Sales

One of the key benefits of customer retention is repeat sales (Figure 15.3). In addition to the base profit derived from sales, profits are also acquired from increased purchase frequency and interest rates applied to higher balances on charge accounts (for firms that offer credit services). An added bonus of retaining existing

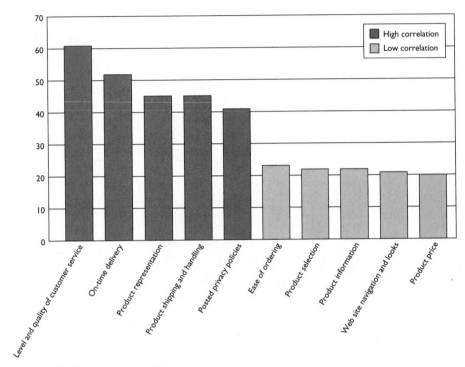

**Figure 15.3**   **Why E-Shoppers Come Back**
The correlation between online shoppers' ratings of merchants in selected categories
and their likelihood of buying again from the same site (100 = perfect correlation;
0 = no correlation).
Source: BizRate.com

customers is that existing customers are willing to pay more for a firm's offering.
This occurs because customers become accustomed to the firm, its employees,
and the manner in which the service is delivered. Subsequently, a relationship
develops that lowers the customer's risk. In essence, repeat customers are willing
to pay more for purchase situations in which the uncertainty of the outcome is
lessened or removed (see Services in Action 15.4).

Increasing customer retention rates can have a profound effect on a firm's
profitability. For example, past studies have shown that a 5 percent increase in
retention rate can translate into 85 percent higher profits for a branch bank, 50
percent higher profits for an insurance broker, and 30 percent higher profits for an
auto-service chain.[7]

## Profits from Reduced Operating Costs

Past research has indicated that it costs three to five times less to keep a customer
than to get a new one.[8] The trusting relationship that develops between customers
and the firm makes existing customers more receptive to the firm's marketing
efforts and, therefore, easier to sell new services to. This, in turn, lowers the cost of
the firm's marketing efforts.

SERVICES 15.4

ACTION   **Visa and American Express Guarantee Zero Liability Protection for Online Shoppers**

Credit card companies are encouraging customers to use their credit cards when shopping online. One method to increase credit card usage is to promote the added value of guaranteed privacy. Effective April 4, 2000, Visa's new zero-liability policy took effect. This policy provides the holder of any Visa credit or debit card 100 percent protection against fraud. Protecting shoppers against fraud is a good way to ease their privacy fears and to promote their credit card usage, but it is also good for consumers. According to Visa's new policy, if your credit card number is stolen while shopping online or in a store, you pay nothing (not even the traditional first $50). American Express also offers total protection for its customers making purchases online.

Source: Adapted from Carol Schultz, "Something for Today," *Colorado State University Cooperative Extension Service* (July–August 2000), 2.

Overall, long-term customers tend to have lower maintenance costs. Existing customers become accustomed to the company, employees, and procedures; therefore, they ask fewer questions and have fewer problems and require less attention. The airline price war that took place in the summer of 1992 presented a few unforeseen problems for the airlines. On one hand, the lower prices did achieve their desired effect—increased sales. Many of these sales, however, were to passengers who had never flown before and who were unfamiliar with ticketing practices, baggage handling, and typical airline behavior. Services such as complimentary beverages had to be explained to new passengers who were unfamiliar with the term *complimentary*. In one instance, a passenger requested instructions on how to "roll down her window." The result of adding new customers to the mix was stressed-out and overworked flight attendants and lower-than-average quality service to existing customers.

## Profits from Referrals

Another benefit of customer retention is the positive word-of-mouth advertising generated by satisfied customers. Existing customers are necessary in order for a firm to develop a reputation that attracts new business. Satisfied customers often refer businesses to their friends and family, which, in turn, reinforces their own decision. As discussed in Chapter 4, personal sources of information are particularly important to services consumers because of intangibility and the perception of increased risk associated with service purchases. New business attributed to current customer referrals can be dramatic. For example, a leading home builder in the United States has found that 60 percent of its business is based on referrals from past customers.[9]

## CUSTOMER RETENTION TACTICS

Firms that embrace a defection management philosophy engage in customer retention tactics that should be routinely implemented on a per-customer basis. Unfortunately, prior research suggests that two thirds of customers defect because they feel that companies are not genuinely concerned for their well-being. That's the bad news! The good news is that the opportunity exists to demonstrate to customers that the firm really cares about them. Because of the lack of consistent customer service that customers experience, firms that effectively communicate customer retention as a primary goal are noticed. Consequently, a firm's defection management efforts should serve to successfully differentiate the firm from its competitors. Effective tactics for retaining customers include the following practices.[10]

### Maintain the Proper Perspective

Managers and employees of service firms need to remember that the company exists to meet the needs and wants of its consumers. Processing customers like raw materials on an assembly line or being rude to customers is incredibly shortsighted. Companies such as USAir employ slogans such as, "The U in USAir starts with you, the passenger." Credos such as this affect customer expectations and reinforce to employees exactly where the firm's priorities lie.

Interacting with the public is not an easy task, and, unfortunately, employees occasionally fail to maintain the proper perspective. The same questions may have to be asked over and over, and not every customer is polite. Maintaining the proper perspective involves a customer-oriented frame of mind and an attitude for service. Employees need to remember that every customer has his or her own personal set of needs and that the customer's, not the employee's, expectations define performance.

### Remember Customers between Calls

Contacting customers between service encounters is a useful approach in building relationships with the service firm. The key is in making customer contact sincere and personal. Typical approaches include sending birthday, get-well, and/or anniversary cards, writing personal notes congratulating customers for their personal successes, and keeping in touch with consumers concerning the performance of past services rendered and offering assistance if necessary. The goal of this tactic is to communicate to customers that the firm genuinely cares for their well-being.

### Build Trusting Relationships

Trust is defined as a firm belief or confidence in the honesty, integrity, and reliability of another person. In the service environment, three major components of trust are (1) the service provider's expertise, (2) the service provider's reliability, and (3) the service provider's concern for the customer. Strategies for building trust include

- Protecting confidential information (see Services in Action 15.5)
- Refraining from making disparaging remarks about other customers and competitors

ERVICES 15.5
N

ACTION **Confidentiality Issues on the Net**

One of the biggest obstacles that keeps consumers from purchasing products on the Internet is concern about confidentiality. Customers must trust that the sensitive financial and personal information that is transmitted to Web merchants is kept confidential. In turn, businesses must be certain that payment information collected from consumers over Web storefronts is indeed valid. Additional precautions must be taken by merchants to ensure that confidential consumer databases are not compromised by hackers or misused by malicious employees.

The challenge of operating a secure Web site is very real. The number of companies that have been attacked by hackers jumped 92 percent from 1997 to 1998. In addition, CERT, which monitors reports of computer network security breaches from around the world, has registered a steep rise in the number of reported incidents in the past few years.

Netscape summarizes security threats as follows:

- *Unauthorized access:* Accessing or misusing a computer system to intercept transmissions and steal sensitive information
- *Data alteration:* Altering the content of a transaction—user names, credit card numbers, and dollar amounts—during transmission
- *Monitoring:* Eavesdropping on confidential information
- *Spoofing:* A fake site pretending to be yours to steal data from unsuspecting customers or just disrupt your business
- *Service denial:* An attacker shuts down your site or denies access to visitors
- *Repudiation:* A party to an online purchase denies that the transaction occurred or was authorized

Source: http://www.ecommerce.ncsu.edu/ec.html

- Telling the customer the truth, even when it hurts
- Providing the customer with full information—the pros and the cons
- Being dependable, courteous, and considerate with customers
- Becoming actively involved in community affairs

## Monitor the Service Delivery Process

After the service has been requested, monitoring the service delivery process should be a key tactic in the firm's customer retention efforts. Because of the inseparability of services, the customer is involved in the delivery process. Although the customer's involvement may decrease the efficiency of the delivery process, vital information can be obtained regarding satisfaction levels prior to the final result of the service. Consequently, service providers that monitor the service delivery process are able to compensate for service inadequacies and influence customer perceptions of service quality prior to completion. Incidentally, this is not true in the manufacturing sector, where the customer has little or no input into the production process prior to the completed product.

Obvious examples would involve a restaurant that regularly communicates with its customers throughout their meal or the owner of firm who contacts a customer with questions about a recent purchase. Proactively seeking customer feedback throughout the process builds customer perceptions of trust and facilitates maintaining customers for life. Note, however, that asking for too much feedback can become an annoyance to the customer.

## Properly Install Equipment and Train Customers in Using the Product

Proper installation of equipment and training of customers save a lot of headaches in the long run. Customers should not have to become frustrated over not under-

**Figure 15.4**
**An Example of
Discretionary
Effort**

BP OIL COMPANY
101 PROSPECT AVENUE, WEST
CLEVELAND OH 44115

September 18, 1996

K DOUGLAS HOFFMAN
WILMINGTON NC 28409

RE: 04122

Dear K DOUGLAS HOFFMAN:

We are very concerned about the devastation from the recent hurricane in your area. We hope you have not been personally affected.

If you have, we know how disruptive and financially burdensome such a loss of property is. We'll be happy to give you additional time to pay any balance that may be due on your credit card account with no finance charges or late fees.

Just write a short note at the bottom of this letter to let us know how you wish to extend payment over the next few months. Or, you may call us toll free at 1-800-883-5527 to work out an arrangement.

We realize this is a small gesture but we wanted to offer a helping hand to you as one of our valued customers.

BP Oil Company

Credit Card Account Number: 04122

Payment Plan:

standing how to use something or, worse, improperly use the product, which may result in damage and further dissatisfaction. Simply dropping off the product and leaving customers to fend for themselves reinforces the idea that the company is not genuinely concerned for the customer's well-being.

## Be There When You Are Needed Most

When a customer returns a product that is in need of service and repair, don't crawl under a rock and hide. Every firm should stand behind what it sells and ensure that every transaction is handled to the customer's satisfaction. Most customers are realistic and understand that nothing lasts forever. Many times customers are simply looking for advice and alternative solutions to problems and are not looking for someone to blame. Expressing a sincere concern for the customer's situation reinforces the firm's customer retention efforts.

## Provide Discretionary Effort

Discretionary effort is behavior beyond the call of duty. It's the Procter & Gamble salesperson who voluntarily bags groceries at the grand opening of a new grocery store. It is the hotel that sends items misplaced by customers to their homes at no charge. It is the oil company that recognizes the special needs of its customers during difficult times (Figure 15.4). Discretionary effort involves countless personal touches—the little things that distinguish a discrete business transaction from an ongoing relationship.

# IS IT ALWAYS WORTHWHILE TO KEEP A CUSTOMER?

Although saving every customer at any cost is a controversial topic and opinions are divided, some experts believe that the customer is no longer worth saving under the following conditions:[11]

- The account is no longer profitable.
- Conditions specified in the sales contract are no longer being met.
- Customers are abusive to the point that it lowers employee morale.
- Customer demands are beyond reasonable, and fulfilling those demands would result in poor service for the remaining customer base.
- The customer's reputation is so poor that associating with the customer tarnishes the image and reputation of the selling firm.

Other experts believe that although these criteria are valid, a more appropriate strategy is to retreat but keep the lines of communication open. Overall, retention efforts should focus on retaining the most profitable customers. Although zero defection is an admirable goal worth pursuing, the investment in customer retention and service recovery programs may not be economically justified in every case. Moreover, it is argued that focusing too heavily on customer retention efforts can harm the firm in the long run if customer acquisition and development efforts are completely overlooked in the process.[12]

# EMERGING CUSTOMER RETENTION PROGRAMS

Several relatively new marketing programs have surfaced that typify the recent interest in customer retention strategies, such as frequency marketing, relationship marketing, aftermarketing, service guarantees, and defection management. The discussions that follow illustrate the importance of customer retention within each of these programs.

## Frequency Marketing

**frequency marketing**
Marketing technique that strives to make existing customers purchase more often from the same provider.

The primary goal of **frequency marketing** is to make existing customers more productive.[13] Consequently, customer retention is a critical component in frequency marketing efforts. In short, frequency marketing combines the use of data collection, communications, recognition, and rewards to build lasting relationships.

The first step in implementing a frequency marketing program is to collect data on the firm's best customers and to determine their level of relationship with the firm. The level of relationship pertains to the number of different services the customer purchases. For example, bank customers may have a relationship with their bank not only through checking accounts, but also through savings accounts, car loans, investments, or a home mortgage.

The next step is to communicate with customers on a personal level. Communications need to be interactive to the point that customers can ask questions and establish a relationship with the firm and action-oriented in that the firm's communications incite customers to respond. Personal communications demonstrate to customers that the firm recognizes the importance of their patronage. When reward programs are developed that prompt customers to act, the communications become action-oriented. Perhaps the most successful frequency marketing programs of all time are the frequent-flier programs. Airlines such as American, Continental, Delta, Northwest, Southwest, TWA, United, and USAir have developed frequent flyer programs designed to reward passengers for flying with one airline. Passenger loyalty is rewarded with credit for "miles," which can be redeemed for discounted fares, free flights, and upgraded seating from coach to first class.

In addition to appealing to the pleasure traveler, frequent-flier programs are the easiest way for airlines to compete for business travelers who often travel 10 to 12 times a year or more. Because of the nature of their activities, business travelers often book flights at the last minute and pay higher fares than pleasure travelers. To attract the more profitable business flier segment, most airlines now assign their best customers, customers who fly more than 25,000 to 30,000 miles a year, to premium memberships that include reservation hotlines, early boarding, bonus mileage, and frequent upgrade privileges.[14]

The frequent-flier programs have become so popular that they are now referred to as the "Green Stamps of the 1990s." In addition to redeeming miles for airline-associated discounts, miles are increasingly being redeemed for things other than flights, such as free nights at hotels, savings bonds, restaurant meals, cruises, and merchandise from a variety of retailers. This new way to redeem miles has been accompanied by new ways to earn the miles as well. Other businesses, such as credit card and telephone companies, have signed on with the airlines and typically pay an airline 2 cents per mile to help retain their own customers as well as attract new ones. Travel experts report that frequent-flier program members earn, on average, 40 percent of their miles without flying and redeem 10 percent of their miles for things other than free trips.[15]

## Relationship Marketing

Another relatively new marketing term that typifies the newfound interest in customer retention efforts is relationship marketing. **Relationship marketing** is the union of customer service, quality, and marketing. More specifically, the relationship marketing perspective takes place on two levels: macro and micro.[16] At the macro level, firms engaged in relationship marketing recognize that the marketing activity impacts customer markets, employee markets, supplier markets, internal markets, and influencer markets (such as financial and government markets). Simultaneously, at the micro level, relationship marketing recognizes that the focus of marketing is changing from completing the single transaction and other conquest marketing practices to building a long-term relationship with existing customers.

Proponents of relationship marketing believe that their firm's products will come and go; consequently, the real unit of value is the long-term relationship with the customer. For example, construction and agricultural equipment manufacturer John Deere & Co. measures its success in terms of generations of farming families that have used its products. Baxter International, a $9 billion health care products and services company, has also embraced the relationship marketing concept.[17] Baxter International actually offers to share the business risk with some of its customers by jointly setting sales and cost reduction targets and sharing the savings or extra expenses.[18]

Overall, relationship marketing emphasizes the importance of customer retention and a concern for quality that transcends departmental boundaries. Relationship marketing broadens the definition of the customer from final consumer to all the groups (e.g., suppliers, employees, influencer markets, etc.) that are integral components in bringing the good or service to the marketplace. Efforts to retain the relationship with all these types of customers are at the core of the relationship marketing concept.

**relationship marketing**
Marketing technique based on developing long-term relationships with customers.

## Aftermarketing

A third marketing concept that embraces customer retention efforts is aftermarketing.[19] **Aftermarketing** emphasizes the importance of marketing efforts after the initial sale has been made. Aftermarketing techniques include the following:

- Identifying customers and building a customer database so that customers can be easily contacted after the sale has been completed
- Measuring customer satisfaction and continuously making improvements based on customer feedback
- Establishing formal customer communication programs—for example, newsletters that convey information such as how the company is using customer feedback in its continuous improvement efforts

**aftermarketing**
Marketing technique that emphasizes marketing after the initial sale has been made.

- Creating an aftermarketing culture throughout the firm that reinforces the importance of maintaining a relationship with the customer after the initial sale

An industry that has made some of the biggest strides in aftermarketing is the automobile industry. Customers are frequently contacted by sales and service personnel after a vehicle has been purchased or after service has been completed on a vehicle. Generally, customers have been very impressed by the dealer's concern in an industry that has historically focused on the quick sell.

Weyerhaeuser, the paper giant, has taken aftermarketing even further by requiring some of its employees to actually work at their client's operations sites for a week. One aftermarketing success story involved the placement of a bar code on newsprint rolls the company regularly shipped to its consumers. Weyerhaeuser employees in the field noticed that the bar code would regularly stick to its customers' high-speed presses. The problem was solved by merely moving the bar code a few inches. Weyerhaeuser later found that other customers had experienced similar problems but had never complained. Placing employees in the field to see personally how customers use the company's products has been beneficial for both Weyerhaeuser and its customers.[20]

## Service Guarantees

One of the most innovative and intriguing customer retention strategies to be developed in recent years is the service guarantee.[21] Although guarantees in and of themselves are not particularly new, they are very new with respect to services, particularly professional services. Overall, service guarantees appear to facilitate three worthwhile goals:

- Reinforce customer loyalty
- Build market share
- Force the firm offering the guarantee to improve its overall service quality

As discussed in Chapter 13, service quality consists of five dimensions: reliability, responsiveness, assurance, empathy, and tangibles. Although each dimension is a crucial component of the service delivery process, experts contend that "customers value reliability above all other dimensions." Consequently, a firm's efforts to enhance its reliability may serve to significantly differentiate the firm from its competitors.

In theory, the offering of a service guarantee to customers should ensure to customers that the firm is reliable. Simply stated, reliability is "the ability to perform the service dependably and accurately." The service guarantee lowers the risk generally assumed by service customers by "overcoming client concerns about the highest value for the money."

### CHARACTERISTICS OF SUCCESSFUL GUARANTEES

In general, successful guarantees are unrestrictive, stated in specific and clear terms, meaningful, hassle free when invoked, and quick to be paid out. On the other hand, mistakes to avoid when constructing a guarantee include (1) promising something that is trivial and normally expected, (2) specifying an inordinate number of conditions as part of the guarantee, and (3) making the guarantee so mild that it is never invoked.

## TYPES OF GUARANTEES

In general, there are three types of guarantees: (1) the implicit guarantee, (2) the specific result guarantee, and (3) the unconditional guarantee.

The **implicit guarantee** is essentially an unwritten, unspoken guarantee that establishes an understanding between the firm and its customers. Although the guarantee is not specified, customers of firms that offer implicit guarantees are ensured that the firm is dedicated to complete customer satisfaction. Consequently, a partnership spirit is developed between the firm and its customers based on mutual trust and respect.

**implicit guarantee**
An unwritten, unspoken guarantee that establishes an understanding between the firm and its customers.

The trade-offs associated with an implicit guarantee strategy are intriguing. On the positive side, because the guarantee is implicit, no explicit specifications state exactly what the firm will do should the guarantee need to be invoked. Consequently, the service firm can tailor the payout of the guarantee to fit the magnitude of the service failure. Hence, an implicit guarantee may not result in an all-or-nothing type of arrangement. Other benefits associated with the implicit guarantee strategy are that (1) it avoids the appearance of a tacky marketing ploy compared with an explicit guarantee; and (2) it avoids stating publicly the possibility that the firm on occasion may not fulfill its promises. In sum, an implicit guarantee is thought to be the "classy" way of pursuing a guarantee strategy.

An implicit guarantee also has its drawbacks. Because an implicit guarantee is unspoken and unwritten, "a firm pursuing an implicit guarantee strategy has to earn its reputation by repeated acts of goodwill communicated to potential clients via word of mouth, a time-consuming process."[22] Hence, an implicit guarantee does little to differentiate a firm early in its business life cycle. In addition, because the guarantee is implicit, new customers may be unaware of the firm's stance on customer satisfaction and may not bring problems to the firm's attention.

Another type of guarantee is a specific result guarantee. A **specific result guarantee** is considered milder than an explicit unconditional guarantee because "the conditions for triggering the guarantee are narrower and well defined, and the payouts are less traumatic."[23] In contrast to an unconditional guarantee, which covers every aspect of the service delivery process, a specific result guarantee applies only to specific steps or outputs.

**specific result guarantee**
A guarantee that applies only to specific steps or outputs in the service delivery process.

On the positive side, specific result guarantees are most easily applied to quantitative results. For example, FedEx guarantees overnight delivery. Moreover, by guaranteeing a specific result as opposed to an overall guarantee, the firm may be able to state its commitment to a particular goal more powerfully. On the negative side, a specific result guarantee may appear weak compared with an unconditional guarantee, and customers may perceive this as the firm's lack of confidence in its own abilities.

**unconditional guarantee**
A guarantee that promises complete customer satisfaction and, at a minimum, a full refund or complete, no-cost problem resolution.

An **unconditional guarantee** is the most powerful of the three types of guarantees. The unconditional guarantee "in its pure form promises complete customer satisfaction, and, at a minimum, a full refund or complete, no-cost problem resolution for the payout."[24] In general, offering unconditional guarantees benefits the firm in two ways. First, the firm benefits from the effect that the guarantee has on customers. More specifically, customer-directed benefits associated with unconditional guarantees include the following:

- Customers perceive they are getting a better value.
- The perceived risk associated with the purchase is lower.
- The consumer perceives the firm to be more reliable.
- The guarantee helps consumers decide when comparing competing choices; consequently, the guarantee serves as a differential advantage.
- The guarantee helps in overcoming customer resistance toward making the purchase.
- The guarantee reinforces customer loyalty, increases sales, and builds market share.
- A good guarantee can overcome negative word-of-mouth advertising.
- The guarantee can lead to brand recognition and differentiation; consequently, a higher price can be commanded.

The second benefit of the unconditional guarantee is directed at the organization itself. A necessary condition for a firm to offer an unconditional guarantee is that it must first have its own operations in order. If not, the payouts associated with an unconditional guarantee will eventually bankrupt the firm. Organization-directed benefits of offering unconditional guarantees include the following:

- The guarantee forces the firm to focus on the customer's definition of good service as opposed to the firm's own definition.
- In and of itself, the guarantee states a clear performance goal that is communicated to employees and customers.
- Guarantees that are invoked provide a measurable means of tracking poor service.
- Offering the guarantee forces the firm to examine its entire service delivery system for failure points.
- The guarantee can be a source of pride and provide a motive for team building within the firm.

As with the other types of guarantees, a number of risks worth discussing are associated with unconditional guarantees. First, guarantees may send a negative message to some customers, thereby tarnishing the image of a firm that offers a guarantee. Some customers may ponder why the firm needs to offer the guarantee in the first place. For example, customers may consider whether the guarantee is because of failures in the past or out of desperation for new business. Another drawback to unconditional guarantees involves the actual payout when the guarantee is invoked. Customers may be too embarrassed to invoke the guarantee; consequently, the guarantee may actually motivate customers not to complain. Other potential problems associated with the payout involve the amount of documentation the firm requires in order to invoke the guarantee and the time it takes for the actual payout to be completed.

## MINIMIZING THE RISK OF A PAYOUT

Obviously, the primary purpose of a guarantee is to communicate to customers that the firm believes in what it provides and that it is committed to customer satisfaction. Ideally, firms that employ a guarantee strategy will seldom have the guarantee invoked. Firms implementing a guarantee strategy can minimize the event of a payout by

- Fully understanding the customer's needs prior to service delivery
- Tracking and monitoring the firm's performance throughout the service delivery process
- Limiting the payout so that it pertains to the key activities and not to minor details (e.g., the firm is refunding the entire amount of the project because the doughnuts were stale at one of the meetings)
- Specifying up front who has the authorization to approve a payout (i.e., upper management or contact personnel)
- Specifying prior to service delivery the amount involved in the payout

## THE PAYOUT

When a guarantee is invoked, the question then turns to the amount of the **payout.** Although a full refund or doubling the customer's money back in some instances may make sense, these types of refunds may be out of proportion for small mistakes. In general, the amount of the payout ultimately should depend on the cost of the service, the magnitude of the service failure, and the customer's perception of what is fair.

> **payout**
> The amount of money or resolution a service firm spends in order to fulfill an invoked guarantee.

In 1989 the Hampton Inn chain offered an unconditional guarantee to its customers.[25] "The policy states that any guest who has a problem and is not satisfied by the end of the stay will receive one night's stay at no charge." Incidentally, the guarantee is paid out when the guest settles the account and is not a voucher for a future stay. The impact of the guarantee has been overwhelmingly positive. Employees immediately took notice of and responsibility for correcting potential service problems. Moreover, overall quality standards in the hotels have noticeably changed. As a result, employee morale has increased, and employee turnover has decreased.

During the first few months of the program, fewer than one tenth of 1 percent of customers invoked the guarantee. By 1991 only 7,000 guests, representing $350,000 in sales, had used the guarantee. Of the guests who have invoked the guarantee, 86 percent say they will return, and 45 percent have already done so. The CEO of Hampton Inn believes that these numbers prove that most guests will not take unfair advantage of the guarantee, and this fact coupled with the positive impact on employee morale has meant that the guarantee has had a very positive effect on the firm's bottom line.

## PROFESSIONAL SERVICE GUARANTEES

As a final note, guarantees as they relate to professional services deserve special consideration.[26] Experts in the area of guarantees believe that guarantees are most effective for professional service providers under the following conditions:

- *Prices are high.* Professional service prices easily approach the five- and six-figure range. Guarantees may alleviate some of the risk associated with such costly decisions.

- *The costs of a negative outcome are high.* Simply stated, the more important the decision and the more disastrous a negative outcome, the more powerful the guarantee.
- *The service is customized.* As opposed to standardized services, where outcomes are fairly certain, customized services are accompanied by a degree of uncertainty. The guarantee helps to alleviate some of the risk associated with the uncertainty.
- *Brand recognition is difficult to achieve.* It is difficult to successfully differentiate professional services. For example, an eye exam or dental services are fairly consistent from one provider to the next. In cases like these, the unconditional service guarantee may successfully differentiate the service from the competition.
- *Buyer resistance is high.* Because of the expense of many professional services and the uncertainty of the outcome, buyers of professional services are highly cautious. An unconditional guarantee may help in overcoming customer reservations and making the sale.

## DEFECTION MANAGEMENT

**defection management**
A systematic process that actively attempts to retain customers before they defect.

Another way of increasing the customer retention rate is by reducing customer defections. The concept of defection management has its roots in the total quality management (TQM) movement. **Defection management** is a systematic process that actively attempts to retain customers before they defect. Defection management involves tracking the reasons that customers defect and using this information to continuously improve the service delivery system, thereby reducing future defections. Cutting defections in half doubles the average company's growth rate. Moreover, reducing the defection rate by even 5 percent can boost profits 25 percent to 85 percent, depending on the industry (Figure 15.5).[27]

### Zero Defects versus Zero Defections

**zero defects model**
A model used in manufacturing that strives for no defects in goods produced.

Since the acceptance of total quality management by the manufacturing sector, the guide to follow has been the **zero defects model.** Although appropriate within the manufacturing sector, where specifications can be identified well ahead of production, the zero defects model does not work well in the service sector.[28]

Service customers carry specifications in their minds and can only approximate their desires to a service provider. For example, customers often show hairstylists pictures of a desired hairstyle and request a similar style for themselves. The picture is an approximation of a desired result—it does not specify exact lengths to be cut nor specific degree of curve for curls.

Another obstacle to applying the zero defects model in the service sector is that each consumer has his or her own set of expectations and corresponding specifications. As one hairstylist stated, "They [some consumers] come in here with two spoonfuls of hair and expect to leave here looking like Diana Ross!" Consequently, specifications that are available in the service sector frequently cannot be standardized for all customers. As a result, the service provider must be able to adapt to each set of expectations on the spot.

Percent Increase in Customer Value*

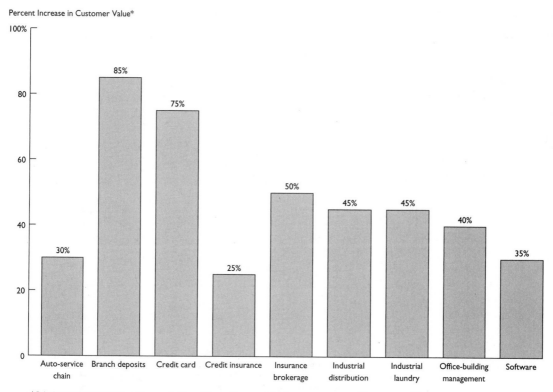

*Calculated by comparing the net present values of the profit streams for the average customer life at current defection rates with the net present values of the profit streams for the average customer life at 5% lower defection rates.

**Figure 15.5**    **Reducing Defections 5 Percent Boosts Profits 25 to 85 Percent**
Source: Frederick F. Reichheld and W. Earl Sasser, Jr., "Zero Defections: Quality Comes to Services," *Harvard Business Review* (September–October 1990), 110.

Because of the unique properties of the service delivery system, the zero defects model used in the manufacturing sector is out of touch with the realities of the service sector. A more appropriate philosophy for service firms would be **zero defections.** In contrast to the "defect pile" of unsellable goods for the manufacturing sector, the "defect pile" in the services sector consists of customers who will not come back.

**zero defections**
A model used by service providers that strives for no customers defections to competitors.

## The Importance of Defection Management

Businesses commonly lose 15 percent to 20 percent of their customers each year.[29] In some industries, the rate is much higher. For example, the cable television industry loses in excess of 50 percent each year,[30] the cellular phone industry experiences turnover at a rate of 30 percent to 45 percent per year,[31] and customer defections in the pager industry range from 40 percent to 70 percent annually.[32] Reducing customer defections is associated with immediate payoffs. In the credit card industry, for example, a 2 percent decrease in defections has the same net effect on the bottom line as a 10 percent decrease in cost (Figure 15.6).[33]

**Figure 15.6    A Credit Card Company's Defection Curve**

Source: Frederick F. Reichheld and W. Earl Sasser, Jr., "Zero Defections: Quality Comes to Services," *Harvard Business Review* (September–October 1990), 109.

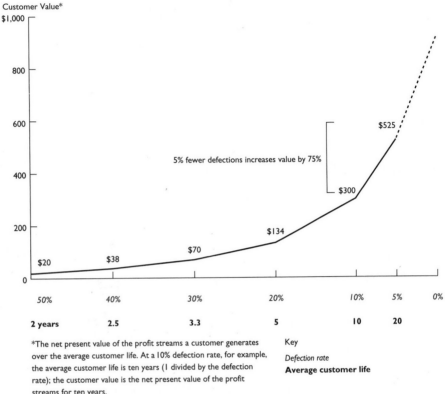

*The net present value of the profit streams a customer generates over the average customer life. At a 10% defection rate, for example, the average customer life is ten years (1 divided by the defection rate); the customer value is the net present value of the profit streams for ten years.

Key

*Defection rate*
**Average customer life**

Another reason that monitoring customer defections is important is the disturbing possibility that customer defection rates may not be directly associated with customer satisfaction ratings.[34] One would think that satisfied customers would be easily retained. Although the idea is intuitively appealing, receiving high satisfaction marks from current customers does not necessarily translate into undying customer loyalty. On average, 65 to 85 percent of defectors say they were satisfied or very satisfied with their former provider.[35] Why, then, do customers defect (see Services in Action 15.6)?

## Defector Types

**price defectors**
Customers who switch to competitors for lower priced goods and services.

Customers defect for a variety of reasons.[36] **Price defectors** switch to competitors for lower priced goods and services and are probably the least loyal of any customer type. Many businesses that pursue a customer retention philosophy are willing to sacrifice price defectors to avoid constantly discounting their own products and services. In particular, firms that differentiate themselves from competitors based on factors such as reliability, responsiveness, empathy, assurance, and the effective management of the tangible evidence that surrounds the service are generally able to retain customers without constantly discounting their products.

ERVICES 15.6

ACTION    **Loyalty and Satisfaction Are Not
Necessarily Related**

Although intuitively higher levels of customer satisfaction would be
expected to be associated with higher levels of customer retention, the relationship does not always necessarily exist. Consider the following cases
where (1) customers are not satisfied, yet they are retained; and (2) customers are satisfied, yet they defect to competitive offerings.

**Low Satisfaction/High Retention**

- Regulated monopoly or few substitutes (e.g., hospitals, airlines)
- Dominant brand equity (e.g., Microsoft)
- High cost of switching (e.g., physicians, financial institutions)
- Proprietary technology (e.g., Microsoft)

**High Satisfaction/Low Loyalty**

- Commodity products or little or no differentiation (e.g., rental cars)
- Consumer indifference (low involvement) (e.g., car wash, dry cleaner)
- Many substitutes (e.g., lawn care service)
- Low costs of switching (e.g., trash collection services)

Source: John E. G. Bateson and K. Douglas Hoffman, *Managing Services Marketing,* 4th ed.
(Fort Worth, Tex.: The Dryden Press, 1999).

**Product defectors** switch to competitors who offer superior goods and services. As such, product defectors are the most difficult to bring back to the fold
once they leave. For example, it is difficult to imagine returning to a provider of
inferior service once a superior provider is found. The secret to minimizing product defectors is to not become complacent with today's successes and ignore the
changing needs of customers. Innovations and continuous improvement are critical in the battle of retaining product defectors.

**Service defectors** defect because of poor customer service. Contrary to other
defector types, firms that are plagued by service defectors are actually providing
existing customers with reasons to take their business elsewhere. Inadequately
informed personnel, unfulfilled promises, and unacceptable employee behavior are
typical reasons customers flee to the competition. Service failures like these combined with inadequate employee responses to those failures can lead to service
defections. Whereas other defector types are primarily externally driven, service
defectors leave as a result of problems with the internal operations of the firm.

**Market defectors** exit the market because of relocation or business failure
reasons. Customers, both individuals and businesses, who move out of the market area would be considered market defectors. Similarly, companies that go out

**product defectors**
Customers who switch
to competitors who
offer superior goods
and services.

**service defectors**
Customers who defect
because of poor
customer service.

**market defectors**
Customers who exit the
market because of relo-
cation or business
failure.

of business and are no longer in the market for goods and services are market defectors.

**Technological defectors** switch to products outside the industry. Typical examples of technological defections include the switch from lamp oil to electricity and from rail to air transportation. As is the case with product defections, technological defections may occur as a result of the complacency of the firm. Successful firms are often lulled into a false sense of security and fail to react to technological developments outside their own industry. For example, the manufacturers of vinyl albums who were caught off guard by the development and consumer acceptance of the compact disc lost much of their business through technological defections.

**Organizational defectors** result from political considerations inside the firm. In some instances, organizational defections will occur as a result of reciprocal buying arrangements. For example, an engineering firm may switch its paper products purchasing to a firm that sells the brand of paper products marketed by the pulp and paper mill that retains the engineering firm's services. In other instances, organizational defections may occur as the result of friendships that develop through civic clubs, country clubs, and a variety of other social and business gatherings.

**technological defectors**
Customers who switch to products outside the industry.

**organizational defectors**
Customers who leave because of political considerations inside the firm, such as reciprocal buying arrangements.

## The Defection Management Process

Although customer defections are frustrating for many firms, defection rates are measurable and manageable.[37] Defections indicate where profits are heading as well as specific reasons that customers are leaving. Information obtained by analyzing defections can assist firms in reaching the goal of continuous improvement.

The key to defection management is the creation of a zero defections culture within the firm. Everyone in the firm must understand that zero defection is a primary goal of the organization. To establish this primary goal, the firm's first step in the defection management process is communicating to its employees the importance of retaining current customers and the benefits obtained by reducing defections. The earlier discussions in this chapter outline the importance and benefits of customer retention that should be conveyed to employees.

The zero defections goal communicated to employees must have supporters at all levels, starting at the top of the organization. It is critical that upper management lead by example and that managers "walk what they talk." Managers who talk customer service in employee meetings and then bad-mouth customers in the backroom will never successfully implement a zero defections culture within their firm.

The second step in creating a zero defections culture is to train employees in defection management. Defection management involves (1) gathering customer information; (2) providing specific instructions about what to do with the information; (3) instructing employees in how to react to the information; and (4) encouraging employees to respond to the information.

The third and perhaps most critical step in the defection management process is to tie incentives to defection rates. Simply stated, if the firm truly values reducing defections, the reward structure should reinforce customer retention efforts.

Firms such as MBNA, as mentioned in Services in Action 15.2, are dedicated to customer retention and have developed reward systems consistent with their customer retention efforts. It is MBNA's policy to talk with every customer who wishes to drop its services. MBNA's employees earn up to 20 percent of their salaries in bonuses associated with customer retention efforts. As a result of the reward structure and these extra communication efforts with customers, MBNA retains 50 percent of customers who call with an intent to end the relationship.[38] Another great example is State Farm Insurance. State Farm agents receive the same commission for securing renewals as they do for signing up new customers.[39] As a company, State Farm recognizes the value of customer retention and rewards employees for their customer retention efforts.

Finally, firms successful in defection management also carefully consider creating switching barriers that discourage defections.[40] A customer switching banks is subjected to the time-consuming task of closing one account at the old bank, opening a new account at the new bank, and sometimes paying for new checks to be printed. Switching to a new dentist may require the cost of new x-rays, and switching to a new physician may translate into completing extensive patient information forms and enduring an extensive physical exam. The key to successfully implementing switching barriers is to develop low entry barriers and non-manipulative yet high exit barriers.

Overall, the key to defection management is the realization that customer defections are measurable and manageable. Too often, firms simply write off customers who no longer request their services. Defection management focuses on retaining customers before they defect and determining the reasons for defections when they do occur. In sum, defectors are a valuable source of information regarding the firm's operations, its employees, and its future.

## SUMMARY

As a result of stagnant markets, increased competition, the rising costs of marketing, changes in channels of distribution, and the ever-changing needs of consumers, the concept of customer retention has increased in importance. Customer retention refers to focusing the firm's marketing efforts toward its existing customer base. Hence, in contrast to seeking new customers, firms engaged in customer retention efforts work to satisfy existing customers in hope of further developing the customer-provider relationship.

Customer retention is associated with a variety of benefits, including the profits derived from initial and repeat sales, the profits from reduced operating costs, and the profits from referrals. Typically, existing customers make more efficient use of the supply of service available and often prefer to stay with one provider over long periods to reduce the risk associated with service purchases.

A number of effective customer retention tactics were presented in this chapter. These strategies include maintaining the proper perspective and remembering that the company exists to serve the needs of its customers; maintaining contact with customers between service encounters; building trust between the firm and its customers; monitoring the service delivery process; properly installing products and training customers in how to use the products they purchase; being available when problems occur; and being willing to expend discretionary effort when needed.

Not all customers may be worth keeping. In general, however, firms focusing their efforts on customer retention programs such as frequency marketing, relationship marketing, aftermarketing, service guarantees, and defection management have found their efforts to be worthwhile and highly profitable.

# Key Terms

| | |
|---|---|
| Aftermarketing | Price defectors |
| Conquest marketing | Product defectors |
| Customer retention | Relationship marketing |
| Defection management | Service defectors |
| Frequency marketing | Specific result guarantee |
| Implicit guarantee | Technological defectors |
| Market defectors | Unconditional guarantee |
| Organizational defectors | Zero defections |
| Payout | Zero defects model |

# Discussion Questions

1. Why has conquest marketing become an acceptable form of business for many of today's firms?
2. Discuss the problems associated with conquest marketing.
3. Discuss the steps associated with frequency marketing as they relate to frequent-flier programs.
4. How have changes within service distribution channels had an impact on customer retention?
5. Discuss the distinction between zero defects and zero defections.
6. How do service defectors differ from other defector types?
7. Is it always worthwhile to retain a customer?
8. Discuss the characteristics of successful guarantees.
9. What are the trade-offs associated with using implicit guarantees?

# Notes

1. Robert E. Wayland and Paul M. Cole, "Turn Customer Service into Customer Profitability," *Management Review* (July 1994), 22–24.
2. Rahul Jacob, "Why Some Customers Are More Equal Than Others," *Fortune* (September 19, 1994), 218, 220.

3. Terry G. Vavra, *AFTERMARKETING: How to Keep Customers for Life through Relationship Marketing* (Homewood, Ill.: Business One Irwin, 1992), 2-6.
4. Ibid., 1.
5. Ibid., 2-6.
6. Michael W. Lowenstein, "The Voice of the Customer," *Small Business Reports* (December 1993), 57-61.
7. Frederick F. Reichheld and W. Earl Sasser, Jr., "Zero Defections: Quality Comes to Services," *Harvard Business Review* (September–October 1990), 105-111.
8. Barry Farber and Joyce Wycoff, "Customer Service: Evolution and Revolution," *Sales and Marketing Management* (May 1991), 44-51.
9. Reichheld and Sasser, "Zero Defections," 107.
10. Adapted from Barton A. Weitz, Stephen B. Castleberry, and John F. Tanner, Jr., *Selling: Building Partnerships* (Homewood Ill.: Irwin, 1992), 330-340.
11. "Is Customer Retention Worth the Time, Effort and Expense," *Sales and Marketing Management* 143, no. 15 (December 1991), 21-22.
12. Wayland and Cole, "Turn Customer Service," 24.
13. Richard Barlow, "Building Customer Loyalty through Frequency Marketing," *The Bankers Magazine* (May/June 1990), 73-76.
14. Jim Ellis, "Frill-Seeking in the Clouds," *Business Week* (September 13, 1993), 104-105.
15. Adam Bryant, "Airlines' Frequent-Flier Miles Not Just for Flying Anymore," *Sunday Star-News,* August 21, 1994, p. 10A.
16. Martin Christopher, Adrian Payne, and David Ballantyne, *Relationship Marketing* (Oxford: Butterworth-Heinemann, 1991).
17. Jacob, "Why Some Customers," 222.
18. Ibid., 215.
19. Vavra, *AFTERMARKETING,* 1.
20. Jacob, "Why Some Customers," 222.
21. Adapted from Christopher W. L. Hart, Leonard A. Schlesinger, and Don Maher, "Guarantees Come to Professional Service Firms," *Sloan Management Review* (Spring 1992), 19-29.
22. Ibid., 29.
23. Ibid., 28.
24. Ibid., 20.
25. "Service Guarantees Yield Surprising Results," *The Cornell H.R.A. Quarterly* (February 1991), 14-15.
26. Hart, Schlesinger, and Maher, "Guarantees Come," 20.
27. Reichheld and Sasser, "Zero Defections," 110.
28. Ron Zemke, "The Emerging Art of Service Management," *Training* (January 1992), 37-42.
29. Reichheld and Sasser, "Zero Defections," 108.
30. "How Five Companies Targeted Their Best Prospects," *Marketing News* (February 18, 1991), 22.
31. *The Cellular Telephone Industry: Personal Communication* (Silver Spring, Md.: Herschel Shostack Assoc., 1992), 122.
32. *The Pager Industry: ProNet Annual Report,* 1989.
33. Reichheld and Sasser, "Zero Defections," 108.

34. Lowenstein, "The Voice," 57.

35. Patricia Sellers, "Keeping the Buyers," *Fortune* (Autumn–Winter 1993), 56–58.

36. Glenn DeSouza, "Designing a Customer Retention Plan," *The Journal of Business Strategy* (March–April 1992), 24–28.

37. Reichheld and Sasser, "Zero Defections," 105.

38. Larry Armstrong, "Beyond May I Help You?" *Business Week/Quality* (1991), 100–103.

39. Sellers, "Keeping the Buyers," 58.

40. DeSouza, "Designing," 27.

## chapter 16

# Putting the Pieces Together: Creating the Seamless Service Firm

## CHAPTER OBJECTIVES

The purpose of this chapter is to tie together the information presented in this book in a meaningful manner. In order to provide service excellence, the individual components of the firm must act in unison to create a "seamless" organization. The firm will not act as one if the current culture of the organization is based on departmentalization and functionalism. Consequently, creating and supporting a customer-focused organizational culture is critical. Finally, by conducting a service audit, a seamless service culture is fostered as personnel throughout the organization come to appreciate the challenges faced and the contributions made by everyone involved in the firm's final service delivery effort.

After reading this chapter, you should be able to:

- Compare and contrast the concept of seamlessness with departmentalization and functionalism.
- Discuss the historical weakness of marketing in service firms.
- Explain the basic concepts of the three-tiered model of service firms.
- Explain what is meant by the firm's culture.
- Discuss methods that may lead to cultural change.
- Discuss the basic components of a service audit.

"What is needed now is to surround these individuals with the system—a logically and tightly connected seamless set of interrelated parts—that allows people to perform their jobs well."

Benjamin Schneider and
David E. Bowen

# Introduction

**seamless service**
Services that occur
without interruption,
confusion, or hassle to
the customer.

Creating a **seamless service** organization means providing services without interruption, confusion, or hassle to the customer.[1] Seamless service firms manage to simultaneously provide reliable, responsive, competent, and empathetic services and have the facilities and resources necessary to get the job done. Seamlessness applies not only to the provision of services but also to service recovery efforts pertaining to core system failures, implicit/explicit customer requests, and employee behavior.

Seamlessness thrives on tightly connected interrelated parts within the service delivery system. Functionalization and departmentalization kills seamlessness. For example, consider the following three memos sent to a young manager of a branch bank on the same day:[2]

*From the marketing department:*
We shortly will be launching a new advertising campaign based on the friendliness of our staff. This is in direct response to the increasingly competitive marketplace we face. Please ensure that your staff members deliver the promises we are making.

*From the operations department:*
As you are aware, we are facing an increasingly competitive marketplace and, as a result, our profits have come under pressure. It is crucial, therefore, that we minimize waste to keep our costs under control. From today, therefore, no recruitment whatsoever will be allowed.

*From the personnel department:*
Our staff members are becoming increasingly militant. This is due, in large part, to the availability of alternative employment with our new competitors. We currently are involved in a particularly delicate set of negotiations and would be grateful if you could minimize any disruptions at the local level.

These instructions from the three different departments obviously conflict with one another. To obey the operations department means no recruitment and therefore an increase in the workload of contact personnel. The increased workload will most likely be a hot topic during labor negotiations and could be disastrous for the personnel department. Finally, the increased workload in all probability will have a negative effect on staff morale. Given the inseparability of the service, the staff's low morale will be visible to customers and will negatively affect customer satisfaction levels.

If this particular branch bank is marketing oriented, the young manager will attempt to trade off the three sets of instructions, giving added weight to the marketing department's instructions. It should be stressed that in service firms it is nearly impossible to be totally marketing oriented. Customers cannot be given everything they want because of the constraints imposed by the firm's service delivery system. For example, in a restaurant setting, every customer cannot be seated and served immediately upon arrival because of seating and available service (personnel) constraints.

If this branch is operations oriented, added weight will be given to the operations department's set of instructions. The young manager may relay marketing's request to the vice president of operations and ask for clarification. The operations vice president, in turn, may fire off an abusive memo to his or her counterpart in marketing. The memo may ask why marketing was sending memos directly to the branches at all and suggest that in the future all other requests made by marketing be cleared by operations.

Firms that continue to cling to functional and departmental mindsets are often besieged by internal conflict as departments compete against one another for resources instead of pulling together to provide exceptional service. Seamlessness is "tooth-to-tail" performance—a term commonly used in the armed forces. "The personnel out front in the trenches need to be backed up with coordinated supplies, information resources, personnel reinforcements, and so on."[3] Similarly, the primary efforts of the service firm should focus on the service delivery process and on the personnel providing customer services.

The conflict that often occurs among marketing, operations, and human resources is not personal.[4] It is a result of their different cultures, which are functions of each department's goals, planning horizons, departmental structure, and people-management systems, as well as the specific individuals in each department. For example, marketing tends to have a longer planning horizon, is less rigidly and hierarchically organized, and tends to reward innovation and creativity compared with its operations counterparts.

In comparison with goods-producing firms, turf wars among departments are more prevalent in service firms because of lack of inventories. Inventories, which provide a buffer between marketing and operations in goods-producing firms, are for the most part nonexistent in service firms. In a service firm, production and consumption often occur simultaneously in a real-time experience.

## THE HISTORICAL WEAKNESS OF MARKETING IN SERVICE FIRMS[5]

Service firms often find themselves in a three-cornered fight among marketing, operations, and personnel (human resources) (Figure 16.1.) Somehow, marketing always seems to lose this fight, since marketers tend to have less influence in service companies than in goods companies (see Services in Action 16.1).

**Figure 16.1**    **The Three-Cornered Fight for Control**
Source: John E. G. Bateson, *Managing Services Marketing: Text and Readings,* 3rd ed. (Fort Worth, Tex.: The Dryden Press, 1995).

S E R V I C E S *16.1*
N
A C T I O N

### Getting the Firm's Act Together: The Haves and Have Nots

In the preface of this text, you were warned that you may never view your service experiences as customers in the same way again. By now you should understand the fundamentals of providing good service and be very aware of when poor service is delivered to you personally. In the effort to regain some control or vent frustrations, students often seek out their instructors, who they feel will lend them a sympathetic ear. For good or ill, service instructors often find themselves playing the role of an advice columnist as they listen to one student-generated customer service story after another. Based on the stories told, the two service incidents below are typical of firms that have their act together and those that do not.

## One of the Have Nots

This first incident is about a customer who wanted to drop off his laundry at a local dry cleaner. The firm's advertising promised, "In by 9:00, out by 5:00." The customer entered the dry cleaner at 8:45 A.M. and gave his laundry to an employee, who recorded all the usual information such as name and telephone number. The employee then asked when the customer would like to pick up his laundry. The customer responded that he would like to take advantage of the firm's prompt service offer and get his laundry back that afternoon at 5:00 P.M. The employee then informed the customer that the truck that picks up the day's laundry and delivers it to the firm's main operations site had already arrived and departed. The customer pointed out to the employee the promise of the firm's sign, and the employee responded that she was just an employee and there was nothing she could do for him.

Frustrated, the customer asked to speak to the manager. The employee responded that she was the firm's only representative at that particular site. The customer then asked for the owner's telephone number and for permission to use the laundry's telephone. The employee complied with both requests. Upon reaching the owner, the customer explained his situation. Without any form of apology, the owner responded by saying that he had bigger problems to worry about than what his sign promised and suggested that next time the customer bring his laundry earlier. The owner further suggested that if the customer really wanted his laundry done by 5:00 P.M., "the customer" should drive halfway across town to the firm's main operations and drop off his laundry there. As the customer continued to press the owner to make good on the firm's service promise, the owner hung up on the customer.

## One of the Haves

The second incident concerns a customer who lived in an area that took a direct hit from Hurricane Bertha in July 1996. By coincidence, the customer had left town three days earlier to visit family in the Midwest and was not at home when the hurricane ripped through the area. Damage caused by the storm was widespread and consisted primarily of downed trees and branches. Shortly after the storm, the customer was in touch with neighbors who informed him that his house had survived but that the yard was full of debris.

Returning to his home two days later, the customer was surprised to see that his entire yard had been cleaned up by his neighbors and that the debris had been hauled off to a local dump site. The customer was grateful to have such good neighbors. Another surprise was that the customer's State Farm insurance agent had left his card inside the doorframe of the house. The agent made a personal trip to the customer's home to see whether the customer and his family required any assistance. In other words, the agent arrived before the customer even attempted to track him down during a period in which the customer believed that getting through to his insurance agent would be next to impossible. Apparently, this type of personalized treatment is part of State Farm's culture—its corporate offices sent an additional 200 agents into the area to assist in assessing and settling claims. In addition, local radio stations aired public service announcements to inform property owners of simple procedures and locations at which to contact insurance personnel.

Although it sounds a bit "corny," when the customer compared the actions of his neighbors with the service he received from his State Farm agent, the company's corporate slogan rang true: "Like a good neighbor, State Farm [was] there!"

At this point it is necessary to understand the differences among marketing orientation, marketing function, and the marketing department. **Marketing orientation** means that a firm or organization plans its operations according to market needs. The objectives of the firm are to satisfy customer needs rather than merely to use production facilities or raw materials.[6] Marketing orientation is clearly an attitude that puts the customer's needs first in any trade-off. Firms do not require a formal marketing department in order to have a marketing orientation.

**Marketing functions** in a firm include tasks such as the design of the product, pricing, and promotion. Decisions in these areas are made in order for the organization to operate, but they need not necessarily be made by people with marketing titles nor by individuals in a formal **marketing department**—the department that traditionally works on marketing functions in the company.

In a typical goods company, the distinctions among marketing orientation, marketing functions, and the marketing department are not necessary. They are,

**marketing orientation**
A firm's view toward planning its operations according to market needs.

**marketing functions**
Tasks such as the design of a product, its pricing, and its promotion.

**marketing department**
The formal department in an organization that works on the marketing functions of the company.

however, necessary in service firms, where a formal marketing department may not necessarily exist. Because the service product is an interactive process, it may be more appropriate to leave the different functional decisions to different departments.

The variety of relationships between marketing and other functions within the organization can be illustrated by the **customization/customer contact matrix** depicted in Figure 16.2. One axis of the matrix relates directly to the degree of contact the firm has with its customers. The higher the level of customer contact, the higher the level of inefficiency because of the uncertainty introduced by customers. This idea is based largely on the concept of inseparability and the participation of consumers in the service delivery process. The second axis relates to the amount of customization of the service available to consumers. Once again, we would expect the "low" state to be preferable for efficiency purposes because it would allow the service delivery system to operate as a production line free from outside influences. A variety of businesses are introduced into the cells to illustrate how the matrix is used.

For example, a travel agency can operate in a number of cells simultaneously. Booking an airline ticket by telephone for a business traveler fits into the low/low cell. But the same travel agency could just as well operate in a different cell if it also maintained a retail operation. From within the retail operation, both high and low customization are possible, depending on whether the customer is a business traveler wanting a ticket or a vacationer planning a multistop European trip.

From an operations perspective, the ideal cell is the low/low cell. In this cell the degree of customization is minimized so that large parts of the organization can be isolated and run like any other manufacturing plant.[7] In addition, the level of customization is also minimized so that the operating system is focused on a limited range of output and its efficiency increased.[8] A move into this cell, however, can have major implications for marketing. Customers may be seeking contact and customization and be willing to pay a premium for them.

A top-quality French restaurant might fit into the high/high cell. Compared with McDonald's, this is a different business with a different formula (but, interestingly

**customization/ customer contact matrix**
A table that illustrates the variety of relationships between marketing and other functions within the organization.

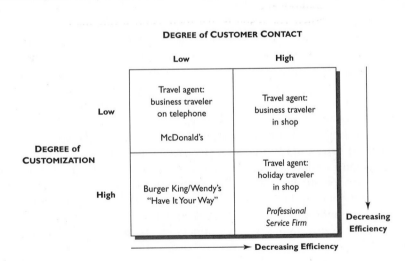

**Figure 16.2**
**The Customization/ Customer Contact Matrix**
Source: John E. G. Bateson, *Managing Services Marketing: Text and Readings*, 3rd ed. (Fort Worth, Tex.: The Dryden Press, 1995).

the target segment may be the same person on a very different occasion). The loss of efficiency implied by the high/high cell is compensated for by the price that can be charged.

The importance of the matrix and this discussion is to show how different cells suggest alternative roles and places for the marketing departments of firms operating within them. Two contrasting examples are the provision of legal services by a traditional law firm and by a franchised firm such as Hyatt Legal Services.

Operationally, the traditional firm will fit into the high/high cell in the matrix. The firm's attorneys will be in intensive contact with clients and will customize each service to meet the needs of each individual client. Except for routine cases, there will be little opportunity for economies of scale in this type of legal firm.

From a marketing point of view, the service product in the high/high cell often is created in the client's offices, away from the home firm of the attorney. In such situations, it is clear that a central marketing department has little influence over the final product and that most of the marketing needs to be delegated to the field offices, if not to the individual attorneys themselves. The selling function is done by consultants or professionals, so that too must be delegated.

The alternative is a firm such as Hyatt Legal Services. This firm represents a clear attempt to move the operating system away from the inefficiency of the high/high cell toward the low/low or at least the high contact/low customization cell. By reducing the types of cases handled, operations can be simplified and economies of scale generated. These economies, in turn, can be passed on to the customer through lower fees.

The marketing implications of moving the operation from a high/high cell to a more standardized outcome are relatively straightforward. The service is branded in order to add value for the consumer in a market that traditionally is not heavily branded. The firm depends on systematization and, from an operations point of view, implies centralization. We therefore would expect to find a strong centralized marketing department as well. Clearly, many service firms do not operate in the low/low cell of the matrix, even though they may wish to do so. For many service firms, therefore, the traditional combination of marketing functions in a marketing department breaks down. The result is that there is no strong marketing group to drive a marketing orientation in the organization. The weakness of the marketing function is compounded by the strength of the operations group and the linkages between them.

## MOVING BEYOND DEPARTMENTALIZATION AND FUNCTIONALIZATION: THE THREE-TIERED MODEL OF SERVICE FIRMS[9]

Seamless service is based on a **three-tiered model** of the service organization (Figure 16.3). Traditionally, organizations are organized by functions such as marketing, human resources, and operations management. In contrast, the three-tiered model consists of a customer tier, a boundary tier, and a coordination tier. Success is based on the effective management and integration of the three tiers.

**three-tiered model**
A view of service organizations that reconfigures traditional departmental functions into a customer tier, a boundary tier, and a coordination tier.

**Figure 16.3**

**The Three-Tiered Services Model**

Source: Benjamin Schneider and David E. Bowen, *Winning the Service Game* (Boston: Harvard Business School Press, 1995), 244.

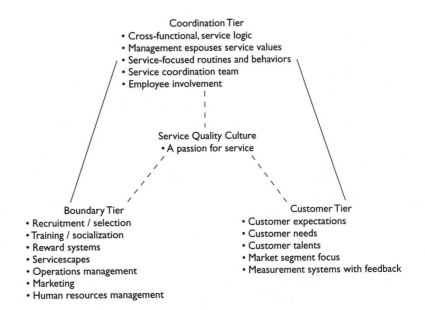

Coordination Tier
- Cross-functional, service logic
- Management espouses service values
- Service-focused routines and behaviors
- Service coordination team
- Employee involvement

Service Quality Culture
- A passion for service

Boundary Tier
- Recruitment / selection
- Training / socialization
- Reward systems
- Servicescapes
- Operations management
- Marketing
- Human resources management

Customer Tier
- Customer expectations
- Customer needs
- Customer talents
- Market segment focus
- Measurement systems with feedback

## The Customer Tier

**customer tier**
The tier in the three-tiered model that focuses on customer expectations, needs, and competencies.

As we have discussed throughout the book, attracting and retaining customers is the lifeblood of every service organization. Without customers, the service firm has no reason to exist. The **customer tier** focuses on customer expectations, needs, and competencies. To provide seamless service, management must have a deep understanding of each of these areas from the customer's perspective (see Services in Action 16.2).

**expectations**
Consumer expectations pertaining to the service delivery process and final outcome.

**Expectations** have been discussed throughout this book and are an integral component in developing customer satisfaction evaluations. As firms have realized the importance of customers, experts believe that businesses now have a fairly good understanding of their customers' expectations but not necessarily of their customers' needs and competencies. At a minimum, service firms must meet customer expectations in order to provide customers what they want, when they want it, and where they want it so that the firms can strategically differentiate themselves from competitors and stay in the service game.

**needs**
Security, esteem, and justice; often unrecognized as needs by customers themselves.

**Needs** are distinguished from expectations in that customers are generally aware of their expectations but are often unaware of what they need. Chapter 12 provided ample examples of products that met with great success such as minivans, personal computers, and cellular phones, despite early customer research indicating that customers did not feel a need for these products. Service experts believe that firms must deliver three key customer needs in order to deliver service excellence:[10]

1. Security: The need to feel secure and unthreatened by physical, psychological, or economic harm.
2. Esteem: The need to feel that one's self-esteem is maintained and enhanced by others.

ERVICES 16.2
N
ACTION

## The Ten Commandments of Customer Service

1. **Bring 'em back alive.** . . . Ask customers what they want and give it to them again and again.
2. **Systems, not smiles.** . . . Saying please and thank you doesn't ensure you'll do the job right the first time, every time. Only systems guarantee that.
3. **Underpromise, overdeliver.** . . . Customers expect you to keep your word. Exceed it.
4. **When the customer asks, the answer is always yes.** . . . Period.
5. **Fire your inspectors and customer relations department.** . . . Every employee who deals with clients must have the authority to handle complaints.
6. **No complaints, something's wrong.** . . . Encourage your customers to tell you what you're doing wrong.
7. **Measure everything.** . . . Baseball teams do it. Football teams do it. Basketball teams do it. You should too.
8. **Salaries are unfair.** . . . Pay people like partners.
9. **Your mother was right.** . . . Show people respect. Be polite. It works.
10. **Japanese them.** . . . Learn how the best really do it; make their systems your own. Then improve them.

Source: Paul B. Brown and Carl Sewall, *Customers for Life* (New York: Bantam, 1998).

**3.** Justice: The need to feel fairly and justly treated.

Examining and understanding customer needs is the foundation of building a competitive strategy that differentiates the firm from its competitors and of providing service excellence.

**Competencies** are the contributions customers bring to the service production process. Service firms that excel look beyond their employees as their only human resources. Throughout much of this book, we have discussed the consumer's involvement in the service delivery process. The customer influences the type and length of demand and often is a major determinant in the success or failure of the final outcome. Consequently, appealing to the "best customers" can be a source of competitive advantage.

**competencies**
The contributions customers bring to the service production process.

As an example, Dayton Hudson, the retailer, pursued a strategy that specifically targeted customers who spent more than $1,500 per year in their stores. By involving these customers in designing a program that would attract and retain their business, a special card was developed that entitled the holder to special discounts, free alterations, gift wrapping, free parking, and presale sales days. The information for designing the program was obtained through survey data, which consisted of more than 2,000 detailed responses from targeted clientele.[11]

## The Boundary Tier

**boundary tier**
The tier in the three-tiered model that concerns itself with the individuals who interact with the customers—the boundary spanners.

Whereas the customer tier deals with customer expectations, needs, and competencies, the **boundary tier** concerns itself with the individuals who interact with the customers—the boundary spanners. The boundary tier is where the customer meets the organization and where the critical incidents or "moments of truth" occur. Service personnel in the boundary tier must be more flexible, communicative, able to deal with stress, and willing to take initiative than their manufacturing counterparts. To the customer, personnel in the boundary tier are the organization and occupy a two-way communication role-from the organization to the customer, and from the customer back to the organization.

The key to successfully navigating the boundary tier is to avoid the "human resources trap." This trap makes the fatal flaw in judgment of placing the full burden of "moments of truth" on boundary-spanning personnel. The firm's nonpersonal services, such as the physical facility, the accuracy and timeliness of billing, and all the support staff who enable the boundary personnel to perform their jobs, must be in place and working together in order for the firm to provide seamless service. Ultimately, boundary personnel are only as good as the service delivery system that supports their efforts.

## The Coordination Tier

**coordination tier**
The tier in the three-tiered model that coordinates activities that help integrate the customer and boundary tiers.

The **coordination tier** is the responsibility of upper management and involves coordinating the activities that help integrate the customer and boundary tiers (see Services in Actions 16.3 and 16.4). Management's most important concerns pertain to (1) defining a target market and developing a strategy for effectively attracting this market; (2) ensuring that the boundary tier has the support necessary to meet the expectations and needs of the customer tier; and (3) ensuring that the expectations and needs of boundary-tier personnel are also being met.

**internal logic**
Implicit and explicit principles of individual departments that drive organizational performance.

The primary challenge of the coordination tier is to get the various departments within the organization to work with one common goal in mind—serving the customer. Before attempting to integrate the various departments of the firm, it is important to understand that each department is driven by its own **internal logic**—implicit and explicit principles that drive organizational performance.[12] Each department's logic is internally focused on departmental needs and creates seams in the service delivery process. For example, consider the logic behind the following functions: operations management, marketing, and human resources.

**operations logic**
The reasoning that stresses cost containment/reduction through mass production.

**Operations logic** is driven by the goal of reducing or containing costs through mass production or the use of advanced technologies. Operations and marketing are often in conflict with each other, which creates seams in service delivery. Whereas marketing is concerned with identifying and understanding customer needs and providing goods and services that meet those needs, operations is concerned with how these products and services will be produced and delivered. In essence, marketing is concerned with the management of demand, whereas operations is concerned with the management of supply. Marketing attempts to focus on meeting demand in the most effective manner in terms of product form, location, price, and promotions, whereas operations is primarily

SERVICES 16.3
IN
ACTION    **Southwest Airlines' 11 Primary Attitudes**

*We are not an airline with great customer service. We are a great customer service organization that happens to be in the airline business.*

Colleen Barrett, Southwest Airlines executive

1. Employees are number one. The way you treat your employees is the way they will treat your customer.
2. Think small to grow big.
3. Manage in the good times for the bad times.
4. Irreverence is okay.
5. It's okay to be yourself.
6. Have fun at work.
7. Take the competition seriously, but not yourself.
8. It's difficult to change someone's attitude, so hire for attitude and train for skill.
9. Think of the company as a service organization that happens to be in the airline business.
10. Do whatever it takes.
11. Always practice the Golden Rule, internally and externally.

Source: Kevin Freiberg and Jackie Freiberg, *Nuts! Southwest Airlines' Crazy Recipe for Business and Personal Success* (Bard Press: Austin, TX).

concerned with meeting demand in the most cost-effective manner. Typical goals of operations management and marketing concerns regarding these goals are displayed in Table 16.1.

The major challenge for operations in a service setting is the involvement of customers in the production process. Compared with raw materials in a pure manufacturing setting, customers are unpredictable and decrease the efficiency of the delivery system. Operations would like to remove the customer from the production process as much as possible, whereas marketing promotes the importance of the customer in the production process. Consequently, operations and marketing must establish a point of equilibrium between the variety and depth of products marketing would like to offer and the cost effectiveness of meeting that demand through efficient operations.

Whereas operations management is internally focused, marketing is externally focused on meeting the expectations and needs of consumers. Ideally, the **marketing logic** is to provide customers with options that better enable the service offering to meet individual consumer needs. Although ideal for customers, providing numerous options leads to serious cost inefficiencies in a firm's operations.

In addition to often being in conflict with operations, marketing may also find itself in conflict with human resources, creating additional seams in service delivery. For example, marketing would like to staff all personnel positions with

**marketing logic**
The reasoning that stresses providing customers with options that better enable the service offering to meet individual needs.

SERVICES 16.4
IN
ACTION    **The Nine Drivers of Service Success**

## Values-Driven Leadership

Values-driven leaders articulate the company's "reason for being," define the meaning of organizational success, live the company's values in their daily behavior, cultivate the leadership qualities of others in the organization, assert core values during difficult times, continuously challenge the status quo, and encourage employees' hearts with caring, involvement, participation, opportunity, fairness, and recognition.

## Strategic Focus

Sustainable service requires a core strategy—a definition of the business—that focuses organizational attention, guides business design decisions, channels execution, and galvanizes the human spirit.

## Executional Excellence

A customer does not experience a strategy; a customer experiences the execution of the strategy—that is, the "total product."

## Control of Destiny

Freedom to act is as important to a company's success as it is to an individual employee's success. Excellent service companies preserve their freedom to act; they chart their own course and pursue it with minimal distraction and interference.

## Trust-Based Relationships

Customers trust companies to keep their promises, as do employees and business partners. Promises kept strengthen commitment; promises broken weaken commitment.

## Investment in Employee Success

Top service companies create their own success by first creating successful employees. They compete for talented people with compatible values and then continually invest in their service skills and knowledge and their sense of inclusion in the organization.

## Acting Small

Excellent service companies—even if they are large—find ways to act small with customers. They find ways to leverage the "build-to-order" potential of a service, to tailor it to the preferences and personality of the individual customer.

## Brand Cultivation

A service brand tells the essential, capsulized story of a service: What it is and why it matters. The purpose of the brand not only is to define the service but also to differentiate it, to establish a distinct personality, and to connect customer and company emotionally.

## Generosity

Caring, giving people—the kind of people who make the best servers—want to be part of a company with a heart. Once on the job, they are energized by the company's contribution to the quality of life both inside and outside the corporation.

Source: Adapted from Leonard L. Berry, *Discovering the Soul of Service* (New York: The Free Press, 1999).

individuals who, in addition to being technically competent, possess strong interpersonal skills that enable the organization to better communicate with its customers. Marketing would argue that hiring personnel who possess well-developed interpersonal skills in addition to being technically competent is free. In turn, human resources would argue that obtaining and keeping highly trained and personable personnel is much more expensive than hiring people who simply adequately perform their roles in the organization. Furthermore, human resources will point out that certain market segments can be served by personnel who are simply civil with customers and who perform their duties adequately. This point is valid. Does the customer really want a McDonald's worker to engage the customer in a lengthy conversation about the weather, community happenings, and family matters, or would the customer rather have a simply civil employee take the order and deliver the food in a speedy manner? Moreover, the food is more likely to be less expensive when provided by adequate as opposed to superior personnel because of the savings in labor costs.

**Human resources logic** is to recruit personnel and to develop training that enhances the performance of existing personnel. In the service encounter, operations, marketing, and human resources are inextricably linked. Figure 16.4 depicts the link between operations and human resources. This figure, which compares the degree of customer contact with production efficiency, reveals that no such

**human resources logic**
The reasoning that stresses recruiting personnel and developing training to enhance the performance of existing personnel.

TABLE 16.1

## Operations and Marketing Perspectives on Operational Issues

| Operational Issues | Typical Operation Goals | Common Marketing Concerns |
|---|---|---|
| Productivity improvement | Reduce unit cost of production | Strategies may cause decline in service quality |
| Make-versus-buy decisions | Trade off control against comparative advantage and cost savings | "Make" decisions may result in lower quality and lack of market coverage; "buy" decisions may transfer control to unresponsive suppliers and hurt the firm's image |
| Facilities location | Reduce costs; provide convenient access for suppliers and employees | Customers may find location unattractive and inaccessible |
| Standardization | Keep costs low and quality consistent; simplify operations tasks; recruit low-cost employees | Consumers may seek variety, prefer customization to match segmented needs |
| Batch-versus-unit processing | Seek economies of scale, consistency, efficient use of capacity | Customers may be forced to wait, feel "one of a crowd," be turned off by other customers |
| Facilities layout and design | Control costs; improve efficiency by ensuring proximity of operationally related tasks; enhance safety and security | Customers may be confused, shunted around unnecessarily, find facility unattractive and inconvenient |
| Job design | Minimize error, waste, and fraud; make efficient use of technology; simplify tasks for standardization | Operationally oriented employees with narrow roles may be unresponsive to customer needs |
| Learning curves | Apply experience to reduce time and costs per unit of output | Faster service is not necessarily better service; cost saving may not be passed on as lower prices |
| Management of capacity | Keep costs down by avoiding wasteful under-utilization of resources | Service may be unavailable when needed; quality may be compromised during high-demand periods |
| Quality control | Ensure that service execution conforms to predefined standards | Operational definitions of quality may not reflect customer needs, preferences |
| Management of queues | Optimize use of available capacity by planning for average throughput; maintain customer order, discipline | Customers may be bored and frustrated during wait, see firm as unresponsive |

Source: © 1989 by Christopher H. Lovelock. Reprinted with permission from Christopher H. Lovelock. Christopher H. Lovelock, "Managing Interaction Between Operations and Marketing and Their Impact on Customers," in Bowen et al. (eds.) *Service Management Effectiveness* (San Francisco: Jossey Bass, 1990), p. 362.

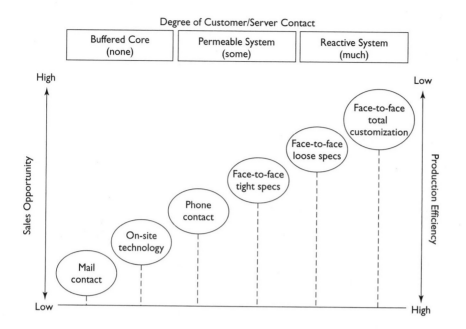

**Figure 16.4**
**Link between**
**Operations and**
**Human Resources**
Source: R. B. Chase
and W. E. Youngdahl,
"Service by Design,"
*Design Management
Journal* 9 (Winter
1992), 12. Adapted
from R. B. Chase
and N. J. Aquilano,
*Production
and Operations
Management:
A Lifecycle Approach*
(Homewood, Ill: Irwin,
1991).

person as the perfect service employee exists. Characteristics of the "right employee" depend on the characteristics of the particular job in question. Some employees will need to be people oriented, whereas others will need to be more task oriented to process "things" instead of "people."

The importance of service firm personnel as they interact with customers throughout the service delivery process highlights the link between human resources and marketing. In services, human resources are the only source of quality control. Consequently, the hiring, training, and reward structures developed by human resources will ultimately play a major role in how employees interact with the firm's customers.

Despite the opportunity to make major contributions to the firm's overall service effort, human resources departments are often stuck in their own production orientation and have difficulty getting their own acts together, let alone helping the organization provide superior service. Human resources' production-oriented activities include mistakes such as using the same employee evaluation forms for everyone in the firm even though the jobs may be very different, conducting canned employee training programs that never change from year to year, and using generic employee selection procedures for a variety of jobs that actually require different skill sets. In contrast, service-oriented human resources programs would be co-designed and co-taught with relevant managers, and evaluation forms would be thought of as coaching and evaluating devices rather than as rating forms used solely for compensation decisions. Overall, the service-oriented human resources department would work much more closely with its customers—the firm's employees—and form an ongoing, interactive, long-term relationship in pursuit of supporting those who serve the firm's final consumers.

**Figure 16.5**
**Cultural**
**Framework**
Source: John E. G.
Bateson, *Managing
Services Marketing:
Text and Readings*
(Fort Worth, Tex.: The
Dryden Press, 1995).

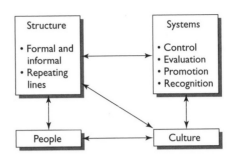

## BUILDING THE SERVICE LOGIC THROUGH CULTURAL CHANGE

**culture**
The shared values and
beliefs that drive an
organization.

The service logic stitches the departmental and functional seams together in order to help the firm provide flawless service. However, before this can happen, the firm's organizational **culture** must be customer focused. The firm's culture reflects the shared values and beliefs that drive the organization—the formally written, the unwritten, and actual occurrences that help employees understand the norms for behavior in the organization. In short, organizational culture establishes the "dos and don'ts" of employee behavior and provides the basis on which various employee behaviors can coalesce.[13]

Figure 16.5 presents a simple framework for considering the options available when implementing cultural change in the service organization.[14] The figure suggests that culture is internally linked to and partly an outcome of three organizational components: structure, systems, and people. **Structure** relates to the formal reporting channels normally represented in an organizational chart (such as frontline employees reporting to middle managers, who report to regional managers, who report to national managers, who report to the chief executive officer).

**structure**
The formal reporting
hierarchy normally
represented in an
organizational chart.

**systems**
People-management
systems of control,
evaluation, promotion,
and recognition.

The **systems** component of the framework refers to the people-management systems utilized for control, evaluation, promotion, and recognition. Evaluation and promotion systems include both formal and informal components. For example, management by objectives would be a formal component, whereas "What do I really have to do around here to get noticed?" would be an informal part of the system. Recognition systems focus on formal and informal rewards as well, ranging from formal rewards such as company trips to informal "pats on the back" such as lunch with the boss.

The other two major components of the culture framework are the people who work in the organization and the firm's current culture. Creating a more customer-focused organization can be accomplished by altering any one of the four components, structure, systems, people, and culture, individually or together.

### Changing Culture through Structure

The organization's culture is a function of its structure. Changing culture through structure, however, is a slow process because in many instances it takes years to successfully implement an organizational change in structure. In the effort to create a more customer-focused organization, two approaches to changing the culture through structure have been tried: (1) using the marketing department as a change agent, and (2) restructuring the firm around the servuction system model.

## MARKETING DEPARTMENT AS CHANGE AGENTS

Marketing departments can be created in order to simply change the current orientation of the firm by creating a customer advocate within the organization. There is a real danger in this approach, however. Once the marketing department has been created, other departments may quickly transfer the complete responsibility for customer satisfaction to the marketing department.[15] Moreover, this transfer is likely to create open warfare among departments in the organization.[16]

Consider again the logic of the operations and the marketing departments. Operations departments, by their very nature, tend to be cost driven. Their focus is on evaluating the operation to find costs to save and procedures to simplify. This outlook tends to have a short time horizon. Marketing, by comparison, is looking for product enhancements in order to create a competitive advantage. The creation of such an advantage is not something that firms can expect to achieve in the short run.

The coordination of conflicting departments such as marketing and operations often requires the use of unconventional management techniques. To allow the logic of the different groups to mesh and to allow them to understand one another, a number of strategies have been suggested by organizational-behavior theory. **Interfunctional task forces** are a classic way of forcing individuals with diverse viewpoints to work together and to develop a better understanding of one another's perspectives. In the same way, **interfunctional transfers** can create informal networks of individuals from different departments who understand and trust one another.

For example, operations managers who are promoted to run a marketing department will face initial problems. Their orientation is toward operations, but their new roles require a marketing perspective. If such a transfer can be achieved successfully, the result is usually a general manager who makes rational and clear trade-offs between operations and marketing. Moreover, it also creates a marketing person who has direct contacts in the operations group and who can overcome many of the traditional barriers to change.

Once the organization has achieved a strong customer orientation, the marketing department can shrink. For example, in the early 1980s, many professional service firms created marketing departments in this way. The departments focused on advertising but also on research and customer satisfaction surveys. The result was a shift in the culture of the firm and the recognition of the importance of the customer's needs and expectations.

## RESTRUCTURING AROUND THE SERVUCTION MODEL

A number of service firms have explicitly or implicitly restructured around the servuction model. For example, one major airline has all departments that have direct customer contact report to the head of marketing. Only engineering and the flight crew (pilots) report to the head of operations. Combining all customer-contact departments with the marketing group has reversed the arguments from

**interfunctional task forces**
Problem-solving group in which individuals with diverse viewpoints work together and develop a better understanding of one another's perspectives.

**interfunctional transfers**
Moving, via promotion or transfer, an employee from one organizational department to another to foster informal networks among departments.

"It will cost too much; it is inefficient" to "The customer needs this; how can we make it happen?"

## Changing Culture through Systems

The firm's culture is also a function of the systems put in place that control, evaluate, promote, and recognize the firm's personnel. A number of approaches have been used to change culture through these systems. Some firms, for example, have started to give bonuses to managers at all levels based on the firm's customer satisfaction scores. The firm's overall research effort can be tailored to measure satisfaction down to the branch level, and managers can be rewarded for improved scores. Unfortunately, the problem with this approach is that only part of the customer's satisfaction is under the control of management. The customer's expectations can be raised by competitive offerings, and satisfaction scores can drop as a consequence.

Another approach has been to introduce revenue into branch manager targets. A major New York bank wanted to change the retail branch manager orientation from one of considering only costs and security to one of considering customers first. The bank introduced a revenue-based performance evaluation system. For the first time, managers had to worry about where the customers came from and had to stop thinking of them as "people who made a mess of my branch." Early successes by a few managers produced interesting results. Up to 20 percent of managers left the company, claiming that this was not what they were hired to do. The balance of the managers woke up the bank's sleeping central marketing department to demand help in getting more customers. The long-term result of the change in the system was an increase in customers as well as in bad debt. The managers discovered that money is an easy product to sell, and the bank discovered it needed to revamp its credit control function.

Planning systems can also be used to change the orientation of companies. Formal marketing planning can drive organizations through the logic of marketing and can force them to develop an understanding of consumers' needs. Such planning exercises can eventually become mind-numbing, but for the first two or three cycles, the process can be educational for all personnel involved. This approach is all the more powerful if combined with training and/or direct attacks on culture.

## Changing Culture through People

Outsiders increasingly are being brought in to the marketing departments of service firms to try to change the orientation. Such an approach must be supplemented with the development of training programs inside the firm. Operations people need to be trained in marketing, and marketing people need to understand all the areas discussed in this book.

## Changing Culture Directly

Culture-change programs are becoming increasingly popular. These programs range from broad-scale educational activities to highly empowering personnel in

## TABLE 16.2

**Categorizing Culture Change Initiatives**

| Empowerment | Group | |
| --- | --- | --- |
| | Mixed | Family |
| **Low** | "Putting the Customer First" | "Orientation Change" |
| **High** | "Change the Way You Work" | "Change the Way We Work" |

Source: John E. G. Bateson, *Managing Services Marketing: Text and Readings,* 3rd ed. (Fort Worth, Tex: The Dryden Press, 1995).

order to re-engineer the firm's entire service delivery process around the customer. Table 16.2 provides a simple way to categorize such activities. Along one axis is the nature of the groups used. Mixed groups are cross-sectional or interdepartmental; family groups can be a department or a naturally occurring group based on process, such as all the individuals involved in loading a particular flight with passengers. The second axis deals with the level of empowerment given to employees. Low levels of empowerment imply that individuals will change their behavior but that the group will have no authority to change the processes and systems of the organization. High-level empowerment implies an ability to change the organization during the event or series of events. The slogans in the cells represent the hypothetical titles of such change programs, which often involve one or more meetings.

The top left cell refers to **"putting the customer first"** programs that take place in mixed groups within the organization. Seated together in sessions, personnel are lectured to and motivated to put the customer first. Through role playing, they are encouraged to recognize the importance of customers and change their behavior accordingly.

These types of programs can be very successful. To be successful, however, the new behavior needs to be reinforced on the job. If management and front-line personnel do not share the same level of enthusiasm and dedication toward the goal of creating a customer-oriented organization, the value of the lessons learned can be wiped out within hours. Without commitment to change, the new behaviors learned will be trivialized by colleagues, the old behaviors will be reinstated quickly, and the value of the program will be a total loss.

The top right cell, **"orientation change,"** overcomes these problems by processing personnel by family groups whose members can reinforce one another on the job. Both cells, however, focus on changing attitudes and individual behaviors. Changing organizational processes and systems are not part of these programs. This potentially produces role conflict as desired individual behaviors are stopped by organizational constraints such as the physical environment or the current operating system.

**"putting the customer first"**
The element of the culture change initiative that teaches personnel to put the customer first.

**"orientation change"**
The element of the culture change initiative that teaches "families" of personnel to reinforce one another on the job.

**"change the way you work"**
The element of the culture change initiative that allows personnel to break the rules in the context of serving their customers.

**"change the way we work"**
The element of the culture change initiative that teaches personnel to flowchart their activities and to re-engineer the process to better serve their customers.

**"Change the way you work,"** in the lower left cell, draws on the empowerment ideas described in detail in Chapter 10. It implies active empowerment of the personnel attending the program. Personnel are allowed to break the rules in the context of serving their customers. Because of the mixed group, however, this type of initiative is focused on the individual rather than on process-level empowerment.

The lower right cell, **"change the way we work,"** refers to initiatives that draw on many of the ideas in this book. Groups are in families and can be asked to flowchart their activities. They can then be asked to re-engineer the process to better serve their customers. The level of excitement in such groups is matched only by the anxiety of their bosses. Empowerment at this level really does place the boss in the role of coach and facilitator, and that is exactly what the boss's role should be. In creating a seamless organization, it is not management's job to force or dictate to employees to deliver service excellence. "Management's job is to put together a system that actually makes it possible to deliver quality service."[17]

## THE TACTICAL QUESTIONS RELATING TO SEAMLESSNESS: CONDUCTING A SERVICE AUDIT[18]

**service audit**
A series of questions that force the firm to think about what drives its profits and suggests strategies for competitive differentiation and long-term profitability.

One helpful approach in creating a seamless organization involves conducting a service audit that addresses a number of questions. The **service audit** directs the firm to think about the forces that drive its current profits and suggests strategies that have been discussed throughout this book that lead to competitive differentiation and long-term profitability. Moreover, the active involvement of front-line and top management personnel in conducting the audit facilitates the change in culture necessary to make the transition from the traditional manufacturing-management approach to an employee- and customer-focused, service-oriented approach.

### The Service Audit: The Profit and Growth Component

#### 1. HOW DOES THE FIRM DEFINE CUSTOMER LOYALTY?
Traditional measures of customer loyalty involve repeat sales, purchase frequency, and increases in amounts purchased. The firm also needs to consider the depth of the relationship. For example, the depth of a customer's banking relationship would be defined by types of transactions and accounts such as savings, checking, certificates of deposit, car loans, home mortgages, savings bond programs, safety deposit box rentals, and so on.

#### 2. DOES THE FIRM MEASURE PROFITS FROM REFERRALS?
Customer loyalty and satisfaction should also be measured in terms of the customers' willingness to refer the firm to friends, family, and colleagues. Given the importance consumers place on personal sources of information when selecting from among competing services, encouraging referrals or at least creating an atmosphere where customers freely inform others of the firm's services is crucial.

## 3. WHAT PROPORTION OF THE FIRM'S DEVELOPMENT FUNDS ARE SPENT ON RETAINING CUSTOMERS AS OPPOSED TO ATTRACTING NEW ONES?

As discussed in Chapter 15, the benefits of customer retention are clear. Current customers generate referrals, are less expensive to market to, purchase more services more frequently, are knowledgeable about the firm's operating system and therefore are more efficient users of the system, and are a great source of information about how the firm can better serve its targeted markets. Unfortunately, under traditional models of management, firms spend the majority of their resources on obtaining new customers while neglecting their existing customers.

## 4. WHEN CUSTOMERS DO NOT RETURN, DO WE KNOW WHY?

Service firms that excel pursue the bad news as well as the good. Traditionally, customer satisfaction assessments are obtained from current customers, who tend to rate the firm toward the more positive end of the scale. Uncovering the reasons customers defect reveals potentially fatal flaws in the firm's service delivery system that other customers have yet to discover and of which the firm may have been unaware. Consequently, contacting customers who have defected provides the firm with the opportunity to make improvements. Moreover, contacting customers who defect makes a positive impression that the firm cares about its customers and may actually lead to recapturing some lost customers.

## The Service Audit: The Customer Satisfaction Component

## 5. IS CUSTOMER SATISFACTION DATA COLLECTED IN A SYSTEMATIC MANNER?

In Chapters 12 and 13 we discussed a number of methods for assessing customer satisfaction and service quality. The key to successful measurement is consistency so that current assessments can be compared with past benchmarks. Satisfaction measurement should also occur on a regular basis and not only when problems arise. Catching minor problems early through periodic customer satisfaction surveys enables the firm to adjust the service delivery system before major gaps in service occur.

## 6. WHAT METHODS ARE UTILIZED TO OBTAIN CUSTOMER FEEDBACK?

The service quality information system discussed in Chapter 13 reveals a number of important methods of obtaining customer feedback on a variety of issues. The active solicitation of customer complaints, after-sale surveys, customer focus-group interviews, mystery shopping, and total market service quality surveys should be used in conjunction with employee surveys. Too often, employees are left out of traditional customer feedback loops even though they are exposed to vast amounts of information about customers' daily interactions with the firm.

## 7. HOW IS CUSTOMER SATISFACTION DATA USED?

Is the information used at all, or is it stuffed in the bottom drawer of a manager's desk? Customer satisfaction data needs to be shared with employees who provide the service. Front-line employees should feel they are an active part of the firm's overall goals and take pride in improvements in customer satisfaction scores. The data should reveal company strengths that can be used for promotional purposes and weaknesses that can be corrected through training programs or by redesigning the service system itself.

## The Service Audit: The External Service Value Component

### 8.  HOW DOES THE FIRM MEASURE VALUE?

One key to providing superior customer service is to define service value from the customer's perspective. Traditional approaches define value internally and frequently miss what is really important to customers. Remember, buyers' perceptions of value represent a trade-off between the perceived benefits of the service to be purchased and the perceived sacrifice in terms of the total costs to be paid.

### 9.  HOW IS INFORMATION ON CUSTOMER PERCEPTIONS OF THE FIRM'S VALUE SHARED WITHIN THE COMPANY?

Keeping customer information in the hands of top management does little to improve the service effort on the front line. By sharing information about customer perceptions with the front line, the employees become sensitized to the behaviors and outcomes that are really important to customers. Improvements made in these specific areas should increase customer satisfaction scores. Similarly, sharing the information with operations, marketing, and human resources personnel should assist each area in understanding the customer's perception of the entire service delivery process.

### 10.  DOES THE FIRM ACTIVELY MEASURE THE GAP BETWEEN CUSTOMER EXPECTATIONS AND PERCEPTIONS OF SERVICES DELIVERED?

Once customer perceptions are obtained, a comparison with customer expectations is vital in assessing customer satisfaction. Customer perceptions alone do not tell the full story. This point was made particularly clear in Chapter 13 regarding the SERVQUAL scale. Perception scores alone merely reflect whether customers agree with the statement, not whether what they are evaluating is really important to them. Including expectation measures increases the managerial usefulness of the information. Given that making improvements often involves a financial investment, comparing expectations with perceptions assists the firm in allocating resources to the most appropriate areas.

### 11.  IS SERVICE RECOVERY AN ACTIVE STRATEGY DISCUSSED AMONG MANAGEMENT AND EMPLOYEES?

Although many firms will spend vast amounts of time and effort to deliver the service right the first time, little discussion centers on appropriate courses of action for employees to take when things do not go according to plan. Consequently, employees are left to fend for themselves while dealing with unhappy customers, and it is apparent that employees often do a poor job in service recovery efforts. Chapter 14 stresses the benefits of both service failure and service recovery analysis. Actively tracking failures and recoveries identifies failure points in the system and allows the firm to minimize their occurrence by training employees in service recovery techniques.

## The Service Audit: The Employee Productivity Component

### 12. HOW DOES THE FIRM MEASURE EMPLOYEE PRODUCTIVITY?

If the firm does not measure what it really believes is important, employees will never pay attention to it. In addition, if productivity is measured simply in terms of output and outcomes and not by the behaviors used to achieve these outcomes, the firm may actually be rewarding employees for anti-customer-oriented activities. For example, the employee may be very curt with one customer so that a quick sale can be transacted with another customer who already knows what he or she wants. Service productivity measures such as timeliness, accuracy, and responsiveness need to be developed to reinforce these types of customer-oriented behaviors.

## The Service Audit: The Employee Loyalty Component

### 13. DOES THE FIRM ACTIVELY PURSUE STRATEGIES TO PROMOTE EMPLOYEE LOYALTY?

Employee loyalty to the organization is often visible to customers and directly influences customer evaluations of the firm. When employees feel more positive about the firm, customers feel more positive about the services the firm delivers. Preaching that employees are the firm's most important asset and then laying off employees in large numbers during periods of downsizing sends a hypocritical message to both employees and customers.

### 14. DOES THE FIRM SET EMPLOYEE RETENTION GOALS?

Although rarely is 100 percent the correct level, employee retention saves the firm funds in terms of recruiting and training costs. Additionally, customers prefer the continuity of interacting with the same personnel over time so much that the firm's personnel may be its key differential advantage over competitors. When service personnel do leave, their regular customers often seek them out at their new places of employment.

## The Service Audit: The Employee Satisfaction Component

### 15. ARE EMPLOYEE SATISFACTION MEASURES LINKED TO CUSTOMER SATISFACTION MEASURES?

Employee satisfaction is linked to increases in productivity and external service value. External service value is linked to customer satisfaction and the additional benefit of customer loyalty. The net effects of customer loyalty are increased revenues and profitability for the firm. The outcomes associated with employee satisfaction—external service values, customer satisfaction, customer loyalty, revenue growth, and increased profitability—provide feedback and reinforce the company's internal service quality and employee satisfaction.

## 16. ARE CUSTOMER AND ORGANIZATIONAL NEEDS CONSIDERED WHEN HIRING?

Southwest Airlines invites panels of customers to help select flight attendants. Customers are so sold on the idea that some take off time from their own work schedules to be on the selection team. Hiring people with good job skills is important in manufacturing. Hiring people with good job skills and good interpersonal skills is vital in services.

## 17. ARE EMPLOYEE REWARD PROGRAMS TIED TO CUSTOMER SATISFACTION, CUSTOMER LOYALTY, AND QUALITY OF EMPLOYEE PERFORMANCE?

Service firms wishing to enhance the customer focus of their employees must implement behavior-based reward systems that monitor employee activities and evaluate employees on aspects of their job over which they have control. Traditional, outcome-based reward systems often discourage the development of long-term relationships with the firm's customers in pursuit of short-term profitability.

## The Service Audit: The Internal Service Quality Component

### 18. ARE EMPLOYEES AWARE OF INTERNAL AND EXTERNAL CUSTOMERS?

The ideal service firm should work seamlessly as a team. Each member of the team should understand fully how individual performance affects the performance of other team members as they provide superior service to external customers. Consequently, employees need to understand that the firm's external customers are not the only ones who are depending on their efforts.

### 19. DO EMPLOYEES HAVE THE SUPPORT NECESSARY TO DO THEIR JOBS?

Does the firm just talk about providing superior service, or does it talk about it and back up it with the support necessary to get the job done right? Over the past few years, Taco Bell, a fast-food franchise, has emerged as a firm with some fairly progressive service strategies. Personnel are supported by the latest advances in information technology, self-managing team training, effective food service equipment, and work scheduling that enhances employee performance.

## The Service Audit: The Firm's Leadership Component

### 20. DOES THE FIRM'S LEADERSHIP HELP OR HINDER THE SERVICE DELIVERY PROCESS?

Service personnel frequently find that, even though they want to provide good service, their hands are tied by overbearing, conservative upper-management types. Frequently, upper management is far removed from the front line of the operation and has lost touch with the realities associated with daily service interactions. The leaders of successful firms act as enablers, coaches, and facilitators, and they are participatory managers who listen to employees and encourage creative approaches to solving old problems.

## 21. IS THE FIRM'S LEADERSHIP CREATING A CORPORATE CULTURE THAT HELPS EMPLOYEES AS THEY INTERACT WITH CUSTOMERS?

Top management sets the tone and provides the resources that support personnel who interact with customers. The links in the service-profit chain discussed in Chapter 10 reveal that employee satisfaction and customer satisfaction are directly related. Top management's job is therefore to create an organization culture in which employees thrive.

### The Service Audit: The Measurement Relationship Component

## 22. HOW DO THE PRECEDING MEASURES OF SERVICE PERFORMANCE IN THE SERVICE AUDIT RELATE TO THE FIRM'S OVERALL PROFITABILITY?

The preceding components of the audit provide strategic measures that aid the provision of superior service. Ideally, the contribution of each measure should be related to the firm's bottom line. Relating these measures to the firm's overall profitability provides a resounding message throughout the company that service and quality pay!

## SUMMARY

In pursuit of service excellence, the individual departments and functions of the firm must act in unison to create a seamless organization. The firm will not act as one if the current focus of the organization is on departmental and functional needs. The three-tiered model of service firms offers an alternative view of how the organization should focus its efforts by segmenting the operation into a customer tier, a boundary tier, and a coordination tier. The goal is to have those in the coordination tier work in harmony with personnel in the boundary tier so that customers experience seamless service.

Creating and supporting a customer-focused organizational culture is critical when developing a seamless operation. The firm's culture drives employee behavior and directly influences the quality of the firm's service delivery system and subsequent consumer evaluations of the firm's service effort. Firms can change the existing culture of the organization by changing the firm's structure, people-management systems, and/or key personnel, or they can change the culture directly through broad-based educational activities or re-engineering the firm's entire service delivery process.

Finally, by conducting a service audit, a seamless service culture is fostered as organizational personnel throughout the organization come to appreciate the challenges faced and the contributions made by everyone involved in the firm's final service delivery effort. The service audit deals directly with such issues as profit and growth, customer satisfaction, external service value, employee productivity, employee loyalty, employee satisfaction, internal service quality, leadership, and measures that assess the impact of each of these issues on the firm's bottom line.

The service audit also provides a framework for combining the materials that are discussed throughout this book. In closing, we hope that this book has helped develop your understanding of the special challenges involved in the marketing and management of service operations. With challenge comes opportunity, and as you well know, there are plenty of opportunities in the business community to make the service encounter a more productive and pleasant experience for everyone involved—customers and employees alike. The time has come to make a difference, and we look forward to writing about the difference you made in future editions of this book.

# Key Terms

Boundary tier
"Change the way we work"
"Change the way you work"
Competencies
Coordination tier
Culture
Customer tier
Customization/customer
  contact matrix
Expectations
Human resources logic
Interfunctional task forces
Interfunctional transfers
Internal logic

Marketing department
Marketing functions
Marketing logic
Marketing orientation
Needs
Operations logic
"Orientation change"
"Putting the customer first"
Seamless service
Service audit
Structure
Systems
Three-tiered model

# Discussion Questions

1. Discuss seamlessness as it relates to "tooth-to-tail" performance.
2. Discuss the fight for control among marketing, operations, and human resources personnel.
3. Define the following terms: marketing orientation, marketing functions, and marketing department. Why is it necessary to distinguish among these terms when discussing service firms? Relate your answer to the customization/customer contact matrix.
4. Discuss each tier of the three-tiered model of service firms separately and then as a combined unit.
5. What is the importance of organizational culture?
6. Explain the relevance of interfunctional task forces and interfunctional transfers as they relate to corporate culture.
7. Discuss the four approaches to directly changing culture as presented in the text.
8. What are the key components of a service audit?

# Notes

1. Benjamin Schneider and David E. Bowen, *Winning the Service Game* (Boston: Harvard Business School Press, 1995), 1–16.

2. This section adapted from John E. G. Bateson, *Managing Services Marketing*, 3rd ed. (Fort Worth, Tex.: The Dryden Press, 1995), 636–645.

3. Schneider and Bowen, *Winning the Service Game*, 199.

4. Bateson, *Managing Services Marketing*, 636–645.

5. Ibid.

6. C. Gronroos, "Designing a Long-Range Marketing Strategy for Services," *Long Range Planning* 13 (April 1980), 36.

7. R. B. Chase, "Where Do Customers Fit in a Service Operation?" *Harvard Business Review* 56, no. 6 (November–December 1978), 137–142.

8. W. Skinner, "The Focused Factory," *Harvard Business Review* 52, no. 3 (May–June 1974), 113–121.

9. Schneider and Bowen, *Winning the Service Game*, 1–16.

10. Ibid.

11. Ibid, 43.

12. Jane Kingman-Brundage, William R. George, and David E. Bowen, "Service Logic-Achieving Essential Service System Integration," *International Journal of Service Industry Management* 6, no. 4 (1995), 20–39.

13. Cynthia Webster, "What Kind of Marketing Culture Exists in Your Service Firm? An Audit," *The Journal of Services Marketing* 6, no. 2 (Spring 1992), 54–67.

14. Bateson, *Managing Services Marketing*, 636–645.

15. Gronroos, "Designing a Long—Range Marketing Strategy," 36.

16. C. H. Lovelock, E. Langeard, J. E. G. Bateson, and P. Eiglier, "Some Organizational Problems Facing Marketing in the Service Sector," in J. Donnelly and W. George, eds., *Marketing of Services* (Chicago: American Marketing Association, 1981), 148–153.

17. Schneider and Bowen, *Winning the Service Game*, 8.

18. This section was adapted from James L. Heskett, Thomas O. Jones, Gary W. Loveman, W. Earl Sasser, Jr., and Leonard A. Schlesinger, "Putting the Service-Profit Chain to Work," *Harvard Business Review* (March–April 1994), 165–174.

# *part four*

# CASES

*case 1*

# Emmy's and Maddy's First Service Encounter*

August 16, 1995. Our day began at 5:20 A.M. Hurricane Felix was predicted to hit the Carolina coast by the end of the afternoon, and I, like most of the other folks in southeastern North Carolina, had spent much of the previous day preparing the house for the upcoming storm. However, my wife and I had one extra concern that the others did not. My wife was six months pregnant with twins, and the prospect of spending lots of time in the car in the attempt to remove ourselves from harm's way was not particularly attractive. We had decided to wait until after my wife's doctor appointment at 9:00 A.M. to make a decision on whether we should leave or stay at home and ride out the storm. We never made it to the doctor appointment.

At 5:20 A.M. I was awakened by the fear in my wife's voice. Her water had broken, and the twins who were due on November 16 had apparently made up their collective minds that they were going to be born 13 weeks early. As first-time parents, we understood that our next move would be to go to the hospital; however, we were unsure as to the best mode of transportation given our particular situation. We had been informed by doctors that multiple-birth pregnancies were high-risk pregnancies and that every precaution should be taken. We quickly called the hospital and asked for advice. The hospital suggested that my wife take a shower, shave her legs, and pack some essentials and that it would be appropriate for us to drive ourselves to the hospital. Too stressed out to take any chances, we passed on the shower advice, quickly threw some things together, and drove to the hospital immediately.

## THE EMERGENCY DEPARTMENT

Upon our arrival at the hospital, we drove to the emergency entrance, and I quickly exited the car to find a wheelchair. I was immediately confronted by a security

---

*Originally published as K. Douglas Hoffman, "Rude Awakening," *Journal of Health Care Marketing,* 16, no. 2, 14–22, 1996.

guard who had been previously engaged in a casual conversation with another gentleman. I was informed that I could not leave my car in its current position. In response, I informed the security guard that I needed a wheelchair and would move the car after I was able to move my wife inside. The security guard pointed his finger in the direction of the wheelchairs. I grabbed the first wheelchair I could get my hands on and headed back out the sliding doors to assist my wife. At this point the security guard informed me that I had grabbed a juvenile-sized wheelchair. I headed back inside and grabbed a much larger wheelchair. I returned to the car, assisted my wife into the wheelchair, and headed back inside. The security guard, while continuing with his other conversation, instructed me to leave my wife with the triage nurse in the emergency department so that I could move my vehicle. I said goodbye to my wife and went to move the vehicle. When I returned, the security guard informed me that they had taken my wife to the maternity ward, located on the third floor.

My wife's encounter with the triage nurse was apparently short and sweet. The triage nurse had called for an orderly to move my wife to the maternity ward. On her way to the third floor, the orderly asked my wife whether she was excited about having the baby. She responded that she was scared to death because she was only six months pregnant. The orderly replied that there was "no way [she was] having a baby that early that [would] survive."

## THE MATERNITY WARD

As I exited the elevator on the third floor, I headed for the nurses' station to inquire about my wife's current location. I was greeted by several smiling nurses who escorted me to my wife's room. On my way I met another nurse who had just exited my wife's room. This nurse pulled me aside and informed me of the orderly's remarks. She continued on to assure me that what he said was not only inappropriate, but more importantly, inaccurate. She also informed me that my wife was very upset and that we needed to work together to help keep her calm. This particular nurse also informed us that she herself had given birth to a premature child, who was approximately the same gestational age as ours, a couple of years earlier.

By this time it was between 6:00 and 6:30 A.M. The resident on duty entered the room and introduced himself as Dr. Baker. My wife gave me this puzzled and bewildered look. The clinic where my wife is a patient consists of five physicians who rotate their various duty assignments. Dr. Baker is one of the five. However, Dr. Baker was 30 to 40 years older than the resident who had just introduced himself as Dr. Baker. What had happened was that the resident was nervous and had introduced himself as Dr. Baker rather than as Dr. Baker's assistant. Realizing his mistake, he embarrassingly reintroduced himself and informed us that Dr. Baker was the physician on call and that he was being contacted and kept informed of my wife's condition.

The resident left the room and soon reappeared with an ultrasound cart to check the positions of the babies. This time he was accompanied by a person I assumed to be the senior resident on duty. For the next 30 minutes or so, I watched the junior resident attempt to learn how to use the ultrasound equipment. He consistently reported his findings to us in sentences that began with, "I think. . . ."

Several times during this period my wife voiced her concern over the babies' conditions and the location of Dr. Baker. We were reassured by the residents that Dr. Baker was being kept informed and were told that being upset was not going to help the babies' conditions. After about 30 minutes I informed both residents that despite their advice for us to stay calm, they were not exactly instilling a lot of confidence in either one of us. The senior resident took over the ultrasound exam at this time.

Dr. Baker arrived at the hospital somewhere between 7:00 and 7:30 A.M. He apologized for not being there earlier and mentioned that he was trying to help his wife prepare for the ensuing hurricane. Sometime during this same time period, it was shift-change time for the nurses and also for Dr. Baker. New nurses were now entering the room, and now Dr. Johnson was taking over for Dr. Baker. By approximately 8:00 A.M. Dr. Baker had pulled me aside and informed me that after conferring with Dr. Johnson, they had decided that if my wife's labor subsided she would remain in the hospital for seven to ten days, flat on her back, before they would deliver the babies. It was explained that with each passing day the babies would benefit from further development. Their lungs were of particular concern.

Upon being admitted to the maternity floor, my wife had immediately been hooked up to an EKG to monitor contractions. Because of the small size of the babies, the contractions were not severe. However, as far as my wife and I could tell, the interval between contractions was definitely getting shorter. We were not overly alarmed by this, since we figured we were in the hospital and surrounded by health-care providers.

Between 8:00 and 8:30 A.M. two other nurses entered the room with lots of forms for us to complete. Because we were having twins, we needed duplicates of every form. The forms covered the basics: names, addresses, phone numbers, social security numbers, and insurance information—all the same questions that the hospital had sent to us weeks earlier, which we had completed and returned. The nurses asked us the questions, we supplied the information, and they wrote the responses.

By 8:30 A.M. Dr. Baker was informing me that, because of one of the babies' breach position, they would deliver the babies by caesarean section. Wondering whether the schedule had been moved up from a week to ten days, I asked when he thought this would be happening. He replied, "In the next hour or so." He then commented that labor had not subsided and that Dr. Johnson would be delivering the babies.

As my wife was being prepared for the operating room, I stood in the hallway outside her room. I noticed another physician limping down the hall with one foot in a cast and a crutch underneath one arm. He stopped outside my wife's room and began to examine her medical charts. He introduced himself as Dr. Arthur (he had broken his foot while attempting to change a tire). Dr. Arthur was the neonatologist, which meant nothing to me at the time. I eventually figured out that my wife had her set of doctors and that my unborn children had their own set of health care providers. Dr. Arthur asked to speak to my wife and me together. This is when he told us that 90 percent of babies such as ours survive and that 90 percent of those survivors develop normally. He was a calm, pragmatic individual who encouraged us to ask questions. He continued to explain that the babies would spend their next few months in the hospital's neonatal intensive care unit (NICU) and that, if all went well, we could expect to take them home within two weeks of their due date (November 16, 1995).

By 9:00 A.M. all hell had broken loose. My wife had dilated at a quicker pace than had been anticipated; the contractions had indeed been occurring at more frequent intervals. Some orderlies and nurses grabbed my wife's bed and quickly rolled her down the hall to the delivery room. I was thrown a pair of scrubs and told to put them on. I was further told that they would come back and get me if they were able. For 10 to 12 very long minutes I sat on a stool in an empty hospital room by myself, watching the Weather Channel track hurricane Felix. The volume on the television had been muted, and the only thing I could hear was a woman screaming from labor in the next room. Suddenly a nurse popped her head in the door and said that a space had been prepared for me in the delivery room.

## THE DELIVERY ROOM

As I entered the delivery room I was overwhelmed by the number of people involved in the process. Myself included, I counted 12 very busy people. I was seated next to my wife's head. She had requested to stay awake during the procedure. My wife asked me whether the man assisting Dr. Johnson was the junior resident. Sure enough, I looked up to see the junior resident wearing a surgical gown and mask with a scalpel in his hand. I lied and told her no.

Suddenly, we realized that we had not finalized our choices for names. Somehow, what we couldn't decide despite months of discussion we decided in 30 seconds. Our first baby girl, Emma Lewis (Emmy), was born at 9:15 A.M. Emmy weighed 2 pounds and was 14.5 inches long. Our second baby girl, Madeline Stuart (Maddy), was born at 9:16 A.M. and weighed 2 pounds, 2 ounces and also measured 14.5 inches long. Both babies were very active at birth, and their faint cries reassured my wife and me that they had at least made it this far.

Upon being delivered from their mother, the babies were immediately handed to Dr. Arthur and his staff, who had set up examination stations in the delivery room. Each baby had her own team of medical personnel, and I was encouraged by Dr. Arthur, who hopped on one foot across the delivery room, as I watched him examine the girls. The neonatal staff examining the girls "ooohed and aaahed" and almost in a competitive manner compared measurements about which baby had better vitals in various areas. Dr. Arthur then suggested that I follow the girls to the NICU to watch further examinations. He also made sure that my wife got a good look at both babies before they were wheeled out of the delivery room in their respective incubators. My wife and I said our goodbyes, and I was told I could see her again in the recovery room in about 20 to 30 minutes.

## THE RECOVERY ROOM

The recovery room and the delivery room are contained within the maternity ward on the third floor of the hospital. The NICU is located on the fourth floor, which is designated as the gynecological floor. The staff on the third floor is geared for moms and babies. The staff on the fourth floor, outside the NICU, is geared for women with gynecological problems.

After receiving the "so far, so good" signals from both my wife's and my babies' doctors, I was permitted to rejoin my wife in the recovery room. It was a basic hospital room with the exception that a nurse was assigned to the room on a full-time basis. One of the hospital volunteers from the maternity floor had taken pictures of each of the babies and taped them to the rails of my wife's hospital bed. The nurses of the third floor maternity ward asked my wife whether she would like a room on the fourth floor so that she could be closer to her babies when she was ready to start walking again. She agreed and spent the next four days in a room on the fourth floor.

Hurricane Felix stayed out to sea and moved up the coastline, missing us completely.

## THE FOURTH FLOOR

My wife's private room on the fourth floor was small, dingy, and dirty. From an emotional standpoint, the staff on the fourth floor were not prepared to deal with our situation. In fact, one nurse, after discussing the situation with my wife, asked whether we were going to have the babies transported to a major university medical center three hours away.

My wife's quality of care on the fourth floor was sporadic. Some of the nurses were good and some were inattentive—slow to respond to the patient's call button and blaming nurses on other shifts when medications and other scheduled or promised care (e.g., providing the patient with a breast pump) were not provided on a timely basis. Although it might seem trivial to many, the breast pump represented my wife's primary contribution to the care of her babies. It was the only thing she could control. Everything else was out of her hands. My wife was instructed to begin pumping as soon as she felt able, yet because of her location away from the maternity ward, obtaining a breast pump was difficult and became a sore point for my wife.

After receiving a courtesy call by the hospital's patient representative, my wife expressed her concerns. Shortly thereafter, personnel were changed, the quality of care improved, and we were moved to a much larger room on the third afternoon.

## THE NEONATAL INTENSIVE CARE UNIT

The NICU (pronounced "nick-u") is located in an isolated area of the fourth floor. The primary purpose of the NICU is to provide care for premature babies and for full-term babies requiring special care. The number of babies cared for each day throughout our stay typically averaged 12.

Emmy and Maddy spent approximately seven weeks in the NICU. The staff made every effort to explain the purpose of every piece of machinery and every tube that seemed to cover the babies' bodies. I was repeatedly told that I could and should ask questions at any time and that the staff understood that it was an overwhelming amount of information; hence, it was understandable and acceptable to ask the same questions day after day. The staff had made signs welcoming each of the babies in bright neon colors and taped them above each of their stations. For ease of access, the girls had not yet been place in incubators. They laid in what looked like large in/out baskets with raised borders. We celebrated weeks later when they finally had enough tubes removed so that they could be moved into incubators, what we called "big-girl beds."

During the first three days, I walked into the NICU to find baby quilts at each of the girls' stations. A local group called Quilters by the Sea had sewn the quilts; apparently they regularly provide the quilts for infants admitted to the NICU. For some reason that I still cannot explain today, the fact that someone outside the hospital who I did not know cared about my girls touched me deeply. The signs the staff had made and the babies' patchwork quilts humanized all the machines and tubes. Somehow, I was no longer looking at two premature infants—I was looking at Emmy and Maddy.

Throughout the girls' stay in the NICU, the quality of care delivered was primarily exceptional. The staff not only excelled at the technical aspects of their jobs but also were very good in dealing with parents. Some of the personal touches included numerous pictures of each of the girls for us to take home, homemade birthday cards with pictures from the girls for Mom and Dad on their birthdays, baby stickers on their incubators, and notes of encouragement from staff when a milestone, such as weighing 3 pounds, was achieved. We arrived one day and found pink bows in the girls' hair. The nurses even signed Emmy's and Maddy's names on the foot cast worn by the baby boy in the next incubator.

Parental involvement in the care of all the infants was encouraged, almost demanded. I had somehow managed to never change a diaper in my life (I was 35 years old). I was threatened, I think jokingly, that the girls would not be allowed to leave the NICU until I demonstrated some form of competency with diaper changes, feedings, and baths. The primarily female staff made me feel at times that my manhood was at stake if I was not able to perform these duties. Personally, I think they all wished they'd had the same chance to train their husbands when they'd had their own babies. I am now an expert in the aforementioned activities.

As for the babies' progress, some days were better than others. We celebrated weight gains and endured a collapsed lung, blood transfusions, respirators, alarms caused by bouts with apnea and bradycardia, and minor operations. Throughout the seven weeks, many of the staff and three neonatologists became our friends. We knew where one another lived, we knew about husbands, wives, boyfriends, and kids. We also heard a lot about the staff's other primary concern, scheduling.

## THE GROWER ROOM

Sometime after the seventh week, we "graduated" from the NICU and were sent to the Grower Room. The Grower Room acts as a staging area and provides the transition between the NICU and sending the babies home with their parents. Babies who are transferred to the Grower Room no longer require the intensive care provided by the NICU but still require full-time observation. As the name indicates, the Grower Room is for feeding and diaper changing, administering medications, and recording vital statistics—basic activities essential for the growth and development of infants. The Grower Room held a maximum of four infants at any one time.

The Grower Room was located in a converted patient room located in the back corner of the second floor, which is designated as the pediatric floor of the hospital. In general, the Grower Room was staffed by one pediatric nurse and visited by the neonatologists during rounds. As parents who were involved in the care of their babies, being transferred to the Grower Room meant that we had to establish new relationships with another set of health care providers all over again.

Compared with the "nurturing" culture we had experienced in the NICU, the Grower Room was a big letdown. One of the first nurses we were exposed to informed us that the nurses on the second floor referred to the Grower Room as "The Hole," and that sooner or later they all had to take their turn in "The Hole." We asked the reasons for such a name, and the nurse explained that because the room was stuck back in the corner, the rest of the staff seldom allowed the "grower nurse" to take a break, and because of the constant duties involved, the grower nurse could never leave the room unattended. It was also explained that some of the nurses simply did not feel comfortable caring "for such small little babies." We quickly found that this attitude had manifested itself in a lack of supplies specifically needed for smaller babies, such as premature-sized diapers and sheepskin rugs inside the incubators.

Furthermore, it quickly became apparent that friction existed between the NICU and the Grower Room. The Grower Room was very hesitant to request supplies from the NICU and on several occasions would delay informing NICU that an occupancy existed in the Grower Room. The reason for delay was so that the Grower Room nurse could catch up on other duties and avoid having to undertake the additional duties involved in admitting new patients. The "successful delay" would pass on these activities to the nurse taking the next shift. Apparently, the friction was mutual, since one of the nurses in the NICU commented to us on the way out of the NICU, "Don't let them push you around down there. If you don't think they're doing what they should, you tell them what you want them to do."

When the Grower Room was in need of supplies for our babies and others, I (on more than one occasion) volunteered to ask for supplies from the NICU. Although my foraging attempts were successful, I definitely got the feeling that there was some reluctance on both sides for me to do this. I suspected that the Grower Room nurses did not want to ask for any favors, and the NICU staff felt that it was not their job to keep the Grower Room stocked with supplies. Moreover, I suspect that the NICU and the Grower Room operate from different budgets. Stocking the Grower Room is not one of the objectives of the NICU's budget. However, from my side, my babies needed supplies, and I did not care about either department's budget.

After a few dark days, we established new relationships with the Grower Room personnel and became very involved with the care of our babies. After spending seven weeks in the NICU, we felt more familiar with each baby's personal needs than some of the Grower Room staff were. Recognizing our level of involvement, most of the staff looked forward to our visits, since it meant less work for them. By now we had learned to ask lots of questions, to double-check that medications had been provided, and to develop a working relationship with Grower Room personnel. Looking back, it was almost as though we and the Grower Room staff trained each other. At the conclusion of our Grower Room experience, my wife and I felt that we had met some good people, but also that the quality of the experience was far lower than what we had grown accustomed to in the NICU.

## NESTING

Once the babies had "graduated" from the Grower Room, our last night in the hospital was spent "nesting." Friends of ours joked that this must have involved searching for twigs, grass, and mud. The nesting rooms were located on the second floor of the hospital, in the same general location as the Grower Room. Nesting allows the parents and the babies to spend a night or two together in the hospital before they go home. During the nesting period, parents are solely responsible for all medications, feedings, and general care of the infants. The nesting period allows the parents to ask any last-minute questions and to smooth the transition from, in our case, nine weeks of hospital care to multiple infant care at home.

The nesting room itself was a small patient room that consisted of one single bed and a fold-out lounge chair. By now the babies had been moved from their incubators to open, plastic bassinets that were wheeled into the room with us. Each baby remained attached to a monitor that measured heart and breathing rates. To say the least, space was limited, but for the first time in nine weeks, the four of us were alone as a family.

Throughout the 22 hours we nested, we were frequently visited by neonatologists, nurses who continued to take the babies' vital signs, the babies' eye doctor, social workers who were assigned to all premature baby cases, hospital insurance personnel, and a wonderful discharge nurse who was in charge of putting everything together so that we could get out the door. Nine weeks to the day after we had entered the hospital, we took our two 4-pound babies home.

## Exercises
..............................................................................................................................................

1. Develop a molecular model for this hospital.
2. Using the Servuction model as a point of reference, categorize the factors that influenced this service encounter.
3. How do the concepts of inseparability, intangibility, and heterogeneity apply to this case?
4. Discuss corrective actions that need to be taken to ensure that subsequent encounters run more smoothly.
5. How would you measure customer satisfaction in this situation?

# Epilogue

As of August 1996, Emmy and Maddy both weighed approximately 18 pounds and appeared to be in good overall health. One of the NICU nurses we met at the hospital helps us out in our home on a regular basis, and we have kept in touch with many of the NICU staff as well as with Dr. Arthur. The charges for our hospital stay were more than $250,000. This bill did not include any of the physicians' (e.g., neonatologists, eye doctors, surgeons, or radiologists) charges. Emmy recently returned to the hospital for a cranial ultrasound, which is an outpatient service (the results were negative for brain bleeds, and Emmy is fine). Despite her previous lengthy stay in NICU, we once again had to provide the hospital with all the insurance information. Ironically, the only information the outpatient service had about Emmy was that her "responsible party" was Maddy.

In terms of our overall experience, we are thankful for the lives of our babies and for the health of their mother. We are particularly grateful to the staff of the NICU and to Dr. Arthur.

# Managing the Service Experience: "Police Gas Mile High Fans"*

It's football season once again sports fans, and it's yet another opportunity to demonstrate the difficulty of managing the service encounter. Like most service encounters, a football game is a shared experience, since other fans can greatly impact the level of enjoyment an individual derives from the event. This particular game between Colorado State University (CSU) and the University of Colorado (CU) at Mile High Stadium (the home of two-time defending Super Bowl champions the Denver Broncos) was no different—except for the fact that the game ended in a police action in which fans were doused with pepper spray and tear gas. Hence the headline: "Police Gas Mile High Fans."

ESPN's *Sportscenter* reported the story approximately as follows: At the request of the Denver Broncos, police dressed in riot gear marched down the sidelines with four minutes left in the game to the Colorado State University student section to protect the field and the goal posts. (CSU was in the process of upsetting its longtime intrastate rival CU to the tune of 41–14, and there were not many CU fans remaining in the stands at this point. The police were informed that CSU students were planning on storming the field.) In response to the armed police presence, CSU students began pelting the police with everything from ice-filled soft drink cups to the occasional can of corn and chili. In response to the pelting and the attempt by a handful of students to take the field, the Denver police began pepper spraying the offending students and eventually launched tear gas canisters into the stands to dissuade others from charging the field. In response to the

---

*Denver Post* headline, September 5, 1999.

gassing, most fans hurriedly headed for the exits while others threw the tear gas canisters that had landed in the stands back on the field, aiming for the police. By the time the melee was over, fans young and old, the CSU pep band, players and coaches, the police, and the media were all suffering from the effects of tear gas.

The reputations of the CSU fans and the Denver police were both tarnished by the event.

## WHAT TO DO NEXT YEAR?

Now it's your turn! Currently there is much talk about whether the CSU/CU game should even be played at Mile High Stadium. In fact, the mayor of Denver, the Denver police, and members of both schools' administrations are meeting this week to discuss the future venue for this game. For years the game had been played at each school's home campus, and this was only the second time the teams had met in Denver (the inaugural meeting was the year before). Below is listed a number of factors that might aid you in making the following decisions: (1) Should the two teams continue to meet at Mile High Stadium; and (2) If so, how would you manage this encounter so everyone doesn't leave crying again?

- Beer was sold at the game and tailgating was permitted in the parking lot starting at 12:00 noon. The game began at 5:00 P.M.
- Staging the game at Mile High promoted the game as a Colorado event instead of as a campus event. The last two games were sellouts. Seating at Mile High is approximately 76,000, while seating at CSU is approximately 36,000.
- Since the game has been played at Mile High, the two respective colleges have been less involved in the management of the game itself. When games are played on campus, each school manages traffic flow, parking, crowd control, and so on.
- The University of Colorado's locker room was located beneath the CSU student section.
- The Denver police have repeatedly used pepper spray and tear gas on sports fans in other situations, including post-game celebrations of the Avalanche and Broncos championship games.
- A chain-link fence stood between the field and the stands.
- College students on a number of campuses are becoming less intimidated by police.
- The Denver Broncos organization and the police denied earlier reports that the Broncos had requested police to protect the field and the goal posts.
- Before kick-off, CU was ranked fourteenth nationally. In contrast, CSU was picked to finish sixth in the newly formed Mountain West Conference.
- National television coverage dictates when the game is played, and the additional revenues generated by coverage contribute greatly to the schools' athletic funds.
- Fans sitting in the alumni section at the game stated, "There was no way to escape, no warning [about the tear gas or mace], there was no way to help friends."[1]

- The CSU band director was inundated with pepper spray while attempting to help injured students. The spray permeated his uniform, blinded him, and began to burn his skin. "I asked the event staff for help but no one was responding. I told the band to start running up the seats and get out as fast as they could."[2]
- The Denver police department continues to avidly defend its actions in response to drunken and overzealous fans. Although many have criticized the action taken by police, many others credit the police for preventing a potential riot.

# Exercises

1. What would your recommendation be? Continue to play at Mile High or stay on campus?
2. If the game continues at Mile High, what suggestions would you provide?
3. Do you think that the fact that the fans who were originally targeted by police were college students as opposed to a "traditional adult population" factored into the actions taken by the police?
4. What unique steps does your school take to manage the sporting event experience?

# Notes

1. Lyle, L'Shawn, "Students Express Anger," *The Rocky Mountain Collegian,* 108, no. 12, September 8, 1999, p. 1.
2. Olson, Eric, "CSU Band Members Speak Out Against Denver PD," *The Rocky Mountain Collegian* 108, no. 12, September 8, 1999, p. 1.

*case 3*

# SpaceDisk Inc.: Establishing a Global Internet-based Infrastructure Service Targeted at ISPs, ASPs, and Private End-Users

SpaceDisk, Inc., started out as a provider of free virtual disk space on the Internet in January 1999. It was hoping to generate revenues from subscriptions and advertising. Within one year, and reacting to changing conditions, SpaceDisk transformed itself into a company with a global marketing strategy to become the world's largest Distributed Applications Platform (DAP) provider. It was then aggressively rolling out a revolutionary Internet infrastructure platform that placed applications on fast local servers directly hooked on to the Internet service provider's (ISP's) backbone networks; it thereby bypassed the heavy traffic on the Internet. The company also established links with firms like Sun Microsystems and IBM to develop applications and maintain its server network. This case study shows the development of SpaceDisk's business model from just offering free disk space on the Internet to becoming a high-value-added provider of DAP infrastructure services within less than eight months.

## INTRODUCTION

In January 1999 S. Mohan incorporated SpaceDisk, Inc, his latest venture. Based in San Jose, California, SpaceDisk was aiming to become the global backbone for the next generation of Internet-based applications. The company claimed to be the world's first Internet DAP provider. SpaceDisk hoped to attract 20 million users, a large number of the world's top 100 ISPs, and leading content (from music, to video, to training) and application software providers (ASPs) to their latest offer of a proprietary, secure Internet DAP.

Mohan envisioned installing a seamless and efficient pipeline that offered powerful value propositions to three parties. First, SpaceDisk offered users fast access to their personal files (including E-mail, photos, and music clips) and to their applications (from word processing to accounting packages), which could be bought, rented, or paid on a per-use basis. SpaceDisk saw its service as the logical extension on of the current servers sitting on local area networks (LANs), where nowadays much of the software and data files are stored on servers. Mohan envisages that in the future this software and data would be sitting on secured servers on high bandwidth networks using SpaceDisk's DAP infrastructure. This would also allow users who were then not linked to servers (e.g., home users, small office/home office [SOHO], small and medium enterprises [SMEs]) to use SpaceDisks to have virtual servers for their software and files.

Second, ISPs could use SpaceDisk to create a loyal and more engaged customer base as well as new revenue streams. The ISPs could offer SpaceDisk as a value-added service to their subscribers. At the same time SpaceDisk reduced the ISPs' international telecom charges, since all these applications and files would be sitting on SpaceDisk servers directly linked to the ISP's backbone network. This way the ISP would not have to pay international data traffic fees (which was in contrast to fees incurred by users who, for example, accessed their Hotmail accounts in the U.S.).

Third, SpaceDisk offered ASPs a worldwide potential client and user base. ASPs could use the subscriber base of SpaceDisk (and subscribers of SpaceDisk's partner ISPs) to distribute their software to millions of users worldwide. This is also where SpaceDisk saw the greatest revenue potential. Users already were used to paying for software and high-value-added content, and purchase, subscription, and usage revenues would then be split between the ASPs, the ISPs (who would own the subscribers and would bill the fees with their normal internet access invoices), and SpaceDisk, who would provide the servers and the infrastructure (i.e., its DAP).

This case study describes the path and challenges SpaceDisk encountered from its initial idea of simply offering free storage space on the Internet with a revenue model mainly based on advertising and selling of merchandise, to the novel concept of its DAP. More information on SpaceDisk and its holding company, e.Com Services, can be found at www.spacedisk.com, www.myspacedisk.com, and www.ecom.com.sg.

## THE INITIAL PRODUCT CONCEPT: MYSPACEDISK

In the early stages of SpaceDisk's entry into e-business its business model was rather simple. A free "virtual disk space" server branded MySpacedisk was introduced to allow private users to store and access their files remotely. Mohan explained, "MySpacedisk allows anyone to save, organise, and retrieve files, including image, sound, music and video files [using our servers] via the Internet. Users' information can be stored indefinitely in MySpacedisk in a safe and secure manner. Also, all these files can be viewed and downloaded from any Internet-connected PC. Users of MySpacedisk will only have to register and join as a member. Members can then access their storage space on our servers. Apart from sending and storing one's own files into the remote server, users can also send files to another MySpacedisk or Internet user much like sending E-mail to someone else today."

A further value proposition was the creation of shared server space. MySpacedisk allowed multiple users to be authorized to share files and folders. Interested target groups for this application could be students (especially at higher levels) working on projects, freelancers, SOHO workers, or consultants working from different locations on the same case. It could also be a substitute to free homepages on the Web. This service was open to anyone who liked to have his or her own "close-by" storage space on the Internet. That is, to be able to use this service, one did not have to be a subscriber of one of SpaceDisk's ISP partners.

The idea of "accessing anywhere" would be especially attractive to Internet users who accessed the Internet from multiple locations and needed access to their stored information. A survey (published on the Internet site estats.com) showed that whereas 45 percent of Internet users access the Web only from home, there were 47 percent who accessed the Web from multiple locations such as home, school, and workplace. This potential usage of the Internet from various locations spurs the need for accessing the same information from different places. In such a case, hard drives are useless (unless they reside on a notebook and are carried around), and floppy disks need to be carried everywhere and have severe capacity limitations. MySpacedisk hoped to become an obvious solution, since it could be accessed from anywhere and was close to the user—almost like a virtual hard disk.

MySpaceDisk aimed at providing members with a service of collecting and keeping their valuable information in a safe and secure site for as long as they wished. They would not have to worry about corrupted floppy disks, crashing hard disk drives, or their storage mediums becoming obsolete, since MySpaceDisk would handle all these issues. The company offered a capacity of 25 megabytes (MB) for free and charged a small fee for users who need more capacity. Starting January 2000, in the face of increasing competition, MySpaceDisk increased the storage space allocated to each charter member (existing individual members and members of partner ISPs) account, which automatically received 40 MB of space free. New applicants continued to receive 25 MB free.

Mohan felt that MySpaceDisk was unique in the Internet world, not only because it provided large amounts of storage space, but also because it offered storage with unparalleled ease-of-use, bundled with a range of features for users, which at the time the service was designed (in 1998) could not be found on any other Internet site.

## POTENTIAL APPLICATIONS OF MYSPACEDISK

Mohan saw tremendous application potential for MySpaceDisk because it allowed users to define their own uses for the platform. He explained further, "We will, in addition to its basic functions, create a number of 'killer' applications that enable users to maximise the potential of SpaceDisk. For example, we intend to create a Music Library, an Image Library, and an electronic Book Shelf (for storing e-books)." In April 2000, MySpaceDisk introduced the Media Album, an application jointly developed with CoolConnect, a Singaporean firm that ran a network of virtual communities. The Media Album allowed SpaceDisk users to upload images and organize them into "albums" for easy viewing. SpaceDisk intended to develop more such applications with CoolConnect in the near future.

Mohan elaborated that, with emerging online video and music streaming technologies, Internet users everywhere eventually would require a safe place to store, classify, and later retrieve music, without worrying about storage mediums and longevity issues. Traditional hard disk and floppy media are not suitable for long-term storage; rewritable compact disks (CD-RW) are useful, but when standards change, and they usually do, currently used CD-Rs and CD-RWs will become obsolete.

In May 2000 MySpaceDisk launched Space Explorer 2.1, an easy one-click system that simplified the uploading and downloading of files to and from MySpaceDisk servers. A customized icon appears on the Windows desktop, and users can simply drag and drop files in the familiar Windows folder format. This integration into the Windows desktop interface simplified the management of files in MySpaceDisk, since there was no need to manually access the MySpacedisk Web site. The access was done in the background, and the user could manage their MySpaceDisk drive in a similar way to their current C or D drives.

Future applications in the pipeline were a quick search feature that would allow users to search their own SpaceDisk or the Web for information on a particular topic. This would enable them to easily access information and to store, retrieve, and distribute information more quickly. Mohan planned to license an existing search engine like AltaVista or Excite and integrate it into SpaceDisk.

## REVENUE MODEL FOR MYSPACEDISK

In the initial start-up phase of SpaceDisk, Mohan was looking at two main revenue streams: first, subscription to premium services from MySpacedisk, and second, advertising revenue.

First, MySpacedisk's major selling point was planned to be the provision of free space on the Internet along with a set of tools that helped people organize and manage their data more efficiently. Having looked at the potential usage base, SpaceDisk decided to segment its users into different membership types, with the amount of space provided as the main service- and price-differentiating factor. Subscription fees to server space of more than the free 40 MB per user were planned to at least initially form a relatively large percentage of SpaceDisk's revenues.

Second, like many high-traffic sites, MySpaceDisk hoped to sell advertising space in the form of banners, sponsorships, and the like. This was the most common model but the hardest to execute, being located in Asia, given that even popular Web sites, such as the homepages of large ISPs like Pacific Net and SingNet, in Singapore generate less than 1 percent of their revenues from advertising.

# CHALLENGES FACED BY MYSPACEDISK

SpaceDisk had encountered a number of challenges that seriously threatened its initial business model, and which eventually led SpaceDisk to the development of its DAP-based service. The key challenges were increasing competition, low potential advertising revenues, and problems in getting subscription revenues.

## Intensifying Competition

Although MySpacedisk was one of the first companies to offer free storage space on the Internet, this idea was copied and improved within a few months by several other start-ups. Since SpaceDisk launched its innovative MySpaceDisk service, dozens of competitors have responded with similar offerings. New start-ups such as MySpace.com (not related to MySpaceDisk) offer up to 300 MB free. From a narrow perspective, the value proposition seems the same—to increase membership by providing free storage space. Many of these firms have also launched desktop-integrated "drag and drop" software similar to SpaceDisk's Space Explorer 2.1.

## Lackluster Advertising Revenues

The initial excitement over Web advertising has taken a setback after high revenues failed to materialize. This is partly due to the over-saturation of the market with many Web sites vying for the same advertising dollars. More so, click-through rates (the percentage of visitors who click on an advertisement) as low as 1 percent challenge the effectiveness of Web advertising. Many Web surfers have learned to ignore marketing pitches on the Net. Perhaps as a result of these developments, advertising rates per 1,000 contacts on the Internet had been collapsing from around US$20 at the beginning of 1999 to in some cases as low as less than US$1 per 1,000 page hits by mid-2000. This crash in advertising rates made advertising-based business models unattractive for all but the largest players. SpaceDisk had to rebuild its business model.

Furthermore, the launch of Space Explorer 2.1 in May 2000 meant that users were then bypassing the company's Web site and uploading/downloading files directly from their desktop. This reduced the page views received by MySpaceDisk.com and made it even less attractive for advertisers.

## Problems in Getting Subscription Revenues

A problem faced by MySpaceDisk was that of raising subscription revenues from individual users. There was nothing stopping them from signing up and opening more than one account to gain additional storage space, apart from the inconvenience of having to deal with several accounts. Thus if this service were priced too highly, potential users would have found it more worthwhile to simply open several accounts. This problem could be attributed to the "gift culture" of the Internet. Historically, Internet users have been pampered with freebies and are now unwilling to pay for information and products unless they see a high value-add (Testerman et al 1998).

With business users, however, this problem was perceived as less critical. This was because businesses would require far more storage space than individual users, and it was neither efficient nor feasible for them to continually set up new accounts to obtain more space. A consideration was to have two pricing schemes—one for individual users, with smaller incremental storage space, and another for business users with higher capacity.

Mohan did not expect many members to pay for MySpaceDisk, mainly because connection speeds still made it difficult to upload and download very large files, since they held up dialup lines for a long time. However, he expected that to change in the medium-term future with the adoption of DSL and cable-speed Internet access.

## ADDING MORE VALUE: THE DEVELOPMENT FROM MYSPACEDISK TO DAP

The initial launch of MySpaceDisk was a success, and the company achieved a client base of more than one million subscribers within six months after its launch; this user base and name recognition were valuable assets. However, the rapid evolution of the Internet and the challenges faced by MySpaceDisk led Mohan to push the development of more value-added services than just free disk space. In addition, the revenue models also had to be realigned with recent market developments, which meant moving away from advertising models and less reliance on subscription fees for storage space.

## THE REVISED PRODUCT CONCEPT: DISTRIBUTED APPLICATIONS PLATFORM

The Internet infrastructure up to the year 2000 was designed to publish static information. However, Web-enabled applications, Internet appliances, wireless Internet tools, streamed video/audio, and demand user-specific (versus mass-published) content pushed the infrastructure beyond what it was capable of delivering. The result was a "World Wide Wait." The global Internet network linked private and public computer networks in a complex arrangement of Internet data centers (IDCs) or exchanges, which were the congested "centers" of the Internet.

All IDCs were interconnected through network access providers (NAPs). This "peering relationship" allowed data from one ISP to be transferred to another ISP without a direct connection. Most slow Internet connections were a result of congestion at the various IDCs and NAPs. A solution that emerged to relieve this congestion was the dedicated network. By directly linking major data centers around the world, these networks literally hopped over the Internet. However, the data still had to go through the data centers joining the queues of information before showing up on the user's screen (Figure 1). SpaceDisk had an idea of how its initial concept of disk space on the Internet could reduce this problem and developed its SpaceDisk Platform.

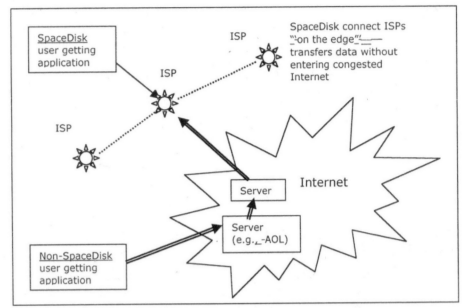

**Figure 1**       DAP Allows Bypassing of Congested Center of the Internet

## THE SPACEDISK DAP

Using its network Sun computers, the SpaceDisk DAP platform provided the base infrastructure. Each SpaceDisk cluster was composed of a configuration of servers, a computing array, a storage array, and network connectivity. The entire network was monitored and maintained on a real-time basis from IBM's network operations centers in the United States and Singapore. The Space Driver applications platform interface (API) was the software platform on which programs were run (e.g., MySpaceDisk and Sun Starportal). Mohan added that this was just the beginning, since SpaceDisk would be offering more and more applications and services. On top of this hardware platform, the company provided an open-source SpaceDisk applications programming interface (S-API) (Figure 2). SpaceDisk had chosen to make the S-API widely available to encourage innovation; thus everyone from large enterprises to individuals interested in software development could create Web-enabled, bandwidth-intensive programs that could be delivered by the SpaceDisk platform (*Business Wire,* 2000).

## STORAGE ON LOCAL SERVERS FOR QUICK ACCESS

SpaceDisk effectively reversed the current Internet infrastructure model. Instead of routing data through the center of the Internet as mentioned earlier, SpaceDisk linked up with ISPs and IAPs (Internet access providers) to place its servers on their backbone networks all around the world. The SpaceDisk servers could be likened to sitting on the edge of the Internet, avoiding the congested center. For

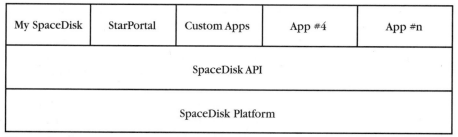

| My SpaceDisk | StarPortal | Custom Apps | App #4 | App #n |
|---|---|---|---|---|
| SpaceDisk API | | | | |
| SpaceDisk Platform | | | | |

**Figure 2**     **SpaceDisk DAP Platform**

example, users in Asia or Europe did not need to download their E-mail or data files from central servers sitting somewhere in the United States, but would only need to access their MySpaceDisk account sitting on the backbone of their local ISP. This translated into access speeds of 20 to 100 times faster (possible access speeds of below 20 ms) because the files come directly from a local server.

Storing data or content in the center of the Internet makes a lot of sense for standardized data that is being retrieved by many people from around the world. However, for customized or personal data, such as Microsoft Word files, E-mails, and personal music files, it makes more sense to provide the storage space close to the user. In anticipation of greater demand, SpaceDisk had been aggressively building capacity. John MacGilvary, SpaceDisk's senior vice president of sales and marketing, said, "SpaceDisk's networks can currently store one petabyte (1,000 terabyte) of information, or 83 pages of text for every person on earth" (Chng, 2000).

## DEVELOPMENT OF NEW AND TIE-INS WITH EXISTING APPLICATIONS

The fact that SpaceDisk provided capacity close to the user allowed for the introduction of new applications. SpaceDisk could develop the DAP for both applications and personal content. SpaceDisk had teamed up with Sun Microsystems as a technology partner to deploy an ASP infrastructure that would deliver Sun's Starportal office productivity suite through the ISPs (*Business Wire* Jan. 2000). With the collaboration between Sun and SpaceDisk, Sun hoped that the Starportal product would be made available globally within one year. The Starportal initiative was Sun's latest step in completing a strategy to provide complete end-to-end software solution to the industry, including tools, client software, middleware, and mission-critical software for the data center. Starportal software provided word processing, spreadsheet, presentation graphics, and other office software tools to any Web browser (and, in the future, portable devices). Starportal is based on the award-winning StarOffice suite, which was made available for Solaris operating environment, Windows, Linux, and OS/2 (*Business Wire* April 2000). More information can be obtained from www.sun.com/staroffice.

Custom business applications could also be provided on the ASP platform. SpaceDisk was working with other ASPs and independent software vendors to expand their offerings. In-house applications by SpaceDisk itself were MySpaceDisk and Media Album, with future applications for multimedia playback and storage in the works.

Defined simply, the DAP allowed Internet users to work from anywhere in the world (as long as they had access to an Internet-enabled PC) just like they would on their desktop PC. Users could access their personal files (downloaded from MySpaceDisk) and work on them using applications available online from the ASPs. Thus instead of carrying a notebook computer around, an executive could access and work on his files with his software remotely, on any computer. Of course, download times of the personal files would be faster at the home base where the Internet storage space is closest to the user.

## WORKING WITH INTERNET SERVICE PROVIDERS

SpaceDisk had established partnerships with ISPs serving more than 3.6 million customers and prospective SpaceDisk members. Through SpaceDisk these ISPs had found an innovative way to increase customer loyalty, provide a valuable new service, and add new sources of revenue.

By becoming the world's first DAP, SpaceDisk added value to the ISPs and its customers mainly through the provision of enhanced performance and reduction in connectivity costs. The ISP did not have to route access to SpaceDisk to outside their backbone network and did not have to pay international telecommunications fees. At the same time SpaceDisk allowed ISPs to provide content and applications (e.g., MySpaceDisk, StarPortal, other online applications) that enhanced the Internet experience. These value-added services leveraged on SpaceDisk's worldwide network of servers that promise 24/7 uptime.

In Asia, SpaceDisk had announced plans to roll out its DAP service to 4.9 million users starting in January 2000 (*ASP News* 2000), in a bid to become the world's largest ASP infrastructure. The company had agreements and memorandums of understanding in place for initial deployment with a number of Asia-Pacific ISPs. These ISPs included Singapore Telecom (Singapore, 300,000 subscribers), Dacom Corp. (South Korea, 2.3 million subscribers), Internet Knowledge Service Centre Co. (Thailand, 330,000 subscribers), and VADs Sdn. Bhd. (Malaysia, 490,000 subscribers). SpaceDisk planned to enter similar agreements with North American, European, and South American ISPs throughout the year 2000.

The ISPs were crucial partners because they provided the backbone networks on which the SpaceDisk servers resided. By July 2000 SpaceDisk would have launched 40 such networks in 21 countries (SpaceDisk 2000), and it aims to deploy 400 networks in 50 countries by December 2001.

## DELIVERING VALUE TO USERS

SpaceDisk offered considerable value to private users, SOHOs, and smaller SMEs. Using the DAP to access to data and applications online, any small firm could transform itself into a high-tech office within a short time. The set-up costs would be

minimal compared with the corporate firm having to build its own Intranet to provide employees with an application library and storage space. As Internet access
speeds within ISP networks become faster (e.g., via broadband connections from
the user to the ISP backbone network), it will become more convenient to use
software and access data files over the Internet.

## SPACEDISK'S NEW DAP-BASED REVENUE MODEL

### SpaceDisk ASP Rentals (Reseller Agreements)

A major portion of SpaceDisk's revenue was planned to be generated from the sale
and rental of applications over the DAP. SpaceDisk saw itself as an efficient platform for distributing software. With the proliferation of home PC users and small
and medium enterprises, the demand for online software rentals and trials was also
expected to increase dramatically. This was considered especially true for software
that is not heavily used enough to justify the purchase of a full license.

Apart from providing access to application software, SpaceDisk's DAP could
also be used to sell or provide access to a wide range of data (from video and
music files to financial data and corporate databases).

SpaceDisk planned to serve as the distribution infrastructure for application
and content providers and share the distribution revenues with the ISPs. The ISPs
would provide access to their subscriber base and would bill their subscribers for
the services used. The original main sources of revenue (subscription revenue for
disk space and advertising revenues) were sidelined by the revised business model.

## THE FUTURE AND CRITICAL SUCCESS FACTORS

Much of SpaceDisk's success came about as a result of the strong product and technology that SpaceDisk brought to the market, as well as the timely execution and
introduction of its DAP to the Asia-Pacific region. There is a great demand for an ASP
service that provides fast download times for its applications and stored data.
However, just as for its initial MySpaceDisk product, Internet competition is fierce
and there are few barriers of entry into SpaceDisk's market. It seems that three factors would be critical for SpaceDisk's success: first, the rapid deployment of a worldwide DAP infrastructure; second, the signing up the majority of the world's 100
largest ISPs; and third, gaining the distribution from ASPs for their high-value applications and from high-value-added content providers. Having established a critical
mass with end-users, ISPs, and ASPs and content providers would then make
SpaceDisk and attractive solution provider and partner for any of the sides involved.
Users would have access to highly attractive applications and content, ASPs and
content providers could distribute to a large number of users, and ISPs would generate additional revenues. This network effect would make SpaceDisk the preferred
provider for each of the parties involved, thereby effectively erecting barriers of
entry for newcomers, which in turn would protect its future revenue streams. Have
a look at their Web site to see whether they have been moving into this direction.

# Exercises

1. What are SpaceDisk's value propositions for its various potential user markets (e.g., home users and SMEs) and for ASPs and for ISPs?
2. What existing services and products is SpaceDisk substituting? What would be their competitive reaction to SpaceDisk's offer on the Web, if any?
3. Which user segments would you focus on first, and what would you recommend SpaceDisk do to penetrate these segments?
4. How could SpaceDisk develop a competitive advantage to prevent others from copying their DAP, ASP, and MySpaceDisk services (e.g., potential competitors such as Yahoo, America Online, or Microsoft)?

# Notes

SpaceDisk Inc, "SpaceDisk.com Launches ISP Benefit Program," Press Release, October 24, 1999.

SpaceDisk Inc, "SpaceDisk Sets Global Rollout Goals," Press Release, April 2000.

"SpaceDisk Launches onto Asia/Pacific: SpaceDisk Rolls Out to 4.9 Million Internet Users—First Step in Building World's largest Application Service Provider Infrastructure," *ASP News,* January 26, 2000.

"SpaceDisk Selects Sun as a Technology Partner to Deploy Applications Service Provider Infrastructure," *Business Wire,* January 26, 2000.

"SpaceDisk Appoints Michael Yap as Chairman; a Global Leader of the Future Brings IT Expertise and Influence," *Business Wire,* April 7, 2000.

Grace Chng, "Space for Everyone," *ComputerTimes,* February 2, 2000.

"eAdvertising Report," *e-Marketer,* December 1999.

"SpaceDisk Partners with ISPs for Application Services," *Newsbytes News Networks,* January 31, 2000.

Joshua O. Testerman et al, *Web Advertising and Marketing,* 2nd ed. (Roseville, California: Prima Publishing, 1998), 86–87.

Jochen Wirtz and S. Mohan, "E.Com Services—Launching SpaceDisk, an Innovative Internet-based Service," in *Principles of Marketing: An Asian Case Book* (Singapore: Prentice Hall, 2000), 162–168.

Souk Yee Wong, "Technopreneur: e.Com Is for e-Commerce," *Asian Entrepreneur,* December 1999.

# Web Sites

SpaceDisk Pte. Ltd.: www.SpaceDisk.com
MySpaceDisk Inc.: www.mySpaceDisk.com
E.Com Services Pte. Ltd.: www.ecom.com.sg
Sun Microsystems Inc.: www.sun.com/staroffice
E-Marketer: www.estats.com

# Source

Jochan Wirtz, Associate Professor, Department of Marketing, Faculty of Business Administration, National University of Singapore. Wirtz is also one of the minority private equity investors in E.Com Services Pte. Ltd., the current holding company of SpaceDisk Inc.

The author gratefully acknowledges the time and input provided by S. Mohan, founder of e.Com Services and CEO of SpaceDisk, Inc, and the research assistance of Sim Siew Lien and Adrian Tan Khiang Loong throughout the case development.

# case 4

# Airlines Attempting To Get a "Leg Up" on the Competition*

In it's biggest move since the introduction of business class over two decades ago, major airline carriers are now considering offering consumers more legroom. Airlines who are offering more legroom are hoping that this added perk will provide a differential advantage that is valued by consumers and subsequently will lead to higher profits. Consumers like Harry Dodge, a retired oil services company owner, agrees: "I have taken some transcontinental flights and developed some painful cramps in my legs. I swore I would never fly again. This extra room in coach will make a big difference for me."

Two of the major corporations leading the charge are United Airlines and American Airlines; however, their mutual goal of increasing profits is obtained through different routes.

## UNITED'S STRATEGY

United is dividing its coach section of the airplane into two classes—premium (referred to as economy plus) and economy. Passengers wanting the extra legroom will have to pay for it. For example, a United Flight from New York to Chicago would cost $1602 for first class, $1094 for economy plus, and $324 for the cheapest economy fare. However, even passengers who do not want to pay for the extra legroom may be affected. By increasing the amount of space between the rows of seats, planes will now have fewer rows and fewer seats. Consequently, fewer

---

*Source: "Plane Seats Get Bigger, Cost More: Airlines Betting Fliers Will Pay Extra for Added Legroom, *Rocky Mountain News*, February 28, 2000, pp. 2A, 31A.

economy seats will be available (best guess estimates are that United will reduce its economy seating by 5 percent), and customers will have to pay an additional 20 percent for the next available discount fare. In addition, some airlines are considering increasing the baggage-weight limit for higher-paying passengers, thereby reducing the limits for baggage and carry-ons for budget passengers.

United is betting on the continuation of a booming economy and that passengers will be willing to pay for the extra legroom. It also feels that by creating the economy plus class, the airline can serve more business class customers. Business travelers only purchase 20 percent of all airline tickets but account for more than 50 percent of the industry's profits. United is hoping that by attracting more business travelers it will rely less on budget travelers, whose fares do not always cover the costs of running an airline.

United's strategy evens the playing field in the sense that "you get what you pay for." On many of today's flights a business traveler seated in coach who had to book a flight on short notice may have paid triple what the budget passenger paid who is seated next to him. Richard Branson of Virgin Atlantic agrees: "Why should someone pay full-coach fare and get the same exact service as someone who paid $99 for the same ticket? There is no other industry where that happens."

## AMERICAN'S STRATEGY

American Airlines is currently implementing a $70 million plan that refurbishes its fleet by providing "economy passengers more legroom than they have had on any domestic carrier in 20 years." American's strategy is to remove two rows of seats in coach cabins (each row takes up 37 inches) and provide each of the remaining 21 rows in a typical Boeing 737 with 3 extra inches. The extra room is provided at no additional charge. Samuel Buttrick, an airline analyst at Paine-Webber, calls this approach "a big win for consumers . . . but it's not a way to increase profitability. What's good for the customer is not always good for the airline industry." Upon completion of the refurbishment project, American Airlines will have 6.4 percent fewer economy seats.

American believes that by offering the additional room at no cost its airline will become the number one choice for budget-minded consumers. According to American's Mike Gunn, executive vice president for marketing and planning, "By having a better product throughout coach, we think that we will be the first call that discount travelers make. We also expect to attract more business travelers who are willing to pay a higher-yielding fare."

## COMPETITIVE REACTION

British Airways is also increasing its legroom and is following a strategy similar to United by creating two different classes of coach section seats. Their premium coach seats will be called "world traveler plus." British Airways has yet to announce how its newest seating section will be priced.

Continental Airlines has characterized the latest moves made by British Airways, United Airlines, and American Airlines as "fads." According to Gordon M. Bethune, CEO of Continental Airlines, "We believe at Continental in giving people what they will pay for . . . and at the end of the day, many passengers want to pay the cheapest air fare. There's more to a good product than a few inches of extra legroom. That's a dumb approach by a bunch of mediocre airlines."

Other carriers, such as Delta Air Lines, are taking a "wait and see" attitude and like Delta are selecting to evaluate "various options" before jumping into anything too hastily. According to a recent Delta passenger survey, the most important criteria passengers consider when selecting an airline are flight schedule, price, and frequent flyer miles. The president of Air Travelers Association, David S. Stempler, agrees: "Seat size and the quality of meals are way down the list." Many other industry consultants are unsure whether the move to more legroom will be adopted universally across the industry.

## Exercises

1. Survey three fellow students and three business people and ask them to list and rank the top five criteria they consider when booking flights. Is legroom a consideration?
2. Referring back to the text (Chapter 4) and the managerial implications of multi-attribute models, how are United, American, and British Airways attempting to influence consumer decision making?
3. Discuss the fundamental differences in pricing strategy between United and American. Which pricing strategy is superior?
4. Discuss the reaction by competitive airlines. If you managed Delta Air Lines, what would you do? Would your suggestion differ if you managed Air Canada?

# The Case of Jim Bakker and PTL*

Jim Bakker created PTL, a Christian-oriented syndication network, in 1977. Before that time, Bakker had spent seven years working for the Christian Broadcast Network (CBN) owned by Pat Robertson. Bakker was not well educated in theology; he had dropped out of North Central Bible College after only three semesters. However, he was a natural on television, where he preached seed-faith and prosperity theology. These theological philosophies had originated with Oral Roberts in the 1940s and by the 1980s were widely embraced by most evangelists.

The seed-faith philosophy taught that if the believers served and gave to God, they would be rewarded by God with an abundance of material needs. Prosperity theology, also known as "health and wealth theology," asserted that God wanted the whole man, including his finances, to be healed. Those practicing prosperity theology recommended that believers pray for a specific outcome or object. Indeed, Bakker recommended that if his supporters prayed for a camper, they should specify the color; otherwise, they were asking God to do their shopping.

Bakker, then, did not preach hard work, saving, and responsible planning. Instead, he subscribed to the belief that the Spirit willed financial miracles as well as the actions of its followers. Bakker sermonized only on the love of God and ignored the topic of sin. This religious philosophy apparently appealed to a wide cross-section of middle-class Americans, since Bakker's congregation grew rapidly. Only 20 percent of Bakker's supporters came from his own Assemblies of God Pentecostal faith; the remainder came from other Pentecostal denominations, other Protestant denominations, and the Roman Catholic Church. Their contributions and support made PTL one of the three wealthiest and most popular media ministries in the nation. Consequently, by 1984 PTL served 1,300 cable systems and 12 million homes and had accumulated $66 million in revenues and

---

*Source: This case written by Judy A. Siguaw, Associate Professor of Marketing, Cornell University, and K. Douglas Hoffman, Professor of Marketing, Colorado State University.

$86 million in assets. PTL also had 900 people on the payroll and enormous operating expenses and debt.

Bakker often prayed with his television audience for the financing of specific projects—an evangelical university, a PTL show in Italy or Brazil, or the "Christian Disneyland" labeled Heritage USA. When the money for these projects poured in from viewers, however, Bakker would use the funds for something else because that was the way he had been moved by the Spirit. Because of this style of financial management, PTL debts mounted.

Thus it was in 1983 that Bakker conceived the idea of selling lifetime partnerships for donations of $1,000 or more. The lifetime partnerships entitled the contributors to three free nights of lodging and recreation at Heritage USA for the remainder of their lives—a package previously valued at $3,000. The funds from the lifetime partnerships were to be designated for completion of construction at Heritage USA. Unfortunately, Bakker sold lifetime partnerships to more donors than he could accommodate at Heritage USA. Further, as the number of lifetime partnerships sold escalated, contributions to the general PTL fund diminished. In order for PTL to continue, funds from the lifetime partnerships had to be diverted for everyday operating expenses. Consequently, construction on the lodging facilities at Heritage USA were never completed.

Bakker's followers were aware of where their contributions were being channeled. *The Charlotte Observer* regularly reported the financial actions of PTL and the Heritage USA construction cost overruns as well as Bakker's purchases, which included three vacation homes, gold-plated bathroom fixtures, an air-conditioned doghouse, and vast amounts of clothing and jewels. Indeed, Bakker would display the headlines on television to demonstrate the hostility of the press. His followers never wavered. They supported and even endorsed Bakker's materialistic lifestyle and promises of financial miracles. After all, Bakker was only acting out what he preached—a religion with standards of excess and tenets of tolerance and freedom from accountability. As a televangelist, he was free to preach what he pleased, and people were free to listen or not. No one coerced monetary contributions from Bakker's supporters—they willingly sent in funds and did not hold Bakker accountable for the disbursement of those funds.

Further, the government was aware of Bakker's actions. Bakker and his PTL operation were extensively investigated in separate incidences by the Federal Communications Commission, the Justice Department, and the Internal Revenue Service beginning in 1979. Even though the agencies had substantial evidence of misconduct involving millions of dollars, no efforts were made to stop Bakker, and none of the agencies moved toward indictment.

Bakker was allowed, indeed encouraged, in his behavior because he personified the culture of the 1980s. No government agency or public outcry arose to stop him until after Bakker, fearing reprisal concerning his affair with Jessica Hahn, resigned from PTL. Bakker's actions could hardly be called covert because they had taken place in plain sight, exemplifying the religious philosophy he and his followers had daily espoused.

In 1987, almost a decade after noting apparent misconduct in the operations of PTL, the federal government charged Jim Bakker with 24 counts of fraud and conspiracy, alleging that Bakker had bilked his supporters.

# Exercises

1. What service properties inherent in religious groups contribute to consumer vulnerability?
2. Which types of moral philosophies could be argued to be the basis for Bakker's actions?
3. What are the ethical issues involved?
4. What factors, other than moral philosophies, may have influenced the ethical behavior of Jim Bakker?
5. What have been the consequences of Bakker's actions?
6. What strategies would you suggest to help control future abuses by other religious leaders?

# Notes

Henry G. Brinton, "Pray TV," *The Washington Monthly* (April 1990), 49–51; Charles Colson, "The Pedestal Complex," *Christianity Today,* February 5, 1990, p. 96; Frances Fitzgerald, "Reflections: Jim and Tammy," *The New Yorker,* April 23, 1990, pp. 45–48; and Kim A. Lawton, "The Remnants of PTL," *Christianity Today,* October 6, 1989, pp. 36–38.

# case 6

# For Innovative Service, Run for the Border*

While the vast majority of other food franchises have remained in the traditional management mode by focusing on more advertising, more promotions, more new products, and more new locations, Taco Bell has been focusing on the customer. Taco Bell believes that the company should be organized to support what the customer truly values—the food and the service delivery system.

Unlike other food franchises, Taco Bell has shifted its operation from manufacturing to assembly. Backroom tasks such as cleaning heads of lettuce, slicing tomatoes, shredding cheese, and making taco shells has been outsourced to other operations. As a result, labor's primary focus is now on serving customers as opposed to preparing food. In contrast, much of the remainder of the industry is expanding its on-site food manufacturing operations by offering products such as freshly baked biscuits and pizzas. Firms pursuing this strategy have complicated their operations and have placed their emphasis on production as opposed to service delivery.

Other changes within Taco Bell's operations have included a total revamping of the firm's managerial hierarchy. This change has translated into managers who coach and counsel rather than direct and control. In addition, a renewed emphasis on selecting and training public contact personnel has also occurred. An investment in advanced technology has also helped move Taco Bell and its employees to the forefront. Unlike other companies that utilize technology to monitor, control, and sometimes replace their employees, Taco Bell provides technology to employees as a resource to assist them in their duties.

Taco Bell has also recognized the importance of employee morale and loyalty to customer perceptions of service quality. To enhance employee morale, Taco Bell

---

*Source: Leonard A. Schlesinger and James L. Heskett "The Service-Driven Service Company," *Harvard Business Review* (September–October 1991), 71–81. Reprinted by permission of Harvard Business Review. Copyright © 1991 by the President and Fellows of Harvard College.

offers front-line employees higher-than-average wages compared with those throughout the rest of the industry. Moreover, because of a generous bonus system, managers are able to make 225 percent more than their competitive counterparts. Such actions have not only improved employee morale but have also resulted in lower employee turnover rates and an improved caliber of recruits.

Taco Bell's training efforts are also unique. Managers are encouraged to spend half their time on developing employees in areas such as communication, empowerment, and performance management. As a result, the majority of Taco Bell employees now feel they have more freedom, more authority to make decisions, and more responsibility for their own actions.

Overall, the consequences of Taco Bell's restructuring efforts to improve its service delivery systems have been overwhelmingly positive. In times of stagnant market growth for the rest of the industry, sales growth at company-owned Taco Bells has exceeded 60 percent, and profits have increased by more than 25 percent per year. In comparison, McDonald's U.S. franchises have increased their profitability during this same period at a rate of 6 percent. What makes the 25 percent increase in profits even more amazing is that Taco Bell has decreased the price on most menu items by 25 percent! Strategies such as these have led to value-oriented perceptions of Taco Bell that surpass competitive offerings.

## Exercises

1. In order to provide seamless service, service firms must balance the needs of their operations, marketing, and human resource departments. Discuss how improvements at Taco Bell have been shared by these three departments.
2. How do the actions taken by Taco Bell relate to the various components of the service-profit chain presented in Chapter 10?

case 7

# e.Com Services: Launching SpaceDisk, an Innovative, Internet-based Service*

e.Com Services Pte Ltd focuses on developing and providing Internet-based services, such as e-commerce, Internet telephony gateway services to various Asian countries, on-line ticketing for performances and cinemas in Singapore, and innovative international calling card services. S. Mohan, senior vice president of e.Com Services, is in the process of developing a global marketing strategy to attract 4 to 5 million users to their latest of a series of innovative Internet-based services, SpaceDisk. More information on e.Com Services can be found at www.ecom .com.sg and www.spacedisk.com.

## THE PRODUCT CONCEPT: SPACEDISK

Mohan explained, "SpaceDisk will allow anyone to save, organize, and retrieve files, including image, sound, music and video files to the service via the Internet. The

*Source: Jochen Wirtz is Assistant Professor, Department of Marketing, Faculty of Business Administration, National University of Singapore. S. Mohan is Senior Vice President of e.Com Services. e.Com's Web site can be found at: www.ecom.com.sg. This case was prepared as the basis for class discussion rather than to illustrate effective or ineffective handling of an administrative situation. e.Com Services considered some data in the case confidential; therefore the data was manipulated in such a fashion as to be acceptable to e.Com Services. The authors gratefully acknowledge the research assistance of Sim Siew Lien throughout the case development. Copyright © 1999 by Jochen Wirtz and S. Mohan. The authors retain all rights. Not to be reproduced or used without written permission from one of the authors.

information can be stored indefinitely in SpaceDisk in a safe and secure manner. Also, all these files can be viewed and downloaded from any Internet-connected PC. Users of SpaceDisk will only have to register and join SpaceDisk as a member. Members can then access their storage space on SpaceDisk. Apart from sending and storing one's own files into the SpaceDisk, users can also send files to another SpaceDisk or Internet user much like sending email to someone else today."

SpaceDisk was aimed at providing members with a service of collecting and keeping their valuable information in a safe and secure site for as long as they wish without having to worry about corrupted floppy disks, crashing hard disk drives, or their storage mediums becoming obsolete, since all of these issues would be handled by SpaceDisk. Mohan felt that SpaceDisk was unique in the Internet world, not only because it provided large amounts of storage space, but also because it offered storage with unparalleled ease of use, bundled with a range of features for users that could not be found on any other Internet site.

## POTENTIAL APPLICATIONS

Mohan saw tremendous application potential of DiskSpace because it allowed users to define their own uses for the platform. He explained further, "We will, in addition to its basic functions, create a number of 'killer' applications that enable users to maximize the potential of SpaceDisk. For example, we intend to create a Music Library, an Image Library, and a Book Shelf."

Mohan elaborated that with emerging online video and music streaming technologies, Internet users everywhere eventually would require a safe place to store, classify, and later retrieve music. "Imagine if you could do this using SpaceDisk. A one-stop repository of all your music files. You no longer would have to worry about storage mediums and longevity issues." The Image Library would be similar to the Music Library but designed for images, photographs, digital videos, and the like.

With the advent of electronic books, users would need a place to store these as well, and Book Shelf was designed as the ideal site for this application. Traditional hard disk and floppy media are not suitable for longer-term storage; rewritable compact disks (CD-R) are useful, but when standards change, and they usually do, currently used CD-Rs will become obsolete.

## MAIN SERVICE FEATURES

For the first version of DiskSpace, Mohan and his team identified a few key features to be launched; more advanced features were planned for the medium term future. They planned to include the following features in version 1.0:

### Easy 'One Click' Upload/Download of Files to/from SpaceDisk

Uploading and downloading files to/from SpaceDisk was designed to be intuitive and easy. Users needed only right click to select the file and then choose the location to save the file in. The rest of the operation was done in the background by the application, invisible to the user. The application was fully integrated into the user's Windows interface. This means that SpaceDisk appears as an icon on the Windows File Manager or Explorer interface much like a floppy or disk drive, allowing users to simply click and drag files to and from their SpaceDisk folders, an extremely convenient feature for an Internet application.

## Intelligent Classification and Storage Agent

A key strength and differentiation of this product from other Web sites was the intelligent agent. Once members registered, they could provide a brief list of topics they are interested in. The task of the agent was to monitor incoming information to the member's SpaceDisk and match, classify, and store the incoming data in the appropriate folders. This agent performs two functions. To the member, the agent helps in classification and storage. To e.Com Services, the agent allowed a gradual build-up of a user profile. This profile was considered to be highly valuable and could be used to sell, advertise, and provide a marketing database to advertisers and companies selling products on the site.

In addition, members had the ability to keep the information "live" by continuously adding more information on a topic, or they could decide that they would like to delete a topic altogether. Users also could pack information or files and send them to other users or to other locations on the Internet.

## Large Amount of Storage Space (Including E-mail)

Unlike Internet sites that provide free home pages, SpaceDisk offered its members a stable and secure site that is a repository for their data. SpaceDisk planned to offer a capacity of 25 megabytes (MB) for free, and charge a small fee for users who need more capacity. With SpaceDisk, users would no longer need to use cumbersome file transfer protocol (FTP) applications to transfer files between destinations. Also users would no longer be restrained by the size of a floppy disk when needing to transport files from one location to another. They could simply upload files into their SpaceDisk and later retrieve them from another location to their local hard disk drive.

Mohan felt strongly that one of the most important services to be integrated into SpaceDisk was E-mail, because it is an important feature that Internet users today use extensively. Mohan planned to license an existing Web-driven E-mail suite that could be easily integrated into SpaceDisk.

## Security for Private Information

An individual's SpaceDisk would be divided into two areas: a "private space" and a "vault." The private space could either be shared with friends or used individually and would be protected at the first level by a password. Members would have the option to define whom they allowed into the private space, which enabled the space to be shared by a group—for example, by a team working on a project. The vault, however, would be protected by a product called Netprotect, developed by CET Technologies, involving a high-level encryption system that allowed users to store their private and sensitive information without fear of break-in and tampering.

## Quick Search Features in SpaceDisk and in the Web

The quick search feature allowed users to search their own SpaceDisk or the Web for information on a particular topic. This would enable them to easily access information and to store, retrieve, and distribute information more quickly. Mohan planned to license an existing search engine like AltaVista or Excite and integrate it into SpaceDisk.

## REVENUE MODEL

Like most Internet community sites, e.Com Services' revenue model was a combination of paid subscription, advertising, and e-commerce for value-added services (see the business plan in Table 1 for details). For the greatest effectiveness, SpaceDisk was looking to create relationships to support other specialist providers who were on the Net selling products and services. For example, e.Com Services had an agreement with Amazon.com in which whenever an Internet user

### TABLE 1

**Business Plan**

|  | Year 1 Dec '99 | Year 2 Dec '00 | Year 3 Dec '01 | Year 4 Dec '02 |
|---|---|---|---|---|
| **Subscriber Target Numbers** | | | | |
| Estimated new members | 75,000 | 304,688 | 1,064,074 | 2,679,766 |
| Estimated total members | 75,000 | 379,688 | 1,443,762 | 4,123,528 |
| Estimated total page hits | 2,500,000 | 18,281,250 | 79,563,516 | 232,246,398 |
| **Revenue** | | | | |
| Subscription fees | 150,000 | 1,064,063 | 4,256,285 | 12,295,584 |
| Advertising revenues | — | 75,938 | 795,635 | 2,322,464 |
| Commissions from merchandise sales | — | 2,393,930 | 16,695,607 | 59,124,778 |
| Total Revenues | 150,000 | 3,533,931 | 21,747,527 | 73,742,826 |
| **Cost** | | | | |
| Cost of software and hardware | 437,500 | 817,969 | 2,905,576 | 7,571,088 |
| Cost of connection | 20,000 | 50,000 | 80,000 | 80,000 |
| Staff cost | 401,250 | 802,500 | 1,337,500 | 2,140,000 |
| Marketing cost | 75,000 | 304,688 | 1,064,074 | 2,679,766 |
| Cost of merchandise sold | — | 2,034,840 | 14,191,266 | 50,256,062 |
| General & administrative | 53,500 | 133,750 | 184,575 | 278,200 |
| Write-off of development cost | 92,000 | — | — | — |
| Total Cost | 1,079,250 | 4,143,747 | 19,762,991 | 63,005,116 |
| Profit (Loss) | (929,250) | (609,816) | 1,984,536 | 10,737,710 |

## TABLE 2

### Pricing Schedule

| Type of Subscriber | Amount of Space Provided | Cost of Space (Version 1.0) | Estimated Percentage of User Base |
|---|---|---|---|
| Member | Up to 25 MB | Free | 95 |
| Silver Member | Up to 450 MB | US$29/yr | 4 |
| Gold Member | Up to 900 MB | US$59/yr | 1 |
| Platinum Member | Unlimited | US$295/yr | 0.1 |

from e.Com's site jumped immediately to Amazon's site and purchased a book from Amazon.com, e.Com Services received a 15 percent commission on that sale. The site was designed to entice members to continually use the services offered within the domain and those of its partners. Already, Mohan saw the need to bundle services in addition to SpaceDisk's key features to attract and retain users.

e.Com planned to offer its members point-based incentives that could be accumulated whenever they log on to SpaceDisk, introduce new friends, buy products from participating service providers, and so on. These points could then be exchanged for gifts, discounts, or premium services.

### Subscription and Premium Services

SpaceDisk's major selling point was to be the provision of free space on the Internet along with a set of tools that helped people organize and manage their data more efficiently. Having looked at the potential usage base, e.Com Services decided to segment its users into four different membership types (Table 2). Mohan planned to base pricing on the amount of desired disk space.

Mohan did not expect many members to pay for SpaceDisk, mainly because connection speeds still made it difficult to upload and download very large files, since they held up dialup lines for a long time. However, he expected that to change in the medium term future. Nevertheless, initially subscription fees were expected to form a relatively large percentage of all revenues. This would fall in the medium-term future to around 20 percent to 30 percent at most. e.Com did not see premium services as a significant revenue generator, and expected only 5 percent to 10 percent of revenue to come from such services.

### Advertising

This was the most common model but the hardest to execute, being located in Asia. Given this fact, after the pilot phase, Mohan felt that SpaceDisk had to be launched in the United States. Advertising revenue was planned to account for 10 percent to 20 percent of the site's revenues. Mohan expected to receive a total of US$0.01 in advertising revenue per site hit.

## Ecommerce and Commissions from Merchandise Sales

This was an emerging revenue stream for sites like SpaceDisk. The major applications at this time included direct marketing of products and auction-type applications. This was expected to account for 40 percent of the revenue stream initially, growing to about 60 percent in the long term. The explicit and implicit data collected via the intelligent agent were considered a powerful asset for targeted cross-selling. A commission-based structure was planned for orders placed by SpaceDisk's customers for partners' products and services.

## NEXT STEPS AND MARKETING STRATEGY

Mohan was looking at a number of ways to market SpaceDisk. The fastest and most cost-effective way to build SpaceDisk's membership base was thought to be via joining other virtual communities (VC) programs and sharing subscriber bases with them. VCs are a collection of Web and portal spaces that agree to work together to share their members and generate more users. This was considered to be effective in initially kick-starting the project. Mohan had identified two VC programs that welcomed SpaceDisk's participation. With these VCs, SpaceDisk had the opportunity to immediately market to a potential membership base of some 600,000.

But VC programs were only one of the means considered by Mohan. He also planned to implement a viral marketing strategy, whereby SpaceDisk's current members were to introduce new members by emailing them SpaceDisk's universal resource locator (URL), with SpaceDisk included as a recipient as well, using a so-called carbon copy. SpaceDisk planned to use incentives to members to introduce their friends.

In addition, Mohan intended to spend a portion of his funds on banner advertising and banner swaps with other Web sites. These were designed to increase public awareness and to build brand recognition and brand equity for SpaceDisk.

Mohan's goal was to attract 4 million subscribers within two years of launch. He expected many of these subscribers to come from advanced countries with high Internet penetration.

## *Exercises*

1. What is SpaceDisk's value proposition? What existing services and products is it substituting? What would be their competitive reaction to SpaceDisk, if any?
2. Who would be the main target customers for SpaceDisk?
3. How would you price this service? Do you agree with e.Com Services' revenue model?
4. What would be the best way of reaching its target market and signing up members?
5. How could e.Com Services gain a competitive advantage to prevent others from copying this service (e.g., Yahoo or Amazon.com)?

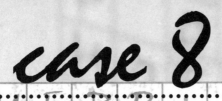

# case 8

# The Trials and Tribulations of Online Communications

The quality of communications a firm offers its customers is one of the many supplemental services that add value to the total benefit package. Presented below is the complete and verbatim dialogue between a customer attempting to order a wok and the customer service department of the manufacturer (The West Bend Company) who sells the wok. Keep in mind that each response had the complete string of messages.

```
  Company [that received the order]:

Thank you for your order!
Order #: ID XXXXXXXXXXXXx
Placed On: 01/15/2001

Billing Information
Bill Johnson Rte. 4, Box 781 Maysville, VA 24567
US

Shipping Information
Bill Johnson Rte. 4, Box 781 Maysville, VA 24567
US

Contents of your cart:
---------------------------------------------------------------
Item 1: 79566 - 6-Quart Electric Wok
for $46.40 qty: 1 total: $46.40
---------------------------------------------------------------
```

Payment method: Master Card
Credit Card Information:
Name on card: Bill Johnson
Card Number: XXXXXXXXXXXXX
Expiration Date: XXXXXXXXXXXXXXX
Shipping method: Priority Mail USPS

Total cost for your order:
Item Total: $46.40 Shipping: $8.00 Tax: $2.09
Order Total: $56.49

---

*Customer inquiry:*
*When can I expect delivery?*

---

Company response:

Thank you for contacting The West Bend Company. Our
customer service department will provide a reply to
your e-mail in the order it was received. We
apologize for the inconvenience but due to extreme
holiday demand you may experience a delay of several
days for a response.

The West Bend Company is closed Saturdays and Sundays,
please do not expect a response on those days.

Phone (262)334-6949 (Business Hours 8:00 a.m.- 4:00 p.m.
M-F Central Standard Time)
Fax (262) 306-7026
E-Mail: housewares@westbend.com
Housewares

---

Company response (during office hours):

I'm sorry I am unclear what you are looking to be
delivered.
Denise
Housewares
Phone (262) 334-6949 (Hours 8:00 A.M. - 4:00 P.M.
M - F Central Standard Time)
Fax (262) 306-7026
E-Mail: housewares@westbend.com

*Customer reply:*

*I placed the following order (this is the confirmation I received):*

*Thank you for your order!*
*Order #: ID1511-115416-10802636*
*Placed On: 01/15/2001*

*Billing Information*
*Bill Johnson Rte. 4, Box 781 Maysville, VA 24567*
*US*

*Shipping Information*
*Bill Johnson Rte. 4, Box 781 Maysville, VA 24567*
*US*

*Contents of your cart:*
-----------------------------------------------------------------------
*Item 1: 79566 - 6-Quart Electric Wok*
*for $46.40 qty: 1 total: $46.40*
-----------------------------------------------------------------------

*Payment method: Master Card*
*Credit Card Information:*
*Name on card: Bill Johnson*
*Card NumberXXXXXXXXXXXX*
*Expiration Date: XXXXXXXXX*
*Shipping method: Priority Mail USPS*

*Total cost for your order:*
*Item Total: $46.40 Shipping: $8.00 Tax: $2.09*
*Order Total: $56.49*

---

Company response:

We moved our warehouse this week and will began to
ship out the middle of next week. You should see
your slow cooker 7 to 10 days after that. I am sorry
for this late ship date. Hold on it coming.
Denise
Housewares
Phone (262) 334-6949 (Hours 8:00 A.M. - 4:00 P.M.
M - F Central Standard Time)
Fax (262) 306-7026
E-Mail: housewares@westbend.com

Customer response:

That's not acceptable. Is there anything that can be done to turn it around sooner? And, by the way, it's not a slow cooker, it's a WOK. I paid for USPS Priority Mail, which means I'm supposed to receive the package in two to three days. I'm sorry for your moving inconveniences, but I was expecting the package, at the very least, within a week of placing the order.

Company response:

I'm sorry your not happy but my hands are tied on this matter.
Denise
Housewares
Phone (262) 334-6949 (Hours 8:00 A.M. - 4:00 P.M.
M - F Central Standard Time)
Fax (262) 306-7026
E-Mail: housewares@westbend.com

Customer response:
Please cancel my order.

All communications ended at this point.

# Exercises

1. Evaluate the above communication from (a) the customer's perspective and (b) the company's perspective.
2. Based on the information provided, do you believe the company is more human resource, marketing, or operations oriented? Please explain.
3. What suggestions would you make to improve the flow of communication between provider and customer?

# case 9

# Electronic Banking Services: High-Tech, Low-Touch?*

## PROFILE OF A HIGH-TECH BANK

MeritaNordbanken is one of the leading financial services groups in the Nordic and Baltic Sea. With Finland and Sweden as its base, the group develops and markets a broad range of financial products and services for private individuals, companies, institutions, and the public sector (see the organizational chart at the end of the case).

The customer base comprises about 6.5 million private individuals and more than 400,000 companies and institutions, which are serviced through 735 branch offices and 1,000 Swedish post offices. Customers also have access to an extensive network of bill payment ATMs and cash dispensers. Almost 2 million customers use MeritaNordbanken's network banking services, which include its telephone bank and PC/Internet bank.

MeritaNordbanken's vision is to assist its customers to grow by acting as their leading banking partner, the best supplier of electronic banking services and the most cost-effective financial service institute.

## EXPLAINING THE IMPORTANCE OF NETWORK BANKING

The Internet has revolutionized the way that businesses operate, and the financial world has not been spared. Financial services and online banking services are

---

*Source: Stephan Martin, MBA candidate, Helsinki School of Economics and Business Administration.

among the industries that flourished rapidly from an estimated US$240 million to US$22 billion by the turn of the century. Internet banking, online share trading, and online mortgage and insurance services are all recording phenomenal growth. Online financial transactions have a clear cost advantage compared with traditional transactions. A brief look at MeritaNordbanken personnel data illustrates this point:

## Number of employees at MeritaNordbanken

|  | 31-Dec-98 | 31-Dec-97 |
|---|---|---|
| Retail operations | 14,171 | 14,824 |
| Asset management | 238 | 196 |
| Corporate | 1,312 | 1,214 |
| Markets | 615 | 656 |
| Central staff units (incl. service units) | 2,096 | 2,063 |
| **Banking operations, total** | **18,399** | **18,986** |
| Real estate | 270 | 381 |
| Subsidiaries (other subsidiaries and companies in temporary ownership) | 1,130 | 1,239 |
| **MeritaNordbanken Group, total** | **19,799** | **20,606** |

Source: http://www.merita.fi.

From 1997 to 1998 MeritaNordbanken's personnel have declined by 653 employees in retail operations (the front-line staff of banks) and by 807 for the whole group. This reduction in the number of personnel is illustrative of the cost savings generated by the rapid development of online banking services of the MeritaNordbanken Group.

In parallel to the development of the Internet is the development of electronic commerce (e-commerce). One of the most critical elements enabling e-commerce is the banking and financial service sector. Where e-commerce has developed, the banking and credit facilities are the major enablers of payment facilities for online transactions. To a large extent, e-commerce transactions rely on the intermediary role of banks, credit card companies, and other financial institutions, which must be interconnected. Banks thus provide an infrastructure that links local and national businesses with global banking network. Banks also give consumers, small businesses, and local communities access to financial resources and services that will allow them to participate in e-commerce.

Another aspect that illustrates the growing importance of internet banking services is the increased automation of data-entry and integration of systems within organizations, which is eliminating data redundancy and errors caused by data manipulations. These improvements are believed to help raise productivity in organizations.

Finally, the ability to provide better consumer service is also underlined as one of the factors contributing to the development of online banking. Direct communication with customers enables businesses to tailor their products and services to the individual preferences of their customers. An example of this phenomenon is the proliferation of Web sites providing individualization and personalization capacities to their online visitors. Businesses may provide their customers with personalized information and additional services that help them retain the loyalty of their customers. Customers also benefit from the ability to seek information and shop, pay their bills, consult their accounts, and transfer money at any time of day.

## INTERNET BANKING AT MERITANORDBANKEN

In a recent statement, available on the bank Web site, Hans Dalborg, the chief executive officer of the MeritaNordbanken group, declared, "We have clearly exceeded our internet banking goals for 1999, and we are ready to move forward. MeritaNordbanken is the number one bank in the world in terms of monthly logons, and we plan to stay at the top."

Services through data networks are deeply rooted in the MeritaNordbanken Group. They began in 1982 with automatic telephone payments and were expanded to PC services in 1984, GSM (cellular network) in 1992, the Internet in 1996, and TV in 1998. Today almost all banking services can be carried out over the Internet.

By late 1998 the bank counted half a million customers using its data networks. The customer base today has grown to 1.1 million. Monthly log-ons to the solo services on the Internet amount to 3 million. Nearly 4 million bills are paid via the Internet every month, and the figure is constantly growing. The proportion of share purchase and sale orders and mutual fund transactions over the Net has periodically reached 61 percent and 10 percent, respectively, in Finland. The growth of online banking is expected to grow even more in the foreseeable future (Figure 1).

**Figure 1**     Internet Banking Goals for 2000–2001

- 5 million log-ons per month
- 6 million bill payments per month
- 2 million Internet banking clients (early 2001)

Source: http://www.merita.fi

## HOW NETWORK SERVICES CREATE CUSTOMER VALUE

Network services make it possible to handle routine items such as payments as well as sophisticated services regardless of the time or location, with various types of technical tools. Customers can save time and money and receive reports that provide a much better overview of assets, loans, cash flow, and transactions. "Customers with an Internet connection are more satisfied with their bank than other customers, which illustrates that customer value is appreciated," says Bo Harald, executive vice president. Customer value also arises through a growing service content, clarity, user-friendliness, and volume-tolerating reliability.

# INTERNET SOLO SERVICES: A CUSTOMER PERSPECTIVE

The Finnish Bank has a simple interface and is available in three languages (Finnish, Swedish, and English). The benefit for prospective customers is that one can test the online banking service with the training function. Interested customers may experience directly the types of services offered by the online bank by logging in with a generic customer number and password.

The Internet bank service provides a rapid overview of all the user accounts (current, investments, and even loans). By clicking on any of these accounts, the user can have a detailed list of all debits and credits that occurred from each of his accounts as well as the name of the payee or payer. Transaction can be set both in Euros and Finnish Marks.

Furthermore, the online bank permits users to invest in high interest account or directly on the stock and bond market. However, some of the instructions on how to proceed are still not available in English.

Merita bank also offers the ability to pay bills online. The online payment form is simple and user-friendly. It requires the account number and name of the recipient. A unique reference number is inserted and the user enters the due date as well as the amount of the bill. There is an option which allows users to receive a receipt for a small fee.

Basic online services such as account monitoring and payments are available to Merita customers for about 120 marks a year (about $20). More complicated services (share trading, lending, investments) are available for an additional 540 marks a year (about $45) plus an additional charge for each buying and selling transaction.

The bank also displays clearly its policy with matters regarding security of transactions and the protection of customer data. Encryption software is used to protect data sent across networks and the little lock logo at the bottom of the browser attests that it is doing so.

For customers who do not have access to the Internet at home, the physical bank has several PCs at the disposition of its customers. These are also used to train and educate customers to use the bank's system. It is not uncommon to see an elderly customer alongside an employee teaching the basics of Internet banking.

Finally, a telephone number is provided to customers who wish to contact an employee should they face any problems during their online experience.

# FUTURE PROSPECTS

Certain of its advance in terms of network banking services, MeritaNordbanken continues its progression by adding further services via the Internet. For example, up to 16 percent of credit applications are currently sent to the bank via the Internet. This trend, explains Bo Harald, is "something which has revolutionized the old thinking that personal service is always indispensable in negotiations on household loans."

In addition to new services, Merita is pioneering the use of the latest technologies for its wireless banking services. Basically, the bank plans to offer all services currently available with the online Solo services directly to its customers' mobile phones. A wireless application protocol (WAP) enabled mobile telephone can be used for account and credit card transaction monitoring, account-to-account transfers, and bill payments. It also enables shopping at MeritaNordbanken's virtual marketplace, the Solo Mall, already familiar to Internet banking customers. All these services were free of charge until the end of February 2000. Thereafter a monthly charge of FIM 4.00 was introduced. Stock trading will be the next service to be made available via WAP phones.

## Exercises

1. Analyze the impact of internet banking on the components of the services marketing mix.
2. Is the servuction model still a valid framework to explain a customer's experience?
3. Evaluate the role of customers as partial employees.
4. How should future services be promoted?

## ORGANIZATIONAL CHART

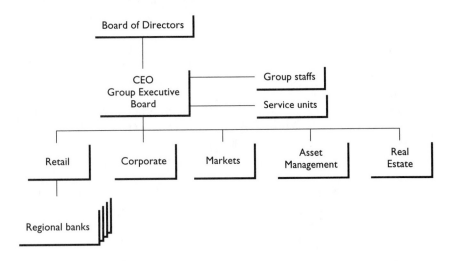

# O'Keefe Associates*

The partner meeting of O'Keefe Associates, a preeminent management consulting firm, had gotten under way, and Kevin O'Keefe, the founding father of the firm, had just announced that he would be removing himself from all decision-making positions. He would be passing control of the firm to its vice presidents, the new partners of the firm.

Recent events had made this departure inevitable, and it had been expected for some time. Despite this, Aviva Katz felt a lump form in her throat, and she quickly reached for the glass of Dom Perignon in front of her. In her haste, she knocked it clean across the shining mahogany into the lap of Henning Amelung, who, even as he felt the wetness permeate his clothes, directed his gaze calmly at her, waiting for an apology. She had half a mind to not offer one but decided to leave personal battles for another day, for today belonged to Kevin O'Keefe, the patriarch who had started the firm 18 years ago. She gestured an apology to the unruffled Henning and her mind started to churn. Kevin's departure meant that the vice presidents had to quickly regroup and decide the immediate fate of the firm. The consulting industry had been declining for the past two years, and O'Keefe Associates had borne the brunt of the downturn because of their connection with a recent, well-publicized lawsuit. The right moves now could stem client erosion, reverse reputation damage, and set the firm on the course to rejuvenation; the wrong moves would mean a slow demise.

## BRIEF HISTORY OF O'KEEFE

"I've watched this firm grow just like I've watched my own children, and perhaps with as much love and care. This makes the decision I face even more difficult. But like most painful decisions, it is inevitable."

Kevin O'Keefe had stepped into the management consulting world with the start-up Boston Consulting Group (BCG). Industry watchers and insiders attributed his meteoric rise within BCG to an undying commitment to his clients' bottom line. He succeeded in consistently doing so by coming up with unorthodox ideas and

*Source: Copyright © 1996 by Professor Brian Wansink.

ensuring that his recommendations were able to be implemented. In 1971 he left BCG with three of his colleagues to form O'Keefe Associates. In an interview at a later date, he gave the following reason for his move: "Paul [another O'Keefe founding father] and I were bringing in about half the revenue for the firm. We operated independently and, over time, drifted away from everyone at BCG. Finally, my entrepreneurial urge got the better of me and I decided to start O'Keefe Associates."

Kevin had built a strong reputation for himself. His clients openly commended him. He earned the respect of colleagues and competitors after creating the highly effective O'Keefe Model for strategy formulation, which was first published in the Harvard Business Review and won the award for the year's best article. When he moved out on his own, his clients decided to continue retaining him. At the same time, three of his colleagues, Paul Vivek, John Hartmann, and Ted Chesner, decided to join him. They decided to split up the ownership of the firm based on the projected revenues each could bring. Consequently, Kevin held 37 percent ownership, Paul 33 percent, and John and Michael 15 percent each.

O'Keefe Associates focused on high-level corporate and business-unit strategy consulting and shied away from industry specialization. Charging the highest billing rates in the industry, they introduced the concept of relationship consulting[2] and focused on a single client in each industry. In return, they asked that their clients not engage any other consulting firm. This one-to-one relationship set the firm apart in the industry and gave CEOs the assurance that their company's secrets and strengths would not be exposed to potential and existing competitors.

Each of the partners had the potential to be a powerful rainmaker at most firms in the industry; together they formed a powerhouse. They leveraged Kevin's reputation and warm personality very effectively with clients as well as with potential recruits at the top three business schools in the United States. As a start-up that promised to reach stellar heights, O'Keefe Associates attracted the topmost talent at schools. As a consulting firm that brought a unique proposition to the table, they attracted Fortune 500 clients from all industries. The result was the perfect high-growth formula, and by 1980, a mere nine years after its birth, O'Keefe Associates had registered itself on the radar of the bigger, more established consulting firms.

As it grew, O'Keefe Associates won friends as well as enemies. While about 80 percent of clients had nothing but praise for them, others felt they had been poorly served. In response to a question asking for their opinion of the firm, respondents had this to say:

> O'Keefe has the brightest talent in the industry. Moreover, their people are not snobs like most consultants are. They mix well with our employees, come up with truly innovative out-of-the-box ideas, and work at convincing all levels of our hierarchy. They know how to address bottom-line concerns and they know how to produce bottom-line results. If I were stranded on a remote desert island, the one thing I'd want with me is an O'Keefe consultant.

—*CEO of a Fortune 500 chemicals company*

O'Keefe may be good intellectually, but they have been inconsistent in dealing with us. Some of the advice they gave us set the company back 10 years. Once when I needed support to defend one of their recommendations to my CEO, they just did an about-face on me, like they had never made the recommendation! They leave me with the feeling that they would do anything to save their own necks!

—*SBU Manager of a Fortune 500 manufacturer*

One of the probable reasons for this variation in quality of service was the growth rate: O'Keefe could not grow its people into experienced consultants fast enough to serve the needs of the entire client base. As a result, some clients suffered. Business media, which thrives on reporting the "out of the ordinary," picked up on stories disgruntled clients had to tell. The ensuing bad press hurt O'Keefe's image, and, by many accounts, they managed to survive only because clients found it impossible to change consultants as a result of contractual obligations and costs involved in getting new consultants up to speed. Over the next two years or so, the founding partners worked hard at avoiding similar embarrassment by building good relations with the media, convincing clients with success stories to speak out, and implementing rigorous recruiting and training procedures. Their efforts at improving quality and cleaning up the image of the firm worked, and they were able to continue commanding the highest billing rates in the industry.

## O'KEEFE'S ORGANIZATION

O'Keefe Associates was organized like most other partnerships. After inception, part of the firm's ownership was given to employees via the employee stock ownership plan (ESOP), primarily as an incentive for them to help the firm grow. The four founding fathers continued to hold most of the equity in the firm, and vice presidents held the rest (about 10 percent). The 27 vice presidents, all officers of the firm, reported to the partners and managed the activities of 68 managers while having complete responsibility for relationships with two to seven clients each (depending on the size of the clients). Managers were responsible for one to three cases that were staffed by senior associates, associates, and research associates (RAs). Senior associates helped in conducting the case while assuming responsibility for case modules.[3] Associates managed case modules. RAs helped case teams analyze data and came up with helpful insights. They were high-performing undergraduates, while associates were the top graduates of the three most highly rated business schools in the country. A typical case team was made up of one vice president, one manager, two senior associates, four associates, and two RAs. Turnover among associates and RAs was high, with about 50 percent of recruits staying on until the three-year mark, at which they made senior associate. Senior associates made manager within about two years. Managers who showed an aptitude for managing client relationships were promoted to vice president after about three years. Base compensation at all levels was high (an associate started at $70,000 a year plus a $30,000 sign-up bonus) and above industry norms. Top performers earned annual bonuses of up to about 50 percent of the base salary.

# THE MANAGEMENT CONSULTING INDUSTRY

Although the management consulting industry can be entered easily by engaging any one client, it is one of the toughest service industries to survive in. The following characteristics explain why.

Consultants face the toughest business problems. Consulting firms have high billing rates, and each engagement costs the client a lot of money and other resources. Consequently, businesses tend to call in consultants if they offer innovative solutions (e.g., CSC Index's reengineering, BCG's Matrix) or if the management is perplexed about a certain problem. Problems that perplex upper management are tough to solve, since the upper management of large businesses is made up of very bright people.

Convincing management about recommendations is an arduous task. The bright people who make up senior management have known their business and industry well for many years. As a result, all recommendations have to be thoroughly supported, and all levels of the client's hierarchy have to buy in to them.

In many cases, it is difficult to measure results. The nature of the problems is such that it is difficult to discern the impact of a recommended solution. The result of adopting a recommended strategy may not be visible for years. Observed outcomes could be the result of factors other than the recommendation. Even when the result can be distinctly identified, it is impossible to tell whether a better recommendation could have been made. This also leads to difficulty in discerning the quality of advice.

Good employees are hard to come by. Employees are the largest constituent of the costs incurred by a consulting firm and are the factor that allows a firm to distinguish itself. Consequently, the recruiting process is rigorous and expensive (see Exhibit 1). Also, since many firms end up competing for the same people, recruitment yields[4] are lower than in other industries.

It is difficult to retain employees. After expending a great number of resources on recruiting, consulting firms face the challenge of retaining employees. This is primarily because consultants lead high-pressure lives plagued with immovable deadlines and consequently long hours. Many recruits burn out quickly, while others leave because of lifestyle issues.

Consultants are always viewed as expendable. If profits come under severe pressure, businesses will first dispense with consultants. This can lead to consulting firms' facing costs without getting revenues; this pressures them to cut costs by laying off employees. This action not only results in the loss of superior resources but also creates a poor reputation for future recruiting efforts.

It is important to be differentiated, clearly positioned, and well reputed. Only distinguishable firms are consistently able to attract talented employees as well as clients; others succumb to vagaries of the economy or to competition.

The management consulting industry can be divided into five categories:[5]

1. *Pure strategy advisors:* These are small firms that provide high-cost advice to corporate and business-unit management (O'Keefe belongs in this category). The competition is strong, though courteous. These firms compete for the topmost talent and compensate their employees extremely well. Their costs are consequently the highest among all segments. Examples of this category are The Boston Consulting Group, LEK Partnership, and Bain & Company.

2.  *Traditional management consultants:* These firms consult in all areas and are somewhat diversified in that sense. They offer strategy consulting services as well as advice in functional areas. These are large in size, and competition between them is keen but polite. Examples are Booz, Allen & Hamilton, McKinsey & Co., and Arthur D. Little.

3.  *Accounting firms (Big 6):* These firms are recent entrants looking for new sources of revenue. They have well-established client relationships as a result of their accounting services and are now trying to leverage these relationships. Traditionally, these firms dealt in functional areas such as accounting and information services. Through acquisitions of specialist strategy boutiques and in-house expansion, they are now encroaching on the territory of management consultants. Competition among these firms is high, and costs are relatively low. Examples are Andersen Consulting, Coopers & Lybrand, and Deloitte Touche.

4.  *Human resource firms:* These are mid-sized firms designing compensation packages for clients. Their costs are low because they do not recruit at top business schools. Competition in this category is intense. Examples are Sibson & Co. and Johnson & Higgins.

5.  *Specialized firms:* These firms advise clients in specialized areas (e.g., financial services). Their costs are at a level between those of accounting firms and traditional firms. This category includes sole practitioners (college professors, retired executives, etc.). Competition in this category is fierce. Examples are Oliver Wyman & Co. and Marketing Corporation of America (MCA).

The management consulting industry enjoyed spectacular success and grew at the rate of about 20 percent annually through the last decade.[6] This boom attracted many new entrants. A downturn in the U.S. economy started the current decline two years ago. Financially strapped clients started terminating engagements prematurely, and recent entrants started falling like ninepins. New engagements were being given to the lower-priced accounting firms.[7] Faced with global competition and technological changes, clients looked for help from specialists, and the demand for the services of generalists crashed. The industry began to consolidate, with outside buyers recognizing an opportunity to buy several firms and merge them. Summarily, the industry was experiencing change like it had never experienced before, and the foreseeable future did not seem to promise any stability.

## CUSTOMERS

O'Keefe's clients were CEOs or divisional heads of Fortune 500 companies seeking advice on strategy formulation or implementation. They engaged O'Keefe because they looked for top-quality advice and an exclusive relationship. Client business units typically had revenues greater than $100 million, since smaller operators could not afford O'Keefe's billing rates.

Customers for the management consulting industry cut across all industries and come in all shapes and sizes. Some require ongoing advice, whereas others call in consultants on an "as needed" basis. Matters on which they need advice range from corporate strategy to operational improvement. Some clients have substantial in-house capability to implement recommendations, whereas others need ongoing support and help during implementation. Without variation, all customers pay top dollar and demand top performance.

## RECENT OCCURRENCES AT O'KEEFE ASSOCIATES

The last two years had brought rough times to O'Keefe Associates. The decline in the consulting market resulting from the economy-wide decline had forced clients to cut engagements and stretch receivables to the maximum. This placed tremendous financial pressure on O'Keefe, but the company was able to handle it reasonably well by finding new clients. However, as the market decline commenced, an employee at the Canadian office was named as a co-defendant in a lawsuit brought by client shareholders against client management for undervaluing a recent divestiture.

The lawsuit was fairly complicated. In it the shareholders claimed that some senior managers were part owners of the closely held acquiring firm. By undervaluing the divestiture, management had cheated shareholders for personal gain. The O'Keefe consultant claimed he was innocent and had no knowledge of any wrongdoing. His name was finally dissociated from the lawsuit, but only after he had agreed to testify against client management. The scandal had been well publicized by the popular and business press, and O'Keefe's reputation had been badly damaged. Moreover, the Canadian client had engaged 40 O'Keefe consultants, who were suddenly left without a case to work on. The loss in revenue and poor market conditions had forced O'Keefe to lay off 65 employees.

The story did not end there. The firm was also in deep financial trouble. During the growth years (O'Keefe revenues grew at about 40 percent annually), the firm's financial needs had been met through internally generated cash and limited bank borrowing. Seeing the steady, low-debt-burden growth of the firm, the founding partners had decided to cash in on their success by selling their holdings to the ESOP. To compensate them, the ESOP had to borrow heavily from various banks, and this placed a heavy debt burden on the firm. In the current downturn, it became impossible for the firm to meet its debt commitments; it was brought to the verge of declaring bankruptcy. Rumor also had it that Kevin O'Keefe had conducted negotiations to sell the firm to an outside buyer but that they had been unable to see eye to eye.

Facing the combined onslaught of reduced business and financial distress, O'Keefe had no choice but to cut costs further. A second round of layoffs was followed by a third. The crisis that ensued had finally forced Kevin O'Keefe to step down as managing director. It had also been decided that the firm would restructure its debt after the founding fathers agreed to revalue the firm and return some of the money they had taken from the ESOP. Consequently, the debt burden would become somewhat more manageable. Challenges that still faced the vice presidents included the following:

- The Canadian lawsuit and financial trouble had severely hurt the firm's reputation among current and potential clients. Consequently, there was a danger of losing more clients without gaining any.
- The skeletal staff remaining was barely able to service the needs of clients. Experienced consultants had been retained, but associates and RAs (who had been laid off) were sorely needed. However, the layoffs had hurt O'Keefe's reputation on college campuses, and potential recruits were largely ignoring the firm.
- Remaining consultants were insecure in their positions, and morale was low. There was a danger that many more would leave very soon if nothing was done to address their concerns. Those leaving first would probably be the best, since they would be in high demand.

The departing leadership had left a void, and the firm needed to establish direction quickly.

## O'KEEFE NOW

After Kevin's departure the first order of business for the new partners was to elect a new leader for the firm. The partner meeting for this election had been scheduled already, and the two vice presidents that were expected to be nominated for managing director were Aviva Katz and Henning Amelung. The following profiles characterize these two well.

## AVIVA KATZ

Aviva was one of the earliest employees of O'Keefe Associates. Prior to attending Harvard Business School, she was a nurse with the U.S. Army. She had dazzled professors and fellow students at Harvard with her intellectual prowess and sharp wit. During her summer job at O'Keefe, she was convinced that she wanted to come back and share in and contribute to the success of the firm. Once there, she quickly won the confidence of the founding fathers and built a strong client base in the consumer products area. Through the late seventies and early eighties, Aviva was the top revenue earner for the firm. More recently, she had cut back on work hours to spend more time with her family. Aviva was well respected and fondly liked by most colleagues. For many, she was the ideal choice for managing director.

## HENNING AMELUNG

The descendant of a wealthy German family, Henning Amelung had graduated from the Amos Tuck School and joined the firm in 1981. Within the first two years he distinguished himself and won accolades for creative solutions that helped in turning around some steel industry clients. Seeing his penchant for finance, Kevin O'Keefe allowed him to start a venture capital subsidiary, which turned out to be a great success. Although Henning drew respect from colleagues and clients, he had a reputation for being a ruthless driver of case teams. One RA had this to say about his experience working with Henning:

> Its almost as though you are a piece of machinery. Your feelings do not exist, you are tireless, and you respond without questioning. That's how he treats you. I was told when I joined that vacation is considered sacred by all at O'Keefe and by and large I have found that to be true. But Henning considers nothing sacred except the directions he gives you. If I'm assigned to another case with him, I'm quitting!

Henning was an extremely hard worker and expected others to follow suit. His entrepreneurial success, "nose for the money," and drive made him a strong candidate for managing director.

## AVIVA'S PLATFORM

Aviva was acutely aware that in making their choice for managing director, partners would consider the nominee's views about the future strategy of the firm. Consequently, she was confident she would win, since she felt her stick-to-historical-strengths perspective was more popular. Salient aspects of this viewpoint included the following:

- Maintain the one-client-per-industry offering. This had helped in setting the firm apart from the rest of the industry and had helped their initial growth. No other firm had built this capability, and it promised O'Keefe a competitive advantage.
- Remain general management consultants. The firm had built a reputation for being generalists and had the talent pool to support that position. Specialization in functional or industry areas mean (a) building expertise in them, probably by hiring experienced people,[8] and (b) dealing with functional management instead of the top management that O'Keefe had customarily dealt with.
- Maintain a wide geographical presence. During its high-growth years, O'Keefe had expanded nationwide and internationally by establishing offices in 16 cities. This had been done to (a) be closer to clients to create a stronger partnership with them and (b) reduce travel requirements for employees. Many partners felt that both issues were extremely important and that O'Keefe should not change this position in any way.

Whereas Aviva espoused these views, she had heard from colleagues that Henning's view was markedly different and was based on the premise that the firm's situation would not improve without radical change. He felt that O'Keefe's strategy had been appropriate for entry and initial growth but that now it had to adapt to the times and the competitive environment. Hearsay had it that his views included the following:

- O'Keefe should accept more than one client per industry. In the past they had turned away business to honor their one-client-per-industry policy, and there was no telling how much revenue had been foregone. Some partners felt that in the current situation, they could not afford to be picky and turn away more business.

- O'Keefe should be general management consultants with specialized strengths in some areas. Specialization was important as the market demand was heading in that direction. But there were very few general management firms left in the marketplace, and although there was a temporary lull in demand, many industry watchers expected it to bounce back. Keeping the general management strength would mean carrying some employees and partners without adequate business to keep them busy. Building specialization would mean training senior staff and hiring experienced people.

- Operations should be consolidated geographically; service coverage should be maintained. Because prestigious firms buy or rent prestigious office space, O'Keefe's lease and mortgage payments were astronomical. Although most internal services were centralized in Washington, D.C., some office staff and services were required to support each location. The current level of business in most offices did not justify maintaining them.

Aviva realized that Henning's perspective was not altogether without merit; however, she was confident that the majority of partners wanted the firm to continue doing what it knew best. She was sure that the discussion about respective platforms prior to the vote would position her well. There was, however, the possibility of the group's digressing to the issue of the firm's reputation. In the recent past, Aviva had been very vocal about her stand on this issue and had discovered, much to her surprise, that the majority opposed her views. Although she had tried to tone down her stand on the issue, a complete about-face would not have reflected well on her. Besides, she did feel very strongly about her beliefs. She advocated the following positions:

- O'Keefe must rebuild its reputation through high-quality advice and renewed commitment to client bottom lines, much the way it had done in the past. The resulting favorable word-of-mouth will ensure reestablishment of O'Keefe's reputation.

- To regain high visibility in a positive light, O'Keefe's partners and employees should publish their work in business periodicals and journals, form alliances with prominent universities, and encourage employees to become involved in community services.

- Under no circumstances should O'Keefe increase starting salaries to become more attractive on campuses. This would be self-defeating because potential recruits would see this as a sign of weakening reputation.[9] Besides, this would necessitate revising salaries for all employees, resulting in higher costs when the firm least needed them.

She was sure that Henning saw the merit in her position on the reputation issue. Her sources had informed her, though, that he had opportunistically aligned himself with the perceived majority, which favored the following positions:

- Undertaking a concerted advertising effort via advertisements indicating that O'Keefe was still a strong player. Placed in eminent business periodicals, these would emphasize O'Keefe's past successes and current strengths by quoting clients. They would assert that O'Keefe had always focused on bottom-line results. Such a strategy had recently been executed by Andersen Consulting with significant success.

*   Actively promoting positive word-of-mouth. This could be done by targeting champion CEOs and offering O'Keefe's services with a guarantee or at concessional terms. Champions would be high-profile entrepreneurs or executives who are quoted in the media often and are respected for their opinions.

*   Offering new recruits higher starting salaries and bonuses. Money was a strong motivator, and there would be a salary level beyond which recruits would have a very hard time declining offers. O'Keefe's weakened reputation was no secret; not raising salaries was not going to fool anyone.

Aviva was critical of these views, especially the aggressive promotion of word-of-mouth. Arranging for a quid pro quo with senior level executives was unthinkable. Even if one were arranged, how could O'Keefe offer guarantees? In case of success stories, how could they be sure that O'Keefe would get the desired exposure? She just did not think it was possible to implement these ideas, and even if it were, she felt they would not go down well with clients.

The partners' meeting was still about an hour away, and Aviva decided to go get some coffee. When she returned she found Michael Silfen, a rising star and currently a manager, waiting for her. Aviva was Michael's mentor[10] and had also worked with him in the past. They shared a strong, positive relationship.

"Hi, Michael! What can I do for you?"

"Hi, Aviva, Something's come up and I need your advice, that is if you have the time."

"I have a few minutes. What's up?"

"Well, it's like this. A headhunter cold-called me about two weeks ago. We struck up a conversation, and to cut a long story short, I have received a very, very attractive offer from a competitor. I'm torn between memories of the good times and the sheer frustration of being here now. Any ideas about what I should do?"

Aviva heaved a quiet sigh. This was going to be a long evening, and the battle had already begun.

# Exercises

1. Identify the strengths and weaknesses and the opportunities and threats that are faced by O'Keefe Associates.
2. Who will be voted managing director?
3. What should the firm's strategy be going forward?
4. How should the firm handle its reputation problem?
5. What should Aviva say to Michael Silfen? If you were in his shoes, would you take the competitor's job offer?

# Notes

1. O'Keefe and O'Keefe Associates have been used synonymously.
2. Relationship consulting means that the client and the consulting firm maintain an ongoing relationship as opposed to having a relationship for the term of an engagement only.
3. Managers usually divided a case assignment into related tasks known as case modules.
4. Recruitment yield is defined as the ratio between the number of recruits accepting the firm's offer and the total number of offers given out by the firm. At 66 percent, O'Keefe's ratio was one of the highest in the industry.
5. Shankar Suryanarayanan, "Trends and Outlook for US Consulting," *Journal of Management Consulting* 5, no. 4 (1989), 4–5.
6. Ibid.
7. Ibid.
8. This would be a marked departure for O'Keefe. Prestigious firms traditionally hired fresh MBAs and groomed them to fit the firm's culture. Although there had been instances of competitors' relaxing this rule, many within O'Keefe were quite opposed to doing so.
9. Although high salaries were important to recruits, many surveys had shown that firm reputation and prestige were the topmost considerations.
10. O'Keefe had a mentoring system in which new associates were assigned to mentors, usually vice presidents. These mentors advised new associates on matters regarding performance, social adjustment, and career planning.

# Exhibit 1

## The Consulting Recruiting Process

Consulting firms have a rigorous recruitment process. This process is also costly, since employees have to be pulled off cases to visit campuses to conduct interviews and select candidates. Candidates selected on campus then visit the office of the hiring firm and are interviewed by more employees. The following is an excerpt from a guide to interviewing with consulting firms.

Most consulting firms conduct case interviews. The primary purpose of these interviews is to get an idea of how well you break a problem down and then logically try to solve it. Because of the nature of the interview, they also get to see how you think on your feet and how well you keep your composure. At times, they also get to see how quickly you bounce back after making mistakes.

In addition to problem-solving ability, interviewers make judgments about your ability to work in teams and lead at client sites. Usually, the last question the interviewer has to answer on the evaluation form is, "Would you like this person to be on your team tomorrow?"

Consulting firms recruit through a multi-round process. Some firms have three rounds, whereas others have only two. In the first round, you interview with one person, and in subsequent rounds you have back-to-back interviews with two to three people. Each of these interviews ranges from 30 to 45 minutes.

In addition to other factors, doing well at case interviews requires skill. Like all other skills, this one can be learned by practice.

## Anatomy of a Case Interview

An interview typically begins with 10 minutes of resume-based discussion. During this, the usual set of questions (why consulting, etc.) are asked. Following this, the interviewer presents a business case and asks you general and specific questions. Your analysis will probably be guided in the direction your interviewer wants you to go, so do not ignore comments or instructions. With each additional insight, the interviewer will probe deeper and push you to the next issue. Although there is no right answer to any case, you will generally be expected to take a stand (state a hypothesis) at the end of the case. You should base this stand on what your analysis reveals, any assumptions you want to make, and any input the interviewer gives you. The following are examples of case questions:

1. An overseas construction firm wants to establish its presence in a growing regional U.S. market. What advice would you give it?
2. A major airline is considering acquiring an existing route from Tokyo to New York. How can it determine whether the route is a good idea?
3. An Israeli travel agent has been extremely successful. His primary source of revenue is customers who fly to and from the United States. He manages to fill up more than two planeloads on a daily basis. Given his success, he is considering buying an aircraft and flying the U.S.–Tel Aviv route himself. What advice would you give him?
4. How would you compare the airline industry with the baby food industry? In which would you invest your own money?

# Passenger-Induced Turbulence*

The service encounter is often a shared experience where customers can have a profound impact on each other's overall experience. Nowhere is this more evident than sharing an airplane with hundreds of other customers. During the late 1990s and continuing into the second millennium, the popular press has been full of stories that describe incidents of "air rage" or "passenger-induced turbulence." Areas known to contribute to disruptive behavior include alcohol abuses, sexual misconduct, smoking in nonsmoking areas, failure to following boarding instructions, violating carry-on baggage restrictions, and a variety of other confrontations dealing with lapses in creature comforts, crew training, and food quality.

Clearly the airlines are concerned and are part of the problem. During the summer of 2000, the CEO of United Airlines publicly apologized to the airline's customers during United's stalled contract negotiations with employees. Numerous flights were canceled or delayed. United admitted in television commercials that their airline had failed to deliver on its basic promise—to service its customers. The voice of the customer is being heard loud and clear as customers are letting the airlines know when violations of customer service occur. Air traveler complaints are up 25 percent, and the number of incidents involving passengers interfering with flight crews has more than tripled over the last 10 years. However, the airlines themselves are not totally to blame for what's going on in the skies. Clearly some customers are out of control.

One of the more recent problems deals with increasing numbers of passengers having sex in their seats or in airplane restrooms. "It's uninhibited up there these days," says psychologist Christina Lawrence, a former United Airlines flight attendant. Airline consultant, Agnes Huff, agrees: "People used to be discreet. But

---

*Source: Asra Q. Nomani, "In the Skies Today, a Weird New Worry: Sexual Misconduct," *The Wall Street Journal,* June 10, 1998, p. A1; Frances Fiorino, "Passengers Who Carry Surly Bonds of Earth Aloft," *Aviation Week and Space Technology* 149, no. 5 (1998), 123.

more and more passengers these days are pushing the limits." In one case involving a South African Airways jumbo jet, a couple disrobed and began having sex in full view of other customers. Flight attendants summoned the captain, who was quoted as saying, "This plane is not a shag house!"—South African slang for bordello. In another incident, numerous members of a company sales group became intoxicated and began to expose themselves to other passengers. One couple, who was part of the group, consummated their office romance on the plane while being cheered on by other members of the group. The captain cut off liquor sales, but the group continued to drink by opening their own personal bottles of liquor, which had been purchased at the duty-free shop before boarding. In yet another incident, the flight attendant of a Delta Air Lines flight felt compelled to knock on the door of the plane's bathroom. Inside, a Southern California women was having sex with her boyfriend. After the passenger responded that she would "be out in a second," the frustrated flight attendant began citing federal rules that do not allow the plane to land unless all passengers are seated.

The policing of customer misconduct aboard planes is a tricky issue. According to one flight attendant, "At 37,000 feet, you don't have the option of throwing people out like you can in a cocktail lounge."

## Exercise

1. As the airline's training director, how would you instruct employees to handle situations that involve disruptive customers?

# Giordano*

Giordano is a retailer of casual clothes in East Asia, Southeast Asia, and the Middle East. In 1999 it operated outlets in China, Dubai, Hong Kong, Macao, Philippines, Saudi Arabia, Singapore, South Korea, and Taiwan. Giordano's sales grew from HK$712 million (US$91.28 million) in 1989 to HK$3092 million (US$396.41 million) in 1999.[1] This case describes the success factors that allowed Giordano to grow rapidly in some Asian countries. In addition, the case looks at three imminent issues that Giordano faced in maintaining its success in existing markets and in its plan to enter new markets in Asia and beyond. The first concerns Giordano's positioning. In what ways, if at all, should Giordano change its current positioning? The second concerns the critical factors that contributed to Giordano's success. Would these factors remain critical over the coming years? Finally, as Giordano sought to enter new markets, the third issue of whether its competitive strengths could be transferred to other markets needs to be examined.

## COMPANY BACKGROUND

Giordano was founded by Jimmy Lai in 1980.[2] To give his venture a more sophisticated image, Lai picked an Italian name for his retail chain. In 1981 Giordano

---

"We are committed to provide our customers with value-for-money merchandise, professional customer service and comfortable shopping experience at convenient locations."

Giordano's Corporate Mission

*Source: Jochen Wirtz is an Associate Professor with the Department of Marketing, Faculty of Business Administration, National University of Singapore. Copyright © 2001 by Jochen Wirtz. Not to be reproduced or used without written permission. This case was prepared as the basis for class discussion rather than to illustrate effective or ineffective handling of an administrative situation. The author acknowledges the generous support in terms of time, information and feedback on earlier drafts of this case provided by Charles Fung, Chief Operating Officer and Executive Director of Giordano (Southeast Asia). Furthermore, the author gratefully acknowledges the input by Ang Swee Hoon, who co-authored earlier versions of this case published in the *Asian Case Research Journal* 4, no. 2 (2000), 145–167, and in Ang et al, *Principles of Marketing: An Asian Casebook* (Prentice Hall, Upper Saddle River, NJ, 2000), 80–87. Finally, the author would also like to acknowledge the excellent research assistance of Jerome Sze Wee Kho, who gathered much of the data and assisted with the write-up.

started in Hong Kong selling casual clothes manufactured predominantly for the United States market by a Hong Kong–based manufacturer, the Comitex Group. Initially Giordano focused on wholesale trade of high-margin merchandise under the Giordano brand in Hong Kong. In 1983 it scaled back on its wholesale operation and started to set up its own retail shops in Hong Kong. It also began to expand its market by distributing Giordano merchandise in Taiwan through a joint venture. In 1985 it opened its first retail outlet in Singapore.

However, in 1987 sales were low, and the business became unprofitable. Lai realized that the pricey retail chain concept was unprofitable. Under a new management team, Giordano changed its strategy. Until 1987 Giordano exclusively sold men's casual apparel. When it realized that an increasing number of female customers were attracted to its stores, Giordano changed its positioning and started selling unisex casual apparel. It repositioned itself as a retailer of discounted casual unisex apparel with the goal of maximizing unit sales instead of margins, and sold value-for-money merchandise. Its shift in strategy was successful. Its sales almost quadrupled, from HK$712 million (US$91.28 million) in 1989 to HK$3092 million (US$396.41 million) in 1999 (see Table 1).

# TABLE 1

## Financial Highlights (Amounts Expressed in HK$ Millions)

| (Consolidated) | 2000* | 1999 | 1998 | 1997 | 1996 | 1995 | 1994 |
|---|---|---|---|---|---|---|---|
| Turnover | 1,661.4 | 3092.2 | 2,609.2 | 3,014.4 | 3,522.0 | 3,482.0 | 2,863.7 |
| Turnover increase (%) | 16.2% | 18.5% | 13.4% | 14.4% | 1.2% | 21.6% | 22.7% |
| Profit after tax and minority interests | 173.3 | 360.0 | 76.1 | 68.0 | 261.2 | 250.2 | 195.3 |
| Profit after tax and minority interests increase (%) | 31.1% | 375.0% | 11.9% | 74.0% | 4.4% | 28.1% | 41.9% |
| Shareholders' fund | NA | 1,250.8 | 1,111.1 | 1,068.9 | 1,138.3 | 911.7 | 544.5 |
| Working capital | 701.1 | 762.3 | 700.6 | 654.2 | 670.3 | 496.0 | 362.0 |
| Total debt to equity ratio | NA | 0.5 | 0.3 | 0.3 | 0.4 | 0.7 | 0.9 |
| Bank borrowings to equity ratio | NA | 0 | 0 | 0 | 0 | 0 | 0.1 |
| Inventory turnover on sales (days) | 28 | 28 | 44 | 48 | 58 | 55 | 53 |
| Return on total assets (%) | NA | 18.8% | 5.3% | 4.8% | 16.5% | 16.4% | 18.8% |
| Return on average equity (%) | NA | 30.5% | 7.0% | 6.2% | 25.5% | 34.4% | 39.1% |
| Return on sales | NA | 11.6 | 2.9 | 2.3 | 7.4 | 7.2 | 6.8 |
| Earning per share (cents) | 24.5 | 51.3 | 10.8 | 9.6 | 36.9 | 38.8 | 30.9 |
| Cash dividend per share (cents) | 8.5 | 34.5 | 4.5 | 5.0 | 16.0 | 13.5 | 11.0 |

Note: NA indicates data were not available at time of publication.

*2000 figures are for the first six months of Giordano's 2000 financial year, ending June 30, 2000. Percentages for 2000 were calculated over the figures for same period in the previous year.

# MANAGEMENT VALUES AND STYLE

## Being Entrepreneurial and Accepting Mistakes As Learning Opportunities

The willingness to try new ways of doing things and learning from past errors was an integral part of Lai's management philosophy. The occasional failure represented a current limitation and indirectly pointed management to the right decision in the future. To demonstrate his commitment to this philosophy, Lai took the lead by being a role model for his employees: "Like in a meeting, I say, look, I have made this mistake. I'm sorry for that. I hope everybody learns from this. If I can make mistakes, who the hell do you think you are that you can't make mistakes?" Lai also strongly believed in empowerment—if everyone is allowed to contribute and participate, mistakes can be minimized.

## Treating Employees As an Asset

Besides the willingness to accept employees' mistakes, another factor that contributed to the success of Giordano was that it had a dedicated, trained, ever-smiling sales force. It considered front-line workers to be its customer service heroes. Charles Fung, Giordano's chief operations officer and executive director for Southeast Asia, said, "Even the most sophisticated training program won't guarantee the best customer service. People are the key. They make exceptional service possible. Training is merely a skeleton of a customer service program. It's the people who deliver that give it form and meaning."

Giordano had stringent selection procedures to make sure that only those candidates who matched the profile of what Giordano looked for in its employees were selected. Selection even continued into its training workshops. Fung called the workshops "attitude training." The service orientation and character of a new employee was tested in these workshops. These situations, he added, were an appropriate screening tool for "weeding out those made of grit and mettle."

Giordano's philosophy of quality service could be observed in its overseas outlets as well. Its Singapore operations, for example, achieved ISO 9002 certification. Its obsession with providing excellent customer service was best described by Fung: "The only way to keep abreast with stiff competition in the retail market is to know the customers' needs and serve them well. Customers pay our paychecks; they are our bosses. . . . Giordano considers service to be a very important element [in trying to draw customers] . . . service is in the blood of every member of our staff."

According to Fung, everyone who joined Giordano, even office employees, worked in a store for at least one week as part of his or her training. "They must understand and appreciate every detail of the operations. How can they offer proper customer assistance—internal and external—if they don't know what goes on in operations?"

In Singapore, for instance, Giordano invested heavily in training its employees. In 1998 it spent 3.9 percent of its overall payroll on training, with each employee receiving an average of 224 hours of training per year. It had a training room complete with one-way mirrors, video cameras, and other electronic paraphernalia. A training consultant and seven full-time line trainers conducted training sessions for all new sales staff, and existing staff was required to take refresher courses. Its commitment to training and developing its staff was recognized when it was awarded the People Developer Award in 1998.

However, providing training programs was not as important as ensuring the transfer of learning from the workshops and seminars to the store. As Fung explained, "Training is important. Every organization is providing its employees training. However, what is more important is the transfer of learning to the store. When there is a transfer of learning, each dollar invested in training yields a high return. We try to encourage this [transfer of learning] by cultivating a culture and by providing positive reinforcement, rewarding those who practice what they [learned]."

For Giordano, investment in service meant investment in people. Giordano paid high wages to attract and keep its staff. Giordano offered what Fung claimed was "one of the most attractive packages in an industry where employee turnover is high. We generally pay more than what the market pays." With higher wages, there was a lower staff turnover rate. Together, the higher wages and Giordano's emphasis on training had resulted in a corps of eager-to-please sales force.

Managing its vital human resources (HR) became a challenge to Giordano when it decided to expand into global markets. To replicate its high service quality positioning, Giordano needed to consider the HR issues involved when setting up retail outlets on unfamiliar ground. For example, the recruitment, selection, and training of local employees might require modifications to its formula for success in its current markets because of differences in culture, education, and technology of the new countries. Labor regulations would also affect HR policies such as compensation and providing welfare. Finally, expatriate policies for staff seconded to help run Giordano outside their home country and management practices needed to be considered.

## Simplicity and Speed

Giordano maintained a flat organizational structure. Fung believed that "this gives us the intensity to react to market changes on a day-to-day basis." Giordano followed a relaxed management style, where management worked closely with line staff. There were no separate offices for higher and top management, but rather their desks were located next to their staff's, separated only by shoulder-high panels. This closeness allowed easy communication, efficient project management, and speedy decision making, which are all critical ingredients to success amidst fast-changing consumer tastes and fashion trends. Speed allowed Giordano to keep its product development cycle short. Similar demands in quickness were also expected of its suppliers.

## KEY COMPETITIVE STRENGTHS

Giordano's home base, Hong Kong, was flooded with retailers both big and small. To beat the dog-eat-dog competition prevalent in Asia, especially Hong Kong, Lai felt that Giordano must have a distinctive competitive advantage. Although many retail outlets in Hong Kong competed almost exclusively on price, Lai felt differently about Giordano. Noting successful Western retailers, Lai astutely observed that there were other key factors for success. He started to benchmark Giordano against best practices organizations along four key areas: (1) computerization (from The Limited), (2) a tightly controlled menu (from McDonald's), (3) frugality (from Wal-Mart), and (4) value pricing (from Marks & Spencer) (Ang 1996).

The emphasis on service and the value-for-money concept had proven to be successful. Lai was convinced that the product was only half of what Giordano sells. Service was the other half, and Lai believed that service that was the best way to make customers to return to Giordano again and again. Lai said, "We are not just a shirt retailer, we are not just an apparel retailer. We are also a service retailer because we sell feeling. Let's make the guy feel good about coming into [our stores]" (Ang 1996).

## SERVICE

Giordano's commitment to excellent service was reflected in the list of service-related awards it had received. It was ranked number one by the *Far Eastern Economic Review,* for being innovative in responding to customers' needs, for three consecutive years—1994, 1995, and 1996. And when it came to winning service awards, the Giordano's name kept cropping up. In Singapore, it won numerous service awards over the years. It was given the Excellent Service Award in three consecutive years: 1996, 1997, and 1998. It also received three tourism awards: Store of the Year in 1991, Retailer of the Month in 1993, and Best Shopping Experience—Retailer Outlet in 1996. These were just some of the awards won by Giordano (Table 2).

How did Giordano achieve such recognition for its commitment to customer service? It began with the Customer Service Campaign in 1989. In that campaign, yellow badges bearing the words "Giordano Means Service," were worn by every Giordano employee. The "Giordano Means Service" philosophy had three tenets: We welcome unlimited try-ons; we exchange—no questions asked; and we serve with a smile. The yellow badges reminded employees that they were there to deliver excellent customer service.

Since Giordano's inception, several creative, customer-focused campaigns and promotions had been launched to extend its service orientation. For instance, in Singapore, Giordano asked its customers what they thought would be the fairest price to charge for a pair of jeans and charged each customer the price that they were willing to pay. This one-month campaign was immensely successful, with some 3,000 pairs of jeans sold every day during the promotion. In another service-related campaign, customers were given a free T-shirt for criticizing Giordano's service. More than 10,000 T-shirts were given away. Far from only being another brand building campaign, Giordano responded seriously to the feedback collected. For example, the Giordano logo was removed from some of its the merchandise, since some customers liked the quality but not the "value for money" image of the Giordano brand.

$\boxed{\text{T}\text{A}\text{B}\text{L}\text{E}}$ 2

## Recent Giordano Company Awards

| Award | Awarding Organization | Category | Year(s) |
|---|---|---|---|
| Excellent Service Award* | Singapore Productivity and Standards Board | — | 1996, 1997, 1998 |
| Tourism Award | Singapore Tourism Promotion Board | Best Shopping Experience | 1996 |
| American Service Excellence Award | American Express | Fashion/Apparel | 1995 |
| ISO 9002† | SISIR | — | 1994 |
| People Developer Award | Singapore Productivity and Standards Board | — | 1998 |
| Ear Award | Radio Corporation of Singapore | Listeners' Choice (English Commercial) | 1996 |
| Ear Award | Radio Corporation of Singapore | Creative Merits (English Jingles) | 1996 |
| Top Advertiser Award‡ | Radio Corporation of Singapore | — | 1994 |
| 1999 HKRMA Customer Service Award | Hong Kong Retail Management Association | — | 1999 |

Note: Awards given to the Giordano Originals Singapore.

*ISO 9002 refers to the guidelines from the Geneva-based International Organisation for Standardisation for companies that produce and install products.

†To be nominated for the Excellent Service Award, a company must have had, among other things, significant training and other programs in place that ensured quality service. These included systems for recognizing employees and getting customer feedback.

‡The Top Advertiser Award was given to companies in different categories that spent the most on advertising during a year. When Giordano received the award, an advertising and promotions budget of S$3 million was considered to be a lot. However, by 1999 the market was more competitive and many big players were spending more than S$8 million on advertising and promotions.

Against advice that it would be abused, Lai also introduced a no-questions-asked and no-time-limit exchange policy, which made it one of the few retailers in Asia outside Japan with such a generous exchange policy. Giordano claimed that returns were less than 0.1 percent of sales.

To ensure that every store and individual employee provided excellent customer service, performance evaluations were conducted frequently at the store level, as well as for individual employees. The service standard of each store was evaluated twice every month, and individual employees were evaluated once every two months. Internal competitions were designed to motivate employees and store teams to do their best in serving customers. Every month Giordano awarded the Service Star to individual employees, based on nominations provided by shoppers. In addition, every Giordano store was evaluated every month by mystery shoppers. Based on the combined results of these evaluations, the Best Service Shop award was given to the top store.

# VALUE FOR MONEY

Lai explained the rationale for Giordano's "value for money" policy. "Consumers are learning a lot better about what value is. Out of ignorance, people chose the brand. But the label does not matter, so the business has become value driven, because when people recognize value, that is the only game in town. So we always ask ourselves how can we sell it cheaper, make it more convenient for the consumer to buy, and deliver faster today than yesterday. That is all value, because convenience is value for the consumer. Time is value for the customer."

Giordano was able to consistently sell value-for-money merchandise through careful selection of suppliers, strict cost control, and resisting the temptation to increase retail prices unnecessarily. For instance, to provide greater shopping convenience to customers, Giordano in Singapore located its operations in densely populated housing estates in addition to its outlets in the traditional downtown retail areas.

# INVENTORY CONTROL

In markets with expensive retail space, retailers would try to maximize every square foot of the store for sales opportunities. Giordano was no different. Its strategy involved not having a back storeroom in each store. Instead, a central distribution center replaced the function of a back storeroom. With information technology (IT), Giordano was able to skillfully manage its inventory and forecast demand. When an item was sold, the barcode information identifying size, color, style, and price was recorded by the point-of-sale cash register and transmitted to the company's main computer. At the end of each day, the information was compiled at the store level and sent to the sales department and the distribution center. The compiled sales information became the store's order for the following day. Orders were filled during the night and were ready for delivery by early morning, ensuring that before a Giordano store opened for business, new inventory was already on the shelves.

Another advantage of its IT system was that the information was disseminated to production facilities in real time. Such information allowed customers' purchase patterns to be understood, and this provided valuable input to its manufacturing operations, resulting in fewer problems and lower costs related to slow-moving inventory. "If there is a slow-selling item, we will decide immediately how to sell it as quickly as possible. When the sales of an item hits a minimum momentum, we pull it out, instead of thinking of how to revitalize its sales." Giordano stores were therefore well stocked with fast-moving items and customers were happy, since they were seldom out of stock of anything.

The use of technology also afforded more efficient inventory holding. Giordano's inventory turnover on sales was reduced from 58 days in 1996 to 28 days in 1999, allowing it to thrive on lower gross margins. Savings were passed to customers, thus reinforcing its value-for-money philosophy. Despite the lower margins, Giordano was still able to post healthy profits. Such efficiency became a crucial factor when periodic price wars were encountered. Giordano was able to carve out ever-greater slices of the market, because it was easy money competing against companies that were used to relying on high gross margins to make up for slow inventory turnover.

Besides the use of IT and real-time information generated from the information system, Giordano's successful inventory control was achieved through the close integration of the purchasing and selling functions. As Fung elaborated, "There are two very common scenarios that many retailers encounter: slow-selling items stuck in the warehouse and fast-selling popular items that are out of stock. Giordano tries to minimize the probability of the occurrence of these two scenarios, which requires close integration between the purchasing and selling departments."

But more than technology and inventory control, Giordano had another competitive edge over its competitors. As Fung explained, "In the 1980s and early 1990s, when few retailers would use IT to manage their inventory, the use of IT gave Giordano a leading edge. However, today, when many retailers are using such technology, it [IT] is no longer our real distinctive competitive strength. In a time when there is information overload, it is the organizational culture in Giordano to intelligently use the information that sets us apart from the rest." This was further explained by Lai: "None of this is novel. Marks and Spencer in Britain, The Gap and Wal-Mart in America, and Seven-Eleven in Japan have used similar systems for years. Nowadays, information flows so fast that anybody can acquire or imitate ideas. What matters is how well the ideas are executed." Indeed, with rapid development in Internet and Intranet technologies, packaged solutions (e.g., Microsoft Office, point of sale [POS] and enterprise resource planning [ERP] software), and supporting telecommunications services (e.g., broadband Internet access), acquiring integrated IT and logistics technology has become easier and more cost-effective than ever before. Hence, a competitive advantage based on technology and its implementation is likely to become smaller and more difficult to maintain in the medium- to long-term future.

## PRODUCT POSITIONING

When a business becomes successful, there is always a temptation to expand into more products and services to meet customers' needs. However, Giordano recognized the importance of limiting its expansion and focusing on one specific area. Fung said, "Focus makes the business more manageable: positioning in the market, keeping the store simple, better inventory management. And we can get the best out of limited resources." Simplicity and focus were reflected in the way Giordano merchandised its goods. "You'll see no more than 100 items in a Giordano store. We have 17 core items; other retailers have 200 to 300 items. Merchandising a wide range of products causes retailers to take a longer time to react to market changes."

Giordano's willingness to experiment with new ideas and its perseverance despite past failures could also be seen in its introduction of new product lines. Its venture into mid-priced women's fashion, Giordano Ladies, clearly illustrated this. With its line of smart blouses, dress pants, and short skirts, the company was hoping to attract young, stylish women and benefit from the fatter profit margins enjoyed in more upscale niches of women's clothing—about 50 percent to 60 percent compared with 40 percent for casual wear. Giordano, however, wandered into a market crowded with seasoned players. Although there were no complaints about the look or quality of the line, it had to vie with more than a dozen established brands already on the racks, including Theme and Esprit. It also failed initially to differentiate its new clothing line from its mainstream product line, and even tried to sell both through the same outlets. Nevertheless, it persisted in its efforts and Giordano Ladies made a successful comeback. In 1999 it took advantage of the financial troubles facing rivals such as Theme, as well as the post–Asian currency crisis boom in many parts of Asia, to aggressively re-launch its Giordano Ladies' line, which met with great success. As of June 30, 2000, the reinforced Giordano Ladies focuses on a select segment, with 14 stores worldwide offering personalized service (e.g., staff are trained to memorize names of regular customers and recall past purchases). It also had plans to expand its five more Giordano Ladies outlets in Hong Kong, Taiwan, and Middle East.

Giordano recently began to reposition its brand by emphasizing sensible but more stylish clothes and broadening Giordano's appeal by overhauling the stores and apparel. For instance, a large portion of its capital expenditure (totaling HK$56.9 million in the first six months of 2000) went to renovations of its stores to enhance shop ambience. This indicated its intention to reinforce its image and to position it in line with its globalization strategy and changing consumer needs. Giordano's relatively mid-priced positioning worked well—inexpensive yet contemporary looking outfits appealed to Asia's frugal customers, especially during the Asian economic crisis. However, over time this positioning became inconsistent with the brand image that Giordano tried hard to build over the years. Says one of Giordano's top executives, "The feeling went from 'this is nice and good value' to 'this is cheap.' When you try to live off selling 100-Hong Kong-dollar shirts, it catches up with you" (*AsiaWeek*, October 15, 1999).

Nevertheless, while it gradually re-marketed its core brand as a trendier label, Giordano continued to cater to the needs of customers who favored its value-for-money positioning. In 1999 it launched a new product line, Bluestar Exchange, to cater to the needs of its budget-conscious customers, after successfully prototyping in Hong Kong and Taiwan. The good market responses to this new line, which targeted mainly families (similar to Gap's Old Navy), triggered plans to expand from the 14 Bluestar stores in Hong Kong and 3 in Taiwan, to 20 in Hong Kong, 15 in Taiwan, 2 in Singapore, and up to 100 in Mainland China (including franchised stores).

## AGGRESSIVE ADVERTISING AND PROMOTION

Fung said, "Giordano spends a large proportion of its turnover on advertising and promotions. No retailer of our size spends as much as us." For the past five years, Giordano in Singapore had been spending about S$1.5 million (HK$6.675 million) to S$2 million (HK$8.9 million) annually on its advertising and promotional activities. It won the Top Advertiser Award from 1991 to 1994 (see Table 1). Up to June 30, 2000, total advertising and promotion expenditure for the Group amounted to HK$41.5 million, or 3 percent of the Group's retail turnover. In addition to its big budget, Giordano's advertising and promotion campaigns were creative and appealing. One such campaign was "Round the Clock Madness Shopping" with the Singapore radio station FM93.3 on May 1, 1994. Different clothing items were discounted between 10 percent and 60 percent at various times beginning at midnight. For example, jeans were offered at a 20 percent discount from 12 A.M. to 1 A.M., while polo shirts and T-shirts were given a 30 percent discount from 1 A.M. to 2 A.M., and then shorts were sold at a 40 percent discount from 2 A.M. to 3 A.M. To keep listeners awake and excited, the product categories on sale at each time slot were only released at the specified hour, so that nobody knew the next items that would be on this special sale. Listeners to the radio station were cajoled into coming to Giordano stores throughout the night (Ang 1996). In 1996 Giordano won the Singapore Ear Award. Its English radio commercial was voted by listeners to be one of the best, with the most creative English jingle.

Another success was its "Simply Khakis" promotion, launched in April 1999, which emphasized basic, street-culture style that "mixed and matched" and thus fit all occasions. In Singapore, within days of its launch the new line sold out and had to be re-launched two weeks later. By October 1999 more than a million pairs of khaki trousers and shorts had been sold. This success could be attributed partly to its clearly defined communications objectives, as Garrett Bennett, Giordano's executive director in charge of merchandising and operations, said: "We want to be the key provider of the basics: khakis, jeans and the white shirt." Elsewhere in the region, sales were booming for Giordano despite only moderate recovery experienced in the retail industry. Giordano's strength in executing innovative and effective promotional strategies helped the retailer to reduce the impact of the Asian crisis on its sales and take advantage of the slight recovery seen in early 1999. Aggressive advertising and promotions also played a significant role in the successful re-marketing of its core brand and re-launch or introduction of sister brands, Giordano Ladies, Giordano Junior, and Bluestar Exchange.

## THE ASIAN APPAREL RETAIL INDUSTRY

Severely hit by the Asian crisis from 1997 to 1999, the Asian retail industry went through dramatic restructuring and consolidation. Many retailers reduced the number of shops in their chains or closed down completely. Almost everyone in the industry implemented cost-cutting measures while at the same time cajoling reluctant customers with promotional strategies. Yet there was a silver lining, as the more competitive firms were able to take advantage of lower rentals and the departure of weaker companies. Some firms, including Giordano, worked toward strengthening their positioning and brand image to better compete in the long run. Some retailers also explored opportunities or accelerated their presence in markets that were less affected by the Asian crisis—mostly in markets outside Asia.

During the crisis and for the immediate future, until a full recovery set in, industry analysts predicted that opportunities would continue to be driven by value. Thus Giordano's value proposition appeared appropriate during these times. It was not surprising, then, that in spite of its problems, Giordano was ranked the fourteenth most competitive company overall in Asia by a regional business magazine (*Asia Inc.*, June 6, 1997). It even won a place on Forbes Global's 1999 list of the World's 300 Best Small Companies, together with eight other Hong Kong companies, indicative of world-class performance. Giordano's performance was credited to its management's swift cost-control strategies in the areas of rents, outsourcing, inventory control, cash management, and overseas travel. The economic downturn had indeed revealed management's flexibility and responsiveness in making decisive moves.

The retailing environment was becoming more dynamic than before, a change that was perhaps led by growing sophistication of tastes and rapid advancements in the media, communications, and logistics environment. Giordano's response to these trends would be the key to its ability to compete in the future, especially as these trends seem to "commoditize" Giordano's current competitive edge in IT, stock control, and logistics.

## GIORDANO'S COMPETITORS

Until recently, Giordano's main competitors for low-priced apparel were Hang Ten, Bossini, and Benetton. However, its shift in positioning and the squeeze of the retailing sector, caused by the crisis, pushed more upmarket firms such as Esprit and Theme to compete for Giordano's value-for-money segment. Table 3 provides a list of their Web sites for more information regarding their product lines and operations. Table 4 shows the relative positioning of Giordano and its competitors: Gap, Bossini, Hang Ten, Baleno, Esprit, and Theme. Financial data for Giordano, Esprit and the Gap are shown in Table 5. Table 6 shows the geographical areas these firms operate in.

Hong Kong–based firms Bossini, Hang Ten, and Baleno were generally positioned as low-priced retailers offering reasonable quality and service. The clothes emphasized versatility and simplicity. But while Hang Ten and Baleno was more popular among teenagers and young adults, Bossini had a more general appeal. Their distribution strategies were somewhat similar, but they focused on different markets. For instance, according to Fung, while Hang Ten was only strong in Taiwan, Baleno was increasingly strong in China and Taiwan. On the other hand, Bossini was very strong in Hong Kong and relatively strong in Singapore but had little presence in Taiwan and China.

## TABLE 3

**Web sites of Giordano and its Closest Competitors**

| Firm | Website Address |
|---|---|
| Baleno | www.baleno.com.hk |
| Bossini | www.plateadas.com/bossini |
| Esprit | www.esprit-intl.com |
| Gap | www.gap.com |
| Giordano | www.giordano.com.hk |
| Hang Ten | www.hangten.com |
| Theme | www.theme.com.hk |

## TABLE 4

### Competitive Positioning

| Firms | Positioning | Target Market |
| --- | --- | --- |
| Giordano and Gap | Value for money<br>Mid-priced but trendy fashion | Unisex casual wear for all ages<br>(under different brands) |
| Hang Ten | Value for money<br>Sporty lifestyle | Casual wear and sportswear, teens<br>and young adults |
| Bossini | Low price (comparable to<br>Giordano) | Unisex apparel, both young and<br>old (30s) |
| Baleno | Value for money<br>Trendy, young-age casual wear | Unisex appeal, young adults<br>Ladies' casual, but also other |
| Esprit | More upmarket than Giordano<br>Stylish, trendy | specialized lines for children<br>Ladies' smart fashion, ladies' |
| Theme | Upmarket, stylish | business wear |

## TABLE 5

### Competitive Financial Data for 1999: Giordano, Esprit, and Gap (Amounts Expressed in HK$ Millions)

|  | Giordano<br>(in HK$ m) | Esprit<br>(in HK$ m) | Gap<br>(in HK$ m) |
| --- | --- | --- | --- |
| Turnover | 3,092 | 5,994 | 90,756 |
| Profit after tax and minority interests | 360 | 430 | 8,791 |
| Working capital | 762 | NA | 3,470 |
| Return on total assets (%) | 18.8% | NA | 24.6% |
| Return on average equity (%) | 30.5% | NA | 59.2% |
| Return on sales (%) | 11.6% | 7.2% | 9.7% |

Sources: *Annual report 1999*, Giordano International; *Financial Highlights 1999*, Esprit International; and *Annual report 1999*, Gap.

Note: Esprit reports its earnings in Euro and Gap in US$. All reported figures have been converted into HK$ at the following exchange rate (as of Nov. 2000): US$1 = Euro$1.16 = HK$7.8.

Esprit is an international fashion lifestyle brand, principally engaged in the image and product design, sourcing, manufacturing, and retail and wholesale distribution of a wide range of women's, men's, and children's apparel, footwear, accessories, and other products under the Esprit brand name. The Esprit name was promoted as a "lifestyle" image and products were strategically positioned as good quality and value for money—a position that Giordano was occupying. As of 1998 Esprit had a distribution network of more than 6,500 stores and outlets in 40 countries in Europe, Asia, Canada, and Australia. The main markets were in Europe, which accounted for approximately 62 percent of 1998 sales, and in Asia, which accounted for approximately 27 percent of 1998 sales. The Esprit brand products were principally sold via directly managed retail outlets, wholesale customers

# TABLE 6

**Geographical Presence of Giordano and Current Competitors**

| Country | Giordano | Hang Ten | Bossini | Baleno | Esprit | Theme |
|---|---|---|---|---|---|---|
| *Asia* | | | | | | |
| HK/Macao | X | X | X | X | X | X |
| Singapore | X | X | X | — | X | X |
| South Korea | X | X | NA | — | X | X |
| Taiwan | X | X | NA | X | X | X |
| China | X | X | NA | X | X | X |
| Malaysia | X | X | NA | — | X | X |
| Indonesia | X | X | NA | — | NA | X |
| Philippines | X | X | NA | — | NA | X |
| Thailand | X | X | NA | — | NA | X |
| *World* | | | | | | |
| U.S. and Canada | — | X | X | — | X | X |
| Europe | — | X | X | — | X | X |
| Japan | — | X | NA | — | X | X |
| Australia | X | X | NA | — | X | X |
| **Total** | **740** | **NA** | **NA** | **125** | **8,470** | **200** |

Note: Data are as of 1999.

X indicates presence in the country/region; — indicates no presence; NA indicates data not available at time of publication.

(including department stores, specialty stores, and franchisees), and by licensees in relation to products manufactured under license, principally through the licensees' own distribution networks.

Theme International Holdings Limited was founded in Hong Kong in 1986 by Chairman and Chief Executive Officer Kenneth Lai. He identified a niche in the local market, for high-quality, fashionable ladies' business wear, although it subsequently expanded into casual wear. The Theme label and chain was in direct competition with Giordano Ladies. From the first store in 1986 to a chain comprising more than 200 outlets in Hong Kong, China, Korea, Macao, Taiwan, Singapore, Malaysia, Indonesia, the Philippines, Japan, Thailand, Canada, and Holland, the phenomenal growth of Theme was built on a vertically integrated corporate structure and advanced management system. However, its ambitious expansion proved to be costly in view of the economic crisis, with interest soaring on high levels of debt. In 1999 the company announced a HK$106.1 million net loss for the six months to September 30, 1998, and it closed 23 retail outlets in Hong Kong, which traded under its subsidiary The Clothing Shop. Theme International has since been acquired by High Fashion International, a Hong Kong-based fashion retailer specializing in up-market, trendy apparel.

In general, although these firms had slightly different positioning strategies and targeted dissimilar but overlapping segments, they all competed in a number of similar areas. For example, all firms heavily emphasized advertising and sales promotion—selling fashionable clothes at attractive prices. Almost all stores were also primarily situated in good ground-floor locations, drawing high-volume traffic and facilitating shopping, browsing, and impulse buying. However, Giordano clearly distinguished itself from its competitors with its high-quality service and cost leadership, which together provided great customer value that none of its competitors was able to match.

In a study by *Interbrand* on top Asian marquees, Giordano was Asia's highest-ranking general apparel retailer. It was ranked number 20. The clothing names next in line were Australia's Quicksilver at number 45 and Country Road at number 47. However, Giordano as a world label was still far off. As a spokesperson on consumer insights for advertising agency McCann-Erickson said, "It is a good brand, but not a great one. Compared to other international brands, it doesn't shape opinion."

A threat from United States–based Gap was also looming. Giordano was also aware that the American retailer was invading Asia. Gap was already in Japan. After 2005, when it is expected that garment quotas will be abolished, imports into the region should become more cost effective. Hence, Giordano had to examine whether its intention to shift toward a higher position from its current value-for-money position was viable.

## GIORDANO'S GROWTH STRATEGY

As early as the 1980s Giordano realized that it was difficult to achieve substantial growth and economies of scale if it operated only in Hong Kong. The key was in regional expansion. By 1999 Giordano had opened 740 stores in 23 markets, out of which Giordano directly managed 317 stores (Table 7). Until 2000, four markets dominated its retail and distribution operations—Hong Kong, Taiwan, China, and Singapore (Table 8).

Giordano cast its sights on markets beyond Asia, partially driven by its desire for growth and partially trying to reduce its dependence on Asia, which was shown all too clearly during the crisis. In 1999 Giordano opened four outlets in Melbourne, Australia, and planned to add 15 to 20 more stores by 2000. The slow speed of expansion in Australia, caused by problems in locating good retail space (most leases are for 4 to 5 years), might be overcome by acquiring chain stores there. Plans for setting up stores in Europe in October 2000 were already in the pipeline, and South Africa and South America were also under consideration. However, Giordano did not intend to enter the U.S. market in the next 2 to 3 years because of keen competition.

Although the crisis made Giordano rethink its regional strategy, it was still determined to enter and further penetrate new Asian markets. This determination led to the successful opening of 253 stores in Mainland China in 1999, 10 of which were directly managed by the Giordano Group. It opened three stores in Jakarta and planned to open another 12 in 2000, and might even venture into India and Japan. In contrast, it was reducing its reliance on Hong Kong by opening fewer new stores, as the pace of recovery in the Hong Kong retail sector was relatively slow compared with other Asian markets. Instead, it would utilize its cash reserves for expansion into high growth markets like China and Malaysia.

Giordano's success in these markets would depend on its understanding of these markets and consumer tastes and preferences for fabrics, colors, and

# T A B L E 7

## Operational Highlights for Retail and Distribution Division
## (Figures Year-End Unless Specified)

|  | 1999 | 1998 | 1997 | 1996 | 1995 | 1994 | 1993 |
|---|---|---|---|---|---|---|---|
| Number of retail outlets |  |  |  |  |  |  |  |
| Directly managed by the Group | 317 | 308 | 324 | 294 | 280 | 283 | 257 |
| Franchised | 423 | 370 | 316 | 221 | 171 | 77 | 481 |
| Total number of retail outlets | 740 | 678 | 640 | 515 | 451 | 360 | 738 |
| Retail floor area directly managed |  |  |  |  |  |  |  |
| by the Group (sq. ft.) | 301,100 | 358,500 | 313,800 | 295,500 | 286,200 | 282,700 | 209,500 |
| Sales per square foot (HK$) | 8,400 | 6,800 | 8,000 | 9,900 | 10,500 | 10,600 | 12,600 |
| Number of employees | 6,237 | 6,319 | 8,175 | 10,004 | 10,348 | 6,863 | 2,330 |
| Comparable store sales |  |  |  |  |  |  |  |
| Increase/(decrease) (%) | 21% | (13)% | (11)% | (6)% | 8% | (9)% | 15% |
| Number of sales associates | 2,026 | 1,681 | 1,929 | 1,958 | 2,069 | 1,928 | 1,502 |

# T A B L E 8

## Regional Highlights

|  | Taiwan 1999 | Hong Kong 1999 | China 1999 | Singapore 1999 | Malaysia 1999 |
|---|---|---|---|---|---|
| Net Sales (HK$ millions) | 953.1 | 681.7 | 543.7 | 349.2 | 66.6 |
| Sales per sq. ft. (HK$) | 6,000 | 9,400 | 22,500 | 13,800 | 3,600 |
| Comparable store sales increase (%)* | 31% | 8% | 4% | 48% | 69% |
| Retail floor area (sq. ft.) | 165,700 | 100,000 | 24,700 | 24,400 | 20,400 |
| Number of sales associates | 827 | 441 | 350 | 228 | 115 |
| Number of outlets |  |  |  |  |  |
| Directly managed | 178 | 61 | 10 | 27 | 23 |
| Franchised | 0 | 0 | 243 | 0 | 11 |

*Note: Figures as compared with previous financial year.

advertising. In the past Giordano relied on a consistent strategy across different countries; elements of this successful strategy included its positioning and service strategies, information systems and logistics, and human resource policies. However, tactical implementation (e.g., promotional campaigns) was left mostly to local managers in their respective countries. A country's performance (e.g., sales, contribution, service levels, and customer feedback) was monitored by regional headquarters (e.g., Singapore for Southeast Asia), and the head office in Hong Kong. Weekly performance reports were made accessible to all managers. In recent years it appeared that as the organization expanded beyond Asia, different strategies had to be developed for different regions or countries.

# Exercises

1. Describe and evaluate Giordano's product strategy.
2. Describe and evaluate Giordano's current positioning strategy. Should Giordano reposition itself against its competitors in its current and new markets, and should it have different positioning strategies for different geographic markets?
3. What are Giordano's key success factors (KSF) and sources of competitive advantage? Are its competitive advantages sustainable, and how would they develop in the future?
4. Could Giordano transfer its key success factors to new markets as it expanded both in Asia and the other parts of the world?
5. How do you think Giordano had/would have to adapt its marketing and operations strategies and tactics when entering and penetrating your country?
6. What general lessons can be learnt from Giordano for other major clothing retailers in your country?

# References

"Aiming High: Asia's 50 Most Competitive Companies," *Asia Inc.*, June 6, 1997, pp. 34–37.

Swee Hoon Ang, "Giordano Holdings Limited," in John A. Quelch, Siew Meng Leong, Swee Hoon Ang, and Chin Tiong Tan (Eds.): *Cases in Marketing Management and Strategy: An Asian-Pacific Perspective*. (Upper Saddle River, New Jersey: Prentice Hall, 1996), 182–190.

"An All-New Dress for Success," *AsiaWeek* 25, no. 41 (October 15, 1999).

"And the Winning Store Is, Again," *The Straits Times (Singapore)*, December 2, 1995.

"Asia: Giordano Plans Expansion," *Sing Tao Daily*, June 29, 1999.

"Asian IPO Focus: Analysts See Little to Like in HK's Veeko," *Dow Jones International News*, April 12, 1999.

Cecille Austria, "The Bottom Line," *World Executive's Digest*, December 19, 1994, pp. 17–20.

"Casual-wear Chain Prospers on Cost-Cutting Regime" *South China Morning Post*, October 15, 1999.

"China: HK Companies Commended by Forbes for Best Practices," *China Business Information Network*, November 12, 1999.

Mark Clifford, "Extra Large," *Far Eastern Economic Review*, December 2, 1993, pp. 72–76.

"Company Looks Outside Asia," *Dow Jones International News*, August 12, 1998.

"Creditors Push Struggling Theme Fashion Outlet into Liquidation," *South China Morning Post*, March 11, 1999.

Esprit International, *Financial Highlights 1999*.

"Fashion Free-Fall," *The Asian Wall Street Journal*, November 9, 1998.

"Giordano 12-mth Target Price Raised to 16.00 HKD," *AFX (AP)*, May 16, 2000.

"Giordano's After-tax Earnings Soared in First Half," *The Asian Wall Street Journal*, July 27, 1999.

"Giordano Comes out of the Cold," *Business Week*, May 31, 1999.

"Giordano Details $700 Million Expansion," *South China Morning Post*, December 4, 1999.

"Giordano Dreams up Sale for Insomniacs," *Business Times (Singapore)*, May 6, 1994.

"Giordano Expects to Set Up Ops in Europe October" *AFX (AP)*, June 19, 2000.

Giordano Holdings Limited, *Annual Report 1993.*

Giordano Holdings Limited, *Annual Report 1997.*

Giordano International Limited, *Annual Report 1998.*

Giordano International Limited, *Annual Report 1999.*

Giordano International Limited, *Interim Results 2000.*

"Giordano Intl 1998 Net Profit," *AFX (AP)*, March 25, 1999 (from Dow Jones Interactive).

"Giordano Out of the Running to Buy Theme: High Fashion International Emerges as Favourite in Race for Control," *South China Morning Post*, November 25, 1999.

"Giordano Predicts Further Growth as Net Profit Reaches $46.3 Million," *The Asian Wall Street Journal*, March 3, 2000.

"Giordano Scores with Smart Moves," *The Straits Times (Singapore)*, September 11, 1993.

"Giordano Seeks to Acquire Chain Stores in Australia," *AFX (AP)*, February 8, 2000.

"Giordano Spreads its Wings," *The Straits Times (Singapore)*, March 13, 1994.

"Good Service Has Brought Giordano Soaring Sales," *Business Times (Singapore)*, August 6, 1993.

"High-end training to Get More Funding," *The Straits Times (Singapore)*, October 1, 1998.

"HK Bossini International Fiscal Year Net Profit HK$17.6 Million Vs HK$45.5 Million Loss" *Dow Jones Business News*, July 16, 1999.

"HK Giordano Gets Green Light to Reopen in Shanghai," *Dow Jones International News*, June 9, 1999.

"Hong Kong: High Fashion to Takeover Theme," *Sing Tao Daily*, November 26, 1999.

"Hong Kong Retailer Raced to New Markets, Spurring Everbright Loan," *The Asian Wall Street Journal*, April 7, 1998.

"Hubris Catches up to Theme," *The Globe and Mail*, April 7, 1998.

"In HK: Retail Shares Win Praise Amid Companies' Losses," *The Asian Wall Street Journal*, June 25, 1999.

Frances Huang, "Interview," *AFX (AP)*, September 16, 1998 (from Dow Jones Interactive).

Gap, *Annual Report 1999.*

Quinn D. Mills and Richard C. Wei, *Giordano Holdings Ltd.* (Cambridge, Mass.: Harvard Business School, 1993).

"Old Loss Masks Giordano Growth," *South China Morning Post*, March 5, 1999.

"Service Means Training," *The Straits Times (Singapore)*, October 7, 1998.

"Simple Winning Formula," *Business Times (Singapore)*, August 6, 1993.

"The Outlook for Asian Retailing," *Discount Merchandiser* (May 1999).

"Theme International Unit to Close 23 Stores," *The Asian Wall Street Journal*, August 4, 1998.

"US News Brief: Benetton Group," *The Wall Street Journal Europe*, December 17, 1998.

"What Is the People Developer," *The Straits Times (Singapore)*, September 30, 1998.

## Notes

1. The exchange rates at the time the case was written (October 2000) were US$1 = HK$7.80 and S$1 = HK$4.45.

2. Mr. Jimmy Lai left the management of Giordano and has not been directly involved in the running of Giordano since 1991. He is now managing his new venture, a Hong Kong publication called *Next Magazine*.

# case 13

# Roscoe Nondestructive Testing*

After nine months, Grover Porter, president of Roscoe Nondestructive Testing, Inc. (Roscoe), was beginning to question the success of his new quality improvement program (QIP). Initiated in March 1991, the QIP had produced substantial increases in recent customer satisfaction surveys; however, none of that satisfaction seemed to be fueling a return to growth in either revenue or number of clients. Porter anticipated Roscoe's second down year in a row as the company continued to lose major customers, and he was eager to reestablish the growth that had preceded the last two years of decline.

It was hard to believe that the cyclical downturn in the pulp and paper industry had pushed the boiler inspection business to competing solely on price. Porter still felt that there was room in the industry for a quality service at a fair price, but the ineffectiveness of the QIP had prompted Porter to reconsider adjusting Roscoe's pricing structure.

## I. THE NONDESTRUCTIVE TESTING INDUSTRY

Nondestructive testing (NDT) involves the examination of materials to discover microscopic cracks, corrosion, or malformation, using inspection techniques that do not damage the material under scrutiny. Common inspection techniques include the use of x-rays, ultrasonics, and electrical eddy currents.

NDT is used in a wide variety of applications, including the examination of aircraft parts, tanks and vessels of various shapes and sizes, and welds of all kinds.

---

Roscoe primarily uses ultrasonic thickness measuring devices to determine the thickness of metal plating.

NDT technicians are certified by area of expertise (e.g., ultrasonic) and accumulated skill and experience (Levels I–III). Technicians certified in more than one inspection technique are a treasured resource in most firms. They were generally employed by four types of companies:

1. "Mom and pop" labs usually employ fewer than 25 people and provide a single type of inspection service to a small number of customers. These firms are the low-cost providers and are quite willing to bid at cost simply to keep busy. Many are often tied to a single client who wields considerable control over pricing and delivery.

2. Nationwide companies have labs around the country and a high degree of name recognition. These firms also provide inspection services to a large number of different industries; however, individual offices usually serve a narrow segment of the market.

3. Specialty firms target very narrow market segments that require specific needs. These firms make large capital investments in the latest inspection equipment and employ the highest-skilled technicians. Barriers to entry into these specialized markets are high, so specialty firms have traditionally achieved high levels of profitability.

4. Although much larger than the mom and pop labs, regional firms lack the name recognition and market strength of the nationwide companies. These firms employ up to 150 technicians and have the resources to tackle the largest inspection jobs. Roscoe is a regional firm, operating primarily in the central southern part of the United States.

All in all, management of NDT firms has been historically uninspired, driven mainly by owner-operators who managed to survive the lean years.

## HISTORY OF ROSCOE

Roscoe was founded in 1973 by Hans Norregaard in Roscoe, Louisiana. After 30 years as an NDT technician, Norregaard decided to set up shop for himself amid many of the pulp and paper mills located in western Louisiana. Roscoe focused on the inspection of large boilers, a service designed to monitor the corrosion of the boiler walls. Inspections conducted every two to three years provided mills with sufficient warning to replace weakened, corroded plates in boiler walls before a catastrophic accident occurred.

In 1980 Norregaard sold the company to National Inspection Services (NIS) for $1.75 million. NIS was a subsidiary of Swanson Industries, a large diversified holding company. At that time, NIS brought in Chad Huerlmann (a Harvard MBA) to manage the company. Huerlmann was eager to run a small business and viewed the Roscoe acquisition as a great opportunity.

The company continued well for four years, until the pulp and paper industry bottomed out again. Hampered by misguided directives and burdened by corporate overhead, Roscoe's low-cost position no longer protected it from the growing price pressure facing NDT companies in the pulp and paper industry. Also, Huerlmann failed to establish an effective relationship with the technicians in the company, and many resigned or left the NDT industry altogether. By 1984 Swanson Industries decided to divest of NIS altogether, and Roscoe was once again up for sale.

At that time Hans Norregaard and a longtime business associate, Grover Porter, decided to get back into the NDT business. Together, they bought back Roscoe for about 35 cents on the dollar. They were convinced that by offering an improved inspection service for a fair price, they could rebuild the company's reputation and good fortunes.

After dismissing Huerlmann, Hans and Grover began building a new management team for Roscoe. A new controller, Jane Bottensak, was hired away from MQS Inspection. Ted Witkowski, a staff professional engineer (PE) out of Texas A&M who had previously worked for Exxon, was also taken on. Both men thought Ted would bring some much-needed technical backbone to the company. Also, longtime technician, Ed Brown, was promoted to operations manager. Finally, Roscoe began recruiting technicians from the best vocational tech schools in the country.

In 1987 Hans Norregaard retired, and Grover Porter became president. Roscoe was back on track.

In 1990 Roscoe encountered a downturn in both revenues and customers. Many mills simply decided not to release bids as often as they used to. Although Roscoe always lost some contracts to lower bidders, Porter felt the recent slow-down in the pulp and paper industry exacerbated Roscoe's situation by forcing mills to be more cost conscious. Still, Porter felt that there must be room for the services that Roscoe offered: "Hans and I have put together a great management team over the last three years and our technicians are some of the best in the industry. Roscoe offers an efficient, quality inspection service and we feel that we can price accordingly." However, the recent loss of established customers caused Grover Porter to question the validity of Roscoe's purported "high-quality" service.

## CUSTOMER PROFILES

Although boiler inspections in pulp and paper mills have been standard practice for many years, mills differed widely on the representative who interacted with Roscoe's inspection team. This contact could be almost anyone from the plant manager down to a purchasing agent. The following descriptions illustrate many of the problems that have plagued Roscoe recently.

George McDonald at the Franklin Paper Company was a typical plant manager who reigned over his plant like a king over his castle. Like any other plant manager, McDonald was primarily concerned about controlling costs and was hostile to the idea of boiler inspections in general. Because inspections could be conducted only during plant shutdowns, McDonald was unhappy about the lost production time:

> Besides the $85,000 inspection fee, my plant is idle during the two days it takes your team to complete the job. At 750 tons per day, I pay an additional opportunity cost of over $330,000 every day you are in my plant. A boiler will

last 20 years without exploding and if it wasn't for corporate HQ, I would never bother with the inspections. Besides, the only thing that I ever get out of it is an "OK" and a pile of figures that I can't make head nor tail of.

International Paper's plant in Longview, Texas, was one of the few clients that maintained their own NDT department. As with other mills, the department consisted of only one retired NDT technician who interacted with service providers like Roscoe. Bob Kapala typified the kind of NDT person often found in paper mills. He was friendly and eager to help but was actually often more of a hindrance. The last thing a technician wanted was someone looking over his shoulder all the time.

After the inspection was completed, Bob would combine the recent inspection data with a pile of past data and attempt to find trends in corrosion patterns. The fact that different inspection firms provided data in different formats complicated Bob's task.

Jim Bulgrin at the Rockton Paper Mill in Texarkana, Texas, presented a different problem. Bulgrin, a recent graduate of Georgia Tech, had been hired into the mill's engineering services department seven months ago. As one of Roscoe's team supervisors described him, Bulgrin was "as wet behind the ears as a newborn calf." But he was eager to learn and was on top of every detail.

Problems arose when Jim noticed that thickness readings on one section of a boiler were considerably greater than when inspected two years before. After confronting the technicians, who ended up getting very angry, Jim eagerly reported the discrepancy to his boss. It was later discovered that a new plate had been welded onto the boiler in that area, but Roscoe lost the contract with Rockton.

Pulp mill supervisors, like Billy Dunlap at the Lufkin Pulp Mill, were Roscoe's most common contact inside a mill. Dunlap has been cajoling his boiler along for the past 15 years and did not take easily to anyone mistreating his "baby."

Finally, the inevitable contact is the purchasing representative who files the paperwork with accounting. Lucy Boyle, in purchasing at Lufkin, was never happy about processing paperwork relating to inspection services:

> Corporate headquarters requires us to file additional paperwork for one-time expenses greater than $50,000. With inspection fees well over $75,000, I end up processing over three times more paperwork than normal. My life doesn't return to normal until the mill goes back on-line.

## A PRELUDE TO ACTION

In January 1991, while attending the Nondestructive Testing Managers Association meeting in Las Vegas, Grover Porter was still struggling with the question of what defined a quality service. As it turned out, one of the speakers in the New Business Segment of the conference presented a talk on the components of service quality. And in that same month a number of articles describing quality improvement programs at major aerospace inspection firms ran in both the ASNT and AWS Journals.[1]

At the monthly staff meeting in February, Porter discussed his concerns regarding the level of service provided by Roscoe. "As you all know, we've lost a bunch of accounts in the last few months. I suspect our service quality is not what it should be, and I've been thinking about a quality improvement program. If we don't do something soon, we may be forced to reduce our fees."

Bottensak, the controller, nodded her head in agreement and commented that something had to be done. "Let's go for it! None of us need reminding that 1990 was a bad year, but it looks like this year will be even worse. That's not great for our bonuses!"

Ted Witkowski, the staff PE, and Ed Brown, the operations manager, were extremely skeptical. Ted explained,

> Look, we have the best-trained technicians out there with top-of-the-line equipment. They make some mistakes now and then, but when a boiler inspection requires 20,000 readings, that will happen. Besides, the mill has to look at the readings over an entire area and not just a single point. It's not reasonable to inspect every point twice. The mills couldn't afford the cost or the downtime.

After further discussion, Porter suggested that they first conduct a short customer survey to determine whether there were any areas for improvement. No one resisted the idea, so Porter spent the weekend composing the survey, and Bottensak pulled together a mailing list of Roscoe customers from the last five years. On Monday morning, 357 surveys were dropped in the mail.

## THE SURVEY RESULTS

By the first week of March, Porter had collected 82 responses. With only three responses returned in the last four days, Porter felt his sample was as big as it was going to get and asked Jane Bottensak to aggregate the results into a single report (Exhibit 1). The next morning, Jane walked into Porter's office with a grin:

> Grover, look's like we got something here. I ignored 11 of the responses since they obviously knew nothing about our work. I reckon those surveys didn't even reach the right contact in the mills. Anyway, that left 71 responses. I pulled all the results together to determine the frequency distributions and from what I can see it seems our people skills need work. Even our office staff could use some improvement.

Porter was surprised that the accuracy of inspection data and time to completion rated so highly, considering that business was so tough these last months. But then he recalled that the speaker at the NDTMA Conference last month emphasized the importance of the people aspect in service quality.

Unfortunately, Roscoe did not attract the type of people blessed with an abundance of social grace. The environment around a boiler is not pleasant. There is constant noise, grime, and heat. And if there was a reason to climb inside the boiler, the technician found himself struggling through cramped areas with his equipment and his flashlight. Once out, his clothing and equipment were coated with a black muck that not even Ultra-Tide could remove. Thus although technicians survived the conditions on-site, they did not necessarily do so quietly.

At the March staff meeting, Porter announced his plans for Roscoe's Quality Improvement Program.

## THE QUALITY IMPROVEMENT PROGRAM

The three elements that Porter decided to include in the QIP were initial training, a bonus reward system, and customer surveys at the conclusion of every job. He recognized that the QIP had to be more than a one-shot deal to be successful and felt that the proposed combination of training, surveys, and bonuses would establish the lasting, fundamental changes Roscoe needed.

Training was provided by ABS Consultants of Madison, Wisconsin, who specialized in teaching customer contact skills for industrial service companies. Training consisted of guided roundtable discussions and role playing, through which technicians and office staff explored not only customers' perceptions of Roscoe, but also their perceptions of the customers as well.

ABS also had Ed Brown put together some services guidelines that went beyond the traditional level of service. Brown explained one aspect of the - guidelines:

> For example, while on-site, we need to emphasize constant visual inspection of the customer's plant and equipment. If a technician sees some insulation hanging off a section of piping, we expect that person to make a note in his report to the client. It doesn't take much time, and our customers appreciate the extra effort.

Technicians also earned bonus points that were cashed out at the end of the year for $25 per point. Every time a client requested a particular technician to be part of the on-site inspection team, that person received a bonus point. Also, after each job the client filled out a customer satisfaction survey. At the end of the year, the surveys were ranked, and for each instance that a technician's team was in the top 5 percent, that technician received a bonus point.

Porter also gave a cash bonus to technicians who passed their certification tests and advanced a level. Achieving Level II earned a $150 cash bonus, while reaching Level III earned $500, since this was the most difficult level to achieve. Finally, the customer satisfaction surveys were compiled monthly and the statistics displayed in the shop area.

## ANOTHER DISAPPOINTING YEAR

Jane Bottensak wrapped up her part of the December staff meeting:

> Well, as I predicted, 1991 is going to be a disappointing year. Revenues were down again and profits were negligible. However, our performance wasn't as bad as I expected, so maybe the quality improvement program was more successful than I thought. But, I think we will still need to reevaluate our fee structure for the coming year.

Ted Witkowski agreed that the program was a success and commented that Roscoe had a record number of technicians certified at Levels II and III. Even Ed Brown conceded that customer satisfaction ratings had improved dramatically over the second half of 1991 (Exhibit 2):

> Most of the experienced technicians are excited about the program. They have been around Roscoe a number of years and have established their families in the area. On the other hand, some of the younger folks have not committed as easily. Part of that is the fact that less-experienced workers get smaller bonuses, on average. But, also, the younger technicians are more mobile and easily move from company to company. Overall, our work force is providing a better service to the customer.

However, regardless of how well the quality improvement program increased customer satisfaction, unless it could support new growth in the company, Grover Porter could only deem the program a failure.

In light of the continued downturn in the pulp and paper industry, Porter felt resigned to restructure the company's pricing policies. And that would mean big changes for Roscoe.

## Exercises

1. Evaluate Roscoe's progress with the quality improvement program.
2. Evaluate Roscoe's customer survey.
3. With respect to the QIP and the survey, is Roscoe doing all it can do?
4. Who is Roscoe's customer?
5. What price changes should Roscoe make?
6. Using the service quality gap model as a point of reference, which gaps appear to be the largest for Roscoe, knowledge, standards, delivery, and/or communications?

## Notes

1. Trade journals of the American Society of Nondestructive Testing and the American Welding Society.

# Exhibit 1

Dear Roscoe Customer,

In an effort to provide you with the best inspection service possible, we would like your opinion of Roscoe and the people who work for us. Simply check the appropriate column on the survey and drop it in the mail within the enclosed stamped envelope. Your cooperation is truly appreciated.

Grover Porter
President

## Roscoe Customer Satisfaction Survey (March 1991)

| Questions | Poor | Below Average | Average | Above Average | Excellent |
|---|---|---|---|---|---|
| **On-Site Inspection Team** | | | | | |
| Accuracy of inspection data | 1.3% | 5.9% | 15.3% | 34.7% | 42.8% |
| Time to complete inspection | 2.9 | 4.8 | 8.4 | 45.6 | 38.3 |
| Knowledge of technicians | 1.5 | 11.5 | 25.6 | 33.3 | 28.1 |
| Willingness to make an extra effort | 24.6 | 26.0 | 23.6 | 13.5 | 12.3 |
| Courtesy of technicians | 26.1 | 30.3 | 18.7 | 16.2 | 8.7 |
| Degree of individualized attention | 17.6 | 29.6 | 38.2 | 9.9 | 4.7 |
| Willingness to make an extra effort | 13.7 | 30.1 | 42.9 | 8.3 | 5.0 |
| Conveys trust and confidence | 9.2 | 28.3 | 34.7 | 23.8 | 4.0 |
| Organization of team supervisor | 4.2 | 25.6 | 37.2 | 29.9 | 3.1 |
| **Accounting Department** | | | | | |
| Accuracy of billing | 3.4 | 8.3 | 16.1 | 55.8 | 16.4 |
| Promptness of billing | 9.8 | 43.9 | 21.7 | 16.5 | 8.1 |
| Courtesy of staff | 6.9 | 24.7 | 38.6 | 13.5 | 16.3 |
| Willingness to help | 22.7 | 25.6 | 38.1 | 8.9 | 4.7 |
| **Overall Performance of Roscoe** | | | | | |
| Ability to deliver the promised service | 2.7 | 15.6 | 18.5 | 39.4 | 23.8 |
| Variety of services that meet your needs | 2.3 | 13.2 | 48.8 | 26.5 | 9.2 |
| Overall service value for your money | 12.7 | 34.1 | 43.2 | 7.8 | 2.2 |

Recorded percentages are the frequency distribution of 71 responses compiled by Jane Bottensak, RNDT's controller. An average was taken for respondents who checked adjacent ratings (e.g., poor and below average).

# Exhibit 2

## Roscoe Customer Satisfaction Survey (November 1991)

| Questions | Poor | Below Average | Average | Above Average | Excellent |
|---|---|---|---|---|---|
| **On-Site Inspection Team** | | | | | |
| Accuracy of inspection data | 1.0% | 4.2% | 2.1% | 24.8% | 55.9% |
| Time to complete inspection | 1.4 | 6.3 | 7.1 | 60.0 | 25.2 |
| Knowledge of technicians | 0.9 | 12.1 | 20.5 | 37.4 | 29.1 |
| Willingness to make an extra effort | 11.9 | 18.2 | 36.5 | 27.8 | 5.6 |
| Courtesy of technicians | 9.3 | 8.9 | 55.3 | 16.3 | 10.2 |
| Degree of individualized attention | 2.1 | 16.7 | 45.9 | 30.1 | 5.2 |
| Willingness to make an extra effort | 9.8 | 17.6 | 40.3 | 30.4 | 1.9 |
| Conveys trust and confidence | 3.8 | 22.7 | 39.8 | 30.6 | 3.1 |
| Organization of team supervisor | 0.0 | 11.9 | 31.8 | 44.7 | 11.6 |
| **Accounting Department** | | | | | |
| Accuracy of billing | 1.5 | 10.4 | 19.6 | 44.2 | 24.3 |
| Promptness of billing | 13.5 | 33.4 | 25.6 | 18.5 | 9.0 |
| Courtesy of staff | 7.9 | 17.8 | 33.4 | 35.1 | 5.8 |
| Willingness to help | 8.6 | 29.4 | 30.3 | 24.6 | 7.1 |
| **Overall Performance of Roscoe** | | | | | |
| Ability to deliver the promised service | 0.0 | 13.2 | 23.1 | 44.2 | 19.5 |
| Variety of services that meet your needs | 7.4 | 13.5 | 56.1 | 15.3 | 7.7 |
| Overall service value for your money | 10.2 | 31.2 | 47.1 | 11.5 | 0.0 |

Compilation of 17 customer satisfaction surveys for inspections completed during November 1991. An average was taken for those respondents who checked adjacent ratings.

BLUEPRINTS

BATESON

CONCEPT

CUSTOMER

SYSTEM

SERVICE PROCESS

# Is This Any Way to Run an Airline?*

HOFFMAN

The following letters are detailed accounts of an actual service encounter and the company's response to the service failures.

July 23, 200x

Dear Customer Service Manager:

Through the Carolina Motor Club my wife and I booked round-trip first-class and clipper-class seats on the following World Airlines flights on the dates indicated:

    1 July World Airlines 3072 Charlotte to Kennedy
    1 July World Airlines 86 Kennedy to Munich
    21 July World Airlines 87 Munich to Kennedy
    21 July World Airlines 3073 Kennedy to Charlotte

We additionally booked connecting flights to and from Wilmington and Charlotte on Trans Air flights 263 (on 1 July) and 2208 (on 21 July).

The outbound flights 3072 and 86 seemed pleasant enough, especially since World Airlines had upgraded our clipper-class seats on flight 86 to first class. However, midflight on 86 we discovered that we had been food poisoned on flight 3072, apparently by the seafood salad that was served in first class that day (it seemed warm to us and we hesitated to eat it but unfortunately did so

*Source: Richard A. Engdahl and K. Douglas Hoffman, "World Airlines: A Customer Service Air Disaster," in Carol A. Anderson, *Retailing: Concepts, Strategy, and Information* (Minneapolis/St. Paul: West, 1993), 215–218.

anyway). My wife was so ill that, trying to get to the restroom to throw up, she passed out cold, hitting her head and, we discovered over the next few days, apparently damaging her back. The flight attendants were very concerned and immediately tried to help her, but there was nothing they could do except help her clean herself up and get the food off her from the food trays she hit. In addition to the nausea and diarrhea, she had a large knot on her head and headaches for several days. Her lower back has been in constant pain ever since. I, too, was very ill for several days. A nice start for a vacation! But it gets worse.

During the long layover between flights at Kennedy, there was a tremendous rainstorm, and our baggage apparently was left out in it, a situation that we discovered when we arrived at our first night's lodging and discovered ALL of our clothing was literally wringing wet. In addition, four art prints we were bringing as gifts for friends were ruined.

The return flights were better only in that we did not get poisoned; instead we did not get fed! Flight 87 out of Munich was apparently short-handed and, due to our seating location, the flight attendant who had to do double duty always got to us last. We had to ask for drinks; there were no hot towels left for us; the meals ran out and we were given no choice but an overdone piece of gray meat with tomato sauce on it. We tasted it, but it was odd tasting and, given our experience on flight 3072, we were afraid to eat it.

Flight 87 was delayed in boarding due to the slowness in cleaning the aircraft (according to an announcement made) and also due to the late arrival of the crew. In addition, the flight was further delayed due to a heavy rainstorm, which backed up traffic for take-off. However, had the flight boarded on time it would have not lost its takeoff priority and could likely have taken off two hours sooner than it did. We might have been able to make our connection in Charlotte. Onboard the flight, the plane was the dirtiest and in the most disrepair of any aircraft I have ever flown on—peeling wall coverings, litter on floor, overhead bins taped shut with duct tape, etc. As a first-class passenger I asked for some cold beer while we were waiting for the rest of the passengers to board; it was warm. We were quite hungry, having not eaten much in the past 12 hours, and asked for some peanuts; there were none; the plane had not been stocked. I asked for a pillow and blanket for my wife; there was none. What a great first-class section! There were only three flight attendants for the whole plane, and I felt sorry for the pregnant one who had to do double duty in first class and the rear cabin. She was very sympathetic to the poor conditions; I don't see how you keep employees when they are treated like that.

Due to the excess delay at Kennedy, flight 87 was very late and we could not make our connection from Charlotte to Wilmington. As it turned out, we would have barely been able to make it if the flight had been on time because World Airlines had changed not only the flight numbers but also the flight times on the Kennedy-Charlotte leg of our journey—AND WE WERE NEVER NOTIFIED OF THIS CHANGE UNTIL WE ARRIVED AT THE AIRPORT! I deplaned in Raleigh to try to alert the people meeting us in Wilmington that we would not be in that night; however, it was too late and they had already gone to the airport. The gate attendant at Raleigh assured me that World Airlines would put us up for the night in Charlotte, so I returned to the plane. However, when we arrived in Charlotte, the World Airlines representative refused to take care of us stating that, since we had not booked the Wilmington-Charlotte portion of our trip through World Airlines, "it is not our problem." Furthermore, he tried to wash his hands of it, saying we had an "illegal connection" due to the times between flights and that he wouldn't provide lodging and meals. After I pointed out to him at least three times that the connection was not illegal when booked and World Airlines changed its flight times without notifying us, and further made it clear that not only was I not going to go away, but that there was going to be a lot more said about the matter, he finally capitulated and gave us a voucher.

After traveling for 24 hours, receiving lousy service, poor food, no amenities, it is a real pleasure to run into an argumentative SOB like your agent in Charlotte. He should be fired!!! As first-class passengers we have been treated like cattle! But, it does not end here.

Upon arriving in Wilmington the next morning, only two of our four bags arrived with us. We had to initiate a baggage trace action. Our missing bags were finally delivered to our house around 3:00 p.m. on 23 July. And SURPRISE, they were left out in the rain at Kennedy again and EVERYTHING was so wet that water poured out of the pockets. I poured water out of the hairdryer. All of our paper purchases, maps, guide books, photos, souvenir brochures, etc. are ruined. I don't know yet if the dryer, radio, electric toothbrush, voltage converters, etc., will work—they are drying out as this is being written. In addition, my brand new bag now has a hole in the bottom of a corner where it was obvious that World Airline baggage handlers dragged it on the tarmac (obviously a water-logged duffle-bag-size piece of luggage is too heavy to lift).

As near as I can figure, we have lost at least a roll of color prints (irreplaceable); approximately $100.00 in travel guides and tour books, many souvenir booklets, brochures, menus, etc.; $100.00 in art prints; $50.00 in damage to luggage; an unknown amount in electronics that may not work; a lot of enjoyment due to pain and suffering resulting from illness and injury (bill for x-rays enclosed); and all sense of humor and patience for such inexcusable treatment by an airline.

If there is to be any compensation for what we have suffered it should be in monetary form. There is no recapturing the lost time and pleasure on the vacation. The art, books, etc. (except for the photos) can be replaced . . . assuming we should make such a trip again. But if we do, you can be assured we would not choose World Airlines.

In closing, I am particularly angry and adamant about this whole fiasco as we wanted this vacation to be special and treated ourselves to the luxury of first-class treatment . . . which we got everywhere except on World Airlines . . . it is almost unbelievable how poorly we were treated by your airline, almost a perfect negative case study in customer service. I have purposely tried to mention every little nit-picky thing I can recall because I want you to realize just how totally bad this whole experience has been!

In disgust,
J. Q. Customer

## WORLD AIRLINE'S RECOVERY STRATEGY

The following is World Airline's actual response to the customer's letter. The first letter was written by the claims manager, and the second by the customer relations manager.

September 25, 200x

Dear Mr. and Mrs. Customer:

This letter confirms the settlement agreed upon during our phone conversation just concluded.

Accordingly, we have prepared and enclosed (in duplicate) a General Release for $2,000.00. Both you and your wife should sign in the presence of a Notary Public, have your signatures notarized, and return the Original to this office, keeping the copy for your records. As soon as we receive the notarized Release, we will forward our draft for $2000.00.

Again, our sincerest apologies to Mrs. Customer. It will be most helpful for our Customer Relations staff if you included with the Release copies of all available travel documents.

Very truly yours,
Claims Manager

October 12, 200x

Dear Mr. Customer:

Let me begin by apologizing for this delayed response and all of the unfortunate incidents that you described in your letter. Although we try to make our flights as enjoyable as possible, we obviously failed on this occasion.

Our claims manager informs me that you have worked out a potential settlement for the matter regarding the food poisoning. We regret you were not able to enjoy the food service on the other flights on your itinerary because of it. I assure you that such incidents are a rare occurrence and that much time and effort is expended to ensure that our catering is of the finest quality.

Fewer things can be more irritating than faulty baggage handling. Only in an ideal world could we say that baggage will never again be damaged. Still, we are striving to ensure baggage is handled in such a way that if damage should occur, it will be minimized.

Flight disruptions caused by weather conditions can be particularly frustrating since, despite advanced technology, accurate forecasts for resumption of full operations cannot always be obtained as rapidly as one would wish. These disruptions are, of course, beyond the airlines' control. Safety is paramount in such situations and we sincerely regret the inconvenience caused.

We make every reasonable effort to lessen the inconvenience to passengers who are affected by schedule changes. Our practice is, in fact, to advise passengers of such changes when we have a local contact for them and time permits. We also try to obtain satisfactory alternative reservations. We are reviewing our schedule change requirements with all personnel concerned and will take whatever corrective measures are necessary to ensure that a similar problem does not arise in the future.

You made it clear in your letter that the interior of our aircraft was not attractive. We know that aircraft appearance is a reflection of our professionalism. We regret that our airplane did not measure up to our standards since we place great emphasis on cabin maintenance and cleanliness. Please be assured that this particular matter is being investigated by the responsible management and corrective action will be taken.

As tangible evidence of our concern over your unpleasant trip. I have enclosed two travel vouchers, which may be exchanged for 2 first-class tickets anywhere that World Airlines flies. Once again, please accept our humble apology. We hope for the opportunity to restore your faith in World Airlines by providing you with completely carefree travel.

Sincerely,
Customer Relations Manager

## EPILOGUE

World Airlines filed for bankruptcy within 24 months of this incident.

## Exercises

1. Categorize the failures that occurred above utilizing the three failure categories depicted in Figure 14.1.
2. What is your assessment of the firm's recovery efforts based on the concepts of distributive, procedural, and interactional justice?

# case 15

# The SpaceDisk
# Service Guarantee

SpaceDisk is a young high-tech firm with leading-edge technology in the business-to-business (B2B) market. S. Mohan, SpaceDisk's CEO, felt that besides technology, excellence in service delivery and high customer satisfaction would be key success factors in SpaceDisk's aggressive growth strategy. To build a customer-driven culture and to communicate service excellence credibly to the market, SpaceDisk aimed to harness the power of service guarantees.

SpaceDisk described itself as an edge service provider (ESP), aiming to become the global backbone for the next generation of Internet-based applications. The company claimed to be the world's first Internet distributed applications platform (DAP) provider, improving current and upcoming congestion problems on the Web. SpaceDisk's main value proposition to Web site operators, portals, Internet service providers (ISPs), and application service providers (ASPs) was to allow them to serve their customers faster. Specifically, the access time for downloading and uploading files of SpaceDisk's customers could be improved by up to 1,000 percent. This was achieved by locating servers at the "edge of the Internet" and thereby delivering content from servers located close to the user. To view a demonstration of SpaceDisk's value proposition go to http://www.spacedisk.com /solutions.html.

Faster and more reliable services were becoming critical, as the widespread use of multimedia and other large files increased exponentially. The value proposition clearly was attractive, but how could SpaceDisk convince prospective clients that its technology and service actually could deliver what they promised? Mohan felt that a quality of service (QoS) guarantee would be a powerful tool to make its promises credible and at the same time push his team to deliver what has been promised. John MacGilvary, SpaceDisk's senior vice president of Sales and Marketing, and Mohan spearheaded the development of the QoS guarantee. They finally launched the QoS guarantee shown in Exhibit 1. The e-mail in which the official launch of the guarantee was announced to all staff is provided in Exhibit 2.

# *Exercises*

1. Evaluate the design of SpaceDisk's guarantee, shown in Exhibit 1. How effective will it be in communicating service excellence to potential and current customers? Would you recommend any changes to its design or implementation?
2. Will the guarantee be successful in creating a culture for service excellence within SpaceDisk? What else may be needed for achieving such a culture?
3. Do you think customers might take advantage of this guarantee and "stage" service failures to invoke the guarantee? If yes, how could SpaceDisk minimize potential cheating on its guarantee?

# *Exhibit 1*

## SpaceDisk's QoS Guarantee

The SpaceDisk Quality of Service Guarantee defines SpaceDisk's assurance and commitment to providing the Customer with no less than full satisfaction with our Service.

If you are not 100% satisfied with any aspect of our service, SpaceDisk will credit up to 100% of the fees for the month affected according to the sole judgment of the Customer. Specifically, we guarantee the following:

### 1. Performance

At any one time, SpaceDisk guarantees that the performance in uploading and downloading content, as a result of using the Service, will be no less than 200% of that which is achieved by a benchmark origin site being accessed from the edges of the Internet, details of which will be available online at all times for Customers to view at www.spacedisk.com/performance. The performance test will be continuously conducted and verified by an independent performance-testing agency.

### 2. Service Availability

SpaceDisk guarantees 100% service availability, excluding Force Majeure and Scheduled Maintenance for Customers who have opted for our replication services.

### 3. Customer Service

SpaceDisk will notify the Customer two (2) days or more in advance of Scheduled Maintenance, which will be no more than 48 hours per annum. If the Service becomes unavailable for any other reason, SpaceDisk will promptly notify the Customer and take all necessary action to restore the Service.

SpaceDisk will provide the Customer with a response to any inquiry in relation to the Service no more than two (2) hours from the time of receipt of the query by SpaceDisk Customer Service.

### 4. Security and Privacy Policy

SpaceDisk has complete respect for the Customer's privacy and that of any Customer data stored in SpaceDisk servers. Using SpaceDisk's service, Customers do not need to provide any end-user private details for the data being stored. All information provided to SpaceDisk by the Customer is stored for the Customer's sole benefit. SpaceDisk will not share, disclose or sell any personally identifiable information to which we may have access and will ensure that the Customer's information and data are kept secure.

SpaceDisk will ensure that the Customer's information and data are kept secure and protected from unauthorized access or improper use, which includes taking all reasonable steps to verify the Customer's identity before granting access.

## Exhibit 2

### The E-mail to All SpaceDisk Staff Announcing the Launch of the QoS Guarantee

Dear Team,

I am pleased to forward to everyone our industry-leading Quality of Service (QoS) guarantee. Please read it over very carefully. You will find it to be very aggressive, and it puts the ownership on everyone in this company to deliver. Customers don't want a Service Level Agreement (SLA), they just want their network up and running all the time. That is why we have created this no questions asked guarantee. This type of guarantee has proven successful in other industries where service is key to success (e.g., Industry Leaders such as Gartner Group, LL Bean, Nordstroms, etc.).

As a member of the SpaceDisk team, you are key to our client's satisfaction.

Thanks in advance for your support in making our clients and ourselves successful.

Warmest Regards,

John J. MacGilvary
SVP Sales & Marketing
SpaceDisk, Inc.

# case 16a

# Westin Hotels in Asia: Global Distribution*

The Westin Stamford & Plaza Hotel is a five-star business and an incentives, conventions, and meetings (ICM) hotel in the heart of Singapore. It opened in 1986 with more than 2,000 rooms and 70,000 square feet of meeting and banquet space. The hotel had been enjoying high occupancy rates of above 80 percent until mid-1997, benefiting from Singapore's position as an Asian business and ICM hub. Its sister hotels, The Westin Banyan Tree in Bangkok and The Westin Philippine Plaza in Manila, were similarly blessed with high occupancies and buoyant markets just prior to June 1997. The economic crisis that hit Asia in mid-1997, however, took the wind out of the Asian markets. Business and ICM arrivals into the three countries declined by some 10 percent to 25 percent in 1998. The three Westin hotels saw their occupancies fall by 10 percent to 20 percent, as well as a sharp decline in average room rates. To compound things, the pre-crisis economic boom had seen a proliferation of five-star hotel developments in the three cities. Travel management trends in Asia were also undergoing rapid changes. Many of the hotels' corporate clients were not local companies but multinational

"No Boundary, No Limits"

Mission statement of
Starwood Hotels & Resorts
Worldwide Inc., parent
company of the Westin Hotels.

*Source: Jochen Wirtz, Department of Marketing, Faculty of Business Administration, National University of Singapore; and Jeannette Ho Pheng Theng, student, Department of Marketing, and Director of Revenue Management, The Westin Stamford & Westin Plaza Hotels, Singapore. The authors greatly acknowledge the generous support in terms of time, information, and feedback provided on earlier drafts of this case by David Shackleton, Vice President, Operations, Central Region for Starwood Asia Pacific; and Philip Ho, Managing Director, Distribution and Revenue Management Asia Pacific. Furthermore, the authors would like to acknowledge the assistance of Cindy Kai Lin Koh and Sim Liew Lien in writing up the case. This case was prepared as the basis for class discussion rather than to illustrate effective or ineffective handling of an administrative situation. Westin considered some data in the case confidential; therefore the data was manipulated in such a fashion as to be acceptable to Westin.

corporations (MNCs), which were increasingly centralizing their purchases of travel-related services at overseas corporate headquarters, giving them more bargaining power.

In view of the shrinking market conditions, intense competition, and changing travel management trends, the three Westin hotels in Asia had to critically reassess their own marketing and distribution strategies. A new opportunity presented itself in late 1997, when Westin's parent company, Starwood Hotels & Resorts Worldwide Inc., acquired ITT Corporation, which owned the Sheraton Hotels & Resorts, St. Regis Luxury Collection, Four Points Hotels, and Caesars World brands of hotels and casinos. This acquisition made Starwood the largest hotel and gaming company in the world, with more than 650 hotels in 73 countries employing more than 150,000 employees. Uppermost in the mind of vice president of operations for the three Westin Hotels, David Shackleton, was the need to leverage the size and global marketing strength of Starwood, to develop new business for his hotels and gain market share from the competitors. Further information on Westin and Starwood can be found at www.westin.com and www.starwood.com.

## TRADITIONAL MARKETING AND DISTRIBUTION STRATEGIES

Until the past five years, local companies, local MNC offices, and local travel agents in Asia were the key decision makers, negotiating rates with the local hotels and selecting venues for corporate meetings, company incentives, and company social functions and making hotel reservations for their overseas guests. The marketing and distribution strategies of the three Westin hotels in Asia were thus predominantly focused on the local markets, and sales team efforts were concentrated on servicing and cultivating local decision makers. Well-staffed reservation departments were also important, since direct bookings with the hotels via fax and phone were the preferred method of making reservations.

Advertising and promotional (A&P) activities to build brand awareness and reach the end customer for the three Westin hotels were also highly decentralized at individual properties and rarely coordinated across sister hotels. Because A&P expenses can be prohibitive, individual hotels tended to target their campaigns at the local market and allocated only a limited proportion of their budgets to overseas advertising.

Moreover, because each individual property was responsible for its own cost and revenue figures, each hotel would focus its sales and marketing efforts on selling its own rooms and facilities. There was minimal cross-selling of other Westin hotels worldwide. In other words, there was no cost-effective and concerted effort by all Westin hotels to reach out to travelers.

## TRAVEL MANAGEMENT TRENDS

Because travel decisions are being made increasingly closer to the travel dates, decisions about hotel choice and the actual reservations are made closer to the customer. The traditional approach of relying on one's local offices or travel agents takes too long. Hence hotels that can provide their global customers easier and faster access will have a competitive edge.

Local secretaries' and the individual business traveler's power to select hotels have also been diluted. The three Westin hotels in Asia saw an increasing trend of their multinational corporate clients centralizing their global hotel room rate negotiations at a corporate head office in order to reduce cost through global volume purchasing and to increase bargaining power. Corporate travelers can only select a hotel that is on the approved listing. The change in corporate travel policies and practices is a result of management's concern with their rising travel and entertainment (T&E) costs. *The 1991 American Express Survey of Business Travel Management* reported that 60 percent of the 1,564 companies surveyed agreed that rising T&E costs is one of management's top concerns.

Corporate clients were also increasingly turning to travel management companies (TMCs) for a total travel solution. The TMCs, such as American Express and Carlson Wagon Lit, are able to handle all airline, hotel, and other travel arrangements. They mainly use global distribution systems (GDS, global reservation systems containing extensive information on airfares, hotel rates, etc.) such as Galileo, Sabre, and Amadeus, for hotel reservations. The Westin Stamford & Plaza in particular had seen an increase in the number of reservations coming in via the GDSs. This reservation channel brings in about 27 percent of the hotel's transient (non-group) revenue. Even wholesale travel agents, who had traditionally booked directly via fax and phone, were increasingly turning to the use of GDS to improve efficiency and obtain instant confirmation.

On this issue, Mr. Shackleton said,

> This trend of centralising travel management is not new in USA, Europe nor Australia, but we in Asia are just beginning to feel the impact. Many MNCs have now organised their home grounds and are extending their centralised management and purchase of travel services to their Asian offices. With the Asian economic crisis dampening demand from large traditional markets like Japan, Indonesia, Malaysia and Hong Kong, we certainly need to grow our markets out of USA, Europe and Australia. We need to reassess our marketing and distribution strategies, in order to align ourselves with these changes and to be effective in reaching out to these decision makers overseas. Competition among the international hotel chains is very keen. Once we have been selected onto a corporate listing, the battle is far from over. We still have to incentivise the travel managers overseas to select our hotels in Asia over Hyatt, Marriott and the Shangri-Las who are also listed. The individual business travelers can still choose between hotels on the approved list. Another development is that meeting and conference planners increasingly need a quick turnaround in exploring possible destinations, checking meeting space and room availability, and finally negotiating the piece of business. Our current process takes days or weeks and is becoming unacceptable to demanding clients.

## STARWOOD'S GLOBAL MARKETING AND DISTRIBUTION STRATEGIES

Since Starwood's acquisition of the ITT corporation in late 1997, a key issue had become to examine how Starwood and its individual properties, such as the Westin, could leverage Starwood's size, geographic coverage, and brand diversity?

## Global Selling and Cross-Selling

Roberta Rinker-Ludloff, vice president of Starwood Global Sales, quoted Henry Ford: "Coming together is the beginning. Keeping together is the progress. Working together is success." Starwood's strategy had been composed of global selling, cross-selling, and improving customer service.

Starwood had formed more than 30 global sales offices (GSOs) around the world to manage customer relationships with key global accounts. These GSOs provided a one-stop solution to corporate travel planners, wholesalers, meeting planners, incentive houses, and mega-travel organizations by addressing all accommodation issues, including global room rate negotiations, corporate meetings, and events planning at any of Starwood's 650 hotels worldwide.

Besides the GSOs, each hotel had its own sales team. With more than 2,000 sales managers from individual properties making sales calls and meeting clients daily, how could Starwood produce synergy and leverage these activities? Team Hot was the answer—a new program to harness the tremendous power of cross-selling across its 650 hotels in an efficient and automated way. Team Hot provided incentives for hotel sales and catering managers to cross-sell other resorts and hotels under the Starwood umbrella. Program participants needed to anticipate their clients' accommodation and catering needs outside their own hotel and then send the lead to the relevant property(s) via the Internet. For leads that result in confirmed business, participants received points redeemable for airline tickets, room nights, and other rewards. Starwood aimed to generate an additional US$225 million in revenue in 1999 through Team Hot.

Overseas guests no longer wanted to make long distance calls to hotels for reservation, preferring to call a local toll-free telephone number instead. Starwood had set up nine central reservation offices (CROs) worldwide to provide one-stop total customer service for the guests, including hotel reservations worldwide, enrollment and redemption of Starwood's loyalty program, general customer service, and others. With the toll-free numbers, guests only needed to remember one number to book any Starwood hotel.

## Technology and Automation

Whether it's the individual customer, the travel agent, or corporate travel planner, all prefer and are likely to stay with hotels that are easy and quick to book, provide immediate response to customer queries, and have rates that are reasonably competitive and up-to-date. Traditional booking methods via direct faxes and phone calls to the hotel were fast on the decline, since they were cumbersome and required customers to remember multiple phone and fax numbers. Meeting and conference planners increasingly needed quick turnaround and prompt servicing. Starwood used technology and automation to improve the quality of customer service and efficiency. The emphasis was on automating reservations and information provision to the customer.

Starwood's Internet capabilities were continuously upgraded, and cutting edge concepts such as electronic brochures were being pioneered and tested. Individual and corporate clients could gain instant access to information on the facilities and amenities provided by any of the 650 Starwood hotels, and could make online reservations and payment, all at a click of a mouse. Corporate clients could even book their own confidential negotiated rates through the Internet. The Internet has great potential in creating value to both travelers and hotels. The revenue from bookings through Starwood's Web sites increased 280 percent in 1998 and more than US$48 million worth of meeting leads were received through the Web sites in the first nine months of 1998.

Starwood also developed its own internal central reservation system called Starlink. Starlink contained up-to-date property information and data on rates and availability for each of the 650 hotels and fed the information interactively to all the major GDSs. Seamless interface between Starlink and the GDSs ensured that all Starwood hotel services were instantly available and up-to-date at more than 400,000 travel agents worldwide.

Starwood had also enlisted the help of technology to make their mobile global sales force more responsive to corporate clients. Its Corporate Travel Information System software enabled the global sales manager to negotiate worldwide corporate rates with clients and print and sign the contracts all in one visit. The Global Sales Force Automation software would soon allow the notebook-armed global sales managers to negotiate and close group deals all in a single day. GSOs could check hotel availability, propose pricing, explore alternative dates, negotiate the contracts, close the business deal, and immediately book guest and meeting rooms. It is a system designed to keep all necessary information at a manager's fingertips and certainly to impress the client.

## Concerted Marketing Effort

Individual properties also needed to create more awareness in overseas markets. To share the burden of high advertising and marketing costs, Starwood hotels clustered together and shared advertising space. Certain rates and promotions were also branded across all hotels within a chain in order to facilitate global advertising. All Westin hotels in Asia Pacific, for example, offered advance purchase discounts that have been branded as the Westin Valuestays Promotions.

# ALIGNING INDIVIDUAL HOTELS TO STARWOOD

How can the three individual hotels in Asia leverage the marketing muscles of Starwood to help them address the trend of centralized corporate purchasing for hotel services and to grow their markets from United States, Europe, and Australia?

With more than 650 properties to sell, and Asia being in recession, it would not be surprising if very little of the global sales efforts was being spent to promote hotels in Asia to Americans and Europeans. To compound things, many of the global sales managers and central reservation agents were heritage Sheraton, and were thus not well acquainted with the Westin hotels. David Shackleton believed that the first priority would be to restructure the sales and marketing teams at his hotels to align them with the global Starwood marketing structure. Hence, besides traditional relationship marketing to the local companies and corporate secretaries, the hotel sales and marketing teams were now asked to also "market" their individual properties to the GSOs and CROs. Each hotel sales manager was responsible for cultivating close working relationships with specific global sales managers. Hotel sales managers needed to prioritize and discuss their global sales objectives with the GSOs, and ensure that all leads provided by them were followed up promptly. The hotel reservation and distribution marketing managers needed to ensure that property information, rates, and availability were constantly kept up to date in all the various distribution systems, such as Starlink, the Internet, and the GDSs. Monthly reports on local sales and marketing activities were provided to the GSOs via electronic media. Hotel promotional collaterals were regularly distributed to the GSOs and CROs to heighten their awareness of the three Westin properties. Familiarization trips were also planned for the GSO and CRO managers to acquaint them with the hotel service experience and enable them to sell the hotels more effectively.

# Exercises

1. Apart from the preferential rates and good service, what other strategies can Starwood hotels employ to encourage selection and loyalty from corporate travel managers and event planners?
2. Even after corporate travel managers have selected and negotiated with individual hotel chains, the individual corporate traveler can still choose among the various chains listed in his company's directory. How can Westin and the other Starwood brands differentiate themselves from other hotel chains and make themselves the top choice of the corporate traveler?
3. In the long term, would it be more effective for the three Westin hotels in Asia to focus their distribution strategy on intermediaries (travel agent or corporate travel managers), or should they employ multi-channel distribution strategies?
4. What are the key challenges facing the three hotels in their move to leverage Starwood's marketing and distribution programs?

# case 16b

# Primula Parkroyal Hotel: Positioning and Managing for Turnaround*

Primula Parkroyal Kuala Terengganu (PPR), a hotel on the east coast of peninsular Malaysia, was going through a strategic change exercise after a new management took over in 1996. In June 1997 Rodney Hawker, PPR's general manager, was working on the 1998 marketing plan for the hotel. As input into this marketing plan, he needed to decide what target customer segments to focus on and how the hotel should be positioned to compete effectively with other hotels in Kuala Terengganu as well as with hotels in other destinations. The Asian financial crisis was beginning to unfold with dropping arrival numbers. The situation was further aggravated by the

*Source: Aliah Hanim M. Salleh is Associate Professor of Marketing, Faculty of Business Management, Universiti Kebangsaan Malaysia. Jochen Wirtz is Assistant Professor, Department of Marketing, Faculty of Business Administration, National University of Singapore. Copyright © 1999 by Aliah Hanim M. Salleh and Jochen Wirtz. The authors retain all rights. Not to be reproduced or used without written permission from one of the authors. This case was prepared as the basis for class discussion rather than to illustrate effective or ineffective handling of an administrative situation. Primula Parkroyal has approved this case for publication with disclosure of the hotel's name.

The case authors gratefully acknowledge Rosiati Ramli, Zakiah M. Mohamed, and Zaleha Abd. Shukor, who together with the main author interviewed all personalities in this case and drafted an earlier version in Bahasa Melayu. The data gathering was funded by a Universiti Kebangsaan Malaysia research grant for a case research project, headed by Dr. Nik Rahimah Nik Yacob, and the write-up was partially funded by the National University of Singapore. Finally, the authors acknowledge the valued assistance of Sim Siew Lien for assisting in writing the case.

intense competition from the many new resorts and hotels that had mushroomed in the state during the past four years. Furthermore, PPR's service levels and staff morale needed to be improved. Behind this backdrop, Hawker had the objective of reinstating the hotel's position as the premier quality hotel in Kuala Terengganu.

## MANAGEMENT TAKEOVER AND REFURBISHMENT

The hotel is located on a beach off the South China Sea in Kuala Terengganu, the capital of Terengganu, a northeastern state of peninsular Malaysia. Terengganu is an oil-rich state with a population of about 850,000, comprising mostly Malay Muslims. PPR was one of the first four-star hotels to be built along the eastern coast of peninsular Malaysia in the eighties. As of 1997, PPR had a total equity of RM[1] 1.6 million, and total assets of RM3.1 million. However, being owned by a state government agency, it incurred millions of RM in accumulated losses, and the state government aimed at making the hotel profitable as well as at improving the state's tourism infrastructure.

In March 1996 Southern Pacific Hotel Corporation (SPHC) took over PPR's management. SPHC had won a "12-plus five-year contract" to manage the hotel, after successfully outbidding several other large hotel management operating companies from the Asia-Pacific region. Hawker asserted that a unique factor favoring SPHC's interest in PPR was Terengganu's unspoiled beaches, waterfalls, lakes, and untapped potential as an attractive tourist destination in Malaysia. This was seen relative to Penang and Langkawi, both of which were expected to reach saturation as tourist destinations. PPR was also the only hotel in Kuala Terengganu that enjoyed both a resort image (with its beach location) and a business image, being so close to town.

In managing the strategic change of the hotel, SPHC focused on the following key priorities: upgrading the quality of the hotel's physical facilities, re-marketing and positioning the hotel, training staff, and changing the work culture. Permodalan Terengganu Berhad (PTB), the Terengganu state government's investment arm, became the new owner just before this management takeover. Under the terms of a profit-sharing agreement between PTB and SPHC, PTB financed an initial RM11 million to be used for physically upgrading and refurbishing the hotel. In recognizing the need to motivate its staff to deliver quality services, rebuilding a new staff canteen was the first renovation work done. Other work included renovating 72 guest rooms in the double-storey wing with access to the beach, and 150 deluxe rooms in the hotel's eleven-storey tower block. A new tea lounge was opened adjoining the reception area and coffee house facing the beach. The entire swimming pool area was also re-landscaped, befitting a world-class business resort hotel.

## COMPETITION

Table 1 shows PPR's main competitors in the vicinity of Kuala Terengganu, and Table 2 presents their market shares. The tables show PPR's strong position in terms of positioning (i.e., excellent city and beachfront location), quality of service and facilities (the only four-star hotel in the area). This strong positioning also translated into a 41.7 percent share revenue of the total market in Terengganu.

TABLE 1

## Comparative Characteristics of Primula Parkroyal versus Competitors

|  | Sutra Beach Resort | Seri Malaysia | Permai Park Inn | Primula Parkroyal |
|---|---|---|---|---|
| Location | 38 km from town center; beachfront | In town | 5 km from town center | 3 km from town center; beachfront |
| No. of rooms | 120 chalets/rooms | 145 rooms | 131 rooms | 150 deluxe rooms, 27 suites, & 72 guest/family rooms |
| Affiliation/owner | SPR Management | Gateway Inn Management | Kemayan Resorts | SPHC/Permodalan Terengganu Bhd. |
| Market segment mix | Private, corporate, government, groups | Groups, private, government | Corporate, government, travel agents/ tour groups | Corporate, government, travel agents/ tour groups |
| Service positioning | Three-and-a-half-star deluxe resort, medium priced | Two-and-a-half-star "value-for-money" budget hotel chain | Three-star town hotel, "bed & breakfast" image | Four-star beach-cum-business resort |
| Occupancy rate for 1997 (est.) | 40% | 55% | 50% | 49% |
| Rooms sold 1997 (est.) | 16,790 | 30,113 | 23,908 | 44,805 |
| Average room rate 1997 (est.) | 125 | 80 | 92 | 137.91 |
| F&B Outlets/ conference facilities | • Merang Restaurant<br>• R-U Tapai Lounge<br>• Conference Hall (350 pax)<br>• Karaoke Lounge | • Sekayu Café (a la carte menu except Sunday & Friday)<br>• Lunches | • Café-in-the-Park<br>• Conference hall (250 pax) | • Bayu Lounge<br>• Cascade Grill<br>• Rhusila Coffee House<br>• 1 Ballroom<br>• 7 Meeting rooms |
| Physical facilities & services | • Business center<br>• Tennis court<br>• Souvenir shop<br>• Swimming pool | • Business center<br>• Swimming pool<br>• Shopping arcade<br>• Gymnasium<br>• Tea/coffee-making facilities in rooms | • Retail stores | • Business center<br>• Koko Nut Klub<br>• Swimming pool<br>• Health center<br>• Tennis & volleyball<br>• Iron & ironing board<br>• Tea/coffee-making facilities in rooms |

Source: Primula Parkroyal internal reports and authors' observations during site visits.

TABLE 2

**Market Share Among Competing Hotels/Resorts: March–December 1996**

| Hotel | No. of Rooms | Capacity (Room Nights/ Year) | Rooms Sold | Occupancy Rate (%) | Average Room Rate | Room Revenue (RM) | Actual Share % Rooms | % Revenue |
|---|---|---|---|---|---|---|---|---|
| Primula Parkroyal | 247 | 75,582 | 34,453 | 46 | 130.04 | 4,480,268 | 34.2 | 41.7 |
| P. Park Inn | 131 | 40,086 | 18,039 | 45 | 87.81 | 1,478,369 | 17.9 | 13.8 |
| Seri Malaysia | 150 | 45,900 | 24,327 | 53 | 68.33 | 1,743,781 | 24.1 | 16.2 |
| Sutra Beach Resort | 100 | 30,600 | 10,710 | 35 | 116.00 | 1,242,360 | 10.6 | 11.5 |
| Tanjung Jara Beach | 115 | 35,190 | 13,372 | 38 | 135.00 | 1,805,220 | 13.2 | 16.8 |
| **Total** | **743** | **227,358** | **100,901** | **44.38** | **106.54** | **10,749,998** | **100** | **100** |

Source: Primula Parkroyal 1997 business plan.

## MARKET SEGMENTS

PPR reached the following target segments: commercial guests (30.1 percent of room nights), individual travelers (29 percent), government (17.1 percent), conference (13.7 percent), and tour groups and sports (15.2 percent) (Table 3). Table 4 shows the food and beverage (F&B) revenues by segment for May 1997. An internal report indicated that PPR enjoyed a lion's share of the commercial market in Terengganu, giving it a higher average yield than its competitors. This report forecasted a 16.8 percent growth in this segment for 1998.

Guests of SPHC hotels in the Asia-Pacific region could obtain special discounts and other privileges through the Pacific Privilege Card membership program. This Pacific Privilege market was PPR's largest supporter in its private (individual travelers) segment. Although this program was low-yielding, it produced volume. The private segment was anticipated to become the hotel's biggest segment over time. PPR planned to increase its share with a low-season promotion drive and intensive customer database marketing.

The conference market was primarily supported by the Malaysian government. This segment was projected to increase by 30 percent. A sales executive based in Kuala Lumpur and Kuala Terengganu was in charge of promoting PPR as a conference destination focusing on the government segment. To cushion reductions in government spending as a result of the Asian crisis, promotions were mostly targeted at senior departmental officers, who were less severely restricted in their hotel choice.

## ROOM SALES

According to Cik[2] Norshidah, one of three sales personnel working in the Marketing and Sales Department, sales were conducted by SPHC's Kuala Lumpur

# T|A|B|L|E 3

## Summary of Room Revenues for January–December 1997 (Planned)

| 1997 Budget | |
|---|---|
| No. of rooms available | 90,885 |
| No. of rooms occupied | 44,805 |
| Occupancy (%) | 49.3 |
| Average tariff (RM) | 137.91 |

| Customer Segment | Rooms Occupied | | Average Tariff | Room Revenue |
|---|---|---|---|---|
| | RM | % | RM | RM |
| Commercial: | | | | |
| • Corporate | 8,590 | 19.2 | 153.10 | 1,315,100 |
| • Corporate conference | 2,270 | 5.1 | 126.09 | 286,220 |
| • Others | 2,615 | 5.8 | 148.51 | 388,350 |
| **Subtotal Commercial** | **13,475** | **30.1** | **147.66** | **1,989,670** |
| Private: | | | | |
| • Rack | 255 | 0.6 | 227.88 | 58,110 |
| • FITs | 9,555 | 21.3 | 149.15 | 1,425,100 |
| • Other discounts | 3,165 | 7.1 | 125.42 | 396,950 |
| **Subtotal Private** | **12,975** | **29.0** | **144.91** | **1,880,160** |
| Others: | | | | |
| • Govt.—govt. FITs | 7,190 | 16.0 | 135.69 | 975,600 |
| • Conference | 3,860 | 8.6 | 137.05 | 529,000 |
| • Sports | 1,625 | 3.6 | 117.05 | 190,200 |
| • Embassies & others | 515 | 1.1 | 185.00 | 17,575 |
| • Tour groups | 5,165 | 11.6 | 115.57 | 596,900 |
| **Subtotal Others** | **18,355** | **40.9** | **130.05** | **2,309,275** |
| **Total** | **44,805** | **100.0** | **137.91** | **6,179,105** |

Source: Primula Parkroyal internal management report.

Note: FIT stands for frequent independent travellers.

head office, which collectively promoted the Parkroyal chain. Room sales were the responsibility of the Rooms Division, headed by Clive Murray. Because rooms can be sold at steep discounts, SPHC used both occupancy rates and average room rates to measure the yield of its rooms. Adlin Masood headed the Public Relations Department, which planned and executed cultural, sports, and social events and the hotel's public relations activities throughout the year. Adlin's work supported not only room sales, but help bring in the crowds for the F&B outlets, as well as servicing the conference and tour group guests.

Out of RM11.7 million in total operating revenue planned for 1997, RM6.18 million were expected to come from room revenues (see Table 3). Seventy-seven

## TABLE 4

**Room and F&B Revenues by Segment for May 1997**

| Customer Segment | No. of Clients | Room Nights | % | Room Revenue (RM) | F&B Revenue (RM) |
|---|---|---|---|---|---|
| **Commercial** | | | | | |
| Corporate | 658 | 489 | 11.00 | 77,074.71 | 13,357.82 |
| Corporate-conferences | 970 | 488 | 10.59 | 50,938.76 | 5,847.02 |
| **Subtotal Commercial** | **1628** | **977** | **21.59** | **128,013.47** | **19,204.84** |
| | | | | | |
| **Private** | | | | | |
| Private individuals | 1268 | 729 | 15.83 | 107,169.69 | 27,796.45 |
| Other discounts | 907 | 593 | 12.87 | 41,342.11 | 13,030.61 |
| **Subtotal Private** | **2175** | **1322** | **28.7** | **148,511.8** | **40,827.06** |
| | | | | | |
| **Government-related** | | | | | |
| Govt. conferences | 1176 | 625 | 13.57 | 62,940.12 | 17,587.53 |
| Govt. groups | 16 | 8 | 0.17 | 1,080.00 | 0.00 |
| Government | 650 | 437 | 9.49 | 65,298.63 | 9,087.21 |
| Embassies | 9 | 5 | 0.11 | 790.00 | 584.33 |
| **Subtotal Govt-related** | **1851** | **1075** | **23.34** | **130,108.75** | **27,259.07** |
| | | | | | |
| **Others** | | | | | |
| Tour groups | 807 | 359 | 7.79 | 36,284.53 | 2,830.95 |
| Tour agents | 195 | 110 | 2.39 | 13,593.87 | 6,679.12 |
| Sports | 1192 | 521 | 11.31 | 44,159.38 | 17,661.43 |
| Internal use | 228 | 165 | 3.58 | 0.00 | 734.26 |
| Daily use | 0 | 0 | 0 | 1,165.00 | 288.53 |
| Long-term use | 101 | 73 | 1.58 | 8,863.60 | 1,471.52 |
| Employee offers | 7 | 5 | 0.11 | 0.00 | 97.12 |
| **Subtotal Others** | **2530** | **1233** | **26.76** | **104,066.38** | **29,762.93** |
| **Total** | **8184** | **4607** | **100.00** | **510,703.40** | **118,063.90** |

Source: Primula Parkroyal internal management report.

percent of room revenues were planned to be net contribution, which compared with an actual net contribution of 70 percent for the time from January to May 1997. A breakdown of room and F&B revenues for each customer segment for May 1997 is provided in Table 4.

PPR's beach location fronting the South China Sea made it vulnerable to seasonal fluctuations of demand. During peak holiday periods of June, July, and August, the occupancy rate was expected to reach 62 percent to 63 percent (with average room rates of RM143). In contrast, demand could go as low as 31 percent to 34 percent (with average room rates dipping to RM125) in the off-peak monsoon season of December, January, and February (Table 5). During the peak season, the occupancy rate could reach 100 percent on weekends and public holidays.

## TABLE 5

**Monthly Average Room Occupancy Rates January–December 1997 (Planned)**

| | 1997 | | 1996 | |
| | Occupancy | Average Rate | Occupancy | Average Rate |
| Month | (%) | (RM) | (%) | (RM) |
| --- | --- | --- | --- | --- |
| January | 31.3 | 125.22 | Not Available | Not Available |
| February | 33.8 | 125.44 | Not Available | Not Available |
| March | 43.0 | 135.85 | 26.9 | 134.47 |
| April | 51.8 | 135.70 | 43.6 | 123.42 |
| May | 58.6 | 140.87 | 46.6 | 142.23 |
| June | 63.0 | 142.66 | 47.9 | 127.04 |
| July | 62.3 | 142.97 | 49.8 | 122.29 |
| August | 60.2 | 143.47 | 56.4 | 128.03 |
| September | 58.3 | 143.08 | 31.6 | 131.25 |
| October | 56.5 | 141.52 | 51.6 | 132.20 |
| November | 38.3 | 134.93 | 47.4 | 131.36 |
| December | 36.4 | 125.07 | 35.3 | 126.64 |

Source: Primula Parkroyal internal management report.

## TABLE 6

**Sales and Marketing Expenses (Cost Center)**

| Sales and Marketing Expenses | Jan–May 1997 |
| --- | --- |
| Salaries & related expenses | 70,216 |
| Staff benefits | 11,987 |
| Promotional expenses | 50,261 |
| Other expenses | 92,027 |
| **Total Expenses** | **224,491** |

Source: Primula Parkroyal internal management report.

According to Hawker, PPR's occupancy rate had not increased very much since the management takeover. Table 5 compares the 1997 planned occupancy and average room rates against 1996 figures. The sales and marketing expenses for January to May 1997 are shown in Table 6.

## HOTEL OPERATIONS

PPR's business was organized into two main departments, which operated as separate profit centers: the Room Division, which included the front office operation, and the Food and Beverage Department.

## ROOM DIVISION AND FRONT OFFICE OPERATIONS

The hotel's front office operations were managed by Encik[3] Radi. This department was responsible for managing room reservations and setting room prices, as well as for arranging every activity their guests engaged in throughout their stay. The department received room reservations either directly from individual guests or from tour operators or event sponsors. Other functions of the department included managing the reception counter and room services, porter and concierge services, and recreational support. The Room Division's income statement is shown in Table 7, with the main cost item being staffing (21.1 percent of gross room revenue).

Encik Radi was fully aware that personal interactions with his front office staff are the key drivers of guest satisfaction. He strongly believed that his staff needed to be developed and trained to increase service levels, especially because no formal front office training had been conducted since 1992 under the previous management. Radi felt that job rotation, for example, between reception and reservation personnel, as well as cross-training (in other Malaysian Parkroyal hotels), could be carried out to develop skills and enrich jobs. Also there was a need to motivate and retain his front office staff, to contain the high turnover rates in the department. He noted that staff motivation was low, and turnover and absenteeism were high. Radi had 35 front office staff at the end of 1997.

Another key area of concern was to manage room capacity more effectively. In particular, the occupancy rate had to be increased throughout the year, but especially so during the low seasons (the monsoon months). Also, because 83 percent of the hotel's room nights were currently occupied by Malaysians, Radi believed that more efforts should be made to attract Malaysian tour groups, rather than tying up high promotional expenses in attempting to bring in more foreign tourists.

TABLE 7

### Income Statement for Rooms Division (Profit Center)

| Room P&L from Jan. to May 1997 | RM | | % of Revenue |
|---|---|---|---|
| **Room Income** | | 1,827,807 | 100.0 |
| Staff expenses | | | |
| Salaries & wages | 212,565 | | 11.6 |
| Overtime | 9,129 | | 0.5 |
| Employee benefits | 165,216 | | 9.0 |
| Subtotal: Staff expenses | 386,910 | | 21.1 |
| Other expenses | 161,242 | | 8.9 |
| **Total Expenses** | | 548,152 | 30.0 |
| **Net Contribution** | | 1,279,655 | 70.0 |

Source: Primula Parkroyal internal report

# FOOD AND BEVERAGE DEPARTMENT

Harry Thaliwal, a Malaysian with a Swiss qualification in hotel management, was appointed the F&B manager. Previously he was attached to Parkroyal properties in Sydney and Kuala Lumpur. With 75 staff reporting to him, Thaliwal was responsible for the kitchen, four F&B outlets, conference facilities, and banquet services.

In general, F&B outlets contribute about 30 percent to 35 percent of a hotel's operating revenue. In the past, lunch buffets were offered only when the occupancy rate was considered high enough to sustain it. Thaliwal saw the potential to attract locals and other tourists not residing at PPR to the hotel for the breakfast, lunch, tea, and dinner/supper buffets, served throughout the day. With the introduction of a new set of menus for the buffets, PPR managed to attract a significant number of non-hotel guests, which pushed F&B's contribution to more than 50 percent of total operating revenue. Sixty percent of the F&B clientele were non-hotel guests; 20 percent of breakfast buffets, 40 percent of lunch and dinner buffets, and 90 percent of the high-tea and supper buffets were consumed by guests not residing at the hotel. The department's P&L statement is presented in Table 8.

Because banquet services accounted for about 50 percent of F&B revenue, more effective planning and marketing of the hotel's banquet services, F&B outlets, and conference rooms were planned. To facilitate more efficient booking of banquets, Thaliwal introduced a system for managing event scheduling and ruled that all requests on quotations were to be answered within 24 hours of a client's inquiry. Also, on-the-job training of the chefs and their cross-training with Kuala Lumpur's Parkroyal were conducted. This was necessary because the menus had not been changed for the past 12 years before the management change.

Thaliwal also observed that a significant number of waiters and waitresses were reluctant to interact with foreign guests, mostly because of a lack of confidence in their English language proficiency. Also, an adequate sense of urgency to

## TABLE 8

**Profit and Loss Statement for Food & Beverage (Profit Center)**

| P&L Food & Beverage (Jan. to May 1997) | RM |
|---|---|
| Revenues | 1,809,670 |
| Less cost of goods sold | (679,517) |
| **Gross revenues** | **1,130,153** |
| **Expenses** | |
| Total wages | 460,314 |
| Employee benefits | 230,285 |
| Other expenses | 193,293 |
| **Total Expenses** | **883,892** |
| **Net Profit (Loss)** | **246,261** |

Source: Primula Parkroyal internal report.

response to guests' requests had to be instilled. Improving service standards had become a key challenge. Viewing customer complaints seriously, Thaliwal introduced lucky draws to encourage guests to fill in comment cards as a continuous system of soliciting customer feedback. Analyses of customer comments were made regularly to keep service standards in line with the guests' expectations.

Thaliwal implemented many changes, which targeted upgrading service quality. They included restructuring of job positions by promoting several staff to supervisory levels, enriching jobs by deploying staff for both room service and reception duty, and cutting manpower and energy costs by merging the coffee house and bar operations. Thaliwal also replaced a karaoke lounge located on the hotel rooftop by a banquet room, since the former was underutilized and was incurring losses.

Thaliwal also implemented a proper inventory and storage system for hotel supplies (including food and beverage items). The system was designed to ensure that there are sufficient supplies, particularly of fresh produce, to meet the daily needs of all F&B outlets, and to avoid excessive overstocking of certain room supplies. The use of kitchen supplies was tightly controlled by Thaliwal and the chief chef. The ordering process for new hotel supplies also needed a revamp. Thaliwal terminated all contracts requiring tenders for food and room supplies. Also, tenders for hotel supplies were now open every six months, in contrast to the previous system of once in three months. The suppliers of food and room materials were evaluated on price, quality, and services rendered.

Upon the request of PTB, which ran all its operations based on Islamic principles, income from alcoholic beverages were treated separately from income from other hotel operations. As Table 9 illustrates, the special accounting treatment was made to "cleanse" the hotel revenues (Islamic principles prohibit profiteering from

## TABLE 9

### Profit from Liquor Sales

| Profit from Liquor Sales (May 1997) | RM |
|---|---|
| **Revenue** | |
| Liquor sales | 21,295 |
| Less cost (33.27% of liquor sold) | (7,085) |
| **Gross Revenue** | **14,210** |
| **Expenses** | |
| Management/license fees (2% of liquor revenue) | 426 |
| Portion of F&B expenses relating to liquor sales (4.6% of F&B expenses) | 9,071 |
| **Total Expenses** | **(9,497)** |
| **Liquor profit (GOP)** | **4,713** |
| Deduct: Incentive fee (6% of GOP) | (283) |
| **Transfer to liquor profit reserve** | **4,430** |

Source: Primula Parkroyal internal report.

the sale of liquor). Therefore, PTB's share of the profit generated from alcoholic beverages was not absorbed into PTB's group profits. Instead, this portion was given on a yearly basis to Baitulmal, a public welfare agency.

## HUMAN RESOURCE DEVELOPMENT

SPHC appointed Encik Rohaizad as the manager of the Human Resources Department (HRD) three months after the management takeover. He found himself in the following situation: low levels of staff training, absence of staff exposure to other hotels' operations and services, and high absenteeism (Table 10). Rohaizad saw changing the work culture as his top priority, with the need to instill service orientation and a strong work ethic across the ranks. Staff size was trimmed from 350 to 315 after the management takeover.

To upgrade skills and advance career development, training programs were conducted at three levels. At the preliminary stage, knowledge of the hotel's service offerings and training targeted at instilling service orientation and greater work ethics were conducted. Next, customer complaint handling and related skills training was done. Lastly, for middle management and above, specific courses, such as management accounting and industrial relations, were conducted. Despite the training, changing work culture and attitude remained imperative. For instance, during the last rainy season, among the 10 employees that were sent to the Penang-Parkroyal Hotel for cross-training, four returned before the training was completed.

Besides problems with employees' work attitude, Rohaizad also found difficulty in recruiting hotel personnel in the predominantly Muslim state. This was possibly due to the Muslim religious code that prohibits Muslims from serving or consuming alcoholic drinks. Rohaizad believed that the people's low level of awareness of the various employment benefits, such as free meals and transport to and from work, also contributed to their reluctance to work in the hotel/catering industry. Rohaizad conducted career lectures and participated in exhibitions aimed at Terengganu youths and secondary school graduates to recruit new personnel.

Hawker pondered the formulation of the 1998 business plan. The worsening economic crisis made it crucial for Hawker to decide on the positioning of the

## TABLE 10

### Human Resource Statistics (July–December 1996)

|                    | July | Aug. | Sep. | Oct. | Nov. | Dec. |
|--------------------|------|------|------|------|------|------|
| Employee strength  | 292  | 304  | 305  | 301  | 305  | 308  |
| Days absent        | 65   | 66   | 128  | 78   | 88   | 125  |
| Employee turnover  | 24   | 17   | 6    | 13   | 9    | 3    |
| New employees      | 17   | 30   | 8    | 7    | 12   | 6    |

Source: Primula Parkroyal HRD records.

hotel, to identify PPR's primary target segments, and to develop strategies that
could smooth the severe seasonal demand fluctuations. Also, work attitudes and
the culture of staff had to be critically assessed in order to achieve a high-quality
positioning.

# Exercises

1. What should PPR's positioning be to differentiate it from its competitors?
2. What should be its target markets for the coming year(s)? Should they be the
   same for peak and off-peak seasons?
3. How could PPR improve room revenue during all seasons?
4. What are PPR's key challenges to achieve its target positioning and improve
   room revenues?
5. What actions would you recommend PPR take over the next 12 months?

The following websites may provide useful information for the case analysis:

- Primula Parkroyal: http://www.sphc.com.au/hotels/parkroyl/pprimula.html
- Asia Travel Hotels and Resorts Reservation Service:
  http://asiatravel.com/malaysia/primula/index.html
- Introduction to Terengganu: http://terengganu.gov.my/intro.htm
- Information on Tourism in Malaysia: http://tourism.gov.my/
- Malaysia Home Page: http://www.visitmalaysia.com
- SPHC Home Page: http://www.sphc.com.au

# Notes

1. RM = Malaysian Ringgit, Malaysia's currency. The exchange rate was US$1 =
   RM3.8 at the end of 1998.
2. Cik is the Malay equivalent of the title Miss.
3. Encik is the Malay equivalent of the title Mr.

# Exhibit 1

**Primula Parkroyal Calendar of Events**

| 1998 Proposed Activities | Reasons for Proposed Activities | Special Occasions |
|---|---|---|
| January<br>Convention packages special | ЖЖ | • New Year's Day<br>• Hari Raya Puasa |
| February<br>Chinese New Year special<br>Convention packages special | ЖЖ | • Chinese New Year |

| Month / Activities | | Events |
|---|---|---|
| March<br>Malay Foods Festival | | • End of Ramadan |
| April<br>Cultural Fest | | • Hulu Terengganu Cultural Fest |
| May<br>Cultural Fest<br>Sports Extravaganza<br>Family packages special<br>Turtle viewing season | | • Terengganu Theatre Festival<br>• Dungun Cultural Fest<br>• National Taekwondo Championship<br>• Beach carnival<br>• Attracting families on vacation |
| June<br>Sports Extravaganza<br>Family packages special<br>Cultural Fest<br>Fishing competitions<br>Turtle viewing season | | • Marang Cultural Fest<br>• Squid Fishing Fiesta<br>• Boat and Marina Show<br>• Attracting families on vacation |
| July<br>Sports Extravaganza<br>Cultural Fest<br>Turtle viewing season | | • Terengganu Beach Games<br>• Kemaman Cultural Fest |
| August<br>Sports Extravaganza<br>Cultural Fest<br>Turtle viewing season | | • Kenyir Kayak Regatta<br>• Terengganu Literary Week<br>• International Long Boat Race |
| September<br>Sports Extravaganza<br>Cultural Fest<br>Lantern Festival<br>Turtle viewing season | | • Beach Festival '98<br>• Terengganu Gathering of Performing Arts<br>• Mid Autumn Festival |
| October<br>Sports Extravaganza | | • Cultural Gathering<br>• Terengganu Open Traditional Dance Competition |
| November<br>Conventions packages special<br>Family packages special | | • Crafts, Arts & Textiles Expo<br>• Batik & Craft Festival<br>• Attract families on vacation |
| December<br>Magic Show<br>Convention packages special<br>Family packages special<br>Christmas promotion | | • School holiday treat for children<br>• Christmas<br>• Attract families on vacation |

Legend:

Monsoon season

Turtle viewing season

School holidays

Peak periods

# index

# credits

## Photo Credits

P. 11 © PhotoDisc, P. 28 © PhotoDisc, P. 38 © PhotoDisc, P. 70 © PhotoDisc, P. 93 © PhotoDisc, P. 109 © PhotoDisc, P. 114 © PhotoDisc, P. 137 © PhotoDisc, P. 144 © PhotoDisc, P. 173 © PhotoDisc, P. 176 © PhotoDisc, P. 200 © AP/Wide World Photos/Ric Feld, P. 215 Harcourt photo/Annette Coolidge, P. 252 © PhotoDisc, P. 275 © PhotoDisc, P. 305 © PhotoDisc, P. 317 © PhotoDisc, P. 328 © PhotoDisc, P 344 © PhotoDisc, P. 360 © PhotoDisc, P. 369 © PhotoDisc

## Literary Credits

Services in Action 1.4   From "Sales Smarts Rule Internet," *USA Today*, January 19, 2000, pp. IB, 2B. Copyright © 2000, *USA Today*. Reprinted by permission.

Services in Action 3.2   From "Mya Desires Your Attention," by Tobey Grumet, *Revolution*, Vol. 1, No. 5, July 2000, p. 25. Reprinted by permission.

Services in Action 3.3   From "Delighting the Global Customer," by Lisa Yorgey, *Target Marketing*, Vol. 23, No. 2, February 2000, pp. 104-106. Copyright © 2000 *Target Marketing*. Reprinted by permission of North American Publishing Co.

Services in Action 5.3   From "Presto Chango! Sales are Huge!" by Jeremy Kahn, *Fortune*, March 2, 2000, Vol. 141, No. 6, pp. 90-96. © 2000 Time, Inc. All rights reserved.

Services in Action 5.5   "Honest Mistake Worth $35,000 Fails to Tempt Auditor," by Kim Folstad, *Denver Rocky Mountain News*, February 28, 2000, p. 6A. Reprinted with permission of the *Rocky Mountain News*.

Services in Action 6.2   Reprinted by permission of Harvard Business Review from "The Service-Driven Service Company," by Leonard A. Schlesinger and James L. Heskett. *Harvard Business Review*, Sept/Oct 1991, pp. 71-81. Copyright © 1991 by the President and Fellows of Harvard College; all rights reserved.

Services in Action 6.3   From "10 Top Stores Put to the Test," by David Ward, *Revolution*, Vol. 1, No. 5, July 2000, pp. 66-74. Reprinted by permission.

Services in Action 7.1   From, "Priceline.com: An On-line Auction Where the Price is Always Right," by Mike Troy, *Retailing Today*, Vol. 39, No. 9, May 8, 2000, pp. 93-94.

Services in Action 7.2   From "Good Buys," by Mara Janis, *Adweek*, Vol. 41, No. 10, March 6, 2000, pp. 58-64. Copyright © 2000 ASM Communications, Inc.

Services in Action 7.3   From "Ethnic Pricing Means Unfair Air Fares," *The Wall Street Journal*, December 5, 1997, pp. B1, B14. Copyright © 1997 Dow Jones and Co. Inc. Reprinted by permission via the Copyright Clearance Center.

Services in Action 8.1   From "Moving Targets," by Mark Dolley, *Revolution*, Vol. 1, No. 5, July 2000, pp. 14, 62-64. Reprinted by permission.

Services in Action 8.2   From "Taco Bell Rings in New Age of Publicity Stunts," by Bob Lamons, *Marketing News*, Vol. 30, No. 11, 1996, p. 15. Reprinted by permission of American Marketing Association.

Services in Action 8.3   From "Web-Influenced Offline Sales Dwarf E-commerce," by Adam Katz-Stone, *Revolution*, Vol. 1, No. 5, July 2000, pp. 8-9. Reprinted by permission.

Services in Action 8.4   From "E-turns: Caveat Emptor," by Becky Ebenkamp, *Brandweek*, Vol. 25, No. 41, January 10, 2000, p. 25. Copyright © 2000 ASM Communications, Inc.

Services in Action 9.3   From "Plane Seats Get Bigger, Cost More," appeared in *Denver Rocky Mountain News*, February 28, 2000, p. 2A, 31A, taken from David Morrow "Airlines Cut Seats to Add to Profits," *New York Times*, February 28, 2000.

Services in Action 10.1   From "Sales Smarts Rule Internet," *USA Today*, January 19, 2000, pp. IB, 2B. Copyright © 2000, *USA Today*. Reprinted by permission.

Services in Action 10.2   Excerpt from *Managing Services Marketing: Text and Readings*, 4/e , by John E.G. Bateson and K. Douglas Hoffman, © 1999 The Dryden Press.

Services in Action 10.3   "Customers from Hell," by Ron Zemke and Kristen Anderson. Reprinted with permission from the February 1990 issue of *Training* Magazine. Copyright © 1990, Bill Communications, Minneapolis, MN. All rights reserved. Not for resale.

PP. 281, 282, 283, 284, 285   Drawings from "Customers from Hell," reprinted with permission from the February 1990 issue of *Training* Magazine. Copyright © 1990, Bill Communications, Minneapolis, MN. All rights reserved. Not for resale.

Figure 11.1   From "Why Service Stinks," by Diane Brady, *Business Week*, October 23, 2000, pp. 120-121. Reprinted from *Business Week* by special permission, copyright © 2000 by The McGraw-Hill Companies, Inc.

Table 12.1   From "Consumer Satisfaction, Dissatisfaction and Complaining Behavior," by Keith Hunt in *Journal of Social Issues*, Vol. 47, 1991, pp. 109-110. Copyright © 1991 The Society for the Psychological Study of Social Issues. Reprinted by permission.

Services in Action 12.2   From "We're Listening," by Vicki Escarra, *SKY*, February 2000.

Table 12.2   From "America's Most Admired Companies," by Geoffrey Colvin, *Fortune*, Vol. 141, No. 4, February 21, 2000, p. 108. Copyright © 2000 Time, Inc. all rights reserved.

Table 12.3   From "America's Most Admired Companies," by Geoffrey Colvin, *Fortune*, Vol. 141, No. 4, February 21, 2000, p. 108. Copyright © 2000 Time, Inc. all rights reserved.

Table 12.4   From AMA Management Briefing, *Blueprints for Service Quality: The Federal Express Approach*, AMA Membership Publications Division, 1991. Reprinted by permission of the American Marketing Association.

Figure 12.2   From "Measuring Customer Satisfaction: Fact and Artifact," by R. Peterson and W. Wilson, *Journal of the Academy of Marketing Science*, Vol. 20, No. 1, 1992, pp. 61, 65. Copyright © 1992 by Sage, Inc. Reprinted by permission of Sage Publications.

Table 12.5   From "Measuring Customer Satisfaction: Fact and Artifact," by R. Peterson and W. Wilson, *Journal of the Academy of Marketing Science*, Vol. 20, No. 1, 1992, pp. 61, 65. Copyright © 1992 by Sage, Inc. Reprinted by permission of Sage Publications.

Table 12.6   From "Measuring Customer Satisfaction: Fact and Artifact," by R. Peterson and W. Wilson, *Journal of the Academy of Marketing Science*, Vol. 20, No. 1, 1992, pp. 61, 65. Copyright © 1992 by Sage, Inc. Reprinted by permission of Sage Publications.

Figure 12.7   From "The Nature and Determinants of Customer Expectations of Service," by Valerie A. Zeithaml, et al., *Journal of the Academy of Marketing Science*, Vol. 21, No. 1, 1993, pp. 1-12. Copyright © 1992 by Sage, Inc. Reprinted by permission of Sage Publications.

Table 13.2   From "Improving Service Quality in America: Lessons Learned," by Leonard L. Berry et al., *Academy of Management Executive*, Vol. 8, No. 2, 1994, pp. 32-52. Reprinted by permission of Academy of Management via Copyright Clearance Center.

Figure 14.1   From "The Service Encounter" by Mary Jo Bitner et al., *Journal of Marketing*, January 1990, pp. 71-84. Reprinted by permission of American Marketing Association.

Figure 15.5   From "Zero Defections: Quality Comes to Services," by Frederick F. Reichheld and W. Earl Sasser, Jr., *Harvard Business Review* (September-October 1990), p. 110. Reprinted by permission of *Harvard Business Review*. Copyright © 1990 by the President and Fellows of Harvard College; all rights reserved.

Figure 15.6   From "Zero Defections: Quality Comes to Services," by Frederick F. Reichheld and W. Earl Sasser, Jr., *Harvard Business Review* (September-October 1990), p. 109. Reprinted by permission of *Harvard Business Review*. Copyright © 1990 by the President and Fellows of Harvard College; all rights reserved.

Table 16.1   © 1989 by Christopher H. Lovelock. Reprinted with permission from Christopher H. Lovelock. "Managing Interaction Between Operations and Marketing and Their Impact on Customers" in Bowen et al. (eds.), *Service Management Effectiveness* (San Francisco: Jossey Bass, 1990), p. 62.

Figure 16.1   From *Managing Services Marketing: Text and Readings*, 3/e, by John E.G. Bateson, © 1995 The Dryden Press.

Figure 16.2   From *Managing Services Marketing: Text and Readings*, 3/e, by John E.G. Bateson, © 1995 The Dryden Press.

Figure 16.3   Reprinted by permission of Harvard Business School Press, *Winning the Service Game*, by Benjamin Schneider and David E. Bowen. Boston, MA 1995, p. 244. Copyright © 1995 by Harvard Business School Publishing.

Figure 16.4   From "Service by Design," by R.B. Chase and W.E. Youngdahl, *Design Management Journal*, vol. 9, Winter 1992, p. 12 adapted from R.B. Chase and N.J. Aquillano, *Production and Operation Management: A Lifecycle Approach*, © 1991 Irwin.

Figure 16.5   From *Managing Services Marketing: Text and Readings*, 3/e, by John E.G. Bateson, © 1995 The Dryden Press.

Table 16.2   From *Managing Services Marketing: Text and Readings*, 3/e, by John E.G. Bateson, © 1995 The Dryden Press.

## Cases

Case 3   "SpaceDisk Inc," by Jochen Wirtz. Copyright © 2000 by the author. The author retains all rights. Not to be reproduced or used without written permission from the author.

Case 7   "e.Com Services: Launching SpaceDisk," by Jochen Wirtz and S. Mohan. Copyright © 1999 by the authors. The authors retain all rights. Not to be reproduced or used without written permission from the authors.

Case 10   "O'Keefe Associates" © 1996 Brian Wansink.

Case 12   "Giordano," by Jochen Wirtz. Copyright © 2001 by the author. The author retains all rights. Not to be reproduced or used without written permission from the author.

Cased 13   "Roscoe Nondestructive Testing" © 1995 Brian Wansink.

Case 16a   Jochen Wirtz and Jeannette Ho Pheng Theng, "Westin Hotels in Asia: Global Distribution." Copyright © 1999 by the authors. The authors retain all rights. Not to be reproduced or used without written permission from the authors.

Case16b   Aliah Hanim M. Salleh and Jochen Wirtz, "Primula Parkroyal Hotel," by Aliah Hanim M. Salleh and Jochen Wirtz. Copyright © 1999 by the authors. The authors retain all rights. Not to be reproduced or used without written permission from the authors.